STUDIES IN MODERN BRITISH RELIGIOUS HISTORY

Volume 17

Religion, Reform and Modernity in the Eighteenth Century

Thomas Secker and the Church of England

The eighteenth century has long divided critical opinion. Some contend that it witnessed the birth of the modern world, while others counter that England remained an *ancien régime* confessional state. This book takes issue with both positions. It argues that the former overstate the newness of the age and largely misdiagnose the causes of change. The latter, by contrast, rightly point to the persistence of more traditional modes of thought and behaviour, but downplay the era's fundamental uncertainty and misplace the reasons for and the timeline of its passage. The overwhelming catalyst for change is here seen to be war, rather than long-term social and economic changes.

Archbishop Thomas Secker (1693–1768), the Cranmer or Laud of his age, and the hitherto neglected church reforms he spearheaded, form the particular focus of the book; this is the first full archivally-based study of a crucial but frequently ignored figure.

ROBERT G. INGRAM is Assistant Professor of History in the Department of History, Ohio University.

STUDIES IN MODERN BRITISH RELIGIOUS HISTORY

ISSN 1464–6625

General editors
Stephen Taylor
Arthur Burns
Kenneth Fincham

This series aims to differentiate 'religious history' from the narrow confines of church history, investigating not only the social and cultural history of religion, but also theological, political and institutional themes, while remaining sensitive to the wider historical context; it thus advances an understanding of the importance of religion for the history of modern Britain, covering all periods of British history since the Reformation.

*Previously published volumes in this series
are listed at the back of this volume.*

Thomas Secker (1693–1768)

From a portrait in Lambeth Palace Library by an unknown artist

Religion, Reform and Modernity in the Eighteenth Century

Thomas Secker and the Church of England

ROBERT G. INGRAM

THE BOYDELL PRESS

First published 2007
The Boydell Press, Woodbridge

ISBN 978–1–84383–348–2

The Boydell Press is an imprint of Boydell & Brewer Ltd
PO Box 9, Woodbridge, Suffolk IP12 3DF, UK
and of Boydell & Brewer Inc.
Mt Hope Avenue, Rochester, NY 14620, USA
website: www.boydellandbrewer.com

A CIP catalogue record for this book is available
from the British Library

This publication is printed on acid-free paper

Printed in Great Britain by
Biddles Ltd, King's Lynn, Norfolk

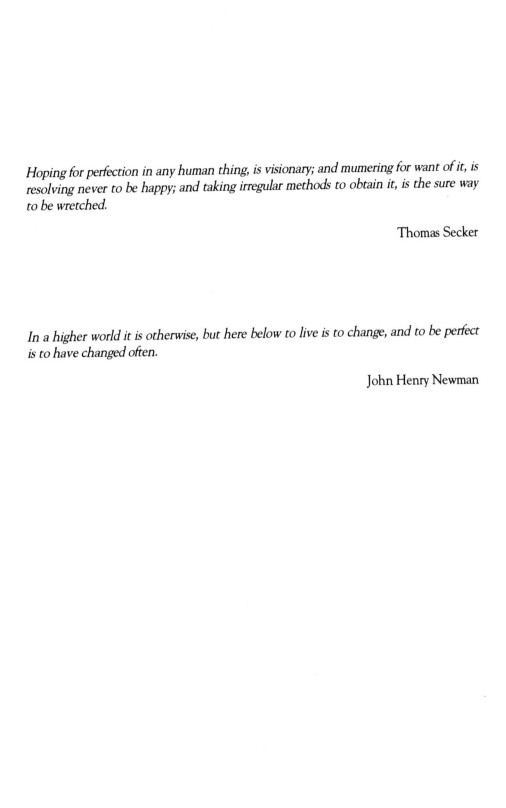

Hoping for perfection in any human thing, is visionary; and mumering for want of it, is resolving never to be happy; and taking irregular methods to obtain it, is the sure way to be wretched.

Thomas Secker

In a higher world it is otherwise, but here below to live is to change, and to be perfect is to have changed often.

John Henry Newman

CONTENTS

PREFACE

This book is about religion, reform, and modernity. More specifically, it is about Thomas Secker (1693–1768), the orthodox church reform effort which he spearheaded, and the lessons that reform effort tells us about eighteenth-century England. Historians need some sort of intellectual glue to hold together the swaths of time we study, or else the past risks becoming just a jumble of chaotic events. Religious change and the attendant political conflict serve as an important cohesive for studies of sixteenth- and seventeenth-century England, while the birth of the modern world does so for the eighteenth. Yet where sixteenth- and seventeenth-century English men and women were clearly concerned with Protestantism, popery, and arbitrary government, it is not evident that those living during the eighteenth century were preoccupied by modernity. Put another way, while recent historians of sixteenth- and seventeenth-century England have tended to address the historical problems which consumed those whom they study, their counterparts examining the eighteenth century have more often let present-day concerns shape their research agendas: rather than subject the eighteenth century to the 'historians' question – where did things stand?', most recent scholars have tended instead to pose the 'solipsistic question...where did I come from?'[1] Indeed, the growing interest in the period has coincided neatly with the increasing scholarly conviction that the eighteenth century gave birth to the modern world. It is our very own creation myth.

To question whether the eighteenth century was the crucible of modernity is not to deny that important transformations took place then. It is merely to suggest that the nature, scope, pace, and causes of that change have been either overstated or misconstrued. This book suggests that Thomas Secker's life possesses a seismographic quality, one which should force us to look afresh at some important aspects of English society during the century after the Glorious Revolution. In particular *orthodox church reform* – itself hitherto unappreciated and, at once, both a reflection of and a response to societal change – elucidates at least two salient points. Firstly, most, including orthodox reform's most strident detractors, looked prescriptively to the past for solutions to current societal problems: the answers for the future lay behind them, not in front of them. It was a way of looking at the world which shared more in common with Renaissance humanists than with the Ecclesiastical

[1]   Paul Halliday, 'Review of David Lemmings, *Professors of Law: Barristers and English Legal Culture in the Eighteenth Century*', H-Albion, H-Net Reviews, Sept 2003.

Commissioners. Secondly, war – rather than any social, economic, or cultural developments – did most to destroy this swivel-headed mindset and the era of which it was symptomatic. The particular manner of the era's demise was not inevitable and what came afterwards was not full-blown modernity. But its passage was yet more proof of Heraclitus's observation that war is 'the father of all things'.[2]

Eight chapters comprise the book. Chapter 1 surveys the historiographical landscape, argues for conceiving of the eighteenth century as an age of reform, and elucidates the reforming mindset before the 1780s. Chapters 2 and 3 chart Thomas Secker's abandonment of Dissent, conformity to the established Church of England, acceptance of orthodoxy, and ascent of the ladder of ecclesiastical preferment. These chapters explain the origins and development of Secker's orthodox reform vision and the reasons that he rose to a position from which he could try to give flesh to that vision. As importantly, they illuminate the salient features of eighteenth-century English religious life. In particular, they point up the effects of legalized religious pluralism, the reasons for religio-political factionalization and heterodoxy's efflorescence during the first half of the eighteenth century, and the nature of the Church's relationship with the state. Chapters 4-8 turn from the chronological to the thematic in order to consider the priorities of orthodox reformers and the outcomes of orthodox reform. Chapters 4 and 5 take up the two most important elements of the orthodox reform agenda – the defence of 'real religion' and the improvement of pastoral provision. Significantly, neither inherently required the support of the English state. Not all orthodox reform, though, was possible without the state's assistance, and Chapter 6 examines more closely the nature of the church-state – and of the Church-Whig – alliance during the mid eighteenth century. It soon becomes evident that theory and practice diverged, sometimes dramatically. For if in theory, church and state were united organically, in practice, the state proved itself to be a less than committed partner in its marriage to the Church of England. In no small part, the state failed to reciprocate the consistent commitment and energy of the established Church because war catalyzed religious liberalization: in order to mobilize the nation to war against the Catholic Bourbons, certain practical concessions had to be made to non-Anglicans in the British Isles and in the North American colonies. In addition to corroding the bonds of union between throne and altar, these developments ensured that the full scope of the orthodox reform agenda was unrealized. One prominent casualty was an American episcopate, an issue taken up in Chapter 7. In the minds of the orthodox, episcopacy was, at the very least, the catholic Church of England's *bene esse* and a bishopless Church in America was wrongly ordered. Yet the heterodox across the

---

[2] Charles H. Kahn, *The Art and Thought of Heraclitus* (Cambridge, 1979), p. 137. I would like to thank Dr. David Berkey for bringing this reference to my attention.

Atlantic world subverted any episcopizing scheme by implicitly – and at times explicitly – raising the spectre of political unrest. As a result, the English state refused to lift a finger, either during the Seven Years War or in its tumultuous and uncertain aftermath, to help introduce Anglican bishops into North America for fear of angering the heterodox. Ironically, during the 1770s the English state would prove more willing to pacify Roman Catholics by removing certain legal barriers than it was to shore up its alliance with the established Church. If war complicated the English state's relationship with the Church of England, so too did it complicate the English Church's relations with churches abroad. The touchstone for eighteenth-century orthodox reformers was the primitive church of the apostolic and patristic fathers, a church whose signal features were its unity and catholicity. Yet Chapter 8 shows that war made clear to the Anglican orthodox that the Church of England could lay few practical claims to being either united or catholic. Instead, relations with churches abroad illuminate the siege mentality which so characterized orthodox Anglican identity during the mid eighteenth century. Insofar as the orthodox were concerned, then, the eighteenth century was at once an age of reform and an age of anxiety.

It has taken me a long time to write this book, and I alone am wholly responsible for all errors which remain in it. What I cannot claim sole credit for is the book's existence, for without the generous help of a host of institutions and individuals, I could not have written it.

The University of Virginia, the English-Speaking Union, the Intercollegiate Studies Institute, the Thomas Jefferson Foundation, the Lewis Walpole Library, the Newberry Library, the Center on Religion and Democracy, Oxford Brookes University, and Ohio University funded my research and writing, and I thank them for helping me keep the wolf from my door for so long. Dozens of archivists and librarians provided invaluable research assistance to me, yet I should single out Melanie Barber (Lambeth Palace Library) and Jan Maxwell (Ohio University Library) for special thanks. At Boydell & Brewer, Caroline Palmer and her staff have helpfully and patiently shepherded the book to press. Grant and Janet Lewison were gracious hosts during a number of extended stays in London.

Parts of this book have appeared in print elsewhere. I am grateful to Boydell & Brewer for allowing me to republish portions of '"The clergy who affect to call themselves orthodox": Thomas Secker and the Defence of Anglican Orthodoxy, 1758-68', *SCH* 43 (2007), pp. 342–53; to the editors of *CROMOHS* for allowing me to republish portions of 'Sykes's Shadow: Thoughts on the Historiography of the Eighteenth-Century Church of England'; and to Sussex Academic Press for allowing me to republish portions of 'Archbishop Thomas Secker, Anglican identity, and relations with foreign Protestants in the mid-eighteenth century', in *From Strangers to Citizens: Immigrant Communities in Britain, Ireland and North America, 1550–1750*, eds. Randolph Vigne and Charles Middleton (2001), pp. 527–38. I would also like to thank Lambeth Palace Library for letting me reproduce a portrait of Secker which it owns and which serves as this book's frontispiece.

At The University of the South, Greg Clark, Brown Patterson, and Tam Carlson set me on the path to an academic career, while the late Martin J. Havran, Erik Midelfort, and Richard Drayton generously and unfailingly supported me at the University of Virginia. I am particularly sorry that Martin Havran did not live to see this book in print: he gave me the free rein to roam in the eighteenth century, when his own field of scholarly expertise lay a century earlier, and I am grateful to him for allowing me to follow my interests where they led me. Among my cohort in Charlottesville, I found truly decent and dependable friends, especially Amy Murrell Taylor, Steve and Melissa Norris, Richard Samuelson, Christof Morrissey, Allyson Creasman, Dave D'Andrea, Andy Morris, Jimmy James Owens, Will Hay, James Guba, and Marshall Shaw.

On the other side of the Appalachian mountains at Ohio University, I have likewise been lucky to be surrounded by enlivening and supportive folks, including Patrick Barr-Melej, John Brobst, Geoff Buckley, Jack Epstein, Walter Hawthorne, Kevin Mattson, Jackie Maxwell, Chester Pach, and Kevin Uhalde. Paul Milazzo and Brian Schoen have been good friends and kindred spirits, as has Bruce Steiner. I am particularly glad to have the opportunity here to thank Bruce for his meticulous reading of my chapter on religion in America and for his spot-on suggestions for improvement. My gratitude for the much else I owe him, I hope he knows full well. Steve Miner and Norm Goda, my two department chairmen at Ohio University, have done much to provide the time and support necessary for me to write this book. I am especially grateful to Norm and Ben Ogles for bringing a greater measure of stability to my family's life by solving a seemingly insoluble two-body problem.

The scholars now working on eighteenth-century religious history are extraordinarily collegial and have been generous to me. Stephen Taylor is incredibly supportive of young scholars, and I very much appreciate him for including this book in his series and for his counsel and assistance across the last decade. Nigel Aston, Jeremy Gregory, and Peter Nockles have also read chapter drafts, written letters of support for grants and jobs, and let me bounce ideas off them for a long time now. Jim Bell, Jeremy Black, Jim Bradley, Arthur Burns, Jeff Chamberlain, Jonathan Clark, Tony Claydon, Bob Cornwall, Brian Cowan, Daniel Cummins, Lucia Dacome, Richard Davis, Grayson Ditchfield, Peter Doll, Geordan Hammond, Joanna Innes, Bill Jacob, Scott Mandelbrote, William Marshall, John Morgan-Guy, Jim Sack, Brian Schoen, Richard Sharp, Jane Shaw, Andrew Thompson, Theo Verbeek, John Walsh, and David Wykes either read drafts of individual chapters, provided me with useful references, helped me to clarify my muddled thinking, or allowed me to read advance copies of their own work. It should be noted that assistance does not imply concurrence, and I am doubly grateful for the help from those who may disagree with some of my arguments.

Other debts of mine to are more personal. Ben Stone, Taylor Fain, and Scott Taylor are irreplaceable friends who, without knowing it, sustained me through darker days than I care to remember. I owe them each a debt I cannot adequately repay. I feel much the same way about my obligations to Charles Perry and Paul Halliday. Charles is a great teacher and a good man. He is also an extraordinarily patient man, one who graciously and gracefully put up with my pestiferous ways as an undergraduate at Sewanee. I am glad he did so because his classes changed the course of my life irrevocably, and he remains for me the touchstone of the scholar-teacher-gentleman. Paul Halliday proved no less patient with me. When he was under absolutely no obligation to do so, Paul saved me from slipping through life's cracks at a time when I was in real danger of doing so, for he realized that while some horses need the whip to run faster, others need just calm words of encouragement. Few today conceive of their responsibilities to students in moral terms, and fewer still can match rhetoric with action. That Paul does so easily and cheerfully has earned him the respect, gratitude, and deep affection of all his students. Paul's newest colleague at the University of Virginia, Patrick Griffin, was mine for a time at Ohio University. Over more bacon cheeseburgers at The Union Bar and Grill than he or his cardiologist will care to think about, Pat let me talk my way to and through my argument, always encouraging me to keep the larger picture in view and to raise my intellectual horizons. Far more important to me, though, has been his steadfast friendship, both on the road to Rome and beyond. Lastly, in light of everything he has done for me, I cannot adequately thank Bill Gibson. Bill first pointed me toward Secker and has since frequently – and rightly – reminded me of Richard Pares's dictum, 'Of the making of a book there must some time come an end'. He is one of the most generous and good-hearted people I know, and I am glad to count him as a mentor and a friend.

My sister and her husband, Kathryn and David Thompson, have been unfailingly supportive, as have my in-laws, the Phillipses. My father, Dr. Glynn Ingram, will likely hold this book in his hands and still not be convinced that it's done. But it is, and that it is owes everything to his unmentioned sacrifices. I hope he accepts this book as a small token of my thanks to him for his authentic selflessness.

I have spent nearly a decade in the company of Thomas Secker. It's been long enough that some friends now ask after him as they do after members of my own family. My family, for their part, assiduously avoid mentioning him, save for my wife's occasional gentle encouragement that I 'just finish the thing'. Way back when, I chose to write about Secker because I thought his life might allow me to address some thorny historiographical problems which bedevil eighteenth-century English historians. I continue to think so. But I have also come to see him as a human being and not just as the key which might unlock the answer to some historiographical riddle. Indeed, the more I have got to know Secker the more I have felt a responsibility to explain him and his age in a way that he and his contemporaries would have understood. I hope this book does just that.

I began the final revisions in earnest during the spring of 2005, right after the birth of my first daughter, Claire, and I am finishing them up just as her little sister, Lucy, nears her ten-month birthday. Not, perhaps, an ideal time to finish up a book? As it turned out, it could hardly have been more propitious, for reasons which Claire and Lucy will likely never appreciate but for which I will always be mindful and grateful. I hope to have future books to dedicate to them. I dedicate this one, though, to their mother, Jill Ingram, who gave me them and so much else besides. To borrow from Graham Greene, 'I used to think I was sure about myself and what was right and wrong, and you taught me not to be sure. You took away all my lies and self-deceptions like they clear a road of rubble for somebody to come along it, somebody of importance, and now He's come, but you cleared the way yourself.' This book is for you, Jill, with love.

Athens, Ohio
August 2007

ABBREVIATIONS

Add.	Additional
AEH	*Anglican and Episcopal History*
ANB	*American National Biography*, eds. John A. Garraty and Mark C. Carnes (Oxford, 1999).
Autobiography	*The Autobiography of Thomas Secker, Archbishop of Canterbury*, eds. John Macauley and R.W. Greaves (Lawrence, KS, 1988).
Beinecke	Beinecke Rare Book and Manuscript Library, New Haven, CT
BIHR	Borthwick Institute of Historical Research, York
BJRL	*Bulletin of the John Rylands Library*
BL	British Library, London
Bodleian	Bodleian Library, Oxford
CCED	*Clergy of the Church of England Database, 1540–1835* [www.theclergydatabase.org.uk]
Charges	Thomas Secker, *Eight Charges delivered to the Clergy of the Diocese of Oxford and Canterbury* (London, 1769).
CMHS	*Collections of the Massachusetts Historical Society*
Cobbett, *PH*	William Cobbett, *The Parliamentary History of England from the earliest period to the year 1803*, 36 vols. (1802–1860).
Egmont Diaries	Historical Manuscript Commission, *Diary of the First Earl of Egmont (Viscount Percival)*, 3 vols. (1923).
EHR	*English Historical Review*
Hardwicke	Philip Yorke, first earl of Hardwicke (1690–1764)
Hearne's Recollections	*Remarks and Collections of Thomas Hearne*, 11 vols. (Oxford, 1885–1921).
Hervey's Memoirs	John, Lord Hervey, *Some Materials Towards Memoirs of the Reign of King George II*, ed. Romney Sedwick, 3 vols. (New York, 1970).
HJ	*Historical Journal*
HMPEC	*Historical Magazine of the Protestant Episcopal Church*
HUO: Eighteenth Century	L.S. Sutherland and L.G. Mitchell (eds.), *The History of the University of Oxford: The Eighteenth Century* (Oxford, 1986).
JBS	*Journal of British Studies*
JEH	*Journal of Ecclesiastical History*
Lectures	Thomas Secker, *Lectures on the Catechism of the Church of England; with a Discourses on Confirmation*, eds. Beilby Porteus and George Stinton (1799).
Literary Anecdotes	John Nichols, *Literary anecdotes of the eighteenth century...*, 8 vols. (1812–1816).

ABBREVIATIONS

Literary Illustrations	John Nichols, *Illustrations of the literary history of the eighteenth century...*, 8 vols. (1817–1858).
LPL	Lambeth Palace Library, London
LRB	*London Review of Books*
LWL	Lewis Walpole Library, Farmington, CT
Memoirs of Isaac Watts	Thomas Gibbons, *Memoirs of Isaac Watts* (1780).
Monthly Repository	*Monthly Repository of Theology and General Literature*
MS(S)	Manuscript(s)
NYRB	*New York Review of Books*
ODCC	F.L. Cross and E.A. Livingstone (eds.), *Oxford Dictionary of the Christian Church* (Oxford, 1997).
ODNB	H.C.G. Matthew and Brian Harrison (eds.), *Oxford Dictionary of National Biography*, 60 vols. (Oxford, 2004).
Oratio	Thomas Secker, *Oratio quam coram Synodo Provinciae Cantuariensis anno 1761 convocata habendam scripseral, sed morbo praepeditus non habuit, Archiepiscopus*, in *The Records of Convocation*, ed. Gerald Bray (Woodbridge, 2006), XII, pp. 315–25.
Oxford Correspondence	A.P. Jenkins (ed.), *The Correspondence of Thomas Secker, Bishop of Oxford, 1737–58* (Stroud, 1991).
OVR 1738	H.A. Lloyd Jukes (ed.), *Articles of Enquiry Addressed to the Clergy of the Diocese of Oxford at the Primary Visitation of Dr. Thomas Secker, 1738* (Banbury, 1957).
Perry, *Massachusetts*	William Stevens Perry (ed.), *Historical Collections relating to the American Colonial Church. III. Massachusetts* (New York, 1969).
Perry, *Pennsylvania*	William Stevens Perry (ed.), *Historical Collections relating to the American Colonial Church. II. Pennsylvania* (New York, 1969).
Perry, *Virginia*	William Stevens Perry (ed.), *Historical Collections relating to the American Colonial Church. I. Virginia* (New York, 1969).
PMHS	*Proceedings of the Massachusetts Historical Society*
Porteus, *Life of Secker*	Beilby Porteus, *A review of the life and character of the Right Rev. Dr. Thomas Secker* (1797).
RHD	Robert Hay Drummond (1711–1776)
SCA	Sheffield City Archives, Sheffield
SCH	*Studies in Church History*
SJ	Herbert and Carol Schneider (eds.), *Samuel Johnson: His Career and Writings*, 4 vols. (New York, 1929).
Speculum	Jeremy Gregory (ed.), *The Speculum of Archbishop Thomas Secker* (Woodbridge, 1995).
TLS	*Times Literary Supplement*
TNA	The National Archives, Kew
TPH	Thomas Pelham-Holles, duke of Newcastle (1693–1768)

ABBREVIATIONS

TRHS	*Transactions of the Royal Historical Society*
Walpole, *Memoirs of George II*	Horace Walpole, *Memoirs of King George II*, ed. John Brooke, 3 vols. (New Haven, CT, 1985).
Walpole, *Memoirs of George III*	Horace Walpole, *Memoirs of the Reign of King George the Third*, ed. G.F. Russell Barker, 4 vols. (1894).
Walpole's Correspondence	W.S. Lewis, *et al.* (eds.), The *Yale Edition of Horace Walpole's Correspondence*, 48 vols. (New Haven, CT, 1937–1983).
WAM	Westminster Abbey Muniment, Westminster Abbey Library, London
WMQ	*William and Mary Quarterly*
WTS	Thomas Secker, *The Works of Thomas Secker, L.L.D., late Lord Archbishop of Canterbury: to which is prefixed a review of his life and character*, ed. Beilby Porteus, 4 vols. (Edinburgh, 1792).

NOTE ON THE TEXT

All dates before 1752 are given in British 'Old Style' (Julian calendar), which was eleven days behind the Continental 'New Style' (Gregorian calendar). The year is taken to begin on 1 January. Unless otherwise noted, the place of publication is London. 'Anglican' is used merely as shorthand to denote allegiance to the Church of England, though it is technically anachronistic for the eighteenth century. Throughout the text, Roman Catholicism is often referred to as 'popery' and Roman Catholics as 'papists': this reflects the eighteenth-century mindset, not this author's own views.

Chapter One

'EFFORTS AT AMENDMENT'

The eighteenth century has long been an era in which historians of England have glimpsed important lessons about their own present. For Victorian whigs and liberals, it was Falstaff to the nineteenth century's Henry V, a debauched and discredited age which stood in stark contrast to their own.[1] 'Modernists' in the twentieth century likewise found the eighteenth century useful for contemporary purposes, fighting in it a proxy war over the purpose of history and the nature of the English state.[2] In the last four decades, the eighteenth century has lost none of its instructive appeal, with historians giving it a place in the manger in the creation story of the modern world.

That story runs something like this. In 1660 or 1688 or 1714 or sometime thereabout, the early modern world ceded way to the modern one.[3] Everywhere one looked, one saw modernity itself either present or fast-approaching over the horizon – we are assured, in fact, that the English 'were obsessed by modernity'.[4] Whether or not eighteenth-century English men and women fixated on modernity is debatable, but there can be no doubt that historians of the period have made elucidating its origins the primary – indeed, seemingly the only creditable – historiographical theme worth pursuing.[5] The Glorious Revolution,

---

[1] Herbert Butterfield, *George III and the Historians* (New York, 1959), pp. 39–190. Annabel Patterson, *Nobody's Perfect: A New Whig Interpretation of History* (New Haven, CT, 2002) aims 'to reinstate a "whig interpretation of history," in defiance of the historiographical orthodoxy that declares such an interpretation archaic and procedurally mistaken'. Jonathan Clark, 'More imperfect than others', *TLS* (13 March 2003), pp. 3–4 offers a trenchant rejoinder. Brian Young, *The Victorian Eighteenth Century: An Intellectual History* (Oxford, 2007) promises to be the authoritative treatment of its subject.

[2] Michael Bentley, *Modernizing England's Past: English Historiography in the Age of Modernism, 1870–1970* (Cambridge, 2005), pp. 144–68. Cf. Victor Feske, *From Belloc to Churchill: Private Scholars, Public Culture, and the Crisis of British Liberalism* (Chapel Hill, NC, 1996), pp. 1–14.

[3] Compare J.H. Plumb, 'The Acceptance of Modernity', in Neil McKendrick, John Brewer, and J.H. Plumb, *The Birth of A Consumer Society: The Commercialization of Eighteenth-Century England* (Bloomington, IN, 1982), pp. 316–34; Miles Ogborn, *Spaces of Modernity: London's Geographies, 1680–1780* (New York, 1998); Richard Price, *British Society, 1680–1800: Dynamism, Containment and Change* (Cambridge, 1999); Alan Houston and Steven Pincus, 'Introduction. Modernity and later-seventeenth-century England', in *A Nation Transformed: England after the Restoration*, eds. Alan Houston and Steven Pincus (Cambridge, 2001), pp. 1–19; Laura Brown, *Fables of Modernity: Literature and Culture in the English Eighteenth Century* (Ithaca, NY, 2001); and Kathleen Wilson, *This Island Race: Englishness, Empire and Gender in the Eighteenth Century* (New York, 2003), pp. 29–53.

[4] Houston and Pincus, 'Introduction. Modernity and later-seventeenth-century England', p. 1.

[5] Peter Lake, 'Retrospective: Wentworth's political world in revisionist and post-revisionist perspective', in *The Political World of Thomas Wentworth, Earl of Strafford, 1621–1641*, ed. J.F. Merritt (Cambridge, 1996), pp. 253–54 argues that the post-war historiography of all early

then, was a modern nationalist revolution, not a religiously inspired *coup d'état*.[6] Drawn after 1688 into a second Hundred Years' war against France, an English fiscal-military state evolved complete with a modern-looking bureaucracy and tax system to finance and direct the war effort.[7] As the state reconstituted itself to permanent war footing, its relationship with those it governed changed – more-nearly representative government founded on contractual theories of government and with greater popular involvement supplanted divine-right monarchy and aristocratic oligarchy.[8] Running parallel to these changes in government was a consumer revolution, which transformed eighteenth-century England's economy, culture, and society.[9] In an increasingly urban, industrial, and commercial world,[10] the modes of behaviour consonant to an agrarian, hierarchical, pre-modern society became less pertinent: polite modes and manners more suited to new social realities – and the middling orders who embodied them – emerged in their stead.[11]

modern England has been shaped 'by various forms of modernisation theory'. Jonathan Scott, *England's Troubles: Seventeenth-Century English Political Instability in European Context* (Cambridge, 2000), pp. 1–19 complains similarly about the historiography of seventeenth-century English politics. Eighteenth-century British historiography is permeated by modernization theory in ways that earlier periods of British history are not. J.C.D. Clark, *Our Shadowed Present: Modernism, Postmodernism, and History* (2003) and idem, *English Society, 1660–1832: Religion, ideology and politics during the ancien regime* (Cambridge, 2000), pp. 1–42 are the latest, and most persuasive, iterations of Clark's sustained assault on the ahistorical nature of 'presentism', an approach to the past of which modernization theory is characteristic. Graham Good, *Humanism Betrayed: Theory, Ideology, and Culture in the Contemporary University* (Montreal and Kingston, 2001), pp. 63–74 examines the problem of presentism from the perspective of literary theory.

[6] Steven Pincus, '"To protect English liberties": The English nationalist revolution of 1688–1689', in *Protestantism and National Identity: Britain and Ireland, c.1650–c.1850*, eds. Tony Claydon and Ian McBride (Cambridge, 1998), pp. 75–104; idem, 'Whigs, political economy, and the revolution of 1688–89', in *"Cultures of Whiggism": New Essays on English Literature and culture in the Long Eighteenth Century* (Newark, DE, 2005), pp. 62–85.

[7] Lawrence Stone (ed.), *An Imperial State at War: Britain from 1689–1815* (1994); John Brewer, *The Sinews of Power: War, Money and the English State, 1688–1783* (Cambridge, MA, 1990).

[8] Nicholas Rogers, *Crowds, Cultures, and Politics in Georgian Britain* (Oxford, 1998); H.T. Dickinson, *The Politics of the People in Eighteenth-Century Britain* (Basingstoke, 1995).

[9] Maxine Berg, *Luxury and Pleasure in Eighteenth-Century Britain* (Oxford, 2005). John Brewer, 'The birth of consumerism', *TLS* (21 October 2004), p. 3 argues that 'the consumer revolution' project was from its outset 'concerned with the origins and development of something that was considered modern. The search for consumer society was a search for modernity, and the emphasis…was on the first signs of what in its maturity was to be a full-blown, modern consumer society.'

[10] Peter Clark (ed.), *The Cambridge Urban History of Britain, II. 1540–1800* (Cambridge, 2000); Roderick Floud and Paul Johnson (eds.), *The Cambridge Economic History of Modern Britain. Volume 1: Industrialisation, 1700–1860* (Cambridge, 2004).

[11] Lawrence E. Klein, 'Politeness and the Interpretation of the British Eighteenth Century', *HJ* 45:4 (2002), pp. 869–98; Jonathan Barry and Christopher Brooks (eds.), *The Middling Sort of People: Culture, Society and Politics in England, 1550–1800* (New York, 1994). J.C.D. Clark, 'The Re-Enchantment of the World? Religion and Monarchy in Eighteenth-Century Europe', in *Monarchy and Religion: The Transformation of Royal Culture in Eighteenth-Century Europe*, ed. Michael Schaich (Oxford, 2007), p. 49 argues that '[t]he real enemy of the history of…religion was the celebratory study of the "middling sort," the argument that unideological, secular, acquisitive urban man provided the world-view of the eighteenth century and after.'

Similarly, the backward-looking classical republicanism consistent with an agrarian world gave way to theories of statecraft and liberal political economy more appropriate to the modern world.[12] The rapid change to English society was spurred along by the bourgeois public sphere – itself a sign of democratization that both heralded and reflected modernity's advent, the public sphere emerged during the eighteenth century and marked the breach with a benighted past.[13] Perhaps not surprisingly, eighteenth-century English men and women thought of themselves as decidedly different from even their most recent forebears. Improvement was the age's leitmotiv;[14] progress was not only possible, but inevitable;[15] and history stopped being cyclical.[16] At the same time, individual and corporate identities modernised.[17] In particular, war, Protestantism, and commerce forged modern British national and imperial identities.[18] Most of all, though, the

---

[12]   Steven Pincus, 'Neither Machiavellian Moment nor Possessive Individualism: Commercial Society and the Defenders of the English Commonwealth', *AHR* 103:3 (1998), pp. 705–36; idem, 'The Making of a Great Power? Universal Monarchy, Political Economy, and the Transformation of English Political Culture', *The European Legacy* 54:4 (2000), pp. 531–45; and idem, 'From holy cause to economic interest: the study of population and the invention of the state', in *A Nation Transformed*, pp. 272–98.

[13]   Jürgen Habermas, *The Structural Transformation of the Public Sphere: An Inquiry into a Category of Bourgeois Society*, trans. Thomas Burger (Cambridge, MA, 1989) and idem, *The Philosophical Discourse of Modernity: Twelve Lectures*, trans. Frederick Lawrence (Cambridge, MA, 1987), esp. pp. 1–22, 336–67 postulate the emergence of the public sphere. Cf. Peter Lake and Steven Pincus, 'Rethinking the Public Sphere in Early Modern England', *JBS* 45:2 (2006), pp. 270–92. Steven Pincus, '"Coffee Politicians Does Create": Coffeehouses and Restoration Political Culture', *JMH* 67:4 (1995), pp. 807–34 is the most forceful articulation of the idea that coffeehouses were emblematic of the emergence in Britain of 'a public sphere in the Habermasian sense'. Cf. Brian Cowan, 'The Rise of the Coffeehouse Reconsidered', *HJ* 47:1 (2004), pp. 21–46 and idem, *The Social Life of Coffee: The Emergence of the British Coffeehouse* (New Haven, CT, 2005).

[14]   Peter Borsay, 'The Culture of Improvement' in *The Eighteenth Century, 1688–1815*, ed. Paul Langford (Oxford, 2002), pp. 183–210.

[15]   David Spadafora, *The Idea of Progress in Eighteenth-Century Britain* (New Haven, CT, 1990).

[16]   Daniel Woolf, *The Social Circulation of the Past: English Historical Culture, 1500–1730* (Oxford, 2003) and Rosemary Sweet, *Antiquaries: The Discovery of the Past in Eighteenth-Century Britain* (2004) elucidate the development of a modern historical consciousness during the eighteenth century. Their work receives support from Jack Lynch, *The Age of Elizabeth in the Age of Johnson* (Cambridge, 2003); Jonathan Brody Kramnick, *Making the English Canon: Print-Capitalism and the Cultural Past, 1700–1770* (Cambridge, 1998); Karen O'Brien, *Narratives of Enlightenment: Cosmopolitan History from Voltaire to Gibbon* (Cambridge, 1997) and idem, 'History and literature, 1660–1780', in *The Cambridge History of English Literature, 1660–1780*, ed. John Richetti (Cambridge, 2005), pp. 365–90.

[17]   Dror Wahrman, *The Making of the Modern Self: Identity and Culture in Eighteenth-Century England* (New Haven, CT, 2004) anatomizes the passage of 'the *ancien regime* of identity' and the subsequent 'making of the modern self'. See Karen Harvey, 'The Century of Sex? Gender, Bodies, and Sexuality in the Long Eighteenth Century', *HJ* 45:4 (2002), pp. 899–916 for the historiography of eighteenth-century gender and sexual identities.

[18]   On British national identity, see Linda Colley, *Britons: Forging the Nation, 1707–1837* (New Haven, CT, 1992); Tony Claydon and Ian McBride (eds.), *Protestantism and National Identity: Britain and Ireland, c. 1650–c.1850* (Cambridge, 1998); and J.C.D. Clark, 'Protestantism, Nationalism, and National Identity, 1660–1832', *HJ* 43:1 (2000), pp. 249–76. On British imperial identities, see Kathleen Wilson, *Sense of the People: Politics, Culture, and Imperialism*

eighteenth century was post-confessional and increasingly secular.[19] Reason was the Enlightenment's epistemological touchstone, and the distancing from, if not the wholesale rejection of, a providential God marked off the eighteenth century as a brave new world.[20] Distil the last forty years of historiography to its essence, and this is it – the master narrative of eighteenth-century English history is a story of becoming whose *teleos* is modernity.[21] And sceptics of this creation story of the modern world are often charged with being right-wing political and religious reactionaries. Could worse a fate could befall a Western academic than to be

in *England, 1715–1785* (Cambridge, 1995); David Armitage, *The Ideological Origins of the British Empire* (Cambridge, 2000); and Eliga Gould, *The Persistence of Empire: British Political Culture in the Age of the American Revolution* (Chapel Hill, NC, 2000). For the view that the eighteenth-century consumer revolution created an 'empire of goods' and, indeed, that consumption united the American colonists during the 1760s and 1770s in ways that ideology alone did not and could not, see T.H. Breen, *The Marketplace of Revolution: How Consumer Politics Shaped American Independence* (Oxford, 2004). But cf. Gordon Wood, 'The Shopper's Revolution', *NYRB* (10 June 2004), pp. 26–30.

19 C. John Sommerville, *The Secularization of Early Modern England: From Religious Culture to Religious Faith* (Oxford, 1992); Kaspar von Greyerz, 'Secularization in early modern England (1660–c.1750)', *Säkularisierung, Dechristianisierung, Rechristianisierung im neuzeitlichen Europa: Bilanz under Perspektiven der Forschung* (Göttingen, 1997), pp. 86–100; Blair Worden, 'The question of secularization', in *A Nation Transformed*, pp. 20–40. Cf. Jeremy Morris, 'The Strange Death of Christian Britain: Another Look at the Secularization Debate', *HJ* 46:4 (2003), pp. 963–76.

20 B.W. Young, *Religion and Enlightenment in Eighteenth-Century England: Theological Debate from Locke to Burke* (Oxford, 1998), p. 5 points to the 'obsessive iteration of "modernity" as a watchword of Enlightenment', while S.J. Barnett, *The Enlightenment and Religion: The myths of modernity* (Manchester, 2003), p. 1 notes that 'modernity and the Enlightenment are so frequently linked that either term almost automatically invokes the other'. Jonathan Sheehan, 'Enlightenment, Religion, and the Enigma of Secularization: A Review Essay', *American Historical Review* 108:4 (2005), pp. 1061–82 is a perceptive, if idiosyncratic, survey of the historiography on the relationship between the Enlightenment and secularization, while B.W. Young, 'Religious History and the Eighteenth-Century Historians', *HJ* 43:3 (2000), pp. 849–68 examines the secularized historiography of eighteenth-century Britain. Clark, 'The Re-Enchantment of the World?', pp. 56–61 perhaps overestimates the gains made by revisionist historiography in rebutting the secularization paradigm, though he acknowledges that '[d]espite much technical scholarship in the last twenty years, older assumptions are deep-rooted. It is still widely held that…religion, [was] destined for destruction' (p. 71).

21 See also, Robert G. Ingram, 'Sykes's Shadow: Thoughts on the Recent Historiography of the Eighteenth-Century Church of England', *CROMOHS* [http://www.cromohs.unifi.it/seminari/ingram_sykes.html] (2006). Eighteenth-century British historiography is not unique in its fixation on modernity's origins. Brendan McConville, *The King's Three Faces: The Rise and Fall of Royal America, 1688–1776* (Chapel Hill, NC, 2006); Christopher S. Celenza, *The Lost Italian Renaissance: Humanists, Historians, and Latin's Legacy* (Baltimore, 2004); and Philip Benedict, *Christ's Churches Purely Reformed: A Social History of Calvinism* (New Haven, CT, 2002), pp. xv–xxvi, 533–46, for instance, anatomize and lament the suffusion of the historiography of colonial America, Renaissance Italian humanism, and Calvinism by modernization theory. For the uses of 'master narratives', see Allan Megill, '"Grand narrative" and the discipline of history', in *A New Philosophy of History*, eds. Frank Ankersmit and Hans Kellner (Chicago, 1995), pp. 151–73.

lumped in with a band of troglodytic 'historian adherents of high-church orthodoxy'?[22]

I

Eighteenth-century English men and women would have been hard-pressed to obsess about modernity since they did not know what it was. To them *modern* meant 'late, recent, not ancient, not antique', and *moderns* were 'those who have lived lately, opposed to the ancients'. To *modernise* was 'to adapt ancient compositions to modern persons or things'.[23] *Modernity*, denoting a radical break with the past and a purposeful rejection of traditional values and beliefs, is a twentieth-century concept whose application to earlier periods tells us far more about recent historians than it does about the people whom they study.[24]

---

[22] Margaret Jacob and Betty Jo Teeter Dobbs, *Newton and the Culture of Newtonianism* (Atlantic Highlands, NJ, 1995), pp. 100–01 characterize Jonathan Clark, the most notable and incisive critic of the modernity *topos*, in this manner. J.C.D. Clark, 'England's Ancien Regime as a Confessional State', *Albion* 21:3 (1989), pp. 450–74 and idem, 'Providence, Predestination and Progress: or, did the Enlightenment Fail?', *Albion* 35:4 are the most succinct and accessible iterations of his arguments, which are fleshed out most fully in idem, *English Society, 1660–1832*. Among the perceptive rejoinders to Clark's work are Joanna Innes, 'Jonathan Clark, Social history and England's "Ancien Regime"', *PP* 115 (1987), pp. 165–200 and Frank O'Gorman, 'Eighteenth-Century England as an Ancien Regime', in *Hanoverian Britain and Empire: Essays in memory of Philip Lawson*, eds. Stephen Taylor, Richard Connors, and Clyve Jones (Woodbridge, 1998), pp. 23–36, as well as special issues of *Albion* 21:3 (1989) and *Parliamentary History* 7:2 (1988). Clark's approach to the historical problems of the eighteenth century, of course, owes much to the revisionist historiography of seventeenth-century Britain. Ronald Hutton, *Debates in Stuart History* (New York, 2004) is a lively, if idiosyncratic, study of revisionism and the historiography of seventeenth-century Britain; Brian Cowan, 'Refiguring Revisionisms', *History of European Ideas* 29 (2003), pp. 475–512 probes more deeply and provocatively into the subject. One of the frequent complaints of Clark's work in particular and of revisionism more generally is the intellectual association with modern political conservatism, an association which is thought by many to vitiate its value. See, for instance, Patrick Curry, 'Towards a post-Marxist social history: Thompson, Clark and beyond', in *Rethinking social history: English society 1570–1920 and its interpretation*, ed. Adrian Wilson (Manchester, 1992), pp. 158–200 and, more generally, Pincus and Houston, 'Introduction. Modernity and later-seventeenth-century England', pp. 9–10.

[23] Samuel Johnson, *A dictionary of the English language… The eleventh edition* (1799). Insight into the ways the early eighteenth-century English thought about what it meant to be modern can be discerned from the celebrated 'battle of the books', for which see Joseph M. Levine, *The Battle of the Books: History and Literature in the Augustan Age* (Ithaca, NY, 1991) and idem, 'Deists and Anglicans: The Ancient Wisdom and the Idea of Progress', in *The Margins of Orthodoxy: Heterodox Writing and Cultural Response, 1660–1750*, ed. Roger Lund (Cambridge, 1995), pp. 219–39.

[24] The *Oxford English Dictionary* cites 1900 as the first use of *modernity* to signify an 'intellectual tendency or social perspective characterized by departure from or repudiation of traditional ideas, doctrines, and cultural values in favour of contemporary or radical values and beliefs (chiefly those of scientific rationalism and liberalism)'. Cf. Raymond Williams, *Keywords: A Vocabulary*

5

To question whether the eighteenth century was the crucible of modernity is not, however, to imply that it was a period of stasis. It was, in fact, a muddled mess whose k variable often seemed to be change itself. But it was a mess that, for many today, makes sense when fit under the penumbra of *modernity*, for doing so gives the swirling change both meaning and direction. Indeed, part of modernity's attractiveness to historians as an organizing principle is the plausible meaning it gives to a century which eludes easy characterization. More to the point, its appeal rests on its ability to explain presentist concerns.[25] Yet while the 'birth of the modern' project might give eighteenth-century England current relevance, it fails to do it full justice. We need to approach the period not with a *teleos* in mind, not preconceiving it as marking a watershed between the early modern and the modern worlds. We need, instead, actively to pursue the concerns of eighteenth-century English men and women, to allow their problems and analytical categories to take precedence over ours.[26] The story of the period then becomes as much about being, as it does about becoming.[27]

Reform helped the mid-eighteenth-century English to navigate their way ahead through the brume. Indeed, as much as the nineteenth century, the

of *Culture and Society* (Oxford, 1976), pp. 174–75; Zygmunt Bauman, 'Modernity', in *The Oxford Companion to the Politics of the World, 2e*, ed. Joel Krieger (Oxford, 2001), pp. 551–53.

[25] Wahrman, *The Making of the Modern Self*, p. xviii argues, 'I have become increasingly convinced that the explosion of interest in the eighteenth century during the last couple of decades…is not unrelated to the frisson caused by the realization that through studying the eighteenth century we can establish a conversation…between the historical bookends of modernity.' Jane Shaw, 'The long eighteenth century', in *A Century of Theological and Religious Studies in Britain*, ed. Ernest Nicholson (Oxford, 2005), p. 236 reckons this holds true for religious historians as well: 'It may be…that the eighteenth century, which witnessed the birth of modernity, holds a particular fascination for our age, which is witnessing the "death" of modernity, and as we struggle with questions of faith and reason at this particular time, we look to the eighteenth century's own struggles with precisely those issues for insight.' Tim Hitchcock, *Down and Out in Eighteenth-Century London* (2004), pp. 238–40; Joanna Innes, 'Not so Strange? New Views of Eighteenth-Century England', *History Workshop Journal* (1991), p. 183; W.A. Speck, 'Will the Real 18th Century Stand up?', *HJ* 34:1 (1991), pp. 203–06; and Claydon, 'The sermon, the "public sphere" and the political culture of late seventeenth-century England', pp. 226–28 note the difficulties that historians have had integrating the old and the new into a coherent vision of eighteenth-century English history.

[26] H.C. Erik Midelfort, *A History of Madness in Sixteenth-Century Germany* (Stanford, 1999) is a model for historians who take seriously the analytical categories contemporaneous to those under historical investigation. Brad Gregory, *Salvation at the Stake: Christian Martyrdom in Early Modern Europe* (Cambridge, MA, 1999), pp. 1–29 articulates an historical approach to religious belief and practice with which I have much sympathy.

[27] Steven Pincus, 'Reconceiving Seventeenth-Century Political Culture', *JBS* 38:1 (1999), p. 111 laments that revisionist 'Denunciations of the politics of a particular kind of progressive history have become in fact strictures against asking questions about historical change. While we might not, for example, any longer unthinkingly embrace liberalism as a good thing, it seems a shame if we are precluded from asking questions about its origins.' To attempt to understand a period of history in terms its contemporaries used does not preclude asking questions about historical change; it is, instead, merely to say that the first task of the historian is, as accurately as possible, to reconstruct the mental world of the past, without which questions of historical change are impossible to ask.

eighteenth century can lay claim to the mantle 'Age of Reform'.[28] We should be clear, however, what precisely we mean by *reform*. We tend today to think of it purely in terms of *achievement*, which means a scorecard is not far behind. In the eighteenth century that means the Wilkesite movement of the 1760s and 1770s and the Association movement of the 1780s were failures – they advocated expanding the electoral franchise, but they 'failed' because they did not achieve it. Edmund Burke's 'economical reforms' of 1780 were, by contrast, a moderate success. He proposed limiting royal patronage in order to curb corruption and some of his measures passed. More likely, though, our gaze turns ahead to the nineteenth century where Catholic emancipation in 1829 pushed forward the cause of religious toleration and where Reform Acts in 1832, 1867, and 1884 cleaned up the political process and opened up the political arena to those previously cut off from the franchise. Because we, perhaps naturally, seem most interested in measuring the success or failure of reform and because nineteenth-century reform efforts produced easily identifiable results, we have tended to view the eighteenth century as an era of 'failed' reform, a missed opportunity.

With our frozen gaze upon reform as achievement, though, we have too often neglected reform as *aspiration*.[29] To what, we might ask, did eighteenth-century reformers aspire? Most commonly, to restoration or reorientation. An unlikely, but apposite, analogue to eighteenth-century English reform would be the Second Vatican Council, a gathering that also aimed for reform through restoration and reorientation. Those who convened in Rome during the mid 1960s to consider reforms of the Catholic Church took two concepts as their lodestars – *ressourcement* ('to return to the sources') and *aggiornamento* ('bringing up to date'). The two were not competing notions but rather were complementary, indeed tethered, understandings of reform. Together they signified a modernization of the Church fuelled, informed, and delimited by past practices and beliefs.[30]

It was by way of considering Vatican II that Avery Dulles has distinguished between 'true and false reform'. 'To reform is to give new and better form to a pre-existent reality, while preserving the essentials', he argues.

Unlike innovation, reform implies organic continuity; it does not add something foreign or extrinsic. Unlike revolution or transformation, reform respects and retains the substance that was previously there. Unlike development, it implies that something has gone wrong and needs to be corrected. The point of departure for reform is always the idea or institution that is affirmed but considered to have been imperfectly or defectively realized. *The goal is to make persons or institutions more faithful to an ideal already accepted.*[31]

---

[28] Joanna Innes and Arthur Burns, 'Introduction', in *Rethinking the Age of Reform: Britain, 1780–1850*, eds. Arthur Burns and Joanna Innes (Cambridge, 2003), pp. 1–70 suggest what makes the seventy years after 1780 a coherent 'age of reform'.

[29] Ibid., p. 1.

[30] See, for instance, Yves Congar, *The Meaning of Tradition* (San Francisco, CA, 2004).

[31] Avery Cardinal Dulles, 'True and False Reform', *First Things* (Aug/Sept 2003), p. 15. Emphasis mine.

Here Dulles makes a point, and a contested one at that, in a contemporary Catholic debate. Yet his distinction between types of reform is suggestive for our purposes since his understanding of the nature of 'true' reform and the dangers of 'false' reform accords closely with the conventional wisdom held by most during the first three-quarters of the eighteenth century.

As a concept, *reform* had a chequered past in England. Most during the eighteenth century associated it with the bloody decades of the mid seventeenth century when the 'world was turned upside down', when subjects murdered their king, when religious anarchy had been loosed on the country ... all in the name of reform. Those bloody decades had taught the English to fear novelty and 'innovation' – in and of itself, newness was a bad thing. The rehabilitation of reform began in the immediate aftermath of the Glorious Revolution, when societies for the reformation of manners sprang up to promote moral and spiritual reform in English public and private life.[32] So too did the court of William III try to legitimate the new regime by using the language of 'courtly reformation'.[33] By the mid eighteenth century, *reform* was enjoying a genuine renaissance, having come to be associated with ameliorative change, though not with innovation.[34] Yet it was a sensibility, akin to a compass whose true north lay in the past, not a programme for systemic destruction. In Samuel Johnson's *Dictionary*, for instance, *reform* and *reformation* shared the same first definition, 'to change from worse to better'. But not just any kind of change, and *reformation*'s second definition – 'the change of religion from the corruption of popery to its primitive state' – gives a clearer sense of the ways contemporaries understood the concept. On this reading, the Protestant Reformation returned the church to the purer condition of the primitive church and rid it of 'popish corruptions and innovations'. There are, to return to Dulles's suggestive formulation, two modes by which this sort of reform might be pursued. On the one hand, there is *restorative reform*, which 'seeks to reactualize a better past or a past that is idealized', while on the other there is *progressive reform*, which 'aims to move ahead toward an ideal or utopian future'. Neither are transgressive, for neither rejects the past; instead they seek either to

---

[32] D.W.R. Bahlman, *The Moral Revolution of 1688* (New Haven, CT, 1957) remains the standard account of its subject. Martin Ingram, 'Reformation of Manners in Early Modern England', in *The Experience of Authority in Early Modern England*, eds. Paul Griffiths, Adam Fox, and Steve Hindle (Basingstoke, 1996), pp. 47–88 provides useful background.

[33] Tony Claydon, *William III and the Godly Revolution* (Cambridge, 1996).

[34] Joanna Innes, '"Reform" in English public life: the fortunes of a word', in *Rethinking the Age of Reform*, pp. 71–97 argues that Edmund Burke's proposals for economical reform in 1780 signalled a linguistic turn after which reform 'became a slogan for a new political project' and came to be associated with a specific set of institutional changes. Cowan, *The Social Life of Coffee*, demonstrates *inter alia* that the early modern English were inherently suspicious of innovation and that new institutions like the coffeehouse had to be legitimated on grounds other than novelty. For a linguistic analysis of *reform* for a later period, see Derek Beales, 'The Idea of Reform in British Politics, 1829–1850', in *Reform in Great Britain and Germany, 1750–1850*, eds. T.W.C. Blanning and Peter Wende (Oxford, 1999), pp. 159–74. Cf. Williams, *Keywords*, pp. 221–22.

'repristinate' or to transcend the past, while at the same time reaffirming the essential nature and goodness of the thing being reformed.[35]

Perhaps surprisingly, none during the eighteenth century were more concerned about reform than those who led the established Church of England, and this book is about the orthodox reform efforts of Thomas Secker (1693–1768), the polymath archbishop of Canterbury and the Cranmer or Laud figure of the age.[36] Indeed, this study contends that *church reform* is an optic through which we can appreciate more clearly the nature of eighteenth-century English society and historical development. This perspective might perhaps strike one as idiosyncratic, even perverse, for the established Church must surely have been a relic of a God-infused, pre-modern world bent on keeping change at bay and on defending the status quo.

There are, however, good reasons to think that someone like Thomas Secker can provide important insights into eighteenth-century English society. The Church of England was the nation's church as established by law and had, if not a legal monopoly on worship after the Toleration Act of 1689, then a legally privileged status. Even at the dawn of the nineteenth century, the Church maintained at least the nominal allegiance of over ninety per cent of the populace, and it retained a privileged, if not unchallenged or even predominant, social, political, cultural, and intellectual role in eighteenth-century society. English bishops and archbishops kept a close eye on what was going on in society – they had to if they hoped effectively to lead their Church. Many had themselves been parish priests so they knew what life was like in the trenches at the frontline. They had vast networks of correspondents scattered across their dioceses and, indeed, often across Europe and the Atlantic world. They sat at the centre of a spider's web of patronage networks in their dioceses and were themselves part of other, national patronage networks. Their episcopal palaces tended to be diocesan command-and-control centres, where a rump of clerical assistants helped them administer their sees. They roamed the halls of Westminster, where they sat in the House of Lords by right of their office, and they allied themselves closely with the

---

[35]   Dulles, 'True and False Reform', p. 15.

[36]   Jeremy Gregory, 'Secker, Thomas (1693–1768)', *ODNB* and Aldred W. Rowden, *Primates of the Four Georges* (1916), pp. 248–309 are excellent sketches of Secker's life and career. Leslie W. Barnard, *Thomas Secker: An Eighteenth Century Primate* (Lewes, 1998) is the only biography of Secker, but Barnard's almost wholesale reliance on Secker's published works, to the exclusion of his enormous archive of unpublished correspondence and papers, vitiates the book: see my review in *AEH* 69:3 (2000), pp. 376–78. A peculiar set of circumstances that temporarily put crucial portions of Secker's archive at Lambeth Palace off-limits to researchers helps account for the relative neglect of this important figure. In the 1970s, Lambeth Palace commissioned R.W. Greaves to edit Secker's autobiography (LPL, MS 2598). Under the terms of that commission, parts of the Secker archive housed at Lambeth Palace Library were made unavailable to the general public until Greaves finished his study. Unfortunately, Greaves died in the 1980s before being able to complete the scholarly edition of the autobiography, though John McCauley, not himself a specialist in early modern British history, did help bring it to print. See Stephen Taylor, review of *Autobiography, JEH* 41:1 (1990), pp. 173–74. I thank Melanie Barber for this information.

nation's rulers. That means that bishops and archbishops had a pretty clear sense of what was going on in their sees and in the nation at large. It also means that they tended to be sensitive barometers of change who allow us to appreciate more clearly just what transformations were afoot in England during the eighteenth century.

None were more interested in or zealous to reform the institution from within than Thomas Secker. A convert to the Church of England from Dissent, a physician with a Continental education, an opponent of theological heterodoxy and a patron of the theologically orthodox, a renowned preacher and model pastor, a committed Whig with the ear of the nation's rulers, a proponent of an imperial, even international, Anglicanism, and a man whose thirty-four-year career on the episcopal bench allowed him both to formulate and implement religious policy, Thomas Secker had the background, beliefs, ambitions, and professional positions that made him a delicate gauge of societal change. He arrived at Lambeth Palace in the spring of 1758 with a reputation for being a zealous churchman. After the amiable Herring's relaxed decade as archbishop and Hutton's abbreviated tenure, contemporaries were anxious to see what kind of leader he would be. It turned out that he shared the reforming zeal of early-eighteenth-century churchmen like Thomas Tenison,[37] William Wake,[38] and Edmund Gibson.[39] During Secker's time on the episcopal bench, though, we see an acceleration in the pace of and an alteration in the nature of change. The tectonic plates of English society shifted uneasily, and at times violently, during the middle decades of the eighteenth century.[40]

---

[37] G.V. Bennett, 'Archbishop Tenison and the Reshaping of the Church of England', in idem, *To the Church of England*, ed. Geoffrey Rowell (Folkestone, 1988), pp. 99–110. Tellingly, Secker took Tenison for his archiepiscopal model: Bodleian, Add. MS A.269, f. 105: Anonymous note in Edmund Gibson-William Nicholson correspondence, n.d.

[38] Sykes, *William Wake, Archbishop of Canterbury, 1657–1737* (Cambridge, 1957), I, pp. 167–80, 222–29.

[39] Stephen Taylor (ed.), 'Bishop Edmund Gibson's Proposals for Church Reform', in *From Cranmer to Davidson: A Church of England Miscellany*, ed. Stephen Taylor (Woodbridge, 1999), pp. 171–202 is a scholarly edition of LPL, MS 2654, ff. 175–81: 'Ecclesia Anglica: Bishop Gibson's thoughts concerning alterations in it', a record of Gibson's proposals which exists only in a Secker transcription. Norman Sykes, *From Sheldon to Secker: Aspects of English Church History, 1660–1748* (Cambridge, 1959), pp. 192–202 glosses this manuscript. Gibson also led efforts to revive the sixteenth-century *Reformatio legum ecclesiasticarum*: Gerald Bray (ed.), *Tudor Church Reform: The Henrician Canons of 1535 and the Reformatio Legum Ecclesiasticarum* (Woodbridge, 2000), pp. cvi-cvii; idem, 'The Strange Afterlife of the *Reformatio Legum Ecclesiasticarum*', in *English Canon Law: Essays in Honour of Bishop Eric Kemp*, eds. Norman Doe, Mark Hill, and Robert Ombres (Cardiff, 1998), pp. 36–47; J.H. Baker, *Monuments of Endlesse Labours: English Canonists and their Work, 1300–1900* (1998), pp. 95–107.

[40] Bob Harris, *Politics and the Nation: Britain in the Mid-Eighteenth Century* (Oxford, 2002) nicely captures the turbulence of mid-eighteenth-century Britain. He argues that the eighteenth-century English lived in 'a world of insecurity and challenge' which led many of them to conclude that 'God had an argument with his chosen nation'. In response to the various international and domestic crises, The English conceived the need for a 'national revival', which entailed both 'moral and social reform' (pp. 6, 10, 16).

II

Thomas Secker's reforming sensibility was entirely of a piece with his age. He was no reactionary who damned reform as an inherently bad thing. But when humans tried to bring about change, he advocated that they be careful and mindful of avoiding 'innovation'. Consider, for instance, his thoughts on political reform, as expressed in a 30 January sermon in 1734. Of those who executed Charles I, he lamented, 'Thus were too many of our predecessors in this nation disposed: extremely miserable under a constitution of government, which they found too late inseparable from their happiness; and so earnest to reform every part of it, that they ruined the whole.' It would be better instead, he continued, to 'esteem [government] then as we ought, and be zealous to preserve it; improve it, if we can really and safely; but not be forward to practice upon it without necessity or some very valuable end. Hoping for perfection in any human thing, is visionary; and murmering for want of it, is resolving never to be happy; and taking irregular methods to obtain it, is the sure way to be wretched.' Certainly time and the change in circumstances might necessitate '[s]ome alterations...but that no wanton or doubtful, much less dangerous trials, ought to be made, the fatal experience of this day fully shews'.[41] Political change, when necessary, should be brought about incrementally, cautiously, and with an eye to the past.

These guiding principles applied equally to religious reform. Secker admitted forthrightly that the established Church stood in need of improvement. 'I am far from being insensible, that our Ecclesiastical Establishment needs to be reformed and improved. And I am far from being against all Efforts at Amendment', he assured a correspondent.[42] His lodestar for church reform, though, was the primitive church, not some platonic ideal of ecclesiastical, liturgical, and theological perfection.[43] 'We must always endeavour not only to maintain the form of the ancient system, but also to restore its strength, as far as divine and human allow,' Secker counselled, and he praised 'those means [by which] the doctors in the first centuries flourished, and the same means are entrusted to us. There is no other way to be respected, and if other ways forward exist, we would not serve the interest of men or attain to eternal life by following them.'[44] Religious amendment,

---

[41]   'Sermon CXXVII. On Reverence of Divine Providence in Governing All the Affairs of Men. A sermon preached in the parish church of St James, Westminster, January 30. 1733–34. [Isaiah 26:9]', in *WTS*, III, pp. 429–30.

[42]   LPL, Secker Papers 7, ff. 150–51: Secker to Theophilus Alexander, 4 Dec 1762.

[43]   On primitive Christianity in eighteenth-century England, see Eamon Duffy, 'Primitive Christianity Revived; Religious Renewal in Augustan England', *SCH* 14 (1977), pp. 287–300; Robert D. Cornwall, 'The Search for the Primitive Church: The Use of Early Church Fathers in the High Church Anglican Tradition, 1680–1745', *AEH* 59:3 (1990), pp. 303–29; Peter Doll, *After the Primitive Christians: The Eighteenth-Century Anglican Eucharist in its Architectural Setting* (Cambridge, 1997); John C. English, 'The Duration of the Primitive Church: An Issue for Seventeenth- and Eighteenth-Century Anglicans', *AEH* 73:1 (2004), pp. 35–52.

[44]   *Oratio*, pp. 361, 366.

when necessary, must be informed by and founded on historical precedent and principle.

Secker acknowledged the possibility of religious improvement. At the level of the individual, he extolled the 'reformation from sin, or improvement in goodness'.[45] It was at the institutional level, though, that his doctrine of religious improvement was most evident and, for our purposes, most relevant. He was, for instance, certain that the established Church of England was the only visible and apostolic church in the British Isles and believed that the Reformation had purified the institution of Roman Catholic corruptions. The Roman church had perverted Christ's teachings so egregiously that 'the instances...of Popish ursurpation, treachery, and cruelty, in every nation of Europe, every nation upon earth, in which popery hath got footing, have been so numerous, that the time would fail me even to name them', he assured an audience at St Mary's, Lambeth, on 5 November 1758.[46] Abandoning *sola scriptura* and the original teachings of the primitive church, the Roman church carried the blame for 'burying every part of religion under a load of rites and ceremonies, that turn it into outward show; and giving it the appearance of art magic by an infinity of absurd superstitions'.[47] In the early sixteenth century, though, the Protestant reformers cleansed the English church, removing centuries of corrupting practices and beliefs, leading Secker to argue that the Church of England had greater claim to catholicity than its Roman counterpart: 'Do we not profess the true catholic faith, that faith which the universal church received from the apostles? We profess it much purer than they.'[48] Elsewhere he contended that, 'The Catholic Church is then the universal Church, spread through the World; and the Catholic Faith is the universal Faith; that Form of Doctrine which the Apostles delivered to the whole Church, and it received.' By these criteria, it was evident to him that the Roman church was but 'one diseased Limb' of the Catholic church, while the Church of England was 'undoubtedly a sound and excellent Member of it'.[49] The Reformation was but the most obvious example of religious progress and improvement in English religious history, and Secker's reform vision was founded on the belief that the established Church of England could improve, if reform were pursued prudently and carefully, using the primitive church as its touchstone.[50] Yet implicit in Secker's vision of

---

[45] 'Sermon XC. The Liberality of the Gospel Scheme, in the Contempt of Partial Distinctions [Galatians 6:15]', in *WTS*, II, p. 568.

[46] 'Sermon CXXXVII. Persecution a decisive evidence of an unchristian spirit. Preached in the parish church of St Mary, Lambeth, November 5, 1758 [John 16:2–3]', in *WTS*, IV, p. 24.

[47] 'Sermon CI. The Sacred Scriptures the only infallible rule of faith and practice [1 Peter 5:12]', in *WTS*, III, p. 93.

[48] 'Sermon CII. The Sacred Scriptures the only infallible rule of faith and practice [1 Peter 5:12]', in *WTS*, III, p. 97.

[49] *Lectures*, p. 113.

[50] Peter Nockles, 'A Disputed Legacy: Anglican Historiographies of the Reformation from the era of the Caroline Divines to that of the Oxford Movement', *BJRL* 83:1 (2001), pp. 121–67 and idem, 'Anglicanism "Represented" or "Misrepresented"? The Oxford Movement, Evangelicalism, and History: The Controversial Use of the Caroline Divines in the Victorian Church of England', in *Victorian Churches and Churchmen: Essays Presented to Vincent Alan*

religious progress was also the idea that the Reformation, and reform itself, would necessarily be unfinished business, that real reform was an destination that might never be reached.[51]

There were, of course, different ways of looking to the past for solutions or legitimation and, therefore, different criteria for judging progress and improvement. Some we might anachronistically call 'radical' reformers found in the past justification for alterations to the religio-political order. Mid-century parliamentary reformers, for instance, argued for an expansion of the franchise on the basis of political rights found either in the ancient constitution or in the primeval state of nature.[52] Likewise, latitudinarians like John Jones and Francis Blackburne did not argue that their proposed religious reforms were innovations but rather insisted that they accorded with original biblical practice.[53] Orthodox Anglican reformers were little different: they found their reforming inspiration in the primitive church, the church of the apostolic and patristic fathers.

What exactly did it mean to be *orthodox* during the mid eighteenth century? Labelling mid-century religious groups is fraught with terminological difficulties, so that it is better to think in terms of religious tendencies rather than coherent religious parties.[54] Samuel Johnson defined *orthodox* as being 'sound in opinion and doctrine; not heretical'; *heresy*, against which orthodoxy was defined, was 'an opinion of private men different from that of the catholic or orthodox church'; and *heterodoxy*, orthodoxy's mirror image, was 'deviating from the established

McClelland, ed. Sheridan Gilley (Woodbridge, 2005), pp. 308–69 examine the contested interpretations of the Reformation by various English religious groups in the late eighteenth and early nineteenth centuries.

[51] Jeremy Gregory's pioneering work on England's Long Reformation (whose 'complete success could never have been achieved') is at once highly instructive and suggestive in this regard. In particular, see Jeremy Gregory, *Restoration, Reformation and Reform, 1660–1828: Archbishops of Canterbury and their Diocese* (Oxford, 2000); idem, 'The Making of a Protestant Nation: "Success" and "Failure" in England's Long Reformation', in *England's Long Reformation, 1500–1800*, ed. Nicholas Tyacke (1998), pp. 307–33; and idem, 'The eighteenth-century Reformation: the pastoral task of the Anglican clergy after 1689', in *The Church of England, c.1689–c.1833: From Toleration to Tractarianism*, eds. John Walsh, Colin Haydon, and Stephen Taylor (Cambridge, 1993), pp. 67–85.

[52] Ian R. Christie, *Wilkes, Wyvill and Reform: The Parliamentary Reform Movement in British Politics, 1760–1785* (1962).

[53] John Jones, *Free and candid disquisitions relating to the Church of England, and the means of advancing religion therein. Addressed to the governing powers in church and state; and more immediately directed to the two Houses of Convocation*, 3rd edn (Dublin, 1750); Francis Blackburne, *The Confessional: or, A full and free inquiry into the right, utility, edification, and success, of establishing systematical confessions of faith and doctrine in Protestant Churches*, 3rd edn (1766).

[54] S.J.C. Taylor, 'Church and State in England in the Mid-Eighteenth Century: The Newcastle Years, 1742–1762' (University of Cambridge Ph.D. thesis, 1987), pp. 215–16; John Walsh and Stephen Taylor, 'Introduction: the Church and Anglicanism in the "long" eighteenth century', in *The Church of England, c.1689–c.1833*, pp. 29–45; and William Gibson, *The Church of England, 1688–1832: Unity and Accord* (2000) illustrate the slipperiness of contemporary religious labels. For the clarity of labels and groupings in a subsequent period, see W.J. Coneybeare, 'Church Parties', ed. Arthur Burns, in *From Cranmer to Davidson*, pp. 213–385.

opinion'. All of this, however, begs the question of what were the standards for soundness of doctrine and catholicity, the answer to which is not to be found in contemporary lexicography.

Much like *Puritan* and *Puritanism* in an earlier period, *orthodox* and *orthodoxy* could be pejorative terms used by one group to tar its opponents.[55] Latitudinarians commonly accused the orthodox of being crypto-papists. 'Hence it became a very difficult thing for an orthodox member of the church of England to attack the church of Rome on any article, without exposing his own church to a disagreeable recrimination', the latitudinarian divine Francis Blackburne contended.[56] In the minds of his opponents, the orthodox cleric was a rigid dogmatic who yearned for 'more Power to enforce our present Canons and Rubricks, or to pin down his subjects to orthodox practice and Profession so called'.[57] And in their application of the established canons and rubrics, the orthodox were supposedly wholly unmoored from principle: 'The scrupulous mortal always labours under an infirmity of mind: the learned, orthodox, and established casuist or confessor, has no such feelings,' Blackburne inveighed.[58] Friend and foe alike considered Thomas Secker to be one of the more notable (or notorious) orthodox figures of the century. His inveterate enemy Blackburne groused that Secker 'was too earnest for his justification to leave his orthodoxy upon conjecture' and that he had 'a predeliction for popish discipline and popish intolerance'.[59] And Blackburne's son later reckoned that Secker 'was animated with the spirit of Laud' and complained of the vindictiveness against his father 'by that part of the clergy who affect to call themselves orthodox'.[60]

As with the seventeenth-century anti-Calvinist descriptions of Puritans, the latitudinarian descriptions of the orthodox should be taken with a grain of salt. Certainly Blackburne and his heterodox kindred were correct that mid-eighteenth-century orthodoxy entailed a defence of old truths (the Apostles' and Nicene Creeds, the Thirty-Nine Articles, the rubric as spelled out in the Book of Common Prayer, for instance). In depicting the orthodox as being unbending, inflexible, and, by implication, unimaginative, though, they over-egged the pudding. For, as J.G.A. Pocock rightly suggests, eighteenth-century orthodoxy, like

---

[55] Peter Lake, 'Anti-Puritanism: The Structure of a Prejudice', in *Religious Politics in Post-Reformation England: Essays in Honour of Nicholas Tyacke*, eds. Kenneth Fincham and Peter Lake (Woodbridge, 2006), pp. 80–97.

[56] Francis Blackburne, *Memoirs of Thomas Hollis* (1780), I, p. 230.

[57] DWL, MS 12.52 (no. 58): Francis Blackburne to Theophilus Lindsey, Jan 1759.

[58] Francis Blackburne, *An historical view of the controversy concerning an intermediate state and the separate existence of the soul between death and general resurrection, deduced from the beginning of the Protestant Reformation to the present times. With some thoughts, in a prefatory discourse, on the use and importance of theological controversy*, 2nd edn(1772), p. lxvii.

[59] Blackburne, *Memoirs of Hollis*, I, p. 228.

[60] Francis Blackburne, *The works, Theological and Miscellaneous, ... of Francis Blackburne ... With some account of the life and writings of the author, by himself, completed by his son, Francis Blackburne, L.L.B., and illustrated by an appendix of original papers* (Cambridge, 1804), I, pp. xxxiii, xxxvi.

reform, was a sensibility regarding change. 'Orthodoxy is not a mere rejection of tensions or an attempt to freeze or deny them; it was a particular way of responding to tensions and seeking to recombine them,' Pocock reckons, 'and this was no less so where it was conservative in the sense that its aimed at maintaining durable and traditional positions.'[61] This point is absolutely crucial to keep in mind, for it usefully reminds us that achieving the aims of eighteenth-century orthodox church reform – conservation, affirmation, and restoration – *necessarily* required flexibility, adaptation, negotiation, and change. In short, no reform, no orthodoxy. Or, as John Henry Newman, one of Secker's unlikely religious heirs, would later famously argue, 'In a higher world it is otherwise, but here below to live is to change, and to be perfect is to have changed often.'[62]

III

Eighteenth-century Anglican church reform is at present a virtual 'non-subject'.[63] To appreciate what church reform entailed requires a consideration of more than figures for clerical residence, provision of the Eucharist, or parish economies. Indeed, Secker's career suggests that church reform could involve much more than the pastoral. In his case, it meant combating those who challenged durable Christian truths. It meant promoting a new translation of the English Bible and being a generous patron of orthodox scholars. It meant working with politicians to protect the ancient rights and privileges of the established Church, but it also meant standing up to his political masters from time to time. It meant meddling in

---

61   J.G.A. Pocock 'Within the margins: the definitions of orthodoxy', in *The Margins of Orthodoxy*, p. 35. Peter B. Nockles, 'Church parties in the pre-Tractarian Church of England, 1750–1833: the 'Orthodox'–some problems of definition and identity', in *The Church of England, c.1689–c.1833*, pp. 334–59 elucidates the meanings of *orthodoxy* for a subsequent period. Cf. Jeffrey S. Chamberlain, 'Moralism, Justification, and the Controversy over Methodism', *JEH* 44:4 (1993), pp. 652–78 on the beliefs of 'mainstream Anglicans' and Ian Green, *Print and Protestantism in Early Modern England* (Oxford, 2000), pp. 557–63 on the theological composition of 'orthodox Protestantism'.

62   John Henry Newman, *An Essay on the Development of Christian Doctrine*, ed. Charles Frederick Harrold (1949), p. 38.

63   Taylor (ed.), 'Bishop Edmund Gibson's Proposals for Church Reform', p. 171. Attention to reform fits uneasily into conventional narratives of English religious history. Constructed by anticlerical contemporaries, endorsed and expanded upon by Victorian reformers, the view of the eighteenth-century Church of England as a torpid institution staffed primarily by trimming vicars of Bray or squarson Woodefordes became conventional wisdom and, despite evidence to the contrary, continues to have legs. Reform has little place in this critical narrative, which emphasizes the Church's worldliness, ineptitude, and corruption. Within the last three decades, a vibrant revisionist critique–one which takes a functionalist approach but which judges the results against the standards of the time–has emerged. These countervailing revisionist narratives, though, have themselves admitted scarce room for a consideration of church reform. Indeed, one gets the sense from much revisionist historiography that the Church was doing its job so well that there was little need for serious alterations, that the institution adapted itself easily to changing circumstances, or that few contemporaries called for reform.

the affairs of Oxford. It meant giving one-third of his income to the poor and badgering the rich to give as much or more to the needy. It meant getting into the pulpit to warn the nation about God's wrath and advising them how they might avoid it. It agitating for the introduction of Anglican bishops in North America. It meant trying to Christianize and Anglicanize Indians and slaves there. What tethered together these seemingly disparate activities was a capacious vision for *orthodox church reform* which aimed to improve the eighteenth-century Church by restoring the practices, teachings, and spirit of the primitive church. It was a back-to-the-future solution. Understanding this requires that we expand the history of church reform in eighteenth-century England beyond the confines of the parish or the diocese.

It also requires that we examine eighteenth-century orthodox church reform on its own terms, rather than survey it from nineteenth-century heights. There was no eighteenth-century analogue to the Ecclesiastical Commission, nor anything like the legislative initiatives of the late 1820s and 1830s which recast church-state relations.[64] The absence of systemic reform has led some to argue that eighteenth-century church reform either did not exist or that it did and failed miserably anyway. Some historians put reform's failure or absence down to the fact that this was an 'age of negligence' in the institution's history;[65] others argue that the Church's leaders suffered from a failure of imagination;[66] and still others blame the paralysis of caution.[67] All of this, though, is to conceive of form in an unduly constricted way and to judge the Church by what came later.[68] Mid-eighteenth-

---

[64] The best treatments of nineteenth-century church reform are Arthur Burns, *The Diocesan Revival in the Church of England, c. 1800–1870* (Oxford, 1999); G.F.A. Best, *Temporal Pillars: Queen Anne's Bounty, the Ecclesiastical Commissioners, and the Church of England* (Cambridge, 1962); Olive J. Brose, *Church and Parliament: The Reshaping of the Church of England, 1828–1860* (Stanford, 1959); Kenneth Thompson, *Bureaucracy and Church Reform: The Organizational Response of the Church of England to Social Change, 1800–1965* (Oxford, 1970).

[65] Peter Virgin, *The Church of England in an Age of Negligence: Ecclesiastical Structure and Problems of Church Reform, 1700–1840* (Cambridge, 1989); Ernest Gordon Rupp, *Religion in England, 1688–1791* (Oxford, 1986), p. 504.

[66] Michael Snape, *The Church of England in Industrialising Society: the Lancashire Parish of Whalley in the Eighteenth Century* (Woodbridge, 2003); Donald Spaeth, *The Church in an Age of Danger: Parsons and Parishioners, 1660–1740* (Cambridge, 2000); idem, '"The enemy within": the failure of reform in the diocese of Salisbury in the eighteenth century', in *The National Church in Local Perspective*, pp. 121–44.

[67] Sykes, *From Sheldon to Secker*, p. x.

[68] Joanna Innes and John Styles, 'The crime wave: recent writing on crime and criminal justice in eighteenth-century England', *JBS* 25:4 (1986), p. 383 argue that the study of many eighteenth-century British institutions have suffered from the 'reform perspective', a teleological approach that judges an institution by reforms implemented later. In this regard, the lasting taint of Victorian censure of the eighteenth-century Church of England cannot be underestimated. B.W. Young, '"Knock-Kneed Giants": Victorian Representations of Eighteenth Century Thought', in *Revival and Religion since 1700: Essays for John Walsh*, eds. Jane Garnet and Colin Matthew (1993), pp. 79–84 illuminates the various 'prejudices and blindspots' among those nineteenth-century critics of the Georgian Church. Maurice Cowling, *Religion and Public Doctrine in Modern England* (Cambridge, 1985), II, pp. 3–100 comes at the problem from a slightly different

century church reform could not look like Victorian church reform because the social, cultural, intellectual, and political conditions in the mid eighteenth century differed completely from those of the early nineteenth century. As such, we can no more blame Secker for not having thought like a Victorian church reformer than we can blame the Elizabethan navy for having invested insufficiently in nuclear submarine technology.[69]

Thomas Secker's life and career offer neither an unobstructed nor an unjaundiced perspective on the age. Nonetheless, viewing the period through his eyes distorts far less than viewing it through the kaleidoscope of modernity.[70] To look at the age from this perspective is to appreciate more fully its overwhelming uncertainty. Eighteenth-century English men and women did not drive toward the bright future of the modern with their eyes on an evenly paved, clearly lighted, unobstructed road. They drove instead with one eye in the rear-view mirror, looking back to a well-lit world whose certainties they knew, and at times feared, and with the other eye on the road ahead trying to peer through a thick fog of uncertainty that was their future. We might know what lay down the road when the fog cleared, but they had no road map and did not know exactly where they were heading. We would do well to sit next to them in the passenger's seat, to view they world as they did, with all its uncertainties, anxieties, and hopes.

What we see is a world defined by God and by war. Eighteenth-century England remained a profoundly religious society. It was, in the narrowest sense, a confessional state with a church established by law. Most English men and women were Anglican, even more were Christian and believed that they lived in God's 'new Israel'. That belief in England's providential destiny only intensified during the late eighteenth and early nineteenth centuries with the decisive defeat of Napoleon's France and the remarkable expansion of the empire. Yet England's confessional state – and the possibilities of orthodox church reform – shrank markedly as a result of war. For by catalyzing religious liberalization, war redefined the state's confessional nature and neutered orthodox reform. Indeed, far more than any -ism or -isation, war transformed eighteenth-century England. Like a gigantic glacier on the move, it slowly, deeply, violently, and, at times, unpredictably tore across the era, leaving little untouched and nothing unchanged.

direction. William Gibson, *The Achievement of the Anglican Church, 1689–1800: The Confessional State in Eighteenth-Century England* (Lewiston, 1996), pp. 5–31 and idem, *The Church of England, 1688–1832: Unity and Accord* (2001), pp. 4–27 highlight the resilience of the Victorian criticism of the Georgian Church.

[69] Arthur Burns, 'English "church reform" revisited, 1780–1840', in *Rethinking the Age of Reform*, pp. 136–62 argues that the 1780s was an axial moment in the concept of *church reform*: 'the terms of "reformation", which the mid-eighteenth century would have been readily available to denote a change involving an internalised moral aspect of the kind implied in a growth of "zeal", [stood] in contrast to the institutional adaptations now more readily associated with the language of "church reform".' See also, idem, '"Standing in the Old Ways": Historical Legitimation of Church Reform in the Church of England, c.1825–65', *SCH* 32 (1997), pp. 407–22.

[70] Brad S. Gregory, 'The Other Confessional History: On Secular Bias in the Study of Religion', *History and Theory* 45:4 (2006), pp. 132–49.

This was Thomas Secker's England, less a world we have lost than one we have forgot.

Chapter Two

BECOMING AN ANGLICAN

Thomas Secker might seem an unlikely Anglican church reformer, not least because he was not reared an Anglican. Instead, he was brought up a Presbyterian and at some point early on espoused Arianism. Why this heterodox nonconformist became an orthodox churchman bears explaining first. He certainly did not blaze new trails in his journey away from nonconformity: the depletion of their ranks, particularly of ministerial candidates like Secker, worried Dissenters during the early eighteenth century. Yet those Protestant nonconformists who conformed to the established Church rarely explained their confessional conversions, leaving hostile contemporaries to impute to them less than flattering motives. This was certainly true of Secker, and, indeed, the closer one gets to the sparse archival record of his early life, the more opaque become both the motive and chronology of his defection. Nonetheless his transit from Dissent to Anglicanism helps to explain some of the salient features of his orthodox reform vision. It also highlights the causes and consequences of the intellectual, political, and religious tumult that so defined the first part of the eighteenth century. For Thomas Secker became an Anglican during an age in which religious pluralism had only recently been legalized, in which religion factionalized the nation's politics, and in which heterodoxy bloomed. His mature religious views forged during this era, Secker took away from it the lesson that errant belief was always something to be confronted head on because if left unanswered, it could horribly contaminate the Church of England and could eat away at the ties which bound church and state together.

Thomas Secker's critics often used his Dissenting background as a cudgel with which to beat him. 'This ArchBp. is a very worthy & honest Man,' thought William Cole, the antiquarian rector of Bletchley, 'but being bred a Dissenter, & among them, contracted such a whining, snivelling & canting Manner, as he never could throw off when he was advanced to the greatest Dignity this Church could afford.'[1] John Gooch, canon of Ely, inelegantly rhymed, 'Where Secker the decent, will go, we can't tell:/But our Tewkesbury Folks will tell you, to Hell,/For deserting the Kirk.'[2] Secker's critics particularly played up his youthful heterodoxy. Cole, for instance, suggested that 'Mr. Secker's Opinions...were wholly deistical'

---

[1] BL, Add. MS 5831, f. 219. Edward Hasted, *The History and Topographical Survey of the County of Kent* (Canterbury, 1797–1801), XIII, p. 511 echoes Cole.

[2] BL, Add. MS 5831, f. 191. In his 'Epilogue to the Satires. Written in 1738, *Dialogue II*', Alexander Pope had written of the circle of friends to whom Secker belonged, 'Ev'n in a Bishop I can spy Desert,/Secker is decent, Rundel has a Heart,/Manners with candour are to Benson giv'n,/To Berkeley, ev'ry Virtue under Heav'n?': Alexander Pope, *Imitations of Horace and An Epistle to Dr. Arbuthnot, and the Epilogue to the Satires*, ed. John Butt (New Haven, CT, 1953), pp. 316–17.

up to a year before he decided to conform.[3] Horace Walpole went even further, arguing that while a student at Oxford, Secker 'was President of an Atheistical Club';[4] the day after Secker's death, he gibed that the archbishop 'had never been a Papist, but almost everything else'.[5] Francis Blackburne explained Secker's orthodoxy as a calculated compensation for the heterodoxy of his youth. 'It was his business to establish a good opinion of his sincerity among his brethren of the establishment at all events,' Blackburne contended, 'which could not be done by such a convert from dissenting principles at so late an hour, but by an apparent zeal for the maxims of church government, and against every attempt to reform the prevailing church system.'[6] In a private letter to John Wiche, Blackburne hinted at even darker secrets in Secker's past. Secker, he assured Wiche, had

> ...held a correspondence with a person of Freedom of thinking, in which he opened himself on the subject of Liberty with so little reserve as to bring himself under suspicions of believing less than his Profession required. The correspondent died, after the elevation of the great man; whose letters by the means of a Trust fell into the hands of a person of real honour who just look'd into them sufficiently to discover their Import; and being then in some acquaintance with the great man, sealed them up and sent them to him, and you may believe he never received a more acceptable present in is Life, except the Crown with two tops. But this is not the hold I have, that is in black and white, an autograph in my custody, and were not the welfare and Peace, of another particular Friend in the Case; it had ere made its appearance.[7]

Following Blackburne's lead, Gilbert Wakefield described Secker as 'a prelate, who thought himself bound, after the example of all profligate converts, to recede as far as possible from the tolerant principles of his dissenting education, that he might remove every suspicion…"of hankering after his old deviations"'. In the event his readers missed the point about Secker's motives, Wakefield likened him to the murderous biblical king Hazael and recounted mockingly how the young Secker responded 'with indignant earnestness' to a suggestion that he would one day adopt Anglicanism out of raw ambition: 'Conform I never can.'[8] To many of his detractors, then, Thomas Secker displayed the zeal of a convert, championing orthodoxy and thwarting ecclesiastical reform to dispel criticism of his heterodox past.

---

[3] BL, Add. MS 5817, f. 192v.
[4] LWL, Horace Walpole's Commonplace Book, II, f. 109. See also, Walpole, *Memoirs of George II*, I, p. 45.
[5] Quoted in James Boswell, *Life of Johnson*, ed. George Birckbeck Hill (Oxford, 1934), IV, p. 29 n. 1.
[6] Francis Blackburne, *Memoirs of Thomas Hollis* (1780), I, p. 227.
[7] DWL, MS 12.45 (no. 100): Blackburne to Wiche, 23 Jan 1767.
[8] Gilbert Wakefield, *The memoirs of the life of Gilbert Wakefield* (1792), pp. 164–65, 166. For the story of Hazael, see 2 Kings 8–13.

In the end, no unified field theory explains when, how, and why Thomas Secker changed his spiritual allegiances and beliefs.[9] Neither naked self-interest nor dogged adherence to principle alone can account for his abandonment of Dissent. Rather, his decisions were shaped at times by principle, at others by careerism, and at others by sheer chance. He was, in other words, like most human beings in being formed and torn by a host of influences.

I

The salient feature of religious life in the England of Thomas Secker's youth was that it was voluntary. Dashing the hopes of those Anglican clergy who steadfastly supported their cause during the 1640s and 1650s, the Stuarts were bent on extending religious toleration, even to Roman Catholics.[10] This was a bridge too far for most of the political nation, who cashiered James II and replaced him on the throne in 1689 with his son-in-law and daughter, William and Mary. Many devoted Anglicans soon realized that the nation had swapped a Roman Catholic monarch determined to impose total religious indulgence for a Dutch Calvinist one determined to put religious disputes quickly to bed so that he could focus on war with the French. His religious theories of monarchy and human society proved irrelevant at the revolution, the hotter sort of Anglican bore the further indignity of having his church 'partially disestablished' by the Toleration Act (1689).[11] Originally intended as a companion to a comprehension bill, the 'Act for exempting their Majesties Protestant subjects, dissenting from the Church of England, from the penalties of certain laws' passed into law without its companion.[12] Anglicans understood the act to apply to the small minority who

---

[9] The extant sources for Secker's early life raise significant interpretative problems. While his substantial archive covers nearly every important aspect of his public life, strikingly little remains to document his first three decades. There is, instead, only brief correspondence between him and his family, contemporary reports in which he is mentioned, and an autobiography. Even those sources that do touch on Secker's early life are problematic. Nowhere in his correspondence, for instance, does he explain in any detail why he conformed to the Church of England, and his autobiography is strikingly perfunctory regarding his spiritual development. Secker's autobiography bears little resemblance to the introspective spiritual autobiographies penned by his evangelical contemporaries: D. Bruce Hindmarsh, *The Evangelical Conversion Narrative: Spiritual Autobiography in Early Modern England* (Oxford, 2005).

[10] For the Restoration Church, see John Spurr, *The Restoration Church of England, 1646–1689* (New Haven, CT, 1991) and R.A. Beddard, 'The Restoration Church', in *The Restored Monarchy, 1660–1688*, ed. J.R. Jones (1979), pp. 155–75. Alexandra Walsham, *Charitable Hatred: Tolerance and Intolerance in England, 1500–1700* (Manchester, 2006) is the most reliable treatment of early modern English religious toleration.

[11] G.V. Bennett, 'Conflict in the Church', *Britain after the Glorious Revolution, 1689–1714*, ed. Geoffrey Holmes (1969), pp. 155–75.

[12] David L. Wykes, 'Introduction: Parliament and dissent from the Restoration to the twentieth century', *Parliament and Dissent*, eds. Stephen Taylor and David L. Wykes (Edinburgh, 2005), pp. 1–26 and Geoffrey Nuttall, '"The Sun-Shine of Liberty": The Toleration Act and the

could not reconcile themselves to the established Church, while Dissenters understood the act as a reprieve from many of the legal disabilities that had attended their nonconformity. Many Anglicans were thus bewildered at the rush of requests for licenses to open Dissenting meeting houses. They recognized belatedly that the levee had been breached, and the next century was to be spent trying to hold off the deluge. All told, the act 'marked the end of the Church of England's claim to be the national church, the single all-inclusive church of the English people, after almost thirty years of struggle'.[13] After 1689, the Church had to compete for members: as an institution, it had inherent market advantages, but the fact nevertheless remained that religious pluralism was legalized after the Glorious Revolution.

Not surprisingly, many Anglicans did not reconcile themselves easily or quietly to the revolutionary religious settlement, meaning that religio-political factionalization marked a second important feature of post-revolutionary English religious life.[14] Many in the Church found ways to come to grips with the new state of affairs. Some low churchmen argued for the church and state as separate but equal, independent but intertwined; but many increasingly propounded the erastian view that the church was subordinate to the state.[15] In general, low churchmen became the clerical arm of the Whig party. Other Anglicans, though, were unable to jettison so easily theories of divine right hereditary monarchy and of the organic link between crown and church. The revolution had 'made a mockery' of the high church doctrines of passive obedience, non-resistance, and divine right. The vocal few who were stung by 'so blatant a denial of [their] political creed' as to be unable in conscience to take the new oaths of allegiance and supremacy were deprived of their livings.[16] For those high churchmen who, through some or another mental contortion, reconciled themselves to the new

Ministry', *Journal of the United Reformed Church History Society* 4:4 (1989), pp. 239–55 examine the act and its effects on Dissenters.

[13] Spurr, *Restoration Church of England*, p. 105.

[14] See, for instance, Craig Rose, *England in the 1690s: Revolution, Religion and War* (Oxford, 1999), pp. 152–94; G.V. Bennett, *Tory Crisis in Church and State, 1688–1730: the career of Francis Atterbury, Bishop of Rochester* (Oxford, 1975); Geoffrey Holmes, *Religion and Party in Late Stuart England* (1975).

[15] William Gibson, *Enlightenment Prelate: Benjamin Hoadly, 1676–1761* (Cambridge, 2004); Rebecca Louise Warner, 'Early Eighteenth Century Low Churchmanship: The Glorious Revolution to the Bangorian Controversy' (University of Reading Ph.D. thesis, 1999), pp. 152–220; Stephen Taylor, 'William Warburton and the Alliance of Church and State', *JEH* 43:2 (1992), pp. 271–86; R.W. Greaves, 'The Working of an Alliance: A Comment on Warburton', in *Essays in Modern English Church History, in memory of Norman Sykes*, eds. G.V. Bennett and J.D. Walsh (Oxford, 1966), pp. 163–80. See also, Andrew Starkie, *The Church of England and the Bangorian Controversy, 1716–1721* (Woodbridge, 2007).

[16] Geoffrey Holmes, *The Trial of Doctor Sacheverell* (1973), p. 22. See also, Robert Cornwall, *Visible and Apostolic: The Constitution of the Church in High Church Anglican and Nonjuror Thought* (1993); George Every, *The High Church Party, 1688–1718* (1956), pp. 61–74; and John Overton, *The Nonjurors* (1902).

oaths,[17] the anger at what had been done to their church did not soon pass, and 'rage of party' between 1690 and 1714 was fuelled in large part by high church rhetoric about the 'Church in danger' – in danger from those who sought to undermine Convocation's independence, to allow 'occasional conformity', to silence the high church firebrand, Henry Sacheverell. As Thomas Secker came of age, the Church of England he knew was one crippled by internecine conflict: small wonder, then, that as archbishop he would try to stamp out the kinds of doctrinal divisions that had given fuel to the fire of party strife during his youth.[18]

One might have thought that as the established Church of England dealt with its own internal dissensions, Dissent would have thrived. It did not because Dissenters were even more divided among themselves than the Anglicans. In the new world of voluntary religion, Dissent, though freed of many previous legal burdens by the Toleration Act, was actually on the wane: nearly everyone recognized that Dissenting congregations were getting smaller and that a growing number of prominent Dissenting ministers and promising ministerial candidates were increasingly, and perhaps unexpectedly, adopting the Anglican mantle.[19] The actual numbers of clerical defections were relatively low. A recent study calculates that thirty-five Dissenting ministers conformed to the Church of England between 1717 and 1732, while an anonymous pamphleteer in 1731 reckoned that fifty had left the Dissenting ranks since 1714.[20] The absolute impact of these defections was not debilitating. It was, instead, the evident promise of those who abandoned Dissent that led to the hand-wringing and public self-examination among religious nonconformists. 'Some of these Gentlemen, who have, of late Years, deserted the Dissenting Interest, are Persons of very considerable Merit, in respect of their natural and acquired Endowments, and the Probity of their Lives,' fretted one pamphleteer.[21] Among those who defected were two future archbishops of

---

[17] John Spurr, '"The Strongest Bond of Conscience": Oaths and the Limits of Tolerance in Early Modern England', in *Contexts of Conscience in Early Modern Europe, 1500–1700*, eds. Harald E. Braun and Edward Vallance (Basingstoke, 2004), pp. 151–65; idem, 'A Profane History of Early Modern Oaths', *TRHS* 11 (2001), pp. 37–63; and David Martin Jones, *Conscience and Allegiance in Seventeenth Century England: The Political Significance of Oaths and Engagements* (New York, 1999).

[18] But cf. William Gibson, *The Church of England, 1688–1832: Unity and Accord* (2001).

[19] While precise figures are unavailable, only an estimated 6.2% of English men and women in the early eighteenth century were Dissenters, with Presbyterians accounting for roughly 3.3% of the populace: Watts, *Dissenters*, pp. 207, 509. But cf. Wykes, 'Introduction', pp. 14–15, which argues that Dissent actually grew until the late 1710s and that the 'decline' was a matter of perception, not reality.

[20] J.T. Spivey, 'Middle Way Men, Edmund Calamy, and the Cries of Moderate Nonconformity (1688–1732)' (University of Oxford D.Phil. thesis, 1986), p. 338; Anonymous, *Some observations upon the present case of the Dissenting interest, and the case of those who have lately deserted it: where in something further is suggested for its support and strengthening, occasioned by some late pamphlets concerning the decay of that interest* (1731), p. 10.

[21] Anonymous, *Some observations upon the present case of the Dissenting interest*, pp. 4–5.

Canterbury, two other bishops, a lord chancellor of Ireland, and a number of prominent Anglican clerical controversialists.[22]

Contemporaries offered a variety of explanations for the defections and for the decline of the Dissenting interest. Strickland Gough, a Dissenting minister who would himself later conform to the established Church, argued that 'ignorance of their own principles, and ill conduct and management of their interests' caused more damage among Dissenters than 'lenity of the government, the want of a persecution to keep us together, [or] the loss of a puritanical spirit'.[23] Philip Doddridge picked up on Gough's suggestion that the Dissenting clergy drove away congregants. Average Dissenters, Doddridge reckoned, were 'plain people, who have not enjoyed the advantages of a learned education, nor had leisure for improvements by after-study'. They demanded that their ministers 'speak to them plainly', and, more importantly, lead them 'that their hearts may be enlarged as in the presence of God, that they may be powerfully affected with those things of religion, which they already know and believe'.[24] Isaac Watts pressed the theme even further: 'I am well satisfied that the great and general reason is the decay of vital religion in the hearts and lives of men, and the little success which the ministrations of the gospel have had of late for the conversion of sinners to holiness, and the recovery of them, from the state of corrupt nature and "the course of this world, to the life of God by Jesus Christ".'[25] For Doddridge, Watts, and others, Dissent had little future if its leaders did not try actively to revive the puritan godliness of the previous century.[26] Interestingly, Secker would later fret openly in his episcopal charges that Anglican clergy were themselves the source of the Church of England's problems: like his friends Watts and Doddridge, he laid the blame many for his church's failures at the door of its own clergy.

---

[22] Prominent defectors from Dissent included John Potter and Thomas Secker (archbishops of Canterbury); Joseph Butler and Isaac Maddox (Anglican bishops); John Bowes (lord chancellor of Ireland); and Henry Owen (biblical scholar). Edmund Calamy, *An Historical Account of My Own Time with Some Reflections on the Times I have Lived in (1671–1731)*, ed. John Towill Rutt (1830), II, pp. 504–06 lists over two dozen other prominent Anglican converts from Dissent. It should be noted that these defectors did not all come from the same generation, but were spread out over a number of decades. Nevertheless, the cumulative effect of the defections worried many Dissenters.

[23] [Strickland Gough], *An enquiry into the causes of the decay of the Dissenting interest* (1730), pp. 3–5. Gough, still a Dissenter when he wrote this pamphlet, published it anonymously and sparked a controversy which is surveyed in Watts, *Dissenters*, pp. 82–93 and Isabel Rivers, *Reason, Grace, and Sentiment: A Study of the Language of Religion and Ethics in England, 1660–1780. Volume I: Whichcote to Wesley* (Cambridge, 1991), pp. 170–73.

[24] Philip Doddridge, *Free Thoughts on the Most Probable Means of Reviving the Dissenting Interest* (1730), in *The Works of Rev. P. Doddridge, D.D.* (Leeds, 1803), IV, p. 213.

[25] Isaac Watts, *An Humble Attempt Towards the Revival of Practical Religion among Christians, By a Serious Address to Ministers and People* (1731), in *The Works of the Rev. Isaac Watts, D.D.* (Leeds, 1813), IV, p. 585.

[26] Abraham Taylor, *A letter to the author of An enquiry into the causes of the decay of the dissenting interests. Containing an apology for some of his inconsistencies; with a plea for the dissenters, and the liberty of the people. To which is added, a short epistle to the reverend Mr. Gough* (1730), unlike many Dissenting commenters, rejected Gough's argument outright.

Contemporaries also tended to blame the restrictiveness of Dissent and credit the latitude of the post-1714 Church of England for the defections of Dissenting ministerial prospects. Edmund Calamy, a prominent chronicler of Dissent, argued that the ultra-Calvinism of nonconforming sects and 'the spirit of imposition working among the Dissenters, which had discovered itself in the proceedings at Salters' Hall, and on other occasions, after the debates about the Trinity grew warm' turned off ministerial prospects.[27] George Hall would later speculate speculate, 'It is not improbable, that Secker was driven into conformity, by the unfortunate differences which existed between the Presbyterian and Independent parties, during his residence at Chesterfield.'[28] Though the Church of England required its clergy to subscribe to the Thirty-Nine Articles, there was more wiggle-room for Anglican clergy regarding contentious doctrinal issues than there was for their Dissenting counterparts.[29] To many, Hoadleian latitudinarianism seemed more 'reasonable' an alternative than 'the more constricting atmosphere of Dissent'.[30] The evidence suggests, however, that the established Church's orthodox Christology, not its theological latitude, might actually have attracted Secker. Tellingly, he took the decisive steps toward Anglican ordination after the Salters' Hall debates. Most of the Presbyterian ministers who attended the 3 March 1719 meeting at Salters' Hall refused to subscribe to the Trinitarian declaration, and their congregations later became unitarian: Secker was at the very same time drifting toward Christological orthodoxy and away from the Arianism of his youth. Watching Dissenting ministers fight to the divide over the central doctrine of Christianity could not have been particularly reassuring to a wavering Dissenter.[31]

Ironically, the education that nonconformist ministerial candidates received in the Dissenting academies later emboldened some to conform to the established Church.[32] The Dissenting academies cultivated intellectual curiosity and

---

[27] Calamy, *An Historical Account of My Own Time*, II, p. 506. See also, [Gough], *An enquiry into the causes of the decay of the Dissenting interest*, pp. 5–6.

[28] George Hall, *The History of Chesterfield; with particulars of the hamlets contiguous to the town, and descriptive accounts of Chatsworth, Hardwicke, and Bolsover Castle* (1839), pp. 120–21. But cf. David L. Wykes, 'After the Happy Union: Presbyterians and Independents in the Provinces', *SCH* 32 (1996), pp. 283–95.

[29] See, for instance, Gilbert Burnet, *An Exposition of the Thirty-Nine Articles of the Church of England* (1699) and Benjamin Hoadly, *The reasonableness of conformity to the church of England, represented to the Dissenting ministers* (1703).

[30] Alan P.F. Sell, 'Presbyterianism in Eighteenth-Century England', *The Journal of the United Reformed Church History Society* 4:6 (1990), p. 357. See also, Rivers, *Reason, Grace, and Sentiment. Vol. I*, pp. 164–204; Watts, *Dissenters*, pp. 391–92; and C.G. Bolam, Jeremy Goring, H.L. Short, and Roger Thomas, *The English Presbyterians: From Elizabethan Puritanism to Modern Unitarianism* (1968), pp. 175–218.

[31] R.O. Thomas, 'The Non-Subscription Controversy amongst Dissenters in 1719: The Salters' Hall Debate', *JEH* 4:2 (1953), pp. 162–86.

[32] David L. Wykes, 'The contribution of the Dissenting academy to the emergence of Rational Dissent', in *Enlightenment and Religion: Rational Dissent in eighteenth-century Britain* (Cambridge, 1996), pp. 99–139; R. Brinley Jones, 'Grace under the Law: Aspects of the History of the Education of Dissenters', *Transactions of the Honourable Society of Cymmrodorion*, New

independence in their students and gave them a firm grounding in biblical history and languages. The earliest academies for religious nonconformists sprang up in 1662 when many of the ejected nonconformist ministers established schools. Many at the academies trained for the Dissenting ministry, while others aimed for secular careers but could not swear to the subscriptions and tests that regulated who could matriculate at Oxford or graduate from Cambridge. The academies tended not to be large, but their curricula were often more innovative than those at Oxbridge; in particular, there was more of an openness to the so-called 'new learning' in the academies than at Oxbridge. John Locke's influence weighed particularly heavily on students in the Dissenting academies. In his *Essay concerning Human Understanding* (1690) and again in *The Reasonableness of Christianity* (1695), Locke argued forcefully against Cartesian theories of innate ideas and for the epistemological primacy of sense, perception, and reason, even when considering the nature and existence of God.[33] Many Dissenters and Anglicans would subsequently found their rejection of orthodox Trinitarian Christianity on Lockean epistemology.[34]

For many, Locke – a professed Christian, if of the Socinian sort – was but the thin end of heterodoxy's wedge. Where Locke worked to explicate the reasonableness of Christianity, others worked to supplant the mysteries Christianity with the certainties of reason. The Arian and Socinian heresies flourished during late seventeenth and early eighteenth centuries, and religious heterodoxy found able and vocal champions in John Toland, the earl of Shaftesbury, Thomas Chubb, Anthony Collins, Matthew Tindal, and a host others.[35] Not only did Nicene Christianity weather 'the full and multifarious

Series 7 (2001), pp. 83–95; and Alan P.F. Sell, *Philosophy, Dissent and Nonconformity, 1689–1920* (Cambridge, 2003), pp. 17–54 are helpful recent introductions to the Dissenting academies. See also, Isabel Rivers, *The Defence of Truth Through the Knowledge of Error: Philip Doddridge's Academy Lectures* (2003). Mordechai Feingold, 'The Mathematical Sciences and New Philosophies', in *The History of the University of Oxford: Seventeenth-Century Oxford*, ed. Nicholas Tyacke (Oxford, 1997), pp. 359–448 and John Yolton, 'Schoolmen, Logic and Philosophy', in *HUO: Eighteenth Century*, pp. 565–92 discuss the curriculum at Oxford, while for Cambridge see John Gascoigne, *Cambridge in the Age of Enlightenment: Science, religion and politics from the Restoration to the French Revolution* (Cambridge, 1989).

33 Wilber Samuel Howell, *Eighteenth-Century British Logic and Rhetoric* (Princeton, 1971), pp. 259–98 elucidates Locke's formative influence on the 'new logic', while Alan P.F. Sell, *John Locke and the Eighteenth-Century Divines* (Cardiff, 1997) surveys eighteenth-century theological responses to Locke.

34 Watts, *Dissenters*, p. 373.

35 H.J. McLachlan, *Socinianism in Seventeenth Century England* (Oxford, 1951); Roland N. Stromberg, *Religious Liberalism in Eighteenth-Century England* (Oxford, 1964); Gerald R. Cragg, *Reason and Authority in the Eighteenth Century* (Cambridge, 1964); Maurice Wiles, *Archetypal Heresy: Arianism through the centuries* (Oxford, 1996); Frederick C. Beiser, *The Sovereignty of Reason: The Defense of Rationality in the Early English Enlightenment* (Princeton, NJ, 1996); James A. Herrick, *The Radical Rhetoric of the English Deists: The Discourse of Scepticism, 1680–1750* (Columbia, SC, 1997); John Marshall, 'Locke, Socinianism, "Socinianism," and Unitarianism', in *English Philosophy in the Age of Locke*, ed. M.A. Stewart (Oxford, 2000), pp. 111–82; and Justin Champion, *Republican Learning:*

assault of a theological revolution',[36] but the Anglican clergy who professed Nicene Christianity came under attack, as well. Early modern England was in theory, if not perfectly in practice, a confessional state. As Justin Champion rightly notes, precisely because 'early modern understandings of the confessional nature of the state insisted that religious orthodoxy was the premise of civil citizenship...politics was infused with Christian meaning'. Anticlericalism during this period was, thus, 'more than the ridiculing of churchmen upon the stage of in the alehouse': when anticlericals challenged religious orthodoxy and mocked the priests who professed it, they were attacking the existing social and political order.[37]

This was the milieu in which Thomas Secker grew up and in which his mature worldview was forged. Church attendance remained legally mandatory, but religious affiliation was wholly voluntary. Politics was incendiary and burned on the fuel of religious grievance and hatred. In most respects, the political situation during this period mirrored the Church of England's own internal politics, for the institution was itself also witness to heated, and at times vicious, internal fighting among churchmen over the legacy and implications of the 'troubles' during the seventeenth century. Surprisingly, though, the established Church's confessional competitors had little success peeling away members from the Church of England and, indeed, Dissent watched its own numbers decline during the first three decades of the eighteenth century. Perhaps the greatest threat to the established Church also appeared to be the greatest threat to English Christianity in general – freethinking of all sorts thrived after the lapse of the Licensing Act in 1695 and was not thought to be refuted successfully by the orthodox until the mid 1730s when Secker's old friend Joseph Butler published his *Analogy of Religion* (1736). Secker, then, grew up in a world in intellectual, political, and religious tumult. As a young man, he was an anticlerical who held heretical religious views: how and why he turned not to freethinking but instead to orthodox Anglicanism tells us much about the orthodox reform programme he tried to effect from the episcopal bench.

II

Born to Thomas and Abigail Secker on 21 September 1693 at Sibthorp, a small village populated by fewer than one hundred in the Vale of Belvoir, Nottinghamshire, Thomas Secker lived an early life marked by both comfort and dislocation. He described his father as 'a Protestant Dissenter; a pious & virtuous

John Toland and the crisis of Christian culture, 1696–1722 (Manchester, 2003) examine the heterodox currents of thought during the period.

[36] Norman Sykes, *From Sheldon to Secker: Aspects of English Church History, 1660–1768* (Cambridge, 1959), p. 219.

[37] Justin Champion, "'Religion's Safe, with Priestcraft is the War": Augustan Anticlericalism and the Legacy of the English Revolution, 1660–1720', *The European Legacy* 5:4 (2000), pp. 547–61, at pp. 548, 549.

& sensible man. He spent much of his time in reading English Books; for he understood no other Language. He declined taking the Office of a minister amongst the Dissenters, though solicited for it: but destined me for that Employment.'[38] A Presbyterian and a butcher's son from Marston, Lincolnshire, the senior Thomas married three times. His first wife died childless, while his second marriage produced a daughter, Elizabeth. Following his second wife's death, he stayed with a friend, the prosperous farmer George Brough in Shelton, Nottinghamshire, where he became taken with Brough's youngest daughter, twenty-three-year-old Abigail, a woman thirty-two years Secker's junior. They married on 18 December 1685/6 and had three children, Abigail-Anna in 1690, Thomas in 1693, and George in 1696.[39] The Seckers lived on a Sibthorp farm, worth £100 per annum and rented from John Holles, duke of Newcastle. The family seem to have been financially secure, and into his late thirties the future archbishop received a comfortable income from a lead mine bequeathed him by his father.[40] Secker's father died in 1700, aged 70; Secker was only seven years old. Soon afterwards, Secker's mother remarried, to William Allen from Swinderby, Lincolnshire, with whom she lived until her death from consumption on 21 January 1707. Though he made 'short visits to [his] Mother at Easter', Secker seems not to have enjoyed close relations with Abigail Allen and, in fact, he had been sent to live with his half-sister Elizabeth and her husband Richard Milnes in Chesterfield, Derbyshire, in 1699, 'at least a year before [his] Father's Death'.[41]

Secker attended some of England's leading Dissenting academies and, like many Dissenting students, changed schools often. Richard Brown, 'a Layman, of irregular life, but a good scholar', was his first schoolmaster. At the free school in Chesterfield, Brown instilled in his young charge 'a competent Knowledge of Latin; & not only of the Greek Prose-Writers, but of Homer & Hesiod, Aristophanes & Sophocles'.[42] By 1708, though, Secker, aged fifteen, had fallen in with a dissolute crowd, 'some of my Acquaintance enticing me, sometimes to drink, sometimes to go to Church'. In response the Milneses transferred him to Timothy Jollie's academy, Christ's College, at Attercliffe, near Sheffield. Jollie (1656/9–1714)[43] attracted a number of pupils who would go on to impressive careers in both church and state, and among the hundred students he taught at Attercliffe were a lord chancellor of Ireland (John Bowes), a Lucasian professor of mathematics at Cambridge (Benjamin Grosvenor), and a host of prominent

---

38 *Autobiography*, p. 2.
39 T.M. Blagg, *The Parish Registers of Shelton, in the county of Nottingham, for the years 1595–1812* (Worksop, 1900), pp. 16, 50; Porteus, *Life of Secker*, pp. 1–2.
40 One contemporary rumour was that 'Bp. Secker was born at Chesterfield of poor Parents, bound Apprentice to a shoemaker but staid not his time out': Bodleian, MS Rawlinson J4° 4.251, f. 255: Unknown to Richard Rawlinson, 12 April 1740.
41 *Autobiography*, pp. 2–3.
42 Ibid., p. 3. Secker seems to have held a lasting respect for Browne. An entry in his account book for 28 September 1766 records a payment of £10.10s being made to 'Mr. Browne ... son of my old schoolmaster': LPL, MS 1483, f. 85.
43 Jonathan H. Westaway, 'Jollie, Timothy (1656/9–1714)', *ODNB*.

Dissenting and Anglican clerics, including Thomas Bradbury, John Evans, and Secker. Yet the staunchly Calvinist Jollie – not considered one of the more rigorous Dissenting schoolmasters – refused to teach mathematics, fearing it would sow the seeds of 'scepticism and infidelity'.[44] Neither did he emphasize the classics, biblical languages, or logic.[45] Secker believed that, largely on account of Jollie's blinkered curriculum, he had squandered the two years he spent at Christ's College: 'I had Lost much of this Learning there, & acquired but little instead of it. For only the old Philosophy of the Schools was taught there: and that neither ably, nor diligently.' Neither, Secker thought, was Jollie a strict disciplinarian – the 'morals of many of the young Men were bad' – and, believing he had spent his time there 'idly & ill', he voluntarily left the school.[46]

Instead of heading to Glasgow after Attercliffe, as he had once planned, Secker followed his friend John Bowes to London, where he lodged with Bowes's family.[47] In London, Secker studied under John Eames (1686–1744), a theological tutor at the Congregational Fund's academy and a teacher known for exposing his students to new ideas in philosophy, logic, and the sciences. Isaac Watts described him as 'the most learned man I ever knew'; an 'Arminian Independent', he was a friend of Isaac Newton and later a fellow of the Royal Society.[48] Secker 'learnt Geometry & Conick Sections', as well as French, under Eames, and it was Eames who first introduced him to Locke's *Essay concerning Human Understanding*.[49] In light of Secker's later interest in medicine, it is suggestive that Eames was the first tutor to teach human anatomy at any of the Dissenting academies.[50]

While in London, Secker met Isaac Watts (1674–1748), a Congregational minister who also lodged with the Bowes family. In 1711, Watts helped Secker, on Eames's advice, to gain admission to Samuel Jones's Gloucester academy. Secker would later thank Watts fulsomely for 'both…advising me to prosecute my studies in such an extraordinary place of education, and [for] procuring me admittance to

---

[44] Quoted in Ashley Smith, *The Birth of Modern Education: The Creation of the Dissenting Academies, 1660–1800* (1954), p. 109.

[45] One contemporary lamented 'the defects in his Institution, as to Classical learning, free Philosophy, & the catholic Divinity': DWL, MS 24.59, ff. 31–32: An anonymous account of the Dissenting Academies from the Restoration of Charles II. Cf. John de la Rose, *A Funeral Sermon Occasion'd by the death of the Reverend Timothy Jollie, Late Pastor of the Congregational Church at Sheffield* (1715). Giles Hester, *Attercliffe as a seat of Learning and Ministerial Education* (1893), pp. 24–28, 59–60; Herbert McLachlan, *English Education under the Test Acts, being the History of Non-Conformist Academies, 1662–1820* (Manchester, 1931), pp. 106–09; and Smith, *The Birth of Modern Education*, pp. 109–11 assess Jollie's curriculum and teaching.

[46] *Autobiography*, p. 3.

[47] McLachlan, *English Education under the Test Acts*, pp. 29–33 discusses the flow of English Dissenting students to Scottish universities.

[48] Smith, *The Birth of Modern Education*, pp. 95–96; Sell, 'Presbyterianism in Eighteenth-Century England', p. 361; Wykes, 'The contribution of the Dissenting academy', p. 115; and Alexander Gordon, 'Eames, John (1686–1744)', rev. Alan Ruston, *ODNB*.

[49] *Autobiography*, p. 3.

[50] McLachlan, *English Education under the Test Acts*, pp. 118–19.

it'.[51] The son of a Welsh minister who emigrated to America, the Presbyterian Jones (1681/2–1719) had been educated in Dissenting academies and on the continent at the university in Leiden. Deciding against entering the ministry, he settled in Gloucestershire to open his school.[52] Secker stayed there from 1711 until 1714, during which time he saw firsthand that while religious nonconformists were tolerated officially, they were not always immune from harassment, official and otherwise. In September 1712, an ecclesiastical correction court accused Jones of inculcating in his students 'seditious and antimonarchical principles...very prejudicial to the present Establishment in Church and State' and, on George I's coronation (20 October 1714), a high church mob attacked Jones's house.[53] The academy soon moved to Tewkesbury.

Despite these disturbances, Secker got a first-rate education from Jones. He 'recovered ... [his] almost lost Knowledge of Greek & Latin; and added to it that of Hebrew, Chaldee & Syriack'. In addition, Jones also gave 'Lectures on Dionysius's Geography; a course of Lectures, Preparatory to a Critical Study of the Bible; & a Course of Jewish Antiquities, besides Logick & Mathematicks'.[54] Clearly Secker and Jones thought highly of each other. Jones 'shews himself so much a gentleman, and manifests so great an affection and tenderness for his pupils, as cannot but command respect and love', wrote Secker to Watts, and in 1713, in the aftermath of the church court present the previous year, Secker loaned Jones £200 to cover the costs of moving the academy from Gloucester to Tewkesbury.[55] An apocryphal story also had Jones standing over Secker while his young student studied, proclaiming that he would one day become archbishop if ever he decided to conform.[56]

In a letter to Watts in the autumn of 1711, Secker described in detail Jones's educational program.[57] Jones, Secker thought, was 'a man of real piety, great learning, and an agreeable temper; one who is very diligent in instructing all under his care, and very well qualified to give instructions, and whose well-managed familiarity will always make him respected'. Unlike Attercliffe's Jollie, Jones ran a tight ship: 'He is very strict in keeping good orders, and will effectually preserve his pupils from negligence and immorality ... I believe there are not many academies freer in general from those vices than we are.' Though 'no great admirer of the old

51   *Memoirs of Isaac Watts*, p. 346: Secker to Watts, 18 November 1711.
52   W.W. 'Biography: some account of Mr. Samuel Jones', *Monthly Repository*, IV (1804), pp. 83–87; David L. Wykes, 'Jones, Samuel (1681/2–1719)', *ODNB*.
53   Gloucester RO, GDR B4/1/1056: articles presented against Samuel Jones of the Parish of St John the Baptist, Gloucester, 1712: quoted in Wykes, 'Jones, Samuel (1681/2–1719)'.
54   *Autobiography*, p. 3; Wykes, 'The contribution of the Dissenting academy', p. 119.
55   *Memoirs of Isaac Watts*, p. 351: Secker to Watts, 18 Nov 1711; *Autobiography*, p. 4.
56   *Monthly Repository* V (1810), p. 401. Richard Brown was also reputed to have said this to Secker, though. *Gentleman's Magazine* (Oct 1768), p. 451 reported that Secker 'acquitted himself so well in his classical exercises there that his master Mr. Brown, had been heard to say (clapping his hand on the head of his pupil), "Secker, if thou wouldst but come over to the church, I am sure thou wouldst be a bishop".'
57   Unless otherwise noted, the quotations in the following two paragraphs are drawn from *Memoirs of Isaac Watts*, pp. 346–52: Secker to Watts, 18 Nov 1711.

Logic', Jones used the Dutch Cartesian Adrian Heereboord's *Ermeneia logica* (1650) as the primary text in logic for his students.[58] As a corrective, though, he took his students systematically through Locke's works on epistemology and logic and the Jansenist Antoine Arnauld's *The Art of Thinking*, both examples of the 'new logic'.[59] On Saturday afternoons, Secker joined other students studying logic with Jones to consider a particular thesis. Interestingly, Secker sat through the logic sequence twice, in part, he noted, 'because I was utterly unacquainted with it when I came to this place'. Jones also taught mathematics, focusing primarily on algebra and Euclid's geometry, and instructed his students in rhetoric by making them read Isocrates and Terence twice weekly.

The religious content of Jones's educational programme lastingly influenced Secker. Jones insisted that his students be fluent in biblical languages. He not only made them 'speak Latin always, except when below stairs amongst the family', but he also had each student translate two verses of the Old Testament into Greek each day and gathered the class every afternoon to read together from the Greek New Testament. Secker learned Hebrew, Chaldee, and Syriac at Tewkesbury, as well. 'I began to learn Hebrew as soon as I came hither,' he wrote to Watts, 'and find myself able now to construe, and give some grammatical account of about twenty verses in the earlier parts of the Bible after less than an hour's preparation.' In addition to drilling his students in biblical languages, Jones also provided his students with a firm grounding in what Secker called 'Jewish Antiquities'. 'The principal thing contained in them are about the antiquity of the Hebrew Languages, Letters, Vowels, the Incorporation of the Scriptures, ancient Divisions of the bible, an account of the Talmud, Masora, and the Cabala,' he wrote to Watts. 'We are at present upon the Septuagint, and shall proceed after that to the

---

[58] Heereboord's *Ermeneia logica* was a substantially revised version of Franco Burgersdijk's *Institutiones logicae* (1626), a textbook which had been commissioned by the States of Holland to be used for secondary education. Both Heereboord and Burgersdijk were used in Oxford and Cambridge during the seventeenth century: Mordechai Feingold, 'The Humanities', in *Seventeenth-Century Oxford*, ed. Tyacke, pp. 294–96, 322; idem, 'The ultimate pedagogue: Franco Burgersdijk and the English speaking academic learning', in *Franco Burgersdijk and his World*, ed. E.P. Bos and H.A. Krop (Amsterdam and Atlanta, GA, 1992), pp. 151–65. Norman Fiering, *Jonathan Edwards's Moral Thought and Its British Context* (Chapel Hill, NC, 1981), p. 38 considers Heereboord's influence on the intellectual development of Secker's near-contemporary, Jonathan Edwards. William Sparks Morris, 'The Young Jonathan Edwards' in *Reinterpretation of American Church History*, ed. Jerald C. Brauer (Chicago, 1968), pp. 29–66 offers a salutary reminder about the ways that Edwards and many of his contemporaries read Locke, Heereboord, and others. See also, Fiering, *Moral Philosophy at Seventeenth-Century Harvard: A Discipline in Transition* (Chapel Hill, NC, 1981), pp. 96–102 and Jonathan Israel, *Radical Enlightenment: Philosophy and the Making of Modernity, 1650–1750* (Oxford, 2002), p. 33 regarding Heereboord. I thank Theo Verbeek for his guidance regarding Heereboord and Dutch philosophy's influence in early modern England.

[59] Antoine Arnauld, *Logic, or, The art of thinking in which besides the common, are contain'd many excellent new rules, very profitable for directing of reason, and acquiring of judgment, in things as well relating to the instruction of a man's self, as of others, in four parts...* (1696; originally published in 1662). For Arnauld's logic, see Steven M. Nadler, *Arnauld and the Cartesian philosophy of ideas* (Princeton, 1989).

Targumim, and other versions, &c.'[60] Jones supplemented his treatment of the 'Jewish Antiquities' with notes from Jacob Perizonius's classics lectures, which he attended as a student in Leiden; his library – 'composed for the most parts of foreign books, which seem very well chosen' – further reflected the influence of a continental education. Furthermore, Jones was characteristic of most Dissenting tutors in encouraging his students' intellectual inquisitiveness. 'We pass our time very agreeable betwixt study and conversation with our tutor,' Secker assured Watts, 'who is always ready to discourse freely on any thing that is useful, and allows us either then or at lecture all imaginable liberty of making objections against his opinion, and prosecuting them as far as we can,' Jones likely intended his educational programme to strengthen his students' religious nonconformity: it did not have that effect on Secker.

In 1714, the twenty-year-old Secker began a period of intense religious introspection that redirected the course of his life. By February, he later noted, 'many Doubts had risen in my mind, concerning Conformity, & many other religious matters'. Though Jones was 'not yet come to his Theological Lectures: it grew daily more doubtful, of what Value they would be: several things become daily more disagreeable'.[61] What those 'several things' were, he never specified; nor did he say why he began to doubt them when he did. It seems likely, though, that the decision of his friend, Joseph Butler, to leave Jones's academy in February 1714, helped catalyze Secker's self-examination, during which Secker's religious views changed markedly. Secker followed Butler out of the door of Jones's academy in June 1714, returning to live with his family in Chesterfield and Nottingham. There he studied under Thomas Hardy, 'first a Clergyman, at this time a Dissenting Minister at Nottingham, & some years afterwards a Conforming Clergyman again'.[62]

Secker's description of Hardy as a future conformist is revealing, for he notes immediately afterwards in the autobiography that the course of religious study he followed under Hardy intensified his religious self-examination, particularly regarding the question of conformity. By the winter of 1714/15, Secker later recounted, 'I studied various Theological subjects, with various Fluctuations & changes of Mind: particularly the Doctrine of the Trinity, in which for some time I agreed very much with Dr. Clarke; the Inspiration of the Scripture, on which I inclined to the Sentimens de quelques Theologiens de Holland; & Subscription to the 39 Articles, concerning which I afterwards had a long Correspondence with

---

[60]   *Memoirs of Isaac Watts*, p. 350: Secker to Watts, 18 Nov 1711. See also, Birmingham University Library Special Collections MS 6/11/3: Notes on Samuel Jones's lectures on Jewish Antiquities derived from Thomas Godwin's *Moses and Aaron*. Jeremiah Jones took these notes in 1713 and appears to have passed them on to Secker later. I thank David L. Wykes for this latter reference.

[61]   *Autobiography*, p. 4. In Secker's eyes at least, the quality of Jones's teaching begun to fall off: in Tewkesbury, Secker contended, Jones 'began to relax of his Industry, to drink too much Ale & small Beer, and to lose his Temper'.

[62]   Ibid. On Hardy, see McLachlan, *English Education under the Test Acts*, p. 12.

Mr. Butler...who went to Oriel College.'[63] In addition, Hardy had Secker 'read...the principal Writers on both sides on the Lay & Ministerial Conformity; & much of the Scriptures, particularly the New Testament in the Original, consulting the Commentators'. In mid 1716, he was still grappling with these issues. During a stay in London that summer, he 'read the Apostolical Fathers, Eusebius' Ecclesiastical History, Whistons Primitive Christianity, & many other chiefly Theological Books'; and in July he wrote his friend John Fox about the lengthy consideration he had made recently of 'whether the prophets really understood their own writing'.[64] In the end, Secker's thoughts on the issue of conformity began to coalesce: 'I was pretty well satisfied of the Lawfulness of conforming to the Church of England as a Layman, but not equally of becoming a Minister in it.' We do not – and likely cannot – know precisely when Secker went through the formal confirmation process; nonetheless it seems unlikely that he did so in 1716. As he himself acknowledged later, 'though I was less inclined to some Singularities of Opinion than I had been, yet I continued favourable to others: nor could be sure how soon, or indeed in what manner, my Judgment might fix'.[65] Secker had, then, made the decisive break away from Dissenting ministerial studies, but he appears in 1716 not yet to have been ready to abandon Dissent itself.

Indeed, Secker's later detractors claimed that between leaving Jones's academy in 1714 and taking up his medical studies in 1716, he served as a pastor in Dissenting congregations. The heterodox John Jones reported that Secker had preached to a small Derbyshire congregation but was 'thought by the elderly and grave people there to be rather too young and airy for such a charge; so he did not continue long in that station'.[66] Francis Blackburne charged that he 'preached a probation sermon to a dissenting congregation somewhere in Derbyshire'.[67]

---

[63]   *Autobiography*, p. 4. Butler ordered his papers burned on his death, so, unfortunately, none of the correspondence between Secker and Butler survives. Samuel Clarke (1675–1729), rector of St James's, Westminster, and a friend of Secker, expressed his Arianizing views on the nature of the Christian godhead most clearly in *Scripture Doctrine of the Trinity* (1712). Richard Simon (1638–1712) was a French biblical scholar usually credited with founding Old Testament criticism. In *Sentiment de Quelques Theologiens d'Holland sur l'Histoire Critique du Vieux Testaments* (1685), he questioned whether Moses had written the Pentateuch. *ODCC*, pp. 1503–04.

[64]   *Autobiography*, p. 5; *Monthly Repository* XVI (Oct 1821), pp. 569–70: Secker to John Fox, 28 July 1716. In light of Secker's mature churchmanship, the choice of books he cites is suggestive, for a high regard for the primitive church was one of the hallmarks of Anglican high churchmanship. On the high church use of patristics during the eighteenth century, see Robert D. Cornwall, 'The Search for the Primitive Church: The Use of Early Church Fathers in the High Church Anglican Tradition, 1680–1745', *AEH* 59:3 (1990), pp. 303–29; and Peter Doll, 'The Idea of the Primitive Church in High Church Ecclesiology from Samuel Johnson to J.H. Hobart', *AEH* 65:1 (1996), pp. 6–43. But cf. G.V. Bennett, 'Patristic Authority in the Age of Reason', *Oecumenica* (1971/2), pp. 72–87.

[65]   *Autobiography*, p. 5.

[66]   *Literary Anecdotes*, III, p. 748: 'Memoirs of Secker by John Jones of Welwyn', n.d.

[67]   Francis Blackburne, *An historical controversy concerning an intermediate state and the separate existence of the soul between death and the general resurrection* (1772), p. 243.

Gilbert Wakefield also contended that Secker preached 'among the sectaries at Bolsover in Derbyshire'.[68] Others made similar claims,[69] though Secker hotly denied the charges: 'I have never officiated as a Minister, or Proposed myself as a Candidate for the Ministry, or received the Sacrament, amongst the Dissenters.'[70] The balance of evidence suggests that these charges are unlikely to have been true. None during Secker's lifetime is recorded to have mentioned him preaching in Dissenting congregations, and, perhaps more significantly, it was not a charge that his apologists ever mentioned, much less refuted. Secker was many things, but a Dissenting minister was not likely one of them.

In addition to recognizing that Secker made his decision to conform against the backdrop of Dissent's decline, it is also bears noting that a number of his close friends were among the defectors. Some conformed after he did. Thomas Hardy, Secker's tutor at Chesterfield, was also a Presbyterian minister in Nottingham and would surprise his congregation in 1727 when he conformed.[71] At the time, Doddridge described Hardy's defection as 'the most considerable conquest which the Establishment has made upon us for several years ... [H]e was a very celebrated scholar, and at the head of the dissenting interest in this neighbourhood.'[72] John Fox, another of Secker's friends, likewise conformed after Secker. Fox was a Presbyterian whose father, like Secker's, had intended him for the ministry. A student of John Eames in London between 1714 and 1716, he befriended Secker and Samuel Chandler, to both of whom Fox later ascribed his increasingly independent thinking on theology. By the mid 1730s, Fox had abandoned Dissent, explaining to Secker in 1736, 'for some years past I have conformed, partly out of regard to public peace, and partly for the sake of paying that respect to the public, which I think it is entitled from every man who can pay it fairly'.[73] Hardy and Fox help locate Secker within a milieu of conform-minded Dissenters.

---

[68] Wakefield, *Memoirs of Gilbert Wakefield*, p. 166.

[69] A manuscript in the possession of John Smith (d. 1810), the Sheffield bookseller who was also the father of the nineteenth-century Congregationalist tutor and scholar John Pye Smith, likewise claimed that that Secker had preached at Bolsover: 'This appears incredible to any one at all acquainted with the principles and practices of Protestant dissenters, when it is considered that Secker studied under Mr. Jollie, as a theological student and that at the close of the time he presented a probationary sermon for the pastoral office at Bolsover in Derbyshire. But the circumstance is put out of dispute by the list of members of Mr. Jollie's church, when the name of Thomas Secker appears in conjunction with the name of other students': BL, Add. MS 24437, ff. 58v-59v. See also, BL, Add. MS 24480, f. 92. I thank David L. Wykes for these references.

[70] *Autobiography*, p. 9.

[71] Calamy, *Historical Account of My Own Life*, II, pp. 500–03 is a detailed contemporary account of Hardy's conversion.

[72] Geoffrey F. Nuttall, *Calendar of the Correspondence of Philip Doddridge D.D. (1702–1751)* (1979), p. 47: Doddridge to Lady Russell, 28 Oct 1727.

[73] *Monthly Repository* XVI (Nov 1821), p. 635: Fox to Secker, June 1736. Fox describes in detail the difficult questions he faced regarding conformity in 'Memoirs of Himself, by Mr. John Fox', *Monthly Repository* XVI (Mar 1821), pp. 129–35; XVI (April 1821), pp. 193–200. See also, Wykes, 'Fox, John (1693–1763)', *ODNB*. Fox's reasons for conforming were precisely those of Benjamin Hoadly's *The Resonableness of Conformity* (1703), a point I owe to Bill Gibson.

It was, however, those like Henry Etough, John Bowes, and Joseph Butler who abandoned Dissent before Secker who served as likely models for him.

Secker met Henry Etough – a lifelong friend, an inveterate Whig, and, soon after the Hanoverian succession, an Anglican cleric – at Attercliffe.[74] Etough decided to conform to the Church of England at least by 1714: he was ordained a deacon on 25 September 1715 and served parishes in Norwich and Hertfordshire until his death in 1757. Etough's seemingly absolute certainty on nearly all matters and his plainspoken advice to Secker in the 1750s about politics and religion make it likely that would have strongly supported Secker's decision to conform.[75]

John Bowes's decision to conform also antedated Secker's. The two met while at Timothy Jollie's academy in Attercliffe where Bowes, like Secker, 'was then intended for a Dissenting Minister'.[76] After leaving Christ's College, they lived together at Bowes's house in London, and when Secker was in Paris in 1719 to study medicine, Bowes spent nearly four months as his guest, recuperating from what appears to have been deep depression.[77] Bowes's decision to abandon Dissent, probably in 1715 or early 1716, disturbed Secker markedly. 'Mr. Bowes is fixed in the Change of his Religion, notwithstanding all I could do,' he lamented. 'I wish he had not forsaken us like Demas.'[78] There is no evidence to suggest that Bowes pressured Secker, but they did have lengthy, at times irreverent, discussions on theological matters between 1715 and 1717. It is suggestive that Secker would make the very same decision as Bowes within a few years of penning his complaint about Bowes's conformity.[79]

Joseph Butler's decision to conform had an even more profound effect on Secker. Butler's father had also determined that his son should enter the Presbyterian ministry and he sent him to Samuel Jones's academy for a clerical education. During his time at Tewkesbury, Butler carried on a secret correspondence with the quasi-Arian divine Samuel Clarke regarding Clarke's Boyle Lectures (1704–05) and his controversial *Scripture Doctrine of the Trinity* (1712); Secker ferried the letters between them.[80] By early 1714, Butler's doubts about entering the Dissenting ministry had intensified to the point that he left Jones's academy and matriculated at Oriel College, Oxford. We do not know

[74] Venn, *Alumni Cantabrigiensis*, II, p. 107; Cambridge University Library, EDR G/1/11 (Register): cited in *CCED. Literary Anecdotes*, VIII, pp. 261–64 sheds light on Etough's personal eccentricities. No early correspondence between Etough and Secker is now extant.

[75] See, for instance, BL, Add. MS 39315, ff. 38–69.

[76] *Autobiography*, p. 3.

[77] SCA, Bagshawe C.330, ff. 13, 14: Thomas Secker to Elizabeth Secker Milnes, 19 July 1719; 6 November 1719.

[78] Ibid., f. 9: Secker to Elizabeth Secker Milnes, n.d.

[79] *Autobiography*, p. 5. See also, S.J. Connolly, 'Bowes, John, Baron Bowes of Clolyon (1691–1767)', *ODNB*.

[80] *Autobiography*, p. 4; Porteus, *Life of Secker*, p. 3. The Butler-Clarke correspondence is reproduced in Samuel Hallifax (ed.), *The Works of Joseph Butler, D.C.L., late Lord Bishop of Durham* (New York, 1860), II, pp. 284–303.

exactly when or why Butler conformed,[81] and his decision to have his executors destroy all of his personal papers after he died means that there remains little evidence to clarify the matter.[82] That Butler's example deeply influenced Secker is clear. During his spiritual introspection in the winter of 1714/15, Secker notes that he worried particularly about 'Subscription to the 39 Articles, concerning which I afterwards had a long Correspondence with Mr. Butler'.[83] And his correspondence repeatedly mentions visiting Oxford between 1716 and 1718, when the two friends 'talked our own Talk without controul'.[84]

During this period, Secker was a theological liberal who embraced both heterodoxy and anticlericalism. During the mid 1710s, Secker concedes in his autobiography, 'I was also acquainted indeed with several Persons, occasionally much given to irreligious Talk,' though he states emphatically that never doubted 'of the Truth of Religion, natural & revealed; & still less being a Disputer against them in Company'.[85] If he did not reject religious belief out of hand, Secker was nonetheless a decided theological liberal. For instance, Secker's opinion of Hoadly and his theology changed fairly dramatically once he had entered into priestly orders. During the 1710s, he was an enthusiastic supporter of Hoadly's work. In late 1716, he recommended Hoadly's *A Preservative against the Principles and Practices of Non-Jurors* (1716) 'if you love the cause of honesty and truth, and have curiosity for so great a novelty, as to see it supported by a dignified clergymen'; a few months he called Hoadly '[t]he best of clergymen [who] grows every day bolder for the truth than ever' and praised his sermons 'against the ceremonies and repetitions of the Common Prayer'.[86] Samuel Clarke, a prominent quasi-Arian who joined Hoadly on the low church wing of early eighteenth-century Anglicanism, was another source of instruction to Secker, and Clarke took it upon himself to introduce his young friend to London society.[87] Secker even jested in 1718, 'I have been labouring to get an Arian ordained by some of our great divines, who know him to be such, and do not much question succeeding.' Around the

---

[81] Butler would have had to subscribe to the Thirty-Nine Articles at matriculation. For the subscription and oath requirements at eighteenth-century Oxford, see J.C.D. Clark, *Samuel Johnson: Literature, religion and English cultural politics from the Restoration to Romanticism* (Cambridge, 1994), pp. 93–99.

[82] Christopher Cunliffe, 'The "Spiritual Sovereign": Butler's Episcopate', in *Joseph Butler's Moral and Religious Thought: Tercentary Essays*, ed. Christopher Cunliffe (Oxford, 1992), p. 38. Samuel Hallifax, 'The Life of Dr. Butler', in *The Works of Joseph Butler*, I, p. xlii retraces Butler's path to conformity without shedding any light on the inner workings of Butler's mind. Norman Sykes, 'Bishop Butler and the Church of His Age', *Durham University Journal* 43:1 (1950), p. 2 adds little to Hallifax's explanation.

[83] *Autobiography*, p. 4. Cf. John Walsh, 'The Thirty Nine Articles and Anglican Identity in the Eighteenth Century', in *Quand Religions et Confessions se Regardent*, ed. Christiane d'Haussy (Paris, 1998), pp. 61–70.

[84] SCA, Bagshawe C.330, f. 4: Secker to Elizabeth Secker Milnes, 26 July 1716.

[85] *Autobiography*, p. 5.

[86] *Monthly Repository* XVI (Oct 1821), pp. 572, 573; Secker to John Fox, 1 Dec 1716; 13 Feb 1717.

[87] See, for instance, SCA, Bagshawe C.330, ff. 8, 11, 13–14: Secker to Elizabeth Secker Milnes, Mar 1716; Nov 1718; 6 Nov 1719.

same time, he argued that Dissenters and Deists shared a common cause, praising a paper 'containing the Joint advice of the Three Denominations to their brethren in the ministry'. It was, he assured John Fox, 'full of the most generous and free principles imaginable, particularly not only precepts of charity to all Christians, but one paragraph express to exhort them to carry it well to the Deists, and maintain their liberties, because any hardship used to them would be contrary both to humanity and the Christian religion'.[88] Secker's theological heterodoxy and his avowed anticlericalism seemed to go hand-in-glove. In 1716, for instance, he argued, 'For as orthodoxy is purely an effect of the former (priestcraft), I think it may very properly be ranged under that same head.'[89] Soon afterwards he pilloried those studying at one of England's priestly laboratories: 'At Oxford the people are all either mad or asleep, and it is hard to say which sort one could learn most from: only the former sort break out sometimes into flights, which, because the by-standers laugh at them, their fellows take for wit.'[90]

It remains the case that we have no idea exactly when or by whom Secker was confirmed into the Church of England. John Fox, Secker's close friend during the mid 1710s, and Beilby Porteus, his first biographer, suggest that Secker conformed sometime in 1720–21. Fox recollected that Secker conformed sometime around 1720, and he chalked up the decision to a lack of sound guidance. 'Mr. Secker…was intended for a Dissenting Minister, but he did not like their principles and practices in a great many things,' Fox remembered. Yet Secker's Arianism put him 'under great difficulty about subscribing the [Thirty-Nine] Articles'. It was Fox's impression that Secker was torn about what to do 'and being under the influence and direction of no parent or guardian' decided to study medicine instead of pursue a clerical career. His subsequent decision to conform to the established Church surprised Fox, then: 'I think there must have been a very great alteration both in his temper and principles, and that very sudden too, otherwise he could never, with any decency or honesty, have stooped to such preferments as I knew he once despised upon the terms they were to be had.'[91]

Beilby Porteus, likewise, located Secker's decision to conform in 1720 or 1721 and reckoned that Secker's own reflections about conformity and the theological divisions in Dissent brought to light by Salters' Hall propelled him from Dissent. '[D]uring the last Years of his Education, his Studies were chiefly turned towards Divinity,' Porteus notes of Secker. 'But though the result of these enquiries was…a well-grounded Belief of the Christian Revelation, yet not being at that Time able to decide on some abstruse speculative Doctrines, nor to determine absolutely what Communion he should embrace', Secker turned 'to pursue some Profession which should leave him at Liberty to weigh these Things more maturely in his Thoughts and not oblige him to declare, or teach publicly, Opinions which were not yet

---

88   *Monthly Repository* XVI (Nov 1821), pp. 633–34: Secker to Fox, 20 May 1718.
89   Ibid. (Sept 1821), p. 507: Secker to Fox, 15 May 1716.
90   Ibid. (Oct 1821), p. 569: Secker to Fox, 28 July 1716.
91   Ibid. (April 1821), p. 194: 'Memoirs of Himself, by John Fox'.

thoroughly settled in his own Mind.' By 1720, Porteus continues, Secker's 'former Difficulties, both with Regard to Conformity and some other Doubtful points, had gradually lessened'. Furthermore, Secker's letters from Paris suggested to Porteus 'that he was greatly dissatisfied with the Divisions and Disturbances which at that particular Period prevailed amongst the Dissenters'.[92]

It seems reasonable, then, to conclude that Secker had not conformed to the Church of England before he took up his medical studies in 1716. Fox was Secker's close friend and exact contemporary, and he notes that he 'constantly corresponded with [Secker] till he had foundation enough to go to Leyden (1720), where he soon took his degree, and then returned to Oxford to make himself known and gain a character'.[93] The implication is that Secker had not yet conformed before leaving for Leiden in early 1721, which jibes fairly neatly with Porteus's chronology of Secker's conformity, as well. What spurred him finally to abandon Dissent was the promise of preferment; what likely propelled him to orthodoxy, though, seems very likely to have been the subject of his medical studies.

III

Nearly two years after leaving Samuel Jones's Tewkesbury academy, Secker moved in the winter of 1716 to London where he began a five-year course of medical studies. Medicine seems initially to have been an interesting diversion for Secker after quitting his training for the Dissenting ministry. In the summer of 1716 when his friends Bowes and Samuel Chandler were going to Flanders and Bath, Secker decided instead to remain in London because 'I have a very good Opportunity of studying natural Philosophy & particularly Anatomy this winter which I know not whether I shall ever meet with again and therefore would willingly improve not. For it is a Study of a great Deal of Pleasure and may be of some use.'[94] By October 1716, he wrote his John Fox, 'I have made a small change in my studies too, from the spirit to the flesh; or in plainer terms, from divinity to anatomy; which, with a little experimental philosophy, and a little good company, will fill up my time this winter.'[95] During the winter of 1716/17, Secker 'went through some Courses of Anatomy...& read the usual Books in the preparatory Sciences' under William Chesleden (1688–1752), an entrepreneurial anatomist whose courses dealt more with natural philosophy and natural theology than with practical surgical

---

92 Porteus, *Life of Secker*, pp. 4–5, 7.
93 *Monthly Repository* XVI (April 1821), p. 194.
94 SCA, Bagshawe C.330, f. 5: Secker to Elizabeth Secker Milnes, 26 July 1716.
95 *Monthly Repository* XVI (Oct 1821), p. 571: Secker to Fox, Oct 1716.

training.[96] From there, Secker moved to King Street, Cheapside, where he put himself for a few months under the tutelage of John Bakewell 'for the Advantage of acquainting my self with Medicines, Prescriptions, and Practice'.[97]

With this preparation, Secker left in 1718 for Paris, where he studied anatomy and obstetrics under some of Europe's leading experts: Jacques-Bénigne Winslow (1669–1760), with whom Secker lodged and whose groundbreaking anatomical work helped establish the cranial neurological network, and Sébastien Vaillant (1699–1722), who conducted lectures and demonstrations which Secker attended.[98] In his own autobiography, Winslow recorded that '[p]ersonal investigations included meticulous anatomical dissections and gross microscopic studies of structure…In this work, the master was usually assisted by a number of his best students.'[99] Secker's note that during this period he 'also learnt to dissect at the Salpetriere' suggests that he probably participated in Winslow's dissections of recently deceased criminals, prostitutes, and homeless poor. It certainly helps explain Beilby Porteus's omission of this point in his life of Secker.

While in Paris, Secker also studied obstetrics and surgery under J.F.A. Gregoire during a time in which obstetric practice was undergoing rapid change. Not only were men becoming involved in the birthing process as 'man-midwifes' (or *accoucheurs*), but improved anatomical knowledge allowed qualified medical practitioners like Gregoire, or indeed Secker, to understand better when intervention was necessary in childbirth.[100] This obstetrical training opened Secker to more criticism later in his life. Horace Walpole called him a 'man-Midwife', while Richard Hill claimed that Secker 'was educated in the profession of a Man-midwife among the Dissenters'.[101] An ecclesiastic *cum* man-midwife would have been disreputable for a number of reasons. Gregoire and like-minded Parsian teachers were among the first to teach their students to administer vaginal exams as part of standard prenatal examinations, something that would have been thought unbecoming of the leader of the established Church of England. The

---

[96] *Autobiography*, p. 5; Anita Guerrini, 'Anatomists and Entrepreneurs in Early Eighteenth-Century London', *Journal of the History of Medicine and Allied Sciences* 59:2 (2004), pp. 219–39'; John Kirkup, 'Cheselden, William (1688–1752)', *ODNB*.

[97] *Autobiography*, p. 6. John Guy, 'Archbishop Secker as a Physician', *SCH* 19 (1982), pp. 130, 135 points out that by 1718, Secker 'was no novice, but already a mature student with some practical experience as well as theoretical knowledge behind him' and argues that he was 'possibly one of the best-trained [doctors] in the England of his day'.

[98] Jan Bondeson, *Buried Alive* (New York, 2001), pp. 51–61; W.L. Tjaden, 'Sebastien Vaillant's Flora of Paris, *Botanicon parisiense*, 1717', *Journal of the Society for the Bibliography of Natural History* 8 (1976), pp. 11–27; Jacques Rousseau, 'Sébastien Vaillant, an Outstanding 18th Century Botanist', in *Essays in Biohistory*, eds. P. Smit and R.J. Ch. V. ter Laage (Utrecht, 1970), pp. 195–228.

[99] Quoted in Guy, 'Archbishop Secker as a Physician', p. 130.

[100] See, Roy Porter, 'The Eighteenth Century', in Lawrence I. Conrad, *et al.*, *The Western Medical Tradition, 800 BC to AD 1800* (Cambridge, 1995), pp. 429–32 and idem, *The Greatest Benefit To Mankind: A Medical History of Humanity* (New York, 1997), pp. 273–74.

[101] LWL, Horace Walpole's Commonplace Book II, f. 109; Richard Hill, *Pietas Oxoniensis: or, a full and impartial account of the expulsion of six students from St Edmund Hall, Oxford* (1768), p. 19.

man-midwife was also a figure widely criticized during the mid-century as either a rakish sexual predator or an ignorant and illiterate brute.[102] Not surprisingly, Porteus claimed that Secker merely attended some of Gregoire's lectures 'but without any Design of ever practicing that or any other Branch of Surgery'.[103]

Taking no degree at Paris, Secker headed for Leiden in January 1721, where within three months of study under Herman Boerhaave (1688–1738), he had written an M.D. thesis on insensible perspiration. In the early 1720s, Leiden was Europe's most innovative medical centre in Europe and Boerhaave its pre-eminent figure, one who drew students from across the continent and the British Isles.[104] A committed Calvinist, Boerhaave accepted Newtonian natural philosophy, with its insistence that the laws of nature were the means by which God acted providentially in this world.[105] He also challenged Galenic humoral theories in favour of a corpuscularian matter theory that saw health as a result of proper hydrostatic pressures, and he encouraged an empirical rethinking of accepted medical truths. His student Secker obliged him in his M.D. thesis *De Medicina Statica*, which challenged the iatromechanist Sanctorius' theories of insensible perspiration.[106] Iatromechanism was a medical mathematics that sought to explain how the human body worked by quantifying the changes which occurred in it. Among the many physiological experiments the Paduan medical professor Santorio Sanctorius (1561–1636) conducted, one concerned the amount of bodily fluid perspired invisibly. By weighing himself throughout the day, calculating both his food intake and subsequent waste, Sanctorius tried to calculate his insensible perspiration. In his Leiden thesis, Secker looked closely Sanctorius' findings and his methodology, accusing him of relying too heavily on Galen and of not basing his conclusions on solid quantitative evidence.

Secker's examination of the seemingly recondite subject of insensible perspiration unexpectedly elucidates his theological development during this period. In his medical thesis, Secker particularly relied on the findings of James Keill's *Account of Animal Secretion* (1708) to highlight the methodological problems in Sanctorius's work on insensible perspiration. Keill (1673–1719) was

[102] Lisa Forman Cody, *Birthing the Nation: Sex, Science, and the Conception of Eighteenth-Century Britons* (Oxford, 2005), pp. 180–89, 202–10.

[103] Porteus, *Life of Secker*, p. 5. Porteus quoted almost verbatim from *Autobiography*, p. 6.

[104] G.A. Lindeboom, *Herman Boerhaave: the man and his work* (1968); idem, *Boerhaave and Great Britain* (Leiden, 1974); idem, 'Boerhaave's Impact on Medicine', in *Boerhaave and His Time*, ed. G.A. Lindeboom (Leiden, 1970), pp. 31–39.

[105] Rina Knoeff, *Herman Boerhaave (1688–1738): Calvinist Chemist and Physician* (Amsterdam, 2002); Ernestine G.E. van der Wall, 'Newtonianism and religion in the Netherlands', *Studies in the History and Philosophy of Science* 35 (2004), pp. 493–514.

[106] Secker's *De Medicina Statica* has never been published in English translation, though one by Judith Phillips is available at Lambeth Palace Library. For a brief analysis of the thesis, see John R. Guy, 'De Medicina Statica. Archbishop Secker, forgotten English Iatromechanist', *Proceedings of the XXVIIIth International Congress for the History of Medicine*, II (1982), pp. 134–37. See also, Santorio Santorio, *Medicina statica: being the aphorisms of Sanctorius, translated into English with large explanations. Wherein is given a mechanical account of the animal œconomy*, ed. John Quincy (1712).

part of a larger circle of Tory Newtonians who found that Newton's natural philosophy 'by providing evidence of God's design and purpose in the universe, could support rather than undermine religious belief'.[107] In particular, as Lucia Dacome has demonstrated in her recent studies of early modern static medicine, many students of insensible perspiration aimed to prove the physical processes of regeneration. 'The story that resulted staged an alliance of medical and religious forces that came together around the evaluation of bodily process and material transformation,' Dacome points out. 'Physicians' accounts of the animal economy of the body offered divines the opportunity to claim that, in spite of putrefactaion and physical dispersion, the human body encoded in itself the capacity to regenerate.'[108] Here was the ultimate fusion of Newtonianism and Nicene Christianity, since, it could be argued, God had established the laws of nature to enable the physical resurrection of bodies, including, pre-eminently, that of Jesus Christ.[109] It is at the very least highly suggestive that Secker wrote his medical thesis on insensible perspiration at precisely the time he was heading into the ministry and shedding the Arianism of his early adulthood.

Some have implied that Secker's medical studies were a kind of displacement activity meant primarily to allow him thinking time to decide whether or not he wanted to take Anglican orders.[110] More likely is that he began his studies in 1716 under William Cheselden as a stop-gap measure, became genuinely interested in medicine, and intended to pursue a career in the field. Two things, however, prompted him to reconsider his plans. First, he realized how costly it would be to establish a medical practice in England. In his autobiography, he wrote of the 'Difficulties & Dangers in the Profession of Physick; especially as my Fortune was too small, to bear any considerable Expence for any long time', a theme he expounded upon at length in a letter to his half-sister in November 1719.

> I must desire my Brother when the Money he has of mine becomes due to send the Interest & £30 of it to Mr. Bowes: the rest of it is at his Service. For I shall be obliged this winter & the next Year to extraordinary Expences besides maintaining myself, which I must go through & fit myself for my Business, the best I can, whatever be the Event. If I had had the good Fortune to have lodge

---

[107] Anita Guerrini, 'Newtonianism, Medicine and Religion', in *Religio Medici: Medicine and Religion in Seventeenth-Century England*, eds. Ole Peter Grell and Andrew Cunningham (Aldershot, 1996), p. 294. See also, idem, 'Keill, James (1673–1719)', *ODNB* and idem, 'The Tory Newtonians: Gregory, Pitcairne, and Their Circle', *JBS* 25:3 (1986), pp. 288–311.

[108] Lucia Dacome, '"With What Body Do They Come?": Resurrecting by Numbers in Eighteenth-Century England', *PP* 183 (2006), pp. 73–110, at p. 92. I thank Dr. Dacome for allowing me to read versions of this article before publication. See also, idem, 'Living with the Chair: Private Excreta, Collective Health and Medical Authority in the Eighteenth Century', *History of Science* 39 (2001), pp. 467–500.

[109] Marc A. Hight, 'Berkeley and Bodily Resurrection', *Journal of the History of Philosophy* (forthcoming, 2007) illumines the ways Secker's friend, George Berkeley, aimed to prove the plausibility of bodily resurrection by way of immaterialism. Berkeley thought materialist defences of the resurrection – such as those proposed by iatromechanists like Secker – were unreliable. I thank Dr. Hight for allowing me to read his article in advance of publication.

[110] Leslie W. Barnard, *Thomas Secker: An Eighteenth-Century Primate* (Lewes, 1998), p. 6.

only £200 in the publick Stocks here when I first came, I might have gained by this Time 4 or £5000: a Sum which would have set me perfectly at least all the rest of Life. But we must never blame ourselves for not doing what nobody could foresee a Probability of Succession. It is true, the Profession of Physick is a Lottery too and perhaps has as many Blanks in it as any other: but it was the only way I had to dispose of myself, and supposing the worst to happen I shall only be obliged to lead a more private Life in a more private way than I needed to have done before I entered upon this Adventure.[111]

On a trip home to England between the time he finished his medical studies in Paris in 1720 and recommenced them in Leiden in January 1721, Secker also made a crucial patronage connection. While Secker had been away in Paris, his friend Joseph Butler had obtained a degree from Oxford, had taken Anglican orders, and had recommended Secker to his friend Edward Talbot, son of the bishop of Salisbury William Talbot. 'Mr. Butler mentioned me to Mr. Talbot, without my Knowledge; who promised, that if I would go into Orders, he would engage his Father to provide for me,' Secker remembered. 'This Offer was made me in or before May 1720.'[112] Though Edward Talbot would soon afterwards die of smallpox (which Secker recalled as 'a grievous Stroke, [that] stagger'd my Resolution'), his father would hold good to his promise to promote the careers of Butler, Secker, and Martin Benson. Clearly the prospect of patronage influenced Secker, as it would many of his contemporaries. Butler, and through him Secker and Benson, had attracted a potentially influential patron in the latitudinarian Bishop Talbot, and the prospect of ecclesiastical preferment probably proved too enticing an offer for Secker to let pass him by. Secker's theological education and interests, the difficulties of establishing a medical practice, Dissent's decline, and Hoadleian latitudinarianism's ascent likely made it seem reasonable to join the Anglican ministry.

With the prospect of a bright future in the ministry now lying before him, Secker needed first to obtain a university degree. 'In this Case an Academical Degree in one of our Universities might probably be of great Use to me,' he recalled later, 'and as I and my Friends apprehended that the Degree of Dr. in Physick at Leyden would help to procure me a Degree at Oxford; I went just before Christmas from London to Rotterdan, & thence to Leyden; suffering very few persons to know, with what particular view I had.'[113] Having got his Leiden M.D. on 7 March 1721,[114] he returned to Oxford where, on the advice of Talbot's chaplain, Thomas Rundle, he enrolled in Exeter College. Secker's own account of his time in Oxford paints the image of an ambitious climber. Though a committed Whig, he 'soon found the Whigs could procure [him] no Academical Favour; & therefore cultivated the Tories', including newfound friends William Delaune, Arthur

---

[111] SCA Bagshawe C.330, f. 14: Secker to Elizabeth Secker Milnes, 6 Nov 1719.
[112] *Autobiography*, p. 6.
[113] Ibid., p. 7.
[114] R.W. Innes Smith, *English-Speaking Students of Medicine at the University of Leyden* (Edinburgh, 1932), p. 207.

Charlett, John Haviland, Samuel Jebb, and Thomas Carte.[115] It would have been hard to fit in with this cast of nonjurors and notorious Jacobites without doing some things that would have been terribly uncomfortable to a supporter of the Hanoverian succession: with almost evident shame, Secker granted, 'With these I often drank the Duke of Ormonds Health; but never the pretenders; nor ever heard them propose it. Yet their meaning seemed intelligible.' As if to make this admission more palatable, he continued, 'I stayed little more at College, than was necessary to keep terms; but went to Brentford & London.'[116]

In July 1721, after less than a year spent at Exeter College, he appealed to the Chancellor that 'contrary to his own inclinations [he] was sent by his guardians to the University of Leyden where he proceeded regularly to the degree of M.D. ... but intending to prosecute his studies in this University, he humbly prays that the degree of B.A. may be conferr'd on him'.[117] Obviously there is a bit of untruth to this plea, for nowhere is there evidence that Secker's family forced him to study medicine. Nonetheless, the Chancellor, Lord Arran, granted Secker his degree, and Talbot, now bishop of Durham, ordained him as a deacon on 23 December 1722 and then as a priest on 10 March 1723 at St James's, Picadilly.[118] After Secker preached his first sermon on 28 March, Talbot took Secker with him to Durham to join Rundle as his domestic chaplain.

IV

Near the end of his life, Thomas Secker had the opportunity to explain why he conformed. In *Pietas Oxoniensis* (1768), Richard Hill accused Secker of training to be a man-midwife. Thomas Nowell rose to Secker's defence and published what he claimed to was Secker's verbatim response.

> His words are these, 'Whereas it is affected in a pamphlet entitled *Pietas Oxoniensis*, p. 19 that a very great dignitary in the church was educated in the profession of a man-midwife among the dissenters: the real fact is this, that the person supposed to be meant was educated first in a public grammar school, then

---

[115] *Autobiography*, p. 8. W.R. Ward, *Georgian Oxford: University Politics in the Eighteenth Century* (Oxford, 1958), pp. 38–130 and the essays by G.V. Bennett (pp. 61–98, 359–400), Paul Langford (pp. 99–128), R.W. Greaves (pp. 401–24), and V.H.H. Green (pp. 425–67) in *HUO: Eighteenth Century* provide important background. See also, J.H. Curthoys, ' Delaune, William (1659–1728)', *ODNB*; R.H. Darwall-Smith, 'Charlett, Arthur (1655–1722)', *ODNB*; Stuart Handley, 'Carte, Thomas (1686–1754)', *ODNB*. For Carte's participation in the Atterbury plot, see Eveline Cruickshanks and Howard Erskine-Hill, *The Atterbury Plot* (New York, 2004), p. 157.

[116] *Autobiography*, p. 8.

[117] Bodleian, MS Rawlinson J4° 4.251, f. 254: Richard Rawlinson's notes concerning Thomas Secker, n.d. Secker's friends had advised him against admitting the real reason he wanted an Oxford degree (i.e., the promise of imminent preferment): *Autobiography*, p. 8.

[118] Ibid., f. 253: Secker to Rawlinson, received 12 Nov 1741.

for five or six years in dissenting Academies, then for two years pursued his studies privately; that in the year 1716, and not before, he applied himself to the study of physic, which he continued till near the middle of 1720, and not longer; that during this time, among many other courses of lectures, he attended (at *Paris* only) one in midwifery; that he never professed, nor practiced, nor intended to practice that, or any other branch of surgery, nor ever acted as a physician, otherwise than occasionally among the poorest of his Parishioners.'[119]

What is notable here is what Secker does *not* say. There is nothing about why he took up his medical studies in the first place nor why he abandoned them in 1720. Nor does he say when or why he conformed to the Church of England. Instead, he merely details the chronology of his medical studies. To the end, he remained maddeningly vague about what motivated him during the 1710s.

Secker's path to conformity contrasts markedly with that of another orthodox churchman and one of his predecessors at Lambeth, John Potter.[120] Potter's father, Thomas Potter, was still alive when his son decided to conform; and John Potter's decision opened up a deep breach between him and his father, who had 'written with not a little Warmness' and accused John 'of to great a love of the World' upon learning of his son's decision to abandon Dissent. 'I am not at all mov'd wth what hard Names may be given' the established Church, John Potter countered. Instead, he was 'very well satisfy'd it is the same, which Christ and his Apostles have prescrib'd ... I can no more comply with any Party of Dissenters, than they with the Church of England.' Asserting at once the primacy of personal conscience and his submission to providence, Potter wrote to his father that his conformity to the established Church 'may happen contrary to yr Expectation & Designs, but God (I question not) has order'd more wisely, that We should have done for our selves, & I trust will do so to the End'. John Potter took his decision knowing it would wound his father, and indeed the two did not meet again for almost twenty years. Secker, by contrast, seems not to have suffered any deep personal injury on account of his confessional conversion. He abandoned Dissent for the established Church out of principle and opportunity, conviction and careerism. The fingerprints of his particular path to conformity were to be seen all over Secker's orthodox reform programme once he became bishop, for he recognized the power of both ideas and incentives in shaping convictions and policies.

---

[119] Thomas Nowell, *An answer to a pamphlet, entitled Pietas Oxoniensis, or, a full and impartial account of the expulsion of six students from St Edmund-Hall, Oxford. In a letter to the author* (1768), pp. 47–48.

[120] Unless otherwise noted, quotations and information in this paragraph are drawn from Stephen Taylor, 'Archbishop Potter and the Dissenters', *Yale University Library Gazette* 67:3–4 (1993), pp. 118–126, in which *inter alia* Taylor reproduces Beinecke, Osborn Files 32.37: John Potter to [Thomas Potter], n.d.

Chapter Three

BECOMING AN INSIDER

Many had ideas about how to reform the eighteenth-century Church of England, but few were in a position to do so. In 1720, not many would have thought it likely that a defector from Dissent would one day become archbishop of Canterbury; only a convert from Catholicism would have seemed a more unlikely candidate. Yet within a decade and a half of his ordination, Thomas Secker was on the episcopal bench and in a position to formulate and implement policy within his dioceses. How did this convert Dissenter become an Anglican insider? It is a necessary question to address because only when Secker wielded considerable power and influence within the established Church could he hope effectively to reform it.

Secker's ascent of the ladder of ecclesiastical preferment also illuminates clearly the organic relationship of church and state in England during the first two-thirds of the eighteenth century. Neither ability, nor connections, nor political influence alone were sufficient guarantees for clerical advancement: it took a mixture of all three. And while Secker was certainly able and hard-working, he needed influential patrons and politically-connected friends to help him weather 'the varying political tempests' in church and state.[1] One of modernity's hallmarks is the secularization of politics which attends legalized religious pluralism and the privatization of religion – the seemingly inevitable result of this secularizing process is the separation of church and state.[2] That separation would have been a concept utterly foreign to Secker and his contemporaries, during whose lives '[r]eligion and politics were not regarded as discrete spheres of activity. The two were inextricably linked in both the theory and practice of government.'[3] This symbiotic relationship between church and state, however, often raised practical, and at times insuperable, barriers to church reform.

---

[1] Norman Sykes, 'The Duke of Newcastle as Ecclesiastical Minister', *EHR* 62:225 (1942), p. 67.
[2] David Hempton, 'Established churches and the growth of religious pluralism: a case study of christianisation and secularization in England since 1700', in *The Decline of Christendom in Western Europe, 1750–2000*, eds. Hugh McLeod and Werner Ustorf (Cambridge, 2003), pp. 81–98; Alan Houston and Steven Pincus, 'Introduction. Modernity and later-seventeenth-century England', in *A Nation Transformed: England after the Restoration*, eds. Alan Houston and Steven Pincus (Cambridge, 2001), pp. 2–10; Philip S. Gorski, 'Historicizing the Secularization Debate: Church, State, and Society in Late Medieval and Early Modern Europe, ca. 1300 to 1700', *American Sociological Review* 65:1 (2000), pp. 138–67.
[3] S.J.C. Taylor, 'Church and State in England in the Mid-Eighteenth Century: The Newcastle Years, 1742–1762' (University of Cambridge Ph.D. thesis, 1987), p. 40.

I

The career path of a typical eighteenth-century English bishop was slow, with steady, incremental progress up the clerical career ladder. Ordination came in his mid to late twenties; a first living and cathedral post in his thirties; an administrative position and a deanery in his forties; and a bishopric in his fifties.[4] How does Secker's career trajectory compare? He was ordained both as deacon and priest before his thirtieth birthday. William Talbot awarded him in quick succession the valuable rectories of Houghton-le-Spring (1724) and Ryton (1727), as well as the third prebend of Durham cathedral (1727). A royal chaplaincy, granted on the recommendation of Thomas Sherlock, followed in 1732, and the prestigious rectory of St James's, Westminster, fell to him in 1733. To much surprise, Edmund Gibson enabled Secker's elevation to the vacant see of Bristol in 1735; Queen Caroline secured his translation to Oxford in 1737. Secker took up the reins of Bristol when he was only forty-two years old, after serving just thirteen years as a priest. Yet he offended both the royal court and Robert Walpole's government, and he languished in the relatively poor see of Oxford for over two decades. His appointment as dean of St Paul's, London (1750) signalled his political rehabilitation, a fact confirmed when George II tapped him for Canterbury (1758).

Secker was an unlikely high-flyer. He did not, for instance, engage in self-recommendation, a practice so prevalent by mid-century that 'it had become not only a tactical disadvantage to appear at court to ask for a place, but a positive offence'.[5] George Lavington, a future bishop of Exeter, learned this lesson after being bypassed for promotion in 1746: 'I am since inform'd that I was wrong; & that custom would have justify'd me in so doing & perhaps decency required it,' he lamented.[6] Nothing, though, suggests that Secker actively politicked for preferment, and only inveterate critics ever accused him of self-promotion.[7]

Secker's personality also rubbed many contemporaries up the wrong way. Certainly he had his admirers, such as the aristocratic parishioner who in 1734 commented favourably on his 'agreeable person and outward behaviour, civility of manners, and discreet behaviour, together with a graceful delivery of his sermons, [which] do all contribute to make him friends and give him friends and give a luster

---

[4] Daniel Ray Hirschberg, 'A Social History of the Anglican Episcopate, 1660–1760' (University of Michigan Ph.D. thesis, 1976), p. 267.

[5] D.R. Hirschberg, 'The Government and Church Patronage in England, 1660–1760', *JBS* 20:1 (1980), pp. 124–27. See also, William Gibson, '"Unreasonable and Unbecoming": Self-Recommendation and Place-Seeking in the Church of England, 1700–1900', *Albion* 27:1 (1990), pp. 43–63; idem, '"Importunate Cries of Misery": The Correspondence of Lucius Henry Hibbins and the Duke of Newcastle, 1741–1758', *British Library Journal* 17:1 (1991), pp. 87–93.

[6] BL, Add. MS 32709, f. 53: Lavington to TPH, 13 Oct 1746.

[7] *Walpole's Correspondence*, IX, p. 318: Horace Walpole to George Montagu, 4 Nov 1760.

to his learning'.[8] Nonetheless, many other contemporaries commented on his aloof, chilly manner. Critics like the Unitarian Gilbert Wakefield thought him 'imperious', and Horace Walpole never tired of complaining about his sycophancy.[9] 'This ArchBp is a very worthy & honest Man', judged the antiquarian William Cole, 'but bring bred a Dissenter, & among them, contracted such a whining, sniveling & canting Manner, as he could never throw off when he was advanced to the greatest Dignity this Church could afford.'[10] Even an ally like Thomas Newton, bishop of Bristol, admitted, 'Whether it was owing to their misrepresentations, or to a certain preciseness and formality in his own behaviour, he was never very acceptable and agreeable at court, nor ever had the due weight and influence there.'[11] Beilby Porteus, another admirer, agreed that 'it must be owned that he was not always equally affable and obliging. There was sometimes a reserve and coldness in his manner, that threw a damp on conversation, and prevented strangers from being perfectly at their ease before him.' Likewise, Secker's 'temper was naturally quick and impatient'.[12] Porteus, who only knew Secker in the last decade of his life, mostly put down Secker's standoffishness to the writhing pain associated with his debilitating gout, to the heavy responsibility that came with his various offices, and to the stress associated with caring for a wife who was constantly ill.[13] Be that as it may, Secker was a prickly pear. It turns out, though, that neither this nor his reticence for self-recommendation stood insurmountably in the way of ecclesiastical preferment.

Secker's career illustrates the absolute centrality of patronage to eighteenth-century English public life.[14] Patronage served as the chief means by which the king's ministers and ecclesiastical leaders promoted their interests, managed government, and shaped public policy. It would also be one of the most powerful tools at Secker's disposal to reform the Church. Patronage systems are not traditionally thought to be one of modernity's hallmarks, and the perceived systematization of patronage under Walpole was – and remains – widely criticized. As early as 1725, the duke of Portland complained that Walpole 'never does anything for nothing', while Bolingbroke took to the pages of the *Craftsman*

---

[8]   *Egmont Diaries*, II, p. 137.
[9]   Gilbert Wakefield, *Memoirs of the life of Gilbert Wakefield* (1792), p. 164; *Walpole's Correspondence*, IX, pp. 318, 321–22: Walpole to Montagu, 4, 13 Nov 1760.
[10] BL, Add. MS 5831, f. 219v.
[11] Leonard Twells (ed.), *The lives of Dr. Edward Pocock, the celebrated orientalist, by Dr. L. Twells; of Dr. Zachary Pearce, Bishop of Rochester, and of Dr. Thomas Newton, Bishop of Bristol, by themselves; and of the Rev. Philip Skelton, by Mr. S. Burdy* (1816), II, p. 161.
[12] Porteus, *Life of Secker*, pp. 107, 112.
[13] Ibid., pp. 112–13.
[14] For the sociological literature regarding patronage, see S.N. Eisenstadt and Luis Roniger, 'Patron-Client Relations as a Model of Structuring Social Exchange' (1980), reprinted in S.N. Eisenstadt, *Power, Trust, and Meaning: Essays in Sociological Theory and Analysis* (Chicago, 1995), pp. 202–38 and Eric Wolf, 'Kinship, Friendship, and Patron-Client Relations in Complex Societies', in *The Social Anthropology of Complex Societies*, ed. Michael Banton (1968, 1969), pp. 1–20.

relentlessly to attack sordid Robinocracy. A popular ballad in 1734 cried that, 'In the Island of Britain I sing of a Kn … t/Much fam'd for dispensing his favour aright,/No Merit could he but what's palpable see,/And he judg'd of Men's Worth by the Weight of their Fee'.[15] Historians since have concurred with Walpole's contemporary critics, with J.H. Plumb most eloquently spelling out the indictment: 'In the eighteenth century, [patronage] scarcely bothered to wear a fig-leaf. It was naked and quite unashamed … It was patronage that cemented the political system, held it together, and made it an almost impregnable citadel, impervious to defeat, indifferent to social change.'[16] Ecclesiastical patronage has come under similar fire. Clerical nepotism rankled some contemporaries.[17] More usually, though, historians have bemoaned the rank politicization of ecclesiastical patronage.[18]

Yet there is another way we might view eighteenth-century patronage in general, and ecclesiastical patronage in particular. Both patrons and clients during the period understood their relationship as one of reciprocal obligation, a view expressed succinctly in 1754 by George Bubb Doddington: 'Service is obligation, obligation implies return', he reckoned. 'Could any man of honour, profess friendship, accept the offer of his friend's whole services, suffer those offers to be carried into execution, avail himself of their whole utility, and then tell him he could not or would not make him any return? Could there be such a character?'[19] To most it seemed perfectly reasonable that crown appointees gave special consideration, if not their actual vote, to the government's interests. Not surprisingly, the duke of Newcastle advised granting crown livings to 'None whom I did not think, most sincerely well affected to His Majesty, and His Government,

---

[15] Quoted in Jeremy Black, *Robert Walpole and the Nature of Politics in Early Eighteenth-Century Britain* (1990), pp. 30–31, 58.

[16] J.H. Plumb, *The Growth of Political Stability in England, 1675–1725* (1967), pp. 188–89. Cf. Quentin Skinner, 'The Principles and Practice of Opposition: The Case of Bolingbroke versus Walpole', in *Historical Perspectives: Studies in English Thought and Society in honour of J.H. Plumb*, ed. Neil McKendrick (1974), pp. 93–128.

[17] William Gibson, 'Patterns of Nepotism and Kinship in the Eighteenth-Century Church', *Journal of Religious History* 14:4 (1987), pp. 382–90; idem, 'Nepotism, Family, and Merit: The Church of England in the Eighteenth Century', *Journal of Family History* 18:2 (1993), pp. 179–90.

[18] Compare Norman Sykes, *Church and State in England in the XVIIIth Century* (1962), pp. 63–65; idem, 'The Church', in *Johnson's England; An Account of the Life & Manners of his Age*, ed. A.S. Turberville (Oxford, 1933), pp. 17–19; Richard Pares, *King George III and the Politicians* (Oxford, 1959), pp. 24–25; Norman Ravitch, 'The Social Origins of French and English Bishops in the Eighteenth Century', *HJ* 8:3 (1965), p. 322; idem, *Sword and Mitre: Government and Episcopate in France and England in the Age of Aristocracy* (The Hague, 1966), pp. 90–132; Hirschberg, 'The Government and Church Patronage in England', pp. 129, 138.

[19] *The Political Journal of George Bubb Doddington*, eds. John Carswell and Lewis Arnold Dralle (Oxford, 1965), p. 281. Cf. Naomi Tadmor, *Family and Friends in Eighteenth-Century England: Household, Kinship, and Patronage* (Cambridge, 2001), pp. 216–36.

and, to the Principles upon which It is founded.'[20] Political allegiance, however, was but one consideration for ecclesiastical patrons, who also paid close attention to a clerical client's merit (as evidenced by his pastoral and administrative abilities) and to his character. The primary aim of high-level ecclesiastical patronage 'was to ensure good government both in the Church and, especially, in the state'.[21] Thus Newcastle also guaranteed 'To recommend none, whose Character as to Vertue, & Regularity of Life, would not justify it.'[22]

II

Until his death in 1730, William Talbot (1659–1730), successively bishop of Oxford, Salisbury, and Durham, served as Secker's chief patron, granting him a domestic chaplaincy, the rectories of Houghton-le-Spring and Ryton, and a prebend of Durham cathedral. Talbot's churchmanship is hard to pin down precisely.[23] He was a leading Whig divine who voted against Sacheverell during his trial and who preached George I's coronation sermon. Both his published writings and his patronage of and friendship with heterodox clerics such as Samuel Clarke and Thomas Rundle likewise testify to his latitudinarianism.[24] Yet it is also the case that Talbot's theology embraced certain high church positions and that he served as patron to evidently orthodox types like Martin Benson, Joseph Butler, and Thomas Secker. What linked these young orthodox Whigs was association with the bishop's son, Edward Talbot. As Secker recalled, '[Joseph] Butler mentioned me to Mr. Talbot without my Knowledge; who promised, that if I would go into Orders, he would engage his Father to provide for me. This offer was made me in or

---

20   BL, Add. MS 32906, f. 387: TPH to Benjamin Hoadly, 31 May 1760.
21   Stephen Taylor, 'The Government and the Episcopate in the Mid-Eighteenth Century', in *Patronages et Clientèlismes, 1550–1750 (France, Angleterrre, Espagne, Italie)*, eds. Charles Giry-Deloison and Roger Mettam (1995), pp. 202, 204. Idem, '"The Fac Totum in Ecclesiastic Affairs"? The Duke of Newcastle and the Crown's Ecclesiastical Patronage', *Albion* 24:3 (1992), pp. 409–33 is the most incisive study of the crown's ecclesiastical patronage during this period, superseding Sykes, 'The Duke of Newcastle as Ecclesiastical Minister', pp. 59–84.
22   BL, Add. MS 32906, f. 387: TPH to Hoadly, 31 May 1760. See also, Mary Bateson (ed.), *A Narrative of the Changes in the Ministry, 1765–1767* (1898), p. 33 in which (29 June 1765) Newcastle spelled out the two qualifications for ecclesiastical preferment: '*First*, that he should always be one of a good, unblemish'd life and character, and such as one of his profession ought to be. *Second*, that he should be, and have always been, most zealously attach'd to the protestant succession in his Royal Family.'
23   William Gibson, 'William Talbot and the Church Parties, 1688–1730', *JEH* 58:1 (2007), pp. 26–48. I thank Professor Gibson for allowing me to read this article in advance of publication.
24   Clarke's quasi-Arianism had prevented him from being elevated to the episcopal bench, and it was widely assumed that Bishop Talbot shared Clarke's heterodox Christology. Rundle introduced the bishop's son, Edward Talbot, to William Whiston and joined with him in membership to Whiston's Society for Primitive Christianity.

before May 1720.'[25] In December 1720, however, Edward Talbot died of smallpox, though not before securing from his father a promise to promote the careers of Benson, Butler, and Secker, a trio bound so closely together through ties of marriage, blood, and friendship 'that it is difficult to treat them separately'.[26]

Educated at Charterhouse and Christ Church, Oxford, Martin Benson (1689–1752) was, unlike Secker, a son of the established Church, his father, John Benson, having been the rector of Cradley, Herefordshire.[27] Following ordination, Benson obtained a prebend of Salisbury (1720), the archdeaconry of Berkshire (1721), a prebend of Durham (1724), a royal chaplaincy (1726), and the bishopric of Gloucester (1735), a living which he held until his death. While travelling on the Continent as a young man, Benson met George Berkeley and, later in Paris in 1719, he befriended Secker. The two remained close friends until Benson's death in 1752.[28] It was Benson who introduced Secker to Berkeley, who often assisted Secker in his pastoral duties in Durham and Oxford, and who served as his chief political ally and confidant during their early parliamentary careers.

One of the things that bound together Secker and Benson was Secker's marriage to Benson's sister, Catherine. She lived in William Talbot's household with Mary and Catherine Talbot, Edward's widow and daughter. In April 1725, Secker proposed marriage, an offer Catherine Benson quickly accepted, and Bishop Talbot wed them at King's Street Chapel, London (28 October 1725). Catherine Secker's perpetual illnesses made for a difficult marriage. By November 1726, Secker sought to exchange his Houghton living because 'I found my Wifes Health, which for some time had not been very good, growing worse. And the Dampness & Gloominess of the Situation was apprehended to be the cause.'[29] After futilely crisscrossing southern England in 1731 searching for somewhere beneficial to her health, he lamented, 'My wife continues to have her usual complaints.' In 1736, he discovered that she had become addicted to painkillers: 'She had taken privately great Quantities of Opiates; of which I knew nothing till now.' Her drug use worried him so greatly during the months following this discovery that he 'scarcely stirred out, even to Church on Sundays'. In the end, Catherine Secker's 'Unwillingness to diminish the Quantity of Opiates &c was overcome with great Difficulty. But they were at length intirely left off.'[30] The fact that he paid the equivalent of two-thirds of his income as bishop of Bristol to his wife's physicians and apothecaries during 1736 alone testifies to the fiscal burden her addiction

---

[25] *Autobiography*, p. 6.
[26] John H. Overton and Frederic Relton, *The English Church From the Accession of George I to the End of the Eighteenth Century (1714–1800)* (1924), p. 107.
[27] Stephen Taylor, 'Benson, Martin (1689–1752)', *ODNB.*
[28] See *Autobiography*, p. 31 for Secker's reaction to Benson's death.
[29] Ibid., p. 11.
[30] Ibid., p. 17.

placed on him. The emotional onus was heavier, and their relationship centred on her frail health until her death in March 1748.[31]

Edward Talbot's widow and daughter, who had moved into Secker's household with Catherine Benson in 1725, stayed on with Secker until his death in 1768.[32] The Talbots had no money to support themselves and relied upon Secker's largesse throughout their lives.[33] In return for Secker's financial support, Mary Talbot likely helped manage the domestic affairs of Secker's household. The Talbots were more than charity cases, though. Catherine Talbot (1721–1770), Secker himself assured her, was 'in stead of a child to my wife and me'.[34] Secker ensured Catherine was liberally educated in modern and ancient languages, and she enjoyed literary friendships with the Bluestockings and Samuel Richardson, among others.[35] Catherine Talbot eventually helped Secker tackle his episcopal duties, serving as both a messenger and an amanuensis.[36]

Into this mix of Seckers, Bensons, and Talbots are to be added Joseph Butler and the family of George Berkeley. Secker's friendship with Butler stretched back to their days in Samuel Jones's Tewkesbury academy.[37] After Butler (1692–1752) left Tewkesbury in 1714, he matriculated at Oriel College, Oxford, where he found that students were obliged to 'mis-spend so much time here in attending frivolous lectures and unintelligible disputations'.[38] It was at Oriel that Edward Talbot, a

---

[31] Robert G. Ingram, 'Nation, Church, and Empire: Thomas Secker, Anglican Identity, and Public Life in Georgian Britain, 1700–1770' (University of Virginia Ph.D. thesis, 2002), pp. 122–25 elucidates the dynamics of Thomas and Catherine Secker's marriage in greater detail.

[32] Ibid., pp. 125–27 examines Secker's relations with the Talbots in greater detail.

[33] Secker paid Mary Talbot 'money as she called for it, leaving the Disposal of it to her, & settling the Balance once a year in her Book, but not entering the Particulars in my own (accounting book)'. For 1760, he noted, 'In Sept , I think, Mrs. Talbot brought back her Daughter from Bristol, much recovered. They had a Coach & a pair of Horses there at my Expence. And in my Account with Mrs. Talbot for this Year I made her a Present of £200, & of £100 every Year since': *Autobiography*, pp. 39–41. In his will, Secker left the Talbot women the income from an investment of £13,000 which amounted to nearly £400 per year for the two of them. This arrangement was to last until after both Mary and Catherine's deaths, at which time the balance of the £13,000 was to be split among the charities listed in Secker's will. LPL, Secker Papers 7, ff. 367–73: Thomas Secker's will.

[34] Beinecke, Osborn MS 53.78: Secker to Catherine Talbot, 1733. See also, Rhoda Zuk, 'Talbot, Catherine (1721–1770)', *ODNB*.

[35] Myers, *The Bluestocking Circle*, pp. 61–81; Montagu Pennington (ed.), *A Series of Letters between Mrs. Elizabeth Carter and Miss Catherine Talbot, from the Year 1741 to 1770: to which are added, Letters from Mrs. Elizabeth Carter to Mrs. Vesey, between the Years 1763 and 1787* (1808); Joyce Godber, *The Marchioness Grey of Wrest Park* (Bedford, 1968); T.C. Duncan Eaves and Ben D. Kimpel, *Samuel Richardson: A Biography* (Oxford, 1971), pp. 357–64.

[36] See, for instance, BL, Add. MS 35639, f. 26: Catherine Talbot to Charles Yorke, n.d.; ibid., Add. MS 46839, f. 4: Talbot to Edward Seymour, duke of Somerset, 14 Nov 1767; ibid., Add. MS 35608, ff. 167, 168: Talbot to Philip Yorke, 2nd earl of Hardwicke, 7 May 1768, [May 1768].

[37] Ingram, 'Nation, Church, and Empire', pp. 128–33 examines Secker's friendship with Butler in greater detail.

[38] Butler to Samuel Clarke, 30 Sept 1717: quoted in Christopher Cunliffe, 'Butler, Joseph (1692–1752)', *ODNB*. Rather than migrate to Cambridge, as he had planned in 1717, Butler remained

fellow of the college, befriended him. Butler's subsequent rise in the Church was precipitous. Ordained into the priesthood in 1718, he was a Rolls Chapel preacher, a prebend of Salisbury, and rector of two wealthy Durham livings before, through Queen Caroline's deathbed nomination, he was elevated to the bishopric of Bristol in 1738.[39] He was later named dean of St Paul's, London (1740) and bishop of Durham (1752).

Secker and Butler remained close friends throughout the 1720s and early 1730s. Both lived in Durham, and in 1725, Secker helped Butler rid himself of an onerous parish living for the 'golden rectory' of Stanhope.[40] Later, in 1732, Secker recommended Butler to Queen Caroline, and in 1733 he proposed to Lord Chancellor Charles Talbot that he take Butler on as a domestic chaplain.[41] Secker also helped Butler edit his *Fifteen Sermons Preached at the Rolls Chapel* (1725) and the *Analogy of Religion* (1736). In particular he helped Butler to clarify his opaque prose. 'I took much Pains in making his meaning easier to be apprehended. Yet they were called obscure,' Secker recalled of *Fifteen Sermons*. With the *Analogy*, though, 'I was somewhat serviceable to him in the Method & Thoughts of this Book; but very much in making the Language of it more accurate & intelligible, which cost me a great deal of time & pains.'[42] So closely were the two men associated that some contemporaries thought that Secker's 'chief merit (and surely it was a very great one) lay in explaining clearly and popularly in his sermons, the principles delivered by his friend, Bishop Butler, in his famous book of the *Analogy*, and in showing the important use of them in religion'.[43]

---

at Oxford to finish out his degree.

[39] Stephen Taylor, 'Queen Caroline and the Church', in *Hanoverian Britain and Empire: Essays in Memory of Philip Lawson*, eds. Stephen Taylor, Richard Connors, and Clyve Jones (Woodbridge, 1998), p. 97.

[40] *Autobiography*, p. 10: The rectory house at Houghton-le-Skerne was dilapidated and required extensive repairs. 'Mr. Butler had neither the Money nor the Talents for that Work', Secker recalled. 'Therefore I persuaded the Bishops ... to give him, instead ... the Rectory of Stanhope, which was of much greater Value, & without such Incumbrance. And his Lordship did it on my Request solely.'

[41] William Coxe, *Memoirs of the life and administration of Sir Robert Walpole, earl of Orford* (1798), I, p. 551; *Autobiography*, pp. 13, 14. Secker's conversation with Queen Caroline was the occasion of the famous exchange he reports in his autobiography: 'A few Days after, she sent for me, & entered into a long & gracious Conversation with me. I took an Opportunity in it of mentioning Mr. Butler to her. She said, she thought he was dead. I assured her he was not. Yet she afterwards asked ABp Blackburne, if he was not dead. His answer was, No, Madam: but he is buried.'

[42] *Autobiography*, pp. 10, 16.

[43] Richard Hurd, *A discourse, by way of general preface to the quarto edition of Bishop Warburton's works* (1794), p. 83. Cunliffe, 'Butler, Joseph (1692–1768)', perceptively observes, 'For Butler, as for Secker, the breadth of his formative education, his journey from dissent to conformity, and his familiarity – through the Talbots – with thinkers and writers on the verge of heterodoxy, such as Whiston and Thomas Rundle, provided additional motivation for a statement of Christian belief that took careful account of criticisms and that was cast in a empirical mould rather than a rationalistic one.'

By the time of the *Analogy*'s publication, though, Secker's friendship with Butler had chilled. Butler's failure to appreciate Secker's efforts to advance his career bothered Secker,[44] while Secker's parliamentary opposition hurt Butler's reputation with Walpole. 'On Easter Monday [1738] ... I preached a Spital Sermon; &, as usual, printed it,' Secker later recalled. 'In it I gave my just praises to the Lord Mayor, Sir John Barnard, who often voted against the Ministry. Sir R. Walpole was offended at this: & Dr. Butler complained to me, that I had hurt him, as being a Friend of mine, with Sir Robert.'[45] Things had got so bad by 1741 that Secker even began to question Butler's integrity. 'He was a serious, & in Matters of Money a generous Man: but in other respects too selfish', Secker recorded privately, 'expecting every one to befriend & serve Him; but seldom thinking himself qualified or obliged to serve others. And that selfish Disregard increased in him greatly from his time of frequenting the Court. This Coldness of his produced a considerable Degree of it in me also towards Him.'[46] By the early 1750s, though, Secker and Butler seemed to have mended their relations, though exactly why is unclear. Whatever the reason, Secker vigorously defended his old friend against posthumous charges of crypto-popery, a subject to which we will later return.

Benson, who died in August 1752, and Butler, who passed away two months earlier, were soon joined in death by their old friend, George Berkeley (1685–1753).[47] Secker and Berkeley first met shortly before Secker's ordination, and Berkeley along with Samuel Clarke introduced Secker to London society. Following their time together at Bath (1727–28), Secker counted Berkeley as 'my good Friend' to the end of his life.[48] Sometimes the Berkeleys, Bensons, Seckers, and Butler gathered in Gloucester to visit together at Benson's episcopal home.[49] Their visits were infrequent, though, since after being named to the Irish see of Cloyne in 1734, Berkeley rarely left his diocese. He retired in August 1752 with his family to Oxford, where his son had just matriculated at Christ Church. Not long afterwards, though, Berkeley died in January 1753 in his lodgings in Holywell Street. The loss of Berkeley, Butler, and Benson within so short a time hurt Secker deeply: 'we have lost in him an ... remaining Friend, after losing within a few months the two that had been still longer & more intimately such'.[50] But Secker took Berkeley's widow and children into his house soon after the bishop's death.

---

[44] *Autobiography*, pp. 14–16.
[45] Ibid., p. 19.
[46] Ibid., p. 22. For analyses of Butler's own voting record in the House of Lords, see Christopher Cunliffe, 'The "Spiritual Sovereign": Butler's Episcopate', in *Joseph Butler's Moral and Religious Thought: Tercentenary Essays*, ed. Christopher Cunliffe (Oxford, 1992), pp. 45–48 and Stephen Taylor, 'The Bishops at Westminster in the Mid-Eighteenth Century', in *A Pillar of the Constitution: The House of Lords in British Politics, 1640–1784*, ed. Clyve Jones (1989), pp. 157–60.
[47] M.A. Stewart, 'Berkeley, George (1685–1753)', *ODNB*.
[48] *Autobiography*, pp. 9, 12, 54.
[49] BL, Add. MS 39311, ff. 27–28: Secker to Berkeley, 1 Feb 1735.
[50] Ibid., f. 69: Secker to Mrs. Anne Berkeley, 16 Jan 1753.

Upon George Berkeley, jr., Secker, one contemporary wrote, placed 'the affectionate attention of a Second father'; and after Secker became archbishop, he helped promote the younger Berkeley's ecclesiastical career.[51] While a student at Christ Church, the bishop's namesake regularly spent weekends at Secker's episcopal lodgings at Cuddesdon in Oxfordshire and remained a close friend of Secker and the Talbot women, even proposing marriage to Catherine Talbot in 1758.[52]

Secker's network of family and friends provide an important context for his public career. The Seckers, Butlers, Bensons, Berkeleys, and Talbots formed a self-sustaining nexus of support and encouragement, providing one another with friendship, confidence, and, when necessary, patronage. Secker, however, outlived many of them and spent the last fifteen years of his life in 'the prudent but duller company of those elder statesmen, Hardwicke and Newcastle'.[53] But before they were Secker's friends, Hardwicke and Newcastle were his patrons, and Secker's path to Lambeth Palace highlights the necessary link between patronage and preferment in eighteenth-century England. It was not a lesson lost on Secker, who himself would use patronage to encourage the cause of orthodox reform.

III

When Bishop William Talbot died in October 1730, Secker preached the funeral sermon in the cathedral at Durham. Talbot's death could easily have sunk Secker's career. Stuck in remote Durham with a prebend, a parish, and a sick wife, Secker surely must have held out slim hopes for the same steady advancement he had enjoyed while his patron was alive. But his career did not stall, as his preaching and administrative abilities earned him new patrons.

While preaching in Bath in 1731, Secker impressed Thomas Sherlock (1678–1761) enough for Sherlock to propel Secker's career in the early 1730s. A noted preacher and controversialist, Sherlock was a singular figure in the early eighteenth century, a divine whose high churchmanship and early Tory sympathies did not bar his eventual promotion to the sees of Bangor, Salisbury, and London.[54] He owed his own elevation to the episcopal bench to the interventions of Queen Caroline of Ansbach (1683–1737), who would also lobby for Secker later in the

[51] BL, Add. MS 46689, ff. 14–18: Memoir of George Berkeley, jr., by a friend

[52] Ibid., ff. 1–9: Diary of George Berkeley, jr., while at Oxford; Myers, *The Bluestocking Circle*, pp. 112–17.

[53] *Autobiography*, p. xv.

[54] Edward Carpenter, *Thomas Sherlock, 1678–1761* (1936). Linda Colley, *In Defiance of Oligarchy: The Tory Party, 1714–60* (Cambridge, 1982), p. 105 highlights the limits of Sherlock's Toryism.

1730s.[55] Within a year of meeting Secker, Sherlock had procured him a royal chaplaincy, which drew Secker into the world of the royal court, itself still central to eighteenth-century English government and religious life.[56] During the period, forty-eight royal chaplains in ordinary served in rotas of four per month, so that Secker was assured of being in residence at court for one month each year. The positions were unpaid, and a chaplain's life at court was not always glamorous. 'The Chaplains Lodgings there had been the Grooms, & were so close to the Stables, that I could hear the Horses move & eat as I lay in Bed,' Secker recalled of his own time spent at Hampton Court.[57] Moreover, the time chaplains in ordinary spent personally with the monarchs diminished significantly after George II allowed only the clerk of the closet, always a bishop, to attend him in his private quarters. Despite these restrictions, contemporaries reckoned that a royal chaplaincy was 'a sure and certain way to greater preferments'.[58] While at court, Secker met some of the eminent divines of the day and rubbed shoulders with the most powerful figures of the British establishment, who were themselves often clerical patrons. During one stay at Hampton Court, for instance, he served alongside Daniel Waterland (1683–1740), a staunch defender of orthodoxy in the debates over Arianism, deism, and the Eucharist.[59] Among the most important people Secker met while serving as royal chaplain, though, were Queen Caroline and Edmund Gibson (1669–1748).

Gibson's influence in the 1720s and early 1730s as bishop of London far outstripped that of the archbishop of Canterbury, William Wake, whose disfavour with the government from 1718 led him into self-imposed exile at Lambeth Palace. 'Walpole's Pope' proved an unlikely patron of Secker: Gibson considered William Talbot and Thomas Sherlock rivals and had worked unsuccessfully to block the latter from elevation to the bench in 1728.[60] Nevertheless, Secker – likely on account of his orthodoxy – sufficiently impressed Gibson for him to lobby George

[55] Norman Sykes, 'Queen Caroline and the Church', *History* 11:44 (1927), pp. 337–38; Taylor, 'Queen Caroline and the Church of England', p. 98.

[56] Henry Bland, the dean of Durham, also recommended Secker to his school friend Robert Walpole for the chaplaincy. Secker was appointed royal chaplain in ordinary on 28 July 1732: *Autobiography*, p. 13. Stephen Taylor, 'The Clergy at the Courts of George I and II', in *Monarchy and Religion: The transformation of royal culture in eighteenth-century Europe*, ed. Michael Schaich (Oxford, 2007), pp. 129–51 is the best treatment of its subject. See also, David Baldwin, *The Chapel Royal: ancient and modern* (1990), pp. 260–71. I thank Professor Taylor for allowing me to read a draft of his article in advance of publication.

[57] *Autobiography*, p. 14.

[58] White Kennett to Arthur Charlett, 11 May 1700: quoted in Sykes, *Church and State*, p. 151. But cf. Taylor, 'The Clergy at the Courts of George I and George II', which argues that the royal chaplaincy declined markedly in prestige by the mid century.

[59] *Autobiography*, p. 14. See also, R.T. Holtby, *Daniel Waterland, 1683–1740: A Study in Eighteenth Century Orthodoxy* (Carlisle, 1966).

[60] Norman Sykes, *Edmund Gibson, Bishop of London, 1669–1748: A Study in Politics and Religion in the Eighteenth Century* (Oxford, 1926), pp. 139–40; Stephen Taylor, '"Dr. Codex" and the Whig "Pope": Edmund Gibson, Bishop of Lincoln and London, 1716–1748', in *Lords of Parliament: Studies, 1714–1914*, ed. R.W. Davis (Stanford, 1995), p. 16.

II to name Secker rector of St James's, Westminster.[61] Gibson's son-in-law, Robert Tyrwhitt, had succeeded Samuel Clarke at St James's in 1729, but 'found that Preaching in so large a Church hurt his Lungs'. Therefore, Gibson 'proposed to the Crown, that he should exchange it for a Residentiaryship of St Pauls, & that I should succeed him'.[62] A prestigious living, St James's was formally constituted a parish by Parliament in 1685 and sat in the middle of one of London's most fashionable neighbourhoods.[63] Christopher Wren had designed the building. From the beginning, its incumbents were men with bright futures in the church: of the first five rectors, Thomas Tenison and William Wake went on to become archbishops of Canterbury; Charles Trimnell served only three years before he was appointed to the bishopric of Norwich; and Samuel Clarke, though never a bishop because of widespread episcopal opposition to his quasi-Arian views, was nonetheless a popular preacher and an influential theologian. For good reason the office was thought to be a 'stepping stone to high office'.[64]

Gibson also proved crucial in obtaining Secker's elevation to the episcopal bench.[65] In mid December 1734, Secker learned that George II had nominated him to the vacant bishopric of Bristol. 'Far from making Application for any

---

[61]   It was widely assumed by both heterodox and orthodox alike that Gibson placed significant weight upon a cleric's theological views. In 1734, Conyers Middleton, himself a heterodox fellow of Trinity College, Cambridge, complained of Gibson's theological litmus tests in a letter to William Webster, editor of *The Weekly Miscellany*: 'Hard fate of the Clergy, to be exposed to the Tyranny of such an Inquisition; that necessarily destroys all improvement in the knowledge; all liberty in thinking; and what is of the greatest use as well as pleasure to liberal minds, all liberality of conversing. For what so instructive in all the Clubs of Clergymen, as to debate with the utmost freedom on every subject; to propose cavils and doubts on all points of Religion to the discussing of the company for mutual information; nay to sustain the part of Sceptic or Infidel for the exercise of their reason and learning, and to enable you to deal the more successfully with men of that character? Nothing could be more entertaining to men of letters; more serviceable to the Church, and useful to Religion, than Societies instituted on this plan. *But such are the terrors of Orthodoxy; and such vengeance threatened to all, who deviate from it; that it destroys all trust and confidence among Ecclesiastics; and to impart scruples against an Established Government;* your best friends will be sure to betray you, for the sake of their own safety; and no wonder; when it is openly maintained by our most favoured Divines; that Apostasy and some kinds of heresy are much greater crimes than Felony or Treason with many other tenets equally absurd and destructive of all civil as well as religious liberty.': BL, Add. MS 32457, f. 101: Middleton to Webster, 9 May 1734. Emphasis mine.

[62]   Secker moved his family into the rectory house in May, was instituted rector on 18 May 1733, and was inducted the next day. *Autobiography*, p. 13; Bodleian, MS Rawlinson J4° 4.251, f. 253: Secker to Richard Rawlinson, received 12 Nov 1741.

[63]   Leslie W. Barnard, *Thomas Secker: An Eighteenth Century Primate* (Lewes, 1998), pp. 13–15; J.P. Ferguson, *Dr. Samuel Clarke. An Eighteenth Century Heretic* (Kineton, 1976), pp. 196–209.

[64]   Barnard, *Thomas Secker*, p. 15.

[65]   The *congé d'élire* and letter missive for Secker were published in the *London Gazette* on 27 Dec 1734 and the *congé* was issued the next day. He was elected to the bishopric of Bristol on 2 Jan 1735 to which royal assent was granted on 9 January. Archbishop William Wake confirmed Secker on 18 Jan and consecrated him on 19 January. Temporalities were finally restored to him on 17 February. John Le Neve, *Fasti Ecclesiae Anglicanae, 1541–1857. VIII: Bristol, Gloucester, Oxford, and Peterborough Dioceses*, compiled by Joyce M. Horne (1996), p. 12.

Thing', Secker wrote his brother-in-law, 'I had not the least suspicion the day before, that I was thought of. And indeed the Account that I was pitched upon gave me uneasiness not pleasure.'[66] The financial burden of being a bishop worried him. 'I have already as much Business in the management of this Parish as I know how to go through,' he fretted to his brother-in-law, 'and the Income of that Bishoprick is so small that it will not in less than four years Time pay the present Expence of coming to it.'[67] While it was an honour to have been elevated to the episcopal bench, Bristol was a notoriously poor see.[68] Indeed, within days of his nomination, Secker explained to viscount Percival that financial concerns required him to retain his livings in Durham and London *in commendam*: 'The revenue of Bristol being no more than £360 a year, out of which he is to pay £27 a year tenths, and maintain a steward, so that the true profits are but £300 per annum, and there is £900 to be paid in first fruits.'[69] Nearly every bishop of Bristol in the eighteenth century was a pluralist of necessity. The lure of the post was too much for an ambitious cleric to refuse, though. 'But all my Friends agree that as it is thus providentially laid in my way I ought to except it', he explained. '[A]nd as it is a mark of his Majestys Regard, to accept it thankfully. This therefore I have accordingly resolved upon, and hope God will enable me to discharge the Duties of the Station I am called to.'[70]

Secker's elevation to Bristol was a chapter in the 'Rundle affair', a controversy which Norman Sykes called 'the most serious ecclesiastical controversy since the banishment of Atterbury'.[71] It involved Secker, his patrons old and new, and prominent figures from his network of friends and family, including his old rival Thomas Rundle (1687/88–1743). Following Elias Sydall's death, Lord Chancellor Charles Talbot had nominated Rundle to fill the vacant see of Gloucester. Talbot

---

[66] SCA, Bagshawe C.330, f. 20: Secker to Richard Milnes, 21 Dec 1734. Elsewhere Secker also emphasized that he had not politicked for the post: 'Thursday, Dec. 19, I have a very unexpected notice by Letter from Bp Gibson, that the King had pitched on me for Bishop of Bristol. I had made no Application for it to any Person; as indeed I never did for any thing, either before or afterwards': *Autobiography*, p. 15.

[67] SCA, Bagshawe C.330, f. 20: Secker to Milnes, 21 Dec 1734.

[68] Sykes, *Church and State*, p. 61.

[69] *Egmont Diaries*, II, p. 137. Because of his pastoral duties in both Bristol and London, though, Secker petitioned George II for a dispensation for non-residence at Durham. 'Only two prebendaries of that church I believe have been bishops from the Restoration till now,' he wrote to the duke of Newcastle whom he asked to submit his request to the king. TNA, State Papers Domestic George II, 36/34/179: Secker to TPH, 18 April 1735. The dispensation was granted on 8 August. *Autobiography*, p. 16.

[70] SCA, Bagshawe C.330, f. 20: Secker to Richard Milnes, 21 Dec 1734.

[71] Sykes, *Edmund Gibson*, pp. 155–61, 265–69; Taylor, 'Queen Caroline and the Church of England', pp. 99–100; T.F.J. Kendrick, 'Sir Robert Walpole, the Old Whigs, and the Bishops, 1733–1736: A Study in Eighteenth-Century Parliamentary Politics', *HJ* 11:3 (1968), pp. 426–28; Christine Gerrard, *The Patriot Opposition to Walpole: Politics, Poetry, and National Myth, 1725–1742* (Oxford, 1994), pp. 27–34; and Alan R. Acheson, 'Rundle, Thomas (1687/8–1743)', *ODNB* survey the Rundle affair from different perspectives. *Hervey's Memoirs*, II, pp. 399–405 and *Egmont Diaries*, II, p. 137 offer contemporary assessments of the episode.

felt the same debt to Rundle that he did to Secker, since both were his father's chaplains and dependants. He had even secured from Queen Caroline a guarantee that Rundle would be elevated.[72] The problem, though, was that Caroline had failed to consult Gibson, who fiercely opposed Rundle's elevation because of heterodox religious views which Rundle himself did not even bother to deny. Thomas Sherlock and seventeen other bishops joined Gibson in united opposition to Rundle's elevation. The timing, for Robert Walpole and Gibson, could hardly have been less auspicious, coming as it did during a period of ministerial instability and rampant anticlericalism in the House of Commons.[73] Furthermore, as Stephen Taylor notes, 'Rundle's promotion threatened to undermine the ministry's ecclesiastical policy. Such an appointment would have been perceived as the abandonment of its declaration that heterodoxy was a bar to preferment in the Church.'[74] To mollify the aggrieved Talbot, the ministry asked him to nominate another candidate: he refused. So, Walpole recommended Martin Benson for Gloucester and Secker for the recently vacated Oxford.[75] The reasons for choosing Benson and Secker were obvious to contemporaries: 'Dr. Benson ... and Dr. Secker ... [were] both of them learned and ingenious men of unexceptional characters, and both of them formerly chaplains to the Lord Chancellor's father, the late Bishop of Durham,' Lord Hervey reckoned. 'This last circumstance was thought to have been weight in the choice of these man, as a sugar-plum to put the taste of those bitters out of my Lord Chancellor's mouth which they had made him swallow by the rejection of Rundle.'[76] As a sop, Rundle was later sent to the lucrative, but remote, Irish see of Derry.[77]

Secker's promotion to Bristol marked a turning point in his career. On the one hand, it thrust him into the centre of the nation's political establishment. Along with twenty-five other English and Welsh bishops, he now sat in the House of Lords. Yet the political independence he and Benson that showed in Parliament during the later 1730s put a brake on his career advancement. Secker's

---

[72] *Egmont Diaries,* II, p. 23.
[73] Stephen Taylor, 'Whigs, Tories and Anticlericalism: Ecclesiastical Courts Legislation in 1733', *Parliamentary History* 19:3 (2000), pp. 329–55.
[74] Taylor, 'Queen Caroline and the Church of England', p. 100.
[75] *Autobiography,* p. 15: 'The Bishoprick was offered first to Dr. Benson, who declined it, and declared against taking any: then to Dr. Mawson, who seemed willing at first, but afterwards refused. Then Bp Gibson, fearing that some Person would be put in, whom he disliked, insisted, after I had been named, that Dr. Benson should take it: & he at last complied. But he first wrote a Letter to the Chancellor, to know, if he had any Objection. He answered with great Civility, but refused to say any thing, which might seem in Favour of Dr. Rundles Adversary: meaning Bp. Gibson. Dec. 24 my Family returned from Bath, & Dr. Benson accepted. But because Glocester had been offered to him, before Bristol was to me, it was thought proper, & I readily consented, that he should be my Senior.'
[76] *Hervey's Memoirs,* p. 405. See also, *Egmont Diaries,* II, p. 137. The move did not wash because Talbot's followers in the commons eventually went over into opposition to Walpole.
[77] Despite Rundle's backbiting during the previous decade, Secker appears to have borne him no ill will. BL, Add. MS 39311, ff. 27–28: Secker to George Berkeley, 1 Feb 1735.

nomination to Bristol also strained his already deteriorating relations with the Talbot family. Finally, while Edmund Gibson might have been thought to have prevailed in the 'Rundle affair', in the long run his involvement actually weakened his position with Walpole, who resented being forced to choose between his lord chancellor and his 'church minister'. The incident provides the backdrop to Gibson's eventual break with Walpole during the Quakers tithe bill controversy in 1736.[78]

With Gibson's influence waning, Secker was lucky to have had the backing of Queen Caroline. Soon after her arrival in Britain in 1714, a circle of clergy formed around the then princess of Wales and her confidante, Charlotte Clayton, later viscountess Sundon.[79] For the most part, the clerics she and Mrs. Clayton favoured – men such as Samuel Clarke, Benjamin Hoadly, William Whiston, Robert Clayton, William Talbot, and Alured Clarke – were decidedly low church. As a result, many Tories and high churchmen accused her of being a patron of latitudinarianism and theological heterodoxy. Though a committed Protestant who was widely popular for having refused on account of religious scruples to marry the Archduke Charles in 1705, she was neither a systematic theological thinker nor an ideologue, and she eventually befriended more orthodox churchmen, such as Wake, Sherlock, and Butler. It seems clear she played a decisive role in Secker's promotion to Oxford in 1737.[80]

Following John Potter's promotion from Oxford to Canterbury in January 1737, George II offered Secker the see of Oxford so that Thomas Gooch (1675–1754) could be slotted into Bristol. Gooch, the orthodox Tory master of Gonville and Caius College, Cambridge, would have been unacceptable in Oxford, just as an Oxford graduate would have been anathema in the diocese of Ely, which included Cambridge. But Secker initially refused the offer 'because the Difference of the Income would not answer the Expence of the Change. It was then offered to Dr. Samuel Lisle [of Wadham College, Oxford] who seemed at first to accept it: but afterwards, on some Difficulty raised about Commendams, declined it.' Oxford was, next to Bristol, the second poorest see in England, bringing in less than £600 a year. Around this time, though, Lord Chancellor Talbot's death vacated the lease of Hook-Norton, which would cost Talbot's heir £500 to renew with Oxford's bishop. This altered the terms of the equation, Secker remembered: 'Bp. Sherlock, zealous for the Promotion of his Brother in Law, Dr. Gooch, urged this to me as a Reason, why I might afford to take Oxford: & so earnestly begged me to

[78] Taylor, '"Dr. Codex" and the Whig "Pope"', pp. 26–27; idem, 'Sir Robert Walpole, the Church of England and the Quakers Tithe Bill of 1736', *HJ* 28:1 (1985), pp. 51–77.

[79] Henry Nettleship (ed.), *Essays by the late Mark Pattison, sometime Rector of Lincoln College* (Oxford, 1889), I, p. 109; Sykes, 'Queen Caroline and the Church', pp. 333–39; and Taylor, 'Queen Caroline and the Church', pp. 82–101 offer differing assessments of Caroline's influence on the distribution of crown patronage.

[80] Hallward Library, University of Nottingham, NE C 1080: Secker to George II, 7 Aug 1750; Walpole, *Memoirs of George II*, I, pp. 45–46.

do it, that I consented, about March 16.'[81] The move to Oxford was not one which Secker relished making. 'I have made an exchange to accommodate other persons,' he lamented to Berkeley, 'which I never thought an advantageous one to myself in point of interest and fear too late it will prove the contrary.'[82] By late spring, Secker was ordaining clergy in Oxford.[83]

Caroline's death in November 1737 robbed Secker of an influential supporter. But, as in such moments earlier in his career, others came to the fore to promote his cause. There was, however, little that either the duke of Newcastle or the earl of Hardwicke could do immediately to help Secker escape the difficult situation in which he found himself with regard to the court and ministry in the late 1730s and 1740s.

Shortly after accepting the bishopric of Oxford, Secker joked, 'To lead in the steps of my predecessor is to be Bishop of Oxford for two and twenty years.'[84] John Potter had served in Oxford from 1715 until his elevation to Canterbury in 1737, and Secker would himself remain there twenty-one years, the second longest tenure in Oxford during the 'long' eighteenth century. Secker's protracted stay in this poor see can be chalked up to his involvement in a dispute between the king and his royal heir in the 1730s and to his independence in the House of Lords before Walpole's fall.

After Secker took up the reins at St James's, Picadilly, Frederick, the prince of Wales (1707–1751), became one of his parishioners, in part because the prince was singularly unwelcome by his parents in the Chapel Royal. Typically of Hanoverian monarchs and their heirs, George II and Frederick were at loggerheads. Frederick resented being reared in Hanover without his parents, and he idolized his grandfather, his own father's late nemesis. More immediately, he resented his father's dithering negotiations to land him a suitable wife and the paltry financial stipend that was only half what George II had been granted while heir. The kettle finally boiled over in the late 1730s, and Frederick established an alternate court first at Norfolk House and then at Leicester House, following his ejection from St James's Palace in August 1737.[85] Association with the prince

---

81   *Autobiography*, p. 18. See also Porteus, 'Life of Secker', *Works*, I, p. xv. There were rumours that Secker's old tutor, John Conybeare, would succeed Potter at Oxford: Margaret Maria Lady Verney, *Verney Letters of the Eighteenth Century from the MSS at Claydon House* (1930), II, p. 124: Lord Fermanagh to Mrs. Stone, 1 Feb 1737.

82   BL, Add. MS 39311, f. 37: Secker to George Berkeley, 29 June 1737.

83   *Congé d'élire* and letter missive for Secker were issued on 4 April 1737 and were published in the *London Gazette* on 23 April. He was elected to the bishopric of Oxford on 13 April, to which royal assent was granted on 2 May. His license to maintain possession of St James's, Westminster, and his Durham prebend were granted on 7 May. Following confirmation by Archbishop John Potter in Bow Church, London, on 14 May, Secker was enthroned on 4 June and his temporalities were restored on 6 June. Le Neve, *Fasti Ecclesiae Anglicanae, 1541–1857. VIII: Bristol, Gloucester, Oxford, and Peterborough Dioceses*, p. 78; Bodleian, MS Rawlinson J4°.251, f. 254: Richard Rawlinson's notes concerning Thomas Secker.

84   BL, Add. MS 39311, f. 37: Secker to George Berkeley, 29 June 1737.

85   Matthew Kilburn, 'Frederick Lewis, prince of Wales (1707–1751)', *ODNB*.

thereafter became synonymous with opposition to the crown and to associate with Frederick and his circle was to incur the king's opprobrium. Aside from christening many of Frederick's nine children and alerting the prince once to rumours of an assassination plot, Secker followed Robert Walpole's advice against waiting upon Frederick at home, 'since Persons who went to the Kings Court, were forbidden going to His. Dr. [Francis] Ayscough pressed me much to come to it, probably by the Princes Direction: but I refused.'[86]

The fatigue of twenty years in power, a dismal war effort against Spain, and a disastrous election in 1741 found Walpole unable to command a majority in the House of Commons. Desperate to hold on to power, he hoped to pick up the allegiance of the MPs allied to Frederick by negotiating a truce between the prince and his father.[87] One measure of Walpole's desperation was that he turned to Secker – who recently had voted against him in important divisions in the Lords – to serve as an intermediary. Egmont thought that Walpole entrusted Secker with the task because 'by being his Royal Highness's parish priest, [he] had access of course to him, without prejudice to his waiting at times on his Majesty'.[88] On 6 January 1742, Walpole's son-in-law, the earl of Cholmondeley, sent Secker to Leicester House with the thankless (and hopeless) task of patching up relations between the feuding royals.[89]

The offer Secker carried to Frederick was direct: if the prince would ask in writing for the king's pardon, publicly renounce opposition, and return immediately to court, George II 'would be reconciled to him, and would add £50,000 a year to his present Income, and would not require any Terms from him in relation to any of those persons, who were in [Frederick's] Service, Councils or confidence, nor retain any Resentment or Displeasure against them'. In addition, the government would pay off Frederick's mountain of debts.[90] Frederick, though, would have no part of any deal which allowed his old foe Walpole to retain power, and he rejected the offer on the grounds that it came from Walpole rather than from the king himself.[91] Frederick probably believed that, should the parliamentary

---

86   *Autobiography*, pp. 21–22, 36. The latitudinarian Ayscough was chaplain and clerk of the closet to Prince Frederick: M. St John Parker, 'Ayscough, Francis (1701–1763)', *ODNB*.

87   John Owen, *The Rise of the Pelhams* (1957), p. 29; John Wilkes, *A Whig in Power: The Political Career of Henry Pelham* (Chicago, 1964), pp. 19–23. See, more generally, Archibald S. Foord, *His Majesty's Opposition, 1714–1830* (Oxford, 1964).

88   *Egmont Diaries*, III, p. 239.

89   On 6 January, Walpole also negotiated with opposition politician George Lyttleton (who negotiated with Frederick's approval) for his 'Security and Protection' from impeachment in return for ministerial places for those politicians in Frederick's circle such as Lyttleton, William Pitt, and the Grenvilles: Robert Harris (ed.), *A Leicester House Political Diary, 1742–3* (1992), pp. 379–80, 385.

90   BL, Add. MS 35587, f. 4: Secker to Hardwicke, 7 Jan 1742.

91   Ibid.; *Egmont Diaries*, III, p. 239. Though Secker was acting on Cholmondeley's directions, it was clear to him that he 'was sent by the Kings Direction with a Message to the Prince of Wales': *Autobiography*, p. 21. Cf. Coxe, *Memoirs of...Sir Robert Walpole*, III, pp. 585–86.

opposition to Walpole form a government, he could secure similar terms without the humiliation of abject submission to his father.[92]

Frederick's rejection of Walpole's offer put Secker in a tricky situation, as the prince himself realized. When Secker was leaving Norfolk House, he stopped him and said

> 'My Lord, I know not what turn or misconstruction may be made to this verbal answer of mine when you shall carry it back, and therefore I think it best, for your justification and mine, that I set down in writing what has passed between us'. Then taking up his pen, he in his own hand wrote all down and having done desired the Bishop to read it, asking him if he had related it truly. The Bishop replied his Royal Highness had done it justly. 'Then', said the Prince, 'we shall both sign it, that it may be a witness for us both hereafter, and here in this cabinet you shall see me lock it up.'[93]

This did not shield Secker from criticism. Some faulted him for not having insisted that Cholmondeley's message to Frederick be put in writing.[94] George II, however, blamed him for not doing enough to convince his son of the errors of his ways, though Secker protested that 'I had no Influence with the Prince'.[95]

In the end, Secker's career suffered in part for having been placed in such an impossible situation. George II punished his messenger for the failure of negotiations. Secker himself later lamented, 'The King thought I might have done more with the Prince than I did: & for that Reason, & for my voting sometimes against the Court, would not speak to me for a Number of Years.'[96] Had Secker been in favour with the court, he would likely have been promoted out of Oxford far sooner; at worst, he would have been given a wealthy deanery to hold *in commendam* as recompense. His voting record in the House of Lords in the waning years of Walpole's ministry, though, ensured that George II would not be willing to give him the benefit of the doubt, for the king considered a vote against Walpole to be a vote against himself. So, Secker remained stuck in one of the poorest English sees with a burdensome London parish to administer as well. And there he would probably have remained but for the determined efforts of two powerful politicians to advance his career.

Secker's connection to Philip Yorke, first earl of Hardwicke (1690–1764) and Thomas Pelham-Holles, first duke of Newcastle (1693–1768) defies easy characterization. He owed his advancement after 1738 almost wholly to them, so he cannot be considered their equal. But neither did Hardwicke and Newcastle

---

[92] Owen, *Rise of the Pelhams*, p. 29.

[93] *Egmont Diaries*, III, p. 239.

[94] Ibid., pp. 238–39: This criticism was made by Sir John Shelley, the duke of Newcastle's brother-in-law. As Shelley was thought to be acting as an agent of Newcastle when he made this remark, it is likely that he parroted a position held by the duke.

[95] *Autobiography*, p. 21.

[96] Ibid.

treat him as a lackey; they trusted his judgment in a wide variety of matters and relied on his friendship and advice in difficult moments in their own careers. Newcastle's influence upon Secker's career has been noted by many, primarily because of his unofficial role as 'Ecclesiastical Minister' from the mid 1730s and because Newcastle was the senior political figure with whom Secker worked most closely during his episcopal career. How Secker came into Newcastle's favour has never sufficiently been explained, though. It would have mattered to Newcastle that Secker's father had rented from the Pelhams in Nottinghamshire; someone so keen to exploit political connections to strengthen his power would not likely have missed the opportunity to draw Secker firmly into his orbit. The earliest correspondence between the two men dates from 1735 when Secker asked Newcastle to convey to the king his request for a dispensation for non-residence for his prebend of Durham.[97] The two likely had met when Secker attended at court as a royal chaplain. But such chance encounters are no basis for the kind of friendship and working partnership which developed between Secker and Newcastle. The most plausible explanation lies in Secker's intimacy with the Hardwicke clan. Hardwicke and Newcastle were close friends, and together with Newcastle's brother, Henry Pelham, they worked as a triumvirate to direct the Whig ministry which succeeded Walpole. It was Hardwicke who most stridently pressed Secker's case for promotion.

The son of a Dover attorney, Hardwicke was a man of unquestionable intelligence and ability. His work regularizing and ordering the judicial branch known as equity and his marriage reform legislation guaranteed his reputation as one of the great eighteenth-century English lawyers.[98] His interests extended beyond the law, though, and this 'accidental politician' was, by some accounts, 'the most important figure in British politics between Walpole's decline and Pitt's rise.'[99] By his thirtieth birthday, he had been elected to parliament, named solicitor general, and knighted. He was lord chief justice (1733) and lord chancellor (1737) soon thereafter.

While likely that Secker met Hardwicke at court during the 1730s, their connection grew closer after the marriage of Hardwicke's eldest son, Philip, to Jemima Campbell in May 1740. Campbell (1722–1797) was the orphaned granddaughter of the Henry Grey, duke of Kent, and split her time between her grandfather's Bedfordshire estate of Wrest and his London homes in Chelsea and St James's Square. Following the duchess of Kent's death in 1729 and the duke's hastily arranged marriage to the daughter of the duke of Portland, Jemima's constant companion was her young aunt, Mary Grey (1719–1761). The duke often sent the motherless girls to his London homes while he spent time with his

97   TNA, State Papers Domestic George II 36/34/179: Secker to TPH, 18 April 1735.
98   See, C.E. Croft, 'Philip Yorke, first earl of Hardwicke – an assessment of his legal career' (University of Cambridge Ph.D. thesis, 1983).
99   Reed Browning, *Political and Constitutional Ideas of the Court Whigs* (Baton Rouge, LA, 1982), p. 151.

new family in Bedfordshire. The duke had evidently asked Secker, as rector of St James's, Westminster, to look in on the girls whenever they were at the Grey house on St James's Square. Before long Jemima, Mary, and Catherine Talbot were boon companions and remained close friends throughout their lives. Secker also seems to have served *in loco parentis* to Jemima and Mary.[100] By the late 1730s, the Secker family would sometimes spend weeks at a time with the girls in Bedfordshire and regularly entertained them as guests at Cuddesdon.[101]

The duke of Kent's failure to produce a male heir by the late 1730s led him to name Jemima his heir, and his old friend, Robert Walpole, pushed through legislation allowing for the ancient title of Kent to pass through the female line.[102] The duke also began to think about a marriage for Jemima, and it was Secker who appears to have played matchmaker by suggesting lord chancellor Hardwicke's eldest son, Philip Yorke (1720–1790). The seventeen-year-old heiress and the twenty-year-old student of Corpus Christi, Cambridge, met and got along well. Within weeks of their first meeting, Secker married them in the duke's Knightsbridge lodgings (22 May 1740). Not long after the wedding, Secker teased the bride, 'Being informed by this mornings Gazeteer that Mr. Yorke is married to a Lady of great merit, and a considerable fortune, but no beauty, I send you some Lillies and Roses to supply that Deficit.'[103] Within a fortnight after the marriage, the duke of Kent died, leaving Secker as one of his executors. Later that summer, the newlyweds spent time with the Seckers at Cuddesdon, and the marriage was, by all accounts, a happy one.[104]

The evidence for Secker's role in arranging the match between Campbell and Yorke is circumstantial rather than conclusive. Horace Walpole thought him directly involved in it: 'He had a service of silver plate given him by Lord Chancellor Hardwicke, for matching his son to the heiress of the Duke of Kent.'[105] Secker's account is more oblique. 'This Match I proposed, by the Duke of Kents Direction, to Lord Hardwicke the Father,' he recorded in his autobiography. 'And on the Completion of it, he made me a Present of a Diamond Ring, which cost him £300; & which I sold again, with his Approbation, for £280, with which I bought several pieces of Silver Furniture. And the Duke gave me 3 dozen Silver plates, worth, I believe, £200'.[106] It seems unlikely that the two nobles would have given Secker gifts totalling far more than the income from Bristol had his role not been crucial.[107]

---

[100] Bedfordshire RO, L30/6/1–2 and L30/9/84/1–9 contain Secker's correspondence with Jemima Campbell and Mary Grey.

[101] *Autobiography*, p. 18.

[102] Godber, *The Marchioness Grey of Wrest Park*, p. 16.

[103] Bedfordshire RO, L30/9/84/5: Secker to Jemima Campbell Yorke [May 1740].

[104] *Autobiography*, pp. 20–21; Bedfordshire RO, L30/9/84/7: Secker to Jemima Campbell Yorke, 6 June 1740; BL, Add. MS 35586, f. 235: Secker to Hardwicke, 18 May 1740.

[105] *Walpole's Correspondence*, XXX, p. 304, n. 66.

[106] *Autobiography*, p. 20.

[107] Secker, however, denied any role in arranging the December 1742 marriage of Lady Mary Grey to

After the wedding, Hardwicke's interest in Secker's career increased. When Secker was dispatched as Walpole's messenger to Frederick, 'Lord Hardwicke sent for me upon it; & I told him frankly all that passed,' recalled Secker.[108] When Sarah, duchess of Marlborough, named Secker her executor in 1744, he turned to Hardwicke for advice, and on several occasions Secker recommended servants Hardwicke might employ.[109] By the end of the decade, Hardwicke had formed such a high opinion of Secker that he was willing to spend his own political capital to press vigorously for Secker's promotion. Indeed, it was Hardwicke, rather than Newcastle, who must be seen as Secker's most important patron after 1740.

Before Hardwicke had secured Secker's nomination to the vacant deanery of St Paul's, London, in 1750 as a *commendam*, there appeared little chance that Secker would be able to rid himself of St James's, Westminster, for a less onerous and more lucrative living. In 1743, the country Whig Samuel Sandys had worked without Secker's knowledge to obtain for him the vacant bishopric of Worcester.[110] There were also rumours afloat in 1746 that Secker might be nominated to an Irish see, which his friend Martin Benson advised him against accepting.[111] When it was suggested in 1747 to George II that Secker might succeed Thomas Herring as archbishop of York, the king did not hesitate: 'I will have no Seckàr.'[112] Edmund Gibson's death in 1748 found Herring writing to Hardwicke regarding the newly vacated see of London, which he thought Joseph Butler, bishop of Bristol, would surely be offered. If, however, Butler was not a candidate, Herring thought Secker should be in line for the position: 'I could wish no objections lay to Oxford, for really as a Clergyman & rector of a Parish, he is an Example of great Pains & Abilities, & I know yr. Lp. thinks, does merit a reward.'[113] Herring even tried to get Secker nominated for the vacant see of Lichfield in late 1749, 'but upon the mention of it to lord G[ower] and earl P[owis], they both flew into a rage of prodigious violence'.[114]

David Gregory of Christ Church, Oxford, 'whom she often saw at my House, but I had not the least Knowledge or Suspicion, that it was intended by either of them, till after they were actually married'. He did work to protect her future, though: 'The Duke of Kent, thinking her unlikely to marry, on account of the Disagreeableness of her Person, would have left her only an Annuity for Life. But the Duchess & I persuaded him to give her a Fortune at her own Disposal: which, if I remember right, was £20,000': *Autobiography*, p. 24.

[108] *Autobiography*, p. 21. See also, BL, Add. MS 35587, ff. 2–5: Secker to Hardwicke, 7 Jan 1742.
[109] *Autobiography*, pp. 26–27; BL, Add. MS 35601, ff. 234, 328: Secker to Hardwicke, 30 Sept 1743, 8 Nov 1744.
[110] *Autobiography*, p. 24.
[111] BL, Add. MS 39311, ff. 52–53: Secker to Benson, 28 Oct 1746.
[112] *Literary Illustrations*, III, p. 479.
[113] BL, Add. MS 35598, ff. 348–51: Herring to Hardwicke, 20 Sept 1748. Secker was not Herring's top candidate; his 'Heart & Judgment' went instead with Matthias Mawson, bishop of Chichester. For the curious circumstances surrounding Thomas Sherlock's translation to the London vacancy in 1748, see Carpenter, *Thomas Sherlock*, pp. 140–45.
[114] BL, Add. MS 35598, f. 440: Herring to Hardwicke, 30 Dec 1749.

Secker's patrons were unable to do anything substantive for him until July 1750, when, on the twentieth of the month, Edward Chandler, bishop of Durham, died while in London. Later that day, Newcastle wrote to Hardwicke, 'This opens a great Succession in the Church, which must naturally have a Train of Consequences.' George II, Newcastle thought, held a high opinion of Butler and might well translate him to Durham. This provided an opening for Newcastle and Hardwicke to press the king to replace Butler with Secker at St Paul's. 'If ... the Deanery of St Pauls would be vacant, and if His Majesty would be pleased to condescend to confer that Dignity on the Bishop of Oxford, it would, in my opinion, be a Promotion universally approved,' Newcastle wrote to Hardwicke. 'Your Grace knows how zealously the Archbishop of Canterbury is in that way of Thinking, without any particular attachment of personal friendship, but merely on account of his great Merit as a Scholar, a Preacher, and in all the Functions of a Clergyman, which he has executed with the most laborious application.'[115] Newcastle's speculation was correct: George II did translate Butler to Durham, upon which he resigned the deanery, and Newcastle and Hardwicke were able to convince the king to give Secker St Paul's. The dean's annual income of £2,000, four times greater than that derived each year from the diocese of Oxford, would have made the position attractive to Secker. It relieved him of the burdens of a large urban parish while still allowing him residence in London and presenting him with a new kind of managerial and spiritual challenge.[116]

But Hardwicke was also aware that George II, who had final say over the dispensation of crown patronage, continued to suspect Secker of association with the Leicester House opposition, an issue Hardwicke addressed directly in his recommendation letter to Newcastle. 'I have formerly told your Grace my opinion concerning some political Faults imputed to him. As to his Conduct in Parliam't several years ago, I will say nothing, but that He has long since declared himself to me entirely convinced of the mischievous tendency of formed oppositions, & has expressed his Resolution in the rightest manner on that subject,' he wrote to Newcastle in the summer of 1750.

> As to some other objections, which I have heard made to his conduct, I verily believe they are ill-grounded; that the appearances, which may have given colour to these objections have been forc'd upon him, and I have sometimes thought of late with a view to do him hurt. Your Grace knows the worthy & strong part, the Bishop acted the last year, in the affair of the University of Oxford, tho' a Standard was set up for them in a certain place; and I know that He has been since very ill-treated & run upon at Oxford for his Behaviour on that occasion.

---

[115] BL, Add. MS 32721, f. 418: TPH to Hardwicke, 20 July 1750.

[116] On 17 November 1750, Herring issued granted Secker a dispensation to hold the deanery of St Paul's and the prebendary of Portpool *in commendam*. Following Secker's election to the deanery on 4 December, Thomas Sherlock confirmed him on 11 December: John Le Neve, *Fasti Ecclesiae Anglicanae, 1541–1857. I: St Paul's, London*, compiled by Joyce M. Horn (1969), p. 6. See also, Guildhall Library, MS 9531/20, ff. 137–47, 339.

For my own part, I never had an opinion in my life, in which I was clearer, than that it is necessary, for the Service & Support of His Majesty's Government, to shew countenance to such Persons, as acted with a becoming Spirit & Zeal on that occasion.[117]

When Newcastle reported to George II that 'the bishop of Oxford had renounced opposition ... the king answered, "I know, Benson has. He acted like a gentleman, and I know, has declared it to be the opposition themselves. He had told Lord Limerick that he would never be for a secret committee again as long as he lived."'[118] Following Newcastle and Hardwicke's intervention, the way soon opened for Secker's translation to the deanery of St Paul's. When the offer came, he eagerly accepted since it allowed him to jettison both St James's and his Durham prebend. 'The Reasons of my Acceptance were, that I found the Burthen of Parochial Business grow heavy upon me; & Part of the Parishioners ungrateful for the Pains, which I sincerely took to serve them in all respects,' he later recollected.[119] Newcastle congratulated Herring 'upon as great, and as reputable Promotions, as ever were made, at one Time, in the Church' while Hardwicke thanked Newcastle for his 'powerful & successful Interposition on behalf of the Bishop of Oxford' and argued that 'You have a great deal of Merit in doing it, not only towards the Bishop of Oxford & his Friends, but the King also, as it shews that Desert will meet with Regard, notwithstanding some little Court Objections.'[120]

Secker's move to the deanery of St Paul's owed most to Hardwicke's intervention on his behalf. It also pointed up the gradual erosion of royal disapproval. Thus, when Butler's death vacated the see of Durham in 1752, Secker's name appeared near the top of the short list of potential successors Herring forwarded to Newcastle.[121] Later in 1755 when it looked like Thomas Sherlock might be fatally ill, Herring quietly approached Secker about the possibility of him succeeding Sherlock as bishop, a prospect that did not initially appeal to Secker.[122] He would not be able to refuse the primacy when it was offered to him in 1758, though.

The very day after Matthew Hutton's death in March 1758, Hardwicke vigorously promoted Secker's candidacy. 'Who should be [Hutton's] Successor is

---

[117] BL, Add. MS 32721, f. 418: Hardwicke to TPH, 20 July 1750.

[118] BL, Add. MS 32722, f. 223: TPH to Henry Pelham, 23 Aug 1750. It should be noted, though, that George II's qualms about Secker were not wholly removed: as late as March 1751 Horace Walpole reported that 'The King would not go to chapel, because Secker Bishop of Oxford was to preach before him: his ministers did not insist upon his hearing the sermon, as they had lately upon his making him Dean of St Pauls': Walpole, *Memoirs of George II*, I, p. 45.

[119] *Autobiography*, p. 28. Secker reiterated this point in a letter of thanks to the king: Hallward Library, NE C 1080: Secker to George II, 7 Aug 1750.

[120] BL, Add. MS 32722, f. 5: TPH to Herring, 1 Aug 1750; BL, Add. MS 32722, f. 108: Hardwicke to TPH, 10 Aug 1750.

[121] BL, Add. MS 32728, ff. 46–50: Herring to TPH, 19 June 1752.

[122] LPL, Secker Papers 7, ff. 92–93: Secker to Herring, 12 May 1755.

undoubtedly a Question of the greatest importance in every respect. I am clearly of opinion that the Bishop of Oxford ought to be the Man, for all kinds of Reasons; and I hope the King will, in his Wisdom, make no difficulties about it,' he wrote to Newcastle.

> However, till That is over, I, who have nothing to do in it, cannot turn my Thoughts to any other. For this reason, I think it will be most advisable for Your Grace to name the Bishop of Oxford singly to His Majesty, not by way of nomination, but by way of Suggestion, as the fittest man; and if the King objects or hesitates, to name no body else to day. I ... cannot help thinking it will be proper for Your Grace to speak to Mr. Pitt on this subject ... If Your Grace thinks it proper, You have my free leave to let His Majesty know that my humble opinion is for the Bishop of Oxford, in the strongest manner.[123]

Newcastle immediately met with George II to recommend Secker for Canterbury, 'and I suggested nobody else', he assured Secker. The king's response was wholly favourable: 'His Majesty was pleased to give so much Attention to what I said, and to express Himself in such a Manner, that, without coming to any Determination, I have just Reason to hope the King will make the Choice I presumed to recommend to Him.'[124] Newcastle, however, was taking the most sanguine view of the meeting, for Secker's earlier opposition to the government in parliament still rankled the king, as Secker later acknowledged in his autobiography:

> The Duke sent me Word, on Monday just before Dinner, that he had proposed me to the King, who said he would consider of it. I returned him a short note of thanks, with Wishes that his Majesty might pitch on a fitter Person. And I neither heard nor said any more of the Matter, till the Duke sent for me on Tuesday to come to him on Wednesday morning, & told me the King had consented, that I should be Abp. And he said he began with describing to the King, who at sort of a Person should be appointed. The King said, I know whom you mean, your Friend the Bishop of St Asaph. The Duke said, No, Sir, I mean the Bishop of Oxford. The King asked Hath not he been connected with Leicester House? The Duke answered, I have made all possible Inquiry, & am fully satisfied, that he never was. And in this he spoke very true ... I believe the Duke advised previously with Bp. Trevor & Bp Drummond about this matter. For he directed me to visit them both, as soon as I could: which I did.[125]

Newcastle also counselled Secker about how to defuse George II's lingering concerns. At the next court levee, Secker was to ask the king for a private

---

[123] BL, Add. MS 32878, f. 276: Hardwicke to TPH, 20 Mar 1758.
[124] Ibid., f. 278: TPH to Secker, 20 Mar 1758.
[125] *Autobiography*, pp. 36–37. See also, BL, Add. MS 32878, f. 280: Secker to TPH, 20 Mar 1758. Newcastle may initially indeed have preferred Robert Hay Drummond, bishop of St Asaph, to Secker for Canterbury. Horace Walpole certainly thought so: 'The Duke of Newcastle had great inclination to give it to Dr. Hay Drummond Bishop of St Asaph, a gentleman, a man of parts, and of the world; but Lord Hardwicke's influence carried it for Secker, who certainly did not want parts or worldliness': Walpole, *Memoirs of George II*, III, p. 14.

audience 'in which you will say, what I am sure will be very proper, both as to what relates to your past and future conduct', Newcastle advised. 'Talk with Openness & Freedom, & desire Leave from Time to Time to wait upon His Majesty. To receive His Commands, to which you shall always pay the greatest Attention.' And before leaving the meeting, 'if your Lordship would add (what is most sincerely true) That you have no connection or Object, but his Majesty & Service'.[126] The king was not the only one with concerns, however, for some thought Secker's ecclesiastical politics, especially his advocacy of an American espicopate, might not sit well with some Dissenters.[127] Nevertheless, Newcastle was satisfied that the fears were overblown. 'He is attached to nobody but myself and my friend Lord Hardwicke,' Newcastle explained to one doubter. 'I sent early to him in relation to his conduct towards Dissenters. He explained himself wholly to my satisfaction and what I am persuaded will be to theirs.' Secker had reassured Newcastle that he got on well with Benjamin Avery and Samuel Chandler, both prominent Dissenting ministers. Nevertheless, Newcastle promised, 'I shall speak to both of them upon the new archbishop's subject, and I shall talk to Dr. Lawrence and to some who are of a different party among the Dissenters; and you may assure them all that I will answer for the new archbishop so far as relates to them.'[128]

Thus, despite some lasting uneasiness about Secker's political behaviour and sporadic criticisms concerning his nomination, George II soon granted his consent to the nomination, and he was translated into office in late April 1758.[129] 'No one will do greater Honour to the station,' Andrew Coltée Ducarel predicted, while an orthodox fellow of Corpus Christi, Oxford, applauded the 'happy omen for the Church, that the indisputably ablest and most well meaning of the whole Bench is at the Helm'.[130] The enormity of his elevation to Canterbury was not lost on Secker. 'I have received the Honour of Your Grace's Letter in the midst of Company, just going to Dinner with me,' he wrote to Newcastle when he first heard news of his nomination, 'and have but a moments Time to say, that I am quite terrified at the unexpected Contents of it; that I shall have great Cause to be pleased, If his Majesty thinks of some worthier Person: that if he should pitch upon me, I must endeavour, through God's help, to appear as little unworthy as I

---

[126] BL, Add. MS 32878, ff. 391–92: TPH to Secker, 27 Mar 1758.
[127] BL, Add. MS 32879, f. 74: J. White to TPH, 5 April 1758.
[128] Ibid., f. 5: TPH to J. White, 1 April 1758.
[129] The *congé d'élire* and letter missive for Secker were issued on 8 Mar 1758 following his nomination by the king in council. He was elected to the archbishopric of Canterbury on 7 April, to which royal assent was granted on 10 April. Following his confirmation on 21 April in Bow Church, London, his temporalities were restored to him on 25 April. John Le Neve and T. Duffus Hardy, *Fasti Ecclesiae Anglicanae* (Oxford, 1854), I, p. 60.
[130] BL, Add. MS 15935, f. 133: A.C. Ducarel to Browne Willis, 27 July 1758; BL, Add. MS 39311, ff. 94–95: Thomas Patten to George Berkeley, jr., 25 Nov 1760 (quoted in *Autobiography*, p. xvi).

can.'[131] After nearly twenty-three years on the episcopal bench, Secker now stood atop the summit of the ecclesiastical hierarchy. The challenges he faced were enormous, not least, to his way of thinking, because unchecked errant belief was both corrosive and incendiary: it weakened the nation during a time of war and it fuelled religio-political strife. Secker's first priority as an Anglican insider, then, was to promote orthodoxy, to stamp out doctrinal diversity, and to combat heterodoxy.

---

[131] BL, Add. MS 32878, f. 280: Secker to TPH, 20 Mar 1758.

Chapter Four

THE CHURCH AND THE ENLIGHTENMENT

Thomas Secker was bearish on England's moral state. 'Christianity is now ridiculed and railed at, with very little reserve: and the teachers of it, without any at all,' he groused in 1738.[1] It was a recurrent theme in his public and private pronouncements on the state of the nation. England's wars abroad and the continuing belief in God's providential intervention in human affairs made the causes and cures of England's moral decline issues of national security.[2] Many argued that new temptations, particularly a thirst for luxury goods, sapped the nation's moral strength.[3] 'We have increased Amusements and Gaieties to a Degree unexampled, just when Providence hath called us most loudly to thoughtful Consideration,' Secker complained, and as a result 'these Indiscretions have produced personal Miseries and national Inconveniences without Number'.[4] Secker, though, thought that theological heterodoxy posed a greater threat than rampant consumerism because errant belief removed a powerful check on human behaviour: '... wrong Belief hath great Power to deprave Men's morals. *Surely then a right one must have some Power to reform them.*'[5] For proof, one needed only to look to the traumatic events of the previous century.

The spectre of the seventeenth century loomed large in the eighteenth century.[6] Secker and his contemporaries 'lived with the memory of the civil wars as

[1]   *Charges* (1738), p. 4. Cf. Joseph Butler, *The Analogy of Religion* (1798; originally published 1737), advertisement.

[2]   Robert G. Ingram, '"The trembling earth is God's Herald": earthquakes, religion, and public life in Britain during the 1750s', *The Lisbon earthquake of 1755: Representations and reactions* (*SVEC* 2005:02), eds. Theodore E.D. Braun and John B. Radner (Oxford, 2005), pp. 97–115; J.C.D. Clark, 'Providence, Predestination, and Progress; or, did the Enlightenment fail?', *Albion* 35:4 (2003), pp. 559–89; W. Speck and D. Napthine, 'Clergymen and Conflict, 1660–1763', *SCH* 19 (1983), pp. 238–46.

[3]   Maxine Berg, *Luxury and Pleasure in Eighteenth-Century Britain* (Oxford, 2005), pp. 31–37; Bob Harris, *Politics and the Nation: Britain in the Mid-Eighteenth Century* (Oxford, 2002), pp. 67–101, 279–81; Christopher J. Berry, *The Idea of Luxury: A Conceptual and Historical Investigation* (Cambridge, 1994), pp. 126–76; John Sekora, *Luxury: The Concept in Western Thought, Eden to Smollett* (Baltimore, 1977), pp. 39–47, 77–109.

[4]   'Sermon preached in 1746, on the Victory at Culloden [2 Cor. 1:9–10]', in Thomas Secker, *Nine sermons preached in the parish of St James, Westminster, on occasion of the war and rebellion in 1745*, 2nd edn (1771), p. 145.

[5]   Thomas Secker, *A Sermon preached before the Incorporated Society for the Propagation of the Gospel in Foreign Parts; at their anniversary meeting in the Parish-Church of St Mary-le-Bow, on Friday, Feb 20. 1740–41* (1741), p. 14. Emphasis mine. See also, idem, 'Sermon XCV. An Explanation and Defence of the Liturgy of the Church of England [1 Cor. 14:15]', in *WTS*, III, p. 2; *Lectures*, p. 32.

[6]   John Seed, 'The spectre of Puritanism: forgetting the seventeenth century in David Hume's *History of England*', *Social History* 30:4 (2005), pp. 444–62; Blair Worden, *Roundhead*

the nightmare from which it was struggling to awake, or if you prefer, to go to sleep again', J.G.A. Pocock rightly notes. 'Its dullest complacency was a blanket spread over that memory.'[7] The eighteenth-century orthodox were particularly aghast at the radical assault on the religio-political order during the previous century and feared a reprise during theirs. In 1734, for instance, Secker warned his audience at St James's, Westminster, that Charles I's execution was 'a most peculiarly instructive example of divine judgments, brought down by a sinful people on their own heads'.[8] In all his providential interventions in human affairs, God teaches 'an awful regard to himself, as moral governor of the world; and a faithful practice of true religion'. And what drew his divine wrath upon England during the 1650s was the abandonment of 'real religion' for 'hypocrisy, superstition, and enthusiasm'.[9] Certainly Laud and his followers might have displayed 'an over warm zeal, and very blameable stiffness and severity', Secker acknowledged. 'But there was also, in the enemies of the church, a most provoking bitterness and perverseness; with a wild eagerness for innovation, founded on ignorant prejudices, which their heated fancies raised into necessary truths; and then, looking on them, as the cause of Christ, they thought themselves bound and commissioned to overturn whatever was contrary to them.'[10]

The lessons to be drawn from the seventeenth-century 'troubles' were relevant because theology and politics remained so tightly and organically intertwined during the eighteenth century. Put simply, theological heterodoxy threatened the religio-political order, theological orthodoxy buttressed it, and the great unravelling of society during the mid seventeenth century proved it.[11] At stake in eighteenth-century religious debate, then, was the survival of both church and state, issues which had heightened importance for a nation at war. Not surprisingly, the promotion and defence of theological orthodoxy were central to Thomas Secker's reform vision. This involved, among other things, careful scrutiny of candidates for ordination, education reforms in the universities, and,

Reputations: The English Civil Wars and the Passions of Posterity (2001), pp. 65–215; J.C.D. Clark, *English Society, 1660–1832: Religion, ideology and politics during the ancien régime* (Cambridge, 2000), pp. 43–123.

7   J.G.A. Pocock, 'Within the margins: the definitions of orthodoxy', in *The Margins of Orthodoxy: Heterodox Writing and Cultural Response, 1660–1750*, ed. Roger Lund (Cambridge, 1995), p. 38.

8   'Sermon CXXVII. Preached in the parish church of St James, Westminster, Jan 30, 1733–4 [Isaiah 32:9]', in *WTS*, III, p. 423. Cf. 'Sermon CXXX. Preached before the House of Lords, in the Abbey-Church of Westminster, on Thursday, May 29, 1739 [Psalm 106:12–13]', in *WTS*, III, pp. 460–71.

9   'Sermon CXXVII. Preached ... [on] Jan 30, 1733–34', p. 425.

10   Ibid., p. 426.

11   A.M.C. Waterman, *Political Economy and Christian Theology Since the Enlightenment: Essays in Intellectual History* (Basingstoke, 2004), pp. 31–54; Justin Champion, '"Religion's Safe, with Priestcraft is the War": Augustan Anticlericalism and the Legacy of the English Revolution, 1660–1720', *The European Legacy* 5:4 (2000), pp. 547–61; Clark, *English Society, 1660–1832*, pp. 318–422.

most importantly, building up a stable of orthodox clerical talent which could be counted to promote and defend 'true religion'.

The intellectual climate during Secker's lifetime was not overwhelmingly supportive of orthodoxy. The lapse of the Licensing Act in 1695 opened the floodgates from the presses, created a sustainable print culture, and served as the English Enlightenment's midwife.[12] As in the sixteenth and seventeenth centuries, religious works dominated the eighteenth-century publishing market; but the end of pre-publication censorship opened the way for heterodox work to stream on to that market, especially as post-publication prosecutions for blasphemy, obscenity, and seditious libel became increasingly rare.[13] Yet it remained a palpably conservative age. England's Enlightenment was not the French Enlightenment's freethinking forerunner.[14] Nor were the scientific breakthroughs of the seventeenth century inherently and necessarily corrosive of religious belief.[15] Indeed it is now almost an historiographical commonplace that the scientific revolution and the Enlightenment 'throve in England within piety',[16] and some historians have pressed even further ahead to argue that the

[12] James Raven, 'Publishing and bookselling, 1660–1780', in *The Cambridge History of English Literature, 1660–1780*, ed. John Richetti (Cambridge, 2005), pp. 11–36; Michael Treadwell, 'The stationers and the printing acts at the end of the seventeenth century', in *The Cambridge History of the Book in Britain. Volume IV: 1557–1695*, eds. John Barnard and D.F. McKenzie (Cambridge, 2002), pp. 755–76.

[13] Isabel Rivers, 'Religion and literature', in *The Cambridge History of English Literature, 1660–1780*, p. 445; Raven, 'Publishing and bookselling, 1660–1780', pp. 16–17; Patrick Collinson, Arnold Hunt, and Alexandra Walsham, 'Religious publishing in England, 1557–1640' and Ian Green and Kate Peters, 'Religious publishing in England, 1640–1695', in *The Cambridge History of the Book in Britain. Volume IV: 1557–1695*, pp. 29–93.

[14] Paul Hazard, *European Thought in the Eighteenth Century: From Montesquieu to Lessing* (1946) and Peter Gay, *The Enlightenment: An Interpretation, The Rise of Modern Paganism* (New York, 1967) are classic expressions of the view that the Enlightenment was a coherent, trans-national intellectual movement that was inherently anti-religious. J.G.A. Pocock, 'The Re-Description of Enlightenment', *Proceedings of the British Academy* 125 (2004), pp. 101–17 and Clark, 'Providence, Predestination and Progress: or, did the Enlightenment Fail?', pp. 559–89 caution against the reification of 'The Enlightenment'. But cf. Louis Dupré, *The Enlightenment and the Intellectual Foundations of Modern Culture* (New Haven, CT, 2005) and John Robertson, *The Case for the Enlightenment: Scotland and Naples, 1680–1760* (Cambridge, 2005), esp. pp. 1–51.

[15] See, for instance, Robert G. Ingram, 'William Warburton, Divine Action, and Enlightened Christianity', in *Religious Identities in Britain, 1660–1832*, eds. William Gibson and Robert G. Ingram (Aldershot, 2005), pp. 97–117; James Force and Sarah Hutton (eds.), *Newton and Newtonianism: New Studies* (Dordrecht, 2004); Loup Verlet, '"F=MA" and the Newtonian Revolution: An Exit from Religion Through Religion', *History of Science* 34:3 (1996), pp. 303–46; Peter Harrison, 'Newtonian Science, Miracles, and the Laws of Nature', *Journal of the History of Ideas* 56:4 (1995), pp. 531–53.

[16] Roy Porter, 'The Enlightenment in England', in *The Enlightenment in national context*, eds. Roy Porter and Miklaus Teich (Cambridge, 1981), p. 6. Cf. Sheridan Gilley, 'Christianity and Enlightenment: An Historical Survey', *History of European Ideas* 1:2 (1981), p. 104.

English Enlightenment was 'decidedly clerical and intellectually conservative'.[17] While *ecrasez l'infame* was not the clarion call of England's Enlightenment, though, the sixteenth and seventeenth centuries nonetheless unleashed intellectual forces – anti-dogmatism and anticlericalism chief among them – which were inimical to orthodoxy. This meant that though the mainstream of English thought remained more traditional than not during at least the first three quarters of the eighteenth century, contemporaries nevertheless violently debated the grounds of religious belief. It is not surprising to find, then, that the orthodox perceived much of the heterodox writing as corrosive of 'true religion' nor to discover that the orthodox fought furiously to rebut what they perceived to be the heterodox threat.

If, as some have recently argued, the Enlightenment 'permanently inured us against one thing: the willingness to accept authority uncritically', then the anti-dogmatists were quintessentially Enlightenment creatures.[18] Anti-dogmatism developed in response to Europe-wide confessional strife, to Laudian formalism, and to the punitive Restoration after 1660. Having witnessed Europe ravaged by war waged over religious truth in the sixteenth and seventeenth centuries, many sought to ground knowledge and certainty on non-transcendental foundations. As a result, scepticism flourished.[19] In the British Isles, anti-dogmatism was a response to the domestic 'troubles': heterodoxy blossomed during the 1640s and 1650s; anti-Trinitarian heresies revived in the decades after the Restoration; and deism, natural religion, and a variety of religious heterodoxies thrived well into the eighteenth century.[20] Anti-dogmatists came in various shapes and sizes and ranged from Tillotson to Clarke, from Burnet to Blackburne, from Locke to Lindsey. In general, they championed *sola scriptura*, discounted tradition, favoured jettisoning man-made articles of faith, and argued for the primacy of individual conscience,

---

[17] B.W. Young, *Religion and Enlightenment in Eighteenth-Century England: Theological Debate from Locke to Burke* (Oxford, 1998), p. 6. See also, J.G.A. Pocock, 'Post-Puritan England and the problem of the Enlightenment', in *Culture and Politics from Puritanism to the Enlightenment*, ed. Perez Zagorin (Berkeley and Los Angeles, 1980), pp. 91–112; idem, 'Clergy and Commerce: The Conservative Enlightenment in England', in *L'età dei Lumi: Studi storici sul settecento europeo in onore di Franco Venturi*, eds. R. Ajello, E. Contese, and V. Piano (Naples, 1985), I, pp. 523–62; idem, 'Conservative Enlightenment and Democratic Revolutions: The American and French Cases in British Perspective', *Government and Opposition* 24:1 (1989), pp. 81–105.

[18] Dupré, *The Enlightenment and the Intellectual Foundations of Modern Culture*, p. ix.

[19] Richard H. Popkin, *The History of Scepticism: from Savonarola to Bayle* (Oxford, 2003).

[20] See, for instance, Christopher Hill, 'Freethinking and libertinism: the legacy of the English Revolution', in *The Margins of Orthodoxy*, pp. 54–72; John Marshall, 'Some Intellectual Consequences of the English Revolution', *The European Legacy* 5:4 (2000), pp. 515–30; idem, 'Locke, Socinianism, "Socinianism", and Unitarianism', in *English Philosophy in the Age of Locke*, ed. M.A. Stewart (Oxford, 2000), pp. 111–82; B.W. Young, '"The Soul-Sleeping System": Politics and Heresy in Eighteenth-Century England', *JEH* 45:1 (1994), pp. 64–81; Nigel Aston, 'The Limits of Latitudinarianism: English Reactions to Bishop Clayton's *An Essay on Spirit*', *JEH* 49:3 (1998), pp. 407–43.

particularly regarding slippery issues of Christology.[21] A more radical anti-dogmatist critique of religious belief came from freethinkers who aimed their artillery at the foundations of Christianity and, at times, of religious belief itself.[22] The gamut of freethinking belief ran from a wholly natural theology to outright atheism. If freethinkers themselves accounted for a negligible percentage of the populace, they punched well above their weight in terms of intellectual influence.[23]

Thomas Secker's work to promote and defend orthodoxy against its heterodox opponents took place in a specific historical context, the mid eighteenth century. A fusillade of orthodox scholarship during the first third of the eighteenth century, culminating in Joseph Butler's *Analogy of Religion* (1736), had repulsed the deist threat, but it did not kill off theological heterodoxy itself. Beginning in the 1750s and crescendoing through the 1760s, a new wave of heterodox work loudly demanded reform in church and state. This time it was anti-Trinitarianism, rather than deism, which served as 'the chief matrix of ideological innovation',[24] and anti-dogmatist quasi-Arians like Edmund Law, Francis Blackburne, and Peter Peckard led the heterodox chorus clamouring for theological, liturgical, and political reform. Secker's own theological views were formed in the crucible of the early eighteenth-century deistic controversy, but his chief opponents during his years on the episcopal and archiepiscopal bench were not the heterodox bogeymen of the early century but their progeny.

The anti-dogmatist assault on orthodox belief during the eighteenth century was one of the wellsprings of a larger anticlerical phenomenon. The demolition of the traditional order in church and state during the mid seventeenth century had catalyzed anticlericalism's growth.[25] And though the traditional order in church and state was restored in 1660, the critics of the establishment did not merely fade away. By the early eighteenth century, anticlericalism was a coherent and powerful language of religio-political opposition, and it remained so well into Secker's primacy. While anticlericals were not carbon copies of one another, nearly all were

---

[21] Young, *Religion and Enlightenment*, pp. 19–44.

[22] See, for instance, Justin Champion, *Republican learning: John Toland and the crisis of Christian culture, 1696–1722* (Manchester, 2003); James A. Herrick, *The Radical Rhetoric of the English Deists: The Discourses of Skepticism, Ridicule and Religion* (Columbia, SC, 1997); Peter N. Miller, '"Freethinking" and "Freedom of Thought" in Eighteenth-Century Britain', *HJ* 36:3 (1993), pp. 599–617; Margaret Jacob, *The Radical Enlightenment: Pantheists, Freemasons and Republicans* (1981). Popkin, *The History of Scepticism* and Jonathan Israel, *The Radical Enlightenment: Philosophy and the Making of Modernity, 1650–1750* (Oxford, 2001) offer a broader perspective on freethinking.

[23] But see S.J. Barnett, *The Enlightenment and religion: The myths of modernity* (Manchester, 2003), which argues that historians have given eighteenth-century deism attention in inverse proportion to its actual significance.

[24] Clark, *English Society, 1660–1832*, p. 368.

[25] Justin Champion, '"May the last king be strangled in the bowels of the last priest": irreligion and the English Enlightenment', in *Radicalism in British Literary Culture, 1650–1830: From Revolution to Revolution*, ed. Timothy Morton (Cambridge, 2002), p. 38.

'grounded in an unfolding tradition of Christian reformism'.[26] Some assaulted the intellectual foundations upon which Christianity based its claims to truth and assailed priests as the purveyors of errant belief; others railed at the privileges which attended the Church's legal establishment; still others accepted Christianity's truth claims but advocated a purely erastian relationship between church and state.[27] Anticlericalism in all its many forms was particularly virulent during the 1730s, at precisely the time when Secker career so precipitously soared upwards – he could not but have been shaped by what he saw.

In the face of their opponents both within and without the Church, the orthodox had a limited number of options. To ignore the attacks would have been folly, while an accommodationist response almost self-evidently guaranteed to produce little fruit. Instead of ignoring the threats or simply hunkering down, many orthodox chose to fight back. As a result, the clerical English Enlightenment was a pugilistic clerical Enlightenment,[28] and the intellectual contretemps often took on the character of a back-alley brawl with few, if any, holds barred.[29] With church courts emasculated and with the state reluctant to stand shoulder-to-shoulder with them to defend orthodoxy, orthodox clergy had to get their hands dirty in intellectual combat. One of Secker's more choleric colleagues, William Warburton, likened the defence of orthodoxy to 'a warfare upon earth'.[30]

One of the leaders of the orthodox counter-offensive was Secker himself. Many at the time believed that he was a vigilant and, if necessary, vengeful leader of the established Church. 'It was commonly said he had two paper books,' asserted one cleric, 'one called the *black*, the other the *white* book; in which he entered down such notices as he received concerning the different characters of each, as they happened to suit the design of either book. Those whose character he found to be bad, he resolved never to promote; nor did, paying no regard to any solicitations made in their behalf.'[31] There is, alas, no evidence that Secker kept detailed lists of the naughty and the nice, but the image of the black and white books raises an important point: the self-identified orthodox and heterodox conceived of the

---

[26] Mark Goldie, 'Priestcraft and the birth of Whiggism', in *Political Discourse in Early Modern Britain*, eds. Nicholas Phillipson and Quentin Skinner (Cambridge, 1993), p. 211.

[27] Nigel Aston and Matthew Cragoe (eds.), *Anticlericalism in Britain, c.1500–1914* (Stroud, 2000) provides a useful introduction to the subject. Stephen Taylor, 'Whigs, Tories and Anticlericalism: Ecclesiastical Courts Legislation in 1733', *Parliamentary History* 19:3 (2000), pp. 329–55 anatomizes an important, if neglected, Tory anticlerical tradition.

[28] J.G.A. Pocock, 'Enthusiasm: The Antiself of Enlightenment', in *Enthusiasm and Enlightenment in Europe, 1650–1850* (*Huntington Library Quarterly* 60:1–2), eds. Lawrence E. Klein and Anthony J. La Vopa (Berkeley and Los Angeles, 1998), p. 12; Young, *Religion and Enlightenment*, p. 6.

[29] A.W. Evans, *Warburton and the Warburtonians: A Study in Some Eighteenth-Century Controversies* (1932) gives a sense of the nature of public intellectual debate during the mid-century.

[30] William Warburton, *Letters from a late eminent prelate to one of his friends* (Kidderminster, 1793), p. 256.

[31] *Literary Anecdotes*, III, p. 751.

eighteenth-century English religious world in Manichean terms. While the orthodox and heterodox shared a desire for restorative religious reform, they diverged over what constituted the durable truths of Christianity. Most of Thomas Secker's contemporaries reckoned that his theology was unimpeachably orthodox.[32] The essence of his faith was belief in scripture, tradition, revelation, and reason as the sources of religious authority; in the Trinity in unity; in the atonement of sin through Christ; in salvation by faith in grace alone; in the providential interaction of God in nature and in human affairs; in the moral obligation to act on belief; and in the necessary role of the visible and apostolic church in the nation's life. He believed, as well, that the history, theology, and liturgy of the established Church of England marked it as the lone authentic representative of the holy catholic church in Britain and its empire. With much of this, particularly regarding the sources of authority and the nature of the Trinity, the heterodox disagreed. Indeed, the heterodox disagreed with the orthodox so violently on these matters that they often accused the orthodox of being crypto-papists, perhaps the worst insult possible in an era of on and off again war with the Catholic Bourbons. '[I]t seems as if the chair of infallibility is to be transferred from Rome to Lambeth,' the heterodox Anglican cleric Thomas Gwatkin groused in 1768. 'In a political view some advantages may be gained by such a change. For certainly it will be attended with some savings to the nation to refer religious disputes to an English Archbishop instead of bringing them before an Italian prelate. Yet I cannot help thinking a good protestant will consider it as a matter equally indifferent, whether he be obliged to regard as infallible the determinations of Pope Clement, or Thomas Secker, Lord Archbishop of Canterbury and primate of all England.'[33]

Secker's response to the heterodox conflation of orthodoxy and popery was at once direct and slippery. '[W]e think the Church of Rome far more heterodox than we do any of the Protestant Churches', he assured Jonathan Mayhew during the mid 1760s. Might this mean that the non-Anglican Protestant churches shared more in common with the Church of Rome than with the Church of England? 'As to other churches, so far as their opinions differ from ours', Secker continued, 'be it in points more or less material, we do indeed think them mistaken, or, if the Doctor [Mayhew] pleases, heterodox.' Nevertheless, he contended that the orthodox were 'without the least contempt of them [i.e., the

---

[32]   Robert G. Ingram, 'Nation, Empire, and Church: Thomas Secker, Anglican Identity, and Public Life in Georgian Britain, 1700–1770' (University of Virginia Ph.D. thesis, 2002), pp. 20–60 and James Downey, *The Eighteenth Century Pulpit* (Oxford, 1969), pp. 89–114 highlight the salient features of Secker's theology. Cf. Jeffrey S. Chamberlain, 'Moralism, Justification, and the Controversy over Methodism', *JEH* 44:4 (1993), pp. 652–78 for the beliefs of 'mainstream Anglicans' and Ian Green, *Print and Protestantism in Early Modern England* (Oxford, 2000), pp. 557–63 for the theological composition of 'orthodox Protestantism' in early modern England.

[33]   Thomas Gwatkin, *Remarks upon the second and third of Three letters against the Confessional by a country clergyman* (1768), p. 43.

heterodox], or breach of brotherly love towards them; and we allow them to think us so, without taking it amiss'.[34] Despite cautiously couched eirenic statements like these, though, Secker spearheaded a spirited, determined, and persistent defence of orthodoxy. He volunteered that heterodoxy and heresy differed from one another,[35] but he did not always act like he believed that.

I

Secker laid much of the responsibility for the spread of heterodoxy on Anglican clerics. The problem, as he saw it, was that '[o]ur clergy have dwelt too much upon mere morality, and too little on the peculiar doctrines of the Gospel'.[36] Only an body of orthodox clergy promulgating orthodox doctrine could prevent the laity from falling into the 'crime of heterodoxy', a theme Secker fleshed out in a planned address to Convocation in 1761. 'It ... is essential that we should succeed in pasturing our flocks as much as possible, and be of one mind, especially in matters of saving faith,' he counselled.

> For there are those who claim to be ours who nonetheless disagree with much of what we teach, particularly concerning the Holy Trinity, the redemption of the human race and the imparting of heavenly grace to the minds of believers. For if the error of those who reject the received teaching concerning these things spreads too far, or if those who fall for such lies are weakened as a result, and lack that conviction of these things which is the source of good works, and the belief that is necessary to have trust in the favour of God engraved on our deepest thoughts, which removes all doubt, we shall be troubled with endless controversies ... . And the beautiful structure of our church will not only be shaken, it will be destroyed, and the soundness of living doctrine will be corrupted.[37]

Worrying that widespread ignorance of Christian teachings might torpedo the Church's pastoral mission, Secker tried to ensure that biblically literate clergy staffed Anglican livings in his dioceses.[38] In 1762, for instance, he delayed Jarvis Kenrick's institution to the vicarage of Chilham on account of Kenrick's biblical illiteracy. 'How he came to be ordained, I know not,' Secker explained to Kenrick's father, who had written a lengthy letter testifying to the quality of his

---

[34] 'An Answer to Dr. Mayhew's Observations on the Charter and Conduct of the Society for the Propagation of the Gospel in Foreign Parts', in *WTS*, IV, p. 533.

[35] Ibid.

[36] *Literary Illustrations*, III, p. 497.

[37] *Oratio*, pp. 361–62.

[38] Jeremy Gregory, 'Standards for Admission to the Ministry of the Church of England in the Eighteenth Century', *Dutch Review of Church History* 83:1 (2003), pp. 283–95 provides some context.

son's Cambridge education. Secker refused to institute Jarvis to Chilham until he had done a crash course on biblical studies because 'the minister of a parish is to teach his people, not mathematicks or natural philosophy, but the word of God: & he appeared to me surprizingly ignorant of the contents of his Bible'. And Secker made it clear to Kenrick's father that the bar Jarvis had been expected to clear was not particularly high. 'I did not ask him hard Questions but such as I hope many illiterate persons in the parish of Chilham can readily answer. Nor did I speak to him in a terrifying manner but with the utmost gentleness, as I believe he will own,' Secker assured Matthew Kenrick.

> Nor did I require sudden & hasty replies from him but allowed him full time. And wn for the present I dismissed him, I gave him advice how he might qualifie himself better ... How cd I treat him with more candor? Surely you wd not have me admit him whilst I think him in my conscience unfit. Persons must have the requisite Qualifications in a competent Degree wn they apply.[39]

Secker instructed Jarvis to read the Bible, William Wake's *Exposition of the Doctrine of the Church of England* (1686), and Isaac Watt's *A Short View of the Whole Scripture History* (1732) before his next examination.[40] Experience with ordinands like Jarvis Kenrick help explain Secker's admonition in his visitation charges, 'It is of the Gospel that you are Ministers: all other Learning will leave you essentially unqualified.'[41]

Secker fretted publicly about clerical ignorance of Christian doctrine, and in his published episcopal charges, he repeatedly encouraged clergy to continue their religious education beyond ordination. In his first charge to the Oxford clergy in 1738, he counselled, 'Giving Instruction requires Knowledge. And therefore, as a competent Degree of it is justly expected of Persons, before they enter into Holy Orders: so, when they enter, the Care of making a continual Progress in it is solemnly promised to them, and covenanted for with them.' As such, he recommended that clergy bone up, first, on the 'Grounds of Religion' and, second, on the 'Doctrines of it', so they could teach their parishioners the 'Proofs of Religion, both natural and revealed ... in the most intelligible and convincing Manner'. The danger of clergy 'being unqualified to give more particular Answers, where they can be given' is that clerical ignorance 'may often prove a great Reproach to us, and a great Stumbling-block to others'.[42] These were themes he continued to harp on after his elevation to Canterbury. In his 1761 Convocation address, for instance, he advised that 'just because we are currently enjoying a time of inactivity, this does not mean that we should neglect theological studies'.[43] And

---

[39] LPL, Secker Papers 3, f. 147: Secker to Matthew Kenrick, 26 April 1762. See also ibid., ff. 145–46: Matthew Kenrick to Secker, 26 April 1762.

[40] Jarvis Kenrick was instituted to the Chilham living later in 1762: *Speculum*, pp. 13–14.

[41] *Charges* (1766), p. 289.

[42] *Charges* (1738), pp. 14, 17, 20.

[43] *Oratio*, p. 364.

in his 1766 charge to the Canterbury clergy, he admonished his clergy 'to complete yourselves in all proper Knowledge: not merely the introductory Kinds, which unhappily are often almost the only ones, taught the Candidates for holy Orders; but those chiefly, which have a closer Connection to your Work'. Though clerics should know 'the Science of Morals and natural Religion', he advised that 'the Doctrines and Precepts of the Gospel require your principal Regard beyond all Comparison'.[44]

Secker realized, however, that Oxford and Cambridge, which together served as England's only seminaries, provided seriously deficient clerical education. 'Many of the Tutors in our Universities have sadly neglected instructing their pupils in Theological knowledge, of which all should have a good Tincture: but all, who are intended for Orders, a very strong one,' he lamented to William Smith in 1760. 'It is indeed the chief thing, that they should learn: the only one absolutely necessary.'[45] Dissatisfied with both the moral and intellectual climate in Oxford and Cambridge, Secker had, by 1739, already begun canvassing his allies in Oxford about ways to improve clerical education there.[46] Taverns and coffee shops abounded, 'tempt[ing] persons to spend their time and money'; tutors' fees were too high; credit was given too freely to students by local tradesmen; and too much money was spent on horses and clothes. As a result, the students had '[l]ess religion', a 'mad love of Liberty & a scorn of everything serious'. As a remedy, Secker suggested that visitors more closely supervise their colleges, for 'when once the Colleges were reformed, that would reform the University'. A kind of tenure system for fellows might also be established to purge the indolent and inept and make way for the industrious and diligent. A closer look should, as well, be given at those admitted to the university, for '[s]uch as our young noblemen now are, it is perhaps better, that there shd not be many of them in the University'.

Most importantly, the theological curriculum stood in need of dramatic reform, chiefly by adding a regular course of lectures in divinity for all university students.[47] Later in his career, Secker promoted Edmund Bentham's candidacy for the regius professorship of divinity at Oxford, hoping that Bentham could successfully bring about curricular reform.[48] While regius professor, Bentham (1706–1776)

---

[44] *Charges* (1766), p. 289.

[45] LPL, MS 1123/II, ff. 290–91: Secker to William Smith, 12 Oct 1760.

[46] LPL, MS 2564, pp. 315–25. In this commonplace book, Secker kept notes on reforms that might improve both the moral tenor of life in the universities and the theological training the students received there. These notes were based upon his own observations and on his conversations with Joseph Atwell and David Gregory, two orthodox Whig churchmen at Exeter and Christ Church colleges. Unless otherwise noted, the information and quotations in this paragraph come from these notes: many of the themes he first outlined in his *Sermon preached before the University of Oxford, at St Mary's, on Act Sunday ... July 8, 1733* (Oxford, 1733). Graham Midgley, *University Life in Eighteenth-Century Oxford* (New Haven, CT, 1996) is an evocative portrait of its subject.

[47] As distinct from the statutory university sermons first instituted during Laud's primacy.

[48] R.W. Greaves, 'Religion in the University, 1715–1800', in *HUO: Eighteenth Century*, pp. 401–10 surveys Secker and Bentham's efforts to reform Oxford's religious curriculum.

introduced, at Secker's suggestion, the first systematic program for prospective ordinands, offering nearly seventy free lectures in 1764 which concerned all aspects of divinity. So that Bentham could 'distribute [books] amongst the poorer part of his Audience', Secker gave him £20 in 1765 and £21 later in 1766 and 1767.[49] In theory, the educational reforms would make for a more learned, more sober pool of potential ordinands. To complement these reforms, Secker advised that the individual colleges screen candidates more carefully before issuing the *testimonia* required for ordination.[50]

Secker hoped that a theologically literate clergy would be prepared to elucidate clearly and persistently orthodox Christianity through catechizing and preaching. A series of questions and answers that explained the basic doctrines of Christianity, catechisms were a staple of early modern English pastoral care.[51] Secker certainly thought catechizing an effective pastoral method. 'The catechism consists of the fundamental articles of the Christian faith and practice,' he advised the Oxford clergy in 1741. 'Without learning these, we know not so much as what it is we profess to be; and there is great Danger that unless Persons learn them at first, they will never learn them thoroughly.'[52] Not surprisingly, he connected catechizing with the nation's religious, social, and political stability:

And that it may be used effectually, the laws of the land, both ecclesiastical and civil, require not only ministers to instruct their parishioners in it, but parents, and masters and mistresses of families, to send their children and servants to be instructed ... For promoting religious knowledge and practice is not only the express design of all church-government, but a matter (would God it were well considered) of great importance to the state also: since neither private life can be happy, nor the public welfare secure for any long time, without the belief of the doctrines and observance of the duties of Christianity, for which catechizing the young and ignorant lays the firmest foundation.[53]

Part of the problem, he believed, was that there was too little catechizing in the established Church.[54] The Anglican canons were explicit on the matter: 'Every parson, vicar or curate, upon every Sunday and holy day, before evening prayer, shall, for half an hour or more, examine and instruct the youth and ignorant persons of his parish in the ten commandments, the articles of belief, and in the Lord's prayer; and shall diligently hear, instruct and teach them the catechism set forth in the book of common prayer.'[55] Even Secker recognized that

---

49 *Autobiography*, p. 50; LPL, MS 1483, ff. 129, 225, 257.
50 LPL, MS 2564, p. 325.
51 Ian Green, *The Christian's ABC: Catechisms and Catechizing in England, c. 1530–1740* (Oxford, 1996), pp. 1–276.
52 *Charges* (1741), p. 48.
53 *Lectures*, pp. 7–8.
54 But see F.C. Mather, 'Georgian Churchmanship Reconsidered: Some Variations on Anglican Public Worship, 1714–1830', *JEH* 36:2 (1985), p. 280.
55 *Anglican Canons* (Canon 59 of 1604), p. 349.

this canonical requirement could not be observed strictly 'during the Winter Season, in the Generality of Country Parishes, or where the Children, being few, were more easily taught'.[56] Nevertheless, he urged the clergy in his dioceses 'to catechise the Children, not only in Lent, but some part of the Summer, when the Days are longer, & the ways & weather better. Indeed there will else be Danger, that what they have learnt one Lent may be forgotten before the next.'[57] Secker was preaching what he practiced. As rector of St James's, Westminster, for instance, he took his own catechetical responsibilities seriously. 'Besides the Lecture on the Catechism once on Week-Days, which I continued through Lent, though former Rectors did not, & so went through the whole, being 39 Lectures, 8 times,' he recorded. 'I went through them also on Sunday Evenings 4 times at St James's Church & twice at Kingstreet Chapel. None of my Predecessors gave this Sunday Evening Lecture.'[58]

There were a number of practical barriers to catechizing, though, which parish priests commonly faced. Many clergy protested that the pervasive illiteracy of their parishioners militated against catechizing. 'There are none in my Parish of sufficient Age, who have not been confirmed; nor of sufficient knowledge I am certain, for very few of their Parents can teach their Children the Catechism, & we have no Schoolmaster in two miles of us,' reported the curate of Godlington.[59] Secker countered complaints like this by arguing that 'The Incapacity of reading was almost general at the Time of the Reformation: yet even in those Days the Clergy were able to teach first Parents and Householders, then by their Means Children and Servants, the Lord's Prayer, the Creed, and the Ten Commandments: and afterwards the rest of the Catechism.'[60]

The degree to which he believed this is testified to by his advice in 1758 to William Gostling, the assistant curate of Harbledown. Shortly after Secker had moved to Lambeth, Gostling sought his counsel about a 'poor man of Anabaptist Parents' in Harbledown who wanted to be baptized. 'He is twenty six years old, & quite illiterate, with the additional misfortune of being very deaf,' Gostling continued, 'but has on this occasion learned the Lords Prayer and Creed, and promises to get farther instructed in Christianity as fast as he is able.'[61] Gostling looked to the archbishop for guidance in the matter. Secker advised him to baptize the man as soon as possible, but not before Gostling had first tried to teach him as much as possible about Christian doctrine.

[56]   *Charges* (1741), p. 49.
[57]   LPL, Secker Papers 6, f. 268: Secker to Lilly Butler, 8 Sept 1761.
[58]   *Autobiography*, p. 29.
[59]   *Oxford Correspondence*, p. 116: Stephen Richardson to Secker, 6 July 1744. For background on literacy, see Adam Fox, *Oral and Literate Culture in England, 1500–1700* (Oxford, 2000).
[60]   *Charges* (1741), p. 54.
[61]   LPL, Secker Papers 3, f. 197: William Gostling to Secker, 16 April 1758.

[H]e must have some competent Acquaintance with the general nature of that Sacram't & with the Commandm'ts as well as with the Creed & Lds Prayer, wch you say he hath learnt. And either before Baptism is possible, or at least as soon as is possible afterwds he must be instructed in the Duty of receiving the Lds Supper. But in all this you must be content if he any way appears to have any tolerable apprehension & suitable Belief of the Gospel Truths wch you deliver to him though he can neither express them with the least accuracy in words of his own nor perhaps repeat exactly those of the Catechism. If he continues in your parish you will endeavour by Degrees to improve him somew't farther in which any serious neighbour of his may be an useful assistant to you.[62]

Most parishioners did not face such barriers to comprehension, though, and Secker expected priests to present those they had catechized for confirmation at his triennial visitations.[63]

Secker thought catechizing of paramount importance when it came to pastoral care at the parish level, but he also recognized the importance of preaching as an instructional tool. 'The sermon as spoken performance was an integral part of eighteenth century society, at all levels from patrician to plebeian,' reckons one recent study of the subject. 'It was as influential a medium as the novel or the newspaper in its ability to reach the literate, and more influential inasmuch as, being a spoken medium, it could reach the illiterate.'[64] This would not have been a point lost on Secker. Horace Walpole was almost alone in criticizing Secker's own sermons, complaining that they were 'moral essays ... as clear from quotations of Scripture, as when he presided in a less Christian society; but what they wanted of Gospel, was made up by a tone of fanaticism that he still retained'.[65] Rather, Secker's sermons and lectures were generally thought to be so efficacious as teaching tools that they continued to be published long after his death.[66] Richard Hurd was no fan of Secker, yet even he grudgingly lauded the clarity, if not the originality, of Secker's sermons.[67] Most others more fulsomely praised his sermons, and many held him up as a model preacher. 'His Lectures and Sermons are written with a rare mixture of simplicity and energy, and contain (what Sermons too

---

[62]   Ibid., f. 198: Secker to Gostling, 17 April 1758.

[63]   LPL, Secker Papers 6, f. 259: Secker to John Young, 20 Mar 1761.

[64]   James Joseph Caudle, 'Measures of Allegiance: Sermon Culture and the Creation of a Public Discourse of Obedience and Resistance in Georgian Britain, 1714–1760' (Yale University Ph.D. thesis, 1996), p. 100.

[65]   Walpole, *Memoirs of George II*, 1, p. 46.

[66]   *Lectures on the Creed, selected from the Lectures on the Church Catechism* (1885) appears to be the latest printing of Secker's works in England; the SPCK published *Five Sermons against Popery* in 1836. In the United States, Isaac N. Whiting of Columbus, Ohio, published Secker's *Lectures on the Catechism of the Protestant Episcopal Church* in 1839 and *Five Sermons against Popery* in 1835. Secker's works were also, it should be noted, reliable sellers which eighteenth-century publishers coveted: Beinecke, Osborn File Folder 18071: John Rivington to Beilby Porteus and George Stinton, 13 Nov 1768.

[67]   Richard Hurd, *A discourse, by way of general preface, to the quarto edition of Bishop Warburton's works* (1794), p. 83.

seldom possess) a great knowledge of life and human nature,' the poet Thomas Warton concluded, while the altitudinarian cleric Ralph Churton reckoned that 'Dr. Secker's transcendent abilities as a practical preacher were universally acknowledged, were strongly attested by those numerous congregations consisting of all ranks of people, that constantly attended his sermons.'[68] After hearing Secker preach for the first time, the earl of Egmont declared, 'His language is fine, yet adapted to the meanest comprehension: his sense strong, his arguments fair and not forced, proposing adversaries' objections, but clearing them with ingenuity. His delivery proper to the pulpit and graceful, and his access and emphasis extraordinary correct, leaving strong impressions in his hearers.' Egmont concluded, 'I take him to be the most accomplished preacher now living.'[69]

In a 1766 visitation charge, Secker explained to the Canterbury clergy how they too might be successful preachers, spelling out in detail how to write and preach sermons that were both enlightening and appealing.[70] Parishioners would tune out a man whom they did not trust, he advised: 'Even Heathens made it a Rule, that a good Orator, if he would persuade, must be a good Man: much more must a Preacher.' Likewise, a good preacher must know not only moral and natural theology, but also 'the Doctrines and Precepts of the Gospel [which] require your principal Regard beyond all Comparison'.[71] Finally, the aspiring preacher should use the works of 'able Divines' as models for their own work. Knowing that many clerics during the period merely read others' sermons as their own, Secker cautioned that clergy should 'not inconsiderately and servilely transcribe' the works of eminent Anglican divines, but should instead 'study, digest, contract, amplify, vary, adapt to their Purpose, improve if possible, what they find in them'.

Upon this foundation, clergy could move to writing their own sermons, the ultimate goal of which was to 'fix them (their parishioners) in the Belief and Practice of what will render them happy now and to Eternity'. Secker advised clergy, first, to choose their texts carefully and then to outline their argument at the sermon's outset. Instead of using flowery language, strive for clarity. 'Your Expressions may be very common, without being low', he assured them, 'yet employ the lowest, provided they are not ridiculous, rather than not be understood.' There is no need 'to prove Things which need not be proved' and certainly avoid 'long or subtle Arguments': instead, 'rest your Assertions on the Dictates of plain good Sense'. When actually delivering the sermon, pay attention to your audience, for most of whom church attendance was a duty and for many of

---

[68]   *Literary Illustrations*, III, p. 482; [Ralph Churton], *A letter to the Lord Bishop of Worcester, occasioned by his strictures on Archbishop Secker and Bishop Lowth in his Life of Bishop Warburton now prefixed to the quarto edition of that prelate's works* (Oxford, 1796), p. 32.

[69]   *Egmont Diaries*, II, p. 209.

[70]   *Charges* (1766), pp. 287–324: unless otherwise noted, quotations in this and the next paragraph are drawn from this charge. For some context, see Caudle, 'Measures of Allegiance', pp. 49–110.

[71]   Cf. G. Gregory, *Sermons*, 2nd edn (1789), pp. xxx–xxxi; Vicesimus Knox, *Christian philosophy: or, an attempt to display the evidence and excellence of revealed religion* (1795), p. 356.

whom sermons were difficult to follow. Speak to be heard because 'audible Exertion is a Mark of Earnestness'; for those without booming voices, 'Distinctness will do much to supply Want of Strength in speaking'. Try to smooth over the edges of 'a provincial Dialect' and avoid 'theatrical Pronunciation'. Try not to read your sermons,[72] and get an outside opinion when you have delivered them to ensure that they came across as you intended. Most importantly, act naturally: 'Every Man's Voice and Utterance, as well as his Face, belongs to himself alone; and it is vain to think either of looking or talking like such or such a one.'

Secker offered such detailed advice to the Canterbury clergy because eighteenth-century England's public sphere was largely a 'preached public sphere'.[73] The pulpit was more effective than print culture for the discussion of politics, and sermons conveyed '"orthodox" loyalism' from the centre to the periphery during the eighteenth century.[74] Not surprisingly, Secker took what opportunities he could to promote orthodox clerics to preach at fasts, thanksgivings, and other prominent public occasions. When the government asked him to nominate someone to preach the fast sermon in 1759, he pushed forward his domestic chaplain, Charles Hall. 'He is a man of worth, good sense & Learning, hath an agreeable manner of speaking, is not usually long, & shall be exhorted to due Brevity on the present occasion,' he averred.[75] Likewise, he nominated the reliably orthodox Edward Bentham to preach the thanksgiving sermon on 5 May 1763.[76] Secker wanted orthodoxy promulgated in sermons, from the pulpits of the remotest parishes church to those of the greatest cathedrals.

---

[72] Cf. James Glazebrook, *The practice of what is called extempore preaching, and the propriety and advantage of that mode of public instruction urged and supported, by arguments deduced from scripture authority, primitive example, historic facts, and the very nature of the office* (Warrington, 1794), pp. 111–14.

[73] Tony Claydon, 'The sermon, the "public sphere" and the political culture of late seventeenth-century England', in *The English sermon revisited: Religion, literature, and history 1600–1750*, eds. Peter McCullough and Lori Anne Ferrell (Manchester, 2000), p. 226. See also, Gerd Mischler, 'English Political Sermons, 1714–1742: A Case Study in the Theory of the "Divine Right of Governors" and the Ideology of Order', *British Journal for Eighteenth-Century Studies* 24:1 (2001), pp. 33–61 and Robert Hole, *Pulpits, Politics and Public Order in England, 1760–1832* (Cambridge, 1989). Françoise Deconinck-Brossard, 'Eighteenth-Century Sermons and the Age', in *Crown and Mitre: religion and society in northern Europe since the Reformation*, eds. Nigel Yates and W.M. Jacob (1993), pp. 105–21 and Downey, *The Eighteenth-Century Pulpit*, pp. 1–29 provide useful context.

[74] James Caudle, 'Preaching in Parliament: patronage, publicity and politics in Britain, 1701–60', in *The English sermon revisited*, pp. 235–63.

[75] LPL, MS 1130/II, f. 185: Secker to William Cavendish, 4th duke of Devonshire, 15 Jan 1759.

[76] Ibid., f. 203: George Spencer, 4th duke of Marlborough to Secker, 12 Apr 1763; ibid., f. 204: Secker to Marlborough, 12 Apr 1763.

II

Thomas Secker hoped that a theologically literate clergy who catechized regularly and preached well might be the foot soldiers in the orthodox fight against heterodoxy. Shaping the culture, though, also meant promoting the orthodox cause in other ways, for teaching orthodox doctrine vigorously and vociferously from parish pulpits was only a partial solution to the problem of heterodoxy. Lambeth needed to provide the strategic vision, the tactical leadership, and the long-range artillery to support the clerical infantry in the parishes.

Secker thought it an important part of his job as archbishop to cultivate orthodox scholarship, to which perhaps his most lasting contribution was in biblical studies, a field of enormous religio-political significance. *Sola scriptura* joined *sola fide* and *sola gratia* to form the bedrock upon which Protestantism rested, so that for a seventeenth-century churchman like William Chillingworth, it was self-evident that 'the Bible, I say, the Bible only, is the religion of Protestants!'[77] In the century intervening between Chillingworth and Secker, though, the Bible's claims to be authentic, truthful, and historically accurate came under assault from both within and the without the Church and from anti-dogmatists and anticlericals alike.[78] In *Tractatus theologico-politicus* (1670), for instance, Baruch Spinoza proposed a biblical hermeneutics founded on reason, not tradition; it aimed to make biblical exegesis a philosophical, not a theological, act; and it saw the task of biblical scholarship as the elucidation of truth, not the buttressing of ecclesiastical authority. Reading the Bible with these interpretative first principles, Spinoza assailed its authenticity, accuracy, and, thus, its divine inspiration, and he opened a breach which was not easily bridged.[79] The French Catholic priest Richard Simon, for instance, agreed with Spinoza that the Old Testament was an evolving document until the ninth century, while nonetheless maintaining that the Bible was divinely inspired. Simon's *Critical History of the Old Testament* (1682) proved enormously influential in England – Newton and Locke had a detailed correspondence about its contents, for instance, and Secker read it while one of Thomas Hardy's students in Nottingham. Simon's work nevertheless was deeply subversive, for by accepting Spinoza's interpretative approach, if not his conclusions, it opened the Bible to further scrutiny.[80] In

---

[77] William Chillingworth, *The religion of protestants a safe way to salvation* (Oxford, 1638), p. 375.

[78] Dupré, *The Enlightenment and the Intellectual Foundations of Modern Culture*, pp. 231–42 and Gerald Bray, *Biblical Interpretation, Past and Present* (Leicester, 1996), pp. 221–69 briefly survey the subject.

[79] J. Samuel Preus, *Spinoza and the Irrelevance of Biblical Authority* (Cambridge, 2001); Richard H. Popkin, 'Spinoza and Biblical Scholarship', in *The Books of Nature and Scripture*, eds. James E. Force and Richard H. Popkin (Dordrecht, 1994), pp. 1–20.

[80] Justin Champion, 'Père Richard Simon and English Biblical Criticism', in *Everything Connects: In Conference with Richard Popkin*, eds. James Force and David Katz (Leiden, 1999), pp. 39–61; idem, '"Acceptable to inquisitive men": Some Simonian Contexts for Newton's

England, Spinozan heremeneutics and Lockean epistemology together provided the more radical anti-dogmatics – deists, atheists, and freethinkers like John Toland, Charles Blount, Anthony Collins, Matthew Tindal, Thomas Morgan, and Thomas Chubb – with the tools de-mystify the Bible.[81] During the late seventeenth and early eighteenth centuries, the furious debate over the Bible elided easily into one over revealed religion itself: those who mocked the divinely-inspired Bible as 'well-invented flam' also sought 'to set aside revealed religion'.[82]

While orthodoxy's defenders rose to defend the Bible against early Enlightenment anti-dogmatists who would strip it – and Christianity – of the supernatural, the cost was no new translation of the Authorised Version (AV) of the English Bible, sometimes known as King James's Bible.[83] And a new translation was, as even orthodoxy's stoutest defenders admitted, desperately needed. The problem with the AV was that there were errors, some of which resulted from bad translation and some of which resulted from printers' and transcribers' errors. This was a political, as well as a religious, problem because the AV was 'a text that carried legal significance', for its very purpose 'was to provide a common text, a lingua franca from which to reinforce decisions about doctrine and organisation, and to orient worship and devotion around a common axis'.[84] The religio-political establishment feared that to admit flaws in the AV might, by implication, be to admit flaws in the establishment of church and state. Though loath to support the production of an new English Bible translation – a subject to which we will return at the end of this chapter – Secker did encourage those whose work aimed to identify errors in the AV, errors that could be rectified when the time was ripe to produce a new AV. In doing so, he tried to use the clerical Enlightenment to defeat the radical Enlightenment.

Secker was the chief patron of the most ambitious orthodox biblical project in the eighteenth century, Benjamin Kennicott's collation of all the known manuscript editions of the Hebrew Bible. Its aim was recover the Old Testament's

Biblical Criticism, 1680–1692', in *Newton and Religion: Context, Nature, and Influence*, eds. Richard H. Popkin and James E. Force (Dordrecht, 1999), pp. 77–96.

81 David S. Katz, *God's Last Words: Reading the English Bible from the Reformation to Fundamentalism* (New Haven, CT, 2004), pp. 116–52; Champion, *Republican learning*, pp. 69–90; Henning Graf Reventlow, *The Authority of the Bible and the Rise of the Modern World* (Philadelphia, 1985), pp. 289–410.

82 Quoted in James Force, Introduction to William Stephens, *An Account of the Growth of Deism in England* (1696) (Los Angeles, 1990), p. iv; John Leland, *A View of the principal deistical writers that have appeared in England in the last and present century, with observations upon them, and some account of the answers that have been published against them. In several letters to a friend* (1754), I, p. iii.

83 Jonathan Sheehan, *The Enlightenment Bible: Translation, Scholarship, Culture* (Princeton, 2005), pp. 31–53.

84 Neil W. Hitchin, 'The Politics of English Bible Translation in Georgian Britain', *TRHS*, 6th series, 9 (1999), p. 72. Cf. Scott Mandelbrote, 'The authority of the Word: manuscript, print and the text of the Bible in seventeenth-century England', *The Uses of Script and Print, 1300–1700*, eds. Alexandra Walsham and Julia Crick (Cambridge, 2004), pp. 135–53.

original text by ferreting out the errors, omissions, and additions. And as David Ruderman rightly notes, the collation project cut 'to the very core of Christian self-identity in eighteenth-century England'.[85] A fellow of Exeter College, Oxford, Kennicott (1718–1783) was a committed Whig in Tory Oxford.[86] When the government's opponents criticized the peace terms of the War of the Austrian Succession, Kennicott preached a thanksgiving sermon to the mayor and corporation of Oxford in 1749 lauding them.[87] When the Jewish Naturalisation Act (1753) ignited a political firestorm, Secker sent Kennicott to scour D'blossiers Tovey's manuscripts on the history of Jews in England for relevant information in support of the measure.[88] And in the hotly contested Oxfordshire election of 1754, Kennicott was one of the leading academic figures helping to organize the Whig 'New Interest'.[89] Though not as blatant as the notorious Richard Blacow, Kennicott was nonetheless a Whig informer whose preferment owed much to his support of Whigs against the entrenched Tory interest at Oxford.[90]

In 1758 the Delegates of the Oxford University Press tapped Kennicott to produce a major biblical collation. The Delegates had asked three Oxford professors 'to recommend such Books, in their different Provinces, as they thought would be most acceptable to the Public, & most for the honour of the University to encourage the Publication of'.[91] Thomas Hunt (1696–1774), the regius professor of Hebrew at Oxford and an enormously influential figure for orthodox biblical scholars there, proposed that the Press should engage someone to collate all of the extant manuscripts of the Old Testament and recommended Kennicott as the man for the task – the Delegates agreed unanimously to Hunt's proposal.[92] Kennicott had learned Hebrew at Oxford under Hunt and Robert Lowth, and by 1748 had begun to realize that the AV Old Testament was littered with errors, some of them serious. 'We must acknowledge that these Sacred Books have not descended to us, for so many ages, without some Mistakes and Errors of the Transcribers,' he

[85] Ruderman, *Jewish Enlightenment in an English Key*, p. 23.

[86] For Exeter College as a Whig bastion in Oxford, see L.S. Sutherland, 'Political Respectability, 1751–71', in *HUO: Eighteenth Century*, pp. 132–41 and R.J. Robson, *The Oxfordshire Election of 1754* (1949), pp. 106–14.

[87] Benjamin Kennicott, *The duty of thanksgiving for peace in general, and the reasonableness of thanksgiving for our present peace. A sermon preach'd at St Martin's in Oxford, before the mayor and corporation, on Tuesday, April 25, 1749. Being the day of thanksgiving for the general peace* (1749).

[88] BL, Add. MS 35592, f. 127: Secker to Hardwicke, 15 Aug 1753. Perhaps this research helps account for Secker's decision in 1753 to give Kennicott the vicarage of Culham, Oxfordshire, and to pay out of his own pocket for Kennicott's admission fees: *Autobiography*, p. 33.

[89] Robson, *The Oxfordshire Election of 1754*, pp. 74, 75; W.R. Ward, *Georgian Oxford: University Politics in the Eighteenth Century* (Oxford, 1958), pp. 192–206.

[90] Sutherland, 'Political Respectability, 1751–71', p. 130. David Greenwood, *William King: Tory and Jacobite* (Oxford, 1969), pp. 234–79 provides background.

[91] LPL, Secker Papers 2, f. 1: Kennicott to Secker, 7 Mar 1758.

[92] Colin Wakefield, 'Hunt, Thomas (1696–1774)', *ODNB*.

reported in 1753.[93] 'For the older any Writings are, the oftener they have been transcribed; the more Mistakes have probably been made by the Transcribers', he later explained. This was particularly the case with the Old Testament, not least because 'several of the Hebrew Letters are very similar; it must have been the more easy for Transcribers to make mistakes.'[94] The aim of a comprehensive collation would be 'to compare Scripture with itself – to explain a difficult Phrase or Passage by a clear one, that bears some Relation to it – to consider the natural force of the Original Words, the Tendency of the Context, and the Design of the Writer – to compare the most ancient Editions of the Original, with one another, and with the best Copies of the most celebrated Versions'.[95] Only by careful comparison of all the extant manuscripts could the errors in the AV Old Testament be identified and, in subsequent editions, expunged; only in this way could the original text of the Hebrew Bible be recovered. By 1757 Secker was encouraging Kennicott to produce this kind of comprehensive collation,[96] and in 1758 the Delegates agreed to publish the project.

Upon receiving the official commission, Kennicott turned immediately to Secker, and, for the next ten years, Secker was his trusted advisor. At turns nervous, fawning, and pushy, Kennicott was not a particularly easy person to help. Secker's primary role was that of fundraiser, for it was uncertain how Kennicott would be paid for his services.[97] At the time of Kennicott's commission, Secker was the bishop of Oxford and he suggested that Matthew Hutton, then the archbishop of Canterbury, should spearhead a subscription drive to raise money for Kennicott's salary.[98] When Secker replaced Hutton as archbishop later that spring, he accepted the responsibility to launch the subscription campaign himself: 'I am very willing to take the part wch I thought was proper for the late Abp of consulting with the other Bps concerning some proper method of encouraging the undertaking proposed to you by the Delegates of the Press,' he assured Kennicott.[99] Good to his word, Secker was the project's first subscriber, contributing generously to the project in the amount of £10.10.0 per year for nine years.[100] Secker also beat the bushes looking for money to support Kennicott's

[93] Benjamin Kennicott, *The state of the printed Hebrew text of the Old Testament considered* (Oxford, 1753), I, pp. 7–8.
[94] Benjamin Kennicott, *The annual accounts of the collation of Hebrew MSS of the Old Testament* (Oxford, 1770), pp. 7, 17.
[95] Kennicott, *The state of the printed Hebrew text of the Old Testament considered*, I, pp. 12–13.
[96] Kennicott, *The annual accounts of the collation of Hebrew MSS of the Old Testament*, p. 9.
[97] OUP granted a three-year subvention of £40, renewable subject to the Delegates' approval. Kennicott's relations with the Delegates were frosty, at best, by the project's completion: Harry Carter, *A History of the Oxford University Press. Volume I to the year 1780* (Oxford, 1975), pp. 410–13.
[98] LPL, Secker Papers 2, ff. 3–4: Secker to Kennicott, 10 Mar 1758.
[99] Ibid., f. 7: Secker to Kennicott, 15 April 1758.
[100] *Autobiography*, p. 41; LPL, MS 1483, ff. 22, 95, 125, 145, 177, 201, 233, 269.

work on the project.[101] Nonetheless, he had from time to time to rein in Kennicott, who was often too forward in soliciting subscriptions. 'I continue to think it very proper, that you shd be encouraged by some preferm't: & particularly some in the Gift of the crown', he wrote to Kennicott in the fall of 1760. 'But I am apprehensive, that a minister may be apt to plead, besides the Multiplicity and Earnestness of other Applications, especially just before a new Parliam't, that you have a large & perhaps still increasing Subscription; that one shd not incur more expence than it will bear; that your work is but just begun, & the Request of a Reward premature; that Ecclesiastical person are the fittest to recompense merit of this sort; or several other things, which do not occur to me.'[102] Kennicott needed reminders like these every so often.

Secker used his clout to secure Kennicott preferments that would provide a reliably steady income, other than subscriptions, so he could keep body and soul together while working on the collations. In 1763, Kennicott thought the Radcliffe librarian, Francis Wise, was on death's door, and he started canvassing for support in the upcoming election to select Wise's replacement.[103] Wise, as it turned out, had another few years in him, not dying until 1767, at which point Kennicott renewed his applications for the office that Richard Rawlinson dubbed 'a fat *sine curâ*'.[104] Kennicott was not Secker's first choice of candidates – the orthodox biblical scholar David Durell was – but once Durell had got a Canterbury prebend, Secker advocated for Kennicott. 'I applied to as many of the Electors, as I could, for Kennicott,' he recalled.[105] In the end, Kennicott beat out two rivals for the position, which paid an annual salary of £120. Not long afterwards, Secker tried unsuccessfully to obtain him a Canterbury prebend.[106]

In addition to drumming up money for Kennicott, Secker helped him keep the big picture in view. From the start, he advised him not to get sucked into a study of vowel points, a particular fixation of the Hutchinsonians.[107] He also loaned Kennicott biblical manuscripts from the library at Lambeth Palace and arranged for him to borrow manuscripts from Cambridge's university library.[108] He tried as well to keep Kennicott focused on the task at hand, collation, rather than on issuing

[101] BL, Add. MS 32902, ff. 104–05, 147: Secker to TPH, 8, 13 Feb 1760. See W.A. Speck, 'Politicians, peers, and publication by subscription, 1700–50', in *Books and Their Readers in Eighteenth-Century England*, ed. Isabel Rivers (Leicester, 1982), pp. 47–68 for context.
[102] LPL, Secker Papers 2, f. 33: Secker to Kennicott, 16 Sept 1760.
[103] BL, Add. MS 38201, ff. 373–74: Kennicott to Charles Jenkinson, 27 Dec 1763; LPL, Secker Papers 2, ff. 74–75: Kennicott to Secker, 12 Mar 1764.
[104] Quoted in Nigel Aston, 'Kennicott, Benjamin (1718–1783)', *ODNB*.
[105] *Autobiography*, p. 62. See also, *Literary Anecdotes*, VIII, pp. 249–50: Charles Godwyn to Mr. Hutchins, 30 Oct 1767.
[106] BL, Add. MS 35068, f. 174: Secker to Philip Yorke, 2nd earl of Hardwicke, 21 May 1768.
[107] LPL, Secker Papers 2, f. 3: Secker to Kennicott, 10 Mar 1758.
[108] Ibid., ff. 61, 217: Secker to TPH, 4 Feb 1762; Secker to Kennicott, 24 Aug 1759.

responses to the Hutchinsonians who sniped at him in print and from the pulpit; and he tried to get Hutchinsonians to temper their criticism of Kennicott.[109]

Alas, Secker did not live to see the published fruits of Kennicott's collation, since it took over two decades to complete the collations. Kennicott's base was in Oxford, where he worked with assistants collating manuscripts.[110] Many of these were to be found in Oxford, particularly at the Bodleian. Cambridge and the British Museum proved willing to lend him manuscripts from their collections so that he could pore over them in Oxford. To collate manuscripts in Continental libraries, Kennicott relied on Paul Jacob Bruns, who visited fifty-two places as his paid research assistant, and the unpaid help of diplomats, English travellers, and fellow scholars, such as Joseph Wilcocks, the English antiquary who lived in Rome.[111] During the course of his research, Kennicott consulted 615 manuscript versions of the Hebrew Bible and 52 printed ones, and he issued ten annual reports between 1760 and 1769 to inform the project's subscribers about his progress.[112]

The first volume of Kennicott's collation, *Vetus Testamentum Hebraicum cum variis lectiionibus*, finally appeared in print in 1776, followed by a second volume four years later. In retrospect, it was a project destined to fall short of its intended aims because Kennicott's methodology was fundamentally flawed and his aims were unrealistic: proceeding as he did it would have been impossible to recover the original wording of the Hebrew Bible.[113] Nonetheless, his project met with more positive reviews among his contemporaries. Robert Lowth (1710–1787) thought *Vetus Testamentum* 'a work the greatest and most important that has been undertaken and accomplished since the Revolution of Letters'.[114] Lowth was not a disinterested critic, for he had taught Kennicott at Oxford and it was he who first encouraged him to question the accuracy of the published Hebrew Bible.[115] Some reckon Lowth was 'the greatest scholar of the Hebrew Bible that England ever

---

[109] Ibid., f. 58: Kennicott to Secker, 3 Dec 1761; Beinecke, Osborn Files: Drawer 34.247: Secker to Thomas Rutherforth, 16 Nov 1761.

[110] Ignatius Dumay assisted Kennicott for four years before falling out with him. He detailed his problems with Kennicott and the methodology of Kennicott's collation in Bodleian, MS Kennicott e.43: I.A. Dumay's observations on Kennicott's Hebrew Manuscripts, n.d. See also, Cecil Roth, 'Salomon Israel, Writing Master in Oxford, 1745 - alias Ignatius Dumay', *Oxoniensia* 28 (1963), pp. 74–78.

[111] Bodleian, MS Kennicott c.13, ff. 106–245 contains the Kennicott-Bruns correspondence. Kennicott's correspondence with others who helped him secure access to Continental manuscripts can be found in his correspondence in Beinecke, Osborn Files, Drawers A-Z, *passim*.

[112] Aston, 'Kennicott, Benjamin (1718–1783)'.

[113] Sheehan, *The Enlightenment Bible*, pp. 183–84; Katz, *God's Last Words*, pp. 204–11; Ruderman, *The Jewish Enlightenment in an English Key*, pp. 23–56; William McKane, 'Benjamin Kennicott: An Eighteenth-Century Researcher', *Journal of Theological Studies*, new series 28:2 (1977), pp. 445–64; Carter, *A History of the Oxford University Press. Volume I to the year 1780*, p. 413.

[114] Quoted in Brian Hepworth, *Robert Lowth* (Boston, 1978), p. 145.

[115] Kennicott, *The annual accounts of the collation of Hebrew MSS of the Old Testament*, p. 7

produced', a reputation he earned for his pioneering theory of parallelism, which posited that the best way to convey the poetic qualities of ancient Hebrew verse was through literal, not metrical, translation.[116] Lowth developed his ideas on parallelism in a series of lectures he gave while professor of poetry at Oxford and which he published as *De sacra poesi hebraeorum* (1753). Lowth would later become successively bishop of St David's (1766), Oxford (1766), and London (1777); he even turned down the offer to become archbishop of Canterbury in 1783. Biblical studies remained Lowth's first love, though, even when he was on the episcopal bench. His signal achievement was a new translation of Isaiah, which allowed him to test against practice his theories regarding Hebrew poetry and proper principles of translation.[117]

Secker thought quite highly of Lowth. His reliably Whig politics recommended him to a Whig bishop of Oxford. In the summer of 1751, for instance, Secker praised Lowth's recent speech promoting the Whig cause. 'You have heard, I presume, that Mr. Lowth made an excellent speech last week, in which he strongly recommended the University of their Duty & Interest in relation to the Government; yet in such a manner, as to be loudly applauded,' he wrote to Nathaniel Forster.[118] But it was Lowth's abilities as a scholar that did most to earn him Secker's fulsome support. When recommending him to Newcastle as a fit candidate for the episcopate, for instance, Secker emphasized to the duke that Lowth was capable of close pastoral supervision of his diocese while at the same time able to 'proceed ... in [his] purpose of serving Religion by Illustrating the Scripture'.[119] Secker also thought Lowth to be an able defender of orthodoxy. In 1764, for instance, Thomas Phillips published a life of Cardinal Pole which, in Secker's view, aimed deliberately at 'Vilifying the Reformation and recommending the Doctrines & Claims of Popery': he first recommended Lowth to rebut him. 'Dr. Lowth would be a perfectly fit man to animadvert on this Book, if he would undertake it, and go through a sufficient Quantity of such Reading, as is requisite for that purpose,' he assured the second earl of Hardwicke.[120] At other times, Secker asked Lowth to recruit orthodox talent.[121] Yet the danger for orthodox

[116] Sheehan, *The Enlightenment Bible*, p. 148; David Norton, *A history of the Bible as literature* (Cambridge, 1993), II, pp. 97–103; Stephen Prickett, 'Poetry and Prophecy: Bishop Lowth and the Hebrew Scriptures in Eighteenth-Century England', in *Images of Belief in Literature*, ed. David Jasper (New York, 1984), pp. 81–103; James L. Kugel, *The Idea of Biblical Poetry: Parallelism and Its History* (New Haven, CT, 1981), pp. 274–86. See also, Scott Mandelbrote, 'Lowth, Robert (1710–1787)', *ODNB.*

[117] Robert Lowth, *Isaiah. A New Translation* (1778, 1779).

[118] BL, Add. MS 11275, f. 111: Secker to Forster, 8 July 1751.

[119] Bodleian, MS.Eng.lett.c.574, f. 67: Secker to Lowth, 5 Dec 1765.

[120] BL, Add. MS 35607, f. 106: Secker to Philip Yorke, 2nd earl of Hardwicke, 5 July 1764. Gloucester Ridley's *A review of Mr. Phillips's History of the life of Reginald Pole* (1766) turned out to be the Secker camp's response to Thomas Phillips, *The history of the life of Reginald Pole* (1764).

[121] David Fairer (ed.), *The Correspondence of Thomas Wharton* (Athens, GA, 1995), pp. 261–62: Lowth to Wharton, 27 Jan 1770.

combatants was that sometimes they might fight one another; and just as he had worked to tamp down the fires that burned in Kennicott's controversy with the Hutchinsonians, so too did Secker work to extinguish the quarrel between Lowth and William Warburton, that most unorthodox of orthodoxy's champions.[122]

While archbishop of Canterbury, Secker did what he could to further Lowth's career. In 1765, he pressed the duke of Newcastle to promote Lowth to a bishopric and reckoned that Lowth was the only person during his archiepiscopate to be elevated to the bench on account of his recommendation.[123] A few years later when David Gregory, the dean of Christ Church, Oxford, fell ill, Secker lobbied aggressively to have Lowth named dean if the position fell vacant, assuring Newcastle, 'I ... know but one man likely to make so good a Dean of Christ Church. I mean the Bishop of Oxford (Lowth).'[124]

From the 1750s until his death in 1787, Lowth was the most prominent member of a group of orthodox biblical scholars, most of whom also fell within Secker's orbit. And Secker's cultivation of Lowth paid dividends, for Lambeth Palace became a centre of orthodox biblical scholarship during Secker's archiepiscopate and remained so long after his death. Jeremy Gregory has noted the degree to which eighteenth-century archbishops of Canterbury created a 'clerical enclave' at Lambeth, the heart of the archiepiscopal administrative machine: Secker clearly hoped to make the library there a welcome home to orthodox biblical scholars, as well.[125] Often they came to consult Secker's manuscripts. While he published no biblical scholarship of his own, Secker kept a series of detailed notes in manuscript study Bibles in which he highlighted errors or explained opaque passages. In a codicil to his will, Secker stipulated that these manuscripts be deposited in the Lambeth Palace library under certain restrictions and for certain purposes: 'I beg therefore, that no one will use any thing which I have said, either to unsettle his own Judgment, or that of any other person. I would not have any part of it published; or even communicated, excepting to such Men of Learning, as the Archbishops my successors, on mature consideration, shall think proper. I promise my self, that under these Restrictions not only some of my just Observations may be useful, but the Examination of my mistakes produce good Effects.'[126] Evidently a number of orthodox biblical scholars found

---

[122] *Autobiography*, p. 53; Bodleian, MS.Eng.lett.c.574, f. 67: Secker to Lowth, 5 Dec 1765; BL, Add. MS 42560, ff. 147, 153: Secker to Warburton, 4, 12 June 1766. Cf. Mark Pattison, 'Life of Bishop Warburton', in *Essays by the Late Mark Pattison*, ed. Henry Nettleship (Oxford, 1889), l, pp. 134–44.

[123] Bodleian, MS Eng.lett.c.574, f. 67: Secker to Lowth, 5 Dec 1765; *Autobiography*, p. 51.

[124] *Autobiography*, p. 62; BL, Add. MS 32985, f. 176: Secker to TPH, 22 Sept 1767.

[125] Jeremy Gregory, *Restoration, Reformation, and Reform: Archbishops of Canterbury and their Diocese, 1660–1828* (Oxford, 2000), p. 33.

[126] LPL, MS 1373, ff. 26–27: Thomas Secker's remarks on the codicil of his will, 8 April 1763. The relevant manuscripts are LPL, MSS 2559–2562 (Secker's notes in interleaved Bible), 2546–2569, 2595–2597 (Secker's reading notebooks), 2574–2575 (Secker's comments on Daniel), and 2578 (Secker's comments in *Biblica Hebraica*).

these notes enlightening. When preparing his translation of Isaiah, for instance, Lowth consulted Secker's marginal notes in his manuscript study Bibles.[127] Lowth particularly praised the 'candour and modesty' of Secker's notes, 'for there is hardly a proposed emendation, however ingenious and probable, to which he has not added the objections, which occurred to him, against it'. Secker's notes, Lowth added, would 'be of infinite service, whenever that necessary work, a New Translation, or Revision of the present Translation, of the Holy Scriptures for the use of our Church, shall be undertaken'.[128] Others in Lowth's circle (including a number of fellows of Hertford College, Oxford) also consulted Secker's biblical manuscripts.

Reconstituted as a college in 1740, Hertford College – where Lowth and Secker associates David Durell, Benjamin Blayney, and William Newcome served as fellows – was the centre of orthodox biblical scholarship in Oxford, one which developed during the 1750s when Secker was bishop of Oxford and one which was sustained when Lowth became bishop there in 1765.[129] A fellow and principal of Hertford College and an accomplished biblical scholar, David Durell (1728–1775) advocated the case for a new translation of the Bible, arguing that the current AV was riddled with infelicitous translations and outright errors.[130] Because many of the errors in the AV resulted from printers' mistakes, rather than from faulty translation, collating the most reliable English Bibles could minimize errors if a new translation was not imminently to be authorized by the king. To that end, Secker helped Durell during the mid 1760s to identify the least inaccurate printed editions of the English Bible so that those published subsequently by Oxford University Press might be as accurate as possible.[131] Secker gave Durell a Canterbury prebend to reward his efforts, and, before Durell's elevation to vice-chancellor of the university, he actively supported his bid to become the Radcliffe librarian.[132] Durell would later deposit some of his manuscripts on biblical subjects in the library at Lambeth Palace.[133]

One of the reasons Durell corresponded with Secker regarding the accuracy of printed English Bibles was that the Oxford University Press wanted during the mid 1760s to publish a definitive AV and marginalia. In the early summer of 1766, the

[127] Robert Lowth, *Isaiah. A New Translation*, 3rd edn (1795), I, p. xci. Lowth repeatedly cited Secker's Lambeth biblical notes as an authority in his translation of Isaiah. For Secker's principles of translation, see *Literary Illustrations*, IV, p. 853: Secker to William Green, 23 Sept 1761.

[128] Ibid., p. xcii.

[129] Scott Mandelbrote, 'Biblical scholarship at Oxford in the mid-eighteenth century: Local contexts for Robert Lowth's *De sacra poesi hebraeorum* (1753)' (forthcoming) anatomizes this network. I am grateful to the author for allowing me to read a draft of this paper in advance of publication.

[130] David Durell, *Critical remarks on the books of Job, Proverbs, Psalms, Ecclesiastes, and Canticles* (Oxford, 1772), pp. v-vi. See also, Nicholas Pocock, 'Durell, David (1728–1775)', *ODNB*.

[131] Mandelbrote, 'The Bible and Its Readers in the Eighteenth Century', pp. 58, 74–75.

[132] *Autobiography*, pp. 55–56, 62.

[133] LPL, MS 2580: 'Philological Remarks on the Major and Minor Prophets by David Durell'.

Delegates enjoined Durell to write to Secker 'begging his Grace to inform him, what Copy of an English Bible his Grace would recommend as a proper Standard for the University Printer'.[134] Secker's response was not particularly illuminating, consisting as it did of a list of the English Bibles in Lambeth Palace's library and the recommendation that the Delegates consult William Wake's papers in Christ Church and read John Lewis's *Complete history of the several translations of the Bible in English* (1730). Secker did try to contact Thomas Broughton, whom either Potter or Herring had 'employed ... to revise a copy, in order to a more accurate Edition than the common ones', and asked Charles Moss to determine the progress of F.S. Paris's similar work in Cambridge. Neither had written back. Secker concluded that, 'Which is the correct edition, I know not: but [the 1611 King James Version] will deserve the chief Regard, excepting where it is evidently wrong printed, or the spelling obsolete.'[135] This told the Delegates nothing, and they decided to find someone who would collate the 1743 and 1760 Cambridge editions, the original 1611 edition, and Bishop William Lloyd's 1701 edition. Durell's Hertford colleague Benjamin Blayney (1727/8–1801) volunteered and Secker did actually give him constructive advice. 'It had been suggested by the late Archbishop of Canterbury, that an improvement might be made in the present editions of the Bible, by taking a number of additional references, of which many useful ones, as he supposed, might be furnished from other editions referred to by him, and particularly from a Scotch edition,' Blayney recollected in 1769. Secker also added other references 'that occurred from his own reading and observation' in order 'to keep clear of mere fanciful allusions ... and to adhere as near as possible to the plan marked out in the former collection made by Bishop Lloyd'.[136] Though most of Blayney's Bibles were destroyed by a fire in the press's bible warehouse in Paternoster Row, London, the Delegates were sufficiently pleased with Blayney's work that his version served as the text against which subsequent Oxford Bibles were compared.[137]

Blayney's next major work was *Jeremiah, and Lamentations. A new translation with notes critical, philological, and explanatory* (1784), during whose preparation he sought the help of Lowth, Kennicott, Durell, and Charles Godfrey Woide. In the preface to this work, though, Blayney apologized for not having had the opportunity to incorporate into the body of his text 'the valuable Notes of the late

---

[134] Oxford University Press Archives, Orders of the Delegates of the Press, II (1758–1794), 12 June 1766. I am grateful to Daniel Cummins of Oriel College, Oxford, for transcribing portions of the Delegates' Orders for me and to Martin Maw, the OUP archivist, for enabling their transcription. 'Diary of David Durell, 1765–68' (unpublished manuscript, private collection), entries for 12, 24, 28 June 1766 also recounts this chain of events. I thank Scott Mandelbrote for bringing Durell's diary to my attention and for providing me with transcribed excerpts from it.

[135] Orders of the Delegates of the Press, II, 24 June 1766: Secker to Durell, 19 June 1766.

[136] *Gentleman's Magazine* 39 (1769), pp. 518, 519: Blayney to the Delegates of the Clarendon Press, 25 Oct 1769.

[137] Carter, *A History of the Oxford University Press. Volume I to the year 1780*, p. 358; Henry Bradley, 'Blayney, Benjamin (1727/8–1801)', rev. Philip Carter, *ODNB*.

Archbishop Secker on the Bible'. During the summer of 1782, before his translation went to press, he travelled to London specifically to consult Secker's manuscripts, but Archbishop Cornwallis, under whose 'immediate authority' they manuscripts were kept, was out of town. By the time Blayney next visited London, most of the translation had gone to press, requiring him to include excerpts from Secker's manuscripts in a long appendix.[138] After his own death, Blayney specifically left his biblical notes to the library at Lambeth Palace to be used 'in the like manner and for the like purposes as the manuscripts of Archbishop Secker'.[139]

William Newcome (1729–1800) was another Hertford fellow in Lowth's and Secker's circle but one who, unlike either Durell or Blayney, was an ecclesiastical high-flyer. Having served as a fellow of the college for over a decade, Newcome was named bishop of Dromore (1766), Osry (1775), Waterford and Lismore (1779), and, finally, archbishop of Armagh and primate of all Ireland (1795).[140] Despite the administrative burden of his episcopal offices, Newcome remained at heart a biblical scholar, producing a slew of works of explication and translation that showed Lowth's influence on him.[141] More than any of the other Oxford orthodox biblical scholars, Newcome made extensive use of Secker's Lambeth material and his works are littered with references to Secker's manuscripts.[142] Like Durell and Blayney, Newcome deposited his notes and manuscript Bibles in Lambeth Palace's library after his death.[143]

The Secker-Lowth circle of orthodox biblical scholars was capacious enough to extend beyond the walls of Hertford College. James Merrick (1720–1769), a biblical scholar and Anglican priest who lived in Reading, received substantive help from Secker and Lowth when translating the Psalms and in a subsequent set of annotations, he included a long appendix which Secker wrote anonymously.[144]

---

[138] Benjamin Blayney, *Jeremiah, and Lamentations. A new translation with notes critical, philological, and explanatory* (1784), pp. vii-viii, 334–61.

[139] LPL, MS 2577, front cover: Blayney's remarks on passages of the Old Testament. Other Blayney manuscripts at Lambeth include, LPL, MSS 2579 (Remarks upon the Minor Prophets compared with Bishop Newcome's version and commentary), 2581–2582 (Metrical version of the Psalms, with brief introductory notes), and 2583–2585 (Critical commentary on the Psalms and Proverbs); 2585–2588 (Notes on Isaiah).

[140] Alexander Gordon, 'Newcome, William (1729–1800)', rev. J. Flavey, *ODNB*.

[141] William Newcome, *An historical view of the English biblical translations: the expediencey of revising our present translation: and the means of executing such a vision* (1792) cites Lowth approvingly throughout.

[142] See, especially, William Newcome, *An attempt towards an improved version, a metrical arrangement, and explanation of the twelve minor prophets* (1785) and idem, *An attempt towards an improved version, a metrical arrangement, and an explanation of the prophet Ezekiel* (1788) both of which cite Secker approvingly throughout.

[143] LPL, MSS 2570–2573: Interleaved folio Bible (Old Testament, excluding Apochrypha only), extensively revised and annotated by William Newcome, n.d.

[144] James Merrick, *Annotations on the Psalms* (Reading, 1768), pp. iii-v, 275–83; William Declare Tattersal, *Improved psalmody* (1794), pp. 4–5; *Literary Anecdotes*, VIII, p. 255: Charles Godwyn to Mr. Hutchins, 15 Aug 1768. Lowth was one of the subscribers to James Merrick, *The Psalms, translated or paraphrased in English verse* (Reading, 1765). Cf. Gregory Sharpe, *A letter to the*

Likewise Secker's domestic chaplain Thomas Wintle (1738–1814) followed the advice of Lowth (who 'first designed the plan') and looked for guidance in Secker's two volumes of manuscript notes on Daniel when producing his own translation of that prophetical book.[145] Even a Roman Catholic like Alexander Geddes (1737–1802) could be drawn into the circle by Lowth, benefit from his and Kennicott's advice, and be granted access to Secker's Lambeth manuscript notes.[146]

The Lowth circle thought highly of Benjamin Kennicott's work, believing that it laid the foundation upon which a new translation of the Bible might be built. Less surprising than Secker's support for their work was his patronage of some of Kennicott's fiercest critics, the Hutchinsonians. The Hutchinsonians took their name from John Hutchinson (1674–1737), whose primary objective was to defend Trinitarian orthodoxy. Worried that Newtonian epistemology led people down the path toward Arianism or even deism, Hutchinson provided an alternative to the Newtonian worldview.[147] In *Moses's Principia* (1724), he argued that the Hebrew Bible contained, in symbolic form, both a true account of Earth's creation and a complete system of natural philosophy. Maintaining that God had punished man in the Tower of Babel by giving him many languages, Hutchinson believed that a careful reading of the Hebrew Bible would reveal hitherto unseen messages, and he took particular aim at Newtonians who sought truth in nature through reason alone. To uncover the original meaning of the Old Testament, the Hutchinsonians advocated a textual approach which argued that readers needed to look past the vowels (a later Jewish add-on, a kind of squid ink meant to obscure the Bible's original meaning) and focus instead on the consonantal skeleton which revealed the Bible's divinely intended, and thus true, meaning.[148] This was an approach to Hebrew studies that found few supporters, least of all among the Lowth-Secker circle.

Right Reverend the Lord Bishop of Oxford, from the Master of the Temple. Containing remarks on some strictures made by His Grace the Late Lord Archbishop of Canterbury in the Revd. Mr. Merrick's Annotations on the Psalms (1769).

[145] Thomas Wintle, *Daniel, an improved version attempted* (Oxford, 1792), pp. ii, xvii, xxvii, xli.

[146] Alexander Geddes, *Dr. Geddes's General answer to the queries, counsils, and criticisms that have been communicated to him since the publication of his proposals for printing a new translation of the Bible* (1790), p. 5; idem, *Doctor Geddes's address to the public, on the publication of the first volume of his new translation of the Bible* (1793), pp. 7–9; idem, *Critical remarks on the Hebrew scriptures* (1800), l, pp. 36, 106, 309, 365, 455. See also, Gerard Carruthers, 'Geddes, Alexander (1737–1802)', *ODNB*.

[147] Katz, *God's Last Words*, pp. 159–65; Derya Gurses, 'The Hutchinsonian defence of an Old testament Trinitarian Christianity: the controversy over Elahim, 1735–1773', *History of European Ideas* 29 (2003), pp. 393–409; C.D.A. Leighton, '"Knowledge of divine things": a study of Hutchinsonianism', *History of European Ideas* 26 (2000), pp. 159–75; idem, 'Hutchinsonianism: A Counter-Enlightenment Movement', *Journal of Religious History* 23:2 (1999), pp. 168–84 ably treat Hutchinsonian biblical hermeneutics. Most of the historiography of Hutchinsonianism has focused almost exclusively on its anti-Newtonian cosmology.

[148] R.A. Muller, 'The Debate over the Vowel Points and the Crisis in Orthodox Hermeneutics', *Journal of Medieval and Renaissance Studies* 10 (1980), pp. 53–72 provides context.

John Hutchinson's own writings were notoriously abstruse and opaque, so the role of explaining his writings to a larger audience fell to his early adherents. The first generation of his popularizers included Alexander Stopford Catcott, Walter Hodges, Duncan Forbes, Robert Spearman, and Julius Bate.[149] It was the second generation of Hutchinsonians, which included George Horne, William Jones of Nayland, and George Berkeley, jr., with whom Secker had close personal dealings.[150]

What did Secker think of the Hutchinsonians? On the face of it, not much. Looking back on the heyday of Hutchinsonianism nearly half a century later, George Horne acknowledged that Secker, one of his own patrons, disagreed with Hutchinson's followers. 'Even Archbishop Secker (then Bishop of Oxford) who was certainly a good and charitable man, had his prejudices against them; which he expressed in a Charge to his Clergy at a Visitation,' Horne admitted.[151] Thus, Secker supported Thomas Sharp (1693–1758) in the *Elahim* controversy during the 1750s. In a series of barbed works, Sharp, the Cambridge-educated archdeacon of Northumberland, challenged the Hutchinsonian Hebraic method, particularly the Hutchinsonian interpretation of the Hebrew word *Elahim*.[152] Alexander Catcott's *The superior and inferior Elahim* (1736) had argued that the Old Testament noun *Elahim* was plural, signalling that God was triune. His intention was to defend Christ's divinity against anti-Trinitarians, but his recourse to the Hutchinsonian Hebraic interpretative method drew upon him the fire of a non-Hutchinsonian orthodox type like Sharp, who laid bare the interpretative problems of the Hutchinsonian *Elahim* in three long works to which Secker gave his editorial eye. 'I read all his Papers before they were printed: & corrected & improved them throughout,' Secker later recalled.[153] Significantly, Secker worked

---

[149] Nigel Aston, 'From personality to party: the creation and transmission of Hutchinsonianism, c.1725–1750', *Studies in the History and Philosophy of Science* 35 (2004), pp. 625–44.

[150] The Anglican evangelical Thomas Haweis provides a good sense of how this second generation of Hutchinsonians was perceived at Oxford: 'They were great Hebraists, following the famed Hutchinson in his peculiar interpretation of the Hebrew; were very high Churchmen; orthodox in their tenets respecting the Trinity; the divinity of Christ & his atonement; venerating the outward forms of the Church almost to Superstition; and entertaining strong Ideas respecting priestly absolution, the imposition of Hands, the Efficacy of Baptism, & the Lord's Supper sacredotally administered': Mitchell Library, New South Wales, Thomas Haweis's MS Autobiography, ff. 28–29.

[151] George Horne, *An apology for certain gentlemen in the University of Oxford, aspersed in a late anonymous pamphlet*, 2nd edn (1799), pp. v–vi.

[152] Thomas Sharp, *Two dissertations concerning the etymology and scripture-meaning of the Hebrew words Elohim and Beerith. Occasioned by some notions lately advanced in relation to them* (1751); idem, *A review and defence of two dissertations concerning the etymology and Scripture-meaning of the Hebrew words Elohim and Berith* (1754); and idem, *Mr. Hutchinson's exposition of Cherubim, and his hypothesis concerning them examined: in three discourses. Wherein also what hath been advanced by some late writers, in support of his doctrine, is occasionally considered* (1755). Gurses, 'The Hutchinsonian defence of an Old testament Trinitarian Christianity', pp. 403–06 surveys Sharp's role in the controversy.

[153] *Autobiography*, p. 30.

behind the scenes, doing what he could to erase his own fingerprints from Sharp's work. 'I have a Copy of my former Letter & of this so that they need not be returned,' he wrote to Sharp in 1754. 'But I wd wish you to burn them after taking any [items] out of them wch you think may be of use to you without writing down whence you took them. For one knows not whose hands Letters or Copies of Letters may sooner or later come, or wt use may be made of them.'[154] Secker's wariness of the Hutchinsonians was evident later when Samuel Johnson, the president of King's College, New York, wrote to him in 1760, asking him to appoint George Horne (1732–1792) as his successor at King's.[155] Secker rejected the suggestion out of hand. 'Mr. Horne ... is, I believe a good man,' he wrote to Johnson, 'but deeply tinctured with Mr. Hutchinson's notions of philosophy and Hebrew, both of which I take to be groundless, notwithstanding a superficial attempt of his to prove a seeming agreement between the former and Sir Isaac Newton, whom Mr. Hutchinson held to be an held to be an atheist.'[156] Secker also thought Kennicott's treatment at the hands of the Hutchinsonians was excessive.

Yet, if Secker did not approve of the Hutchinsonians' biblical scholarship, he nonetheless turned to them to help defend other orthodox positions, and he promoted the careers of Horne, Jones, and the younger Berkeley.[157] What accounts for Secker's support of the Hutchinsonians? Part of it can be put down to the second generation of Hutchinsonians consciously distancing themselves from Hutchinson's cosmology and idiosyncratic approach to Hebrew.[158] The staunch trinitarianism of the Hutchinsonians also appealed to Secker, and while he rejected heterodox Hutchinsonian natural philosophy, he nonetheless valued their spirited defence of other orthodox positions.[159] Whatever the case, Horne rightly noted that 'it is pretty well known, that [Secker's] opinion was greatly altered on the subject, long before the time of his death'.[160]

---

[154] LPL, Secker Papers 7, f. 325: Secker to Sharp, 28 Sep 1754. See also, ibid, f. 320: Sharp to Secker, 8 Oct 1754.

[155] *SJ*, IV, pp. 59–60: Johnson to Secker, 15 Feb 1760.

[156] Ibid., p. 71: Secker to Johnson, 4 Nov 1760. Cf. George Horne, *A fair, and candid, and impartial state of the case between Sir Isaac Newton and Mr. Hutchinson* (Oxford, 1753) in which Horne tried to square the circle.

[157] George Berkeley, *The works of George Berkeley, D.D. late Bishop of Cloyne in Ireland* (Dublin, 1784), I, p. xxii; William Jones, *Memoirs of the life, studies, and writings of the Right Reverend George Horne* (1795), p. 48; *Autobiography*, pp. 33, 49, 54, 68.

[158] Derya Gurses, 'Academic Hutchinsonians and their quest for relevance, 1734–1790', *History of European Ideas* 31 (2005), pp. 408–27; Aston, 'From personality to party', p. 641.

[159] Aston, 'The Limits of Latitudinarianism', pp. 407–33; idem, 'Horne and Heterodoxy', pp. 895–919; idem, 'The Dean of Canterbury and the Sage of Ferney: George Horne looks at Voltaire', in *Crown and Mitre*, pp. 139–60.

[160] Horne, *An apology for certain gentlemen in the University of Oxford*, p. vi.

III

If Secker promoted orthodoxy by cultivating orthodox scholars, he also defended it through more aggressive, and at times coercive, means. Thomas Hollis accused him of persecuting Peter Annet (1693–1769) 'with the bitterest severity' for having published the heterodox *The Free Inquirer*, a charge Secker denied. 'I endeavoured to get the Publication stopped,' he explained, 'but had no Concern in the Prosecution of the Writer.'[161] Quashing publication of material he considered blasphemous was not something he shied away from. In 1764, for instance, he encouraged the earl of Hardwicke to prosecute Thomas Phillips because his apologia for Reginald Pole impugned the established Church of England and promoted popery: 'the Government hath already enough to proceed upon, if it dares be thought to attempt any thing against the Liberty of the Press', Secker reckoned.[162] He likewise made his dispensation for a Kentish clergyman to hold multiple livings contingent upon the applicant 'retracting his assertion in a formal writing under his hand' that miracles did not cease with Christ's death.[163] Edmund Law, the bishop of Carlisle, also believed that Secker 'pursued him and opposed his promotion to the last' for having published works defending mortalism.[164]

Secker's treatment of Peter Peckard (1717–1797) and Francis Blackburne (1705–1787), both mortalists and anti-subscription advocates, gives a fuller sense of the coercive lengths to which he was willing to go and the methods he was prepared to employ to combat heterodoxy. His treatment of them furthermore shines bright light onto the theological issues that divided the orthodox and heterodox within the established Church during the mid century. In them we see the twin poles of England's clerical Enlightenment. Secker, a former Dissenter, found Blackburne's and Peckard's anti-dogmatism subversive, while Blackburne and Peckard, heterodox Anglicans, thought Secker's reliance on any religious authority outside of the Bible was, at best, a betrayal of Protestantism and, at worst, intellectually corrupt. Their squabbles occurred during the 1760s, a time when the heterodox calls for religious and political reform grew louder.[165]

Peckard and Secker disagreed over the state of the soul after death. Secker held the orthodox Protestant view that 'the Souls of all Men continue after Death' and

---

[161] *PMHS* 69 (1947–50), p. 146: Hollis to Jonathan Mayhew, 4 April 1764; *Autobiography*, p. 44. See also, Herrick, *The Radical Rhetoric of the English Deists*, pp. 134–44; idem, 'Annet, Peter (1693–1769)', *ODNB*.

[162] BL, Add. MS 35607, f. 106: Secker to 2nd earl of Hardwicke, 5 July 1764.

[163] Francis Blackburne, *An historical view of the controversy concerning an intermediate state and the separate existence of the soul between death and general resurrection* (1772), p. 246.

[164] John Rylands University Library of Manchester, Theophilus Lindsey Letters, I (unfoliated): Lindsey to William Tayleur of Shrewsbury, 5 June 1784. I thank Grayson Ditchfield for bringing this letter to my attention and for providing me with a transcription of it.

[165] Clark, *English Society, 1660–1832*, p. 378.

that 'their Bodies shall at the last Day be raised up, and re-united to them'.[166] Peckard, on the other hand, adopted the anti-dogmatic mortalist line that between death and final judgment, the soul lay dormant, that at death the whole man died rather than just his physical being.[167] The mortalist controversy was 'a symptomatic clash' between dogmatists and anti-dogmatists during the eighteenth century.[168] What gave the theological disagreement between Secker and Peckard particular purchase was a bureaucratic hurdle that Peckard, the rector of Fletton near Peterborough, had to clear before he could take up a lucrative crown living which had been offered to him in 1760. In order to hold two livings in plurality, he needed Secker to grant him a dispensation: Secker used the opportunity to make Peckard publicly back away from his heterodox mortalist views.

Though Peckard arrived at Lambeth with 'all the common credentials requisite for a dispensation, and in the common forms', Secker made Peckard write lengthy Latin explanations of his earlier writings on mortalism, the heresy which holds that the soul 'sleeps' between death and the body's resurrection.[169] ('Whether the teaching concerning an intermediate state between rewards and punishments is consistent with holy scripture?' and 'Whether the soul is by its nature immortal?' were the questions Secker posed to Peckard.) Displeased with the initial responses in which Peckard had hedged about his views, Secker's chaplain forced him to write two further essays, on the internal and external truths of Christianity. Furthermore, Secker made Peckard submit a new testimonium for dispensation in which was inserted a clause affirming that Peckard 'had not published anything contrary to the doctrine of the church of England'. Peckard, then, was forced to return home to get his paperwork in 'due form', after which Secker grilled him personally. Having read through Peckard's mortalist writings and made extensive notes on them, Secker sat Peckard down, telling him that 'he did not send for me to dispute the point with me, but that he did not require any answer from me. That his present intent was to give me some advice, which he hoped by the blessing of God, might have a good influence on me.' That advice took the form of a monologue, which Peckard was not allowed to interrupt, on the errors of mortalism. Secker ended the lecture requiring Peckard to have yet another

---

[166] Lectures, pp. 127–46.
[167] Peter Peckard, Observations on the doctrine of an intermediate state between death and resurrection: with some remarks on the Rev. Mr. Goddard's sermon on that Subject (1756); idem, Farther observations on the doctrine of an intermediate state, in answer to the Rev. Dr. Morton's queries (1757).
[168] B.W. Young, '"The Soul-Sleeping System": Politics and Heresy in Eighteenth-Century England', JEH 45 (1994), pp. 64–81, at pp. 68–69. Thomas Ahnert, 'The Soul, Natural Religion, and Moral Philosophy in the Scottish Enlightenment', Eighteenth-Century Thought 2 (2004), pp. 233–53 and Norman T. Burns, Christian Mortalism from Tyndale to Milton (Cambridge, MA, 1972) provide further context.
[169] Peckard detailed his treatment by Secker in three letters to Francis Blackburne (dated 3 Nov, 5 Dec, and 6 Dec 1760): Francis Blackburne, The Works of ... Francis Blackburne, M.A ... .; with some of the life and writings of the author (Cambridge, 1804), I, pp. xciv-cvii. Unless otherwise noted, the information from this paragraph is drawn from these letters.

interview with his domestic chaplain. More importantly, he forced Peckard to assent to four articles, which were an effective renunciation of mortalism, and withheld his dispensation 'till he (Peckard) had subscribed a private paper, promising his Grace not to preach or publish any thing against the Doctrine of an intermediate state'.[170] Peckard got his second living, but he never again published in support of the mortalist heresy. Bullying could work.

We know about Peckard's treatment at Secker's hands from a series of letters he wrote to fellow mortalist Francis Blackburne.[171] Secker and Blackburne, though both Anglicans, differed wildly on the sources of religious authority and the autonomy of the individual believer. It was a disagreement brought most starkly into light by their disagreements over the Christian creeds and Anglican religious articles. Blackburne, who occupied the latitudinarian wing of the eighteenth-century Church, believed in scriptural sufficiency and dismissed the Christian creeds and the Thirty-Nine articles because they were man-made formulae. His friend, the latitudinarian Anglican cleric John Jones, had railed against the creeds in his *Free and candid disquisitions* (1749),[172] a tract Blackburne quickly endorsed in an anonymous letter to Archbishop Herring in 1754. There he argued that truth needs to be founded on the Bible alone and rejected the über-Trinitarian Athanasian creed. '[T]he Errors in the Athanasian Creed are many and grievous,' he asserted, and went so far as to contend 'that there is great probability that the Athanasian Doctrine is not conformable to the Doctrine of the Gospel.'[173] To Blackburne's way of thinking, what applied to man-made creeds applied equally to man-made articles of religion, and he lambasted the required clerical subscription to the Thirty-Nine articles. 'The Subscription of so many Ministers every year to Articles of Religion, which many of them understand not, and many others of them believe not,' he warned Herring, '... affords such suspicions of impenetrable stupidity, voracious avarice, and prostituted conscience in the subscribers as will unanswerably fix upon the Church of England, as long as this state of things shall last, all that odium and contempt which reasonable and upright men have for arbitrary impositions, and mean and sordid submissions to them.'[174] For Blackburne, the Bible remained the religion of Protestants, the right of private

---

[170] Peter Peckard, *Subscription. Or historical extracts* (1776), p. 127.

[171] Blackburne, *An historical view of the controversy concerning an intermediate state and the separate existence of the soul between death and general resurrection*, pp. 241–67 highlights his own disagreements with Secker regarding the soul.

[172] John Jones, *Free and candid disquisitions relating to the Church of England, and the means of advancing religion therein*, 3rd edn (1750), pp. 103–30.

[173] [Francis Blackburne], *A letter written by a country clergyman, to Archbishop Herring in the year MDCCLIV* (1771), pp. 15, 18.

[174] Ibid., p. 36.

judgment was inviolable, and religious progress was necessary to complete the unfinished work of the Reformation.[175]

Secker's ideas on these matters differed markedly from Blackburne's. Scripture, tradition, and reason were the sources of religious authority for Secker, and ranked in that order. Clearly the Bible is 'the original charter of our religion', and in it 'the doctrines of our religion are truly and fully conveyed to us'.[176] Yet he parted company with Blackburne in arguing that tradition was also a legitimate source of religious authority.[177] One of his best-selling works provided a detailed, systematic defence of the Apostles' creed, whose ultimate worth, depended on its biblical foundations: '... neither this, nor any other Creed, hath Authority of its own, equal to Scripture; but derives its principal authority from being founded on Scripture. Nor is it in the Power of any Man, or Number of Men, either to lessen or increase the fundamental Articles of the Christian Faith.'[178] Similarly, to Secker's way of thinking, the Athanasian creed's 'doctrines are undeniably the same with those, that are contained in the articles of our church, in the beginning of our litany, in the conclusion of many of our collects, in the Nicene creed, and, as we conceive, in that of the apostles, in the doxology, in the form of baptism, in the numerous passages of both testaments: only here they are somewhat more distinctly set forth, to prevent equivocations'. The main point of the Athanasian creed was simply to rebut those who 'deny in general the Trinity in Unity, or three Persons who are one God'.[179] This was further than Blackburne and like-minded anti-dogmatists were willing to go.

It was, however, the combustible issue of clerical subscription to the Thirty-Nine articles that brought Secker and Blackburne into outright conflict with one another. This was not an arcane issue, because, as John Walsh suggests, the Thirty-Nine articles 'have been the doctrinal mirror in which Anglicans have officially viewed themselves', and during the eighteenth century, 'they were a focus of civic as well as doctrinal identity, for they were welded into the structure of the confessional state'.[180] Calling for the abolition of clerical subscription, then, was an explicit renunciation of the 'confessional principle' which served as the foundation of the relationship between church and state in England. For these reasons and

---

[175] R.S. Crane, 'Anglican Apologetics and the Idea of Progress', in idem, *The Idea of the Humanities* (Chicago, 1967), I, pp. 251–97 considers the latitudinarian Edmund Law's theory of religious progress.

[176] 'Sermon XLI. On the Duty of Reading Scripture [II Tim. 3:16–17]', in *WTS*, I, p. 486; *Lectures*, p. 38.

[177] Ingram, 'Nation, Empire, and Church', pp. 27–34 elucidates Secker's thoughts on religious authority in greater detail.

[178] *Lectures*, p. 40.

[179] 'Sermon XCV. An Explanation and Defence of the Liturgy of the Church of England', pp. 4, 5.

[180] John Walsh, 'The Thirty-Nine Articles and Anglican Identity in the Eighteenth Century' in *Quand Religions et Confessions se Regardent*, ed. Christine d'Haussy (Paris, 1998), pp. 61–70, at p. 61. Dr. Walsh's article is a brief, but excellent, treatment of its subject, and I appreciate him bringing it to my attention.

more, Secker spearheaded the orthodox counter-offensive against Blackburne's *The Confessional* (1766), a work which occasioned the most serious intellectual challenge to the established Church during the mid eighteenth century.

Blackburne first spelled out his anti-subscription views in an anonymous response to William Samuel Powell's Cambridge commencement sermon of 1757.[181] There Blackburne rejected Samuel Clarke's contention that 'every person may reasonably agree to such forms, whenever he can in any sense at all reconcile them with Scripture'.[182] Instead, he believed that this latitudinarian formula for subscription to the Anglican articles proposed by Clarke and seconded by Powell was casuitical: it was, he argued, 'a Defence conducted on such principles as manifestly tend to confound the common use of language'.[183] Blackburne also accused the Church's leaders of blocking efforts to reform subscription requirements. 'A large majority of the clergy, either really are, or affect to be persuaded, that no alterations in the constitution of our church are at all necessary,' he insisted. 'At the head of these are some of the most opulent and dignified of the order. Vigorous opposition from there is certain and formidable, and sufficient to intimidate the few in comparison, who are affected with a different sense of their situation.'[184] Eight years later, Blackburne made a lengthy and systematic assault on the subscription requirements in *The Confessional*. The Church lacked the authority to interfere with the right of private judgment, he argued. 'Lodge your church-authority in what hands you will, and limit it with whatever restrictions you think proper, you cannot assert to it a right of deciding controversies of faith and doctrine,' he asserted, 'or, in other words, a right to require assent to a certain sense of scripture, exclusive of other senses, without an unwarrantable interference with those rights of private judgment which are manifestly secured to every individual by the scriptural terms of Christian liberty, and thereby contradicting the original principles of the Protestant Reformation.'[185] It flowed logically from this understanding of church authority, that requiring clerical subscription to the Thirty-Nine articles was anathema and needed to be jettisoned.

The Confessional sparked a vigorous, at times vitriolic, debate on the very nature of the established Church's status and privileges.[186] Secker thought it posed

---

[181] Francis Blackburne, *Remarks on the Revd. Dr. Powell's sermon in defence of subscriptions, preached before the University of Cambridge on the commencement Sunday 1757* (1758).
[182] Quoted in Martin Fitzpatrick, 'Latitudinarianism at the parting of the ways: a suggestion', in *The Church of England, c. 1689–c. 1833: From Toleration to Tractarianism*, eds. John Walsh, Colin Haydon, and Stephen Taylor (Cambridge, 1993), p. 213.
[183] Blackburne, *Remarks on … Dr. Powell's sermon*, pp. 70–71.
[184] Ibid., p. x.
[185] Francis Blackburne, *The Confessional; or, a full and free inquiry into the right, utility, edification, and success, of establishing systematical confessions of faith and doctrine in Protestant churches. The third edition, enlarged* (1770), p. 50.
[186] On the theology and politics of the subscription controversy, see Young, *Religion and Enlightenment in Eighteenth-Century England*, pp. 45–80; Fitzpatrick, 'Latitudinarianism at

a sufficient threat to the Church to co-ordinate responses to it, and he worked to have a rebuttal in print as soon as possible.[187] William Jones (1726–1800), the Hutchinsonian rector of Pluckley, volunteered to draft a retort, and Secker threw himself fully into the project. Calling off Jones's proposed response to Voltaire's *Dictionnaire philosophique portaif* (1764–69), Secker 'addres'd a long letter to the said Rector full of seasonable directions about the turn and temper of mind to be obser'vd in a reply to such a work, and wherein He offers all the assistance in his Power towards the execution of it'.[188] Secker recalled later, 'I gave him Directions about the Manner of writing, sent him very large Remarks upon it, & furnished him with Books. He made a Beginning, which he sent me, & I returned him Many Corrections on it.'[189]

Jones, however, soon became too ill to continue the project, and Secker 'engaged' Glocester Ridley (1702–1774), 'who had also supplied Mr. Jones with Observations', to draft the response. A good friend of fellow Wykehamist Robert Lowth, Ridley was something of a biblical scholar.[190] In 1761, he published *De Syriacoarum novi foederis versionum*, a study of the sixth-century Syriac version of the New Testament attributed to Philoxenus, which Ridley dedicated to Secker. By the mid 1760s, Ridley had also established a reputation as a reliably orthodox writer, having published on the Eucharist, the operations of the Holy Ghost, and providential theology. He was one of Secker's favourites, and the archbishop contributed significantly to Ridley's quintessentially orthodox *Three letters to the author of The confessional* (1768), noting 'I wrote a great part of each of them, & furnished him all the Help that was in my power.'[191] He even took to the pages of London newspapers to defend Ridley.[192] For Ridley's efforts, Secker nominated him to a lucrative Salisbury prebend (1766) and had a D.D. conferred upon him (1767).[193] It is suggestive that a number of others closely connected to Secker also wrote up defences of subscription during the ensuing controversy. The Hutchinsonians Jones and Horne published against the anti-subscriptionists, as did the political economist Josiah Tucker.[194] While Secker gave Thomas

---

the parting of the ways', pp. 209–27; and G.M. Ditchfield, 'The Subscription Issue in British Parliamentary Politics, 1772–79', *Parliamentary History* 7 (1988), pp. 45–80.

[187] Aston, 'The Limits of Latitudinarianism', pp. 407–33 explains why many Anglicans viewed Blackburne's assault on clerical subscription requirements as a logical follow-up to Robert Clayton's heterodox *An essay on spirit* (1750).

[188] BL, Add. MS 39311, f. 180: Horne to George Berkeley, jr., 17 July 1766.

[189] *Autobiography*, p. 52.

[190] W.P. Courtney, 'Ridley, Glocester (1702–1774)', rev. Bridget Hill, *ODNB*.

[191] *Autobiography*, p. 68.

[192] See, for instance, *London Chronicle* 23 (12–14 April 1768), p. 359 where Secker defended Ridley under the pseudonym 'Oxoniensis'. In particular, he was responding to attacks on Ridley's critique of *The Confessional* by 'Old Milton' and 'Cantabrigiensus', which had appeared in earlier editions of the same paper.

[193] *Autobiography*, pp. 54, 57; *Literary Anecdotes*, VIII, p. 116.

[194] William Jones, *Remarks on the principles and spirit of a work entitled the Confessional* (1770); George Horne, *Considerations on the projected reformation of the Church of England. In a*

Rutherforth some assistance as he drafted his defences of subscription,[195] he did not – as Blackburne charged – secretly commission and edit John Rotheram's *Essay on establishments in religion* (1767).[196]

Blackburne's circle suspected that Secker was orchestrating the mid-century campaign to defend orthodox belief. 'I am told that a certain Abp. Has declared that the Ch. Of E. shall suffer no alteration (for the better, I fear, was here intended) so long as he governs it.' Blackburne's friend John Wiche lamented in 1766, while Blackburne himself groused in 1767, 'No one who is acquainted with the features of that master-workman (Secker) in this Episcopal Fabric, can doubt, but that he intended ... to lock down upon us at home the Hierarchical Yoke.'[197] When Horne took to the pages of the *London Chronicle* to rebut Voltaire in the persona of 'Nathaniel Freebody', Blackburne saw Secker as the orthodox puppet-master, believing that Horne was 'set to work by the Great Man of Kent', and, when Horne ran into opposition, gloated that 'C – t – b – y himself could not save him.'[198] Blackburne was furthermore convinced that Secker coordinated the counter-assault against *The Confessional*: he 'was the prime encourager of, if not the chief instrument in, the principal publications against the book'.[199]

Blackburne's son also suggests that Secker tried to take a more punitive line against his father. Blackburne had published *The Confessional* anonymously but, it seems, Secker used his contacts to ferret out his name: 'When the book was published, it appeared from the clamour that was raised against it, that grievous offence was taken at it by that part of the clergy who affect to call themselves orthodox. The indignation of Archbishop Secker was excessive. His mask of moderation fell off at once. He employed all his emissaries to find out the author, and by the industry of Rivington, and the communicative disposition of Millar, he succeeded.' Edmund Keene, bishop of Chester and Blackburne's diocesan, warned Blackburne that any hopes he held of career advancement would vanish if he did

---

letter to the right honourable Lord North (1772); Josiah Tucker, *An apology for the present Church of England as by law established, occasioned by a petition laid before Parliament, for abolishing subscriptions, in a letter to one of the petitioners,* 2nd edn (Gloucester, 1772).

[195] Beinecke, Osborn Files: Drawer 34.248: Secker to Rutherforth, 30 Jan 1768. Thomas Rutherforth, *A vindication of the right of Protestant churches to require the clergy to subscribe to an established confession of faith and doctrines in a charge delivered at a visitation in July MDCCLXVI* (Cambridge, 1766); idem, *A second vindication of the right of Protestant churches to require the clergy to subscribe to an established confession of faith and doctrines in a letter to the examiner of the first* (Cambridge, 1766); idem, *A defence of a charge concerning subscriptions, in a letter to the author of the Confessional* (Cambridge, 1767). See also, DWL, MS 12.45 (no. 102): Blackburne to Wiche, 4 Sept 1767.

[196] Blackburne, *Memoirs of Thomas Hollis,* I, pp. 326, 406; *Literary Anecdotes,* VIII, p. 194: Rotheram to unknown, 22 Oct 1780.

[197] DWL, MS 12.53 (no. 44): Wiche to Blackburne, 17 Oct 1766; *PMHS* 99 (1987), p. 105: Blackburne to Andrew Eliot, 23 Jan 1767.

[198] DWL, MS 12.45 (no. 100): Blackburne to Wiche, 23 Jan 1767; ibid., MS 12.45 (no. 102): Blackburne to Wiche, 9 Sept 1767.

[199] Blackburne, *Memoirs of Thomas Hollis,* I, p. 406.

not renounce *The Confessional*: 'mentioning the resentment of the Archbishop of Canterbury … [Keene] intimated that if the suspicion which fell upon Mr. B. was groundless, he would do well to silence the imputation, by publicly disavowing the work in print; for that every door of access to farther preferment would otherwise be shut against him'.[200] Blackburne had, however, set his mind against ever again subscribing to the Thirty-Nine Articles; he would remain archdeacon of Cleveland, a post he first took up in 1750, until his death in 1787.

In addition to questioning the need for subscription requirements, Blackburne also accused the Church of England of being soft on Roman Catholicism and accused prominent orthodox clergy of harbouring pro-Catholic sympathies.[201] Here he was influenced by his close friend, Thomas Hollis (1720–1774), an anti-Catholic zealot, radical Whig, and former friend of Secker, who financed *The Confessional*'s publication in the first place. Hollis also coordinated the stream of anti-Catholic pieces by Blackburne, Theophilus Lindsey, William Harris, and Caleb Fleming that appeared in the *London Chronicle* during the late 1760s.[202] Secker, he thought, was too lenient on Catholics, complaining to Jonathan Mayhew that Secker had forsaken the 'hard unsplendid work at home, the watching, *da vero*, against the evil morals, conduct of his own vast Flock, and the alarming growth of Popery'.[203] It was a charge against Secker vitiated by the fact that one of the priests who was a member of the London Association and involved in the Gordon Riots testified that he had read Secker's works as prophylaxis against popery![204] In *The Confessional*, Blackburne also cast aspersions on Archbishop William Wake's correspondence with Gallican Catholics during the early eighteenth century, correspondence which had been aimed at forming ecumenical ties between the Church of England and Gallican Church.[205] Secker had Osmund Beauvoir copy original letters between Wake and Beauvoir's father, who had been domestic chaplain to England's diplomatic representative to France during the late 1710s, and had Edward Bentham make extracts from Wake's papers at Christ Church, Oxford, to clear the former archbishop's name. Then, Secker recalled, 'I methodized both these, & sent what I had done to Dr. [Robert] Richardson, Sir Joseph Yorkes Chaplain at the Hague to be communicated to Mr.

---

[200] Blackburne, 'Life of Francis Blackburne', p. xxxiii.
[201] Colin Haydon, *Anti-Catholicism in eighteenth-century England, c.1714–80. A political and social study* (Manchester, 1993), pp. 180–94 examines this common, if irrational, charge made from within the Church of England by quasi-Arians like Blackburne and old-style republicans like Thomas Hollis.
[202] P.D. Marshall, 'Thomas Hollis (1720–74): The Bibliophile as Libertarian', *BJRL* 66 (1984), 257–59; Caroline Robbins, 'The Strenuous Whig, Thomas Hollis of Lincoln's Inn', *WMQ*, 3rd series, 7 (1950), pp. 406–53; W.H. Bond, *Thomas Hollis of Lincoln's Inn: A Whig and his Books* (Cambridge, 1990); Colin Bonwick, 'Hollis, Thomas (1720–1774)', *ODNB*.
[203] *PMHS* 69 (1947–50), pp. 171–72: Hollis to Mayhew, 24 June 1765.
[204] *The proceedings at the trial of George Gordon, Esquire, commonly called Lord George Gordon, for high treason, in the Court of King's Bench, Westminster; … On Monday and Tuesday, Feb the 5th and 6th, 1781* (1781), p. 27.
[205] Blackburne, *The Confessional*, pp. lxxxvii, xci-xciv.

[Archibald] Maclaine for the Foundation of his Defence of the Abp.'[206] A year later, Secker wrote a number of anonymous letters, which he placed in St *James's Chronicle*, to counter Blackburne's and Caleb Fleming's charges that Joseph Butler had died a Roman Catholic.[207] For all of this, Secker earned Blackburne's lasting enmity. 'The Archbishop', he groused 'was indefatigable in tracing out the anonymous authors of what he called obnoxious books; and sometimes used means to gratify his passion which would not have passed for allowable practice among the horse-dealers in Smithfield.'[208]

IV

It might not have been pretty, but Secker's way planted the seeds of a successful defence of Anglican orthodoxy in the late eighteenth century. For all the modern scholarly fascination with and fixation upon the heterodox, it was the orthodox who won the eighteenth-century fight of ideas, if not in a knockout, then at least in a split decision.[209] Be that as it may, some might be tempted to accuse Secker of suffering from a paralysis of caution or a failure of imagination. Without doubt, he was inherently cautious and unwilling to expose the Church to negative press. The failure to produce a new English translation of the Bible was one result of Secker's caution. Nearly everyone recognized the problems with the 'King James's Bible' (1611) and the need for a new, more accurate translation. By the time Secker assumed the primacy, it had been nearly a century and a half since the AV's publication, a period during which ways of treating and translating ancient texts had moved on considerably and, more importantly, during which most had come to acknowledge the evident errors that littered the text. This was a scholarly issue, but it was also a political one because one of the crucial debates in the English Enlightenment was over the social and intellectual sources of authority. As the foundational document of Christianity and as 'a bulwark of royal and episcopal authority', the AV carried political significance for both church and state, and

---

[206] *Autobiography*, p. 57. Maclaine's defence appeared in a book-length appendix to the second edition of J.L. Mosheim, *An Ecclesiastical History*, ed. and trans. Archibald Maclaine (1768), pp. 45–137. See also, *Literary Anecdotes*, II, p. 40.

[207] *Autobiography*, pp. 58, 61, 178. Joseph Butler, *The analogy of religion, natural and revealed, to the constitution and course of nature ... with a preface by Samuel Hallifax* (1798), pp. xliv-xlviii surveys the controversy in some detail. See also, Joseph Butler, *A charge delivered to the clergy at the primary visitation of the diocese of Durham, in the year MDCCLI ... with a preface by Samuel, Lord Bishop of Gloucester* (1786), pp. xxv-xxix and Francis Blackburne, *A serious enquiry into the use and importance of external religion* (1752).

[208] Blackburne, *Memoirs of Thomas Hollis*, I, pp. 406–07.

[209] Nigel Aston, 'Anglican Responses to Anticlericalism in the "Long" Eighteenth Century, c. 1689–1830', in *Anticlericalism in Britain, c.1500–1914*, p. 122; idem, 'The Limits of Latitudinarianism', p. 433; idem, 'Infidelity Ancient and Modern: George Horne Reads Edward Gibbon', *Albion* 27:4 (1995), p. 561.

Anglican leaders like Secker worried that altering it might let the camel's nose into the tent and embolden the heterodox to demand alterations in the Church itself. Not surprisingly, a wide variety of contemporaries called for a new AV. In 1749, for instance, the latitudinarian John Jones placed a new translation of the Bible and a radical reorganization of its contents atop his comprehensive reform agenda for the established Church, and Archbishop Herring's draft notes on Jones's proposal acknowledged its merits.[210] Other churchmen were not so willing as Herring to give ground. It is telling that the need for a new AV appears nowhere in Edmund Gibson's own comprehensive proposals for church reform dating from the mid 1730s. Secker admitted the problems inherent in translations of the Bible and acknowledged that a new AV might be a good thing, eventually.[211] Nevertheless, he thought Herring had gone too far in agreeing with Jones that a new AV required a systematic reorganization of its contents.[212]

Not surprisingly, then, there appeared no updated translation of the Bible during Secker's primacy largely because Secker himself lacked the stomach for it. In February 1759, Francis Blackburne wrote to Theophilus Lindsey with his explanation of the archbishop's inactivity.

> Pilkington's *Remarks on several passages of Scripture*, where the errors of the Hebrew text are rectified is worth your notice. His aim is at a new Translation of the Bible, which he and Kennicott and others have made appear is much wanted. The present A.B.C. [Secker] set a particular person (very capable) upon collecting instances of erroneous Translations in order ot the setting forward this desirable end: But he was then Bp of Oxford only. Since his promotion, he has told the poor Fellow, his pains might have been spared – For that – *tempora mutanto*. i.e. the Times now that we can look at them from a greater point of Elevation, appear to be not so *ripe* as we thought them upon lower ground: I have the fragment of the Letter he wrote to this man: and shall insert it in the remarks on Ec Hist and if I can meet with it before I write next to you shall have a copy of proper Terms of Taciturnity.[213]

Secker confirmed many of these suspicions when, two years later, he spelled out publicly his reasons for opposing a new translation.

> Rival interpreters appear every day, but they are mostly second-rate and their excessive zeal leaves us much more uncertain than we were before. The essential knowledge of the sacred tongue is reviving, but it has not yet acquired the right talents, and those who cultivate it take delight in their own fantasies. Therefore if we want to achieve something worthwhile, we ought to wait either until these people repent or their error becomes clear, until the tide of looking for new meanings, and this recent madness, I would almost call it, for emendation, by

---

[210] Jones, *Free and candid disquisitions*, pp. 11–23; LPL, Secker Papers 2, f. 165.
[211] *Lectures*, p. 39; *Oratio*, p. 363.
[212] LPL, Secker Papers 2, f. 185.
[213] DWL, MS 12.52 (no. 60): quoted in Hitchin, 'The Politics of English Bible Translation', p. 83.

which honest and not unlearned men are driven to splatter the sacred text with blots recedes, until there is some worthwhile result arrive at, where they can make a comparison between themselves and, along with the most ancient interpretations, the books of the Old Testament written in Hebrew.[214]

If these provisions were met, Secker promised, he would be perfectly willing to promote a new translation. But, he warned, 'the last thing I want is to be the patron of undertakings from which too much quarrelling is likely to arise. These things can wait until an effectual meeting of the synod be called, so that we do not let ourselves stir up internal warfare which will do great harm to the public interest.' This kind of approach meant that hopes for a new AV died during Secker's primacy. He chose instead to promote biblical scholarship by patronizing those who aimed to clear up mistakes in the current AV but who, nonetheless, did not actively demand a new translation and reorganization of the Bible. As we will see throughout the course of this book, Secker often shied away from fights which he knew were right but which, he believed, were unduly risky.

Secker also tended to fight almost exclusively about the status and reputation of the established Church. In retrospect, these might look like intramural squabbles which were important to stamp out doctrinal diversity, defend the institution, and present a unified face to the world, but which did little to address the fundamental questions about the nature of religious belief itself which were arguably of a more subversive nature. Secker's defence of miracles perhaps speaks most eloquently the scope of his imaginative horizons. Protestants had always suspected Roman Catholic miracles, but the mid eighteenth century witnessed a more sustained and trenchant attack on miracles. John Redwood dubbed it 'the great debate of the new age'.[215] David Hume's 'Of Miracles' (1748), which pounded away at miracles as part of a wider assault on revealed religion,[216] and Conyers Middleton's *Free enquiry into the miraculous powers* (1748), which challenged the historical accuracy of patristic miracles, were the two most important sceptical treatments of the miraculous during the mid century.[217] Hume's powerful and searing critique of miracles remains relevant for professional philosophers today,[218] but, as even Hume acknowledged, it was Middleton's work

---

[214] *Oratio*, p. 363.

[215] John Redwood, *Reason, Religion, and Ridicule: The Age of Enlightenment in England, 1660–1750* (1976), p. 145.

[216] David Hume, *An Enquiry concerning Human Understanding*, ed. Tom L. Beauchamp (Oxford, 2000), pp. 83–99. David Wootton, 'Hume's "Of Miracles": Probability and Irreligion', in *Studies in the Philosophy of the Enlightenment*, ed. M.A. Stewart (Oxford, 1990), pp. 191–229 is an excellent study.

[217] There is no modern biography of Middleton, but see John Hunt, *Religious Thought in England from the Reformation to the End of the Last Century* (1873), III, pp. 60–70 and Leslie Stephen, *English Thought in the Eighteenth Century* (1902), I, vi.66–83.

[218] See, for instance, Nicholas Saunders, *Divine Action and Modern Science* (Cambridge, 2002); the symposium on miracles in *Zygon* 37:3 (2002), pp. 701–62; and David Johnson, *Hume, Holism and Miracles* (Ithaca, NY, 1999).

that most provoked contemporaries.[219] While not challenging miracles generally or biblical ones in particular, Middleton's *Free enquiry* nonetheless challenged the reliability of miracles during the patristic age. Middleton's was an early modern approach to the problem, and Secker had a hand in the orthodox responses to it. Thomas Church (1707–1756), vicar of Battersea, published two volumes refuting *Free enquiry*, of which Secker later recalled, 'I gave him a good deal of Assistance in both.'[220] Secker assured the earl of Hardwicke that Church 'hath shewn himself in several Controversies an Orthodox Man, and received an honorary Drs. Degree on that account'.[221]

This same concern to vindicate the historical reliability of miracle reports can be seen clearly in Secker's published defences of the signal Christian miracle, the resurrection of Jesus Christ. Nowhere does he grapple with Hume's contention that 'no human testimony can have such force as to prove a miracle, and make it a just foundation for any such system of religion'.[222] Instead, Secker carefully evaluates the historical evidence surrounding the resurrection, evidence whose merit he subjects to the test of reasonableness. While not accepting the biblical narratives wholly uncritically, Secker nonetheless defends the fact of the resurrection on biblical evidence alone. It was patently clear to Secker that Jesus was not a charlatan who faked his own death. '[I]t is obviously plain, that no impostor would ever have appealed to a method of trying his pretensions, that required his being put to death before it could decide any thing,' he argued, 'and that no enthusiast would ever have conducted himself in so calm and prudent a manner, and taught so rational a doctrine as our Saviour did.'[223] Likewise, the apostles had no incentive to lie when they preached that Jesus rose from the dead on the third day after his death. 'Surely, in these circumstances, if his disciples had acted on worldly motives, their point must have been to provide for their own safety by flight and silence; and thus, for aught that appears, they might have been very safe,' Secker reasoned.[224] Indeed, it defied logic that they would persist in preaching doctrines they knew to be patently false and that would eventually lead to their executions.[225] In the end, Secker saw no way in which the historical credibility of the resurrection could be questioned.

---

[219] 'On my return from Italy, I had the mortification to find all England in a Ferment on account of Dr. Middletons Free Enquiry; while my performance was entirely overlooked and neglected': quoted in John Valdimir Price, 'The reading of philosophical literature', in *Books and their Readers in Eighteenth-Century England*, ed. Isabel Rivers (Leicester, 1982), p. 171.

[220] *Autobiography*, p. 30. Thomas Church, *A vindication of the miraculous powers, which subsisted in the three first centuries of the Christian Church. In answer to Dr. Middleton's free enquiry* (1750).

[221] BL, Add. MS 35592, f. 127: Secker to Hardwicke, 15 Aug 1753.

[222] Hume, *An Enquiry concerning Human Understanding*, p. 184.

[223] 'Sermon LXIX. The Evidence of the Resurrection of Christ [Acts 10:40–41]', in *WTS*, II, p. 324.

[224] Ibid., p. 325.

[225] Ibid., p. 326.

Secker's was not a retrograde approach to the problem of miracles, but neither was it novel. There were churchmen, such as William Warburton, who recognized clearly the potential threat posed by Hume and who tried to defend orthodoxy with the tools of Newtonian natural philosophy.[226] But most of the orthodox thought Middleton, not Hume, posed the greater threat. Secker's private biblical marginalia certainly confirm that he, unlike a Warburton, did not try explicitly to reconcile biblical miracles to Newtonian natural philosophy. Rather, his concern in even his private studies was to see how biblical miracles might plausibly be explained without recourse to Newtonianism. So, for instance, in the margins of his study bible next to the account of Moses parting the Red Sea, he cites a number of historical accounts from Livy to the present about large bodies of water becoming shallow enough to allow people to walk through them. 'The Thames in the winter of 1716 was blown so dry, that great numbers of persons walked over it below bridge [sic], only with the help of boats or planks in some places to keep them from being wet,' he observed.[227] Likewise, against claims that gunpowder caused the thunder, lightning, and trumpet blast that God used to call Moses and his people to meet Him at the foot of Mt. Sinai in Exodus 19, Secker argued that

> It may be added, that there is no cause to think, that [Moses], or any one then, or long after, was acquainted with gunpowder: that the noise & flash of it is very distinguishable from thunder & lightning: that he cd not have fired his powder without letting too many into the Secret. Yet some will still say, that prohibiting Access to the mountain looks suspicious. It shd be observed, that more stress is laid on the loudness of the sound of the trumpet than on any thing else, and that Gunpowder, unless in mines or vast quantities wd not make the mountain quake greatly.[228]

At times, though, he was left to scratch his head. With the biblical Flood, for instance, he could not easily explain how freshwater fish were able to survive in salt water when the seas rose or how all the land creatures on Noah's ark spread out across the earth.[229] For the most part, though, Secker found himself able, through reason, to defend the biblical miracles, something particularly evident in his study edition of the New Testament, where he methodically considered the accounts of Christ's miracles to refute those who would deny them.[230]

In retrospect, it is striking that while Blackburne drove Secker to distraction, Hume did not. Yet perhaps this misses the point. Perhaps Hume, not Secker, was the oddity of the age. Perhaps his critique of miracles matters more to us than it did to his own contemporaries because our own age finds it persuasive while his own

[226] Ingram, 'William Warburton, Divine Action, and Enlightened Christianity', pp. 97–117.
[227] LPL, MS 2559, f. 61v [Exodus 21:14].
[228] Ibid., f. 65v [Exodus 19:16].
[229] LPL, MS 2564, p. 461.
[230] LPL, MS 2562, *passim*.

found it risible.[231] In worrying about Blackburne rather more than about Hume, all Thomas Secker did was to think like a man of his time, and it is hard to see how we could blame him for doing so. It is only in hindsight that we see that thinking like a man of his time had long-term intellectual consequences which the orthodox did not, and could not, foresee. Much the same can be said for the orthodox approach to Anglican pastoral reform – it too was informed by a backward-looking worldview which moderns would find both puzzling and anathema.

---

[231] Isabel Rivers, 'Responses to Hume on Religion by Anglicans and Dissenters', *JEH* 52:4 (2001), pp. 675–95 surveys contemporary reactions to Hume's work on the miraculous. Cf. John Earman, *Hume's Abject Failure: The Argument Against Miracles* (Oxford, 2000).

Chapter Five

THE CHURCH AND THE PARISHIONERS

Thomas Secker's thoughts on how to reform Anglican pastoral provision strongly echoed Gilbert Burnet's *Discourse of the Pastoral Care* (1692), a work written by the bishop of Salisbury in the aftermath of the Toleration Act. Thereafter, many churchmen fretted about how to deal with the confessional competition from Protestant nonconformists. Some advocated legal coercion of Dissenters and pressed for laws banning occasional conformity and regulating the Dissenting academies even more carefully.[1] Others came at the problem from the other end, advocating religious comprehension to obviate the problem of religious nonconformity.[2] Most, though, thought the Church could lure back confessional defectors and retain waverers without at the same time watering down its confessional requirements. Among the latter group, the latitudinarian Burnet argued forcefully that the burden lay with the clergy to convince Dissenters to return to the established Church. The problem, as Burnet saw it, was that churchmen had insufficiently fulfilled their pastoral responsibilities. '[T]he Pastoral Care, the Instructing, the Exhorting, the Admonishing and Reproving, the Directing and Conducting, the Visiting and Comforting the People of the Parish, is generally neglected,' he groused. Church of England ministers, he argued, 'are under more particular Obligations, first to look into our own Ways, and to reform whatsoever is amiss among us, and then to be Intercessors for the People committed to our Charge'. And what was the 'glorious Model' of reform which Burnet put forward? The primitive Church itself: 'the Argument in favour of the Church, how clearly soever made out, would never have its full effect upon the World, till Abuses were so far corrected, that we could shew a Primitive Spirit in our Administration, as well as a Primitive Pattern for our Constitution'.[3] Burnet did highlight specific clerical abuses or shortcomings, yet *Discourse of the Pastoral Care* prescribed clerical moral reformation as the remedy without which all others would fail. If only the clergy took their jobs as seriously as had Gregory of Nazianzus and John Chrysostom, then most of the Church of England's pastoral shortcomings would be remedied.[4]

---

[1]   See, for instance, Henry Sacheverell, *The Political Union. A discourse shewing the dependance of government on religion in general: and of the English monarchy on the Church of England in particular* (Oxford, 1702).

[2]   See, for instance, Benjamin Hoadly, *The common rights of subjects, defended: and the nature of the sacramental test, consider'd. In answer to the Dean of Chichester's vindication of the Corporation and Test Acts* (1719).

[3]   Gilbert Burnet, *A Discourse of the Pastoral Care*, 4th edn. (1736), pp. xi, xiii, 47, 48.

[4]   Ibid., pp. 49–73.

Other bishops during the eighteenth century shared Burnet's vision of restorative reform and joined him in thinking that shoring up clerical standards should be church reform's chief aim.[5] Thomas Tenison counselled Anglican clergy to 'devote themselves to practical religion' rather than to factious politics, and he successfully raised clerical standards in his dioceses.[6] William Wake, Tenison's immediate successor at Lambeth Palace, restructured his diocesan visitations to allow for better supervision of parochial clerical activity,[7] while Edmund Gibson drafted proposals for reform which advocated everything from equalizing diocesan incomes, to tightening clerical residency requirements, to taming the excesses of pluralism, to revising clerical education requirements.[8] Secker's own interest in pastoral reform is evidenced in part by his private papers, which contain the only extant copies of Gibson's proposals and of reform proposals submitted to Archbishop Herring in 1748.[9]

Thomas Secker's pastoral reform efforts, then, were not cut from whole cloth but, instead, were part of a more deeply rooted tradition within the eighteenth-century Church of England.[10] And, as with Burnet, the heart of his restorative

[5] Arthur Burns, 'English "church reform" revisited, 1780–1840', in *Rethinking the Age of Reform: Britain, 1780–1850*, eds. Arthur Burns and Joanna Innes (Cambridge, 2003), pp. 139–42 synopsizes the main church reform proposals between the end of the American Revolution and the mid nineteenth century. It is striking, and telling, that Secker advocated none of them.

[6] G.V. Bennett, 'Archbishop Tenison and the Reshaping of the Church of England', in idem, *To the Church of England*, ed. Geoffrey Rowell (Folkestone, 1988), pp. 99–110 at p. 106. See also, Edward Carpenter, *Thomas Tenison, Archbishop of Canterbury: His Life and Times* (1948), pp. 141–66. Secker apparently took Tenison for his archiepiscopal model: 'Archbishop Secker used to declare that of all his predecessors none discharged the Duties and conducted the business of his See with more judgment and ability than Dr. Tenison', recorded one contemporary: Bodleian, Add. MS A.269, f. 105: Anonymous note in Edmund Gibson-William Nicholson correspondence, n.d.

[7] Norman Sykes, *William Wake, Archbishop of Canterbury, 1657–1737* (Cambridge, 1957), 1, pp. 167–80, 222–29.

[8] Stephen Taylor (ed.), 'Bishop Edmund Gibson's Proposals for Church Reform', in *From Cranmer to Davidson: A Church of England Miscellany*, ed. Stephen Taylor (Woodbridge, 1999), pp. 188–202 is a scholarly edition of the Secker transcription (LPL, MS 2654, ff. 175–81: 'Ecclesia Anglica: Bishop Gibson's thoughts concerning alterations in it'). Norman Sykes, *From Sheldon to Secker: Aspects of English Church History, 1660–1748* (Cambridge, 1959), pp. 192–202 glosses this manuscript. Gibson also led efforts to revive the sixteenth-century *Reformatio legum ecclesiasticarum*: Gerald Bray (ed.), *Tudor Church Reform: The Henrician Canons of 1535 and the Reformatio Legum Ecclesiasticarum* (Woodbridge, 2000), pp. cvi–cvii; idem, 'The Strange Afterlife of the Reformatio Legum Ecclesiasticarum', in *English Canon Law: Essays in Honour of Bishop Eric Kemp*, eds. Norman Doe, Mark Hill, and Robert Ombres (Cardiff, 1998), pp. 36–47; J.H. Baker, *Monuments of Endlesse Labours: English Canonists and their Work, 1300–1900* (1998), pp. 95–107.

[9] LPL, Secker Papers 2, ff. 158–82: Abstracts of papers put into my hands by the ABp of Canterbury Nov 4. 1748.

[10] Jeremy Gregory's work on England's Long Reformation is particularly adept at placing eighteenth-century Anglican pastoral aspirations and reform in a longer and wider perspective; see, especially, his *Restoration, Reformation, and Reform, 1660–1828: Archbishops of Canterbury and their Diocese* (Oxford, 2000). Ian Green, 'Teaching the

reform vision involved the clergy's moral reformation. Clergy should lead 'a blameless life', avoiding 'indulging in pleasures, even the more innocent ones, for it is in the best interests of the clergy to abstain, not only from those recreations which are condemned, but also from those which are looked down upon or which do little good'.[11] Even bishops were not immune from Secker's criticism on this score. Shortly after John Egerton was named bishop of Durham, for instance, Secker 'took the liberty of talking with Egerton ... about riding a-hunting in a jockey cap, & the reproach he brought upon himself as well as indignity to the Bench, by this and other unclerical actions'.[12] Acknowledging that he and the rest of the clergy had 'superintended' the livings under their care 'less carefully and less skilfully' than they ought, Secker exhorted them 'to increase [their] dedication in order to make up ... for the human weakness by which we have sinned'. Clerical moral reformation of this sort would improve pastoral provision, both by raising clerical standards and by modelling appropriate behaviour for the laity. 'For lay people will not tolerate in the clergy things which they easily forgive in one another,' Secker cautioned.

> But if we attend to ourselves and to our doctrine, ... it will be inevitable that our reputation will gradually grow higher and that men will daily perceive more clearly to whom the control of affairs has been given. They will see how much and in how many things our labours can be useful, and then they will not only let us have that power, but will ask and demand that we exercise it for the sake of their commonwealth, so that by common consent we may be able to supply what is lacking to the church.

This would not, Secker conceded, produce immediate results 'for it will be only slowly and with great hesitation that the majority of people will start to respect us'. Nonetheless, there was 'no other way to be respected'. Here, clearly enunciated, was an orthodox vision of restorative pastoral reform which

Reformation: The Clergy as Preachers, Catechists, Authors, and Teachers' in *The Protestant Clergy in Europe*, eds. C. Scott Dixon and Luise Schorn-Schütte (London, 2003), pp. 156–75, 234–27 highlights the pastoral ideals of the reformed priesthood. Quite obviously, this book rejects the idea that there was no substantive efforts at pastoral reform during the eighteenth century. Cf. Peter Virgin, *The Church in an Age of Negligence: Ecclesiastical Structure and the Problems of Church Reform, 1700–1840* (Cambridge, 1989); Donald A. Spaeth, *The Church in an Age of Danger: Parsons and Parishioners, 1660–1740* (Cambridge, 2000); Michael Snape, *The Church of England in Industrialising Society: the Lancashire Parish of Whalley in the Eighteenth Century* (Woodbridge, 2003). Likewise, it rejects the notion that Thomas Secker himself was uninterested in or unconscious of the need for reform of the Church's pastoral provision. Cf. Ernest Gordon Rupp, *Religion in England, 1688–1791* (Oxford, 1986), p. 504; Sykes, *From Sheldon to Secker*, p. x; John H. Overton and Fredric Relton, *The English Church From the Accession of George I to the end of the Eighteenth Century (1714–1800)* (1924), p. 120.

[11] Unless otherwise noted, quotations in this paragraph derive from *Oratio*, pp. 365–66.

[12] G.M. Ditchfield and Bryan Keith-Lucas (eds.), *A Kentish Parson: Selections from the Private Papers of the Revd. Joseph Price Vicar of Brabourne, 1767–86* (Stroud, 1991), p. 81.

advocated moral reform in the clergy, not institutional restructuring, as the key to improving the Church of England's pastoral improvement.[13] And, significantly, it required no help from the English state.

I

Thomas Secker's prescriptions for pastoral reform rested squarely on the foundation of his own pastoral experience. What he knew about life as a country parson he had gleaned first from his parochial assignments in Durham during the 1720s and early 1730s.[14] Shortly after his ordination in March 1723, Secker went north to Durham to serve as one of Bishop William Talbot's domestic chaplains. While his initial duties were limited primarily to reading prayers to the bishop's family or to preaching assize sermons,[15] Secker's appointment in February 1724 to the 'golden' rectory of Houghton-le-Spring – whose yearly income of £550 was worth more than the bishoprics of Bristol, Oxford, or Llandaff – proved that Talbot thought highly of his abilities.[16] Houghton-le-Spring was an extensive,

[13]   Any consideration of the eighteenth-century Church's pastoral performance risks sailing through historiographical waters that, depending on one's point of view, are either roiling or stagnant. Rather than trying to navigate safely the straits between the Scylla of 'optimism' and Charybdis of 'pessimism', though, we shall set an alternate course around them by focusing on pastoral aims rather more than pastoral outcomes. For pastoral aspirations reflected conditions and concerns within the Church and within English society itself. John Walsh and Stephen Taylor, 'Introduction: the Church and Anglicanism in the "long" eighteenth century', in *The Church of England, c.1689–c.1833: From Toleration to Tractarianism*, eds. John Walsh, Colin Haydon, and Stephen Taylor (Cambridge, 1993), pp. 1–3 briefly surveys the optimistic and pessimistic readings of the eighteenth-century Church's pastoral performance (and calls for a new agenda in work on religion). Jeremy Gregory and Jeffrey S. Chamberlain, 'National and Local Perspectives on the Church of England in the long Eighteenth Century', in *The National Church in Local Perspective: The Church of England and the Regions, 1660–1800*, eds. Jeremy Gregory and Jeffrey S. Chamberlain (Woodbridge, 2003), pp. 1–28 offers the most balanced and reliable assessment of eighteenth-century Anglican pastoral provision. Mark Goldie, 'Voluntary Anglicans', *HJ* 46:4 (2003), pp. 977–90 chides historians for continuing to rebut the Victorian bill of particulars regarding eighteenth-century Anglican pastoral provision.

[14]   There are surprisingly few archival sources for Secker's tenure at Houghton-le-Spring, Ryton, or St James's, Westminster. His composition tithe book for Houghton-le-Spring (1724) survives, while his name appears in some of the ecclesiastical records now housed at Durham University Library. For St James's, Westminster, we have primarily official records such as church vestry minutes and churchwarden accounts from which to reconstruct his time there. There are, of course, useful bits about his time in these livings in his *Autobiography*.

[15]   *Autobiography*, p. 9. Secker preached the Assize Sermon at Newcastle in 1723.

[16]   Durham RO, EP/Ho 466: Composition tithe book of Thomas Secker, rector of Houghton, 1724. Talbot also installed Secker as the third prebend of Durham cathedral: *Autobiography*, p. 9; John le Neve, *Fasti Ecclesiae Anglicanae 1541–1857: Volume XI: Carlisle, Chester, Durham, Manchester, Ripon, and Sodor and Man Dioceses* compiled by Joyce M. Horn, David M. Smith, and Patrick Mussett (2004), p. 91.

ancient parish lying to the northeast of Durham city at the head of a vale sheltered by limestone hills on the north and east, and its sandstone, cruciform church dates from the twelfth century.[17] As Secker later remembered it, 'We were all at first much pleased with the Place. The Parish hath ten or a dozen Villages, in which as many Coaches were kept. And the People appeared well satisfied with their Minister.'[18] If Secker found his work at Houghton-le-Spring satisfying, his frail wife found its 'Dampness & Gloominess' unbearable, which explains why he exchanged the picturesque living for the rectory of Ryton in 1727. Ryton had the advantage of allowing Catherine Secker to live in the supposedly healthier climate of the city of Durham; it had the disadvantage of making her husband non-resident in his parish.[19] The requirement that royal chaplains spend at least one month each year in residence at court and his wife's frequent visits to Bath contributed further to his non-residence. While he did his best to fulfil his pastoral obligations – 'I went frequently to Ryton on Saturday, to preach on Sunday; & returned that Evening, or Monday morning,' he later recalled – Secker nonetheless had to pay a resident curate to help him shoulder his parochial duties at Ryton.[20]

Secker's time in Durham also gave him a foretaste of the pastoral challenges and responsibilities of the episcopal life. Living in William Talbot's household provided insight into a bishop's work, and Talbot took Secker with him on his 1725 visitation, asking him to preach the visitation sermon at Berwick on short notice.[21] The 'great deal of pains' which Secker and Martin Benson 'took ... in putting part of the ancient Deeds & Writings of the Church of Durham in Order' in the winter of 1728–1729 seems to have made a particularly deep impression on him.[22] An obsession with the clear and useful organization of ecclesiastical

---

[17] Robert Surtees, *The History and Antiquities of the County Palatine of Durham* (Yorkshire, 1972; first published 1816), p. 145.

[18] *Autobiography*, p. 10. Porteus, *Life of Secker*, pp. 14–15 contends that Secker 'applied himself with Alacrity to all the Duties of a Country Clergyman ... He brought down his Conversation and his Sermons to the Level of their Understandings; he visited them in private, he catechised the young and ignorant, he received his Country Neighbours and Tenants kindly and hospitably, and was of great Service to the poorer sort of them by his Skill in Physic, which was the only Use he ever made of it.'

[19] Secker's retreat into Durham city in 1727 sits uneasily with his admonition to a clergyman four decades later: 'I greatly disapprove the custom which is growing very common amongst clergy that they quit their parishes, for a more sociable life in market towns': LPL, Secker Papers 3, f. 225: Secker to Samuel Weller, 19 April 1763.

[20] *Autobiography*, pp. 12, 13; Porteus, *Life of Secker*, p. 16.

[21] *Autobiography*, p. 10. J.C. Shuler, 'The Pastoral and Ecclesiastical Administration of the Diocese of Durham, 1721–1771, with Particular Reference to the Archdeaconry of Northumberland' (University of Durham Ph.D. thesis, 1975), pp. 86–103 considers Talbot's pastoral administration of Durham during the 1720s.

[22] *Autobiography*, p. 12. At the 14 Sept 1727 meeting of the dean and chapter of Durham, it is recorded that it was 'agreed that any one member of the Body accompanyed [sic] with the Registrar may proceed to the putting the Muniments to order'. There is no further reference in the minutes of the dean and chapter to the reorganization. I am grateful to Roger Norris,

records was one of the hallmarks of his pastoral care.[23] Perhaps this sounds like an arcane point, but Secker understood that defending the rights and privileges of the Church necessitated accurate record keeping and, more importantly, that effective pastoral oversight required current and easily accessible information.[24] This explains the careful scrutiny he gave to the maintenance and organization of diocesan records. Shortly after he took hold of the reins of Canterbury, for instance, he wrote to the archiepiscopal librarian, A.C. Ducarel, to advise him about how best to the catalogue the manuscripts at Lambeth Palace's library. 'I have now had Time to look a little into the first volume of Bp Gibsons Papers, which you left here the other Day,' he wrote to Ducarel. 'And by doing so, I am confirmed in my Opinion, that it would have been much better, before any of them were bound, to put them all, or as many as had chronological marks of any kind, into Order of Time. But particularly those which were written about the same Time, and upon the same Subject, should have been so digested.'[25] He trebled Ducarel's salary in 1759 'for writing the Indexes to the Registers, an useful work, but begun very injudiciously, before my time, & continued in the same manner, almost of necessity afterwards'.[26] Secker also left behind detailed specula of the various parochial livings in Bristol, Oxford, and Canterbury dioceses, and his archiepiscopal records at Lambeth Palace are a model of clarity, having been organized by him into discrete subjects where possible.

Before Secker had the chance to put to use the knowledge of episcopal administration he gained in Durham, he faced the challenge of managing a large London parish, St James's, Westminster. Carved out of the parish of St Martin-in-the-Fields in the late seventeenth century, St James's was an affluent parish staffed by those chosen from among the best and brightest in the established Church. Secker quickly made a name for himself there as a preacher.[27] He nonetheless found the day-to-day management of the parish difficult, for his immediate predecessor had left 'the affairs of [the] parish … in great disorder'. This required Secker to work 'in concert with others, to put the accounts of the several officers into a regular method [and] dr[a]w up a set of … rules to direct

---

    deputy librarian of the Durham cathedral chapter library, for providing me with this information.

23   Cf. Gregory, *Restoration, Reformation, and Reform*, p. 11.
24   *Charges* (1750), pp. 123–61.
25   LPL, MS 2214, f. 22: Secker to A.C. Ducarel, 20 Aug 1758. See also, LPL, MS 2214, f. 24: Ducarel to Secker, 22 Aug 1758; *Literary Anecdotes*, V, p. 290; ibid., VI, p. 394. Upon moving to Lambeth, Secker also badgered Edward Bentham to provide him with a summary of William Wake's papers in Christ Church, Oxford's library and William Sancroft's papers in the Bodleian Library. Secker hoped that the papers of these two former archbishops of Canterbury would help him settle questions of precedent when they arose. See the correspondence between Bentham and Secker (1759–61) in LPL, MS 1133, ff. 1–12. Sykes, *William Wake*, I, pp. 4–5 summarizes the exchange.
26   *Autobiography*, p. 40. See also, LPL, MS 1483, ff. 25, 29.
27   *Egmont Diaries*, II, p. 209.

them better for the future'.[28] Selecting the personnel to staff the various chapels and lesser offices of the parish remained a perennial, often exasperating, issue for Secker and the 25–member vestry. When choosing the schoolmaster of King's Street chapel in 1738, for instance, the earl of Egmont noted that 'The Bishop as Rector of St James' might have named [it] himself, but said he had so ill success with the two preceeding persons that he would not now take it upon him.'[29] To the rector and vestry also fell the duty of supervising the poor relief in the parish.[30] While many a lowly country clergyman dreamed of a living as wealthy and influential as St James's, Secker willingly traded it for the deanery of St Paul's cathedral in 1750. 'The Reasons of my Acceptance', he recalled, 'were, that I found the Burthen of Parochial Business grow heavy upon me; & Part of the Parishioners ungrateful for the Pains, which I sincerely took to serve them in all respects.'[31]

The deanery of St Paul's was among the most prestigious non-episcopal offices in the Church of England.[32] 'It will be *otium cum dignitate*,' Thomas Herring wrote to the duke of Newcastle on learning of Secker's appointment, 'and a handsome retirement to him from a Life and Station of more than ordinary labour.'[33] Yet the dean's duties were not inconsiderable. Chief among his responsibilities was supervising divine services. 'During the whole time, that I was at St Pauls, I went to Church twice every Day, unless something extraordinary prevented me, whether I was in Residence or not', Secker recorded. 'And I engaged the three other Residentiaries to agree, that we would ordinarily preach our Afternoon turns our selves.'[34] He also faced substantive administrative challenges there. While dean, he completely reorganized the chapter's accounts, indexed the cathedral's records, updated and corrected the statute book, resolved lingering disputes concerning the use of the cathedral's churchyard, and engaged in a spirited, often bitter, fight with the cathedral's surveyor, Henry Flitcroft, regarding overcharges for building repairs.[35]

---

[28] Porteus, *Life of Secker*, pp. 21–22.

[29] *Egmont Diaries*, II, p. 470.

[30] Westminster City Archives, D 1759–1760: St James's, Westminster, vestry minutes, 1712–1750 paint a vivid portrait of the varied duties required of the rector and vestry in managing the parish's spiritual and secular affairs. See also, Porteus, *Life of Secker*, p. 22.

[31] *Autobiography*, p. 28, in which Secker details the particularly obnoxious behaviour of parishioners Henry Fane and Thomas Bonney. See also his extraordinary 'Sermon CXXXIV. Preached at the Parish-Church of St James, Westminster, Dec 30, 1750, on Resigning the Rectory' [II Cor. 13:11], in *WTS*, III, pp. 542–57 in which he explained at length the difficulties one faced as rector of St James's, Westminster.

[32] For the history of St Paul's cathedral during the eighteenth century, see the essays by W.M. Jacob, Jeremy Gregory, and Nigel Aston in Derek Keene, Arthur Burns, and Andrew Saint (eds.), St *Paul's: The Cathedral of London, 604–2004* (New Haven, CT, 2004).

[33] BL, Add. MS 32720, f. 217: Herring to TPH.

[34] *Autobiography*, p. 34. See also, Porteus, *Life of Secker*, pp. 44–45.

[35] For the Flitcroft controversy, see LPL, Herring Papers 2, ff. 154–254.

Secker held the deanery *in commendam* with the bishopric of Oxford. He had been nominated to Oxford in 1737 after a two-year stint in the diocese of Bristol, during which time he had 'laid the Foundation of a Parochial Account of the Diocese for the Use of [his] Successors'.[36] Few records remain for his pastoral oversight of Bristol, but those extant for his oversight of Oxford and Canterbury evidence a demonstrable pastoral industriousness. Secker could not have performed his episcopal duties so well had he not surrounded himself with capable people to assist him.[37] For most of the time he was bishop of Oxford, Daniel Burton (d. 1775) served as his domestic chaplain and as chancellor of the diocese. A staunch Whig and an Oxford native, Burton was crucial to Secker's diocesan administration, a formidable task made more difficult for a Whig bishop overseeing a diocese at whose centre lay the Tory bastion of the University of Oxford. The political capital Secker spent to get Burton a canonry of Christ Church, Oxford, shows just how much he valued Burton.[38] Secker also relied on John Potter (diocesan chancellor) and Herbert Beaver (deputy diocesan registrar) in his administration of Oxford diocesan affairs.

During his archiepiscopate, Secker turned to a wider cast of characters for help than he had in Bristol and Oxford. He needed them because he was at once a diocesan responsible for pastoral supervision of Canterbury diocese and the primate of the national Church of England.[39] He was allowed eight domestic chaplains at Lambeth. He kept on Thomas Wray, Charles Plumptre, and Charles Hall after Archbishop Hutton's unexpected death and, in time, added Beilby Porteus, George Stinton, John Fowell, Thomas Wintle, and John Saunders.[40] Each served an important function in the archiepiscopal household. Plumptre's

---

[36] *Autobiography*, p. 16.

[37] *Oxford Correspondence*, pp. xxi–xxiii. This is not to suggest that Secker's relations with his diocesan officers were always harmonious. For his dispute with the Oxford archdeacon's official, Henry Brooke, see Bodleian, MS Top.Oxon.c.209, ff. 14–15. For the role of senior diocesan officials in episcopal administration, see William Gibson, *The Achievement of the Anglican Church* (Lewiston, 1995), pp. 161–64.

[38] For Secker's lobbying on Burton's behalf, see BL, Add. MS 32857, f. 322: Secker to TPH, 2 July 1755; BL, Add. MS 35858, f. 67: Newcastle to Secker, 8 Aug 1755; BL, Add. MS 35858, ff. 108–09: Secker to TPH, 11 Aug 1755; BL, Add. MS 32906, f. 46: Secker to TPH, 13 May 1760; BL, Add. MS 32906, f. 468: Secker to TPH, 3 June 1760. See also, John le Neve, *Fasti Ecclesiae Anglicanae 1541–1857: Volume VIII: Bristol, Gloucester, Oxford and Peterborough Dioceses*, compiled by Joyce M. Horn (1996), pp. 103–05.

[39] Gregory, *Restoration, Reformation, and Reform*, pp. 24–41 and, more generally, idem, 'Archbishops of Canterbury, their diocese, and the shaping of the National Church', in *The National Church in Local Perspective*, pp. 29–52.

[40] This list is derived from A.C. Ducarel, 'History and Antiquities of the Archiepiscopal Palace of Lambeth', in *Bibliotheca Topographica Britannica* (1780–90), II. John Saunders is not listed in Ducarel as an archiepiscopal domestic chaplain, but Secker recorded in his *Autobiography* (p. 67) that he took Saunders on as his chaplain in the spring of 1768. For Secker's treatment of his Canterbury chaplains, see John Eachard, *The Works of John Eachard* (1773), I, pp. 13–14; P.J. Grosley, *A tour of London: or, new observations on England, and its inhabitants .... Translated from the French by Thomas Nugent, LL.D., and fellow of the Society of Antiquaries* (Dublin, 1772), I, p. 278.

long association with the University of Cambridge, for instance, made him well-placed to advise Secker on clerical candidates hailing from there,[41] while Secker trusted Porteus and Stinton enough to name them the executors of his estate. He also valued greatly the work of John Head, his 'very faithful & useful Archdeacon', who did yeoman's work for him on the ground among the clergy in Kent.[42] Together these and others helped Secker to meet his episcopal duties with a vigour and efficiency surpassed by few during the eighteenth century.

II

Secker executed his own pastoral responsibilities with distinction: his job as a bishop was to ensure that the parish clergy in his diocese performed their duties with equal distinction, particularly in what he believed was 'a profane and corrupt age' in which 'religion, and its ministers are, are hated and despised'.[43] To make certain that clergy met his own elevated standards, Secker monitored them carefully. Effective episcopal oversight was both a precondition for and a tool of effective pastoral reform in the eighteenth-century Church. Not only did the processes of oversight – visitations, confirmations, and ordination, and the like – enable bishops to scrutinize their diocesan clergy's pastoral qualifications and performance, it also allowed them to experiment with measures that make might pastoral care more effective in the parish.[44]

English canon law enjoined bishops to follow the medieval custom of triennial visitations.[45] The sheer size of some dioceses – such as Lincoln with its 1,267 parishes – made it logistically and practically impossible for all bishops to

[41] While Secker's other Canterbury chaplains spoke highly of him, Plumptre left his service early, resentful at being 'slighted' by Secker: *Autobiography*, p. 39; BL, Add. MS 5817, f. 192: William Cole's notebook, n.d. Cf. Thomas Wintle, *Daniel; an Improved version attempted* (Oxford, 1792), p. xviii.

[42] *Autobiography*, p. 41.

[43] 'Instructions given to Candidates for Orders, after their subscribing the Articles', in *WTS*, IV, p. 216.

[44] Cf. Scott A. Wenig, 'John Jewel and the Reformation of the Diocese of Salisbury, 1560–1571', *AEH* 73:2 (2004), pp. 141–68.

[45] *Anglican Canons*, pp. 350–51 (Canon 60 of 1603), but see also pp. 230–31 (Canon 7 of 1584) and 572–73 (Canon 9 of 1640). Anglican canon law regarding episcopal visitations clearly reflected proposals in the *Reformatio legum ecclesiasticarum*, for which see Bray (ed.), *Tudor Church Reform*, pp. 404–09. The vicar general or archdeacon were to visit the diocese yearly between the episcopal visitations to admit new churchwardens to their offices and to provide additional oversight of the parochial clergy: E. Garth Moore and Timothy Briden, *Moore's Introduction to English Canon Law* (1985), p. 23. S.J.C. Taylor, 'Church and State in Mid-Eighteenth Century England: The Newcastle Years, 1742–1762' (University of Cambridge Ph.D. thesis, 1987), pp. 124–34; Gibson, *The Achievement of the Anglican Church*, pp. 125–42; and Arthur Burns, *The Diocesan Revival in the Church of England, c. 1800–1870* (Oxford, 1999), pp. 23–27 reliably survey the eighteenth-century visitation.

visit every parish individually, and, even in much smaller dioceses, parochial visitation by bishops was virtually unknown. Instead, they stopped at a dozen or so different churches while touring their dioceses, summoning clergy from the surrounding rural deaneries to meet with them there.[46] Originally designed as a regular occasion to confirm into the Church those who were baptized, episcopal visitations had by the seventeenth century taken on a judicial function as well. Clergy provided proof of their orders and licenses, and the chancellor swore new churchwardens into their offices. Those churchwardens also presented to the visitor violators of canons, statutes, royal injunctions, or the liturgy, who would be tried in a consistory court later.[47] In articles of inquiry issued weeks in advance of the visitation, visitors posed a whole range of questions to churchwardens regarding the state of religion in each parish.[48] Visitors might additionally publish a prescriptive charge in advance of their visitation.

Frustrated by the formulaic responses (*omnia bene*) to the articles of enquiry by churchwardens and recognizing the new pastoral challenges posed by the Toleration Act, some reform-minded bishops of the early eighteenth century restructured the visitation to make it yield more actionable intelligence. In his primary visitation of Lincoln in 1706, William Wake directed questions both to clergy and to churchwardens, a practice his successor Edmund Gibson expanded in his own primary visitation of Lincoln in 1718.[49] This proved to be the basic model of the eighteenth-century visitation. With the gradual emasculation of the ecclesiastical courts, the episcopal visitation became primarily a pastoral tool, allowing bishops to examine regularly the temporal and spiritual affairs of their diocese.[50] Not without reason have eighteenth-century visitations been described as '[t]he keystone of the arch of ecclesiastical administration'.[51]

---

[46] On the other hand, some dioceses, like Rochester, were compact enough to allow the bishop to gather clergy in only three or four centres: Gibson, *The Achievement of the Anglican Church*, p. 130.

[47] Spaeth, *The Church in an Age of Danger*, p. 64.

[48] Kenneth Fincham (ed.), *Visitation Articles and Injunctions of the Early Stuart Church. Volumes I and II* (Woodbridge, 1994, 1998).

[49] Norman Sykes, 'The Primary Visitation of William Wake of the diocese of Lincoln, 1706', *JEH* 2:2 (1951), pp. 190–206; idem, *Edmund Gibson, Bishop of London, 1669–1748: A Study in Politics and Religion in the Eighteenth Century* (1926), pp. 74–76. For an example of visitation articles and returns during the eighteenth century, see R.E.G. Cole (ed.), *Speculum dioceseos lincolniensis sub episcopis Gul: Wake et Edm: Gibson ad 1705–1723* (Lincoln, 1910). For examples of other visitation articles and returns, see S.L. Ollard and P.C. Walker (eds.), *Archbishop Herring's Visitation Returns, 1743* (Wakefield, 1928–9); John R. Guy (ed.), *The Diocese of Llandaff in 1763: The Primary Visitation of Bishop Ewer* (Cardiff, 1991); W.R. Ward (ed.), *Parson and Parish in Eighteenth-Century Surrey: Replies to Bishops' Visitations* (Guildford, 1994); idem (ed.), *Parson and Parish in Eighteenth-Century Hampshire: Replies to Bishops' Visitations* (Winchester, 1995); and Mary Ransome (ed.), *Wiltshire Returns to the Bishop's Visitation Queries, 1783* (Devizes, 1971).

[50] It is notable, however, that even as the church courts declined in effectiveness, Secker could be found in the early 1750s encouraging Oxford clergy to have churchwardens make presentments at visitations: *Charges* (1753), pp. 165–72. For the state of church courts in the

Certainly Secker's visitations formed the bedrock of his administration of the dioceses of Bristol, Oxford, and Canterbury,[52] and he used them to advertise and implement reform.[53] Visitations aimed, he explained to his clergy, 'principally, to give Bishops Opportunities of exhorting and cautioning their Clergy, either on such general Subjects as are always useful, or on such particular Occasions as the Circumstances of Things, or the Inquiries, made at or against these Times point out; and of interposing their Authority, if there be Need; which amongst you, I am persuaded, there will not'.[54] He made particular use of his published visitation charges to admonish and to advise parish clergy about a range of matters from the need to reside in their livings to preparation of the laity for confirmation to the management of church properties. Though he did not strictly fulfil the canonical requirements for triennial episcopal visitations during his tenure in Oxford (1738, 1741, 1747, 1750, 1753) and Canterbury (1758, 1762, 1766), Secker's visitations may nonetheless be considered the gold standard by which others during the period are to be judged.[55]

Secker's visitations normally lasted just under three weeks, allowing him to meet with the parochial clergy and to confirm at around fifteen sites.[56] His visitations of Bristol and Oxford and of Canterbury differed significantly in scale. He toured Oxford on horseback: his retinue for his primary visitation of Canterbury in 1758, by contrast, consisted 'at the least ... of, a Chaplain, two Gentlemen..., a Butler & Cook both out of Livery, two Footmen, Coachmen, Portilion & Helper or Groom, & the Chaplain's Servant upon his Master's Horse'.[57] If the provisions for the first three-night stay near Canterbury are any indication, the archiepiscopal entourage must have been impressive. Secker's host on that occasion remembered,

ABp. Secker having accepted my Invitation to be at my House during his primary Visitation in and near Canterbury sent down for his entertainments there 2 Diz of

'long' eighteenth century, see W.M. Jacob, *Lay people and religion in the early eighteenth century* (Cambridge, 1996), pp. 135–54; Spaeth, *The Church in an Age of Danger*, pp. 59–74.

[51]   Sykes, *From Sheldon to Secker*, p. 15.

[52]   Secker also made certain to visit the archiepiscopal peculiars in Sussex 'because scarce any memory was left, that any Abp [since Tenison] had visited them personally': *Autobiography*, pp. 43–44. For this, see LPL, Secker Papers 6, ff. 193–273.

[53]   Cf. Burns, *Diocesan Revival*, p. 27.

[54]   *Charges* (1758), p. 206.

[55]   Gregory, *Restoration, Reformation, and Reform*, p. 277 points out that Canterbury episcopal visitations were held by tradition every four years. There could be a great deal of regional variation to the patterns: in Winchester, episcopal visitations were held yearly, while in Norwich they were held septennially: William Gibson, '"A Happy Fertile Soil Which Bringeth Forth Abundantly"', in *The National Church in Local Perspective*, p. 115 and W.M. Jacob, 'Church and Society in Norfolk, 1700–1800', in ibid., p. 181.

[56]   *Autobiography*, p. 38; LPL, Secker Papers 3, f. 305: Visitation schedule, June 1762.

[57]   *Autobiography*, p. 21; LPL, Secker Papers 3, f. 286: Henry Hall to Mr. Symondson, 19 May 1758.

Claret, 2 Diz Mountain & 2 doz of Maderia in 3 Hampers. I undertook & did provide for him at Canterbury 6 Hams, 11 Tongues, Pickled Salmon 3 or 2 Pieces, 5 doz of Red Port, 1 Chaldron of Coals, 6 Sacks of Charcoal, 2 of which were carried to Dr. Walroyals to be used in his Kitchen, 1 Barrel of Ale & Barrel of Small Beer, 18 Chickens, 20 Ducks, 2 Geese, Corn to feed the said Poultry which were accordingly fed (by Magdalen who came on purpose) in my yard ... [58]

Philip Yonge, bishop of Bristol, assisted Secker during this 1758 visitation, and it was not uncommon for Secker to receive help during visitations from other bishops. Debilitated by gout in 1762, he entrusted the entire visitation to John Green, bishop of Lincoln, though he received frequent reports from his chaplain during the visitation's progress.[59]

One of the bishop's chief responsibilities during his visitations was to confirm those baptised into the Church. Though not a sacrament in the Church of England, the ancient rite of confirmation was nonetheless important to the orthodox.[60] John Denne, rector of Lambeth, argued, 'We have reason to believe, that we may derive hereby such communications of grace from the Holy Ghost, as are ordinarily requisite for securing all the privileges and advantages of our Baptismal Covenant, for enlightening and sanctifying our souls and for leading us thro' the course of our lives in the knowledge and obedience of God's word.'[61] Secker reckoned that confirmation was 'of such acknowledged Usefulness, that in the Times of Confusion [during the 1640s and 1650s] ... when Bishops were Rejected, some of their Adversaries took upon them to perform this Part of their Function'.[62] In addition to the individual spiritual benefits of confirmation, the rite also had knock-on benefits for the Church. Robert Nelson contended that when those being confirmed realized that only a bishop could perform this rite, they would be 'sensible of their Obligation to live in Episcopal Communion, and convince them that their Obedience is due to such Pastors and Ecclesiastical Governors as are endued with all those Powers that were left by the Apostles to their Successors'.[63] Secker himself speculated that 'perhaps to maintain a due subordination, it was reserved to the highest, by prayer and laying on of hands, to communicate the further measures of the Holy Ghost'.[64] Valuing confirmation's benefits, he confirmed annually in Oxford, rather than triennially as was

---

[58] LPL, MS 2797, f. 15: Anonymous account of Secker's 1758 Canterbury Visitation, July 1758.
[59] *Autobiography*, p. 45; LPL, Secker Papers 3, ff. 306–16: Charles Hall to Secker, 13, 14, 17, 19, 22, 27 June 1762.
[60] Robert Cornwall, 'The Rite of Confirmation in Anglican Thought during the Eighteenth Century', *Church History* 68:2 (1999), pp. 359–72.
[61] John Denne, *A discourse on the nature, design, and benefits of confirmation* (1737), p. 14.
[62] *Charges* (1741), pp. 54–55.
[63] Quoted in Craig Rose, 'The origins and ideals of the SPCK, 1699–1716', in *The Church of England, c. 1688–c. 1833*, p. 183.
[64] 'Sermon CXL. Confirmation of Divine Authority; and its Importance in Promoting Piety and Virtue [Acts 8:17]', in *WTS*, IV, p. 45.

required; and he persistently badgered the parochial clergy to prepare their parishioners properly for the rite.[65]

When parish priests brought forward no candidates for confirmation, Secker was incredulous. 'A Clergyman told me yesterday, that he was desired by you to acquaint me, that upon Inquiry made at every House in your Parish, no persons had offer'd themselves to be presented to me for Confirmation' he wrote to the rector of St Michael, Royal, in 1761. 'Now as your Parish contains 58 Houses, and but 3 Families of dissenters, and yet only 5 persons have been presented to me from thence in 3 years, it doth not seem likely, that this Inquiry was made by a proper person in a proper manner. My Letter directed you to instruct your Parishioners, both publickly & privately in the nature & Benefits of Confirmation. I desire to know, whether you have done so.'[66] Likewise, when the rector of Barnes, Surrey, presented no one for confirmation in 1763, Secker acidly remonstrated with him, 'I think you should have gone to your parishioners and talked with them separately on the Subject of Confirmation, since they did not come to you on what you said to them in general. You should also consider seriously, what is the Reason, that so little Regard is paid to your Instructions.'[67]

Confirming those who did present themselves for confirmation could be physically demanding for bishops. In 1688, for instance, the bishop of Sodor and Man confirmed at the rate of 300 per hour during one four-hour stint at Canterbury, while Robert Hay Drummond confirmed 41,600 during his twelve-year tenure as archbishop of York.[68] Secker noted of his 1738 Oxford visitation, 'At Bloxham particularly I confirmed 6 Hours without ceasing', and he instructed that barrier rails be installed in churches where he was to confirm in order 'to prevent noise and confusion that this Holy Rite may be performed in a most solemn and edifying manner'.[69] By 1758, he had begun to issue admission tickets for confirmations, 'finding no other way effective to keep the People orderly'.[70]

Secker also used his visitation to meet with his diocesan clergy, and he required them to travel to the fifteen or so sites where he was confirming. Oftentimes he provided a communal meal, such as the one for 'all the Heads of Houses, & all the clergy of the Diocese who resided in Oxford' during his primary visitation there in 1738.[71] 'These Meetings were designed', he later explained,

---

[65] See LPL, Secker Papers 7, f. 81: Secker to Minister of Cuddesdon, 26 May 1750 for Secker's instructions regarding preparations for confirmations.

[66] LPL, Secker Papers 6, f. 259: Secker to John Young, 20 Mar 1761.

[67] Ibid., f. 193: Secker to Ferdinando Warner, 22 Sept 1763.

[68] Gregory, Restoration, Reformation, and Reform, p. 279; Gibson, The Achievement of the Anglican Church, p. 147.

[69] Autobiography, p. 19; Oxford confirmation notice of 1738, quoted in W.M. Marshall, 'The dioceses of Hereford and Oxford, 1660–1760', in The National Church in Local Perspective, p. 207.

[70] Autobiography, p. 37. In 1758, for instance, Secker paid for 9,750 tickets to be printed: LPL, MS 1483, f. 13.

[71] Autobiography, p. 19.

'partly to give Clergy Opportunities of conferring with each other, and consulting their superiors, on Matters relating to their Profession.'[72] The clerical gatherings at visitations thus provided the chance to promote diocesan and professional unity.[73]

Inevitably, some chose not to attend the visitation when asked. Bishops of Oxford could normally expect just 75 per cent of the parochial clergy to attend.[74] Though disability was one of the accepted reasons for non-attendance, Secker hounded those with no good excuse for their absence. 'The morning I left Chipping-Norton, I sent to speak with you,' he wrote to the rector of Heythrop in 1738. 'But you did not come to me, though you came before I was gone, to another person in the house where I was. Unless you can give some good acct of this behaviour, I must look upon it as an instance of disrespect.'[75] When the curate of Goodnestone by Wingham protested in 1761 that his patron forbade him attending the episcopal visitation, Secker responded curtly: 'Incumbents are bound by Conscience to obey the Directions of their Superiors in the Church, in all things lawful & honest: and they are not bound in Conscience to obey the Prohibitions of their Patrons to the contrary.'[76]

When the parochial clergy met with him, he expected answers to the detailed list of visitation articles he had sent them beforehand. His drew upon those by Wake and Gibson and were notable for their 'clarity and a rigour in detail'.[77] Falling under twelve heads, the sixty or so questions aimed to elicit from incumbents detailed information about a variety of topics that would allow for better management of the diocese.[78] The questions concerned the size and income of the parish, the presence of Roman Catholics and other religious nonconformists, pastoral provision, residency, charity, and education. When he had received responses to his inquiries, he sorted his correspondence with the clergy into categories and recorded the information from the returns into a diocese book, which he updated regularly and which his successors continued to use.[79] Likewise, he advised parochial clergy to keep accurate terriers and parish registers.[80]

---

[72] *Charges* (1758), p. 206.
[73] Burns, The *Diocesan Revival*, pp. 85–86 makes a similar point about ruridiaconal assemblies in the nineteenth century.
[74] W.M. Marshall, 'The Administration of the Dioceses of Hereford and Oxford, 1660–1760', *Midland History* 8 (1983), pp. 227–28.
[75] *Oxford Correspondence*, p. 4: Secker to James Martin, 8 Aug 1738.
[76] LPL, Secker Papers 3, f. 178: Secker to John Maximilian De L'Angle, 12 Jan 1761.
[77] Ward (ed.), *Parson and Parish in Eighteenth-Century Hampshire*, p. x.
[78] For sets of Secker's Oxford and Canterbury articles of inquiry, *OVR 1738*, pp. 4–5 and *Speculum*, pp. xli-xlii. The questions themselves reflected the bishops' interests and concerns. In the early seventeenth century, for instance, Laudian bishops used them to ferret out Puritans, while after the Restoration, Tory high church bishops used them to seek out religious nonconformists.
[79] Secker's Oxford diocese book has been lost: *Oxford Correspondence*, p. xiv. His Bristol and Canterbury ones, though, can be found in Elizabeth Ralph (ed.), 'Bishop Secker's diocese

Once he had collated and assimilated the material from his visitation, Secker badgered the negligent. The rector of Goodnestone by Faversham complained to Secker that his large family forced him to take up other livings to augment his income and that weekly services in Goodnestone were thus impossible. Secker's response was forthright and unambiguous. 'I am far from delighting to exercise Authority, or to say unpleasing things to any one of my Clergy. But in some Cases, to use the Apostles words, if I sought to please men, I should not be the Servant of Christ,' he replied.

> And therefore I must say, that unless you are content to let your people at Goodnestone have Service every Sunday, or to make way for one that will, you have by no means the Concern which you ought, for their Spiritual welfare or your own. It will be much better for you another Day, Sir, to have brought up your Family with the Strictest Frugality, than to have deprived the Flock of Christ, put under your care, through a Course of years, of one half of the religious Offices, which ought to have been performed amongst them, in order to lay out upon your Family or lay up for them, a few more pounds annually, than you could have done else. I hope you will understand this plain Dealing meant, as it is, for your good...[81]

Oftentimes chastened ministers acceded to his demands, but the case of Goodnestone suggests that immediate change was not always forthcoming, since, Secker noted in his Canterbury diocese book, 'At the Visitation 1758 Service once every Sunday was directed. See Letters afterwards. Sept. 1759 Still only once a fortnight.'[82]

Episcopal leverage was often slight because once someone possessed a living, it proved difficult to remove him except in the most unusual of circumstances.[83] The only instance during Secker's episcopate of a parish priest actually losing his living came in January 1764 when he deprived Samuel Bickley of the vicarage of Bapchild after Bickley had been convicted at the Kent assizes for 'Sodomitical Practices'. Even then, though, Secker gave Bickley £10 'for his present Support'.[84] In practice, the best chance to protect the Church from poorly qualified or scandalous clergy was at the ordination stage. English canon law both enjoined a bishop to ordain four Sundays per year and set up a number of hurdles for

book', in *A Bristol miscellany*, ed. Patrick McGrath (Bristol, 1985), pp. 21–70 and *Speculum*. Secker's friend, Martin Benson, kept similar records: John Fendley (ed.), *Bishop Benson's Survey of the Diocese of Gloucester, 1735–1750* (Bristol, 2000).

80   *Charges* (1750), pp. 138–42; ibid. (1753), pp. 187–90.
81   LPL, Secker Papers 3, f. 177: Secker to Charles Norris, 24 Aug 1758.
82   *Speculum*, pp. 128–29.
83   W.M. Jacob, 'Supervising the Pastors: Supervision and Discipline of the Clergy in Norfolk in the Eighteenth Century', *Dutch Review of Church History* 83 (2004), pp. 296–308. It should be noted, though, that that a parson's freehold could also protect him from episcopal whim.
84   *Autobiography*, p. 49; Gregory, *Speculum*, p. 159; LPL, MS 1483, f. 181. For background on the Bickley case, see LPL, Secker Papers 3, f. 4: Sir Edward Simpson to Dr. Hay, July 1763; BIHR, Bp C&P VII/175/3: Secker to RHD, 28 July 1763; LPL, Secker Papers 3, f. 5: Charles Yorke to Secker, 29 Sept 1763; WAM 64632: Secker to Zachary Pearce, 8 Aug 1763.

ordinands to clear. Deacons had to be at least twenty-three years old; priests, twenty-four. Each had to 'be able to yield an account of his faith in Latin, according to the articles of religion ... and to confirm the same by sufficient testimonies out of the Holy Scriptures'. In addition, each candidate for ordination had to present certificates of title to prove that he had a vacant living awaiting him and testimonials 'of his good life and conversation, under the seal of some college in Cambridge or Oxford ... or of three or four grave ministers, together with the subscription and testimony of other credible persons, who have known his life and behaviour by the space of three years next before'.[85]

The ordination process was one of a bishop's most important duties, for his sole right to ordain in his diocese enabled him to regulate the quality of the body of clergy under his supervision. Few were more rigorous in their administration of the rite than Secker.[86] His published instructions to ordinands and his advice to the bishops of his archdiocese in the 1760s highlight the degree to which he thought moral regeneration a precondition for ordination and the foundation of a successful ministry.[87] 'Therefore inspect your souls thoroughly: and form them, by the help of divine grace, to be duly influenced by the right principle,' he instructed candidates for ordination. As well, he argued that candidates for ordination needed to ensure that they were 'inwardly moved by the Holy Ghost' to enter the ministry and to ensure that their lives served as examples to their parishioners: 'Have you a genuine practical faith in Christ? Are you, on the terms of the gospel covenant, intitled to everlasting life?', he queried.[88] He reiterated these themes in his published charges. 'We are bound to be Patterns of the most diligent Practice of Virtue, and the strictest Regard to Religion', he counselled the Oxford clergy in 1738, 'and we shall never make others zealous for what we ourselves appear indifferent about'.[89] In his final Canterbury charge of 1766, he returned to this theme: 'And here I must begin with repeating, what I need not enlarge upon, for I have done it already, that the Foundation of every Thing in our Profession is true Piety within our Breasts, prompting us to excite it in others.'[90]

While Secker hoped that candidates for ordination took their future responsibilities seriously, he was prepared to deny orders to unsuitable candidates.

---

[85] *Anglican Canons* (Canons 34–35 of 1603), pp. 314–17. See also, Richard Burn, *Ecclesiastical Law* (1763), III, pp. 24–57.

[86] Jeremy Gregory, 'Standards for Admission to the Ministry of the Church of England in the Eighteenth Century', *Dutch Review of Church History* 83 (2004), pp. 283–95.

[87] [Thomas Secker], 'The Archbishop's Directions to the Bishops of his Province, Concerning Orders and Curates, 1759', in John Bacon, *Liber Regis* (1786), appendix I. See also, *Oratio*, p. 362.

[88] 'Instructions Given to Candidates for Orders, after Their Subscribing the Articles', in *WTS*, IV, p. 210. These are reminiscent of Dissenters' standards and echo Secker's own past.

[89] *Charges* (1738), p. 33.

[90] *Charges* (1766), p. 288.

Some he rejected because they did not meet the canonical age requirements.[91] Others, like the dull-witted Jarvis Kenrick, had to bone up on their Latin and their Bible before they could be ordained.[92] Secker vigilantly manned other barriers to ordination, as well. Though a parliamentary act recognized the Moravians as 'an antient Protestant Episcopal Church', for instance, he advised against accepting Francis Okely's ordination into the diaconate by a Moravian bishop. 'Let the Moravian Bishops, if they are Bishops, ordain for their own Congregations,' he wrote to Robert Hay Drummond, archbishop of York. 'We have no proper method of knowing any of them or any of their Acts.'[93] Criminous clergy likewise had to be barred from entering the ministry or taking up Anglican livings. Like Samuel Bickley, Israel Close had been convicted at the Lincolnshire assizes of 'a Sodomitical Attempt, for which he stood in the Pillory' – Secker cautioned Drummond to grant neither Bickley nor Close ecclesiastical employment without first discussing the matter with him.[94] Indeed, though Secker had aided Samuel Bickley after depriving him of Bapchild, he worried that bishops lacked the legal authority to suspend those like him and Close outright from their livings. 'Yet surely a Transition from the Pillory to the Reading Desk & Pulpit is not fitting,' he fretted.[95]

The lengths to which he was prepared to go to bar unqualified candidates from clerical orders is illustrated in the case of Henry Perfect. Within months after assuming the primacy Secker received testimonials that Perfect was a charlatan. In a bizarre letter to Secker in his own defence, Perfect confirmed his reputation as a schemer and a bigamist.[96] He admitted that he had been expelled from Oxford for stealing wood and afterwards had taken lodgings with a man who married a 'common prostitute ... who getting intoxicated, and behaving amiss, in the Village, did ... [him] injury & gave rise to many flying stories'. Perfect's next landlord was a woman who ran a gin shop and in whom he could discern within the first hour 'besides a natural tendency to Idleness, a deal of sluttishness'. The woman, however, clearly had her charms for she eventually infected Perfect with syphilis and married him while he was drunk. The two soon separated, and '[i]n pursuance of this Separation, & on hearing that she was taken up for murthering a bastard Child, & a Supposition that she was hanged for it, he married again'.[97]

---

[91] *Oxford Correspondence*, p. 174: Lancelot Jackson to Secker, 23 Jan 1749. Cf. WAM 64635: Secker to Zachary Pearce, 16 Sept 1763.

[92] LPL, Secker Papers 3, f. 147: Secker to Matthew Kenrick, 26 Mar 1762.

[93] BIHR, Bp C&P VII/175/3: Secker to RHD, 28 July 1763. Cf. Colin Podmore, *The Moravian Church in England, 1728–1760* (Oxford, 1998), pp. 246, 287–88.

[94] BIHR, Bp C&P VII/175/2: Secker to RHD, 10 Mar 1763.

[95] BIHR, Bp C&P VII/175/3: Secker to RHD, 28 July 1763. See also, WAM 64632: Secker to Zachary Pearce, 8 Aug 1763.

[96] Unless otherwise noted, the information in this paragraph is from LPL, Secker Papers 7, ff. 184–95: Henry Perfect to Secker, 3 July 1758.

[97] BIHR, Bp C&P VII/215: Secker to RHD, 27 May 1763. See also, WAM 64623: Secker to Pearce, 6 Sept 1760.

Perfect only later found out that his first wife was still alive. Somewhere along the way, he claimed to have received orders from the now conveniently deceased bishop of Worcester. Unfortunately, Perfect had 'lost his orders in stepping into or out of a post chaise'.[98] With no physical proof of his ordination, he could not assume the Derbyshire living of Beighton promised him by the duke of Kingston. Nor could he take up the curacy of Alkham, Kent, though he was deluded enough to encourage Richard Smith, the vicar, to write to Secker for a reference. 'He says he is not unknown to your Grace, and refers to Mr. Symondson your Secretary for a Character,' wrote Smith to Secker. 'He seems to be a man, who has seen much of the World, and met with many Hardships, and wishes for a quiet retreat where he may rest from his Fatigues. I think Alkham will very well suit him in that Respect, if he has your Grace's Permission to settle there.'[99] He did not obtain Secker's permission, and indeed from 1758 until 1763, Perfect protested his innocence and cast around the episcopate for someone to 're-ordain' him. For the next five years Secker likewise wrote to his fellow bishops to relate Perfect's story and to encourage them to deny him orders.[100] Even with this kind of diligent episcopal oversight, though, candidates were able to receive orders on the basis of misleading testimonials.[101] Still other clerical charlatans sought preferment or, worse yet, actually officiated, on the basis of fraudulent orders.[102]

We should not, of course, assume either that Secker thought like a twenty-first-century professional manager or that completely effective oversight was possible – prescriptive practices, expectations, and technology ensured that neither was the case. Nevertheless, his relatively close supervision of the clergy provided him with a clearer sense of pastoral problems that required episcopal attention, not the least of which stemmed from the Church's economic structure. Rather than advocate systemic solutions to what, in retrospect at least, seem to have been the systemic problems of the ecclesiastical economy, Secker thought that restorative reform was a sufficiently efficacious remedy.

III

The eighteenth-century Church of England's economy was medieval in both origins and structure, and the system of sustaining its clergy – particularly parish

---

[98] The bishop of St Davids, however, later informed Secker that Perfect's 'orders, or what he called such, were pawned at a publick House near Blackheath': BIHR, Bp C&P VII/215: Secker to RHD, 21 May 1763.

[99] LPL, Secker Papers 3, f. 1: Richard Smith to Secker, 16 Dec 1762.

[100] Judith Jago, *Aspects of the Georgian Church* (1997), p. 246 suggests that Samuel Squire, bishop of St Asaph, finally granted Perfect orders.

[101] BIHR, Bp C&P VII/109/3: Secker to RHD, 1 Sept 1763.

[102] WAM 64632: Secker to Pearce, 8 Aug 1763; BIHR, Bp C&P VII 175/5: Secker to RHD, 6 Sept 1763.

priests – was cause for episcopal concern. In particular, marked disparities in incomes often led to pluralism and non-residence, soured relations between parsons and their parishioners, and opened the Church to charges that its clergy paid insufficient attention to their spiritual duties. At its worst, the Church's economy was both systemically dysfunctional and something of a public embarrassment. Nineteenth-century church reformers would address the institution's economic problems by trying to regularize and equalize clerical incomes.[103] They were, however, men of a later age with much different values. In his own age, Secker neither proposed nor desired thoroughgoing restructuring of ecclesiastical financial structures. Instead, he worked within the existing system to maximize ecclesiastical income so that clerical poverty was not an excuse for shirking pastoral responsibilities. More importantly, though, he challenged, prodded, and demanded that parish clergy fulfil their pastoral obligations in spite of financial problems they might have faced. While acknowledging flaws in the Church's economy, he nonetheless aimed to make it work as efficiently as it could. Restorative reform involved reviving primitive clerical ideals, not remaking the institution anew by radically reorganizing the ecclesiastical economy.

We need to appreciate the contexts in which Secker and other church reformers operated and to grasp in the first instance what problems the mid-century Church of England did *not* face. To begin with, the Church's economic activity had drawn fire from many sides long before the eighteenth century.[104] The very nature of the institution's organization and the ways it sustained its clergy made it impossible for the institution not to involve itself heavily in local finance and land management, so that complaints about Church finances were nothing new. In addition, many of the problems which nineteenth-century church reformers worked to eradicate were the products of developments *after* Secker's death. Some, for instance, have argued that its ancient parochial structure rendered the Church ill-equipped to accommodate the urbanization that attended the eighteenth-century population boom.[105] Yet demographic upsurge is not particularly relevant when analysing Secker's career since his death coincided with the initial explosion of the population boom.[106]

---

[103] G.F.A. Best, *Temporal Pillars: Queen Anne's Bounty, the Ecclesiastical Commissioners, and the Church of England* (Cambridge, 1964); Olive J. Brose, *Church and Parliament: The Reshaping of the Church of England, 1828–1860* (Stanford, 1959); Kenneth A. Thompson, *Bureaucracy and Church Reform: The Organizational Response of the Church of England to Social Change, 1800–1965* (Oxford, 1970).

[104] Christopher Hill, *Economic Problems of the Church from Archbishop Whitgift to the Long Parliament* (Oxford, 1956); Laura Brace, *The idea of property in seventeenth-century England: Tithes and the individual* (Manchester, 1998).

[105] But cf. Mark Smith, *Religion in Industrial Society: Oldham and Saddleworth, 1740–1865* (Oxford, 1994).

[106] England's population rose by only 20%, from 6.0 million to 7.1 million people, during Secker's five decades as a cleric; in the half century after his death, the nation's population

There were, nevertheless, serious pastoral problems that Secker and other Church leaders faced during the mid eighteenth century which stemmed directly from the institution's economy: non-residence and pluralism topped the list of them. The failure of parish clergy to reside in their livings particularly concerned Secker. Though some parishes actually supported their priest's request to live outside of the parish,[107] the majority of parishioners disliked clerical non-residence. Secker himself thought continual residence was a *sine qua non* of diligent pastoral oversight. 'It is only living amongst your People and knowing them thoroughly that can show you what is Level to their Capacities and suited to their Circumstances and what will reform their Faults and improve their hearts in true Goodness,' he advised the Canterbury clergy in his 1758 visitation charge. 'Yet this is your Business with them: and unless you perform it every Thing else is Nothing.'[108]

The eighteenth-century Church was not unique in confronting clerical non-residence. Indeed, English canon law had regularly addressed residence requirements for clergy since the early sixteenth century.[109] While the nature and coverage of archival sources make it difficult to render a detailed picture of non-residency across the eighteenth century, it is possible to sketch the broad outlines. In Secker's Oxford, for instance, 51 per cent lived in their parishes in 1738, 16.8 per cent lived nearby, and 19.4 per cent had permanent curates.[110] Four decades later, only 39.4 per cent of Oxfordshire clergy lived in their parishes, while 20 per cent lived nearby, and 16.4 per cent hired permanent curates.[111] This pattern of increasing levels of non-residence generally held across England during the eighteenth century.[112]

---

rose by 70%, from 7.1 million to 12.7 million people: Jeremy Gregory and John Stevenson, *The Longman Companion to Britain in the Eighteenth Century, 1688–1820* (2000), p. 289.

[107] See, for instance, *Oxford Correspondence*, pp. 40–41: John Buswell and Thomas Dandridge to Secker, 19 Sept 1739.

[108] *Charges* (1758), p. 208.

[109] *Anglican Canons*, pp. 20–23 (Canon 8 of 1529), 198–99 (Canon 7 of 1571), 236–37 (Canon 3 of 1597), 327–33 (Canons 41–45 of 1603), 499–500, 504 (Canons 26–28, 36 of 1634). Cf. Burns, *Ecclesiastical Law*, III, pp. 294–318; J.I. Daeley, 'Pluralism in the Diocese of Canterbury during the Administration of Archbishop Parker, 1559–75', *JEH* 18:1 (1967), pp. 33–49.

[110] Marshall, 'The Administration of the Dioceses of Hereford and Oxford, 1660–1760', p. 105.

[111] McClatchey, *Oxfordshire Clergy, 1777–1869*, p. 31.

[112] Cf. Jan Albers, 'Seeds of Contention: Society, Politics and the Church of England in Lancashire, 1689–1790' (Yale University Ph.D. thesis, 1988), pp. 85–93; Carpenter, *Thomas Sherlock*, pp. 128–62; Gibson, *The Achievement of the Anglican Church*, pp. 162–68; Gilbert, *Religion and Society in Industrial England*, pp. 5–7, 97–98; W.M. Jacob, '"A Practice of Very Hurtful Tendency"', *SCH* 16 (1979), pp. 315–26; Jago, *Aspects of the Georgian Church*, pp. 150–60; Sykes, *From Sheldon to Secker*, pp. 189–91, 198–99; Virgin, *The Church in an Age of Negligence*, pp. 191–214; Arthur Warne, *Church and Society in Eighteenth-Century Devon* (Newton Abbot, 1969), pp. 38–43; and Walsh and Taylor, 'Introduction: the Church and Anglicanism in the "long" eighteenth century', pp. 7–9.

Non-residence had no one cause. Some clergy put it down to poor health. 'My ... Excuse for non Residence with regard to my health is most just and true,' the rector of St Michael Crooked Lane pled on his own behalf.

> In May 1754 I had a stroke of the palsy. Soon after that, I received another Shock from the overturning of a Chaise, was much hurt, and confined for some time. Notwithstanding which I resided all the following Winter in the Parsonage house. But I found these two Casualties were attended with the Continuance of such a nervous Disorder of Body and spirits, that my staying longer in that habitation would be ruinous to my health: I was therefore forced to Camberwell for the better Air, & necessary Exercise.[113]

Secker's response to the vicar of Sittingbourne suggests that he was sceptical of this rationale: 'You have pleaded your Health for residing in the parish of Tunstall. I suppose the House and Land, which you have purchased there, to be another motive.'[114] When the vicar of Snave protested that the unhealthiness of his parish forced him into non-residency, Secker advised him to stiffen his spine, since 'some persons have taken Care of the less healthy Parishes, it is most reasonable that Incumbents should Season themselves to such places'.[115] (It was advice he had not taken himself when he was a country priest in Durham.) Some ministers shifted the blame from themselves to family members: the rector of Kencote lived outside of his parish because, he explained to Secker, 'my wife will not consent to live there, upon any Consideration whatsoever'.[116] Another common reason for non-residence was the disrepair of the parsonage, if one existed in the first place.[117] 'I never could be informed of any house ever belonging to a Minister in this Parish,' wrote the vicar of Bromfield to Secker, 'nor was any provision made for his Residence at the dissolution of the Priory.'[118] In Oxford, it was also common for non-resident clergy to point to residence requirements in their colleges as a barrier to living full-time in their cures.

The most common reason for non-residence, though, was pluralism, a practice that topped the list of contemporary complaints against the Church.[119] Pluralism was holding more than one living simultaneously, and because a

---

[113] LPL, Secker Papers 6, f. 256: Thomas Kemp to Secker, 8 Dec 1759. Cf. *Speculum*, p. 246.

[114] LPL, Secker Papers 3, f. 250: Secker to Thomas Bland, 8 Oct 1758.

[115] Ibid., f. 253: Secker to Josias Pomfret, 24 Nov 1758.

[116] *OVR 1738*, p. 64; *Oxford Correspondence*, p. 150: George Underwood to Secker, 31 May 1746.

[117] In Winchester, though, many clergy rented houses in their parishes but were still technically non-resident. I thank Bill Gibson for this information.

[118] LPL, MS 1134/1, f. 82. Tellingly, Secker willed one-sixth of his estate to help build or repair rectories in poor livings in Canterbury.

[119] Jago, *Aspects of the Georgian Church*, p. 150 argues that pluralism 'was part of a syndrome whose other features bred problems. The syndrome was pluralism, non-residence, absenteeism, dispensations, and sinecures, with the effect that many parishioners had no clergymen living among them to minister to their needs.'

pluralist could not live in two places at once, he was necessarily non-resident in one or another of his cures. English canon law provided that livings held in plurality lie no more than thirty miles apart, that the pluralist should reside in each of his livings 'for some reasonable time every year' and that he should provide those benefices in which he did not reside, 'a preacher lawfully allowed, that is able sufficiently to teach and instruct the people'.[120]

Pluralism and non-residence were not, in and of themselves, terminally lethal to the Church's pastoral mission.[121] The compact parish structure in Canterbury, for instance, enabled clergy to serve more than one cure while living near to each.[122] Indeed, near-residence could actually allow for diligent pastoral provision. The vicar of Barsted, for example, explained, 'I do not reside in my Parish, my House being unfit for that purpose. I reside at Maidstone, at the distance of three miles. I perform punctually all the Duties of my Parish my self and am there almost every day of the Week.'[123] Nonetheless, pluralities opened the Church to criticism both from within and without the institution during the mid eighteenth century.[124] As with non-residence, the figures for pluralism during the eighteenth century are incomplete because of sources and coverage. Between 1680 and 1760, the number of pluralists in Oxford doubled from 9 to 22.[125] That had shot up to 63 by the end of the century.[126] This too seems to have been consistent with general trends across the country and the period.[127]

Pluralism was also a condition with many fathers. Some argued that to attract high-calibre clerical talent, better rewards such as lucrative add-on livings were necessary. Earlier in his career, Secker himself seems to have been granted a dispensation to hold multiple livings at once as a reward for merit. Most commonly, though, sheer poverty forced clergy to take on more than one

---

[120] *Anglican Canons*, pp. 326–29 (Canons 41–42 of 1604), but see also pp. 200–01 (Canon 8 of 1571), 228–29 (Canon 5 of 1584), and 234–37 (Canon 2 of 1597) on licenses for plurality of benefices.

[121] Jacob, '"A Practice of Very Hurtful Tendency"', p. 326.

[122] Gregory, *Restoration, Reformation, and Reform*, p. 171; *Speculum*, p. xxi.

[123] LPL, MS 1134/1, f. 54.

[124] See, for instance, J.B., *The Church of England's complaints to the Parliament and clergy against I. Careless non-residents II. Encroaching pluralities. III. Unconscionable simony. IV. Loose prophaneness. V. Undue ordination. Now reigning among her clergy ...* (1737); [Richard Newton], *Pluralities indefensible. A treatise humbly offered to the consideration of the Parliament of Great-Britain. By a presbyter of the Church of England* (1743).

[125] Marshall, 'The Administration of the Dioceses of Hereford and Oxford, 1660–1760', p. 105.

[126] McClatchey, *Oxfordshire Clergy, 1777–1869*, pp. 47–56.

[127] Cf. Albers, 'Seeds of Contention', pp. 85–93; Gibson, *The Achievement of the Anglican Church*, pp. 167–75; Gibson, 'The Hanoverian Church in Southern England', pp. 160–63; Marshall, *George Hooper*, pp. 90–95; W.B. Maynard, 'Pluralism and Non-Residence in the Archdeaconry of Durham, 1774–1856', *Northern History* 26 (1990), pp. 103–30; M.F. Snape, '"Our Happy Reformation": Anglicanism and society in a northern parish, 1689–1789 (University of Birmingham Ph.D. thesis, 1994), pp. 138–71; Sykes, *Edmund Gibson*, pp. 223–24, 229–31; Virgin, *The Church in an Age of Negligence*, pp. 191–214.

living.[128] Secker himself even recognized this in a visitation charge. 'I acknowledge, that the Poorness of some Benefices makes the Residence of a distinct Minister upon each of them impracticable: and therefore they must be served from an adjoining Parish, or a greater Distance; and no more Duty expected, than there is a competent Provision for.'[129] There is little evidence in either Oxford or Canterbury that clergy took on multiple livings to enrich themselves, and in Oxford pluralists usually had 'one very poor benefice'.[130]

Secker did not begrudge these necessary pluralists their need to keep the wolf from the door, but he refused to condone cavalier non-residence among parochial clergy. 'It must not ... be pleaded that however necessary the residence of some minister may be, that of a curate may suffice,' he wrote to the clergy of Canterbury in his primary visitation charge. 'For your engagement is not merely that the several Duties of your Parish shall be done, but that you personally will do them.' Acknowledging that there were 'indeed Cases, in which the Law dispenses with holding two Livings', he warned that much was expected of non-resident clergy under the terms of their dispensation. 'But Persons ought to consider well; supposing they can with Innocence take the Benefit of that Law; whether they can do it on other Terms, than their Dispensation and their Bond expresses, of preaching yearly 13 Sermons, and keeping two Months Hospitality, in the Parish where they reside lease,' he advised. 'For the Leave given them on these Conditions, is not intended to be given them, however legally valid, if the Conditions are neglected.'[131]

Secker's treatment of Charles Hall put to rest any doubts that he was unprepared to enforce the terms of legal dispensations. Hall was one of Secker's favourites, serving as his 'Oxford chaplain' and benefiting from Secker's patronage during the 1760s. Nonetheless, Secker refused to grant him a dispensation of non-residence to hold the rectory of All Hallows, Bread Street and the deanery of Bocking in plurality, which meant that Hall had to give up the former.[132]

Secker harried pluralists to provide adequate care for their cures at least in part to neuter hostile press. In April 1768, for instance, he advised the English bishops to make accurate counts of the non-resident clergy in their dioceses. His reasons are telling: 'I recommended it to them ... partly because such Lists had lately been called for by the Parliament in Ireland; & partly because one Mr.

---

[128] M.F. Snape, 'Poverty and the Northern Clergy in the Eighteenth Century: The Parish of Whalley, 1689–1789', *Northern History* 36:1 (2000), p. 87, however, argues that 'the relationship between poverty and clerical pluralism was clearly an ambiguous one'. For a similar analysis extended into the nineteenth century, see Virgin, *The Church in an Age of Negligence*, pp. 191–214. Taylor, 'Church and State', p. 39 quantifies the levels of clerical poverty by diocese.

[129] *Charges* (1758), p. 213.

[130] Marshall, 'The Administration of the Dioceses of Hereford and Oxford, 1660–1760', p. 103.

[131] *Charges* (1758), pp. 210, 211.

[132] *Autobiography*, pp. 38–39.

Wegg, a Lawyer, & a good but warm man, had a little before sent me a manuscript, addressed to the Society for promoting Christian Knowledge, & exhorting them to prosecute, as a Body, Non-Residents. This he intended to print.'[133] George Wegg, a lawyer from Essex, had come to recognize the problems non-residence might pose when he saw its effects in his own neighbourhood. He explained to Secker that during the early 1750s a Dissenting minister had drawn away many members from the local parish church, which a feckless clergyman led. 'An intimate friend of mine succeeded him,' Wegg explained to Secker, and 'to him I wrote in the year 1753 pressing him to come and reside and endeavour to bring the flock back that had gone astray, or at least to send a resident curate. I had a very civil answer and fair promises, but no performances.' To remedy the situation nationwide, Wegg had thought about seeking a seat in Parliament where he planned 'to attempt some explanation and amendment of the Statutes concerning Residence: a very short Bill I think would cure most of the neglects'. Unfortunately, he could not get a seat in Parliament and now hoped that by bringing the matter to the attention of the bishops, 'they might order their Archdeacons to look more narrowly into those defects and to make out some such Lists as I have attempted, and on their particular returns I thought it not improbable that some such regulations as I have hinted at may be made by the Body collectively'. It was the Church leadership's responsibility to reform the situation. 'I know it is in the power of their Lordships and their Archdeacons to do a great deal towards a Reformation in those particulars', Wegg contended.[134] Wegg also wanted to take the matter to court, but Secker 'wrote a long Letter … to dissuade him; & prevailed on him for the present'.[135] He tried to allay Wegg's fears and assured him that the bishops cared deeply about non-residence themselves, so much so that Secker had recently brought suit against John Pearsall, rector of Warehorn to deprive him of his living on account of non-residence.[136] And, of course, he could point to the efforts that he and other bishops were now taking to get a precise count of non-resident clergy in England and Wales.

While Secker vigilantly monitored his dioceses to ensure that parish worship did not suffer because of pluralism and non-residence, nothing lasting could be done to reduce levels of pluralism until clerical poverty was ameliorated. Secker, like most of his colleagues among the higher echelons of the Church, was unbothered by the sometimes yawning gaps in clerical income. Indeed, he argued, extremely wealthy livings might lure top-flight talent into the Church. 'The few [endowments] that may appear to be larger than was necessary, are in Truth, but needful Encouragements to the Breeding up of Youth for holy Orders,' he assured

---

[133] Ibid., p. 68.
[134] LPL, Secker Papers 7, ff. 167–68: Wegg to Secker, 24 Feb 1768.
[135] *Autobiography*, p. 68.
[136] LPL, Secker Papers 7, f. 172: Secker to Wegg, 2 Mar 1768.

his Oxford clergy in 1747. 'And were they lessened, either an insufficient Number would be destined to that Service, or too many of them would be of the lowest Rank, unable to bear the Expence of acquiring due Knowledge, and unlikely to be treated with due Regard.'[137] John Eachard had made a similar point in the early 1670s.[138] One suspects that struggling curates in Oxford thought differently from their bishop on this matter.

Despite his justification of sometimes stark clerical income disparities, Secker worked aggressively to combat the clerical poverty which nurtured pluralism and non-residence. A benefice's value depended wholly on a number of variables – including the 'accidents of historical endowment, topography, geography, the economy of the parish, and the size of its population' – all of which were outside anyone's ability to control.[139] There were, though, instances when Secker's intervention could make a tangible difference. The poorest clergy were curates, whose income per living averaged no more than £30.[140] To alleviate the plight of curates within his diocese, Secker frequently insisted that tithe owners supply their curates enough upon which to live. 'I have received from Mr. Lewis, your Curate, a Complaint, that you owe him three Quarters salary, and a very improper Letter, written by you to him on that Subject,' he wrote to the vicar of Leysdown. 'You are to pay him the Allowance for which you agreed; & not to send him, against his will, to collect it from other persons ... Whilst he continues to be employed by you, he ought to be well treated.'[141] He reiterated this message in his episcopal charges: 'But if any Minister, who hath either a large Preferment, or two moderate ones, or a plentiful temporal Income, tries to make a hard Bargain with his Brother, whom he employs; and is more solicitous to give the smallest Salary possible, than to find the worthiest Person; it is a Matter of severe and just Reproach.'[142]

While curates depended upon stipends determined and disbursed by others, rectors and vicars had some control over their incomes. In particular, many could manage the incomes of their livings more carefully, especially with regard to tithes.[143] Historians disagree about tithing's impact on lay-clerical relations. Some argue that the 'payment of tithes was the argument over which parsons and parishioners quarrelled most often in the century after the Restoration', while others counter that '[w]hat is at first sight striking is not the reluctance, but

---

[137] *Charges* (1747), p. 89.

[138] John Eachard, *The grounds and occasions of the contempt of the clergy and religion inquired into* (1670). I thank Bill Gibson for this reference.

[139] Gregory, *Restoration, Reformation, and Reform*, p. 148.

[140] Sykes, 'The Church', pp. 25–26.

[141] LPL, Secker Papers 3, f. 224: Secker to Liscombe Maltbe Stretch, 5 Aug 1766.

[142] *Charges* (1758), p. 211.

[143] Robert G. Ingram, 'Nation, Empire, and Church: Thomas Secker, Anglican Identity, and Public Life in Georgian Britain, 1700–1770' (University of Virginia Ph.D. thesis, 2002), pp. 190–91.

rather the willingness, of lay society to pay for the parish clergy'.[144] The evidence from Secker's dioceses illustrates that tithes could frequently be a source of conflict.[145] While he did not dismiss the strain that tithe collection might place on lay-clerical relations, Secker was adamant that parish clergy had to protect and defend their economic interests for the Church to survive. 'Glebe Lands have been blended with temporal Estates: and Pretences set up, that only such a yearly Rent, far inferior to real Value, is payable from them,' he complained in 1750.

> Tithes and other Dues have been denied; under false Colours of Exemptions in some Cases, and of Modus's in many. Every unjust Plea admitted makes Way for more. And thus what was given for the Support of the Clergy in all future Times, is decreasing continually; and becoming less sufficient, as it goes down to them. The Laity, themselves, if they would reflect, must see, that they have by no Means any Cause to rejoice in this .... But whatever they are, we ourselves cannot surely fail to be deeply concerned at the ill Aspect which these Encroachments bear towards Religion in Ages to come. Whoever is indifferent, shews himself very unworthy of what he enjoys from the Liberality of Ages preceding. And whoever is grieved at it, will set himself to consider, not how he can augment the Patrimony of the Church, where it is already plentiful; or any where, by dishonourable Methods ... but how he can retrieve any Part of it, which is illegally or unequitably seized and detained.[146]

To ensure that he had a clear idea of the Church's financial state, he included detailed questions about parish income in his visitation articles, kept careful note of the answers in his diocese books, and followed up with incumbents if their answers raised concerns or questions. Sometimes he actually advised clergy about how to go about recovering income which he believed was properly owed to them. In 1759, for instance, he provided John Clutton with papers relating to questions concerning the land tax on the vicarage of Portslade, Sussex, 'that you may judge of them or ask the opinion of Lawyers concerning them if you think fit'.[147] When Secker moved to Lambeth Palace, he himself took steps to improve the archiepiscopal income. For instance, he had Stiff Leadbetter properly survey the archiepiscopal woods in Kent and hired, in Thomas Carter, an overseer of the woodlands who 'hath sold the Under-Wood, & I believe the Timber, very much better than Mr. Denne (the former overseer) did, & hath prevented great Frauds

---

[144] Spaeth, *The Church in an Age of Danger*, p. 133; Gregory, *Restoration, Reformation, and Reform*, pp. 147–60 at p. 147. Eric J. Evans, 'Some reasons for the growth of English rural anti-clericalism, c. 1750–1830', *PP* 66 (1975), pp. 84–109; idem, *The Contentious Tithe: The Tithe Problem in English Agriculture, 1750–1850* (1976); and idem, 'Tithes', in *Agrarian History of England and Wales*, ed. Joan Thirsk (Cambridge, 1985), V.2, pp. 389–405 most systematically argue for the divisive effect of tithes in English society. But cf. Christopher Clay, '"The Greed of Whig bishops"?: church landlords and their lesees, 1660–1760', *PP* 87 (1980), pp. 128–57.

[145] See, for instance, *Oxford Correspondence*, p. 114: George Sheppard to Secker, 15 June 1744.

[146] *Charges* (1750), pp. 125–26.

[147] LPL, Secker Papers 6, f. 265: Secker to Clutton, 6 Oct 1759.

& Abuses committed by Mr. Denne'.[148] He expected the same thoroughness and diligence from parish priests.

No matter how well parochial clergy might safeguard their ancient rights and privileges with regard to the incomes from their livings, though, Secker understood that the full income from some churches was insufficient to support their incumbent. For this reason, incomes had to be augmented, and it was a subject that took up a good deal of his time and energy as bishop. Livings could be augmented either privately or through Queen Anne's Bounty. Sometimes Secker improved the income of poor livings out of his own pocket. The case of Philip Warham, vicar of Kennington, is illustrative. The archbishop of Canterbury owned Kennington's advowson and leased the parsonage lands to a layman. Under the terms of the lease the lessee was to pay the vicar one quarter of the yearly harvest of wheat and barley. The problem was that Warham, who had been instituted to the vicarage in 1730, had never received his fair due under the terms of the lease; instead, he was paid 32s. yearly, after 8s. had been subtracted for the land tax. The error continued unnoticed when Archbishop Hutton renewed the lease in 1757. Five years later, Secker discovered the error. Upon investigation, he found that Warham had been short-changed because the lessee's subtenant was the person actually responsible for paying the vicar and that the subtenant's lease stipulated that the vicar was owed 40s. per year rather than one quarter of the wheat and barley.[149] Secker advised Warham that 'the Persons, who have been Lessees during your Incumbency ought in Conscience to pay you for the whole time Past'. Thinking them unlikely to do so, though, he promised Warham that if the lease came due to be renewed during his tenure, he would 'not renew it, till Justice be done you' regarding the income. 'And I would have you in the mean time make your Demand, as a matter of Right, and in my Name, but in a very civil manner.'[150] Because the subtenant did not pay Warham's back salary, Secker himself gave Warham £10 as recompense. When the lease came up for renewal in 1764, however, he forgot his earlier promise to Warham to settle the matter of the wheat and barley and renewed the lease without emendation. Apologetic for the mistake, he again made up the difference in Warham's income out of his own pocket.[151] His payment to Warham was not unusual, for he gave outright gifts to other clergy in similar situations, such as the vicar of River, whose pension had lapsed, and Benjamin Waterhouse, vicar of Hollingbourne.[152]

There were also instances in which Secker tried to improve an incumbent's finances by negotiating personally with the leaseholder. The most notable

---

[148] *Autobiography*, p. 41.
[149] *Speculum*, p. 62; LPL, Secker Papers 3, f. 219: Secker's notes on Philip Warham's salary [1766].
[150] LPL, Secker Papers 3, f. 212: Secker to Warham, 2 Oct 1762.
[151] Ibid., ff. 217–18, 220: Secker to Warham, 11, 31 Mar 1766; LPL, MS 1483, f. 211.
[152] *Autobiography*, pp. 43, 51; *Speculum*, pp. 81, 188–89; LPL, MS 1483, ff. 69, 181.

example of this was his negotiations with Philip Stanhope, the fourth earl of Chesterfield, over the lease of St Gregory's Priory. The archbishop of Canterbury controlled the lease, which granted the tenant income from the great tithes of twelve parishes in the diocese and stipulated that he was responsible for the physical upkeep of the churches in those parishes and with paying yearly pensions (incomes) to the incumbents.[153] Chesterfield held the lease but his subtenant, Mrs. Roberts, refused to pay the pensions without first deducting the land tax, arguing that the deduction alone prevented her from losing money on the sublease. When the lease came due for renewal in 1759, Secker took the matter up with Chesterfield, but not before inquiring closely into Mrs. Roberts's finances. 'Either the Answer, which bears the name of Mrs. Roberts, is not hers, or she is unacquainted with the value of the estate and things which have passed in relation to it,' he wrote to Chesterfield. 'For the ABP can not suppose, that she is unwilling to give an exact Account of them.'[154] Though he explained clearly how Roberts had underestimated the value of the estate by over £110 per year and offering 'to make a considerable Abatement in the Fine, on Condition, that a Covenant should be inserted to free from the Land Tax the pensions reserved by that Lease to the Incumbents of several Parishes mentioned in it,'[155] the earl refused to accede, arguing instead that 'because the Estate being held in trust for [him] only for his Life, it was apprehended, that no Act could be legally done, which would lessen the value of it to those who should come after'. Advised by legal counsel that Chesterfield was indeed in the legal right, Secker stepped in to make up the difference of income himself. As he explained to the incumbents in a joint letter, 'it is my intention to pay the Land-Tax for the Incumbents during my own Time, since nothing more is in my power. And Ld Chesterfield hath agreed to accept it from me: so that you are to receive your pension clear from any Deduction on that Account.'[156] This cost Secker £31 a year for the rest of his life. He clearly learned from the Chesterfield incident. 'And in the Renewal of every other Lease, I have obliged the Lessees to pay these Pensions Tax-free,' he noted, 'which for the most Part they ought to have done before, but did not. Now their Obligation is clearly expressed.'[157]

While Secker could help a few poor or unjustly fined clerics within his diocese, his own pockets were not bottomless and there was only so much he could do personally to help impecunious clergy. The organization responsible nationwide for the augmentation of poor livings was Queen Anne's Bounty. The Bounty had been established in 1704 to divert the first fruits and tenths that the

---

[153] Gregory, *Restoration, Reformation, and Reform*, p. 121.
[154] LPL, TR-12, f. 80: Secker's notes concerning St Gregory's priory [1759].
[155] Ibid., f. 93: Secker to Chesterfield, 18 July 1759.
[156] Ibid., f. 96: Secker to incumbents of St Gregory's Priory, 13 Aug 1759.
[157] *Autobiography*, p. 42.

crown had received since 1533 to poor clergy in the established Church.[158] The Bounty drew the poverty line at £50 and augmented those livings under that amount at random by lot. Rather than give poor clerics yearly pensions, the Bounty augmented by investing capital grants of £200 per living into land whose rent would produce a yearly income; in addition, if a private patron gave £200 to augment a living, the Bounty agreed to match that gift. This approach put the Church's finances on a sounder financial basis in the longer term, ensured that rents on the purchased lands would rise along with any improvements in agricultural productivity, and bound Church and society closer together by placing some of the Church's financial security in the hands of private donors.

Secker worked closely with the Bounty while he was bishop. For one thing, he spent a good deal of his own money trying to improve poor livings. Not only did he leave £1,000 in his will to augment five Canterbury livings, but during his time as archbishop, he spent £800 to augment the parishes of Ouere, St Dunstan's, Canterbury, Cliffe near Lewes, and Little Brickhill.[159] There were instances when Bounty augmentation threatened actually to decrease the value of a living, something he worked to avoid. In 1750, for instance, the Bounty augmented the living of the chapel of Wheatley, Oxfordshire, by £200; this stood to increase the annual income of Wheatley's curate by £3–4. Secker worried, however, that when the residents of Wheatley found out that their chapel had been augmented, that they would cease their own £6 yearly contribution, causing the curate's salary to decrease rather than increase with the augmentation. To avert this possibility, Secker advised Nathaniel Forster, Wheatley's curate, to drum up a matching £200 augmentation from the parishioners: 'I would therefore propose to you, to try, whether they could not be induced to do something towards procuring a third Augmentation: which you need not call a third in speaking to them; but only tell them, that if land or money can be got, to the Amount of £200 more to it; and their usual payment of £6 a year ... shall cease for the future.'[160]

Most private augmentations to the Bounty did not require such delicate maneuvering, for the laity frequently looked to relieve clerical poverty. Jeremy Gregory reckons that in Kent 'over two-thirds of the diocesan livings receiving augmentation in the eighteenth century did so to match gifts of money and land given by the laity, as opposed to receiving augmentation by lot'.[161] Secker, though, did work aggressively to funnel private donations to poor livings in his dioceses. When Sir Philip Boetler alerted the Bounty in 1765 that he planned to

[158] Alan Savidge, *The Foundation and Early Years of Queen Anne's Bounty* (1955); Best, *Temporal Pillars*; and I.M. Green, 'The First Five Years of Queen Anne's Bounty', in *Princes and Paupers in the English Church, 1500–1800*, eds. Rosemary O'Day and Felicity Heal (Leicester, 1981), pp. 231–54.

[159] *Autobiography*, pp. 49, 60, 61.

[160] *Oxford Correspondence*, pp. 180–81: Secker to Forster, 1 Feb 1750.

[161] Gregory, *Restoration, Reformation, and Reform*, p. 164.

give £14,000 to it for the augmentations of poor livings, for instance, Secker immediately began working to get Canterbury livings augmented. He asked Lord Romney to talk with Boetler, explaining that 'the Governors are ready to augment such Livings, not exceeding the certified Value of £45 a Year, as he shall chuse, by adding, to the Benefit of each of them, £200 of Queen Annes Bounty to £200 of his Legacy. Now there is a large number of Livings in the Diocese of Canterbury, which come with this Description: and I should be glad to see as many of them, as should be thought reasonable to be augmented.'[162] Romney put off speaking with Boetler because the latter's health was poor, but Secker returned to him four months later with the same request. 'It is now, as I am informed, much better: and therefore I beg Leave to repeat my Application to your Lordship,' he wrote to Romney. 'I am very sorry to hear, that you are at present under a grievous domestick Anxiety, to which may God give a happy Issue. But if it will permit your Lordship to pay a little Attention to this matter, you will greatly oblige [me].'[163] In the end Secker got what he had hoped for in his application to Boetler: 'I recommended to him all those in the Diocese of Canterbury which were capable of Augmentation; & he inserted almost all of them in his list.'[164]

As primate of the Church of England, though, Secker had to keep the national picture firmly in view. To this end, he monitored the activity of the Bounty closely to ensure that it augmented the greatest number of poor livings possible. Thus it came as something of a shock to him when he discovered in early January 1767 that the Bounty had nearly £88,000 of unused funds. In a letter to Archbishop Drummond of York, Secker fretted both that this represented a dereliction of duty by the Board's governors, of which they both were members, and that it threatened publicly to embarrass the Church. 'How can we answer for this Neglect, to the Publick, to the Clergy, to our selves? Ought we not to take immediately the speediest Methods of reducing this enormous Sum of to a moderate one?', he wondered.

> We may join Benefactions with all Sir Philip Boetlers Money: We may draw Lots for the Livings not exceeding £20 a year. These things will take up a good deal, and it must be well consider'd, how much we shall leave. But we must lose no time in Considering & Acting. For what if the House of Commons should get the Start of us; & calls to an Account for our Supineness, before we have taken any Step towards Amendment?[165]

---

[162] LPL, MS 1120, f. 165: Secker to Romney, 5 June 1765.
[163] Ibid., f. 167: Secker to Romney, 10 Oct 1765.
[164] *Autobiography*, p. 56.
[165] LPL, MS 1120, f. 182: Secker to RHD, 8 Jan 1767.

By the end of the month, the Board had augmented 250 livings and, Secker noted, 'hath reduced the unappropriated money to so moderate a Sum, that it can give no Ground for Complaint'.[166]

IV

Clerical residence was not an end in itself. Instead, Secker saw it as only one of the first steps to reform and revitalize the Church's pastoral care, the success or failure of which depended on the clergy themselves. The curates who served in the stead of pluralists concerned him greatly. In rare instances, non-resident clergy did not bother to hire a curate to cover one of their livings. When Secker found out that Frederick Dodsworth had virtually abandoned Minster-in-Thanet, he was apoplectic: 'I never knew, and hoped I never should have known, so scandalous an Omission of Duty in any parish under my Care,' he fumed. 'I cannot in these Circumstances continue your Leave of Absence, and therefore do by this Letter withdraw it, promising myself, that you will keep your Oath of Residence, though other Motives seem to have less weight with you.'[167]

Dodsworth's was an extraordinary case, though, and Secker had primarily to monitor the quality, not the presence, of resident curates. Those who did not reside in their parishes must choose 'a fit Substitute', he demanded. 'And therefore I charge it upon your Consciences, not to suffer Cheapness, Recommendation of Friends, Affection to this or that Person or Place of Education, in short any Inducement whatever to weigh near so much with you, as the Benefit of your People, in chusing Persons to serve your Churches,' he continued.[168] The close-fistedness of incumbents particularly angered him. 'I have received from Mr. Lewis, your Curate, a Complaint, that you owe him three Quarters salary, and a very improper Letter, written by you to him on that Subject,' he chastened Liscombe Maltbe Stretch in 1766.[169] When choosing a curate, he also advised incumbents 'first to inquire after Persons of Merit, already ordained, and if possible ordained Priests, take Care to see their Orders, as well as to examine their Characters, before you think of granting Nominations to others'.[170] Indeed, he expected incumbents to pay the same kind of attention to testimonials and face-to-face interviews when choosing a curate that he did when deciding whether or not to ordain a clerical candidate.[171] Certainly he was

---

[166] *Autobiography*, p. 56; LPL, MS 1120, f. 205: RHD to Secker, 24 Jan 1767.
[167] LPL, Secker Papers 3, f. 234: Secker to Dodsworth, 14 May 1761.
[168] *Charges* (1758), pp. 219–20.
[169] LPL, Secker Papers 3, f. 224: Secker to Liscombe Maltbe Stretch, 5 Aug 1766.
[170] *Charges* (1758), p. 222.
[171] Ibid., pp. 225–30.

unwilling to grant a curate's license without proper testimonials. In 1761, for instance, he wrote to Wheler Twyman about his curate:

> It is very true, that I did ordain Mr. Sayer priest in 1742: and I hope you will let him know that upon a wrong Information I understood your Curates name to be Hughes. I would never put any clergymen to unnecessary Expence or Trouble. But I think producing a Testimonial, countersigned by the Bishop of the Diocese quitted, to be very necessary on coming into another: and such a Testimonial may be procured without any Expence or Trouble worth naming. Therefore I hope my clergy will always take Care to see both the Orders & the Testimonials of those, whom they employ; and give me an Account of them: and that you will do it in this case.[172]

If Secker was going to have to accept curates to serve livings in his dioceses, he was going to make certain that they were properly qualified.

After the quality of the clergy, he was concerned to ensure adequate provision of church services in the parishes. English canon law called for two services each Sunday, what contemporaries called 'double-duty'. The longer service in the morning consisted of prayer, the litany, ante-communion, and the sermon, while the evensong (and catechizing) followed in the afternoon or early evening.[173] How frequently were Sunday services held in the eighteenth-century Church? Historians have long argued that the provision of Sunday services declined steadily throughout the eighteenth century.[174] What is most striking when surveying the visitation returns for Secker's dioceses, though, is not the frequency of pastoral neglect providing regular Sunday services, but the infrequency of pastoral delinquency. In 1738, 85 per cent of Oxfordshire churches had double-duty, while fifty years later, fully 67 per cent did.[175] In Canterbury, rates of double-duty improved markedly during the mid eighteenth century, jumping from 30.3 per cent in 1716 to 43.4 per cent in 1758. Rates of double-duty in Canterbury actually improved markedly during the mid century, jumping from 30.3 per cent in 1716 to 43.4 per cent in 1758, before dropping off in 1806 to 35 per cent.[176] More importantly, remarkably few churches in Oxford or Canterbury were not provided with a service at least once each Sunday.

Secker, however, was dissatisfied with this performance and badgered all of his clergy to offer two services each Sunday. In a sense, he fell into the trap of taking 'regulations for attendance in the 1604 canons as actually descriptive of a bygone age of universal churchgoing, when in fact they were prescriptive, and by

---

[172] LPL, Secker Papers 3, f. 226: Secker to Twyman, 19 Jan 1761.
[173] F.C. Mather, 'Georgian Churchmanship Reconsidered: Some Variations in Anglican Public Worship, 1714–1830', *JEH* 36:2 (1985), pp. 265–66.
[174] Anthony Russell, *The Clerical Profession* (1980), pp. 54–55; Sykes, *Church and State*, p. 238; Overton and Relton, *The English Church (1714–1800)*, pp. 292–93.
[175] Marshall, 'The Dioceses of Hereford and Oxford, 1660–1760', p. 210; McClatchey, *Oxfordshire Clergy, 1777–1869*, pp. 80–82.
[176] Gregory, *Restoration, Reformation, and Reform*, p. 263.

no means always obeyed'.[177] Certainly Secker wanted to make double-duty normative in the eighteenth-century Church. 'I must not conclude this Head without desiring you to remind your People, that our Liturgy consists not only of Morning but Evening Prayer also: that the latter is in Proportion equally edifying and instructive with the former; and so short, that, generally speaking, there can arise no Inconvenience from attending upon it, provided Persons are within any tolerable Distance from the Church,' he exhorted the Oxfordshire clergy in 1741.[178]

Parish priests offered a variety of reasons for not providing two Sunday services. Some argued that poor attendance made double-duty pointless.[179] The rector of Heythrop, for instance, explained that he offered one service each Sunday because 'we can't make up a tolerable congregation without the Assistance of Stragglers from neighbouring Parishes, who will not come till the Afternoon: for wch. reason, tho a Sermon is constantly preached here once every Sunday; public Service was never perform'd here twice in one Lds. Day'.[180] Secker retorted that 'the smallness of your Congregation ought not to hinder you from performing Divine Service in your Church, twice every Sunday, and that your having Popish families in your Parish particularly requisite'.[181] Likewise, when the vicar of Leysdown explained that he held one service each Sunday because he had so few attendants, Secker bluntly replied, 'I yield to Reason: but not to Requests without Reason; and I see none for yours.'[182] The vicar of Boughton explained that sermon-sampling accounted for his offering only one service per Sunday: 'I know of no other Reason but this, why there is not Service twice every Sunday but because my Parishioners had rather go to another church to hear Preaching, than to come to their own to hear Prayers only.'[183] Other clergy protested that they were not paid enough to do double-duty, an excuse Secker refused to countenance. 'The Incomes of Livings were settled on them for the performance of Divine Service,' he wrote to the rector of Goodnestone, 'for which purpose, by Apostolick Appointment, Christians ought to assemble every Lords Day: and by ancient usage as well as by the Law of this Land, the people of every parish ought to assemble twice.'[184] Most often ministers blamed the pressures of pluralism as a reason for not providing two services on Sundays. The rector of Denton, for instance, explained, 'The reason of there not being publick service twice is my having another cure wch I serve myself.'[185] Secker had little patience for those who offered pluralism as an excuse. He chastened the vicar of

[177]   Ibid., p. 255.
[178]   *Charges* (1741), p. 74.
[179]   *OVR 1738*, p. 160.
[180]   Ibid., p. 82.
[181]   *Oxford Correspondence*, pp. 4–5: Secker to James Martin, 8 Aug 1738.
[182]   LPL, Secker Papers 3, f. 223: Secker to Liscombe Maltbe Stretch, 14 Sept 1762.
[183]   LPL, MS 1134/I, f. 43. Cf. *Speculum*, p. 11.
[184]   LPL, Secker Papers 3, f. 176: Secker to Charles Norris, 24 Aug 1758.
[185]   LPL, MS 1134/II, f. 20.

Sittingbourne, for instance, 'concerning the Service of your Parish', which, he noted,

> ... consists of 130 Houses, & is a considerable thorough-fare: & the Income is such, as may well afford the whole Service, which the Law requires: and my Book Informs me, that the whole was performed there a few years ago. Therefore I see no Reason, why you officiate there only once every Sunday. Care may be taken of Borden some other way: and your Circumstances I am told, are good. Whether you have preferment in any other diocese, I know not. You have pleaded your Health for resigning in the parish of Tunstall. I suppose the House and Land, which you have purchased there, to be another Motive. But if you are indulged in that, you should the rather do the whole Sundays Duty, and so make your parish amends for your non-residence.[186]

The careful scrutiny he paid to the frequency of divine service in the parishes in his dioceses frequently paid off in improved performance. During his primary visitation of Canterbury in 1758, for instance, he discovered that services were provided in Ham only on the first Sunday of each month because almost no one lived in the parish; within a year, he had persuaded the minister to provide a service every Sunday, despite the tiny congregation.[187] Yet as we saw earlier in the case of Goodnestone, he did not always succeed in cajoling incumbents to do double-duty.

Secker's high sacramental theology lay behind his exhortations to the parochial clergy to celebrate the Eucharist more frequently. Historians have looked to the frequency of holy communion as a barometer both of the laity's religiosity and of the clergy's diligence. In turn, they have argued that the liturgical emphasis on the Eucharist declined during the 'age of reason' and that this decline spoke poorly of the eighteenth-century Church.[188] This distorts the facts and engages in anachronism. In no Protestant church in England during the eighteenth century was the Eucharist central to spiritual or devotional life, nor did this represent a significant change from earlier eras.[189] It was the Tractarians of the nineteenth century who pressed for weekly communions, and English canon law during the eighteenth century merely stipulated that the 'holy communion shall be administered ... at such times as every parishioner may communicate at least thrice in the year, (whereof the feast of Easter to be one), according as they are appointed by the book of common prayer'.[190] Most of the churches in Secker's dioceses met these minimal standards. In 1738, 60 per cent

---

[186]   LPL, Secker Papers 3, f. 250: Secker to Thomas Bland, 8 Oct 1758.
[187]   *Speculum*, p. 147.
[188]   See, for instance, Sykes, *Church and State*, p. 250; Horton Davies, *Worship and Theology in England from Watts and Wesley to Maurice, 1690–1850* (Princeton, 1961), p. 63.
[189]   Henry D. Rack, *Reasonable Enthusiast: John Wesley and the Rise of Methodism* (1989), pp. 19–21, 417–19; *ODCC*, p. 386.
[190]   *Anglican Canons*, p. 291 (Canon 21 of 1604).

of Oxford parishes had communion quarterly, while in 1758, fully 72 per cent of Canterbury's churches celebrated the Eucharist that often.[191]

Nonetheless, Secker pressed the parish clergy to increase the frequency of holy communion, in part, because he believed that the sacraments were important means of conveying grace.[192] 'The small Proportion of Communicants which I find there is in most of your Congregations, and very small in some, must undoubtedly ... be a Subject of great Concern to you', he admonished the Oxford clergy in 1741.[193] Through careful and persistent ministry, he hoped that the parish churches in his dioceses could 'advance from a quarterly Communion to a monthly one'. Yet he realized that there were often cultural barriers that militated against frequent communion.[194] 'Some imagine that the Sacrament belongs only to Persons of advanced Years, or great Leisure, or high Attainments in Religion, and is a very dangerous Thing for common Persons to venture upon,' he acknowledged. 'Some again disregard it stupidly, because others, they say, who do receive are never the better for it.' So, he tried to offer the clergy practical advice about how to counter those fears. First, they needed to be tenacious in their ministry: 'our complaining of these Prejudices is not enough; but labouring to overcome them is our Business, and we are not to grow weary of it'. In addition, clergy needed to explain the importance of the sacraments clearly in their sermons, and, finally, they needed to recognize that their 'public Instructions on this Head will be much more effectual for being followed by seasonable private Applications'.[195]

V

Among the reasons Secker so carefully scrutinized parochial pastoral provision was that the Church of England lacked a monopoly on religious provision. The

---

[191] Marshall, 'The Administration of the Dioceses of Hereford and Oxford, 1660–1760', pp. 120–21; idem, 'The Dioceses of Hereford and Oxford, 1660–1760', pp. 211–12; Gregory, *Restoration, Reformation, and Reform*, p. 263. Mather, 'Georgian Churchmanship Reconsidered', pp. 272–75 surveys the regional variations regarding the frequency of Eucharistic celebrations.

[192] Ingram, 'Nation, Empire, and Church', pp. 48–50.

[193] Unless otherwise noted, all quotations in this paragraph are taken from *Charges* (1741), pp. 59–63.

[194] Mather, 'Georgian Churchmanship Reconsidered', pp. 272–74 examines why there was a 'reluctance among the laity to communicate' during the eighteenth century.

[195] LPL, Secker Papers 6, ff. 204–05: Secker to Charles Hall, 20 June 1762 illustrates the kind of detailed private advice Secker frequently offered his clergy regarding the instruction of orthodox Anglican doctrine to the laity. Hall had reported that the residents of the Canterbury peculiar, Bocking, Essex, had intentionally abstained from baptizing their children for a number of years; Secker's letter details both the message that Hall should deliver to the residents of Bocking as well as the manner in which to present that message.

Toleration Act freed Trinitarian Protestant nonconformists to worship in their own churches and demoted the Church of England from the national church to the established one. As the eighteenth century progressed, the Church's leaders worried increasingly more about the threats to Christianity posed by Christological heresies than they did about challenges to the established Church by schismatics. Nonetheless, they remained acutely vigilant of confessional competitors.

Considering the pervasive anti-popery of the day, it is unsurprising that Secker vehemently opposed nearly everything about Roman Catholicism.[196] The Church of England, not the Church of Rome, was the only visible and apostolic holy catholic church in England. The Roman church, Secker argued, had perverted Christ's teachings so egregiously that 'the instances ... of Popish usurpation, treachery, and cruelty, in every part of Europe, every nation upon earth, in which popery hath got footing, have been so numerous, that the time would fail me even to name them'.[197] Having ignored the Bible, the papists had buried 'every part of religion under a load of rites and ceremonies, that turn it into outward show; and [given] it the appearance of art magic by an infinity of absurd superstitions, many of them the undeniable remains of Heathenism very little disguised'.[198] Yet while Secker faulted the Church of Rome for abandoning *sola scriptura* and for fetishising tradition, he himself argued from tradition to rebut Catholic charges 'that Protestants, not being of the Roman church, are not of the catholic church'. He likened the Church of England to the primitive one: 'Do we not profess the true catholic faith, that faith which the universal church received from the apostles? We profess it much purer than they,' he asserted.[199] Elsewhere, he spelled out more fully why the Church of England's claims to catholicity trumped those of Rome. 'The Catholic Church is then the universal Church, spread through the World; and the Catholic Faith is the universal Faith; that Form of Doctrine, which the Apostles delivered to the whole Church, and it received,' he argued.

> What this Faith was, we may learn from their Writings, contained in the New Testaments ... Every Church or Society of Christians that preserves this Catholic or universal Faith, accompanied with true Charity, is a part of the Catholic or universal

---

[196] While Secker's anti-popery was by no means unique, his *Five Sermons Against Popery*, given at St James's, Westminster, during the Forty-Five, was enormously popular, going through over a dozen editions by the 1830s. Colin Haydon, *Anti-catholicism in eighteenth-century England, c. 1714–80: A political and social study* (Manchester, 1993) argues that clerical anti-Catholicism waned during the mid-century, though popular anti-Catholicism waxed, which leaves Secker's experience either as anomalous or cautionary.

[197] 'Sermon CXXXVIII. Persecution a Decisive Evidence of an Unchristian Spirit: Preached in the Parish Church of St Mary, Lambeth, Nov 5, 1758 [John 16:2–3]', in *WTS*, IV, p. 24.

[198] 'Sermon CI. Sacred Scriptures the Only Infallible Rule of Faith and Practice [1 Peter 5:12]', in *WTS*, III, p. 93.

[199] 'Sermon CII. Sacred Scriptures the Only Infallible Rule of Faith and Practice [1 Peter 5:12]', in *WTS*, III, pp. 96, 97.

Church; and because the Parts are of the same Nature with the Whole, it may be usual to call every Church singly, which is so qualified, a Catholic Church. Several Notions and Customs, may, notwithstanding, each of them be truly Catholic Churches. But the Church of Rome, which is one of the most corrupted Parts of the Catholic Church, both in Faith and Love, hath presumed to call itself the whole Catholic church, the universal Church: which it no more is, than one diseased Limb ...

The Church of England, then, did not pretend 'absurdly, to be the whole Catholic Church; but is undoubtedly a sound and excellent Member of it'.[200]

Secker's practical pastoral advice was shot through with this same kind of virulent anti-Catholicism. In the aftermath of his visitation of Canterbury's Sussex peculiars, for instance, Secker discovered that the parish of Slidon contained a gaggle of Catholics, nearly one-third of the parish's populace. While there was no public Catholic chapel, the young earl of Newburgh kept a priest resident in his household, making it the epicentre of Catholicism in Slidon. The first line of defence against popery was upright clerical behaviour, so that Secker advised Slidon's rector, Robert Styles Launce, 'to be careful, & prudent in your Conduct'. Yet Launce should also actively fight the Catholic menace. If Newburgh's priest 'makes any Attempts on your people, ... I would have you represent freely & boldly, yet decently, both to him and to my Lord, that Gratitude for the Indulgence, which they enjoy, and Caution to preserve it, should restrain them from all such Enterprizes'. Yoked to these threats should be evangelism. 'You will do well also, whether any popish Book or Tracts are put into the Hands of your parishioners,' he advised Launce, 'and to furnish them regularly with some of the small pieces written in Defence of the Protestant Religion.' Secker even went so far as to express grudging admiration for popish priests: 'I fear the priests of the Church of Rome ordinarily take more pains with their Laity, than we do with ours: which ought not to be. And as they study every way to make Converts, so should we.'[201]

Secker's actions did not match his heated rhetoric. His own chaplain claimed that Secker did not think the numbers of Catholics in England 'to be so great as to afford any just Ground for Apprehension or Alarm'.[202] And, indeed, he supported Lord Radnor's May 1767 parliamentary motion proposing a count of all Catholics in England mainly to safeguard the Church of England's reputation for vigilance against popery. 'I said from the first Mention of it to me, that the Bishops could not possibly oppose it,' he remembered, and his dealings with his

---

[200] *Lectures*, p. 113.

[201] LPL, Secker Papers 6, f. 266: Secker to Launce; *Speculum*, p. 218. For Secker's thoughts on the legal means to prevent Catholic conversions within families, see LPL, Secker Papers 7, ff. 110–17; on the subject of Catholic conversions more generally, Eamon Duffy, '"Poor Protestant Flies": Conversions to Catholicism in Early Eighteenth Century England', *SCH* 15 (1978), pp. 289–304.

[202] Porteus, *Life of Secker*, p. 76.

fellow bishops suggest that, insofar as the Catholic religious census was concerned, insulating the Church from criticism was the most important thing to him.[203] Later that year, Secker and Archbishop Drummond of York reported back to Parliament that out of a nation of 7 million people, they counted 68,000 Roman Catholics, or less than 1 per cent of the nation's populace.[204] In Secker's own diocese, there were only 217 Catholics, or less than one per Kentish parish.[205] This hardly represented a serious challenge to the Church of England, and when the results came in, Secker admitted to the duke of Newcastle, 'What use is to be made of these Returns, I do not know: excepting, that when an inquiry is made hereafter, they will shew, if the numbers be increased.'[206]

Notwithstanding Secker's vocal anti-Catholicism, a former Catholic priest like James Smith could find in Secker a patron. Judging Smith as 'having a good Character, & appearing to be a sincere Convert', Secker received him into the Church of England in 1765, named him rector of Eastbridge, and granted him nearly £90 in addition.[207] He was similarly generous to former Dissenting clergymen who had taken up the Anglican mantle. When Liscombe Maltbe Stretch abandoned Dissent in 1762, for instance, Secker ordained him and gave him the vicarage of Leysdown.[208] Likewise, Secker helped out the former Dissenting minister Joseph Price, giving him £20 in 1766 and granting him the vicarage of Brabourne the next year.[209] A defector from Dissent himself, Secker knew that a warm welcome from within the established Church might draw along other Dissenting ministers.

At the same time, he worked to keep up good connections with Dissenting clergymen. In the first few decades of his episcopal career, he found it easy to do, because he had known Samuel Chandler, Isaac Watts, Philip Doddridge, Nathaniel Lardner, and many Dissenting leaders since he was a young man.[210] With Dissent on the wane in the 1740s, it was likewise easy for him to talk the language of comprehension with Dissenting clergy. 'Indeed it must be and ought to be owned in general that dissenters have done excellently of late years in the service of Christianity,' he assured Doddridge, 'and I hope our common warfare will make us chiefly attentive to our common interest, and unite us in a closer

---

[203] *Autobiography*, pp. 60, 64. For the official instructions to the bishops, see William L. Clements Library, University of Michigan, Lord Shelburne Papers, f. 7: Shelburne to Secker and RHD, 3 July 1767.

[204] *Autobiography*, p. 68.

[205] WAM 64651: Secker to Zachary Pearce, 20 Oct 1767; Porteus, *Life of Secker*, p. 76.

[206] BL, Add. MS 32986, ff. 323–24: Secker to TPH, 9 Nov 1767. Cf. DWL, 12.45 (no. 102): Francis Blackburne to John Wiche, 4 Sept 1767.

[207] *Autobiography*, p. 49; *Speculum*, p. 101; LPL, MS 1483, ff. 173, 175, 179, 183, 191; James Smith, *The Errors of the Church of Rome Detected, in Ten Dialogues* (Canterbury, 1777).

[208] *Autobiography*, p. 46; *Speculum*, pp. 167–68.

[209] *Autobiography*, pp. 51, 57; *Speculum*, p. 97; G.M. Ditchfield, 'Price, Joseph (1736?-1807)', *ODNB*.

[210] Porteus, *Life of Secker*, pp. 77–78.

alliance.'[211] In 1745, he agreed with Doddridge 'in wishing that such things as we think indifferent, and you cannot be brought to think lawful, were altered or left free, in such a manner as that we might all unite'. Nevertheless, he added, 'I see not the prospect of it'.[212]

During his archiepiscopate, Secker continued to try to cultivate the Dissenters. While preparing Samuel Chandler's collected sermons for publication, Thomas Amory contacted Secker to see whether he had any of his old friend's works. Secker replied that he did not hold any of Chandler's sermons but that he did 'desire the Favour of [Amory's] Acquaintance. For I had non left amongst the Dissenting Ministers; & thought it was convenient that I should have some; & had heard a very good Character of Him.' Secker thought the meeting went well, concluding, 'I was very well pleased with him.'[213] Secker's arch-nemesis Francis Blackburne, though, heard quite a different account of the meeting. 'You must have heard of the Abp's Interview with Mr. Amory and the overtures made him to succeed Dr. Chandler in that Prelates good graces,' Blackburne wrote to John Wiche in the late summer of 1767. 'But I am told that Gentleman is not to be so easily overreached.'[214]

A more serious challenge to the Church of England than Old Dissent came from the Methodists, an intra-Anglican group of religious reformers who denied being separatists even as many suspected them of separatism.[215] On the one hand, Secker applauded the Methodist emphasis on the insufficiency of works in gaining salvation.[216] Yet for him the Methodists' *de facto* separation from the established Church and their ostentatious religiosity outweighed their theological merits. As early as 1739 he wrote to his brother about Methodists in Nottingham: 'They all set out at first I believe with a very good intention but have run into Indiscretions and Extravagancies: and some of them, particularly Mr. Whitefield, seem blown up with a vanity which I fear hath and will lead them into mighty wrong behaviour.'[217] Posthumously defending Secker against '[t]he Charge of great personal Prejudices' against Methodists, Bishop Richard Terrick conceded that

---

[211] Thomas Stedman (ed.), *Letters to and from the Rev. Philip Doddridge, D.D.* (Shrewsbury, 1790), p. 278: Secker to Doddridge, 29 Sept 1743.

[212] Ibid., p. 280: Secker to Doddridge, 21 Feb 1745. Geoffrey F. Nuttall, 'Chandler, Doddridge and the Archbishop: a study in 18th century ecumenism', *Journal of the United Reformed Church History Society* 1:2 (1973), pp. 42–56 examines Samuel Chandler's proposals for comprehension during the late 1740s.

[213] *Autobiography*, p. 59.

[214] DWL, 12.45 (no. 102): Blackburne to Wiche, 4 Sept 1767. Cf. BL, Egerton MS 2325, ff. 23–25: Amory to Blackburne, 29 July 1769; Alan Ruston, 'Amory, Thomas (1701–1774)', *ODNB*.

[215] Jeremy Gregory, '"In the Church I will live and die": John Wesley, the Church of England, and Methodism', in *Religious Identities in Britain, 1660–1832*, eds. William Gibson and Robert G. Ingram (Aldershot, 2005), pp. 147–78 explores the problematic nature of Methodist religious identities.

[216] Ingram, 'Nation, Empire, and Church', pp. 53–54.

[217] LPL, MS 1719, f. 15: Secker to George Secker, sr., 11 Sept [1739].

Secker 'had [been] in favour of a regular Established Ministry', that he had preferred 'the regular Members of the Establish'd Church', and that he had guarded 'against those, whose Tenets He thought bore a less friendly aspect to it'. But how, wondered Terrick, could that be considered 'unworthy of the Head of an Established church'?[218]

Secker's fellow clergy often agitated for him to stamp out Methodism. William Warburton, bishop of Gloucester, for instance, sought his approval before ejecting a curate, sympathetic to the Methodists, who allowed a woman to catechize in his church. 'Now it is apprehended, that were he to continue at Stinchcomb, armed with your Grace's beneficence & Continuance, he would treat all inferior authority with still greater insolence,' Warburton complained. 'The sum of all this is that unless your Grace be pleased to intimate your pleasure to him that he should quit my Diocese, I shall be obliged to make vacant the Curacy by Law.'[219]

Secker urged a more cautious approach. For one thing, he recognized that there were many different shades of Methodism. 'The Notions & Behaviour of different sets of Methodists vary so much', he wrote to the vicar of St John's Thanet, 'that without your acquainting me, as I desire you would, of what sort your Methodists are, I cannot well furnish you with proper Books to reclaim them, or to guard others against them.'[220] For whatever reason, he advised ministers in his diocese not to lash out too harshly against the Methodists. In 1759, for instance, he described to the curate of Kenardington the fine line that Anglican clergy had to walk in their parishes when it came to Methodists. 'I apprehend our Duty to withdraw ourselves from them, as Brethren that walk disorderly; and to have no company with them, that they may be ashamed,' he counselled the deacon of Kenardington, 'yet not to count them as Enemies, but admonish them as Brethren; & shew peculiar Tenderness towards such as appear peculiar Objects of it; yet so as not to lessen by such Condescensions our Usefulness amongst our own People.'[221] This was a theme he expanded upon in a 1761 letter to David Price, chaplain of Sheerness. 'But which so ever way you take, I beg you will take Heed to your self, and to your doctrine. Acknowledge what ever is good in any of the Methodists: acknowledge their Intention to be good, if you have Cause, even when they do wrong: say nothing to the Disadvantage of any of them, without being sure that it is true & proper to be divulged,' he wrote to Price.

Represent none of their practices or Tenets as being worse than they are. Preach diligently all those Gospel Truths, beyond which they have gone into Error. Take

---

[218] Westminster College, Cambridge, E/3/1/3: Terrick to Selina, countess of Huntington, 27 April 1771.
[219] LPL, Secker Papers 3, f. 232: Warburton to Secker, 5 Mar 1767.
[220] Ibid., f. 242: Secker to William Harrison, 11 Oct 1765.
[221] Ibid., f. 206: Secker to George Burnett, 6 July 1759.

notice and make a prudent use of their Differences amongst themselves. Affect not to place them or their Notions in a ludicrous Light & beware of ridiculing any Expression of theirs, which doth but so much as seem lacking to any one used in Scripture, or in the common Language of serious persons. Avoid all Levity in your Discourse & Behaviour. Expostulate with them, when occasion offers, strongly but meekly, concerning their Invectives against the Clergy. Speak of them to others, not with Bitterness or Contempt, but with good will & Compassion. Study the Scripture & the 39 Articles assiduously. Pray God earnestly to give you understanding & prudence. And when need requires it consult [me].[222]

Secker's own treatment of the Anglican evangelical and Methodist sympathizer, Thomas Haweis (c.1734–1820), suggests that he practised what he preached. From Cornwall, Haweis was a student at Oxford during the 1750s, when Secker was bishop there. In 1757 Haweis sought ordination, but the vehemently anti-Methodist bishop of Exeter, George Lavington, refused to recognize the testimonials to which he had to assent before Secker could ordain Haweis. Nevertheless, Haweis's good friend, the Hutchinsonian George Berkeley, jr., interceded on his behalf with Secker, who suggested that he would be glad to ordain Haweis in a private ceremony at Cuddesdon if Haweis could find three more people from Exeter to whose testimonials Lavington would not object. This Haweis did, and after his ordination into the diaconate on 9 October 1757, Secker, Haweis remembered, 'invited me to dine with him. In the interval between the time for Dinner, I sat with him in his study & conversed, I believed, for two hours .... He heard me with Candor, in general approved of my Openness; objected to nothing I had said, but added so many checks, cautions and guardings, that when he had done I could not possibly decide what he really meant me to say or do, & what not.'[223] Later, on 19 February 1758, when he ordained Haweis into the priesthood, Secker waived the formal license for his curacy to spare the young priest the associated fees.[224] As curate of St Mary Magdalen, Oxford, Haweis drew scorn upon himself from many quarters of the university for his evangelical sermons and for leading a group of evangelical young men in Oxford. When the new bishop of Oxford, John Hume, refused formally to licence Haweis to his curacy in 1762, Secker's waiver in 1758 came back to haunt Haweis. He turned to the archbishop for help, even offering to submit 300 of his sermons for inspection and examination. He found no assistance forthcoming from Lambeth. Though he 'received [Haweis] with much Civility', Secker was unwilling to intervene in the affairs of Oxford diocese. 'Mr. Haweis, during the time I was your diocesan I always protected you, tho' I had many Complaints preferred against you', Secker told him. 'You have now another diocesan, who must be more competent to judge your Conduct on the Spot than

---

[222] LPL, Secker Papers 3, ff. 246–47: Secker to David Price, 26 May 1761.

[223] Mitchell Library, New South Wales, Thomas Haweis MS Autobiography, ff. 32–37. See also, Edwin Welch, 'Haweis, Thomas (1734?–1820)', *ODNB*.

[224] Haweis MS Autobiography, f. 44.

I can be. You know how much the University is set against you ... but whether you really give the Offence, or they take it I cannot take upon myself to determine.'[225] There were, then, limits to his patience with Methodists, and Haweis had surpassed them. Haweis eventually left Oxford and moved to London, where he later took up the living of Aldwincle.[226]

Though generally tolerant of Methodists, Secker was not above advising the clergy in his dioceses to use sharp tactics if they thought it necessary. 'If the Methodists in your Parish have a place, where they assemble separately for religious worship, neither their Teacher nor they are excepted by the Toleration Act from Penalties against Non-Conformists, unless both he and They declare themselves to be Protestant Dissenters,' he wrote to the vicar of St John's Thanet. 'Not possibly some of them may be unwilling to call themselves Dissenters & to be esteemed such by other Persons. And in that Case, it may be worth while to try, what Effect the Fear of the Law will have upon them.'[227] Howell Harris, the early Methodist divine, even alleged that Secker proposed 'a scheme against the Methodists' to William Pitt and the speaker of the House of Commons in 1762, hoping it might be passed through Parliament.[228]

No evidence remains to substantiate Harris's claim, but the claim itself says much about the religious climate of England during the mid eighteenth century. Nearly everyone recognized that the tectonic plates of English religious life had still not settled, even seven decades after the Toleration Act's passage into law. In addition to religious pluralism, certain structural features of the Church's economy strained its ability to provide pastoral care of the quality many would have liked.

Rather than press for a wholesale restructuring of the ecclesiastical economy, Secker thought that the best way to deal with the challenges Church faced was by way of restorative reform, whose hallmark where pastoral affairs was concerned was a return to the primitive model of priesthood. So, for instance, when he proposed the revival of the ancient office of the rural deans, he hoped to encourage and to enliven clerical self-discipline.[229] Likewise, while he hoped augmentations would help lessen pluralism and non-residence, Secker nonetheless believed that, in the final analysis, clergy had to weigh which was more important, the temporal or the eternal. 'I hope [non-residence] will be rectified by the best Method, beyond Comparison,' he wrote to the Canterbury clergy in 1758, 'your own serious Reflections on what you owe to your Flocks, and

---

[225] Ibid., ff. 67–72.
[226] Cf. Bruce Hindmarsh, *John Newton and the English Evangelical Tradition* (Cambridge, 2001), pp. 89–91 for Secker's treatment of John Newton, the evangelical who sought ordination without a university degree.
[227] LPL, Secker Papers 3, f. 242: Secker to William Harrison, 11 Oct 1765.
[228] Quoted in Frank Baker, *John Wesley and the Church of England* (1970), p. 180.
[229] *Charges* (1753), pp. 186–87. Martin Benson had revived the practice of rural deans in the diocese of Gloucester a decade earlier: BL, Add. MS 39311, f. 50: Benson to Secker, 23 April 1743. See also, Burns, *Diocesan Revival*, pp. 75–107.

what you owe to the great Shepherd of Souls.' While he acknowledged that the clergy were 'expressly permitted by human Laws to be absent from your Cures', he nonetheless reminded them that they were 'answerable to an infinitely higher Tribunal for what God, and not Man alone, hath made your Duty'. At stake, he assured them, was 'the Peace of your own Souls and your final Comfort'.[230] Despite exhortations like Secker's, the eighteenth-century Anglican clergy, or so their nineteenth-century critics thought, had failed miserably to heed them. R.W. Church, the high church dean of St Paul's and historian of the Oxford Movement, adjudged of the pre-Victorian Church of England, 'It was slumbering and sleeping when the visitation days of change and trouble came upon it.' And to blame was a body of clergymen who had taken 'their obligations easily', who were tainted by their 'quiet worldliness'.[231] From the point of view of Dean Church and his contemporaries, restorative pastoral reform was wholly ineffectual. And for many, though certainly not all, the only way to address the pastoral 'abuses' was through utilitarian structural innovation.[232] Neither, though, did many nineteenth-century church reformers particularly approve of the eighteenth-century Church's relationship with the English state, a relationship whose particulars Secker and likeminded orthodox churchmen thought were both normative and necessary.

---

[230] *Charges* (1758), pp. 215–16.

[231] R.W. Church, *The Oxford Movement: Twelve Years, 1833–1845*, ed. G.F.A. Best (Chicago, 1970), p. 11. Whether the Victorian critics of the eighteenth-century Church of England were right in their diagnosis of the pastoral 'diseases' of the previous century remains hotly debated. Compare, for instance, Jeremy Gregory, review of *Doing the Duty of the Parish: Surveys of the Church in Hampshire 1810*, ed. Mark Smith (review no. 508) [www.history.ac.uk/ reviews/paper/gregory.html] with Mark Smith, review of *The Church of England in Industrialising Society. The Lancashire Parish of Whalley in the Eighteenth Century*, Michael Snape (review no. 444), author's response [www.history.ac.uk/ reviews/paper/snaperesp.html].

[232] Best, *Temporal Pillars*; Brose, *Church and Parliament*; and Thompson, *Bureaucracy and Church Reform* best cover the structural church reforms of the mid nineteenth century. But cf. Burns, *The Diocesan Revival* for a parallel movement in church reform.

Chapter Six

THE CHURCH AND THE STATE

Convocation embarrassed many among the orthodox during the eighteenth century. It was the nation's spiritual parliament, in its highest conception the spiritual co-equal to the Parliament at Westminster. In the first decades of the century, though, controversy spilled out from the Houses of Convocation, further fuelling the nation's already combustible political life. The crown subsequently interpreted the royal supremacy to include the power to stop Convocation from conducting substantive business. From 1717 until the mid nineteenth century, the gathering of the clergy in Convocation was purely ceremonial, an act that for many highlighted the Church's emasculation.[1]

The antiquarian-cleric William Stukeley was one of those frustrated with Convocation's crippled state, and in the spring of 1754 he wrote to Archbishop Herring with complaints.[2] 'It is a great grief of mind, whenever I think of that ill-fated day that the convocation gave up their right of granting money to the crown,' because it robbed the Church of England's clergy of political influence. 'Before then, the clergy were on a good footing, had some real worth in the eye of the government,' Stukeley argued. Now, however, they 'are a body suspended merely on the cobweb thread of a minister's favour and ready to be given up to the commons whenever an exigency of affairs affords a colour to it, and there is a pretended want of their church estates'. The opening of the 'floodgate of dissenters'; the 'neglect and desecration of the Sabbath'; 'popery, with its subtleties, triumphant'; and 'the infidelity daily spreading among us, chiefly from the impunity in printing wicked, blasphemous, anti-Christian, atheistic books' predictably followed from Convocation's inactivity. Worse yet, 'the government gives itself no concern about these mischiefs'. The solution, Stukeley insisted, was to revivify Convocation by granting the state £10,000 each year, 'for a clergyman in convocation would have as much power and be as highly esteemed as a member of parliament now is, when he can grant money'. The result, Stukeley contended, would be the clergy's 'person and his doctrine would have its due respect and influence'. Only voluntary clerical taxation would 'save

---

[1] Gerald Bray, *The Records of Convocation. XIX: Introduction* (Woodbridge, 2006), pp. 197–225 and Norman Sykes, *From Sheldon to Secker: Aspects of English Church History, 1660–1768* (Cambridge, 1959), pp. 36–67 detail the fortunes of Convocation during the eighteenth century.

[2] Unless otherwise noted, the quotations in this paragraph are drawn from Gerald Bray, *The Records of Convocation. XI: Canterbury, 1714–1760* (Woodbridge, 2006), pp. 383–85: Stukeley to Herring, 24 April 1754.

religion, morality, even the government, our country, from the impending destruction'.

Thomas Secker's address to Convocation in 1761 frankly acknowledged the criticism from those like Stukeley.[3] 'Since no business has been transacted for a long time now, intelligent people keep asking why we gather together here, with such laughable solemnity (for so they regard it), when we have been given nothing, and will be given nothing to do,' Secker conceded. Nevertheless, he defended Convocation's enforced inactivity. The Church, he argued, inadvertently benefited from having its bishops, deans, archdeacons, and elected parochial clergy gather together and do nothing because it showed the English people 'that they have nothing to fear from us, but rather expect all manner of good things'. Secker recognized, though, that many within the Church found Convocation's inactivity intolerable and that they thought the clergy should agitate for a restoration of 'whatever rights were assigned to earlier synods ... [so] the discipline of the ancient church, which is now in ruins and virtually extinct, may at last be revived and vigorously exercised, for our inertia has long since brought us down'. Yet while those who called for the revival of Convocation were 'generally very religious and highly learned', they had misjudged the situation entirely – 'they do not understand the times we live in, or what our present position is', Secker insisted. For one thing, allied against the Church of England were enemies who would 'drown everything in their outcries' and 'write ... of some supposed tyranny and easily fill the wide-open ears of many with their own imaginings' if Convocation were actually allowed to conduct business. Furthermore, debating the 'thousand specious, or not even specious, plans for reform' threatened to divide the clergy: '[w]hichever way we turn, we shall cause great offence and in the end perhaps never decide anything, or if we do decide on something, be unable to carry it out properly'. Most importantly, though, the nation's secular leaders were loath to unfetter Convocation for fear of what it might unleash. 'They are clearly afraid that if they load themselves up with ecclesiastical matters as well as military ones, they will be overwhelmed by the amount of business,' Secker counselled. 'They are also afraid that something might be upset, either by us or by others. This is why they act as cautiously, or sluggishly you might think, as they do. Nor do I try to do anything about it,' he added. 'Their fears are plausible enough in their way, and so if they are convinced by them, it is not something to be too indignant about.' It was best for the clergy simply to 'be content with the permission granted to us' and bide time.

The reasoning Secker employed in his 1761 Convocation address would not go down well with posterity. In the near future lay Victorian critics, who would

---

[3]   The *Oratio Synodalis* was a Latin sermon which Secker wrote for the opening of the 1761 Convocation. Unless otherwise noted, all quotations cited in this paragraph are drawn from *Oratio*, pp. 315–18. Though Secker did not deliver the sermon because of ill health, he published it subsequently: Norman Sykes, *From Sheldon to Secker: Aspects of English Church History, 1660–1768* (Cambridge, 1959), p. 222.

have excoriated the address as an admission of the Church's impotence and a spineless acceptance of abject subjugation to the state.[4] In the distant future lay those who would find an eighteenth-century churchman's thoughts on politics largely irrelevant, for the separation of church and state is integral to the secularization process which defines modernity.[5] Both understandings would have baffled Secker and for a host of reasons. Firstly, he recognized that there were political realities which the Church of England could not to alter. Secondly, he actually thought that the English confessional state was rightly ordered and that its imperfections were epiphenomenal not essential.[6] He and his orthodox contemporaries believed that the Church of England was at once *in apostolic succession* and *by law established*, which meant that while the Church was 'subject to the jurisdiction to the crown and established by the authority of statutes enacted by the king in parliament', it was not in consequence 'separated from the church that had been in Christ's presence ... but [instead] continued to take part in that church's spiritual activity and its history as a human association'.[7] The eighteenth-century orthodox could hold both ideas in their heads at the same time, even if some later could not. Finally, Secker reckoned that the fate of orthodox church reform hinged on the state's support: without it, he thought, nothing was possible. The mid eighteenth century, however, was a

---

[4]   See, for instance, S.A. Skinner, *Tractarians and the 'Condition of England': The Social and Political Thought of the Oxford Movement* (Oxford, 2004), pp. 87–138; idem, '"The duty of the State": Keble, the Tractarians, and Establishment', in *John Keble in Context*, ed. Kirstie Blair (2004) pp. 33–46; Peter B. Nockles, *The Oxford Movement in Context: Anglican High Churchmanship, 1760–1857* (Cambridge, 1994), pp. 63–103; idem, 'Church and King: Tractarian politics reappraised', in *From Oxford to the People: Reconsidering Newman and the Oxford Movement*, ed. Paul Vaiss (Leominster, 1996), pp. 93–126.

[5]   Alan Houston and Steven Pincus, 'Introduction. Modernity and later-seventeenth-century England', in *A Nation Transformed: England after the Restoration*, eds. Alan Houston and Steven Pincus (Cambridge, 2001), pp. 2–10. More generally, see David Hempton, 'Established churches and the growth of religious pluralism: a case study of christianisation and secularization in England since 1700', in *The Decline of Christendom in Western Europe, 1750–2000*, eds. Hugh McLeod and Werner Ustorf (Cambridge, 2003), pp. 81–98 and Philip S. Gorski, 'Historicizing the Secularization Debate: Church, State, and Society in Late Medieval and Early Modern Europe, ca. 1300 to 1700', *American Sociological Review* 65:1 (2000), pp. 138–67.

[6]   On England's confessional state, see J.C.D. Clark, 'Great Britain and Ireland', in *Enlightenment, Reawakening and Revolution, 1660–1815* (*Cambridge History of Christianity, VII*), eds. Stewart J. Brown and Timothy Tackett (Cambridge, 2006), pp. 54–71; idem, *English Society, 1660–1832: Religion, ideology and politics during the ancien régime* (Cambridge, 2000), pp. 26–34; idem, 'England's Ancien Régime as a Confessional State', *Albion* 21:3 (1989), pp. 450–74. Cf. Jeremy Black, 'Confessional state or elect nation? Religion and identity in eighteenth-century England', in *Protestantism and National Identity: Britain and Ireland, c.1650–c.1850*, eds. Tony Claydon and Ian McBride (Cambridge, 1998), pp. 53–74.

[7]   J.G.A. Pocock, 'Within the margins: the definitions of orthodoxy', in *The Margins of Orthodoxy: Heterodox Writing and Cultural Response, 1660–1750*, ed. Roger D. Lund (Cambridge, 1995), pp. 33–53, at p. 37.

time when the English state was hardly interested in promoting religious reform of the sort Secker advocated, for the pressures of war catalyzed religious liberalization and loosened the ties which bound together church and state.[8] The result was that the established Church far more committed to the union of throne and altar than its partner, the English state. This, suffice it to say, did not augur well for the fate of orthodox religious reform.

I

The appropriate relation of the Church of England to the English state had been a matter for debate since at least the early sixteenth century. On the one hand, the statutes of the Reformation Parliament – which defined the relationship between king and church, between the Church in England and the Church of Rome, and between England and other nations – were decidedly erastian. The Act for the Submission of the Clergy (1534: 25 Henry VIII, c.19) constrained Convocation from doing business 'unless the King's royal assent and licence may be to them be had to make, promulge and execute such constitutions and ordinances as shall be made in the same and thereto give your royal assent and authority', while the Act for the Restraint of Appeals (1533: 24 Henry VIII, c.12) declared that 'this realm of England is an empire ... governed by one supreme head and king ... unto whom a body politic, compact of all Sorts of degrees and people, divided in terms, and by names of spirituality and temporalty, been bounden and owe to bear next to God a natural and humble obedience'.[9] The Henrician Reformation was an act of state; and underlying it was the idea that the Church in England was necessarily, indeed obviously, subordinate to the state.[10]

---

[8] See, for instance, Stephen Conway, *War, State, and Society in Mid-Eighteenth Century Britain and Ireland* (Oxford, 2006), pp. 170–92. For the later eighteenth century, see Stephen Conway, *The British Isles and the War of American Independence* (Oxford, 2000), pp. 239–66; G.M. Ditchfield, 'Ecclesiastical Legislation during the Ministry of the Younger Pitt, 1783–1801', *Parliamentary History* 19:1 (2000), pp. 64–80; idem, 'Ecclesiastical Policy under Lord North', in *The Church of England, c.1689–c.1833: From Toleration to Tractarianism*, eds. John Walsh, Colin Haydon, and Stephen Taylor (Cambridge, 1993), pp. 228–46.

[9] G.R. Elton, *The Tudor Constitution: Documents and Commentary* (Cambridge, 1962), pp. 339, 344. Cf. Henry Chadwick, 'Royal ecclesiastical supremacy', in *Humanism, Reform and the Reformation: The Career of Bishop John Fisher*, eds. Brendan Bradshaw and Eamon Duffy (Cambridge, 1989), pp. 169–204.

[10] G.W. Bernard, *The King's Reformation: Henry VIII and the Remaking of the English Church* (New Haven, CT, 2005); Eamon Duffy, *The Stripping of the Altars: Traditional Religion in England, 1400–1580* (New Haven, CT, 1992), esp. pp. 377–447. Cf. Ethan Shagan, *Popular Politics and the English Reformation* (Cambridge, 2003). Quentin Skinner, 'The state', in *Political Innovation and Conceptual Change*, eds. Terence Ball,

Richard Hooker (1554–1600), by contrast, offered an alternate reading of English church-state relations to the erastian Henrician one.[11] While acknowledging the royal supremacy over the Church of England, Hooker rejected Caesar-papism, the notion that the civil power has absolute supremacy in ecclesiastical matters.[12] Rather, he argued for the essential unity of church and state. 'For the truth is that the Church and Commonwealth are names which import things really different,' Hooker contended. 'But those things are accidents and such accidents and such accidents as may and should always dwell together in one subject.'[13] The unity of church and state, to Hooker's way of thinking, rested not on the erastian subjection of one to the other but on the fact that both institutions derived their authority from God and were, as a result, ultimately subject to him. This, in turn, implied that the purposes of church and state were identical.[14]

For the next two centuries, these sixteenth-century conceptions of church-state relations – the one baldly erastian, the other deeply organicist – formed the poles of English Christian politico-theology. The former thrived in practice during the Interregnum and had wide currency in principle across much of the latter half of the seventeenth century.[15] Yet raw erastianism's attraction waned during the 'long' eighteenth century. The Glorious Revolution, for instance, catalyzed a vibrant critique of erastianism among non-jurors and sympathetic, if conformist, high churchmen.[16] By at least the second quarter of the eighteenth

James Farr, and Russell L. Hanson (Cambridge, 1989), pp. 90–131 anatomizes the linguistic shift by which *state* 'came to be accepted as the master noun of political argument'.

[11] Peter Lake, *Anglicans and Puritans?: Presbyterianism and English Conformist Thought from Whitgift to Hooker* (1988), pp. 145–238 and idem, 'Business as Usual? The Immediate Reception of Hooker's *Ecclesiastical Polity*', *JEH* 52:3 (2001), pp. 456–86 make clear that Hooker's works aimed to shape, not reflect, the English religio-political realities of the late sixteenth century.

[12] John Guy, 'Monarchy and counsel: models of the state', in *The Sixteenth Century, 1485–1603*, ed. Patrick Collinson (Oxford, 2002), pp. 125–26; Howell A. Lloyd, 'Constitutionalism', in *The Cambridge History of Political Thought, 1450–1700*, eds. J.H. Burns and Mark Goldie (Cambridge, 1991), pp. 279–83.

[13] Richard Hooker, *Of the Laws of Ecclesiastical Polity*, ed. Arthur Stephen McGrade (Cambridge, 1997), p. 134.

[14] John Gascoigne, 'Church and State Unified: Hooker's Rationale for the English Post-Reformation', *Journal of Religious History* 21:1 (1997), pp. 23–34. For Hooker's posthumous reception, see idem, 'The Unity of Church and State Challenged: Responses to Hooker from the Restoration to the Nineteenth-Century Age of Reform', *Journal of Religious History* 21:1 (1997), pp. 60–79; Diarmaid MacCulloch, 'Richard Hooker's Reputation', *EHR* 107:473 (2002), pp. 773–812.

[15] John Marshall, 'The Ecclesiology of the Latitude-men, 1660–1689: Stillingfleet, Tillotson, and "Hobbism"', *JEH* 36:3 (1985), pp. 407–27; Jeffrey R. Collins, *The Allegiance of Thomas Hobbes* (Oxford, 2005).

[16] Robert D. Cornwall, *Visible and Apostolic: The Constitution of the Church in High Church Anglican and Non-Juror Thought* (1993), pp. 73–93. But cf. Andrew Starkie, 'Contested Histories of the English Church: Gilbert Burnet and Jeremy Collier', *Huntington Library Quarterly* 68:1–2 (2005), pp. 335–51.

century, the Hookerian vision of an organically united church and state was hegemonic – the 'vast majority of members of the Church of England, both clerical and lay, believed ... not only that a church establishment was necessary, but that church and state were linked in an indissoluble union'.[17] Tellingly, disestablishment was not even an option seriously considered during Thomas Secker's lifetime.[18] Instead, church and state ineluctably coinhered such that the Church 'upheld the "natural" hierarchy of mutual obligations which were thought to provide social cohesion', while the state 'protected the legal Establishment of Christianity as the appropriate agent for the diffusion of benevolence and public morality'.[19] On this view, church and state in England were not unlike conjoined twins, in sharing vital organs but having separate heads.

Secker's views on the proper relationship of church to state placed him squarely within the orthodox mainstream. His, though, was an understanding less the product of systematic reasoning than an acceptance of received wisdom. That prescriptive knowledge rested firmly on well over a thousand years of historical experience. Church and state had, since Constantine the Great,

---

[17] S.J.C. Taylor, 'Church and State in England in the Mid-Eighteenth Century: The Newcastle Years, 1742–1762' (University of Cambridge Ph.D. thesis, 1987), pp. 41–66, at p. 41. See also, A.M.C. Waterman, *Political Economy and Christian Theology Since the Enlightenment: Essays in Political History* (New York, 2004), esp. pp. 31–69; Clark, *English Society, 1660–1832*, pp. 43–123, 232–317; Rebecca Louise Warner, 'Early Eighteenth Century Low Churchmanship: The Glorious Revolution to the Bangorian Controversy' (University of Reading Ph.D. thesis, 1999), pp. 152–219; and Stephen Taylor, 'William Warburton and the Alliance of Church and State', *JEH* 43:2 (1992), pp. 271–86. But cf. R.W. Greaves, 'The Working of an Alliance: a Comment on Warburton', in *Essays in Modern English Church History, in Memory of Norman Sykes*, eds. G.V. Bennett and John Walsh (Oxford, 1966), pp. 163–80; and Sykes, *Church and State*, pp. 284–331.

[18] G.F.A. Best, *Temporal Pillars: Queen Anne's Bounty, the Ecclesiastical Commissioners, and the Church of England* (Cambridge, 1964), pp. 35–37; Edward R. Norman, *Church and Society in England, 1770–1970* (Oxford, 1976), p. 19; David Hempton, *Religion and political culture in Britain and Ireland: From the Glorious Revolution to the decline of empire* (Cambridge, 1996), pp. 3–4; Peter M. Doll, *Revolution, Religion, and National Identity: Imperial Anglicanism in British North America, 1745–1795* (2000), p. 13. See also, idem, 'The Idea of the Primitive Church in High Church Ecclesiology from Samuel Johnson to J.H. Hobart', *AEH* 55:1 (1996), pp. 6–43, at p. 10, which argues that the late eighteenth and early nineteenth centuries witnessed 'the working out of the thinking about episcopacy ... from an episcopal church identified with but hampered by its association with the state, to one that defines its mission in large part as distinct from civil society'. It is telling, as well, that *disestablishment* has nineteenth-century origins: *OED*.

[19] Norman, *Church and Society in England*, p. 15. Furthermore, orthodox theories of church-state relations were not at their heart contractarian, for it was the divine right of governors which undergirded orthodox theories of obligation and obedience: Gerd Mischler, 'English Political Sermons, 1714–1742: A Case Study in the Theory of the "Divine Right of Governors" and the Ideology of Order', *British Journal of Eighteenth-Century Studies* 24:1 (2001), pp. 33–61; Waterman, *Political Economy and Christian Theology*, pp. 41–43, 56–60; Robert Hole, *Pulpits, politics and public order in England, 1760–1832* (Cambridge, 1989), esp. pp. 12–21.

worked together, more or less in union, so that the interdependence of the two had a history stretching back well over a millennium. By the early eighteenth century that necessary interdependence was an idea so deeply ingrained in the Western Christian worldview as to be almost axiomatic; it was also tangibly real in Secker's England. Politics is about exercising power, just as much as it is about obtaining it, and in both theory and fact 'the Church was a political institution, an inseparable part of politics and of the governmental apparatus of the English state'.[20] The ecclesiastical and legal systems so tightly intertwined, for instance, that it was hard even to tell where one began and the other ended.[21] The parish was also the atomic unit of local government, and at the heart of every town and village in the country lay the parish church, which served as the centre of both local religious and civic life. In the localities, the Church distributed poor relief, administered local charities, ran schools, and inculcated Georgian loyalism from its pulpits. The Church likewise claimed an important political role at the centre, where the bishops sat by right of office in the House of Lords. The institution, then, was fully enmeshed in the warp and weave of national political life. It is not surprising that Thomas Secker accepted the propriety of the status quo – it would have been shocking had he not.

Insofar as Secker publicly articulated his thoughts on church-state relations, he did so in his occasional sermons, most often preached at feasts, fasts, and national political anniversaries.[22] Not surprisingly, Secker's expressed conception of church-state relations was religiously grounded. While man entered voluntarily into society, he did so to fulfil a divine purpose. 'We experience an inward propension to assemble and unite,' Secker argued, because '[w]e cannot ... either improve or enjoy ourselves, as God designed, but in society.' Indeed, he continued, government was 'so powerfully conducive to the attainment of these most valuable ends, which doubtless our Maker designed to be attained, [that] the establishment of it in the world ought consequently to be regarded, as a most important law of God and nature, directly flowing from the constitution of things'. The purpose of government, then, was to constrain the 'appetites, the passions, the caprices of men' and to give 'a public direction ... both for defence against external dangers, and for establishing inward order in the community'.[23] Membership in society likewise entailed obligations and duties because 'society cannot subsist, without a due subordination of one part of it to another; that is,

20   Taylor, 'Church and State in England', p. 3.
21   Best, *Temporal Pillars*, pp. 37–43.
22   James Joseph Caudle, 'Measures of Allegiance: Sermon Culture and the Creation of a Public Discourse of Obedience and Resistance in Georgian Britain, 1714–1760' (Yale University Ph.D. thesis, 1996), pp. 192–286; D. Napthine and W.A. Speck, 'Clergymen and Conflict, 1660–1763', *SCH* 19 (1983), pp. 238–46; Françoise Deconinck-Brossard, 'The Churches and the '45', *SCH* 19 (1983), pp. 253–62; H.P. Ippel, 'Blow the Trumpet, Sanctify the Fast', *Huntington Library Quarterly* 44 (1980), pp. 43–60.
23   'Sermon CXXXIX. Duty of Subjection to the Public Magistrate. Preached in the Parish Church of St Mary, Lambeth, October 25, 1761 [Titus 3:1–2]', in *WTS*, IV, p. 33.

without government and obedience'. Consequently, the right to resist society's divinely ordained governors was extraordinarily narrow: 'if they treat us hardly, or manage the concerns of the nation wrongly, we are to bear it with patience'.[24] Even St Paul 'enjoined ... dutiful obedience' to the 'extremely bad' government of 'the cruel and vicious emperor Nero'![25]

Governing the nation's governors was a providential God.[26] For Secker, as for most of his contemporaries, providence explained historical development. 'The same wise and good being, who hath fitted the whole frame of this world to the various wants of his creatures, hath fitted the events of things to our reformation and moral improvement,' he argued during the Anglo-Spanish war of 1739. 'Were they to be considered as events only, it would be folly not to learn from them; but as they are lessons intended by heaven for our instruction, it is impiety also.'[27] When the Pretender enjoyed unexpected success during the initial stages of the Forty-Five, for instance, Secker explained it as God's providential punishment. Had the English not forsaken God, the Jacobites would never have done so well during the war. 'The natural consequences, and superadded punishments of our disregard to him, have appeared very plainly for some time, and are daily becoming more visible and sensible,' Secker warned.[28]

God watched so closely over England because it was his chosen nation, the new Israel.[29] And Secker preached that the nation's security and the individual's moral health were symbiotically linked. To be 'truly religious' required the individual Christian to do three things: 'reasonable Government of ourselves, good Behaviour towards our Fellow creatures, and Dutifulness to our Maker'.[30] The individual's first obligation was to pay God the reverence due Him. 'But the least apprehension of a perfect being superintending us, must surely magnify

---

[24] Ibid. p. 35.

[25] Ibid., p. 37.

[26] Françoise Deconinck-Brossard, 'Acts of God, Acts of Men: Providence in Seventeenth- and Eighteenth-Century England and France', *SCH* 41 (2005), pp. 356–75; Jonathan Clark, 'Providence, Predestination and Progress; or, did the Enlightenment Fail?', *Albion* 35:4 (2004), pp. 559–89; William E. Burns, *An Age of Wonders: Prodigies, politics and providence in England, 1657–1727* (Manchester, 2002), pp. 149–84; John Spurr, '"Virtue, religion, and the government": the Anglican uses of providence', in *The Politics of Religion in Restoration England*, eds. Tim Harris, Paul Seaward, and Mark Goldie (Oxford, 1990), pp. 29–47. But cf. Kaspar von Greyerz, 'Secularization in Early Modern England (1660–c.1750)', in *Säkularisierung, Dechristianisierung, Rechristianisierung in neuzeilichen Europa*, ed. Hartmut Lehman (Göttingen, 1997), pp. 90–95.

[27] 'Sermon CXXX. Preached before the House of Lords in the Abbey-Church of Westminster, on Thursday, May 29, 1739 [Psalm 106:12–13], in *WTS*, III, p. 460.

[28] 'Sermon CXIX. Preached on a General Fast [1 Peter 5:6]', in *WTS*, III, p. 309.

[29] Bob Harris, *Politics and the Nation: Britain in the Mid-Eighteenth-Century* (Oxford, 2002), pp. 290–95; Conway, *War, State, and Society in Mid-Eighteenth-Century Britain and Ireland*, pp. 173–75. But cf. Steven N. Zwicker, 'England, Israel, and the Triumph of Roman Virtue', in *Millenarianism and Messianism in English Literature and Thought, 1650–1800*, ed. Richard H. Popkin (Leiden, 1988), pp. 37–64.

[30] *Lectures*, p. 1.

beyond expression the sense, how very imperfect we are,' Secker admonished, 'and convince us, that the utmost reverence, of which we are capable towards such a one, if such a one there be, will fall vastly short of what we owe.'[31] Because the English lived in 'thoughtless and irreligious times,' he advised that they first strengthen their own faith. 'The duty ... of the generality of Christians, in regard to the enemies of their faith and practice, besides pitying them and praying for them, goes little further, than first securing themselves, and those who belong to them, from the contagion,' Secker counselled.[32] But, he feared, innate human depravity might thwart people from fulfilling their religious duties. 'And in proportion as the frame of any moral agent is compounded of superior and inferior principles, the more he will be obliged to disregard and deny the lower, in order to follow the dictates of the higher,' he reckoned. 'But wretched man, fallen and sinful, lies under a heavier necessity of this kind.'[33]

This propensity to sin both exposed the individual sinner to eternal damnation and endangered the nation. Secker pointed to the especially malign consequences for the nation of two pernicious individual sins – the decline of religious zeal and the pursuit of luxury.[34] Many refused to acknowledge God's providence. 'Acknowledging a Sovereign Lord of the world, without standing in awe of him is doubtless a most astonishing inconsistency', Secker fretted, 'and yet I conceive it will appear, on inquiry, the main source of those great and many sins, for which we are met here to express our concern.'[35] Others thirsted unslakeably for luxury. 'We have encreased amusement and gaieties to a degree unexampled, just when providence hath called us most loudly to thoughtful consideration,' Secker groused. Not surprisingly, 'these indiscretions have produced personal miseries and national inconveniences without number'.[36] Some argued that an economic system which produced 'superfluities' unintentionally benefited society – Secker countered that 'national wealth, and private plenty of the conveniences of life are desirable in communities, but luxury and extravagance destructive to them'.[37]

---

[31] 'Sermon CXVIII. Preached on a General Fast [1 Peter 5:6]', in *WTS*, III, p. 294.

[32] 'Sermon CXXXVI. Preached in the Church of St Mary-le-Bone, December 4, 1754 at the Yearly Meeting of the Religious Societies [Malachi 3:16]', in *WTS*, III, p. 579.

[33] 'Sermon LXVIII. The Meaning of the Expression, of Taking Up the Cross [March 8:24]', in *WTS*, II, p. 307.

[34] Maxine Berg and Elizabeth Eger, 'The Rise and Fall of the Luxury Debates', in *Luxury in the Eighteenth Century: Debates, Desires and Delectable Goods*, eds. Maxine Berg and Elizabeth Eger (Basingstoke, 2005), pp. 7–27.

[35] 'Sermon CXVIII. Preached on a General Fast', p. 295.

[36] 'Sermon CXXII. Preached in 1746, on the Victory at Culloden [2 Cor. 1:9–10]', in *WTS*, III, p. 355.

[37] 'Sermon CXXIV. Preached on a General Fast [Psalm 122:6],' in *WTS*, III, p. 381. Cf. Bernard Mandeville, *The Fable of the Bees*, ed. Philip Harth (1970); Jill Phillips Ingram, *Idioms of Self-Interest: Credit, Identity, and Property in English Renaissance Literature* (New York, 2006).

By explicitly linking individual and corporate sin, Secker opened the way for the established Church of England to play a necessary role in the nation's life. The sins of a nation required God's temporal punishment as proof of his power and mercy; consequently, protecting individuals and the nation from God's providential punishment required clerical guidance.[38] 'For promoting religious Knowledge and Practice is not only the express Design of all Church Government, but a matter ... of great Importance to the State also,' he argued, 'since neither private Life can be happy, nor the public Welfare secure for any long time, without the Belief of the Doctrines and Observance of Christianity.'[39] While any Christian church might promote these beliefs, the innate virtues of the Church of England were, to Secker's way of thinking, self-evident: 'our religion ... is undeniably the most rational and worthy of God, the most humane and beneficial to men, the furthest from being either tyrannical or burdensome, the freest from superstition, enthusiasm, and gloominess of any in the world'.[40]

Secker unequivocally connected the health of the body politic directly to the status of the established Church. The Church of England 'is established with such care, that the support of it is inseparable from that of the civil government', he contended, 'yet happily with such moderation, as to bear hard on none who dissent from it'.[41] The beneficial effects of this mutually supportive relationship between the civil and religious authorities were evident to him. '[A] right belief in God, and his various dispensations towards men, promotes, beyond all things, both the virtue and the happiness of mankind,' he averred. People thus were 'guarded, at once, from the dreadful evils both of impiety and superstition; and carefully taught to discharge the duties, and bear the afflictions of human life'.[42] In his instructions to ordinands, Secker spoke forthrightly about the application of the principle of subordination to church-state relations: 'Without union there cannot be a sufficient degree either of strength or beauty: and without subordination there cannot long be union. Therefore obey, as the apostle directs, them that rule over you; and promote their honour, their credit, their influence.'[43]

Thomas Secker envisioned the English church-state like a piece of tongue and groove furniture. In theory, no glue or nails was needed to bind the parts because they fit together neatly, tightly, almost perfectly. The piece's sturdiness came not so much from the individual parts but from the strength of their union. Theory, suffice it to say, sometimes fell short of practice, all the more so because

---

[38] 'Sermon CXXII. Preached in 1746, on the Victory at Culloden', pp. 346–58.

[39] *Lectures*, pp. 7–8.

[40] 'Sermon CXX. Preached on the Occasion of the Rebellion in Scotland in 1745 [2 Samuel 10:12]', in *WTS*, III, p. 320.

[41] Ibid.

[42] 'Sermon CXXXIX. The Duty of Subjection to the Public Magistrate. Preached in the Parish Church of St Mary, Lambeth, 25 October 1761 [Titus 3:1–2]', in *WTS*, IV, pp. 33–34.

[43] 'Instructions given to Candidates for Orders after their Subscribing the Articles', in *WTS*, IV, p. 213.

England during Secker's adulthood was a one-party state dominated by the Whigs.[44] In that political world the established Church had a significant voice because, despite a long history of Whig anticlericalism, Edmund Gibson worked during the 1720s with Walpole and others to forge a Church-Whig alliance that proved remarkably durable.[45]

The terms of the alliance were seemingly clear-cut. The state inculcated 'true religion', which meant protecting and promoting the Church of England. In return, the Church inculcated Georgian loyalism – which, the orthodox argued, entailed fostering orthodoxy – and helped the Whigs govern the nation.[46] While it may have been that 'in the actual working of the constitutional partnership of ecclesiastical and temporal jurisdictions, the temporal held a firm superiority', both sides in the church-state – and in the Church-Whig – alliance accepted that they had reciprocal obligations.[47] Perhaps inevitably things were not all sweetness and light in relations between church and state, and tempers flared up when one partner in the alliance thought the other had failed to uphold its end of the mutual bargain. The story of religion and politics during Secker's time on the episcopal bench was about managing the (increasing) tensions in the relationship; and the fate of orthodox reform depended on the Church's success in dealing with them, for without the state's support, Secker reckoned, orthodox reform was a dead-letter. That often required the Church to accept compromises

---

[44] But see Linda Colley, *In Defiance of Oligarchy: The Tory Party, 1714–60* (Cambridge, 1982).

[45] Norman Sykes, *Edmund Gibson, Bishop of London, 1669–1748: A Study in Politics and Religion in the Eighteenth Century* (Oxford, 1926), pp. 83–122 remains the most thorough examination of Edmund Gibson's role in reconciling the Church to the Whigs. See also, Stephen Taylor, '"Dr. Codex" and the Whig "Pope": Edmund Gibson, Bishop of London, 1716–1748', in *Lords of Parliament: Studies, 1714–1914*, ed. R.W. Davis (Stanford, CA, 1995), pp. 9–28. Until quite recently, historians took a rather dim view of the Church-Whig alliance. Geoffrey Holmes, *Religion and Party in late Stuart England* (1975), pp. 29–30 argues that the Walpolean regime subjugated the Church. Roy Porter, *English Society in the Eighteenth Century* (1990), p. 173 likewise contends, 'Yet if the Church had a strong grip on society, government had a stronger grip upon the Church ... [After 1717] the Church had no independent, corporate spiritual leadership of its own, for prelates were generally thick as thieves with the politicians who were their nursing fathers.' Cf. Jeffrey S. Chamberlain, *Accommodating High Churchmen: The Clergy of Sussex, 1700–1745* (Urbana and Chicago, 1997), which argues that the Tory clergy of Sussex in the 1700s transferred their allegiance to the Whigs by the 1730s not out of base self-interest but for a variety of other reasons, including the fact that the Whigs had convinced many that they were the most able and committed defenders of the established Church. Jeremy Gregory, *Restoration, Reformation, and Reform, 1660–1828: Archbishops of Canterbury and their Diocese* (Oxford, 2000), pp. 97–98 echoes Chamberlain's findings. Reed Browning, *Political and Constitutional Ideas of the Court Whigs* (Baton Rouge, LA, 1982) and H.T. Dickinson, *Liberty and Property: Political Ideology in Eighteenth-Century Britain* (New York, 1977), pp. 57–90, 121–162 survey the ideological content of Georgian Whiggism.

[46] Hannah Smith, *Georgian Monarchy: Politics and Culture, 1714–1760* (Cambridge, 2006), pp. 161–89.

[47] Best, *Temporal Pillars*, p. 43.

– such as Convocation's suspension – which were unpalatable to some, then and later.

II

The fundamental fact of English political life during the mid eighteenth century was the predominance of the Whigs, and Thomas Secker's political influence derived from his intimacy with the most powerful among the Old Corps Whigs. His relationships with Newcastle and Hardwicke transcended that of patron and client. The prospective benefits of such close association between Secker and two of the members of the Pelhamite triumvirate were evident. Newcastle and Hardwicke thought an alliance with a well-respected cleric like Secker brought credit to the government and girded the Church-Whig alliance.[48] For his part, Secker believed that his friendship with the Pelhamites assured the Church an influential voice in shaping public policy.

Yet equally clear prospective disadvantages attended so personal an attachment to the Pelhamite Whigs. If Secker's political influence depended on his friendship with Newcastle and Hardwicke, that influence would surely weaken if the they went into opposition against the king's government, as both did after George III's accession in 1760. The young king took up the crown determined not to depend upon the Old Corps Whigs to conduct his business in Parliament, and Newcastle's was the most prominent scalp he took.[49] With his patron and friend out of power after 1762, Secker worked to preserve friendly relations with the king's ministers, which at times required him to walk a tight line. In 1767, for instance, he stayed away from the House of Lords, 'partly

[48] This principle could even apply to those who were not card-carrying Whigs. In 1747, for instance, Newcastle implored the high churchman (and sometime Tory) Thomas Sherlock to become the new archbishop of Canterbury; when Sherlock refused, Newcastle helped secure Sherlock's translation to the vacant see of London in 1748 on account of 'the dignity that attends the Government in having such a man resident at Fulham': Edward Carpenter, *Thomas Sherlock, 1678–1761* (1936), pp. 136–39; William Gibson, *The Achievement of the Anglican Church, 1689–1800: The Confessional State in Eighteenth Century England* (Lewiston, 1996), p. 87.

[49] Secker had been one of the leading voices encouraging Newcastle to remain at the Treasury upon George III's accession: Philip C. Yorke, *The life and correspondence of Philip Yorke, Earl of Hardwicke, Lord High Chancellor of Great Britain* (New York, 1977), III, p. 307: Hugh Valence Jones to the duchess of Newcastle, 28 Oct 1760. For Newcastle's opposition, see Reed Browning, *The Duke of Newcastle* (New Haven, CT, 1975), pp. 291–335; W.M. Elofson, *The Rockingham Connection and the Second Founding of the Whig Party, 1768–1773* (Montreal and Kingston, 1996); Stephen Michael Farrell, 'Divisions, Debates and "Dis-ease": The Rockingham Whig Party and the House of Lords, 1760–1785' (University of Cambridge Ph.D. thesis, 1993), pp. 141–96; and Paul Langford, *The First Rockingham Administration, 1765–1766* (Oxford, 1973).

unwilling to vote against either my old Friend, the Duke of Newcastle, or the Kings Ministers with whom I must frequently have Business to transact. The Duke approved my Conduct.'[50] Some derided Secker for courting the king's new ministers while at the same time, as they saw it, being disloyal to his old friend. 'The Archbishop, conscious of not having been at Newcastle's last levee, and ashamed of appearing at Lord Bute's first, pretended he had been going by on his way from Lambeth,' Horace Walpole wrote to George Montague in the early summer of 1762, 'and upon inquiry had found out it was Lord Bute's levee, and so had thought he might well go in – I am glad he thought he might as well tell it.'[51]

On the whole, though, Secker navigated skilfully through the political shoals since neither George III nor his prime ministers punished him for his close association with the Old Corps Whigs. Secker got on well enough with Bute and found the king's favourite helpful at times.[52] While there was little warmth of feeling between Secker and George Grenville, that owed to a conflict of personalities not a lack of royal favour. The only one of the king's prime ministers during the 1760s whom Secker personally disliked was William Pitt. 'How many more Caprices he may have, private & publick, if he gets into power again, no one can foresee,' Secker complained to Newcastle in 1766. 'But he hath shewn abundantly, both formerly & of late, that nothing less than full power will suffice him. And I dread to think what in that plentitude he may attempt. Perhaps at present he is a little mortified & sunk: but is he not capable of recovering himself, & talking in a quite different strain, as soon as ever an Opportunity appears?'[53] Even still Secker got on professionally with Pitt and managed to prosecute the Church's business during his ministry.

By allying themselves so closely with the Whigs, churchmen like Secker opened themselves up to the criticism of later generations that they had prostituted themselves through their sordid erastianism. Secker would have countered that the Church was an independent spiritual body, that the Whig party had committed itself to supporting the Church wholeheartedly, and that an alliance with the ruling regime, so long as it did not compromise the Church's integrity or independence, was actually in the best interests of both church and state. Indeed because the Old Corps Whigs had, with rare exceptions, proved themselves stalwart defenders of the established Church, the Church best served its interests by supporting and encouraging loyalty to the Whig regime and the house of Hanover. Nowhere was it more important to do so than in England's fractious clerical nursery, the University of Oxford.

---

[50] *Autobiography*, p. 60.
[51] *Walpole's Correspondence*, X, p. 35: Walpole to Montagu, 8 June 1762.
[52] *Autobiography*, p. 43.
[53] BL, Add. MS 32974, ff. 17–18: Secker to TPH, 16 Feb 1766.

III

Oxford was not a hotbed of Georgian loyalism during the mid eighteenth century. Unlike Cambridge, where more widespread ministerial patronage and a tradition of political heterodoxy had combined to create a Whig-friendly environment,[54] Oxford solidly allied itself not just with the proscribed Tories, but with the Jacobites, whose ostensible goal was to overturn the Hanoverian succession.[55] Because the university served as one of the nation's two clerical training grounds and because Oxford joined the City of London as one of the acknowledged centres of opposition to the Old Corps, the Hanoverian kings and their ministries worked hard to alter the opposition culture there. The limited scope of the crown patronage in Oxford made it difficult to pack the colleges with those sympathetic to the government, and only Christ Church, Merton, Wadham, and Exeter colleges could be counted as firmly in the Whig camp.[56] Thus a Whig bishop of Oxford's brief extended well beyond the pastoral supervision of his diocese to include an active political role in advancing Whig interests in the overwhelmingly Tory university and county.

Only sure hands were allowed to take up the diocesan reins of Oxford. Besides having studied at the University, prospective bishops needed to have demonstrated unquestioned loyalty to the Whig regime; the political acumen to report accurately on Oxford's political life; and the fortitude to promote patiently and skilfully the government's policies and agenda in a hostile climate. Scholarly ability also helped the credibility of candidates for the Oxford episcopate. It is telling that the two bishops of Oxford between the '15 and the '45 – John Potter and Thomas Secker – were later elevated to Canterbury. By the end of the eighteenth century, Oxford had shrugged off its mantle as the centre of anti-Georgian political sympathies and purposefully allied itself with the government against the challenge from Dissent.[57] Though the Whig conquest of Oxford came after Secker's death, it built upon the foundations he helped to lay.

Secker's first substantive involvement in the University's political life came when the vice-chancellor invited him to preach the Act Sermon during the

---

[54] D.A. Winstanley, *Unreformed Cambridge: A Study of Certain Aspects of the University in the Eighteenth Century* (Cambridge, 1935); John Gascoigne, *Cambridge in the age of the enlightenment: science, religion, and politics from the Restoration to the French Revolution* (Cambridge, 1989), pp. 71–114; and Peter Searby, *A History of the University of Cambridge, Volume III: 1750–1870* (Cambridge, 1997), pp. 386–422 explore the political world of eighteenth-century Cambridge.

[55] R.J. Robson, *The Oxfordshire Election of 1754* (1949); W.R. Ward, *Georgian Oxford: University Politics in the Eighteenth Century* (Oxford, 1958); *HUO: Eighteenth Century*, pp. 99–190, 401–68; and J.C.D. Clark, *Samuel Johnson: literature, religion, and English cultural politics from the Restoration to Romanticism* (Cambridge, 1994) anatomize the political world of eighteenth-century Oxford.

[56] L.S. Sutherland, 'Political Respectability, 1751–1771', in *HUO: Eighteenth Century*, p. 133.

[57] L.G. Mitchell, 'Politics and Revolution, 1772–1800', in ibid., pp. 163–90.

summer of 1733.[58] Secker's sermon was a call to Georgian loyalism. On the afternoon of 8 July from the pulpit of St Mary's, Oxford, Secker expounded upon 'the advantages of right Education' and the consequent 'duty of endeavouring, that these advantages may be obtained'.[59] The first half of the sermon uncontroversially extolled the virtues of a Christian education. In its second half, though, Secker suggested '[t]hat all persons concerned should endeavour with united care, in their several stations, that these advantages may be effectually obtained; especially in the places dedicated to that purpose'. Secker was no Sacheverell who breathed fire; instead he emphasized that the Hanoverians were friends of religion. 'The publick care, in this respect, we must ever gratefully own, continued through a long succession of our Princes; and flourishing still in its height, under the Administration of a King, zealous for the happiness of his people, and resolute to maintain all the rights of his subjects,' he reassured his audience. 'Next to those who assur'd and experience'd Protection, we cannot but thankfully acknowledge the gracious Munificence of his Royal Consort; therefore bountiful to Religion and learning, because she most intimately knows their value, and most affectionately esteems them.'[60] This was a mantra of those promoting Whig Anglicanism during the mid eighteenth century. Lest his audience think that inculcating Toryism and Jacobitism among the students was a way to safeguard sound learning and buttressed morals against heterodoxy or anticlericalism, Secker counselled the dons 'conscientiously [to] teach that dutiful obedience and honour, which Christianity requires all subjects to pay; and which the happiest subjects in the world ought to pay with the chearfullest gratitude'. The good teacher 'will discourage with all possible care, the rage of party zeal; which warm and unexperienc'd minds too often mistake for publick spirit', he continued.

> Admitted in this fair disguise, it possesses the whole man; tinctures his way of thinking on almost every subject; leads him to hate and injure worthy persons, to admire and associate amongst very bad ones; with whom this immoral temper stands in the stead of all merit, whilst indeed it hinders the acquiring of any. As life goes on, these evils increase: of which all the world complains, but unhappily indulges them at the same time; instead of each curbing, on its own side, the eagerness and keenness of so malevolent a principle. Young persons should therefore be reminded, that the seats of learning are purposefully secreted from the busy scenes of life; that the time for engaging in those will come but too soon, and meanwhile the generous ardour of youth should be exerted in making the preparation of useful knowledge and virtuous habits; but ever tempered with such

---

[58] Convenience also recommended Secker, for he, like most Act preachers during the period, was intercepting for a doctorate in divinity the day he preached his sermon: Greaves, 'Religion in the University, 1715–1800', in *HUO: Eighteenth Century*, p. 413; *Hearne's Recollections*, XI, p. 227.

[59] Thomas Secker, *A sermon preach'd before the University of Oxford, at St Mary's, on Act Sunday in the afternoon, July 8. 1733* (1733), p. 4.

[60] Ibid., p. 14.

mildness and diffidence concerning matters, of which they need not judge yet, as they will every day see more necessary in order to judge and act right.[61]

Secker's Oxford Act sermon, like so much else in his career, was shot through with moderation. He might easily have inveighed against the university on the occasion, proving his loyalist *bona fides*. Instead, he affirmed his loyalty to the crown, while also gently, if firmly, pressing Oxford to drop its opposition to the house of Hanover since, he argued, the two Georges had proved themselves champions of true religion and virtue. And he did all of this in the language of high church Toryism that was his audience's mother tongue. It was an adroit performance, and even sceptical contemporaries judged Secker's Act sermon extraordinarily skilful.[62] No less an avowed Jacobite than Thomas Hearne admitted its distinction, describing it as 'rather an Essay than a Sermon, but 'tis very handsome and neat, and proper enough for the Auditory, notwithstanding his speaking in commendation of King George and Queen Caroline'.[63]

While bishop of Oxford, Secker steered the same cautious course, pressing the Whig cause firmly, but not so stridently that he might alienate important figures in the university and diocese. Shortly after his consecration in 1738, he made it a point in his initial visit to Oxford as its bishop to cultivate cordial relations with the influential there, inviting 'all the Heads of Houses, & all the Clergy of the Diocese who resided in Oxford, to dine with me'.[64] His political skill, not to mention his patience, would nonetheless be tested repeatedly during his twenty-year episcopal tenure.

The 1740s were not a high point of good relations between the government and Oxford, and the inaction of the clergy and gentry of Oxford during the Jacobite rebellion of 1745 contrasted poorly with the ostentatious support of the house of Hanover by their counterparts in Yorkshire.[65] What did the government expect of the Anglican hierarchy during this crisis? First, bishops needed to ensure the loyalty of their diocesan clergy to the house of Hanover.[66] Once it became clear in September 1745 that the Jacobite army posed a real threat to church and state, Secker responded immediately, sending 'a circular

---

[61] Ibid., p. 20.

[62] *Hearne's Recollections*, XI, pp. 231, 238, 241.

[63] Ibid., p. 243. Cf. *Autobiography*, p. 14 for William Webster's criticism of the sermon in the *Weekly Miscellany*; Secker subsequently noted that Webster 'found me afterwards for several Years one of his most liberal Supporters'.

[64] *Autobiography*, p. 19.

[65] Paul Langford, 'Tories and Jacobites, 1714–1751', in *HUO: Eighteenth Century*, pp. 119–20; Jonathan Oates, *York and the Jacobite Rebellion of 1745* (York, 2003).

[66] Smith, *Georgian Monarchy*, pp. 165–69. More was expected from bishops of the northern dioceses, whose roles as members of the civil administration were also emphasized by government leaders: Taylor, 'Church and State in England', pp. 157–58.

printed Letter to my Clergy upon it immediately'.[67] On 15 October he presided over a meeting of many of the leading landowners and clergy of Oxfordshire at which most, in imitation of other counties across England, entered into an association for the defence of the constitution in church and state. Associations had originated in the 1580s, and in times of public crisis were ways to profess ostentatious loyalty to the crown.[68] But a distrust of associations was a hallmark of the country platform to which many Tories ascribed.[69] This was particularly true in Oxford where Toryism flourished, and fewer than ten senior figures in the University (most of them Whigs) actually joined the association. University Tories followed county Tories and abstained on the grounds that 'it was improper to make free grants to the Crown without parliamentary authority'.[70] Corralling such a contrarian group must have seemed a thankless task.

Surprisingly less nettlesome for Secker was preparing an address to the king from the notoriously Tory Oxfordshire clergy in the fall of 1745. When it became clear in mid September that the rebellion was a serious crisis, eighteen dioceses, both universities, Convocation, and the dean and chapter of Ely presented addresses of loyalty to the king.[71] Rather than spontaneous outpourings of support from the lower clergy, these addresses were 'a testimony to the activity of the bishops'. They nonetheless proved fairly reliable indications of the clergy's loyalty to the Crown.[72] Oxford did not rally actively to the Pretender's call, and Secker was so pleased with the positive responses from the Oxfordshire clergy which met the circulated address that he commended them in his 1747 diocesan charge for 'the unanimous Zeal you expressed against [the rebellion] ... Your Behaviour and that of the whole Clergy, on this trying Occasion, hath abounded with Proofs of Loyalty and Affection to the Government.'[73]

---

[67] *Autobiography*, p. 26. Robert Harris, *A Patriot Press: National Politics and the London Press in the 1740s* (Oxford, 1993), pp. 198–99 places the episcopal circular letters in the context of anti-Jacobite propaganda in the fall of 1745.

[68] Edward Vallance, *Revolutionary England and the National Covenant: State Oaths, Protestantism and the Political Nation, 1553–1682* (Woodbridge, 2005), pp. 17–27.

[69] Robson, *The Oxfordshire Election of 1754*, pp. 1–13; Linda Colley, *In Defiance of Oligarchy: The Tory Party, 1714–60* (Cambridge, 1982), pp. 39–40; Eveline Cruickshanks, *Political Untouchables: the Tories and the '45* (1979), pp. 84–85; Paul Langford, *A Polite and Commercial People: England, 1727–1783* (Oxford, 1989), p. 203. At issue was a longstanding constitutional question regarding parliamentary supply.

[70] Langford, 'Tories and Jacobites', p. 120; Ward, *Georgian Oxford*, p. 166. For a full list of the subscribers to the Oxford Association, see *An Authentick Copy of the Association entered into by Part of the Nobility, Gentlemen and Clergy of the County of Oxford, at the Time of the Late Unnatural Rebellion in ... 1745, together with the names of persons who subscribed thereto* (Oxford, 1745).

[71] There were a total of 307 loyalist addresses published in the *London Gazette* between September 1745 and April 1746: Harris, *A Patriot Press*, p. 190. The Oxford address, a copy of which may be found in *London Gazette* 8478 (22–26 Oct 1745)was presented to the king on 26 October 1745.

[72] Taylor, 'Church and State in England', pp. 150–52.

[73] *Charges* (1747), p. 87.

This spirit of amity was fleeting at best, illusory at worst, though, for the Blacow affair of 1748 threw into full public view the conflict between the Whig ministry and the Tory rank and file of the University.[74] In the years after the '45, drunken and rowdy scholars had regularly toasted 'King James III'. University officials, aware of this, left the offenders unpunished and hoped nothing leaked into the newspapers. In 1747, though, two drunk undergraduates pressed their attacks on the crown too far. On 23 February, a fractious Whig don from Brasenose named Richard Blacow heard 'Rioters' outside Winter's coffeehouse 'shout aloud God bless king James, Prince Charles, damn King George, and other Treasonable and Seditious Expressions'. When Blacow grabbed one of the group, a Balliol student named John Whitmore, to take him to the Proctor, the group struck Blacow and one, James Dawes, cried 'I am the man that dare say God bless King James the 3d and tell you my name is Dawes of St Mary Hall.'[75] Blacow subsequently collected witnesses and reported the incidents to Vice-Chancellor John Purnell, who took no action against them. The government, however, arrested, tried, and convicted both of the students and even brought charges against Purnell himself. Riots subsequently erupted in the university. The ambitious Edward Bentham tried to demonstrate his worth to the Old Corps Whigs by publishing *A Letter to a Young Gentleman* (1748), which excoriated William King, the university's leading Jacobite.[76] Secker encouraged Bentham insofar as he could. 'In the beginning of 1748, Dr. Bentham published, without his name, & without my Knowledge, a Letter to a young Gentleman, by a Tutor and Fellow of a College at Oxford. It relates to the political notions and Disturbances there,' he recalled. 'I sent him Corrections and Improvements, which he used in a 2d and 3d Edition, to which his name was put. Towards the End of that Year he published, with his Name, A Letter to a Fellow of a College, which I saw in manuscript, & corrected & enlarged very much.' For his efforts, Secker 'recommended him for a Canonry of Christ Church'.[77] King responded to Bentham's open letter by savaging him in print.[78] This unseemly sniping tarnished the university's reputation and raised the government's ire.

---

[74] Langford, 'Tories and Jacobites', pp. 120–21; Ward, *Georgian Oxford*, pp. 170–73; and Robson, *The Oxfordshire Election of 1754*, pp. 3–4.

[75] BL, Add. MS 35887, f. 24: M. Sharpe to Hardwicke, 4 Nov 1748; Richard Blacow, *A letter to William King, LL.D. Principal of St Mary Hall in Oxford. Containing a particular account of the treasonable riot in Oxford in Feb. 1747* (1755), pp. 7–13.

[76] Nigel Aston, 'Bentham, Edward (1707–1776)', *ODNB*.

[77] *Autobiography*, p. 27. See also, BL, Add. MS 39311, f. 58: Bentham to Secker, 27 May 1748.

[78] William King, *A Proposal for publishing a poetical translation of the Rev. Mr. Tutor Bentham's Letter to a young gentleman of Oxford* (1749); idem, *A poetical abridgement, both in Latin and English, of the Reverend Mr. Tutor Bentham's Letter to a young gentleman of Oxford* (1749). In the latter pamphlet, King pilloried Bentham as 'Half a Casuist, half Lawyer, half Courtier, half Cit/Half a Tory, half Whig (may I add, half a Wit?)' (p. 43). See also, David Greenwood, *William King: Tory and Jacobite* (Oxford, 1969), pp. 183–92.

Hoping further to embarrass Oxford at this moment, the University of Cambridge took the unprecedented step of addressing the king on the Treaty of Aix-la-Chapelle (1748), beating even the Houses of Parliament to the punch. Oxford had to follow suit, but their impolitic address mentioned the recent riots which followed Whitmore and Dawes's convictions. In a stunning blow to the university, the king rejected the address, deeming it 'not a Proper one for Him to receive'.[79] It was a move which Secker had actually encouraged. 'Many Persons in that University having given just Offence to the Governmt, & an Address from thence having been drawn up, which appeared unsatisfactory,' he remembered. 'A Meeting was held at the Duke of Newcastles, at which I was, to consider whether the King shd be advised to receive it. Bp Sherlocks Opinion principally produced a Resolution, that he shd not.'[80] The government's desire for retribution did not stop there, though, for ministers and the episcopal bench seriously debated whether to subject the university to a royal visitation. 'I was also at a meeting ... to consider abt a Visitation of the University,' Secker recalled, '& probably a Bill wd have been brought into Parliamt for that Purpose, if there had not been some Movements of the Prince of Wales's Friends to form an opposite Party'.[81] The threat achieved its effect, for June 1749 found Secker writing to Hardwicke that Oxonians 'have certainly been put in Fear: enough I believe to make all of them present cautions of affronting the Government and some of their careful to pay it Respect'.[82]

Secker's political talents in Oxford were crucial to the government's successful handling of the uproar aroused by the so-called 'Jew Bill' of 1753. The run-up to the parliamentary elections of 1754 witnessed heated Whig-Tory animosity in Oxford. The repeated complaints from Oxford clergy about the recently enacted Jewish Naturalization Act (1753: 26 Geo. II c.26) blindsided Secker during his visitation of the diocese in the summer of 1753. 'I am at present in the midst of my Visitation: and I find, that the bill for permitting Jews to be naturalized hath not only raised very great Clamours amongst the ignorant & disaffected, but hath offended great numbers of better understandings & dispositions, and is likely to have an unhappy influence on the Election of next Year,' Secker warned Hardwicke in June 1753. 'I have done my best to quiet the Clergy.'[83]

---

[79] Quoted in Langford, 'Tories and Jacobites', p. 122.
[80] *Autobiography*, p. 27. Ward, *Georgian Oxford*, p. 175 suggests that Secker's old Exeter tutor, John Coneybeare, 'persuaded Secker ... to present the whole discussion (regarding the drafting of the address) in a bad light to the ministry', causing it to be rejected. The abortive Oxford address was printed in *Gentleman's Magazine* (Jan 1749), pp. 20–21.
[81] *Autobiography*, p. 27.
[82] BL, Add. MS 35590, f. 301: Secker to Hardwicke, 7 June 1749.
[83] BL, Add. MS 35592, f. 84: Secker to Hardwicke, June 1753.

In the spring of 1753, the earl of Halifax had introduced into the House of Lords a bill easing naturalization of Jews born in England.[84] The bill was not technically a government bill, though it had the Pelhams' support. Its central provision regarded the sacramental test for naturalization: 'Be it therefore enacted … that persons professing the Jewish religion may, upon application for that purpose, be naturalized by Parliament without receiving the Sacrament of the Lords' Supper, the said Act of the seventh year of the reign of King James the First, or any other law, statute, matter, or thing to the contrary in any wise notwithstanding.'[85] With the sacramental test removed, naturalized Jews could actually hold full property rights and hope for commercial equality in the marketplace. The Jew Bill first came before the House of Lords on 3 April 1753 and passed without significant debate through both houses of Parliament by 22 May. As news of the bill's passage spread, though, a motley group – London merchants, Whigs and Tories opposed to the Pelhamite ministry, and many Anglican clergy – rallied the country against it, so that the issue dominated the nation's politics in 1753–54.[86] Secker lamented the 'astonishing spirit of Rage & Bitterness, which is gone forth on this Occasion'.[87] Ideology did not bind together the Jew Bill's opponents – raw political considerations and blind bigotry did, for everyone understood that opposition politicians merely wanted the issue as a cudgel with which to beat the Old Corps. Opposition to the act 'began in the Town in order to hurt a particular Gentleman, who serves for the City of London, and has since been industriously propagated in the Country with the same View, I mean the approaching Elections', Hardwicke groused to Secker in early July.[88]

Because Secker was the ministry's frontline defence against the Oxford clerical assault on the Jew Bill, he consulted Hardwicke frequently about how to respond to critics from within the university and the diocese. Some in Oxford worried that Jews would snatch up freeholds in England; others complained that Jews had not been formally readmitted to the kingdom after their expulsion by Edward I in 1290; others thought that Jews should be allowed privileges in only a limited part of the kingdom; others worried that the country would be deluged by Jewish immigrants eager to naturalize; still others argued that Jews should remain

[84] Thomas W. Perry, *Public Opinion, Propaganda, and Politics in Eighteenth-Century England: A Study of the Jew Bill of 1753* (Cambridge, MA, 1962); G.A. Cranfield, 'The *London Evening Post* and the Jew Bill of 1753', *HJ* 8:1 (1965), pp. 16–30; David Katz, *The Jews in the History of England, 1485–1850* (Oxford, 1994), pp. 240–83; Dana Rabin, 'The Jew Bill of 1753: Masculinity, Virility, and the Nation', *Eighteenth-Century Studies* 39:2 (2006), pp. 157–71.

[85] Quoted Perry, *Public Opinion, Propaganda, and Politics*, p. 47.

[86] J.C.D. Clark, *The Dynamics of Change: The crisis of the 1750s and English party systems* (Cambridge, 1982), p. 12; Brian Hill, *British Parliamentary Parties, 1742–1832: From the Fall of Walpole to the First Reform Act* (1985), pp. 79–80.

[87] BL, Add. MS 35592, f. 102: Secker to Hardwicke, 6 July 1753.

[88] Ibid., f. 93: Hardwicke to Secker, 3 July 1753.

without the franchise and be barred from sitting in Parliament. Secker cautioned Hardwicke that the law's opponents were largely impervious to reasoned argument – 'telling persons, that as they [Jews] never have attempted it, they probably never will, or if they did, would be refused, doth not give Satisfaction'.[89] Nonetheless, he deployed Hardwicke's legal arguments in support of the bill, which the lord chancellor appreciated. 'Your Lordship has acted a very worthy part in endeavouring to undeceive your Clergy in your Visitation, and I make no doubt you will continue to exert yourself in the same way,' Hardwicke thanked Secker.[90]

Secker attacked the Jew Bill's opponents from other directions, as well, and put to work some of his protégés to undermine the opposition arguments regarding the law. The Jew Bill's opponents drew much of their ammunition from D'Blossiers Tovey's recent history of the Jews in England.[91] Yet Hardwicke thought Tovey had cited apocryphal historical manuscripts; hoping to prove them apocryphal, Secker directed Edward Bentham and Benjamin Kennicott to examine the manuscripts Tovey used and to report their findings.[92] Secker's promotion of clerical talent likewise paid off when Thomas Church forwarded him a work which supported the Jew Bill. 'Dr. Church hath very unexpectedly sent me a manuscript, which he hath written to prove, that the Jews Bill is not prejudicial to Christianity: and begs my Opinion, by which he saith he will be ruled, whether he shall publish it or not', Secker wrote to Hardwicke. 'It will make a moderate pamphlet, is written sensibly enough, and with good Temper, though not with much Spirit or Elegance.' Significantly, Secker added that Church 'hath shewn himself in several Controversies an Orthodox Man, and received an honorary Drs. Degree on that account, possibly his name might have weight with some persons'.[93] Yet neither Thomas Church nor any of Secker's other protégés produced anything sufficiently persuasive to dissuade the Jew Bill's opponents.   Sometime in early November 1753 the ministry concluded that the Jew Bill jeopardized the ministry's chances in the forthcoming parliamentary elections. A face-saving retreat seemed the only viable option. The Pelhams aimed to rob their opponents of the issue – Newcastle would move for repeal with Secker seconding his motion.[94] Secker recognized clearly that even this would be insufficient to assuage the clergy, which explains why, before the Parliament met, he asked Hardwicke to retain the language from the original bill which had barred Jews from holding Anglican advowsons. 'I must intreat your Lordship to

[89]   Ibid., f. 84: Secker to Hardwicke, June 1753.
[90]   Ibid., f. 93: Hardwicke to Secker, 3 July 1753.
[91]   D'Blossiers Tovey, *Anglia Judaica: or the history and antiquities of the Jews in England, collected from all our historians, both printed and manuscript, as also from the records in the Tower, and other public repositories* (Oxford, 1738).
[92]   BL, Add. MS 35592, f. 127: Secker to Hardwicke, 15 Aug 1753.
[93]   Ibid.
[94]   BL, Add. MS 32733, f. 255: Secker to TPH, 14 Nov 1753.

indulge me a few words more about Jewish patronages: for indeed the longer I think of them, the less I am reconciled to them,' he importuned Hardwicke. 'They are unfit in themselves: and will be a Dishonour to the Church of England, such as no other church in any Christian Country suffers, as ever did,' he complained.

> We have Laws against Popish patronages: and though the Danger from Jewish may not be so great, yet the shame of them is much greater. It was not known before, that there were such in the Nation: but now it is universally known: and persons will either fear or pretend Fears that the Jews may set themselves to purchase more Advowsons, either for profit or Revenge. The Parliament and the Bishops in particular have been treated very injuriously for passing this Act. But new Reproach will fall upon us, and with such Appearance of Justice, that those of our Bench will not be able to hold up their Heads under it, if we concur without necessity in repealing a Clause, which every body owns to be a good one, and many think the only good one.

The government risked losing its episcopal supporters, Secker warned, if the bill's parliamentary opponents proposed repealing the Jewish advowson clause first – in that instance, 'the Bishops must divide against their Friends'.[95]

Secker reiterated these private warnings in his parliamentary speech in favour of repeal. While noting that he found nothing inherently wrong with the original bill, Secker assured the assembled Lords that he was willing to vote for the repeal, but on one condition: 'I cannot consent to the repeal of that part of it which disables any Jew to purchase advowsons, or any thing that may give him a right to intermeddle in affairs relating to the Church: and therefore I cannot agree to the leaving out the exception or proviso contained in the Bill now before us.' Just as 'the Turks would be far from looking upon any man as a true mussulman, if he proposed that the Imaum or Sheik of any of their mosques should be chosen or named by the Christians', so too would English Christians look askance at anyone presented to a living by a Jew.[96] To mollify the episcopal bench, Newcastle made sure to exempt the Jewish advowson clause in his motion to repeal.[97] By 20 December the king had given the repeal his assent.

The Jew Bill's repeal successfully defused the issue, restoring calm before the 1754 election. The repeal proved successful, that is, nearly everywhere but Oxford, where it remained one of the central issues of 'the most notorious county election of the century'.[98] There had been no contest in the county since 1710, but the Whigs and Tories fielded rival candidates in 1754. The duke of Marlborough, Lord Macclesfield, and Lord Harcourt supported Sir Edward

---

[95] BL, Add. MS 35592, f. 192: Secker to Hardwicke, 12 Nov 1753.
[96] Cobbett, *Parliamentary History*, XV, pp. 114–17.
[97] Perry, *Public Opinion, Propaganda, and Politics*, p. 148.
[98] Sir Lewis Namier and John Brooke (eds.), *The Houses of Commons, 1754–1790* (1964), I, p. 356.

Turner and Lord Thomas Parker for the Whigs, while Lord Philip Wenman and Sir James Dashwood stood for the Tories. Because the Whigs were weak in Oxford, a victory by one or both of their candidates would have been a public relations coup for the party. That is why the government committed over £7,000 to the Whig cause and why the Tories spent £20,000 of their own. The high stakes also explain why over a year before the contest, Hardwicke recruited Secker to electioneer. He need not have asked, for Secker had already begun actively to politick for the Whigs.[99] He recognized his own limitations to sway clerical voters, though. 'The small property I have in Oxfordshire is either in the hands, or in the neighbourhood of persons, whom I cannot influence; excepting some, which is in the Management of the Duke of Marlboroughs steward. I have no preferments to give the clergy,' Secker lamented to Hardwicke. 'I cannot promise or threaten to behave to them according as they vote. If my Opinion will be of any weight with them, I have declared it from the first: and given Sir Edward Turner and his Friends leave to Plead it, wherever they think it will be of use. If your Lordship thinks I should appoint any person to make a more formal Declaration in my name next week, it shall be readily done.'[100] This contrasts strikingly with his admonition to Oxford clergy in 1747 that 'Benefices ought neither to be given nor accepted with any Condition or Promise, than that of doing our Duty in Relation to them'.[101] Despite his earlier disavowal of placing overt political pressure on the clergy, Secker did precisely that in the run-up to the 1754 election, as his 1753 Oxford charge clearly endorsed the Whigs. 'The other Subject, on which I would speak to you, is the Contest about Representatives for this County in the next Parliament,' he wrote to his clergy. 'Let no one be alarmed. I need not, and I do not mean, to give you at a Meeting of this Nature, my Opinion which of the Candidates that you ought to prefer.' Nonetheless, he urged them 'to regard, in the first Place, the inseparable Interests of the excellent Church we are members of, and, its only human Support, the just and gracious Government we live under; than other subordinate Considerations'.[102] Secker made an even more ostentatious point when he ensured that his June 1753 confirmation in Henley coincided with the canvass there.[103] Inexplicably, though, he skipped the important September Chipping Norton races, where candidates for both parties and their supporters met to socialize and plan strategy. Secker's absence, however, did not prevent Tories from reporting that he 'was there in a laced Coat'.[104] At the poll, finally taken in April 1754, the voters returned the Tory candidates to Parliament. Secker could

---

99   In 1738, he tried to work through his brother-in-law to help him sway the votes of two family friends: SCA, Bagshawe C.330, ff. 23–24: Secker to Richard Milnes, 1 Sept 1738.
100 BL, Add. MS 35592, f. 30: Secker to Hardwicke, 8 Feb 1753.
101 *Charges* (1747), p. 93.
102 *Charges* (1753), p. 197.
103 *Jackson's Oxford Journal* (June 1753), 9.3.3.
104 *Autobiography*, p. 33.

console himself that if the majority of Oxford clergy did not vote for the Whigs, those who held their livings from the Crown and from him actually did vote solidly in favour of the Whigs.[105] That might have been all that could be expected from him.

The events of 1753–54 convinced the government that it had to pay closer attention to Oxford. 'As to a certain party, which your Lordship describes, I am sorry they have deceived your hopes, but am glad you now see them in their true colours,' Hardwicke wrote to Secker in the election's aftermath. 'I have long seen that spirit; and great industry has been used to keep up that spirit, where you see the exertion of it, in order to hold out that place as the garrison and fortress of Toryism and Jacobitism.'[106] As if further proof were needed of Hardwicke's point, just months later Secker passed along reports of raucous fights between Jacobites and Whigs in Corpus Christi College.[107]

Secker's involvement in Oxford politics continued even after his elevation to Canterbury.[108] One of his first orders of archiepiscopal business regarding Oxford was to convince George II to accept the university's address to him in the summer of 1758. In its preparation, Secker 'did use some Endeavours first, that the Address might be inoffensive and dutiful'.[109] He also lobbied the king personally. 'I took great personal Pains with him to persuade him to receive it kindly,' Secker recorded. 'I could not prevail on him to speak to the Persons, who presented it. But he read it afterwards: & then directed me to return the University Thanks for it from him.'[110] In convincing the king to accept the address, Secker paved the way to the closer relations between crown and university that developed by the end of the century.

Newcastle hoped that Secker might continue to monitor the university for the government as its chancellor following Lord Arran's death in December 1758. A staunch Tory, if no Jacobite, Arran had held the office since 1715, and the court was eager to nominate a Whig replacement and place at the head of the university a more favourable governor. Newcastle settled upon Secker as Arran's replacement. 'But the Bp. of Durham [Richard Trevor], by the Advice, I believe, of Dr. Dickens, got himself proposed, without consulting the Duke or me,'

---

[105] Robson, *The Oxfordshire Election of 1754*, pp. 83–85 analyzes clerical voting patterns in the election.
[106] BL, Add. MS 35593, f. 3: Hardwicke to Secker, 3 Sept 1754.
[107] Ibid., ff. 79–83: Secker to Hardwicke, 16 Dec 1754.
[108] After his elevation to Canterbury, Secker took an interest in Kentish electoral politics as well, reporting to Newcastle what information he and his colleagues had gathered: BL, Add. MS 32906, f. 338: Secker to TPH, 28 May [1760]; 32916, ff. 278–79: Secker to TPH, 23 Dec 1760; 32917, f. 406: Secker to TPH, 19 Jan 1761; 32920, f. 253: Secker to TPH, 16 Mar 1761. As archbishop, Secker also served as the visitor of All Souls College, Oxford: LPL, MS 1155; Codrington Library, Oxford, Injunctions, Mandates, Letters 261–262. More generally, see G.D. Squibb, *Founder's Kin: Privilege and Pedigree* (Oxford, 1972).
[109] BL, Add. MS 32884, f. 420: Secker to TPH, 18 Oct 1758.
[110] *Autobiography*, p. 38. See also, BL, Add. MS 32884, f. 418: TPH to Secker, 18 Oct 1758.

Secker remembered. 'I believe the Duke spoke very strongly to him on the Occasion for he made his Excuses to me with Tears in his Eyes. I did not in the least wish to be proposed, or resent his Behaviour, but directed my Friends to vote for him'.[111] The contest between Trevor, whose Tory background did not bar him from being the court's candidate, and earls of Westmorland and Lichfield proved heated, though after Lichfield withdrew and threw his support behind Westmorland, the latter won the contest easily.[112] Lichfield had not withdrawn willingly, though, and upon Westmorland's death in 1762 was nominated as the court's candidate for the vacant chancellorship. Secker's protégés Benjamin Kennicott and David Gregory were among the Whig whips in the university who were asked to lobby on behalf of Lichfield. There were, though, a number of objections to Lichfield, and Secker's own attempts to reassure his colleagues and friends seem half-hearted at best. 'Undoubtedly fitter Persons might have been proposed, and I presume amongst the Kings Servants: but this Man alone hath been proposed from thence,' he wrote to George Berkeley, jr., 'and it is very material to shew, that a place at Court is not consider'd as a Disqualification, indeed to have a Chancellor that is possessed of some Interest there: and I know not, that Lord Lichfield is so much less fit than either of the two Candidates, as to overbalance this Argument in his Favour.'[113] Lichfield eventually won the contest, but needed the overwhelming support of Whig strongholds like Exeter and Christ Church colleges to prevail.[114]

At Cambridge, Newcastle used patronage successfully to 'strengthen and consolidate the whig ascendancy in the university,' but at Oxford Whig predominance had not yet been established.[115] This helps explain why Secker took such an active interest in vacancies within Oxford long after he ceased to be the diocesan there. Placing sympathetic folks in influential administrative positions might, the government hoped, change Oxford's political culture. Perhaps Secker's most vigorous intervention concerning the crown's patronage dealt with the vacant regius chair of divinity in 1763. 'I have been at your Door this morning to acquaint you with the Death of Dr. Fanshaw, Canon of Christ Church, and the Kings Professor of Divinity in the University of Oxford,' he wrote to George Grenville on 31 May 1763. 'It is a matter of very great importance, that he should have a proper Successor.' Secker recommended the reliable Whig, Edward Bentham, the canon of Christ Church. 'He is a man of unblemished Character in every respect, a very good Scholar and Divine: hath always been a hearty Friend to the Government; and shewed his Regard to his

---

[111]   *Autobiography*, p. 40.
[112]   Ward, *Georgian Oxford*, pp. 207–09; Sutherland, 'Political Respectability', pp. 144–46.
[113]   BL, Add. MS 39311, f. 119: Secker to Berkeley, 23 Sept 1762. See also, BIHR, Bp. C. & P. VII/109/2: Secker to RHD, 30 Aug 1762.
[114]   BL, Add. MS 39315, f. 74: Kennicott to Secker, 23 Sept 1762; Ward, *Georgian Oxford*, pp. 218–23; Sutherland, 'Political Respectability', pp. 151–54.
[115]   Gascoigne, *Cambridge in the age of the Enlightenment*, pp. 103–13.

present Majestys Administration in the Sermon, which he had the Honour of preaching before him last Thursday,' he reassured Grenville. 'He was many years a most highly & deservedly esteemed Tutor: he hath been very useful in his present Station: and I am certain will discharge every part of the professors Office, (from which he hath no Avocation) ably, diligently and conscientiously. This, I am verily persuaded, is the Opinion, which every one, who knows him, entertains of him.'[116] Bentham ended up being inconvenienced by the promotion, though. 'I have got Dr. Bentham against his will, the professorship of Divinity,' Secker confided to Drummond afterwards, 'for who might have got it else, I could not tell ... But they have, I think very unkindly forced Dr. Bentham to quit his good House for an extremely bad one, and to become Junior Canon ... I am sorry for poor Bentham: but I am glad for the University.'[117] It was worth it to Secker for an ally to be the regius professor, especially when he was amenable to reforming religious education at Oxford.

In support of his old friend Benjamin Kennicott's successful bid for the librarianship of the Radcliffe Library in 1766, Secker was equally brazen: 'I applied to as many of the Electors, as I could, for Kennicott,' he remembered, and his personal intervention with the university's lord chancellor turned at least one vote in Kennicott's favour.[118] This was Secker's reward to Kennicott for the heavy lifting he had done on the ministry's behalf in many battles in Oxford through the years and for his collation of Hebrew scriptures. Even in the last year of his life, Secker remained interested in Oxford affairs, recommending and campaigning for Thomas Randolph – an ardent defender of clerical and lay subscription – to become Lady Margaret chair of divinity. 'I ... am told my Recommendation got some Influence,' Secker recorded with some satisfaction.[119]

Secker's role in the Whig conquest of Oxford was not decisive, yet neither was it unimportant. He had provided the state with reliable information and counsel in times of crisis there. He had championed solid Whigs, if not always exceptional scholars, for important vacancies within the university. Above all, he tried to ensure that the political temperature in Oxford did not rise too high. These were, admittedly, moderate measures, but even near the end of his tenure

---

[116] BL, Stowe 119, f. 152: Secker to Grenville, 10 May 1763. Spencer Cowper recorded that Bentham had been recommended for a prebend of Durham in November 1752 as 'a Tory, but a man of extraordinary good character, and very moderate, and who has served the Gvt very much at Oxford in opposition to his more violent Brethren': quoted in Ward, *Georgian Oxford*, p. 172, n. 19.

[117] BIHR, Bp. C.&P. VII/175/2: Secker to RHD, 31 May 1763.

[118] *Autobiography*, pp. 62–63.

[119] Ibid., p. 67. See also, Thomas Randolph, *The reasonableness of requiring subscription to articles of religion from persons to be admitted to holy orders, or a cure of souls, vindicated in a charge delivered to the clergy of the diocese of Oxford, in the year 1771* (Oxford, 1771); idem, *An answer to a pamphlet entitled Reflections on the impropriety and inexpediency of lay-subscription to the XXXIX articles, in the University of Oxford* (Oxford, 1772); idem, *An answer to a pamphlet, entituled, Considerations on the propriety of requiring a subscription to articles of faith* (Oxford, 1774).

as bishop of Oxford, the university and community had become less hostile to the Whigs. 'And though I be among the Children of men that are set on Fire,' he wrote to Archbishop Herring in 1755, 'they have given me but little disquiet and one may hope will rather grow cooler than hotter'.[120] That this moderating trend continued throughout the rest of the century is a testament in part to Secker's persistent, if understated, attempts to change the culture of Oxford from within. By trying to re-orient the university community away from the Tories and toward the Whigs, Secker believed that he was actually fulfilling part of his responsibilities to protect and defend the Church by promoting loyalism and championing orthodoxy. If these were important tasks for the Church to do in Oxford, they were equally important at the epicentre of English political life, the royal court.

IV

The Georgian royal court served at least three important political functions during Secker's time on the episcopal bench.[121] It was a point of contact between the aristocracy, the established Church, and the monarch, the three groups who together governed eighteenth-century England.[122] In addition, the political class flocked there to obtain or maintain the position, influence, and prestige that came only by access to the king.[123] Finally, the royal court was an important venue for the performance of authority.

The established Church of England maintained a presence at court out of necessity and self-interest. Bishops held a number of high-profile positions within the royal household, serving as dean of the chapel royal, clerk of the closet, and

---

[120] LPL, Secker Papers 7, f. 92: Secker to Herring, 12 May 1755.

[121] For the continued political importance of the royal course, see Hannah Smith, 'The Court in England, 1714–1760: A Declining Political Institution?', *History* 90:297 (2005), pp. 23–41; J.C.D. Clark (ed.), *The memoirs and Speeches of James, 2nd Earl Waldegrave, 1742–1763* (Cambridge, 1988), pp. 1–21; idem, *Revolution and Rebellion: State and society in England in the seventeenth and eighteenth centuries* (Cambridge, 1986), pp. 71–83. More generally, see John Adamson, 'The Making of the Ancien-Régime Court, 1500–1700', in *The Princely Courts of Europe: Ritual, Politics and Culture under the Ancien Régime, 1500–1750*, ed. John Adamson (1999), pp. 7–42. But cf. R.O. Bucholz, *The Augustan Court: Queen Anne and the Decline of Court Culture* (Stanford, CA, 1993), p. 250.

[122] Cf. G.R. Elton, 'Tudor Government: The Points of Contact. III: The Court', *TRHS*, 5th series, 26 (1976), pp. 211–28.

[123] Leicester House, the seat of the reversionary interest, proved the alternate magnet to some aspiring to political power: Robert Harris (ed.), 'A Leicester House Political Diary, 1742–3', in *Camden Miscellany*, 4th series, 44 (1991), pp. 373–411; Aubrey N. Newman (ed.), 'Leicester House Politics 1750–60: From the Papers of John, Second Earl of Egmont', in *Camdem Miscellany*, 4th series, 23 (1969), pp. 85–228; idem, 'Leicester House Politics, 1748–1751', *EHR* 76:301 (1961), pp. 577–89.

lord almoner; many lesser clergy frequented court as royal chaplains.[124] Anglican clergy also baptized, wed, crowned, and buried royals. Yet the king and his ministers expected far more from the Church than its mere confessional presence at the royal court. The crown wanted the Church's leadership to help shape and disseminate Georgian loyalism, particularly ensuring that a loyalist message blared from the nation's pulpits during times of national crisis. The archbishop of Canterbury also served as one of the king's privy councillors, and his participation in council deliberations was supposed to be substantive rather than ceremonial.[125] Finally, as nearness to the king increased the political standing of politicians, so cordial relations with the monarch enhanced the Church's prestige and influence.

High politics often turns on the interplay of personalities, and this was especially so in the hothouse world of the eighteenth-century royal court. Secker's parliamentary opposition of the late 1730s and his ill-fated role as intermediary between George II and Frederick, prince of Wales, damaged his relations with the house of Hanover. When Secker presented one of his anti-Jacobite sermons to the king in October 1745, for instance, George II 'did not vouchsafe to speak' to him and 'received, with the same Silence' an address Secker presented to him from the Oxfordshire clergy.[126] Even in the spring of 1751, after the king's animosity for Secker had begun to cool, he still 'would not go to chapel, because Secker, Bishop of Oxford was to preach before him: the ministers did not insist upon his hearing the sermon, as they had lately upon his making him Dean of St Paul's'.[127] Nevertheless, relations between Secker and George II gradually improved during the late 1750s.[128] The new reign which commenced in 1760 promised a clean slate, and George III's early assurances 'that he thought it his principal Duty to encourage & support Religion & Virtue' heartened his archbishop of Canterbury.[129] At times, Secker was overly eager to curry the new king's favour. '[T]he Archbishop has such hopes of the young King, that he is never out of the circle,' Horace Walpole harrumphed in November 1760. 'He trod upon the Duke's foot on Sunday in the haste of his

[124] For the holders of the episcopal offices, see *Officials of the Royal Household, 1660–1837. Part I: Department of the Lord Chamberlain and associated offices*, compiled by J.C. Sainty and R.O. Bucholz (1997), I, pp. 55–57.
[125] Stephen Taylor, 'The Bishops at Westminster in the Mid-Eighteenth Century', in *A Pillar of the Constitution: The House of Lords in British politics, 1603–1784*, ed. Clyve Jones (1989), p. 138.
[126] *Autobiography*, p. 26.
[127] Walpole, *Memoirs of George II*, p. 45.
[128] *Autobiography*, p. 42.
[129] LPL, MS 1130/1, f. 30: Secker's account of George III's accession [1760].

zeal; the Duke said to him, "My Lord, if your Grace is in such a hurry to make your court, that is the way.'"[130]

But did it really matter one way or the other? Looking back, much of Secker's activity at the Georgian royal court – itself surely a pre-modern deformity doomed to extinction in the progressive evolution of English political institutions – might seem meaningless at best, pernicious at worst. Neither Secker nor his contemporaries would have been able to fathom this view. For them, the royal court's importance was simply a fact of political life; and, for those in positions of power, association with the court was not optional. Secker had an interrelated set of aims that he hoped to gain by participating in life at court – promoting orthodoxy and Georgian loyalism; demonstrating the Church's loyalty to the Hanoverians; and, thereby, strengthening the state's support for the established Church.

Monitoring and regulating the royals' religious life topped his list of concerns at court, for if the English monarchs were unobservant, why should their citizens be otherwise? From Secker's point of view, then, it was imperative to ensure that the royal family followed orthodox Anglican liturgical practices. Not long after Queen Charlotte (1744–1818) arrived in England, for instance, Secker learned that some took offence at her behaviour in the chapel royal. 'After I came from Court yesterday, I was told, that the Queen did not kneel at any part of the Service at the Chapel last Sunday, and that many persons present had taken Offence at the Omission,' he wrote to the duke of Devonshire in September 1761. 'I believe the foreign Protestant, as well as our Dissenters, more usually stand, than kneel, at their publick prayers: and the two postures are certainly indifferent. But your Grace knows, what stress the people sometime say upon such things: & doubtless her Majesty would chuse to follow our Customs.'[131] Secker advised that she simply follow the king's lead during services, since she herself did not yet speak English.[132] Secker also promoted orthodox belief at court by promoting the cause of orthodox clerics there. When asked to nominate preachers for fasts and thanksgivings at court, for instance, he put forward reliably orthodox protégés such as Charles Hall and Edward Bentham.[133] When Princess

---

[130] *Walpole's Correspondence*, IX, p. 318: Walpole to George Montagu, 4 Nov 1760. See also, Walpole, *Memoirs of George III*, I, p. 16; Paget Toynbee and Leonard Whibley (eds.), *Correspondence of Thomas Gray* (Oxford, 1935), II, p. 711: Gray to Brown, 8 Nov 1760.

[131] LPL MS 1130/I, f. 123: Secker to William Cavendish, 4th duke of Devonshire, 19 Sept 1761.

[132] Charlotte seems to have been unwilling to heed Secker's advice, though, for on 20 Sept 1761, the duke of Devonshire noted, 'The King spoke to the Queen to kneel at Chapel: she did not': Peter D. Brown and Karl W. Schweizer (eds.), *The Devonshire Diary. Memoranda on State of Affairs, 1759–1762* (1982), p. 131.

[133] Secker nominated Charles Hall to preach a fast sermon in early 1759: LPL, MS 1130/II, f. 183: William Cavendish, 4th duke of Devonshire to Secker, 15 January 1759; ibid., f. 185: Secker to Devonshire, 15 January 1759; ibid., f. 186: Devonshire to Secker, 16 January 1759. He nominated Edward Bentham to preach a thanksgiving sermon before the court on

Amelia (1710–1786) wanted Secker to appoint a 'proper Chaplain to come every Day to read Prayers to preach On Sundays and to administer the Sacrament once a Month at her House',[134] he proposed William Bell, whom he later commissioned to write an orthodox defence of revealed belief.[135]

The royal court, no less than the urban parish, was a site of confessional competition, as the birth of the prince of Wales in 1762 illustrates. On 12 August 1762, Queen Charlotte gave birth to George, prince of Wales, at St James's Palace.[136] In a private meeting in the royal closet on 23 August 1762, Secker and the king debated whether the Church of England's clergy should send an address of congratulation upon the prince's birth. Upon being informed by Secker 'that Diocese Addresses of mere Compliment had not been made, excepting on Accessions', George III 'said, that was a sufficient Answer to all that could be said on the other side: & continued to decline addresses'.[137] There matters stood until Dissenting minister Samuel Chandler informed Secker not only that many Dissenting ministers had it in mind to deliver a congratulatory address but that he had discussed the matter with Bute, who had agreed to let him know the following day 'whether it would be agreeable to the King'. When informed of the details of Secker's earlier conversation with the king, Chandler allowed that he hoped the request would be denied. If George III granted the request, though, Secker insisted that London's Anglican clergy be allowed to present their address first, despite the fact that Richard Osbaldeston, the bishop of London, would not return to town from Yorkshire until late the next week. The king must have changed his mind, since Bute informed Chandler on 10 September 'that his Majesty will do us the Honour to receive our Congratulations on the birth of the Prince'. To appease the archbishop, though, Chandler agreed to 'wait till the London clergy have presented theirs, in which I hope there will be no delay'.[138] In his letter to Osbaldeston, Secker spelled out the political implications of the situation. 'I think it had been better, if the Dissenters had not addressed; & Dr. Chandler said he was of the same mind,' Secker groused. 'But as they will address, it seems likely, that they, & some of the courtiers, & perhaps some of yr Lps. own Clergy, may find fault, if you do not address. And if the episcopal Address comes first; it will scarce be much, if at all known, that the Dissenters were the first

5 May 1760: ibid., f. 203: George Spencer, 4th duke of Marlborough to Secker, 12 April 1763; ibid., f. 204: Secker to Marlborough, 12 April 1763.

[134] LPL, MS 1130/I, f. 59: Lady Isabella Finch to Secker, 5 Dec 1760.

[135] *Autobiography*, p. 52; B.W. Young, 'Bell, William (1731–1816)', *ODNB*; William Bell, *A Defence of Revelation in general and the Gospel in particular; in answer to the objections raised in a late book entitled, The morality of the New Testament, digested under various heads &c and subscribed, A rational Christian* (1766).

[136] Secker christened him that same night: Christopher Hibbert, *George III* (1997), p. 45.

[137] LPL, MS 1130/I, f. 191: Secker's notes about addressing on the birth of the prince, [Sept] 1762. Unless otherwise noted, all quotations in this paragraph derive from this memorandum. See also, BL, Add. MS 35597, f. 181: Secker to Hardwicke, 6 Sept 1762.

[138] LPL, MS 1130/I, f. 194: Chandler to Secker, 10 Sept 1762.

movers: of if known, yr Lps Absence will account for it.'[139] Chandler and the Dissenters irked Osbaldeston, leading him to complain, 'I do not apprehend the forward zeal of the dissenters shou'd be any rule to us, as I do not remember, it ever has been on the like occasion to our body.'[140] Nonetheless, he drew up an address from the clergy of the London diocese and presented it to the king in advance of the Dissenting address. George III would expect national celebrations upon the births of his children thereafter.[141]

Other court business also required Secker to tread lightly through a political minefield, where one misstep could bring unfavourable attention on the Church. In 1763, for instance, the king's ministers arranged late in 1763 for George III's eldest sister, Augusta (1737–1813), to marry Charles William Ferdinand, hereditary prince of Brunswick in the hope that by it England could thereby ally itself with the house of Brunswick during the Seven Years War.[142] For some reason, though, Bute disliked the Brunswick family, calling them his 'personal enemies'; he particularly loathed the prince, 'whom he accused of using him *cruelly*, as he termed it'.[143] The ministry, therefore, was none too eager to hurry the negotiations, and indeed delayed the treaty's completion as long as possible. When the prince of Brunswick arrived in London on 12 January 1764, he was treated shabbily by the court and placed in Somerset House without guards. The London crowds treated him as a kind of hero, though, and he ostentatiously met with leaders of the opposition, who included among their number not only Pitt but also Secker's chief patron, the duke of Newcastle.[144] Possibly for this reason, Secker was kept on a short leash – he was only informed of the ceremony's date two days beforehand and was asked at short notice to draw up and grant a marriage license for the couple so that they might marry in the council chamber at St James's Palace rather than in public.[145] To strain matters further, by 8 o'clock the morning of the ceremony Secker had not yet received the king's

---

[139] Ibid., f. 195: Secker to Osbaldeston, 11 Sept 1762.
[140] Ibid., f. 196: Osbaldeston to Secker, 11 Sept 1762. See also, ibid., f. 197: Osbaldeston to Secker, 12 Sept 1762; ibid., f. 198: Secker to Osbaldeston, 13 Sept 1762; ibid., f. 199: Osbaldeston to Secker, 13 Sept 1762; and ibid., f. 200: Osbaldeston to Secker, 14 Sept 1762.
[141] WAM, 64633: Secker to Zachary Pearce, 20 Aug 1763.
[142] LPL, MS 1130/I, f. 229: George Montagu Dunk, 2nd earl of Halifax to Secker, 5 Dec 1763. Walpole, *Memoirs of George III*, I, pp. 275–77 describes the wedding and the prince's visit in some detail.
[143] Yorke, *The Life of Lord Chancellor Hardwicke*, p. 400: Joseph Yorke to Hardwicke, 16 July 1762.
[144] Newcastle had resigned from office on account of disputes with Bute over foreign policy and entered into opposition in May 1762. Pitt had resigned in October 1761.
[145] LPL, MS 1130/II, f. 10: Granville Levenson-Gower, earl Gower to Secker, 14 Jan 1764; ibid., f. 11: Secker to Gower, 14 Jan 1764.

warrant required for him to initiate the licensing paperwork.[146] By all accounts the wedding, which he conducted, was itself a tense affair, the king and queen having ordered their servants not to appear in new clothes at the ceremony.[147] Navigating his way through such hostile waters required some skill, for in the interests of the Church, Secker would not have wanted to offend Bute or the king in any way, while his allegiance to Newcastle along with disgust at the court's general pettiness in the affair might easily have led him to complain of his treatment.[148]

What went the furthest to strengthening the state's support for the established Church of England was the active promotion of Georgian loyalism by the Anglican clergy. Loyalty to the Crown might easily be equated with loyalty to the Church, and the vigour with which the Church's leaders expressed and encouraged such loyalty themselves might also work to raise the Church's standing in the eyes of the king and his ministers. The accession of George III in October 1760 and Secker's work on thanksgivings during the Seven Years War illustrate this particularly well. 'It is unfortunately my lot to acquaint Your Grace with the melancholly Event of the Death of the King, our most gracious Sovereign. His Majesty was taken Ill this morning about eight o'Clock & expired in a few minutes', the earl of Holderness wrote to Secker on 25 October 1760.[149] This notice by the secretary of state of George II's death set in motion a train of activity over the next two months aimed at securing George III's position on the throne. Despite the fact that the Jacobite threat had been quashed on the fields of Culloden in 1745, it was nonetheless important to buttress the new king's standing and to endorse his legitimacy. And, as Secker would be central to George III's coronation a year later, so too was he was intimately involved in the pro-Georgian project during the fall of 1760.

Late on the afternoon of George II's death, those privy councillors in and around London gathered at Carlton House to sign the proclamation of George III's accession and to meet as a group with the king.[150] It fell to Secker to notify the new king officially of his grandfather's death 'subjoyning in few words wishes of a happy Reign to him'.[151] Despite the occasion, the formality of the

---

[146] 'As these things will require some time, I mention them now thus particularly to yr Lp, so that no Blame may afterwds lie on [me],' Secker cautioned Gower: LPL MS 1130/II, f. 12: Secker to Gower, 16 Jan 1764.

[147] Walpole, *Memoirs of George III*, p. 276; *Walpole's Correspondence*, XXII, p. 197: Walpole to Sir Horace Mann, 18 Jan 1764.

[148] Secker would actually conduct the baptism of the couple's son two years later: LPL, MS 1130/II, f. 23: Charles William Ferdinand, prince of Brunswick to Secker, 3 Mar 1766; ibid., f. 25: Secker to Brunswick, 3 Mar 1766; ibid., f. 26: William Henry Cavendish Bentick, 3rd duke of Portland to Secker, 6 Mar 1766.

[149] LPL, MS 1130/I, f. 24: Holderness to Secker, 25 Oct 1760.

[150] Since they met on a Saturday, most privy councillors had headed to their country homes on Friday afternoon.

[151] LPL, MS 1130/I, f. 26: Secker's account of George III's accession, [1760]. Secker notified the prince formally, 'it not being thought decent that the compliment on the death of his

proceedings bothered at least one of those in attendance. 'The use of form was never more seen than on this day,' Henry Fox groused, 'when for want of Minister or Clerk of Council who knew anything of it, we waited 4 hours for what might have been prepar'd in one ... About sixe, the Abp (ridiculously enough) acquainted us with the King's death, of which we informed the King, his Grace speaking for us, & that we had signed a Proclamation of His Majesty.'[152] The following day, Secker and the council reassembled at Saville House where they appeared as a group on the steps of the residence jointly to proclaim the new king, from whence they processed into the City. But for some unknown reason Secker decided to go further than the rest of the entourage, to comic results – 'I thought to go on as far as Temple Bar, & then to the House (of Lords), but cut not for the Crowd till I had got to Fleet Ditch ... I believe no lords coach, but mine, went much further than Charing Cross.'[153] Thereafter Secker's duties turned to working privately with the king to modify the royal prayers, planning the royal proclamation against vice and profaneness.[154]

Most importantly, he shepherded the various addresses of loyalty from the dioceses and religious bodies to the king. Addresses were set-piece professions of loyalty or congratulations from a group, ranging from diocesan clergy to charitable organizations to town corporations. Though addresses were staged events, they were not some quaint symbol but were reprinted not only in the English provincial newspapers but also in colonial journals.[155] Typically, a person or committee representing the draft a short text of four or five paragraphs that were appropriate to the occasion to be signed by members of the group. When the signatures had been gathered, the leader of the group, joined sometimes by other members, would present the address to the monarch at court. After presentation, the address and along with the names of its presenters would be printed in the *London Gazette*. Monarchs did not always receive these addresses favourably, though, as the rejected Oxford address of 1749 attests to – and sometimes rival groups even sought to poison the monarch against an address from a particular group.[156] Thus, every stage of the address process from the drafting to the presentation required political acumen, and as archbishop of Canterbury Secker was supposed to guide and assist addressing groups. Most often that guidance took the form of helping properly to word the address. For the Sons of the

---

father should be uttered by the Duke [of Cumberland]': Walpole, *Memoirs of George III*, p. 6. For a description of the somewhat contentious privy council meeting, see Hibbert, *George III*, pp. 33–35.

[152] 'Lord Holland's Memoir', in *The Life and Letters of Lady Sarah Lennox, 1745–1826*, eds. Countess of Ilchester and Lord Stavordale (1901), I, p. 5.

[153] LPL, MS 1130/1, ff. 27–28: Secker's account of George III's accession.

[154] Ibid., ff. 28–30.

[155] Nicholas Rogers, *Whigs and Cities: Popular Politics in the Age of Walpole and Pitt* (Oxford, 1989), p. 14.

[156] Paul D. Halliday, *Dismembering the Body Politic: Partisan Politics in England's Towns, 1650–1730* (Cambridge, 1998), p. 229.

Clergy, he 'put into the Hands of Bp. Yonge a hasty sketch of an Address, merely to intimate, what sort of things [he] thought shd be mentioned', while for the Society for the Propagation of the Gospel in Foreign Parts (SPG) he made 'several Alterations & Additions'.[157] Since some bishops, such as Osbaldeston of London and the eighty-four-year-old Hoadly of Winchester, were disabled, Secker stepped in to present their diocesan addresses himself.[158]

In the months after the accession, Secker also made certain that churchmen took no missteps. At George II's funeral, for instance, he observed that 'I did not put on my Weepers with my other Mourning: & few of the Bishops or other clergy did; & those were chiefly among the younger & gayer.' None of the clergy 'as omitted them now were blamed' for having done so.[159] When the Oxford bishops presented their address, they appeared in their full 'Episcopal Habits' because the Cambridge bishops had done so two days earlier.[160] Secker also ensured that the *London Gazette* published accounts of every clerical address printed to the king.[161]

The efforts of Secker and his fellow bishops at the transfer of power were important symbolically; so too was his work coordinating national feasts and fasts during the Seven Years War. Dating back to the mid sixteenth century, crown-appointed days of fast and humiliation called for God's help during times of national crisis. Fast days were held during the week and on them all work was supposed to cease when local churches held special services to which all were required to attend. During the mid eighteenth century, monarchs most often called fast days to invoke God's assistance during the wars against the French. Feast days, by contrast, were occasions of national thanksgiving and celebration and were inserted into the normal Sunday service to be read after the bills of mortality.[162]

Secker assumed office as archbishop just prior to the *annus mirabilis* (1759), during which the British rattled off a series of victories over the French from Minden to Quebec. Shortly after news of many of these victories, the king would be 'so sensible of the Blessing coronations in the royal family's life of Providence upon the army by her signal victory attained over the French' that he would order Secker to draft a short prayer of thanksgiving in commemoration.[163]

[157] LPL, MS 1130/l, f. 33: Secker's account of George III's accession.
[158] Ibid., ff. 31–32.
[159] Ibid., f. 32.
[160] Ibid., f. 33.
[161] Ibid., f. 34.
[162] Matthew Cragoe, "The hand of the Lord is upon the cattle': religions reactions to the cattle plague, 1865–67', in *An Age of Equipoise? Reassessing Mid-Victorian Britain*, ed. Martin Hewitt (Aldershot, 2000), pp. 191–92; Christopher Durston, '"For the Better Humiliation of the People": Public Days of Fasting and Thanksgiving During the English Revolution', *Seventeenth Century* 7:2 (1992), pp. 129–49; Roland Bartel, 'The Story of Public Fast Days in England', *Anglican Theological Review* 37:3 (1955), pp. 190–200.
[163] LPL, MS 1130/II, f. 85: TPH to Secker, 27 June 1758.

Because these prayers were to be read before every Anglican congregation in England, a great deal of care had to put into their composition so that the wording, the pro-Georgian message, was just right. Normally the king accepted the archbishop's suggestions without alteration, but at other times he made changes he thought fit. On occasion Secker challenged those royal suggestions when they risked over-egging the pudding. In August 1759, for instance, he complained that he believed the form of the thanksgiving prayer suggested by the king overstated the decisiveness of a recent English victory: 'I take the Liberty of troubling yr Lp again with the Form', he wrote to the secretary of state in August 1759, 'because in Consequence of the amendment made at Kennington, I think it will be proper to make another, by omitting the words, cross which I have drawn a Line; since they rather suppose a Deliverance more perfect, than possibly this may have been.'[164] Secker believed that having the churchmen oversell their parishioners on the scope of the victory could undermine the Church's position in the public's opinion. At other times, Secker had to safeguard the liturgical purity of the thanksgiving prayers that he composed. In October 1759, for instance, William Pitt suggested changes in the prayers of thanksgiving for General Wolfe's victory at Quebec. 'At the same time, I will beg your Grace's Indulgence for using the great liberty you are pleased to allow me, and offer a suggestion merely of Political Delicacy, which is that the words with regard to our Allies, *sorrow* and *fear* might perhaps be, not improperly, changed to *Labours* and *Perils* or some better ... words of much Import'.[165] Secker was quick to respond: 'I ... am sure you will give me Leave to observe to you in Return, that the words in Scripture Is. XIV.3, are, *The Lord shall give thee Rest from thy Sorrow & thy Fear*. And indeed our Allies have had great Cause for both. But if you apprehend, that this is not sufficient to secure these Expressions from misconstruction, I am very willing to substitute those, which you have suggested ... '.[166] In the end, though, Pitt acquiesced and left Secker's wording unaltered.[167]

If wrangling like this largely went on behind closed doors, the bishops' participation in parliamentary politics was a decidedly public spectacle. In January 1742, Secker later recalled, 'my Windows in Pickadilly were broken by the Mob, between 2 and 3 in the morning, under Pretence, that they were not illuminated on Admiral Vernons taking Porto Bello'. Yet the mob had targeted Secker's house because he 'had favoured the Court Candidates' for the election of Westminster. It was unclear whether this influenced Secker's subsequent vote in the House of Lords at the end of the month to 'Censure for the Neglect of keeping proper Number of Officers in the Garrison of Minorca'.[168]

---

[164] Ibid., f. 105: Secker to Holderness, 9 Aug 1759.
[165] Ibid., f. 113: Pitt to Secker, 19 Oct 1759.
[166] Ibid., f. 117: Secker to Pitt, 19 Oct 1759. Emphases in the original.
[167] Ibid., f. 115: Pitt to Secker, 19 Oct 1759.
[168] *Autobiography*, p. 21.

V

No aspect of the eighteenth-century Church of England's political activity has come in for more sustained criticism than the episcopate's role in the House of Lords.[169] Because the twenty-six bishops were part of a parliamentary body of around only 200 peers, they were an important potential voting bloc.[170] But because the crown appointed them, bishops were thought by many to be the king's servile pawns. 'The right reverend bench', reckoned the earl of Effingham in 1780, 'were not affected by any fear of losing the very respectable rank and emoluments they held in the state: but still, in some minds, translations to higher dignities and great emoluments might be not entirely overlooked.'[171] Until quite recently, the historiographical conventional wisdom has differed from Effingham's indictment in degree, rather than in kind.[172]

If the earl of Egmont is to be believed, even Secker early on might have found some merit to complaints about the rubber-stamp episcopal voting bloc in the

---

[169] Despite its age, A.S. Turberville, *The House of Lords in the XVIIIth Century* (Oxford, 1927) remains the starting point for the subject. See also, A.J. Rees, 'The Practice and Procedure of the House of Lords, 1714–1784' (University of Wales Ph.D. thesis, 1987). J.P. Parry and Stephen Taylor, 'Introduction: Parliament and the Church of England from the Reformation to the Twentieth Century', in *Parliament and the Church of England, 1529–1960*, eds. J.P Parry and Stephen Taylor (Edinburgh, 2000), pp. 1–13 is the best brief treatment of its subject.

[170] Clergy had sat in the English parliament as far back as Edward I's Model Parliament of 1295. By the eighteenth century the clerical representatives in the House of Lords were the archbishops of Canterbury and York along with the twenty English and four Welsh bishops who sat by appointment of the crown. Their parliamentary seats were not hereditary but neither were they subject to re-election, so that once in the Lords, the bishops were members of the deliberative body until death or resignation from office. Removal from office was rare, associated as it was with the extraordinary parliamentary deprivations of 1642. Only twice during the eighteenth century were bishops forcibly removed from office, once in 1699 when Thomas Watson of St David's was deprived for simony and again when Francis Atterbury's treasonable activities got him dismissed from Rochester: J.V. Beckett and Clyve Jones, 'Introduction: The Peerage and the House of Lords in the Seventeenth and Eighteenth Centuries', in *A Pillar of the Constitution: the House of Lords in British politics, 1640–1784*, ed. Clyve Jones (1989), pp. 11–13.

[171] E.N. Williams, *The Eighteenth Century Constitution, 1688–1815: Documents and Commentary* (Cambridge, 1960), p. 138.

[172] Porter, *English Society in the Eighteenth Century*, pp. 62, 114; Richard Pares, *King George III and the Politicians* (Oxford, 1953), p. 41; Sykes, *Church and State*, pp. 44–61 are emblematic of those who hold that the bishops were the state's servile pawns in the House of Lords. For a distinctly different assessment, which emphasizes episcopal independence and which suggests that the amity between church and state resulted mostly from shared aims, see Taylor, 'Church and State in England', pp. 162–86; idem, 'The Bishops at Westminster', pp. 137–63; William C. Lowe, 'Politics in the House of Lords, 1760–1775' (Emory University Ph.D. thesis, 1975); and idem, 'Bishops and Scottish Representative Peers in the House of Lords, 1760–1775' (1978), in *Peers, Politics and Power: The House of Lords, 1603–1911*, ed. Clyve Jones (1986), pp. 261–81.

Lords: 'I added, it was no less a misfortune that the bishops' bench went everlastingly in a string together for the court measures, for it lost them all reverence, and the present immorality and irreligion of the age has as much owing to that as anything else. He (Secker) freely granted it'.[173] Secker and his brother-in-law, Martin Benson, were quite obviously idealistic young bishops in the 1730s, ones who thought that the episcopate had a responsibility to scrutinize closely legislation which passed through the Parliament, even, and perhaps especially, if the king's ministers backed that legislation. '[I]t is so necessary for supporting the interest of the Church, that the bishops should be present in Parliament, that it is our duty I think to appear there,' Benson explained to George Berkeley in 1738, 'and if we take care to shew that it is not our private interest which brings us thither and rules us there, we may be able to do some good, or at least to hinder a great deal of mischief. A great deal is designed against us, & every opportunity is watched & waited for to put it in execution.'[174] This particular conception of their roles in the House of Lords led both Secker and Benson to vote against Walpole's ministry from time to time; their careers suffered for it, something they surely could have anticipated before casting their opposing votes. That they did so anyway tells us much about their own temperaments,[175] their high conception of the bishop's parliamentary role as a defender of the Church, and their belief that the Church was bound to the English state, not subject to it.

Secker's tenure in the Lords spanned over thirty-three years. He was not necessarily the most diligent attendee. On the meeting days with the greatest political importance between 1742 and 1762, the episcopate accounted for just under 14 per cent of the attendees in a body where they numbered 13.5 per cent of the members.[176] The same pattern of steady, if not extraordinary, attendance continued through the 1760s as well.[177] Secker, though, never ranked among the more frequent episcopal attendees in the Lords. Between 1741 and 1762, he showed up around 22 per cent of the time, an attendance rate which placed him in the bottom one-third of the bench. This is a bit surprising since his oversight of St James's, Westminster, and St Paul's cathedral required his regular residence in London. Despite his move to Lambeth, Secker's rate of attendance in the Lords dropped off even more markedly during the 1760s, as age and infirmity took their toll on him. 'I did not attend any of the long Days at the House of

---

[173] *Egmont Diaries*, III, p. 122.
[174] BL, Add. MS 39311, f. 39: Benson to Berkeley, 7 Feb 1738.
[175] Other bishops privately criticized Walpole's ministry but did not have the public courage of their private convictions. Secker complained of Joseph Butler, for instance, 'He said to me, at the End of the first Session, in which he sat in the House of Lords, that the ministers were both wicked Men & wicked Ministers. Yet he not only always voted with them, but expressed Contempt & Dislike of me for doing otherwise': *Autobiography*, p. 22.
[176] Taylor, 'The Bishops at Westminster', pp. 142–43.
[177] Lowe, 'The House of Lords, 1760–1775', pp. 333–35; G.M. Ditchfield, 'The House of Lords in the Age of the American Revolution', in *A Pillar of the Constitution*, p. 201.

Lords,' he noted of the 1767 session, 'being confined by the Gout in the beginning; and afterwards partly unable to bear the Fatigue, & suffocating Heat of the House.'[178] Around the same time, he explained to Newcastle, 'I am not able, and have not been able for some sessions past, to bear the Heat & Fatigue of long Days in the House of Lords.'[179] An unwillingness to offend his longstanding political allies, as well as a sense of his more wide-ranging political responsibility to the Church, also played into his decision to stay away from Parliament during his archiepiscopate. In 1762, for instance, he absented himself from the Lords rather than vote with Newcastle in the opposition.[180] Likewise in 1767, when Newcastle was once again out of king's ministry, Secker felt his personal obligations and public responsibilities pulling him in two different directions, and, in consequence, thought it most politic to steer clear of Westminster. 'It would be inconvenient to the Publick that I should offend those, with whom I must from time to time transact business of an ecclesiastical nature and with whom I have now such Business of great Consequence depending,' he confided to Newcastle at the time. 'Yet no one can have a stronger Sense of anything than I have of my Obligations to your grace and of the Deference which I owe to your Judgment.'[181]

If Secker's attendance record lagged behind those of his episcopal colleagues, he distinguished himself from them by his involvement in parliamentary debate. Many at the time pilloried the bishops for their mute presence in the Lords. William Pitt mocked the bishops, whose 'eyes were the only eyes in the House who could not meet his' and joked about them 'waking, as your Lordships knows they do, just before they vote, and staring on finding something the matter'.[182] The bishops themselves were aware of their reputation for silence and offered a variety of explanations, ranging from William Warburton's that it would debase the episcopal office for bishops regularly to engage in verbal fisticuffs during debate to Thomas Newton's that bishops entered Parliament unskilled in extempore debate because their oratorical training ground, the Convocation, had been emasculated since 1717.[183] By the time Secker took his seat on the bench, bishops customarily spoke almost exclusively on matters regarding religion. Compared to his episcopal colleagues, Secker was notably active in the Lords. Cobbett's *Parliamentary History* numbers his number of parliamentary speeches at eight.[184] Between 1735 and 1738, all of the other bishops combined spoke ten

---

178   *Autobiography*, p. 60.
179   BL, Add. MS 32982, f. 138: Secker to TPH, [26] May 1767.
180   BL, Add. MS 32945, f. 53: TPH to Devonshire, 16 Nov 1762.
181   BL, Add. MS 32982, f. 138: Secker to TPH, [26] May 1767.
182   *Correspondence of William Pitt, Earl of Chatham* (1838–40), IV, p. 328: Pitt to Shelburne, 27 Feb 1774.
183   Lowe, 'The House of Lords, 1760–1775', pp. 338–39.
184   In 1743, he spoke three times in the debate on the Spirituous Liquors Bill; in 1744, he spoke twice in the debate on the Bill to prevent correspondence with the Pretender's sons; in 1748 he spoke twice in the debate on the Bill for disarming the Scottish Highlands; and

times in the Lords, Benjamin Hoadly speaking eight times and Thomas Sherlock and Isaac Maddox once apiece. It should be noted, though, that Cobbett's figures unintentionally lowball the number of times lords actually spoke.[185] For instance, his *Parliamentary History* does not include one of Secker's speeches in 1765 against the proposed repeal of Hardwicke's Marriage Act, while the published version of his 1748 speech on the bill for disarming the Scottish Highlands bears little resemblance to the manuscript versions preserved in his papers.[186] Nevertheless, we can say with a fair amount of certainty that, with the exception of Hoadly, no one on the bench rivalled Secker's activity in parliamentary debate between the mid 1730s and the late 1760s.[187]

Secker took such interest because the Parliament into which he entered was strikingly hostile to the Church of England. The 1735 session proved relatively quiet, Secker reporting to George Berkeley that 'it does not appear that we shall have any church work this session'.[188] The calm was short-lived, though, for the 1736 session proved to be 'the high-water mark of parliamentary anticlericalism in the first half of the eighteenth century'.[189] As a leading Whig anticlerical Lord Hervey bragged, 'All the considerable debates that passed this year in Parliament were upon church matters, and Parliament, like bull-dogs, sticking close to any

---

in 1753 he spoke once in the debate on the repeal of the Jew Bill: Cobbett, *PH*, XII, pp. 1205–09, 1296–98, 1327–34; XIII, pp. 775–77, 846–48; XIV, pp. 269–70; XV, pp. 114–17.

[185] Mary Ransome, 'The reliability of contemporary reporting of the debates in the House of Commons, 1727–1741', *Bulletin of the Institute of Historical Research* 19:56 (1942), pp. 67–79. There was not official reporting of parliamentary debates during the mid eighteenth century. Ransome shows that the parliamentary reporting in the published monthlies, such as the *Gentleman's Magazine* and *London Gazette*, often inaccurately identified speakers or mischaracterized their remarks. This is unfortunate, since Cobbett's *Parliamentary History* draws heavily from those contemporary published reports. Thus a published version of the speech is likely to be less accurate than the handwritten version of the speech in the speaker's own hand. Where possible in my discussion of Secker's career in the House of Lords, I rely upon his manuscript notes. There are a number of instances, though, when the only surviving copy of his speeches is in Cobbett. I thank Stephen Taylor for his advice on this point.

[186] BL, Add. MS 35879, ff. 326–38; LPL, Secker Papers 7, ff. 348–51; LPL, MS 1349, ff. 159–66.

[187] Secker's manuscripts notes of parliamentary debates between 1735 and 1743 (BL, Add. MS 6043) form the basis of Cobbett's *Parliamentary History* for those years and further testify to Secker's demonstrable interest in proceedings in the Lords. During the debates themselves, Secker took shorthand notes and copied them into longhand sometime later: Cobbett, *PH*, IX, preface. The notebook contains reports on two debates from 1735 before picking up again in April 1738. The reports end in Feb 1743 (1742 on the old calendar).

[188] BL, Add. MS 39311, f. 27: Secker to Berkeley, 1 Feb 1735.

[189] Stephen Taylor, 'Whigs, Tories and Anticlericalism: Ecclesiastical Courts Legislation in 1733', *Parliamentary History* 19:3 (2000), pp. 329–55, at p. 330. Sykes, *Edmund Gibson*, p. 149 memorably argued that 'The clergy were the objects of a series of sharp and damaging attacks during the latter half of the Parliament of 1727–33, which recalled the Reformation Parliament of Henry VIII in its zeal to attack the stronghold of clerical privilege and abuse.'

hold in which they have once fastened, the poor Church this winter was as much worried as Sir Robert had been any other.'[190]

Three bills were introduced into Parliament within two weeks of each other in March 1736 which severely strained the Church-Whig alliance which Walpole and Gibson had forged over the last decade. The first bill, pressed for by the Dissenting Deputies and designed to repeal the Test and Corporation Acts, was dead on arrival, scuttled by a Walpole determined to demonstrate publicly his readiness to defend the Church of England against its enemies.[191] Surprisingly little fuss, though, was put up by the bishops over the Charitable Uses Act (9 Geo. II c. 36), more commonly known as the Mortmain Act, which outlawed granting lands or money to purchase lands unless arranged at least a year before the donor's death. The legislation's supporters intended it to cripple the ability of charitable organizations to receive benefactions of land from individuals at their death. The act directly hurt a number of prominent charitable religious organizations, but it passed through the Lords without division.[192] The Quakers Tithe Bill of the same year, though, did not meet with silent acquiescence from the episcopal bench.[193]

The Quakers were unique among tithe disputants in early modern England in their absolute refusal to tithe.[194] Believing it immoral to pay anyone who ministered the Gospel, they were so serious about non-payment of tithes that a member who paid them could be expelled from the Society of Friends for freely paying them. This presented the Quakers with a serious legal dilemma, though,

---

[190] *Hervey's Memoirs*, II, p. 530.

[191] James E. Bradley, 'The Public, Parliament and the Protestant Dissenting Deputies', in *Parliament and Dissent*, eds. David Wykes and Stephen Taylor (Edinburgh, 2005), pp. 71–90; T.F.J. Kendrick, 'Sir Robert Walpole, the Old Whigs, and the Bishops', *HJ* 11:3 (1968), pp. 433–34; N.C. Hunt, *Two Early Political Associations: The Quakers and the Dissenting Deputies in the Age of Sir Robert Walpole* (Oxford, 1961), p. 85. See also, Andrew Thompson, 'Contesting the Test Acts: Dissent, Parliament and the Public in the 1730s', in *Parliament and Dissent*, pp. 58–70.

[192] Nicholas Cox, *Bridging the Gap: A History of the Corporation of the Sons of the Clergy over 300 Years, 1655–1978* (Oxford, 1978), pp. 60–62; Alan Savidge, *The Foundation and Early Years of Queen Anne's Bounty* (1955), pp. 100–05; Best, *Temporal Pillars*, pp. 104–10. Edmund Gibson and Thomas Sherlock had tried unsuccessfully to have Queen Anne's Bounty and a number of other charitable organizations exempted from the Mortmain Act's provisions. Nearly every major charitable organization in England also petitioned Parliament against the act, but in the end only the universities of Oxford and Cambridge and the colleges of Eton, Winchester, and Westminster were freed from its provisions. Sykes, *Edmund Gibson*, pp. 161–63 and Carpenter, *Thomas Sherlock*, pp. 121–23 chart the clerical opposition to the act.

[193] Hunt, *Two Early Political Associations*, pp. 1–112 and Stephen Taylor, 'Sir Robert Walpole, the Church of England, and the Quakers Tithe Bill of 1736', *HJ* 28:1 (1985), pp. 51–77 are the most reliable guides to the Quakers Tithe Bill controversy.

[194] Eric J. Evans, *The Contentious Tithe: The tithe problem and English agriculture, 1750–1850* (1976), pp. 58–62; G.M. Ditchfield, 'Parliament, the Quakers and the Tithe Question, 1750–1835', *Parliamentary History* 4 (1985), pp. 87–90; and Taylor, 'Quakers Tithe Bill of 1736', p. 57 explain the Quakers' legal position regarding tithes.

because it was illegal to refuse tithe payment and a Friend risked losing all of his property for non-compliance with the law. As a result, a whole series of unwritten practices developed at the local level whereby the Quakers might forfeit their tithes without offending their consciences. For instance, some Quakers permitted tithe owners to enter their fields and harvest their portion of the tithes. The most conscientious Quakers, though, refused to pay tithes until they had gone through prosecution and distraint of property. This was an expensive and lengthy process, mitigated only somewhat by the act of 1696 (7, 8 Wm. III, c. 6), which allowed JPs the option to issue a summary judgment for tithes less than £10. Quakers sought in the 1736 legislation to make the summary proceedings obligatory, rather than optional. Hoping to split the Tories and the opposition Whigs, Walpole's ministry sponsored the bill.[195]

Edmund Gibson spearheaded an episcopate resolutely opposed to the Quakers Tithe Bill, a move that caught Walpole completely off-guard. At a meeting of the bishops to consider what to do about the bill, 'Some were for amending it in Concert with the Ministry, & yielding to it,' Secker, then bishop of Bristol, remembered. But John Potter, bishop of Oxford, 'opposed this earnestly', and the bishops all sent circular letters to their clergy to raise funds to pay for legal counsel against the bill. As the junior member of the episcopate it fell to Secker to collect from each of the bishops the £170 donated by the nation's clergy to pay for legal counsel to advise them in their fight against the bill in Parliament.[196] The Quakers Tithe Bill was anathema to the episcopate for at least three reasons. First, it would make collecting tithes more difficult. Second, the bishops believed that the bill affronted the Church's property rights and feared that its passage into law would lead down a slippery slope to the abolition of all tithes. And, finally, the clergy resented the state meddling with the Church's independence by trying to impose restrictions on ecclesiastical courts.[197]

Secker's speech before the Lords echoed all of these arguments.[198] He opened with an vicious attack on the Quakers. 'The persons whom this bill relates to, plead a Scruple of Conscience against it paying the Clergy what is due to them by the Law of the land, & is demanded only on that Foot,' he complained. 'This you will agree is a very strange Scruple, & the stranger, because this very scrupulous People, who refuse paying to a Clergy, make no Scruple paying to a War, though they reckon it just as Antichristian a Thing as a Clergy.' Furthermore, the Quakers' complaints about the bishops sending circular letters to the clergy in their dioceses rang hollow: the Quakers themselves circulated

---

[195] Taylor, 'Quakers Tithe Bill of 1736', pp. 70–71.
[196] *Autobiography*, pp. 16–17.
[197] Taylor, 'Quakers Tithe Bill of 1736', pp. 64–67.
[198] LPL, Secker Papers 7, ff. 326–33: Secker's remarks on the Quaker Bill [1736]. Unless otherwise noted, all quotations in this paragraph are drawn from these manuscript remarks. This speech is not recorded in Cobbett, *PH*. If Secker did not actually deliver it in the Lords, then the manuscript text, at the very least, reflects his own objections to the bill.

letters and the Dissenting Deputies, who sought the repeal of the Test and Corporation Acts, also lobbied Parliament as a group. Despite the Quakers' hypocrisy, Secker argued, churchmen 'in general have treated them, & do now with great Kindness and Friendliness'. Indeed, he boasted, 'I had the Pleasure of receiving their Thanks at Bristol last year for what I had said in my charge concerning the Proper manner of the clergys recovering their Dues.' If the Quakers Tithe Bill were to be enacted into law, though, it would make gathering tithes 'unsafe or difficult to the Clergy'. Moreover, it would infringe upon the Church's property rights: 'This is a bill relating to Property, & your Lordships will look upon it, as if it were a cause relating to Property & determine it merely upon the merits of the cause.' He reiterated this point later in the speech, stressing that 'A Bill of great Importance it undoubtedly is, as it affects the property in the first Place of all the Clergy in England.'

Secker's response was typical of the Church's reaction to the Quakers Tithe Bill, and a surprised (and infuriated) Walpole tried desperately to salvage the Church-Whig alliance. Various amendments in the Commons failed to sway any of the bishops' votes, though, so it was left to Hardwicke and Lord Chancellor Talbot to kill off the bill in the Lords. Rather than attacking it directly, they argued that the Commons' amendments had made the bill both unclear and contradictory, that there was insufficient time in the session to draft a satisfactory act, and that the bill should therefore be scuttled.[199] This enabled Walpole to claim that the ministry had not abandoned the bill while at the same time signalling that it was alright to vote against it. On the motion to commit on 12 May, fifteen bishops joined Newcastle, Hardwicke, and other prominent Whig lords in a 54–35 vote to defeat the bill.[200] Though he jettisoned Gibson as his ecclesiastical minister as punishment for leading episcopal opposition to the bill, Walpole worked concertedly to mend what damage had been done to the Church-Whig alliance.[201]

Where Secker differed from most of his fellow bishops was in his behaviour after the Quakers Tithe Bill's defeat. While most returned to voting for ministerial measures in Parliament, Secker and Martin Benson opposed the

[199] Taylor, 'Quakers Tithe Bill of 1736', p. 72. Cf. Kendrick, 'Sir Robert Walpole, the Old Whigs and the Bishops, 1733–1736', p. 443.

[200] Cobbett, *PH*, IX, pp. 1219–20. There were, in addition to the fifteen bishops present, six more who had given their proxy support if it were necessary. No bishops supported the motion to commit, and only William Wake, Samuel Hough, Benjamin Hoadly, and John Wynne did not bother to vote or give their proxies to another member of the Lords. Taylor, 'Quakers Tithe Bill of 1736', p. 67. Cf. Kendrick, 'Sir Robert Walpole, the Old Whigs and the Bishops, 1733–1736', p. 443.

[201] Sykes, *Edmund Gibson*, pp. 166–75; Taylor, 'Quakers Tithe Bill of 1736', p. 74; idem, '"Dr. Codex" and the Whig "Pope"', pp. 26–28.

ministry on a number of procedural measures during the next six years.[202] On more significant political divisions between 1736 and 1744, Secker voted against the ministry twice, once in March 1739 against the address to address upon the Spanish Convention (in which only four other bishops joined him in opposition)[203] and again in February 1743 in the vote on the Spirituous Liquors Act (in which he was joined by all of the bishops who voted). In the five other division lists of the period, he is counted a supporter of the government.[204] Analyzing his own voting behaviour during the period, Secker reckoned that he and Benson had 'voted with the Court ... in other Divisions much oftener than otherwise; & sometimes when other Bishops, as Litchfield, Hereford & Lincoln voted against it'.[205] Nonetheless, he gained a reputation as a ministerial opponent, something which helped stall his career for over a decade.

Policies, not personalities, seem to have informed Secker's parliamentary behaviour during this period. Rather than an inherent dislike of Walpole, it was Walpole's prosecution of the war with Spain and his court policies which most bothered Secker.[206] A clue to his thinking is provided in a letter to George Berkeley in the summer of 1737. 'The ministry I believe mean us of the clergy neither any harm nor much good. Many of those who would be thought their best friends indeed are vehement against us and so are many also of their most determined enemies,' he wrote to Berkeley.

> It doth not seem therefore that our strength is in adhering to either party; as indeed I think it never can: but in the honest policy of acting uprightly between both and joyning with neither to do wrong. Those who act thus will neither stand or fall with honour. I see very little prospect that any thing in the Established Church will be altered for the better: for ministers are against all changes and they who complain would be very sorry to see the things which they complain mended. Nor doth there appear any immediate danger of alteration for the worse. And yet

---

[202] A cursory review suggests that out of at least 35 procedural motions during this period, Secker abstained twice and voted against the ministry eight times. BL, Add. MS 6043, *passim*.

[203] Clyve Jones and Frances Harris, '"A Question ... Carried by Bishops, Pensioners, Place-Men, Idiots": Sarah, Duchess of Marlborough and the Lords' Divisions over the Spanish Convention, 1 March 1739', *Parliamentary History* 11:2 (1992), pp. 254–77, at p. 272. Benson joined Secker in opposition.

[204] Though Secker actually supported Walpole's ministry in a bellwether vote against appointing a date for a committee of the whole House on the state of the nation, Benson joined three other bishops in opposition: Clyve Jones, 'The House of Lords and the Fall of Walpole', in *Hanoverian Britain and Empire: Essays in Memory of Philip Lawson*, eds. Stephen Taylor, Richard Connors, and Clyve Jones (Woodbridge, 1998), pp. 119, 130–31.

[205] *Autobiography*, p. 19.

[206] Thus Secker notes that on 13 Feb 1741, 'Bp Benson & I voted against the Proposal in the House of Lords to Address the King to remove Sir Robert Walpole from his Presence & Counsels for ever. But we also voted against the Proposal for censuring the Proposal.' Likewise, he 'did not vote on the 2d reading of the Bill for indemnifying Persons, who should make Discoveries concerning the Earl of Orfords Conduct': *Autobiography*, pp. 21, 23.

considering the increasing disregard to Religion and every thing that deserves the name of principle together with the strange growth of that wild spirit which calls it self zeal for Liberty there would be no occasion to wonder at any shock how great or sudden so ever which might happen either to the Ecclesiastical or the Civil part of the Constitution.[207]

When a pension bill, something of concern to a country-minded cleric like Secker, came before the Lords in the spring of 1740, he was torn between his desire for good government and for the promotion of public virtue. On 18 March, he visited the earl of Egmont to discuss the bill. Secker explained to Egmont that 'he was under great difficulties how to vote on that occasion'. As Secker saw it, 'to oppose the pensioning of members of Parliament would have an ill appearance to the public'. Yet, he reasoned, 'on the other [hand] it was certain many members would perjure themselves, for by the bill they were to swear at the Speaker's table that they had or had not pensions, and it was too much to be feared that many would forswear themselves, which was a snare no conscientious man ought to lay in other men's way'. Egmont assured him that 'gentlemen of education, and who pretended to have regard to their honour, would not in the sight of the Speaker and Parliament swear a falsity, which would come soon to the knowledge of the world'. Secker was decidedly less sanguine about the transparency of government. Furthermore, he worried that corruption might become accepted by the public as a matter of course in government: 'suppose they shown own to the House they had pensions, and confidently glory in it, would not that make pensions a fashionable thing and in time take away the shame of them?'[208] Secker nevertheless ended up supporting the 1740 pension bill. His record thereafter was mixed, helping vote down place and pension bills in 1741 but supporting them in 1742.[209]

The Spirituous Liquors Act of 1743 (16 Geo. II, c. 8) showed that Secker and his fellow bishops were still willing to oppose the government if they believed that parliamentary measures threatened religion and morality.[210] Secker's own opposition is especially notable in light of his friendship and patron-client

---

[207] BL, Add. MS 39311, ff. 37–38: Secker to Berkeley, 29 June 1737. Martin Benson later echoed this cautiously pessimistic assessment later when he wrote to Secker, 'It was measures, not ministers I desired to see changed. And as I had little hope of seeing the former, I have less concern about the latter': BL, Add. MS 39311, f. 49: Benson to Secker, 23 April 1743.

[208] *Egmont Diaries*, III, p. 122.

[209] *Autobiography*, pp. 21, 23. For the 1742 place and pension bills, see also Stephen Taylor and Clyve Jones (eds.), *Tory and Whig: The Parliamentary Papers of Edward Harley, 3rd Earl of Oxford, and William Hay, M.P. for Seaford, 1716–1753* (Woodbridge, 1998), p. 58.

[210] Taylor, 'Bishops at Westminster', pp. 151–53 examines episcopal opposition to the act. See also, Jessica Warner, *Craze: Gin and Debauchery in an Age of Reason* (2003); Lee Davison, 'Experiments in the Social Regulation of Industry: Gin Legislation, 1729–51', in *Stilling the Grumbling Hive: the response to social and economic problems in England, 1689–1750*, eds. Lee Davison et al. (Stroud, 1992), pp. 25–48; Peter Clark, 'The "Mother Gin" Controversy in the Early Eighteenth Century', *TRHS*, 5th series, 38 (1988), pp. 63–84.

relationship with the Pelhamites, then heading the king's ministry. During the first half of the eighteenth century, many thought gin consumption was a serious social problem, one depicted graphically in Hogarth's *Gin Lane*. Parliament first addressed the problem in an act of 1729 that required gin retailers to pay £20 a year for a license and put a duty on gin. Parliament revisited the issue again in a 1736 act that made retailing licenses more expensive (£50 per annum) and that increased the duty on gin to £1 per gallon. While this succeeded in putting gin out of the price range of many poor people, retailers found ways to skirt the law by selling it clandestinely.

By 1743 it had become obvious that parliamentary efforts to regulate gin retailing and consumption had failed and that a new approach was needed. In response, the government sponsored a bill that would substantially lower the duty on gin but would seriously restrict the number of licensed retailers. The bishops, led by Secker and Thomas Sherlock, stridently opposed this measure.[211] While acknowledging that the bill would end the clandestine trade in gin, Secker questioned whether it would reduce consumption. 'On the contrary, the commodity may, by this Bill, be brought cheaper to the consumer; because the distiller, the compounder, and the retailer, especially the latter, will sell at less a profit,' he argued in a speech before the Lords, 'for surely the twenty shillings to be paid by the retailer is not near equal to the risk every clandestine retailer now runs'. Indeed, he worried that with increased consumption, there would follow 'such a considerable revenue, that no administration will be willing to part with it, or consent to any law for redressing the grievance, because it will annihilate, or very much diminish the revenue'.[212] This was a theme he returned to in a later speech in the Lords. 'The only argument which can be offered in defence of this Bill, is the necessity of supporting the expences of war, and the difficulty of raising money by any other method,' he contended. 'The necessity of the war, my lords, I am not about to call into question ... but this I can boldly assert, that however just, however necessary, however prudently prosecuted, and however successfully concluded, it can produce no advantages equivalent to the national sobriety and industry, and am certain that no public advantage ought to be purchased at the expense of public virtues.'[213] Indeed, Secker argued, Parliament had neglected its duty to supervise and regulate the morals of the nation, for 'it is allowed [spirituous liquors] are pernicious to the health, industry, and morals of the people; and what is prejudicial to the morals extends its consequences to the world that shall never end'. Thus, he declared, 'I shall oppose it as destructive to virtue, and contrary to the inviolable laws of religion.'[214] In the end, these arguments changed few minds. Though eighteen other bishops joined Secker in

---

[211] Porteus, *Life of Secker*, pp. 29–30.
[212] Cobbett, *PH*, XII, pp. 1208–09.
[213] Ibid., p. 1334.
[214] Ibid., pp. 1296, 1297.

opposition to the bill, it nevertheless passed into law. Frustrated at having lost, ten bishops, including Secker, entered a formal protest against the bill's passage.[215]

Though on the losing side in the vote on the Spirituous Liquors Act, Secker did not in the future shy away from opposing the government when he believed it to be his religious duty to do so. This was particularly evident regarding Scottish religious affairs during the 1740s. The Episcopal Church of Scotland stood in much different relation to the state than did its counterpart the Church of England.[216] Following the Glorious Revolution, William III had acceded to the abolition of episcopacy in Scotland and its replacement with the Presbyterian church system. In this, William bent to a vocal minority, for much of Scotland continued to support the episcopal ministers. Disentanglement did not proceed quickly, and many kept their parochial cures until their deaths. In 1712, parliament passed a toleration act for Scotland which allowed for prayer-book worship outside parish churches led by pastors ordained by any Protestant bishop. Though most of the Scottish episcopal clergy grudgingly took the required oaths of allegiance and abjuration of the Pretender, they remained 'the most significant single group of men creating and transmitting articulate Jacobite theology', and their parishioners 'produced the vast majority of active participants in every single Jacobite rebellion'.[217] Indeed, by the 1740s, all the bishops were non-jurors, as were most of the lower clergy. The religious situation in Scotland, then, made the Church of England's involvement there fraught with potential problems, but also loaded with potentially powerful religious symbolism.

In November 1743, representatives from the established Church of Scotland approached Secker promoting a parliamentary bill that would provide a state-funded charity for the widows and children of Scottish clergy. (Why the Scots approached him to promote the bill rather than either of the archbishops is suggestive in itself of his parliamentary reputation.) Something akin to such a fund existed in England in the form of the Sons of the Clergy charity. As Secker remembered, though, the representatives who met with him 'fancied the Bishops wd oppose' the bill. And well they might have anticipated opposition coming from the episcopal bench since the established Church of Scotland was a Presbyterian church whose theology and ecclesiology differed markedly from the Church of England. To some surprise, though, Secker actively promoted the bill:

[215] Taylor, 'Bishops at Westminster', p. 153.

[216] Rowan Strong, *Episcopalianism in Nineteenth-Century Scotland: Religious Responses to Modernizing Society* (Oxford, 2002), pp. 1–32; F.C. Mather, *High Church Prophet: Bishop Samuel Horsley (1733–1806) and the Caroline Tradition in the Later Georgian Church* (Oxford, 1992), pp. 116–38; idem, 'Church, parliament and penal laws: some Anglo-Scottish interactions in the eighteenth century', *EHR* 92:364 (1977), pp. 540–72.

[217] Bruce Lenman, 'The Scottish Episcopal Clergy and the Ideology of Jacobitism', in *Ideology and Conspiracy: Aspects of Jacobitism, 1689–1759*, ed. Eveline Cruickshanks (Edinburgh, 1982), p. 36.

'I paid [them] all the Civility & did all the Service I could. No Bp opposed their bill publickly or privately. And we took Care that a Bp shd be present at each of its 3 readings in the House of Lords.'[218] The encouragement given to the Presbyterian ministers by Secker and his fellow bishops could be interpreted as a capitulation to the state, which would have wanted to reward the clergy of the established Presbyterian church for their loyalty and to snub those of the Episcopal Church of Scotland for their non-juring sympathies. However, the bench's support of the Scottish episcopal clergy just five years later, when the reputations of their northern brethren lay at their lowest, undermines these charges of erastianism.

Following the failed Jacobite rebellion of 1745, Parliament passed several acts aimed at extirpating Jacobitism in Scotland and non-jurors among the clergy. One of 1746 (19 George II, c. 38) required all Scottish episcopal members to register their clerical orders with a JP by 1 September 1746, after which only those clergy ordained by English or Irish bishops would be granted licenses to preach. This meant that those who registered before September could have been ordained by Protestant bishops from Sweden, Denmark, or Prussia or even by Scottish non-juring ones. However, in the 1748 Act for Disarming the Scottish Highlands, the government included a clause that would ban *all* Scottish episcopal clergy who had not been ordained by English or Irish bishops, irrespective of whether their orders had been registered before September 1746 or not. This proved too much for the English bishops, who united together in opposition to the bill, opposition that 'was motivated by their concern for ... [the Church's] rights and privileges as an independent society'.[219]

In the debate on the bill in the Lords, Secker led the episcopal opposition.[220] He did not claim, as was reported later, that the clause 'arrogated to the civil authority a power to determine whether a priest has been duly and regularly ordained, or a bishop consecrated, which is a question no true member of the Church of England will allow the civil authority to have anything to do with'.[221] Indeed, the speech he actually gave and the one he was reported to have given bear little resemblance to one another.[222] In his speech of 10 May 1748, though,

---

218 *Autobiography*, p. 23. See also, Porteus, *Life of Secker*, pp. 30–31.

219 Taylor, 'The Bishops at Westminster', pp. 153–56.

220 Secker had recently solidified his anti-Jacobite credentials when, in 1744, he joined Hardwicke and Carteret to speak vigorously in favour of legislation (17 Geo. II c. 39) to attaint the Pretender's sons; the bill passed into law, but not without 'a strong and animated protest'. He also preached a sermon against the Pretender at St James's, Westminster, and later published it: *Autobiography*, pp. 24, 113; Cobbett, *PH*, XIII, pp. 775–77, 846–48; Porteus, *Life of Secker*, pp. 33–34.

221 Cited in G. Grub, *An ecclesiastical history of Scotland from the introduction of Christianity to the present time* (Edinburgh, 1861), IV, p. 38.

222 The text of Secker's speech which was reprinted in *London Magazine* and in Cobbett's *Parliamentary History* differs markedly from the text of the speech found in two places in his private papers: LPL, Secker Papers 7, ff. 342–46, 348–51 and LPL, MS 1349, ff. 159–66. See also, Taylor, 'The Bishops at Westminster', p. 154 n. 91 on the provenance of Secker's

he did vigorously object to the clause's adoption into law, framing his argument against the clause in language that would appeal most directly to the majority in the Lords who were not bishops. He admitted from the outset that the clause did not constitute an attempt by the state to legislate 'the spiritual validity of orders, nor with any legal confirmation of them'. Rather, he believed that the clause undermined the principles of toleration. 'Supposing the Orders given by Nonjuring Bishops ever so valid. Theologically, the State may forbid men's officiating upon them, if the Public Good requires it,' he contended. '[Y]et on the genuine principles of Toleration, the State may and should suffer men to officiate upon them, if it do the Public no harm: just as the other Sects are suffered; some without any orders at all and some with orders from we know not whom.'[223] To Secker's way of thinking, the clause was manifestly unjust upon other grounds as well. Before the 1746 act, the aspiring Scottish episcopal cleric 'understands, that he may legally have them from a Nonjuring bishops. It is therefore natural that he should go to such a one, as the nearest, and the more so because if he goes to an English bishop, he will in all likelihood be refused.' Indeed, Secker averred, 'Bishop Talbot of Durham when I was his Chaplain, 20 years ago, told me that the Bishops of the Northern Parts of this Nation had agreed amongst themselves not to ordain any person for the service of the Episcopal Churches of Scotland.' Under these circumstances 'why might not a man, ever so well affected to the Governmt, apply to a Scotch nonjuring Bishop for orders?'[224] In the end, Secker and his fellow bishops failed to carry the debate. Though the unanimous vote against the clause by all twenty bishops present when the Lords met in committee on 10 May helped defeat it 32–38, the government quickly marshalled its forces and the clause was restored the next day on a 37–32 vote upon the report of the bill.[225]

The clause represented the apex of legal discrimination against the Episcopal Church of Scotland, but later generations of Anglican high churchmen would look to the disestablished Scottish church as an exemplar of an anti-erastian body whose claims were purely spiritual and which 'did not need the buttress of the State to uphold primitive truth'.[226] And though Secker and his fellow bishops could have made their argument against the clause in the Bill for Disarming the Scottish Highlands on secular grounds, they united in opposition to the government in order to protect the Episcopal Church of Scotland's independence.

---

published speech in Cobbett, *PH*, XVI, pp. 270–76. All quotes from that speech here are taken from the version in LPL, MS 1349.
[223] LPL, MS 1349, f. 159.
[224] Ibid., f. 166.
[225] Taylor and Jones (eds.), *Tory and Whig*, p. 83.
[226] Peter Nockles, '"Our Brethren of the North": The Scottish Episcopal Church and the Oxford Movement', *JEH* 47:4 (1996), p. 657.

1748 marked one of Secker's last substantive forays into parliamentary affairs until the 1760s, a decade which witnessed marked episcopal opposition in the Lords.[227] Bute's cider excise went down to defeat on 28 March 1763, with almost half of the bishops present voting against the measure.[228] Two years later, bishops led the opposition which killed off the ecclesiastical estates bill and Thomas Gilbert's bill to alter the poor laws.[229] A number of bishops also voted against the Regency Bill in 1765.[230] Raw political calculations, rather than a rigid adherence to religious principle, helps explain the maverick behaviour. The 1760s was a period of Byzantine complexity in British politics, as a new reign ushered in new rules of allegiance and personnel.[231] In an era of such uncertainty, many bishops found it easiest simply to vote with their patrons, rather than to try successfully to guess who would, in the end, clamber atop the political summit.[232]

What occasioned Secker's re-entry into active parliamentary politicking during the mid 1760s was, in no small measure, a desire to help his old friend and patron, the duke of Newcastle.[233] Newcastle returned to government in 1765 in the first Rockingham ministry.[234] Named lord privy seal, he and Secker were given a free hand with crown religious patronage. 'His Majesty was graciously pleased to say, that he desired I would undertake the Church affairs, that is, the recommending of all Church preferments,' Newcastle recollected. 'I told His Majesty, with the Assistance of the Archbishop of Canterbury I should obey His

---

[227] Lowe, 'Bishops and Scottish Representative Peers', pp. 264–72; Taylor, 'The Bishops at Westminster', pp. 148–51. Secker did speak in support of the repeal of the Jew Bill in 1753: Cobbet, *PH*, XV, pp. 114–17.

[228] Patrick Woodland, 'The House of Lords, The City of London and Political Controversy in the Mid-1760s: The Opposition to the Cider Excise Further Considered', *Parliamentary History* 11 (1992), pp. 57–87; BL, Add. MS 32947: TPH to Secker, 25 Mar 1763.

[229] BL, Add. MS 32965, f. 400: TPH to Secker, 28 Feb 1765; BL, Add. MS 32966, f. 131: TPH to Secker, 31 Mar 1765; Richard S. Tompson, 'Gilbert, Thomas (*bap.* 1720, *d.* 1798)', *ODNB*.

[230] Derek Jarrett, 'The Regency Crisis of 1765', *EHR* 85:335 (1970), pp. 282–315.

[231] Peter D.G. Thomas, *George III: King and Politicians, 1760–1770* (Manchester, 2002) succinctly conveys the political uncertainty of the decade.

[232] Lowe, 'Bishops and Scottish Representative Peers', p. 269.

[233] The pull of personal loyalties for Secker is evident in the spring of 1765, when he broke what appears to have been a twelve-year silence in the House of Lords to deliver a long and spirited defence of Hardwicke's Marriage Act of 1753 (26 George II c. 32) against a new bill to repeal the 1753 act. Hardwicke himself had died in March 1764, but Secker nevertheless felt obliged to defend his old friend's signal piece of legal reform legislation: BL, Add. MS 35879, ff. 326–38: The Archbishop of Canterbury's speech in the House of Lords, on the Second Reading of the Marriage Bill, Wednesday May 8th 1765; R.B. Outhwaite, *Clandestine Marriage in England, 1500–1850* (1995), pp. 112–13. For background on the 1753 act, itself emblematic of restorative reform, see LPL, Secker Papers 7, ff. 267–325; Rebecca Probert, 'The Impact of the Marriage Act of 1753: Was It Really "A Most Cruel Law For Fair Sex"?', *Eighteenth-Century Studies* 38:2 (2005), pp. 247–62; David Lemmings, 'Marriage and the law in the eighteenth century: Hardwicke's Marriage Act of 1753', *HJ* 39:2 (1996), pp. 339–60.

[234] Langford, *The First Rockingham Administration*, pp. 33–35.

Majesty's commands.'[235] When George III talked with Secker about the new arrangements, he told Secker, 'Take Care of Oxford, for the Duke will take care of Cambridge.' This marked a significant change in Secker's public role, for he 'was neither asked nor told any thing by the King, or any of his Ministers' about the disposition of crown ecclesiastical patronage during the Grenville ministry.[236] Newcastle also turned to Secker for help convincing Charles Yorke to join the Rockingham ministry as attorney-general.[237]

More pressing business than ecclesiastical patronage and Yorke's pique faced the Rockingham ministry, though, for it became almost immediately clear to the new government that it had to manage the blowback from America over the Stamp Act.[238] Many thought it self-evident that the provocative act needed to be repealed, but it was hotly debated how to do so without appearing to cave to pressure from the colonies. Secker took a direct hand in formulating a parliamentary strategy for the repeal and played a pivotal role in organizing the bishops to vote for the repeal.[239]

In late January 1766, the second earl of Hardwicke and Newcastle sought Secker's opinion on the five resolutions the ministry aimed to put before Parliament to sugar-coat the bitter pill of repeal. Charles Yorke had taken a leading hand in drafting them and they were thought to represent the views of those less conciliatory and, thus, less willing to accept repeal.[240] Secker advised Hardwicke and Newcastle, the latter of whom was sceptical of both the tone and content of Yorke's resolutions, that their passage was necessary to placate those opposed to repeal; indeed, both needed to meet with Rockingham to '[awaken] him to see, that the Administration had much better secure it self the proposal of Resolutions, than let the Opposition have Credit of it; & much better move for Resolutions which they can maintain as sufficient, than let them be overturned, as feeble & ineffectual, to make place for others, which may be extravagant & mischievous'.[241] Addressing Newcastle's worries about adopting the resolutions, Secker cautioned, 'If the approaching parliamentary storm can be weathered by

[235] Mary Bateson (ed.), *A Narrative of the Changes in the Ministry, 1765–1767* (1898), p. 33; *Autobiography*, p. 50; BL, Add. MS 32969, f. 15: TPH to Secker, 13 Aug 1765. Newcastle elsewhere described Secker as 'My Coadjutor, of my own making': BL, Add. MS 32968, f. 392: TPH to Thomas Townshend, 1 Aug 1765.

[236] *Autobiography*, p. 50.

[237] Ibid., pp. 50–51; BL, Add. MS 32967, f. 359: TPH to Secker, 12 July 1765; BL, Add. MS 35637, f. 194: Secker to Charles Yorke, 20 July 1765; BL, Add. MS 32969, f. 15: TPH to Secker, 13 Aug 1765; John Cannon, 'Yorke, Charles (1722–1770)', *ODNB*.

[238] Edmund S. Morgan and Helen Morgan, *The Stamp Act Crisis: Prologue to Revolution* (Chapel Hill, NC, 1995); Peter D.G. Thomas, *British Politics and the Stamp Act Crisis: The First Phase of the American Revolution, 1763–1767* (Oxford, 1975).

[239] William C. Lowe, 'Archbishop Secker, the Bench of Bishops, and the Repeal of the Stamp Act', *HMPEC* 46:4 (1977), pp. 429–42 is the most detailed study of its subject.

[240] Langford, *The First Rockingham Administration*, pp. 151–52.

[241] BL, Add. MS 35607, ff. 235–36: Secker to Philip Yorke, 2nd earl of Hardwicke, 31 Jan 1766.

such precautions, general methods may be gradually interposed with safety in future proceedings, to prevent Inconveniences from strong Declarations now.'[242]

Secker had sat long enough in the House of Lords and was an astute enough politician to sense the Rockingham ministry's weakness there, and his contacts with his fellow bishops stoked his worry that the episcopal bench would divide over the repeal, absent some show of resolve from the king and his ministers. These fears were borne out when the resolutions came up for votes; in one vote on 6 February, eleven of the sixteen bishops present voted against the ministry. If it could not get the resolutions though the Lords, could the ministry actually get the repeal through?[243]

Because the repeal was a money bill, it had to originate in the House of Commons. Once the repeal had got through the Commons, a divided Lords took it up. Few wanted to risk the sort of constitutional crisis that would follow from the Lords rejecting the repeal, but there was still work to be done to line up the actual votes for repeal. George III's dithering did not help. Rockingham had got a pledge from him in writing that he wanted the Stamp Act repealed, but Newcastle urged Secker to have a personal audience with George, knowing a face-to-face assurance from the monarchy himself might sway episcopal votes.[244] Secker agreed, noting that 'the Bishop of Winchester will vote as he understands the King to be inclined: & so will other bishops'.[245] In their meeting, the king assured Secker that 'he was for the Repeal, of which the Archbishop made very good use with the Bench'.[246] When the final vote on the repeal came in early March, eighteen bishops voted for the repeal, with eight voting against it. Through their efforts, Secker and Newcastle had managed to flip five bishops into the pro-repeal camp, something that had looked entirely unlikely only a month before.[247]

Though enduring yet another bout of gout during the winter 1765–66, Secker threw himself into the effort to whip up episcopal support for the Stamp Act's repeal. In large part, his work can be put down to deep personal loyalty to Newcastle. But more than that explains his motivation. To begin with, Secker, like any archbishop of Canterbury worth his salt during the eighteenth century, was eager to prove that the established Church was willing to fulfil its responsibilities in the church-state alliance. Secondly, American affairs mattered to Secker: an American episcopate had been a publicly-stated aim of his for nearly a quarter of a century and a central concern of orthodox reformers for even

---

[242] BL, Add. MS 32973, f. 332: Secker to TPH, 1 Feb 1766.
[243] Lowe, 'Archbishop Secker ... and the Stamp Act', pp. 434–36.
[244] BL, Add. MS 32974, ff. 5–7: TPH to Secker, 15 Feb 1766.
[245] Ibid., f. 17: Secker to TPH, 16 Feb 1766.
[246] A Narrative of the Changes in the Ministry, p. 52.
[247] Lowe, 'Archbishop Secker ... and the Stamp Act', pp. 438–41. The repeal carried by 12 votes among those present for the vote on 11 March; the margin increased to 34 votes when proxies were counted. Seventeen bishops were present for the vote on 11 March (voting 10–7 for repeal), while 9 voted by proxy (8–1 for repeal).

longer than that. If the American colonists were aflame over the Stamp Act, there would be little opportunity to introduce Anglican bishops there; hence the effort expended to line up the episcopal votes behind repeal was aimed as much at proving something to those in Boston, Philadelphia, and Williamsburg as it was to proving something to those in Whitehall and Westminster.[248] As it turned out, the only people less interested than the average British colonist in an American episcopate were England's governors. For if the time was not ripe during the mid-century wars to plant Anglican bishops in America, the years which followed the wars' conclusion were even less propitious. As was nearly always the case during the period, political exigencies easily trumped ecclesiological imperatives.

[248] But some colonial Anglican ministers worried that the Stamp Act's repeal would actually undermined the Church of England's position in America. See, for instance, Rhodes House, Oxford, USPG B23 (no. 12): Samuel Andrews to SPG, 25 June 1766: 'I do not indeed pretend to say, what Effect the Repeal of the Stamp Act may have here upon a civil Account ... however upon a Religious attest, I fear the Consequence, Especially in this Colony, as the Dissenters have here, the Authority in their own Hands, ... they have an Inclination to distress and even Extirpate the Church, and as they imagine from the late Occurrence, they have Nothing to fear from your Side of the Water, ... it seems those of our Profession, must have a melancholy Prospect before them, unless powerfully supported from Home.'

Chapter Seven

THE CHURCH AND AMERICA

On 20 February 1741, Thomas Secker stepped into the pulpit of St Mary-le-Bow to deliver the 'annual anniversary sermon' to the Society for the Propagation of the Gospel in Foreign Parts (SPG). He had been invited by the archbishop of Canterbury to speak on the occasion, and the audience drew from the great and good of the English governing class.[1] It was Secker's first public airing of his views on the religious situation in America, and, in retrospect, established an interpretative framework that remained consistent for him right through to his death. Things on the other side of the Atlantic were dire, Secker argued. The first European inhabitants 'carried but little Sense of Christianity abroad with them' so that among their descendants there was soon 'scarce any Footsteps of it left, beyond the mere Name'. Americans' religious ignorance and popery's threat spurred the SPG to support missionaries and schoolteachers. 'But at present much remains to be done,' Secker warned.[2]

The Society's first order of business was to Christianize, Protestantize, and Anglicanize the 'heathens' who lived in America. 'Our blessed Lord hath intrusted his Followers, to preserve his Gospel in Purity, where it is; and communicate it, where it is not,' Secker averred.[3] Slaves – who brought with them from Africa 'the grossest Idolatry, and the most savage Dispositions' – suffered under conditions in America that were 'nearly as hard as possible'. 'And thus,' he lamented, 'many thousands of them spend their whole Days, one Generation after another, undergoing with reluctant Minds continual Toil in this World, and comforted with no Hopes of Reward in a better.'[4] American Indians were little better off. Resentful, intemperate, mischievous, lazy, and cannibalistic, the Indians 'consist of various Nations … immersed in the vilest Superstitions, and engaged in almost perpetual Wars against each other, which they prosecute with Barbarities unheard of amongst the rest of Mankind'.[5]

Both spiritual and temporal benefits would accompany the evangelization of the 'heathen'. 'Christian Principles will teach them Dutifulness and Loyalty,' Secker assured his listeners,[6] and an elucidation of the nexus of orthodox belief,

[1]   Troy O. Bickham, *Savages Within the Empire: Representations of American Indians in Eighteenth-Century Britain* (Oxford, 2005), pp. 211–12.
[2]   Thomas Secker, *A Sermon preached before the Incorporated Society for the Propagation of the Gospel in Foreign Parts; at their anniversary meeting in the Parish-Church of St Mary-le-Bow, on Friday, February 20. 1740–41* (1741), pp. 4–6.
[3]   Ibid., p. 23.
[4]   Ibid., pp. 6, 7.
[5]   Ibid., pp. 8–9.
[6]   Ibid., p. 15.

civilized behaviour, and civil obedience constituted the heart of the sermon. Christianity civilized. It might, for instance, make the slaves' 'Tempers milder, and their Lives happier' and would 'undoubtedly restrain [the Indians'] mutual Barbarities ... and dispose them to a settled and orderly Life'.[7] Civil obedience trailed closely behind civilization. Among the recent slave rebels in New York, for instance, only two had received any Christian instruction and only one had actually been baptized.[8] Likewise, the Indians' Christian conversion would be the surest prophylaxis against the French in America. '[E]very single Indian, whom we make a Christian; we make a Friend and Ally at the same Time,' Secker reminded the audience, 'both against the remaining Heathen, and a much more dangerous Neighbour, from whose Instigations almost all that we have suffered by them is allowed to have come.'[9]

In addition to its responsibilities to slaves and Indians, the SPG also had a duty to evangelize the whites in America. Many American colonists vehemently disagreed with Secker on this point. Some there insisted that people would provide for an Anglican minister if they wanted one. 'But this cannot be expected from the Heathen, who are insensible of their Want of them,' Secker countered, 'nor from those of our own People who are too like Heathen, and have not the Sense of it which they ought.'[10] Could it really surprise anyone that most Anglo-Americans lacked proper religious instruction?, Secker asked rhetorically. 'Our Colonies receive from hence a great deal of what is bad. We send them our Malefactors: we send them our immoral and irreligious Customs: we send them our infidel and profligate Books.' In light of this, he concluded, 'we ought to do some Good, where we do so much Harm'.[11] From the SPG's perspective, this meant building up the Church of England's presence in America: 'We acknowledge it, whoever is taught Christianity by our Care, will be taught it as professed in the Church established here by Law. There can be no Teaching at all, but in some particular Form. We think our own the best.' Standing in the Church's way in New England were the Congregationalists, who sought to exclude the Church of England from being introduced, even though the SPG 'settled no Clergyman any where, without the Inhabitants requesting it, and contributing to it'.[12]

In addition to overcoming opposition by its confessional rivals, the Church needed, so its orthodox proponents argued, to replicate the English ecclesiological model and pastoral norms. This meant bishops on the ground in America, not

---

[7]   Ibid., pp. 18, 20. Cf. Patrick Griffin, *American Leviathan: Empire, Nation, and Revolutionary Frontier* (New York, 2007). I appreciate Dr. Griffin for allowing me to read his manuscript in advance of publication.

[8]   Secker, *SPG Sermon*, p. 19. Cf. Christopher Leslie Brown, *Moral Capital: Foundations of British Abolitionism* (Chapel Hill, NC, 2006), pp. 33–101; Jill Lepore, *New York Burning: Liberty, Slavery, and Conspiracy in Eighteenth-Century Manhattan* (New York, 2005).

[9]   Secker, *SPG Sermon*, p. 21.

[10]   Ibid., p. 23.

[11]   Ibid., p. 25.

[12]   Ibid., pp. 29, 30.

least so that 'the primitive and most useful Appointment of Confirmation might be restored; and an orderly Discipline exercised in the Churches'. Foreseeing Dissenting objections that bishops were the thin end of the wedge of an Anglo-American Anglican church-state, Secker reassured his audience that a bishop would not 'encroach at all on the present Rights of the Civil Government in our Colonies; or bring their Dependance into any Degree of that Danger'.[13] The end result of successful SPG missionary work in America 'shall hinder Corruptions of Christianity from prevailing there, and sharing with Profaneness a divided Empire over the Land'.[14] Church and state, then, were both organically linked and mutually supportive. At least that was what the orthodox thought.

Predictably, Secker's SPG sermon was polarizing. The heterodox loathed it. 'It was the coloring bye-view of this Sermon, that first occasioned a fixt dislike in me to Dr. Seckar,' Thomas Hollis explained to Jonathan Mayhew in 1765.[15] 'His Sermon before the Propagators is the *root* Sermon of all misrepresentation, rancour and baseness,' Hollis subsequently groused, 'and must be copied, somehow, by all the Youngling Bshps, during his Life, for commendam.'[16] Francis Blackburne darkly predicted that were the sermon's prescriptions made reality, 'The consequences Frenchmen and Spaniards will tell our posterity with pleasure.'[17] By the same token, the orthodox thought Secker's performance entirely a good thing. Samuel Johnson, later president of King's College, New York, reckoned that Secker 'had outdone all his predecessors in pleading the cause of the Church in America and particularly the necessity of bishops for these remotest parts'; in consequence Johnson 'thought it his duty to write his thanks in particular for that sermon'.[18] When Secker revised the sermon some years later and distributed it to the Oxford diocesan clergy, Philip Bearcroft, the SPG's secretary, wished that 'the Society would send a Copy of it to each Minister of a Parish in the Kingdom. This would inform most effectually those, by their distance from the metropolis, & from other accidents know little of the true intent, & Circumstances of the Society, & furnish them & the most knowing among us with the best arguments to recommend it, at the same time it would enable them to answer all the little Cavils against its good Designs.'[19]

The sermon delighted the orthodox and upset the heterodox because Secker proposed the extension of orthodox religious reform to America. When he said that 'the Hopes and Means of supporting Christianity amongst our own People

13 Ibid., p. 28.
14 Ibid., p. 16.
15 *PMHS* 69 (1956), p. 171: Hollis to Mayhew, 24 Jun 1765. But see Houghton Library, Harvard University, MS Eng 1911 (The Diary of Thomas Hollis), vol. 1, which demonstrates quite clearly that Hollis was a regular visitor at Lambeth Palace and that he and Secker maintained cordial relations during the initial years of Secker's archiepiscopate.
16 *PMHS* 99 (1987), p. 137: Hollis to Andrew Eliot, 25 May 1768. Emphasis in the original.
17 Francis Blackburne, *Memoirs of Thomas Hollis* (1780), I, p. 274.
18 *SJ*, I, p. 30: 'Memoirs'.
19 LPL, MS 1123/I, f. 213: Bearcroft to Secker, 22 Feb 1752.

there, are just the same as here at home,' he meant it.[20] Seventeenth-century Puritans had left England on an errand into the wilderness, hoping to reform life in England by demonstrating the viability of a reformed life abroad.[21] Secker understood the Anglican mission on the western side of the Atlantic in similarly dramatic terms. America during the eighteenth century was akin to the Mediterranean world of the early first century. At the time of Christ's death, there was but a handful of true believers in the risen Saviour and a rump of apostles commissioned by him to spread the gospel. The early Church's task was to hew paths into the spiritual wilderness by evangelization and to erect the ecclesiastical institutions which alone could sustain Christian settlement. The early Christians were an embattled minority in the Mediterranean world, feared, loathed, mocked, and misunderstood, sometimes all at once. What secured the future for them and their Church was the Roman state's protection after Constantine. In eighteenth-century America, the Church of England confronted similar challenges and, so the orthodox thought, required similar solutions.

Yet the Church faced an entirely different set of circumstances in America than it did at home.[22] Anglican leaders feared that demography was destiny. The nature of early colonial settlement meant there were far more non-Anglicans in America than in England: where just over 90 per cent of the populace conformed to the Church in England during the mid 1770s, only 25 per cent did so in America.[23] Scarce numbers of American Anglicans consequently meant that many churches had difficulty sustaining their priests. Without significant and sustained financial assistance funnelled from England through the SPG, there would have been almost no Anglican churches except in colonies where the Church enjoyed a legal establishment.[24] As well as being outnumbered, American Anglicans lacked the institutional structures that undergirded the Church at home. In particular, the absence of bishops to confirm, ordain, consecrate, and supervise de-centralized

---

[20] Secker, *SPG Sermon*, p. 12.

[21] Perry Miller, *Errand into the Wilderness* (Cambridge, MA, 1956), pp. 1–15.

[22] James B. Bell, *The Imperial Origins of the King's Church in Early America, 1607–1783* (New York, 2004); Nancy L. Rhoden, *Revolutionary Anglicanism: The Colonial Church of England Clergy during the American Revolution* (New York, 1999), pp. 10–36; Patricia U. Bonomi, *Under the Cope of Heaven: Religion, Society, and Politics in Colonial America* (New York, 1986), pp. 41–61; Frederick V. Mills, sr., *Bishops by Ballot: An Eighteenth Century Ecclesiastical Revolution* (New York, 1978), pp. 3–34 reliably survey the Church of England's legal and social standing in colonial American society.

[23] Boyd Stanley Schlenther, 'Religious Faith and Commercial Empire', in *The Oxford History of the British Empire. II. The Eighteenth Century*, ed. P.J. Marshall (Oxford, 1998), p. 146. Cf. Patricia U. Bonomi and Peter R. Eisenstadt, 'Church Adherence in the Eighteenth-Century British American Colonies', *WMQ*, 3rd series, 39:2 (1982), pp. 245–86. Secker himself reckoned that a little over 30 per cent of the white populace in Britain's American colonies were 'Episcopalians': LPL, SPG Papers 10, f. 176: Thoughts on the State of the Church of England in America, June 1764.

[24] Cf. Bruce E. Steiner, 'New England Anglicanism: A Genteel Faith?', *WMQ*, 3rd series, 27:1 (1970), pp. 122–35.

Anglican religious life and crippled church growth, while the dearth of American Anglican colleges made it difficult properly to train native clergy.

The colonial Church of England also had to deal with significant lay control over religious life. In England, ministers were nominated to a living by the patron; instituted into the spiritualities of the living by the bishop; and inducted into the living's temporalities by the archdeacon. Once an English clergyman had been installed into a parish living, his freehold helped to protect him, and only his death, resignation, or removal by an ecclesiastical court could vacate the living. In the colonies, by contrast, Anglican parish priests often enjoyed far less security in their livings because many were chosen by the parish vestry, which also doled out their annual salary. To maintain greater control over parish religious life, colonial vestries frequently asked royal governors not to induct priests into their livings, so that clergy effectively performed their duties on year-to-year contracts.[25] This threatened both to rob the colonial Church of its independence and to diminish its social status. Clergy risked no longer being independent purveyors of Christian truths.

Finally, the colonial Church of England never enjoyed the legal status in the American colonies that it did at home. Anglicanism found strongest support in the southern colonies, where by the 1740s the Church of England was established by law in Maryland, Virginia, South Carolinas, and Georgia.[26] Yet even in the Anglican redoubt of Virginia, the absence of towns, bishops, and the colonial government's willingness to recreate an English-style religious establishment weakened the Church there. In the colonies north of Maryland, the Church of England did not enjoy even the watered-down legal establishment it did in the southern colonies. The Ministry Act of 1693 established the Church of England in only four counties in New York, and that was never enlarged. Pennsylvania enforced true religious toleration, while New Jersey had such diverse populations, ethnically and religiously, that English authorities never tried seriously to establish an official church there. Rhode Island was home, in the words of Cotton Mather, to 'Antinomians, Arminians, Socinians, Quakers, Ranters – everything in the world but Roman Catholics and real Christians'. In the New England colonies of Connecticut, Massachusetts, and New Hampshire, it was the Congregationalist church that was established by law. And in the most extreme cases, the Congregationalists used all the legal tools at their disposal – including fines, arrest, and the threat of exile or even execution – to discourage New England colonists from worshipping in non-Congregationalist churches.

---

[25] Bell, *The Imperial Origins*, pp. 125–41 discusses the powers of American vestries; see John K. Nelson, *A Blessed Company: Parishes, Parsons, and Parishioners in Anglican Virginia, 1690–1776* (Chapel Hill, NC, 2001), pp. 33–42 and Rhys Isaac, *The Transformation of Virginia, 1740–1790* (Chapel Hill, NC, 1982), pp. 143–46 for those in Virginia.

[26] Edwin S. Gaustad and Philip L. Barlow, *New Historical Atlas of Religion in America* (New York, 2001) and Rhoden, *Revolutionary Anglicanism*, pp. 15–18 survey the religious geography of Britain's American colonies.

From Thomas Secker's point of view, then, America was a spiritual wilderness at its frontiers and an Anglican wilderness in most of its established settlements. Yet, confident that the Church of England was both primitive and catholic, he aimed to nurture the Church in America where possible and build it where necessary. The heterodox on both sides of the Atlantic, in turn, suspected something sinister was afoot. Thomas Hollis accused Secker of 'proceeding to kindle the flame of AntiReformation in the Colonies', while Andrew Eliot argued that Secker's fixation with establishing bishops was meant 'to prevent any reformation at home'.[27] It was neither the first nor the last time that his ecclesiastical opponents would misread Secker's motives, for it was by reforming abroad that Secker hoped to bolster orthodox reform at home. An unreformed Church in America stood as an implicit indictment of the Church in England. The heterodox surely would ask, if the Church could survive in America without bishops and a sharp-toothed legal establishment, why not in England as well? As a result, American colonial religious policy became a proxy war for the future of the English religio-political order.

The outcome of this particular proxy war was decided in favour of the heterodox because the English state embraced neutralism. When Secker became primate of the Church of England in 1758, he was the first archbishop of Canterbury in decades actively to embrace the idea of an American episcopate. Yet, from the perspective of the king's ministers, the time could not have been worse for such an enterprise. The Seven Years War, with an important theatre in North America, made introducing bishops there impossible between 1756 and 1763. The aftermath of war, though, proved no more a propitious time for the state to embrace plans for an American episcopate, especially after the onset of the Stamp Act crisis. Thus, despite the Church of England's promotion of Georgian loyalism and its steadfast political support for the king's ministries throughout the mid-century, the nation's governors were wholly unwilling to support the orthodox calls for an American episcopate. Whatever the relation of church to state might have been in theory, England's wars ensured that, in practice, it was a partnership of unequals. That, in turn, meant the failure of orthodox programmatic aims both at home and abroad. This was a religio-political fact which the orthodox did not, and perhaps could not, appreciate fully.

I

Secker's knowledge of America came mainly from orthodox Anglican converts who had abandoned Dissent because they believed the Church of England was a

---

[27] *PMHS* 99 (1987), p. 130: Hollis to Eliot, 18 Dec 1767; *CMHS*, 4th series (1858), IV, p. 411: Eliot to Hollis, 13 Nov 1767.

primitive, catholic Church. Samuel Johnson (1696–1772) was Secker's primary correspondent on American affairs. Shortly after becoming archbishop, Secker assured Johnson that 'Some further Attention is required of me now; and I shall endeavour to give it, in the best Manner that I can; depending greatly on the Information, Advice and Assistance of the Missionaries and other Clergy in our Colonies, *but on yours in particular.'*[28] A Yale graduate and tutor and a Congregationalist minister in West Haven, Connecticut, Johnson abandoned Congregationalism for the Church of England in 1722 after intensive reading in Anglican and patristic works in the thousand-volume library donated to Yale in 1716 by Jeremiah Dummer, Connecticut's colonial agent in London.[29] Along with a number of others who had also immersed themselves in the Dummer collection, Johnson concluded 'that the conditions of things here relating to religion was far different from that of the primitive church, and that the Church of England came the nearest to the purity and perfection of those first and purest ages, of any church at this day upon the face of the earth'. In particular, a number of those who had read widely in the Dummer collection reckoned 'that from the facts in Scripture, compared with the facts of the primitive church immediately after, and so downward it appeared very plain that the episcopal government of the church was universally established by the Apostles wherever they propagated Christianity'. This led Johnson and other ministers among the group to 'be considerably dubious of the lawfulness of their ordination' because they not been ordained by bishops.[30] On 13 September 1722, the day after Yale's commencement, Johnson and a handful of fellow 'apostates' met with the college trustees and 'declared themselves in this wise, that they could no longer keep out of the communion of the Holy Catholic Church, and that some of them doubted of the validity, and the rest were persuaded of the invalidity, of Presbyterian ordination in opposition to Episcopal'.[31] Soon afterwards, a small group of Anglican converts sailed for England to seek holy orders in the Church of England. On 31 March 1723,

---

[28] LPL, MS 2589, f. 56: Secker to Johnson, 27 Sep 1758. Emphasis mine.

[29] Peter Doll, 'The Idea of the Primitive Church in High Church Ecclesiology from Samuel Johnson to J.H. Hobart', *AEH* 65:1 (1996), pp. 8–32 is a particularly insightful examination of primitivism's influence on Johnson's intellectual and theological development. See also, Joseph J. Ellis, *The New England Mind in Transition: Samuel Johnson of Connecticut, 1696–1772* (New Haven, CT, 1973), pp. 77–81 and Donald F.M. Gerardi, 'Samuel Johnson and the Yale "Apostasy" of 1722: The Challenge of Anglican Sacramentalism to the New England Way', *HMPEC* 47:2 (1978), pp. 153–76.

[30] *SJ*, p. 13: 'Memoirs'.

[31] Francis L. Hawks and William Stevens Perry, *Documentary History of the Protestant Episcopal Church in the United States ... Connecticut* (New York, 1864), I, p. 58: George Pigot to SPG, 3 Oct 1722. See also, Richard Warch, *School of the Prophets: Yale College, 1701–1740* (New Haven, CT, 1973), pp. 96–125.

Thomas Green, bishop of Norwich, ordained Johnson at St Martin-in-the-Fields in London.[32]

Among the Yale 'apostates' ordained in the spring of 1723 with Johnson was the college's former rector, Timothy Cutler (1684–1765).[33] A man 'of high, lofty, & despotic mien', Cutler graduated from Harvard in 1701 and was called in 1709 to lead the Congregational parish in Stratford, Connecticut, where the SPG had recently set up a mission. Being chosen to take up such a sensitive position testifies to Cutler's abilities, in the eyes of his contemporaries: it made his subsequent conversion to Anglicanism so much the more traumatic for New England Congregationalists. After his Anglican ordination, Cutler returned to Boston as an SPG missionary, to take up the reins of Christ Church; he subsequently distinguished himself even among colonial Anglicans for the heights of his high churchmanship and for his inveterate defence of the Church of England.[34] Henry Caner, a fellow SPG missionary who preached Cutler's funeral sermon in 1765, noted that Cutler 'was inflexible in his principles, these he accounted sacred. And as he had deliberately entertained a high opinion of the constitution of the church of England, so he was ever zealous in its defence.'[35]

Unlike either Johnson or Cutler, Caner (1700–1792) was born in England and emigrated to Connecticut, where he graduated from Yale in 1724.[36] There he came under Johnson's influence, and by the fall of 1726 was determined to receive Anglican ordination and become an SPG missionary.[37] In 1727, he received Anglican orders and returned to Connecticut where he served as SPG missionary to Fairfield. Later he would move to Boston where he served as the rector of King's Chapel; he would remain there until his loyalist sympathies drove him back to England in 1776.[38] Timothy Cutler described Caner as a man 'of unshaken Loyalty to his present majesty and his Illustrious House, of true zeal and courage in

---

[32] Ellis, *The New England Mind in Transition*, pp. 86–87. Bell, *The Imperial Origins*, pp. 142–65 details the making of an eighteenth-century American Anglican churchman, with particular reference to Samuel Johnson and Timothy Cutler.

[33] Allen C. Guelzo, 'Cutler, Timothy', *ANB*, 5, pp. 935–37; Clifton K. Shipton, *Sibley's Harvard Graduates* (Boston, 1937), V, pp. 45–67; Warch, *School of the Prophets*, pp. 96–99, 102–15, 117–21.

[34] Donald L. Huber, 'Timothy Cutler: The Convert as Controversialist', *HMPEC* 44 (1975), pp. 489–96; Frank Lambert, *Inventing the 'Great Awakening'* (Princeton, 1999), pp. 206–07, 212–13, 218.

[35] Henry Caner, *The Firm Belief of a Future Reward a powerful motive to obedience and a good life: a sermon preached at Christ Church in Boston, August 20. 1765. At the funeral of the Rev. Timothy Cutler, D.D ... .* (Boston, 1765), p. 19.

[36] Franklin B. Dexter, *Biographical Sketches of the Graduates of Yale College: October 1701–May 1745* (New York, 1885), I, pp. 296–99.

[37] Hawks and Perry, *Documentary History of ... Connecticut*, I, pp. 109–11: Johnson to SPG Secretary, 16 Sep 1726.

[38] For Caner's disappointment as a loyalist exile, see Mary Beth Norton, *The British-Americans: The Loyalist Exiles in England, 1774–1779* (1974), pp. 51–52; Gregory Palmer, *Biographical Sketches of Loyalists of the American Revolution* (Westport, CT, 1984), p. 137.

the cause of Religion & the Church';[39] and during the combustible 1760s, it was Caner who saw most clearly the nature of the heterodox threat to Church of England in America. For Caner's unwavering defence of the Church, Secker obtained him an Oxford D.D. in 1766.

Johnson, Cutler, and Caner served as Secker's chief points of contact with colonial New England. They shared a high churchmanship forged by and founded on primitivism, something which was not the case with William Smith (1727–1803), Secker's primary source of information about colonial Pennsylvania's religious life.[40] Born into a Scottish Episcopal family, Smith would convert to Presbyterianism before becoming an Anglican churchman in the American colonies. Educated at the university in Aberdeen, Smith left without a degree for New York in 1751 to serve as a private tutor. There, he met Samuel Johnson and vigorously defended Johnson in the controversy surrounding the founding of King's College in the early 1750s. Bearing letters of recommendation from Johnson and other prominent American high churchmen, Smith sailed to England in 1753 for ordination.[41] On his return to America, he had settled in Philadelphia, where Benjamin Franklin secured him a position to teach logic, rhetoric, ethics, and natural and moral philosophy at the Academy of Philadelphia. Never a high churchman in the Johnsonian mould, Smith walked a cautious line during the 1760s and 1770s as Anglo-American relations disintegrated; unlike Caner, he remained in America through the Revolution, but he pursued a course that pleased neither patriots nor loyalists.[42] Others in the colonial Church thought him conniving and overly ambitious.[43] Nonetheless, throughout the 1750s and 1760s, Smith was someone whose advice Secker trusted on Pennsylvania church matters.[44]

In Thomas Secker, the primitive Anglicans found their champion. Even before he became archbishop, they corresponded with him regularly about American affairs and agitated for a variety of issues which they, and in consequence Secker, believed would fortify the Church of England's position in America. Four interrelated sets of concerns shot through the American Anglicans' correspondence: protecting the rights and privileges of the Church of England in America; securing the supply and support of orthodox clergy to staff the Church; expanding the opportunities for Anglican evangelization both at the frontier and

---

[39] Perry, *Massachusetts*, p. 222: Cutler to SPG Secretary, 24 May 1727.

[40] Horace Wemyss Smith, *Life and Correspondence of the Rev. William Smith, D.D.* (Philadelphia, 1880); Frank Gegenheimer, *William Smith: Educator and Churchman, 1727–1803* (Philadelphia, 1943); Robert Lawson-Peebles, 'Smith, William (1727–1803)', *ODNB*.

[41] LPL, MS 1123/1, f. 227: Johnson to Secker, 25 June 1753; ibid., f. 233: Henry Barclay to Secker, 25 July 1753; ibid., f. 235: James De Lancy to Secker, 27 July 1753.

[42] Robert M. Calhoon, *The Loyalists in Revolutionary America, 1760–1781* (New York, 1973), pp. 148–54.

[43] Smith, *Life and Correspondence of ... William Smith*, I, pp. 185–86: Robert Jenney to Secker, 27 Nov 1758.

[44] *Autobiography*, p. 64.

in the established settlements; and, above all else, introducing an American episcopate. As bishop and archbishop, Secker would make them his own. Yet these were just the sort of issues bound to frighten the heterodox, who, on both sides of the Atlantic, feared a conspiracy was afoot to rob them of their rights and privileges.[45] As a result, Anglican colonial religious policy fared poorly and contributed significantly to the dissolution of Britain's American empire.[46]

II

American Anglicans were intent to protect what few legal rights and privileges the Church of England enjoyed there. The Parson's Cause in Virginia illustrates the kind of incursions on Anglican privilege that worried the colonial clergy and the metropolitan religious and political leaders.[47] The English church-state's response likewise reinforced the suspicions held by the heterodox of the orthodox and confirmed for many others the metropole's determination to infringe the political and religious liberty of the colonies.[48] In 1753, 1755, and 1758, the Virginia General Assembly passed the Two-Penny Acts, which consequently cut the salaries of Anglican clergy in Virginia. Since the mid seventeenth century, the Assembly had set clerical salaries to be paid in tobacco, most recently in a statute of 1748. But the Two-Penny Acts, each a one-year measure passed in anticipation of a bad tobacco crop, allowed people to discharge debts owed in tobacco at two pence per pound. Because this rate was below market price, the acts effectively reduced clerical salaries.[49] The Virginia clergy mounted a legal protest in 1759, sending John Camm to represent their case to the bishop of London, the

---

[45] Bernard Bailyn, *The Ideological Origins of the American Revolution* (Cambridge, MA, 1967); Gordon Wood, 'Rhetoric and Reality in the American Revolution', *WMQ*, 3rd series, 23:1 (1966), pp. 3–32; idem, 'Conspiracy and the Paranoid Style: Causality and Deceit in the Eighteenth Century', *WMQ*, 3rd series, 39:3 (1982), pp. 401–41.

[46] James B. Bell, *A War of Religion: Dissenters, Anglicans and the American Revolution* (forthcoming, 2007); J.C.D. Clark, *The Language of Liberty, 1660–1832: Political discourse and social dynamics in the Anglo-American world* (Cambridge, 1994), esp. pp. 296–381. Gordon S. Wood, 'Religion and the American Revolution', in *New Directions in American Religious History*, eds. Harry S. Stout and D.G. Hart (Oxford, 1997), pp. 173–205 trenchantly reviews the secondary literature on the subject. I appreciate Dr. Bell allowing me to read portions of his book in advance of publication.

[47] On the Parson's Cause, see George Maclaren Brydon, *Virginia's Mother Church and the Political Conditions Under Which It Grew* (Philadelphia, 1952), II, pp. 288–320; Richard L. Morton, *Colonial Virginia, II. Westward Expansion and Prelude to Revolution, 1710–1763* (Chapel Hill, NC, 1960), pp. 751–819; Rhys Isaac, 'Religion and Authority: Problems of the Anglican Establishment in Virginia in the Era of the Great Awakening and the Parson's Cause', *WMQ*, 3rd series, 30:1 (1973), pp. 3–36; and Bell, *The Imperial Origins*, pp. 75–81.

[48] Bailyn, *Ideological Origins of the American Revolution*, pp. 252–54.

[49] Perry, *Virginia*, pp. 434–46: Clergy of Virginia to Thomas Sherlock, 29 Nov 1755, 25 Feb 1756.

Anglican official directly responsible for colonial religious affairs, and the Lords Commissioners of Trade and Plantations, know more commonly as the Board of Trade. A Cambridge-educated Yorkshireman, Camm quickly earned a reputation for challenging colonial Virginia's leadership.[50]

Camm arrived in England during the height of the Seven Years War to find the Board of Trade intent on preserving the royal prerogative in the colonies and the Church's leadership equally determined to safeguard the colonial Anglican clergy's rights and privileges. Thomas Sherlock, bishop of London, should have been most intimately involved in the affair, but by the late 1750s he was increasingly frail. In his stead, Secker represented the Church's interest in the appeal. He did this primarily by representing the Church in the Board's deliberations on the matter. Camm brought with him to London a memorial from the Virginia clergy protesting the Two-Penny Acts by which 'the Condition of the Clergy is rendered most distressful, various, & uncertain, after a painful & laborious performance of their Function, in parishes, very wide & extensive'.[51] The Virginia clergy argued that since George II had taken the unusual step of expressly confirming a 1748 Virginia statute setting clerical salaries to be paid in tobacco, it was illegal for the General Assembly subsequently to pass statutes that contravened the 1748 one. In forwarding the matter to the Board of Trade, Sherlock also highlighted the implications which the case had for the royal prerogative. 'As to the Want of Justice & Equity, shewd in this Bill, to the Clergy, the Case is too plain, to admit of any Reflections upon it,' he contended. 'And if the Crown does not, or cannot, support itself, in so plain a Case as is before Us, it would be in Vain for the Clergy to plead the Act confirmed by the King; for their Right must stand, or fall, with the Authority of the Crown.'[52]

The Board of Trade agreed with Sherlock and on 4 July advised George III to disallow the Two-Penny acts for being 'in direct contradiction to ... your Majesty's Instructions'.[53] The matter did not rest there, however, for Camm asked the king not only to disallow the acts, but also to declare them null and void. Upon this point the Board of Trade could not readily decide and asked Secker to confer with Sherlock on the legal precedents and ramifications in advance of a hearing from legal counsel for the disputants.[54] Sherlock's response was equivocal at best, concluding only that 'the Clergy seeks for Redress against an arbitrary Law affecting their Property; and as the same Law is injurious to the King's Right, it is no wonder that they should interest him in it'.[55] Secker's notes of the 3 August Board of Trade meeting on the Parson's Cause make clear that the debate was spirited, with Lord Chancellor Hardwicke and the attorney general vigorously

---

[50] Thad W. Tate, 'Camm, John (21 June 1718–22 May 1779)', *ANB*, IV, pp. 262–63.
[51] LPL, Secker Papers 1, f. 68: Memorial from the Virginia clergy to the Board of Trade [1759].
[52] Ibid., f. 71: Sherlock to Board of Trade, 14 June 1759.
[53] Ibid., f. 73: Board of Trade to George III, 4 July 1759.
[54] Ibid., f. 74: Secker to Sherlock, 27 July 1759.
[55] LPL, MS 2589, f. 107: Sherlock to Secker, 29 July 1759.

arguing that failing to annul the acts would allow the American colonists to think they could contravene the royal prerogative with impunity; as a close ally of Hardwicke, Secker likely wanted the acts voided as well.[56] In the end, the Board of Trade upheld the Virginia clergy's appeal, but only disallowed the act, rather than voiding it.[57] Even this mildly conciliatory ruling provoked outrage from many Virginians, who believed that the crown was using its royal prerogative to muscle in on the authority of the colonial legislatures.[58] Significantly, Virginia Anglicans who defended the Two-Penny Acts resorted to the language of anti-Catholicism as Anglican anticlericalism.[59] Richard Bland, a burgess for Prince George County, thundered, 'I abhor those Accusers who, like Romish Inquisitors, or some late Conventioners, carry on their insidious Practices in the Dark, lest the Day-light should discover the Iniquity of their Transactions.'[60] While metropolitan political and religious leaders thought it their responsibility to defend the rights and privileges of church and state in the colonies, the Board of Trade's decision in the Parson's Cause helped radicalize Virginia's laity. This rotted the ties that bound together the empire. It also made realizing the primitive Church in America even more difficult.

III

How to supply and support orthodox clergy was a pressing problem for the Church of England in America – it was hard to evangelize without evangelists. The obvious long-term solution was to train Americans to staff the Anglican livings in America. Not surprisingly, then, much effort during the eighteenth century went into building and sustaining colleges to train Americans for the Anglican priesthood. Before the early 1740s, the only colleges in America were Harvard, Yale, and the College of William and Mary, the last of which was the only one with an Anglican disposition. Beginning in the mid 1740s, however, there was an mini-explosion of college founding. Presbyterians set up the College of New Jersey at Princeton in 1746, evangelical Baptists founded Brown in 1764, Dutch

---

[56] LPL, Secker Papers 1, ff. 75–78: Secker's notes on debate in Board of Trade on Two-Penny Act, 3 Aug 1759.

[57] Perry, *Virginia*, pp. 458–60: Report from the Lords Commissioners, 4 July 1759; University of Virginia, Alderman Library, MSS 3525–s: Secker to unknown, 27 July 1759.

[58] Gordon S. Wood, *The American Revolution* (New York, 2002), p. 16. Cf. Rhys Isaac, *The Transformation of Virginia, 1740–1790* (Chapel Hill, NC, 1982), pp. 143–57.

[59] James E. Bradley, 'Anti-Catholicism as Anglican Anticlericalism: Nonconformity and the Ideological Origins of Radical Disaffection', in *Anticlericalism in Britain, c.1500–1914*, eds. Nigel Aston and Matthew Cragoe (Stroud, 2000), pp. 67–92 anatomizes the language and illustrates its prevalence among Dissenting circles.

[60] Richard Bland, *A Letter to the Clergy of Virginia* (Williamsburg, 1760), p. 20. Cf. Jack P. Greene (ed.), *The Diary of Colonel Landon Carter of Sabine Hall, 1752–1778* (Charlottesville, VA, 1965), I, p. 264 (18 April 1764).

Reformers established Queens College (later Rutgers) in 1766, and a Congregationalist Indian missionary school formed the rump of Dartmouth (incorporated in 1769). Two colleges were also formed that could train those intending for the Anglican clergy: in the early 1750s, Benjamin Franklin and others set up the Academy and College of Philadelphia, while King's College got off the ground in 1754.[61] Two of the proponents of an American episcopate played important roles in these two colleges, with William Smith serving as provost and tutor in Philadelphia and with Samuel Johnson serving as the first president of King's.[62]

While Secker had little to do with the establishment of these colleges in Philadelphia and New York, he promoted their interests. The first measure of a college was the quality of its instructors, and Secker helped colonial educators, including Samuel Johnson, obtain the Oxford doctorates that brought prestige to their colleges and to the Church of England in America.[63] There were times when this proved difficult, though. When, for instance, prominent American Anglicans asked him to help William Smith obtain an Oxford D.D., Secker responded frankly that Smith's notoriously difficult personality did not make him an easy sale.[64] In the end, Secker and a number of other bishops who had received their degrees at Oxford convinced authorities there to grant Smith his doctorate in divinity.[65]

Secker also steered orthodox faculty in England to the American colleges. Staffing American colleges with properly principled churchmen helped safeguard orthodoxy in the colonies, a concern of Secker's that is clear in his efforts to find a vice-president for King's College in the late 1750s. When New York suffered another smallpox scare in late 1759, Samuel Johnson removed himself from the city to his former parish in Connecticut, where he was unable to supervise closely the affairs of the college. 'I then left my young college in a flourishing state,' he assured Secker, 'but within two or three months, by reason of my absence, and the ill health of one of my tutors, and the want of good conduct in the other, it fell into a very suffering condition.' Thus he sought not only a new tutor, 'but also a gentleman duly qualified for a Vice-president, who can constantly reside, and who would have the highest probability of being my successor'. He wanted the tutor to hail from Cambridge, the new vice-president from Oxford. And, he solicited advice from Secker, an *ex officio* member of the board of governors of King's, suggesting

[61]   Beverly McAnear, 'College Founding in the American Colonies, 1745–1775', *Mississippi Valley Historical Review* 42:1 (1955), pp. 24–44.
[62]   Gegenheimer, *William Smith*, pp. 43–94; Ellis, *The New England Mind in Transition*, pp. 175–217; David C. Humphrey, *From King's College to Columbia* (New York, 1976); Donald F.M. Gerardi, 'The King's College Controversy, 1753–1756 and the Ideological Roots of Toryism in New York', *Perspectives in American History* 11 (1977–78), pp. 147–96.
[63]   See, for instance, LPL, MS 1123/I, f. 159: Secker to Johnson, 8 March 1746; ibid., MS 1123/III, ff. 40–41: Henry Barclay to Secker, 3 June 1761.
[64]   LPL, MS 1123/II, f. 95: Secker to Thomas Moore, 1 Mar 1759.
[65]   Ibid., f. 102: Moore to Secker, 23 Mar 1759.

that he was sufficiently impressed with George Horne's published defence of Hutchinsonianism as to want him as a vice-president.[66] This proposal was a non-starter for Secker, who found distasteful Horne's distinctive flavour of Hutchinsonianism during the late 1750s.[67] Secker did, however, propose Myles Cooper, a fellow of Queen's College, Oxford, as a viable alternative, noting that he came with a reputation for being 'a grave and good man, and very well affected to the government; well qualified for the inferior tutor's place, but not inclined to accept it; not unskilled in Hebrew, and willing to take the vice-president's office; but not of an age for Priest's Orders till next February'.[68] Cooper drove a hard bargain, though. He asked for £20 from the SPG to defray his moving expenses and for a delay before leaving for New York.[69] Once arrived at King's, he complained that his salary fell short of what the college's governors had originally promised.[70] Secker tried to mollify Cooper and persuaded the governing board to increase his salary.[71] The negotiations proved worth it, from Secker's point of view, because Cooper soon became one of America's leading Anglican churchmen, bringing King's more into line with the Oxbridge model, organizing the clergy of the middle colonies, and touring the southern colonies three times to help rally support for a colonial episcopate. He also was a loyalist at the Revolution: indeed, so much was Cooper associated with the king's government that he had to flee America when war broke out.[72]

Without an influx of significant financial support from abroad, the colonial colleges would have little need for orthodox leaders like Cooper, because the endowments were insufficient to enable the American colleges to thrive, much less to expand.[73] Running serious deficits during the early 1760s, the College of Philadelphia and King's College sent William Smith and James Jay abroad to raise funds for them.[74] Finding that their individual solicitations were proving ineffective, Smith and Jay combined forces and sought Secker's help getting a

---

[66] *SJ*, IV, pp. 59–60: Johnson to Secker, 15 Feb 1760. See also, LPL, MS 1123/II, ff. 181–82: Barclay to Secker, 16 Feb 1760.

[67] *SJ*, IV, p. 71: Secker to Johnson, 4 Nov 1760.

[68] Ibid. See also, LPL, MS 1123/III, f. 63: Johnson to Secker, 9 Jan 1762; *SJ*, IV, pp. 76–77: Barclay to Secker, 11 Jan 1762.

[69] *SJ*, IV, pp. 78–80: Edward Bentham to Secker, 11 Mar 1762; ibid., pp. 80–81: Cooper to Secker, 15 Mar 1762; ibid., p. 81: Secker to Cooper, 19 Mar 1762; ibid., III, p. 278: Johnson to Secker, 28 Sep 1763; LPL, MS 1123/III, f. 103: Secker to Lords Treasurer, n.d.

[70] *SJ*, IV, p. 100: Cooper to Secker, 23 June 1763.

[71] LPL, MS 1123/III, f. 208: Secker to Barclay, 19 Sep 1763; *SJ*, IV, pp. 102–03: Secker to Cooper, 19 Sep 1763; ibid., pp. 104–05: Cooper to Secker, 2 Nov 1763.

[72] James B. Bell, 'Cooper, Myles (1736/7–1785)', *ODNB*; Calhoon, *The Loyalists in Revolutionary America*, pp. 259–60; Humphrey, *From King's College to Columbia*, pp. 126–39.

[73] Beverly McAnear, 'The Raising of Funds by Colonial Colleges', *Mississippi Valley Historical Review* 38:4 (1952), pp. 591–612.

[74] LPL, MS 1123/III, f. 95: Johnson to Secker, 12 May 1762; ibid., f. 99: Jay to Secker, 19 July 1762; and ibid., f. 101: Jay to Secker, 21 July 1762.

national church brief in support of the colleges.[75] Secker helped them as he could. Not only did he grant them £60 of his own money, but he worked aggressively to help them raise funds from other sources. 'I procured for those two Colleges a Brief for a Collection throughout England, notwithstanding the vehement Opposition of Ld Granville, President of the Council, who would have excluded New York,' he remembered. 'And I procured for them £300 from the King, by the Favour of Lord Bute.' He also recommended their case to the lord primate of Ireland, who 'amused them with vain Hopes, & neither got any thing for them, nor gave them any thing'.[76] In the end, Smith and Jay raised £6,900 for the colleges, a sum that made their trip a huge success.

Where possible Secker supported American colleges with a decided Anglican presence, but he harried those which refused to accommodate the Church of England. In the case of the College of Rhode Island (later renamed Brown University) in 1767, it simply meant not offering the institution moral or financial support. Its governing board dominated by Baptists, Quakers, Presbyterians, and Independents, the College had little to recommend it to the leaders of the Church of England. 'On laying the Plan before the Bps Dec. 26 they agreed with me, that such a College could be of little or no use to the few Candidates for Orders, which we might have in that Province, & who might better be sent to some other,' Secker recalled, 'but that it tended to Perpetuate the Notions of the Anabaptists there, & on these Accounts was not proper for us to encourage.'[77]

The more aggressive steps Secker took to prevent George Whitefield's Bethesda project from gaining a royal charter as a college point to the complicated confessional rivalries at play in the Anglophone Atlantic world.[78] Bethesda began life in the late 1730s as an orphanage just outside Savannah, Georgia; it soon became a plantation worked by slaves bought with funds raised during Whitefield's American preaching tours. During the late 1750s, Whitefield began to remove the orphans from Bethesda – 'I pity them, but they must blame their parents ... I am determined to take in no more than the plantation will maintain, till I can buy more negroes' – and in 1764 petitioned the Governor and Council of Georgia to establish a college there; the petition got passed along to the privy council in London.[79] Because the matter touched on the issue of religion, the Council asked Secker to read the memorial.

Secker and Whitefield had a history of mutual dislike stretching back across three decades. As early as 1739, Secker complained to his brother that several

---

[75] Ibid., f. 104: Smith and Jay to Secker, 9 Aug 1762. A 'brief' was permission to raise funds from Church of England congregations through requests for funds and collections sent to each parish with the archbishop's permission and sanction.

[76] LPL, MS 1483, f. 101; *Autobiography*, p. 44.

[77] *Autobiography*, pp. 66, 67.

[78] For background, see Mollie C. Davis, 'Whitefield's Attempt to Establish a College in Georgia', *Georgia Historical Quarterly* 55 (1971), pp. 459–70.

[79] Boyd Stanley Schlenther, 'Whitefield, George (1714–1770)', *ODNB*; George Whitefield, *The Works of the Reverend George Whitefield* (1771), III, pp. 472–75.

Methodists, 'particularly Mr. Whitefield, seem blown up with a vanity which I fear hath and will lead them into mighty wrong behaviour'.[80] In late 1740, Secker and Whitefield exchanged letters about Secker's recent SPG sermon – Whitefield not so subtly intimated that Secker was wholly ignorant of America affairs, and Secker did his best to keep his indignation from spilling over on to the page.[81] 'I have accused no persons, nor designed to make any person otherwise thought of, than he was before,' he wrote icily to Whitefield, in bringing the exchange of letters to a close. 'If I have given Occasion to any one to ask himself, whether he is blameable or not, I have only put him upon doing what we all ought to do frequently.'[82] The relationship had not got off on the right foot.

By the time Secker got wind of Whitefield's memorial for a college at Bethesda, rumours of Whitefield's plans had been circulating for years. Samuel Chandler discussed the matter with Secker in the early 1760s, noting that Whitefield had agreed 'that a minister of the Church of England must be at the Head of it'.[83] Later, William Legge, the second earl of Dartmouth and the president of the Board of Trade, brought up the matter with Secker.[84] William Smith, though, had already forewarned orthodox Anglicans in England of Whitefield's plans. In early May 1765, Smith harboured suspicions that Whitefield's college was intended to be 'a nursery of his own particular Tenets, which tend to hurt order and regular ministration of the Gospel'. He promised the SPG secretary that he would 'have some conversation with [Whitefield] on this Head and shall write the Archbishop'.[85] Their conversation only heightened Smith's fears that Whitefield planned to make Bethesda a 'nursery of Methodism', for he advocated that carefully worded language be added to the charter to secure Anglican oversight for the college.[86] Secker took from Smith's guardedly suspicious reports that 'Mr Whitefields Design was to appoint a Number of Persons by Name for the Governors & Managers of his College, who shd fill up Vacancies as they happend, & that thus it wd probably become a Methodist College.'[87] To counter that possibility, Secker proposed that the colony's royal officials should be governors. He did not think he had achieved much success, though: 'Mr. Whitefield hath got such hold of Lord Dartmouth, who was first Lord of Trade till a few Days ago, that I laboured in vain to oppose his scheme for the Orphan House,' he confided to Smith.[88] For whatever reason, though, the matter lay dormant in Council until

---

[80]   LPL, MS 1719, f. 15: Secker to George Secker, sr., 11 Sept [1739].
[81]   The correspondence is to be found in LPL, MS 1123/1, ff. 132–43.
[82]   Ibid., ff. 142–43: Secker to Whitefield, 17 Sept 1741.
[83]   *Autobiography*, p. 64.
[84]   Dartmouth was a thoroughgoing evangelical: Peter Marshall, 'Legge, William, second earl of Dartmouth (1731–1801)', *ODNB*.
[85]   Perry, *Pennsylvania*, p. 381: Smith to Daniel Burton, 8 May 1765.
[86]   LPL, Fulham Papers 8, ff. 19–20: Smith to Richard Terrick, 25 June 1765.
[87]   *Autobiography*, p. 64.
[88]   Smith, *Life and Correspondence of … William Smith*, I, p. 397: Secker to Smith, 2 Aug 1766.

1767, by which time Whitefield had returned to England and formally petitioned George III for a charter.

Secker's opposition to the plan was unequivocal and the means of his opposition entirely predictable: he aimed to blunt the fortunes of a religious rival by quietly exploiting the Church's relationship with the state to scuttle Whitefield's designs. The Council's president himself reckoned that the Bethesda charter should emulate that of King's College, New York, in stipulating that a member of the Church of England should be head of college.[89] Secker concurred that the college's head should always be an Anglican and that 'the Publick Prayers in the College shd be not extempore, but either the Liturgy of the Church of England, or part of it, or some Form approved by the Governors'.[90] He did, however, rather hope that Northington would be the bearer of bad news. 'Mr. Whitefield will think it is my Fault, if you do not yield to his whole Scheme,' Secker assured Northington, 'whereas I want him to fear, that yr Lps Consent to it can not be obtained'.[91] Whitefield could not abide by the stipulations – noting among other things 'that by far the greatest part of the ... collections came from the Dissenters' – and withdrew his application for the royal charter.[92] Perhaps to embarrass his archiepiscopal antagonist, Whitefield later published the correspondence with Secker.[93]

Coming just after the Stamp Act crisis and in the year of the Townshend Acts, the Bethesda controversy played out just as the sinews of empire were beginning to strain and snap under the weight of the problems which attended victory in the Seven Years War.[94] Secker and Whitefield both understood that something larger was at stake in what might now seem like a minor controversy over a royal charter for a college in a peripheral southern colony. To Whitefield's way of thinking, the Council's refusal to grant the charter married concerns about religion and politics: Bethesda came to symbolize Whitefield's own 'struggle for freedom, for independence from the Anglican church'; not surprisingly, he 'linked his fight for liberty with that of the colonists'.[95] For Secker, too, there were weightier issues raised by the charter request. To have allowed Whitefield to turn Bethesda into a royally-chartered Methodist college would have, from Secker's point of view, been confessionally suicidal because it would have laid bare the Church of England's impotence on both sides of the Atlantic: religio-political victories so easily won could not be let to slip by. Recognizing that the Great Awakening had helped to

---

[89] LPL, SPG Papers 11, f. 254: Robert Henley, 2nd earl of Northington to Secker, 27 Aug 1767.
[90] *Autobiography*, p. 65.
[91] LPL, SPG Papers 11, f. 255: Secker to Northington, 28 Aug 1767.
[92] Ibid., ff. 259–60: Whitefield to Secker, 16 Oct 1767.
[93] Ibid., f. 262: Whitefield to Secker, 12 Feb 1768. The correspondence appeared in *The Works of George Whitefield*, III, pp. 472–84. This appeared in print after Secker's death.
[94] Griffin, *American Leviathan*; P.J. Marshall, *The Making and Unmaking of Empires: Britain, India, and America, c. 1750–1783* (Oxford, 2005).
[95] Frank Lambert, *'Pedlar in divinity': George Whitefield and the Transatlantic Revivals, 1737– 1770* (Princeton, 1994), p. 210.

rot away some of the buttresses of traditional religious authority, Secker would also not have wanted to reward its prime mover in America.[96] That both Secker and Whitefield would have thought in these ways is testimony to the heated – even shrill and paranoid – criticism of the English church-state by the heterodox on both sides of the Atlantic. Contributing most to the intensification of the heterodox opposition rhetoric and its increasing dissociation from reality were Secker's old enemies, the Hollisites and their American friend, Jonathan Mayhew, who found the SPG's activities in America not just objectionable, but a threat to both religious and political liberty.

IV

Metropolitan and colonial religious leaders hoped that the colleges in Williamsburg, Philadelphia, and New York would soon produce enough native clergy so that the Anglican ministry in America was self-sustaining. Until then, the Church's pastoral efforts had to be staffed and supervised from abroad. The SPG served as the main tool of the Anglican pastoral mission in America. Founded in 1701 by Thomas Bray to complement the work of the SPCK, the SPG was a royal corporation to ensure that British subjects overseas had access to Anglican worship and to evangelize among non-Christians in British colonies.[97] By the mid eighteenth century most SPG missionaries lived in the northern colonies where the Church of England was not established.

Secker contended that no Anglican mission would succeed without the moral regeneration of the American Anglicans themselves. 'I should have said one more thing about the pamphlet, which is more material than all the rest,' Secker wrote to Samuel Johnson, 'that whatinsoever we are justly accused, clergy or people, we should own it, and mend; which is the only good answer in such cases.'[98] Similarly, he advised Henry Caner that 'no confutation will be effectual unless our missionaries & their people will conscientiously amend whatever Faults can be justly charged upon them'.[99]

The greatest weight of responsibility rested on the clergy's shoulders, and the SPG scrutinized closely the beliefs and behaviour of its missionaries. To begin with, it was necessary to ensure the orthodoxy of SPG missionaries. Some,

---

[96] Wood, 'Religion and the American Revolution', p. 182.
[97] John Woolverton, *Colonial Anglicanism in North America* (Detroit, 1984), pp. 81–106; C.F. Pascoe, *Two Hundred Years of the S.P.G., 1701–1900: Based on a Digest of the Society's Records* (1901); H.P. Thompson, *Into All Lands: An Historical Account of the Society for the Propagation of the Gospel in Foreign Parts: Based on a digest of the Society's Records* (1901); John Calam, *Parsons and Pedagogues: The SPG Adventure in American Education* (New York, 1971).
[98] *SJ*, IV, p. 84: Secker to Johnson, 6 Oct 1762.
[99] Perry, *Massachusetts*, p. 476: Secker to Caner, 6 Oct 1762.

especially converts like Cutler and Caner, were reliably orthodox, but others were not. In 1757, for instance, the Connecticut clergy convened to debate John Beach's heterodox sermon on the 'state of the dead'. Beach (1700–1782) was one of the star SPG missionaries during the first half of the eighteenth century, having converted to the Church of England after serving as a Congregationalist minister in Newtown, Connecticut, for eight years.[100] After Anglican ordination in London in 1732, he returned to Connecticut as an SPG missionary at Newtown and Reading. Ezra Stiles called him 'a high churchman and a high Tory', qualities that recommended him highly to some who led the mother Church.

Beach had fully intended the sermon to rebut the mortalist heresy, espoused by Francis Blackburne and others, but instead produced a rebuttal that was wholly heterodox in its own right.[101] Beach argued that Christ judges the dead immediately after death, that the souls of the saved go immediately to heaven never to be reunited with the body, which was simply the soul's earthly vessel. Though he denied the 'soul-sleeping' system proposed by mortalists, he nonetheless contravened over a millennia and a half of orthodox Christian eschatology by denying the resurrection of the body. This led Congregationalist ministers ostentatiously to adopt the mantle of 'orthodoxy' and complain to the SPG about Beach's sermon. Beach had, they claimed in a letter to the Society in December 1755, 'promulgated some Errors subversive of the Xtian Faith', and they hoped the SPG would 'discountenance such dangerous principles, & prevent for the future the bad consequences of them'.[102] It was humiliating to the SPG to have one of its missionaries justly pilloried by non-Anglicans for his heterodox views. The Society's secretary, Philip Bearcroft, reported William Johnson, 'seems quite stumbled what to think of him. He says he deserves to be turned out immediately, but as he is old and infirm, and been long in the Society's service, it will look a little too hard; however he is resolved to lay the sermon before the Society, as he thinks he is obliged to do by his office, and let them do as they shall think proper.'[103] The Society instead decided to have Secker and the bishops of Peterborough and Norwich study Beach's sermon; their subsequent report, written by Secker, argued that the sermon could undermine the SPG's mission. '[W]e conceive it is contrary to the plain Tenor of Scripture, to the Belief of the Catholick Church in all Ages, to the Creeds received & the Liturgy used by the Church of England, & by Him as a Minister of our Communion,' Secker wrote on

---

[100] Dexter, *Biographical Sketches of the Graduates of Yale College*, I.

[101] John Beach, *A Modest Enquiry into the State of the Dead, by which it appears to the enquirer that there is no intermediate state, but the resurrection immediately succeeds death* (Boston, 1755). Marc Mappen, 'Anglican Heresy in Eighteenth Century Connecticut: The Disciplining of John Beach', *HMPEC* 48 (1979), pp. 465–72 and Bruce E. Steiner, *Samuel Seabury, 1729–1796: A Study in the High Church Tradition* (Athens, OH, 1971), pp. 95–99 survey the episode. B.W. Young, '"The Soul-Sleeping System": Politics and Heresy in Eighteenth-Century England', *JEH* 45:1 (1994), pp. 64–81 provides background.

[102] Quoted in Mappen, 'Anglican Heresy', p. 469.

[103] *SJ*, I, p. 251: William Johnson to Samuel Johnson, 3 April 1756.

behalf of the committee. 'We also think, that as in general the propagation of these Opinions must tend to unsettle & mislead mens Judgments in religious matters, & produce Disquiet & contention: so in particular the propagation of them by one of our missionaries, if disregarded by us, will bring a Reproach on the Society; & hurt the Cause, in which we are engaged.' They advised the Society to send a letter 'to signifie the Societys Disapprobation of the peculiar Tenets of the Book, & their Desire, that, where it is needful, their missionaries would contradict & confute them'.[104] It was clear the Beach incident touched a raw nerve for the orthodox, for Secker highlighted it in a letter to Samuel Johnson soon after moving into Lambeth Palace. 'It will be requisite to know ... if any Missionary is guilty of gross Vices, or teaches false Doctrines; which last I am sorry to say we learnt, in the Case of Mr. Beach, from the dissenters, not from any of our own Church.' The SPG, he counselled Johnson, required missionaries who were 'diligent, wise, Judicious, learned'.[105]

Just as clerical orthodoxy was a concern of the SPG back in London, so too were standards of clerical behaviour and for much the same reason: clerical misconduct reflected poorly upon the Church of England and was, thus, to be avoided. The case of William McClenachan likewise reaffirmed for the orthodox the iron law that conduct and belief were conjoined.[106] All could agree that McClenachan (1714–1766) – an Irishman and former Congregationalist minister in Chelsea, Massachusetts – sailed to England in 1755, received Anglican orders, and returned to the rough edges of the Massachusetts frontier as an itinerant SPG missionary.[107] The stories of McClenachan's subsequent conduct conflict. On McClenachan's telling, he was a determined and orthodox servant of the Church in a land of infidels and Anglican backsliders.[108] Rather than accept a comfortable living in London at St Anne's, Limehouse, he took his wife and eight children to the wilds of America, staying in Boston during the first winter before spring enabled him to move them northeastward to Kennebec. There he performed

---

[104] LPL, MS 1123/II, f. 44: Report of the committee about Mr. Beaches book concerning the Resurrection, drawn up by Thomas Secker, 21 Jan 1757. See also, ibid., ff. 46–54: Papers sent by Thomas Secker to be transcribed for Mr. Beach, regarding Beach's book concerning the resurrection, March 1757. Secker's interest in the case is attested to by the note he adds to the end of this manuscript: 'These papers I sent to Dr. Bearcroft abt the beginning of March, 1757 to be transcribed for Mr. Beach. The Transcript was brought to me by Dr. Bearcroft read over by me and returned to him March 15.'

[105] LPL, MS 2589, f. 80: Secker to Johnson, 27 Sept 1758.

[106] A.M.C. Waterman, 'The nexus between theology and political doctrine in Church and Dissent', in Enlightenment and Religion: Rational Dissent in Eighteenth-Century Britain, ed. Knud Haakonssen (Cambridge, 1996), pp. 193–218.

[107] James F. Cooper, jr., and Kenneth P. Minkema (eds.), The Colonial Church Records of the First Church of Reading (Wakefield) and the First Church of Rumney Marsh (Revere) (Boston, 2006), p. 320 shows that McClenachan resigned his post on 18 Dec 1754.

[108] Unless otherwise noted, the quotations in this paragraph are drawn from Smith, Life and Correspondence of ... William Smith, I, pp. 237–42: McClenachan to Secker, 23 Aug 1760 [received].

double-duty each Sunday, held services on weekdays, and travelled 'no less than 1000 or 1200 Miles every Year, in the Discharge of the several Duties of [his] sacred Function'. His salary was insufficient to support his family, and he begged the Society for relief.[109] 'At length, almost worn out with Fatigue, and myself and Family being daily in Jeopardy of being killed or captivated by the cruel Enemy, [McClenachan] resolved to take a Tour to the Southward, and see what Providence would do for [him].' Providence was kind, for he found a parish in Virginia willing to take him on as a minister. With the promise of employment in hand, he headed back to New England 'to deliver [his] Family from the Danger of the common Enemy', stopping 'at the opulent City of Philadelphia' along the way. There he introduced himself to Robert Jenney, the minister of Christ Church, then the city's only Anglican church. Invited to preach there, McClenachan was asked by some in the congregation to stay on at Christ Church more permanently. But, though the vestry approved the idea and voted him Jenney's assistant, the bishop of London, the orthodox Thomas Sherlock, denied him a license to serve in that position. Furthermore, the Anglican clergy of the Philadelphia area convened in late April 1760 and agreed to bar McClenachan from preaching in any of their churches.[110] The reason? McClenachan put it down to his opponents' pastoral neglect and theological heterodoxy. 'The melancholy Truth is too plain to be doubted: and Dissenters have Reason to say, that, instead of propagating the Errors of Arminius, they are artfully and industriously introducing Deism,' he contended.

McClenachan's complaints of the American clergy loudly echo George Whitefield's complaints of SPG missionaries two decades earlier with good reason: McClenachan, his opponents claimed, had been heavily influenced by Whitefield's brand of revivalism and his most vocal supporters in Philadelphia were eighteen Philadelphia ministers.[111] William Smith spelled out the case against McClenachan most clearly and succinctly in a letter to Secker.[112] McClenachan, Smith wrote to Secker, had exercised a 'double profession', practicing in Boston 'as a Physician, pretending to perform extraordinary Cures, by means of certain Nostra'. Failing to insinuate himself into Christ Church, Boston, as Timothy Cutler's replacement and having run up considerable debts, McClenachan did not

---

[109] LPL, MS 1124/I, ff. 16, 31, 57: McClenachan to SPG, 7 June 1758, 2 Oct 1758, 22 June 1759.

[110] Perry, *Pennsylvania*, pp, 302, 304: Copy of minutes of a convention or voluntary meeting of the episcopal clergy of Pennsylvania, 4, 5 May 1760.

[111] LPL, MS 1123/II, ff. 230–32: Clergymen of Philadelphia to Secker, 24 May 1760. Cf. LPL, MS 1123/I, ff. 138–40: Whitefield to Secker, 28 July 1741. Joseph Tuckerman, later occupant of the Chelsea pulpit, recorded, 'But as a preacher, I am told, that he was quite as eloquent as Whitefield': Mellen Chamberlain (ed.), *A Documentary History of Chelsea, Including the Boston Precincts of Winnissmmet, Rumney Marsh, and Pullen Point, 1624–1824* (Boston, 1908), II, p. 256.

[112] Unless otherwise noted, the quotations in this paragraph are drawn from Perry, *Pennsylvania*, pp. 319–24: Smith to Secker, 1 July 1760.

heed Henry Caner's advice to find a living 'in the back parts of Maryland or Virginia where by good Economy he might maintain his Family & save something to pay his Debts justly'. Instead, he ended up in Philadelphia, where he hoped to remain. There he preached sermons aiming 'to run down the Clergy and persuade the People that he himself was the only sound Divine'. After 'two such extraordinary Sermons charging the whole body of our Church & Clergy with Heterodoxy', even his supporters among the vestrymen of Christ Church, Philadelphia, abandoned him, leaving the Quakers 'who love to divide in order to rule our Church' to let McClenachan use their meeting house for services. Few followed him 'to his Conventicle', but the Quakers remained 'the chief people who contribute to encourage this schism'.

Secker believed McClenachan's clerical opponents – perhaps not surprisingly, considering an earlier SPG disciplinary action – and wrote a detailed rebuttal.[113] It silenced neither McClenachan[114] nor pamphleteers in America, some eager to attack the Church of England at home and abroad. In 1762, an anonymous Presbyterian layman excoriated those who would call the archbishop of Canterbury *your Grace*, 'a Title never given to Christ or his Apostles, and which no Gospel Minister ought to assume, as smelling of rank Popery ... Popery and Prelacy are Synonimous Terms'. Secker also came in for criticism as 'a Deserter from our Church ... gone over to the prelatical Church of England'.[115] In 1764, McClenachan himself published a self-defence in which he implied that his Anglican opponents were crypto-papists. 'You know that I was bred in the Presbyterian Church, and as the Founder of our Sect, made a greater Leap from the Romish Church, than the Establish'd Church has done, by tearing off the Lace at once, and denying the Power of Bishops, of Course we must be hated ... by those who have been bred in that way,' McClenachan began. His enemies –

---

[113] *SJ*, I, p. 251: William Johnson to Samuel Johnson, 3 Apr 1756. The original letter from Secker to McClenachan is to be found in LPL, MS 1123/II, ff. 284–89: Secker to McClenachan, 9 Oct 1760. Secker copied the letter to Smith and Samuel Johnson, though he did not accede to their wishes to publish it: LPL, MS 1123/III, f. 51: Secker to Smith, 10 Oct 1761; ibid., f. 59: Secker to Johnson, 12 Oct 1761. Thomas Bradbury Chandler, *An Appendix to the American Edition of the Life of Archbishop Secker: containing His Grace's letter to the Revd. Mr. Macclanechan, on the irregularity of his conduct; with an introductory narrative* (New York, 1774) published it after Secker's death, with a lengthy preface detailing the conflict and defending Secker's involvement.

[114] On 4 June 1760, McClenachan's supporters signed a formal agreement to erect St Paul's, Philadelphia, and they moved into the building on 25 Dec 1761. In 1762, St Paul's ignored the bishop of London's refusal to grant McClenachan a license to preach. In 1766, the congregation was reported to have looked to George Whitefield to send them a minister and its members were believed to favour an 'independent Church of England': William Wilson Manross, *The Fulham Papers in the Lambeth Palace Library* (Oxford, 1965), pp. 112, 115–17.

[115] *Old covenanting and true Presbyterian layman, A true copy of a genuine letters, sent to the Archbishop of Canterbury, by eighteen Presbyterian ministers, in America: with some remarks thereon in another letter to the congregations of the said ministers* (Boston, 1762), pp. 6, 9.

'Descendants of Popery', both 'implacable and vindictive' – had accused him of theological heterodoxy: 'I am not Heterdoxish in my Divinity, but Orthodoxish,' he countered and insisted that that 'there is a Church, the Members thereof would govern us best, that is better by far than the Church of England, or Quakers either'.[116] It was acutely embarrassing for the SPG and for the Church of England to have a former convert publicly air such views, especially during the mid 1760s when another religio-political crisis was in full flower to the north of Philadelphia, in Massachusetts.

The SPG's missionary brief was a contentious matter during the mid eighteenth century. This was particularly the case in New England, where issues of religious and imperial authority often dovetailed. In 1762, as the Seven Years War was drawing to a close, William Smith argued that the fate of Britain's North American empire hinged on its Protestantization, meaning its Anglicanization. The 'Providence of God seems ... to have in view through us ... bringing the barbarous nations around us, within the pale of Religion and civil Life,' he contended. Things were acutely precarious at the American frontier, 'when Violence is abroad upon the earth, when Popish and Savage Foes have combined against us, and when it behoves every Head to consult, every Hand to act, and every Bosom to be animated, for the public safety'. In the epochal struggle between the forces of religious and political 'Liberty and Slavery', the SPG had a significant role because it had complementary aims of ministering to the white colonists and winning 'over the Heathen-native to the knowledge of God, and a firm attachment to our national interest'.[117] To Anglicanize the colonists and Indian natives was to secure the fortunes of the British empire, Smith argued.[118]

Secker agreed wholly with this view.[119] He said as much in his 1741 anniversary sermon before the Society, and he reiterated it upon becoming archbishop of Canterbury. 'I suspect We ought to have more [missionaries] on the Frontiers ... ,' he wrote to Samuel Johnson in the fall of 1758. 'For Missionaries there might counteract the Artifices of the French Papists, and do considerable Services, religious and political at once, amongst the neighbouring Indians.' Against those who charged that the Society had no business establishing missions

---

[116] [William McClenachan], *A Letter, from a clergyman in town; vindicating himself against the malevolent aspersions of a late pamphleteer letter-writer* (Philadelphia, 1764), pp. 3, 5, 7, 8.

[117] William Smith, *Discourses on Public Occasions in America* (1762), pp. viii-viii, 135.

[118] Bickham, *Savages Within the Empire*, pp. 210–40 argues that this was the official SPG line straight through to the American Revolution. Cf. Eliga Gould, 'Prelude: The Christianizing of America', in *Missions and Empire*, ed. Norman Etherington (Oxford, 2005), pp. 19–39; Andrew Porter, *Religion versus empire? British Protestant missionaries and overseas expansion, 1700–1914* (Manchester, 2004), pp. 16–28; Laura M. Stevens, *The Poor Indians: British Missionaries, Native Americans, and Colonial Sensibility* (Philadelphia, 2004), pp. 111–37; Gerald J. Goodwin, 'Christianity, Civilization and the Savage: The Anglican Mission to the American Indian', *HMPEC* 42:2 (1973), pp. 93–110.

[119] Woolverton, *Colonial Anglicanism*, p. 88 points out that Thomas Bray, the SPG's founder, explicitly rejected the idea of a missionary effort among non-Anglican Protestants, particularly in New England.

in areas settled by white colonists, Secker answered, 'that our Charter was granted for the Encouragement of an Orthodox, that is a Church of England, Ministry'. Some, however, countered that 'the Evils specified in the Charter against which this Orthodox Ministry might be applied, are only those of Infidelity & Popery; and that We have no Right to presume any other ends to have been in View, than are expressed'. Be that as it may, the Church of England 'can urge with Justice, that both these Evils will be best obviated or remedied by the principles of our Church; for the Establishment of which throughout the American Dominions, there are strong Motives of various kinds, to wish most earnestly'.[120]

The debate over the Society's rights and responsibilities moved from the theoretical to the practical when a group of Congregationalist clergy and merchants convinced the Massachusetts General Court to charter a missionary society for the Indians in January 1762.[121] Secker took the establishment of the rival society as an affront to the royally chartered SPG and as an infringement upon the Church of England's legal rights and privileges. He first heard of the New England Society from Henry Caner in October 1762,[122] and immediately wrote to Richard Osbaldeston, bishop of London, advising that counter-measures needed to be taken. 'I went this morning to the Council Office, to inquire about the Act: and found that it hath been referred to the Board of Trade,' Secker wrote to Osbaldeston. 'Whether I shall have notice, when it comes before the Council, or rather the Committee, I know not: having more than once asked that Favour in like Cases, & failed of obtaining it.' Yet he recognized from the start that the establishment of this rival society put the Church of England and the SPG in a tricky political situation: 'Our Society for propagating the Gospel cannot with a very good Grace make any Opposition. It will be said we ought gladly to let others do what we confess we have not been able to do our selves in any great Degree. And if the new Society be likely to lessen our Income, or our Credit, many will like it so much the better. Indeed no serious man can object against the Intention, which the Title of the Act expresses.' Nonetheless, he agreed with Henry Caner that 'another [aim] lies under it'.[123]

That other aim, which worried orthodox churchmen like Caner and Secker, was a concerted and coordinated assault on the Church by the heterodox on both sides of the Atlantic. 'The Dissenters in America are so closely connected with those in England,' Secker warned Samuel Johnson in 1758, 'and Both, with such as under the Colour of Being Friends to Liberty, are many of them Enemies to all Ecclesiastical Establishments and more than a few to the Gospel Revelation; that

[120] LPL, 1123/II, f. 57: Secker to Johnson, 27 Sept 1758.
[121] John E. Sexton, 'Massachusetts Religious Policy with the Indians under Governor Bernard, 1760–1769', *Catholic Historical Review* 24:3 (1938), pp. 310–28 provides useful background on its subject.
[122] Perry, *Massachusetts*, pp. 471–72: Caner to Secker, 9 Aug 1762.
[123] LPL, MS 1123/III, f. 120: Secker to Osbaldeston, 5 Oct 1762.

We have need to be continually on Guard against them.'[124] Caner likewise thought the heterodox intent on thwarting the progress of the Church of England in America, particularly in the aftermath of the Seven Years War. 'The only reason I can give for that bitterness of spirit which seems thus of a sudden to break out among the Dissenters is, that they look upon the war as a near a conclusion, and that a great part of the conquests made in America will probably be ceded to the British Crown,' he wrote to Secker in 1763.

> So remarkable a Crisis, it is natural to imagine, will fall under such regulations as will either greatly establish the Church of England, or the Dissenting Interest, in this part of the world. Their activity is therefore employed to the uttermost, both here and in England, to secure the Event in their favour. And I am sorry to say, that their conduct in this matter is as disingenuous as their diligence is remarkable.[125]

Other American Anglicans linked the health of the Church of England in America with the strength of Britain's empire. 'I am not alone in the opinion', wrote Ebeneezer Dibblee to the SPG in 1765, 'that the Protection, support and encouragement of the Church in the American Colonies, is the highest wisdom, even in point of Civil Policy, and the best Security of this peoples Allegiance and Attachment to the Mother Country.'[126]

In the run-up to the Board of Trade's deliberations of the Massachusetts missionary society, then, Secker hammered home to the bishop of London that the leading lights of the rival group were Dissenters. '[N]o officer under the Government appears to be in the List of the Society,' he pointed out, 'nor do I imagine, that there is one Member of the Church of England amongst them, but there is a considerable number of Dissenting ministers; amongst them one Dr. Mayhew, who hath been a most foul-mouthed Bespatterer of our Church & our Missionaries in print.'[127] Despite the Massachusetts Congregationalist minister Charles Chancy's later protestations that '[w]e have no intention to oppose the Church of England, or do anything that may tend in the least to disserve it', the orthodox were certain that opposing the Church was precisely the aim of the rival society's founders.[128]

Secker's correspondence with Osbaldeston was part of a coordinated political effort aimed to convince the Board of Trade to disallow the Massachusetts-granted charter. It required some delicacy. 'I am of opinion that our Society must not appear against it,' Secker advised Caner. 'But I conceive it may be shewn that several improprieties & Defects in the Present Frame of it, make it unfit for the Royal Assent.'[129] Over the next few months, Secker collected the opinions of

---

[124] LPL, MS 1123/I, f. 58: Secker to Johnson, 27 Sept 1758.
[125] Perry, *Massachusetts*, p. 490: Caner to Secker, 7 Jan 1763.
[126] Rhodes House, Oxford, USPG B23 (no. 123): Dibblee to SPG, 28 Oct 1765.
[127] LPL, MS 1123/III, f. 120: Secker to Osbaldeston, 5 Oct 1762.
[128] *CMHS* 74 (1918), p. 116: Chauncy to Jasper Maduit, 4 May 1763.
[129] Perry, *Massachusetts*, p. 475: Secker to Caner, 6 Oct 1762.

trusted advisors regarding opposition strategies to the New England missionary society. William Smith contended that the Massachusetts act 'seems an Encroachment on the Rights of other American Provinces' and that it 'tends evidently to overturn the Plan and Order settled by his Majesty for the government of the American Indians'.[130] The archbishop of York agreed that 'the main Objections seem to be the Society's meddling wth other Indians besides those near their Colony: & their not being subject to His Majesty's Superintendance for Indian affairs'.[131] Henry Caner and Samuel Johnson thought the new society worth suppressing simply because it was full of 'zealous dissenters'.[132] Smith's arguments were eventually given to Lord Sandys as talking points in the debate within the Board of Trade,[133] and the privy council voted in May 1763 to disallow the Massachusetts General Count act chartering the New England Society. The orthodox could even maintain that they had not had an active hand in subverting the New England missionary society, since, Secker noted, with what must have been some satisfaction, 'No Bishop was present either at the Committee or the Council.'[134] The immediate threat had been seen off, and, in this instance, the rights and privileges of the SPG and the Church of England preserved. The controversy over the New England missionary society, though, was as much about bishops as it was about missionaries. Running through the pamphlet dust-up over the issue was the question of whether or not the Church of England in America needed bishops: the orthodox thought it did, the heterodox thought not. And, given the choice between having Anglican bishops in America and scuttling the charter of the rival society, though, Secker and his fellow orthodox would have taken the bishops. For in the minds of the orthodox, a church without a bishop was not a rightly-ordered church.

V

The mid-eighteenth-century debate over establishing an American episcopate is one of the most exhaustively examined issues in the religious history of the eighteenth century and, indeed, in Secker's own career.[135] Two questions

---

[130] Ibid., pp. 478, 479: William Smith to Secker, 22 Nov 1762.
[131] LPL, MS 1123/III, f. 143: RHD to Secker, 11 Dec 1762.
[132] Ibid., f. 150: Johnson to Secker, 6 Jan 1763; Perry, *Massachusetts*, pp. 482–89: Caner to Secker, 23 Dec 1762.
[133] BIHR, BP C&P VII/175/1: Secker to RHD, 3 Feb 1763.
[134] LPL, MS 1123/III, f. 183: Extracts from the Council books concerning the Act of the Assembly at Boston for a SPCK among the Indians, May 1763.
[135] Notable studies include, Bell, *A War of Religion*; Doll, *Revolution, Religion, and National Identity*, esp. pp. 155–236; Rhoden, *Revolutionary Anglicanism*, esp. pp. 37–63; Stephen Taylor, 'Whigs, Bishops and America: The Politics of Church Reform in Mid-Eighteenth-Century England', *HJ* 36:2 (1993), pp. 331–56; Donald F.M. Gerardi, 'The Episcopate

concerning it, though, are especially germane to this study. Why would the orthodox want bishops in America? And, what did the failure to introduce Anglican bishops into America before 1784 tell us about orthodox reform, the Church of England, and the age more generally?

The orthodox argued that practical necessities and primitive ecclesiology required an American episcopate. Since at least 1638, when William Laud proposed sending a bishop to America, Anglican leaders had argued for a necessary episcopal presence in North American.[136] And it was not a cause which the orthodox alone trumpeted. In 1736, for instance, Samuel Wesley wrote to his brother, John, then in Georgia, to advise him that the Church needed bishops in America if it was to prove a healthy and stable institution. 'You know that a church where there are only presbyters is *res unis aetatis* [an affair of one generation only],' Samuel counselled his younger brother. 'Aim therefore with all your strength at getting bishops on your side of the sea.'[137] The orthodox among Secker's circle would have agreed: the Church in America could only put down deep roots if bishops were resident there because bishops ordained and confirmed; bishops supervised the clergy through regular visitations; and bishops instituted reforms when necessary. Bishops, in short, steered the Church, and it simply proved impossible for the bishop of London – the metropolitan religious leader under whose aegis the American Church fell – adequately to supervise colonial religious affairs.[138] As Thomas Sherlock, bishop of London, freely admitted in 1751, 'for a Bishop to live at one end of the world, and his Church at the other, must 'make the office very uncomfortable to the Bishop, and in a great measure useless to the people'.[139] Beyond mere practicalities, it was also the case that the Church of England's claim to being a primitive church was rooted in its episcopal/apostolical character.

What in the American Church of England required a resident bishop? Ordination, confirmation, and supervision, answered the orthodox, with mantric

Controversy Reconsidered: Religious Vocation and Anglican Perceptions of Authority in Mid-Eighteenth-Century America', *Perspectives in American History*, new series 3 (1987), pp. 81–114; Woolverton, *Colonial Anglicanism*, esp. pp. 220–33; Mills, *Bishops by Ballot*; Steiner, *Samuel Seabury*; Carl Bridenbaugh, *Mitre and Sceptre: Transatlantic Faiths, Ideas, Personalities, and Politics, 1689–1775* (Oxford, 1962); Don R. Gerlach, 'Champions of the American Episcopate: Thomas Secker of Canterbury and Samuel Johnson of Connecticut', *HMPEC* 41:4 (1972), pp. 381–414; and Arthur Lyon Cross, *The Anglican Episcopate and the American Colonies* (New York, 1902).

136 Rhoden, *Revolutionary Anglicanism*, p. 39.
137 Frank Baker (ed.), *The Works of John Wesley: The Bicentennial Edition* (Oxford, 1980), XXV, p. 460: Samuel Wesley, jr., to John Wesley, 29 Apr 1736. I owe this reference to Mr. Geordan Hammond, whose forthcoming University of Manchester doctoral thesis will elucidate John Wesley's attempts to recreate the primitive church in Georgia.
138 Geoffrey Yeo, 'A Case Without Parallel: The Bishops of London and the Anglican Church Overseas, 1660–1748', *JEH* 44:3 (1993), pp. 450–73. Cf. LPL, SPG Papers 10, ff. 175–76: Thoughts on the State of the Church of England in America, June 1764.
139 Perry, *Virginia*, p. 373: Sherlock to Philip Doddridge, 11 May 1751.

regularity in their private correspondence and public writings across the first three-quarters of the eighteenth century. Only a bishop could ordain. In practice, this required all Americans who sought ordination to travel to England for their clerical orders.[140] Someone had to pay for the ministerial candidate's transatlantic voyage; and if a candidate could not afford the Atlantic passage himself, the burden fell either upon a congregation, which might not easily be able to afford the expense, or upon the SPG.[141] The journey proved lethal to many clerical candidates. Some drowned; disease felled others. Hebron, Connecticut, had the misfortune in the mid 1750s of two consecutive ministerial candidates dying of smallpox during their travel to London for ordination.[142] The disease likewise killed Samuel Johnson's son, William Johnson, in June 1756 while he waited in London to return to America, leading his father to lament to George Berkeley, jr., 'I confess I should scarce have thought my dear son's life bestowed … if it could have been a means of awakening this stupid age to a sense of the necessity of sending bishops (at least one good one) to take care of the Church in these vastly wide extended regions.' William Johnson was, his father continued, 'the seventh precious life (most of them the flower of this country) that has been sacrificed to the atheistical politics of this abandoned age'.[143] The 'Trouble, Expences and Hazard of a Voyage to England' for ordination were, Secker noted not long after William Johnson's death, 'a Burthen to them which if *they* [the Congregationalists] were subjected they would think it in supportable'.[144] He suspected, as well, that a resident bishop would do much to improve the quality of Anglican clergy in America since it would make America less of a dumping ground for the underemployed dregs of the English clergy.[145] Still others among the orthodox thought a bishop's presence in America would keep promising ministerial candidates from joining the ranks of Dissent by removing 'the great

---

[140] M.K.D. Babcock, 'Difficulties and dangers of pre-revolutionary ordinations', *HMPEC* 12 (1943), pp. 225–41; Bell, *The Imperial Origins*, pp. 157–58.

[141] LPL, MS 1123/II, f. 36: Timothy Cutler to Secker, 15 Jan 1756; LPL, MS 1124/I, f. 27: Samuel Johnson to SPG, 25 Oct 1758; Thomas Secker, *A Letter to the Right Honourable Horatio Walpole, Esq.; written Jan 9, 1750–1* (1769), pp. 4–5.

[142] Ibid.

[143] *SJ*, II, p. 339: Johnson to Berkeley, 10 Dec 1756. See also, LPL, MS 1123/II, f. 58: Johnson to Secker, 7 Dec 1757.

[144] LPL, MS 2589, f. 60: Secker to Johnson, 25 Oct 1758. Emphasis in the original. See also, LPL, MS 2564, f. 257; Henry Caner, *A Candid Examination of Dr. Mayhew's Observations on the Charter and Conduct of the Society for the propagation of the Gospel in foreign Parts* (Boston, 1763), p. 89.

[145] LPL, SPG Papers 10, f. 174: Thoughts on the State of the Church of England in America, June 1764. This document was likely written by Archbishop Drummond, but it will here be understood as wholly representative of Secker's thinking, not least on account of its postscript, which reads, 'June 1764. Thoughts upon the State of the Church of England in America. Episcopacy. I know not by whom (I think that Drummond drew this State. J.C.) But have seen the original draught with corrections in Abp Seckers hand. This is as corrected by him' (f. 179).

expences and dangers of the Seas that the Americans must encounter with before they can obtain an ordination'.[146]

Bishops were also necessary to confirm. 'Confirmation is an Office of our Church, derived from the primitive Ages,' Secker remonstrated with Horatio Walpole in 1751, 'and when administered with due Care, a very useful one.'[147] The orthodox held a particularly elevated view of confirmation – it was, Secker noted, 'a practice which rightly or wrongly, we hold in high Esteem' – tracing its origins back to the apostolic church.[148] It was at once spiritually and politically efficacious. Frequent confirmations, for instance, held out the promise of a more ordered civil society in Britain's North American colonies. '[T]he people by renewing their baptismal vow in their solemn manner, will be more induced to lead pious & virtuous lives,' Secker reasoned. 'And there is more need of all helps to this, because the first planters, & their Descendants for a long time, had no publick worship: and so did not transmit a spirit of piety & regularity to their posterity: whence there still remains a great looseness of manners in some parts of the plantations.'[149] Presumably confirmation would remedy this. The problem, as Thomas Bradbury Chandler noted, was that 'confirmation can be administered by none but the Bishops. In the Time of the Apostles, this Power was exercised by them – and they conveyed it to those only who were appointed to succeed them – and it has always been confined to the highest Order in the Church.'[150] It was not a responsibility that could be devolved to a mere commissary of the bishop of London.

Lastly, bishops provided the institution a guiding hand. Appointing commissaries and granting royal governors the right to induct incumbents into the temporalities of their livings only partially alleviated other administrative problems that resulted from having no resident bishop. More important than administrative oversight was episcopal supervision of clergy and congregations. 'The Church of England without a Bishop, is, left to the Care of only a few private clergymen who have no Person to over See, or to call them to an Account upon their Misbehaviour, nor to encourage and Support them in the best Cause,' William Sturgeon, the assistant at Christ Church, Philadelphia, complained. 'This leaves them and their respective Congregations to do the best they can, and indeed, sometimes it is bad enough.'[151] Others hoped a bishop would help the Church in

---

[146] Perry, *Pennsylvania*, p. 404: Hugh Neill to Daniel Burton, 19 May 1766.
[147] Secker, *A Letter to … Horatio Walpole*, p. 3.
[148] LPL, MS 2589, f. 60: Secker to Samuel Johnson, 27 Sept 1758; Thomas Secker, *A Sermon on Confirmation. A New Edition* (1795), pp. 18–19; Thomas Bradbury Chandler, *An Appeal to the public, in behalf of the Church of England in America. Second edition* (1769), pp. 17–20. Cf. Robert Cornwall, 'The Rite of Confirmation in Anglican Thought during the Eighteenth Century', *Church History* 68:2 (1999), pp. 359–72.
[149] LPL, MS 2564, ff. 258–59.
[150] Chandler, *An Appeal to the public*, p. 23.
[151] LPL, MS 1123/II, f. 133: Sturgeon to Secker, 29 Nov 1758.

America defend itself against confessional competitors. 'I speak not this as if our condition were easy without a Bishop,' Timothy Cutler assured the SPG in 1724, 'for we need such a one to guide us and protect us from the scorn, insults and hardships we are exposed to.'[152] In the aftermath of the Stamp Act controversy, many colonial Anglicans believed that bishops would strengthen the metropole's hand by repairing the religio-political fabric. 'Besides that unity of an establishment in ye Chh. would naturally (in time) bring about a unity in ye state, and without an establishment of some national Chh. the state will ever by liable to frequent convulsions & in ye end prove fatal to one party or another,' missionary George Craig advised the Society in 1767. 'I am certain ye Chh. of England has observed her loyalty in ye worst of times in ye mother country and why not ye same in ye Colonies of America were she properly [to] invest'.[153] The most sanguine among the American Anglican ministers were convinced that an episcopate would be a powerful antibiotic against the infection of heterodoxy. '[W]ith a Bp here, ye Dissenters wou'd decay and vanish, as Water thrown on ye Ground,' Matthew Graves confidently asserted in 1768.[154]

There were, then, clear practical problems facing the Church of England in America which the orthodox thought could only be remedied by resident bishops. Yet as compelling as these practical problems was an ecclesiological imperative.[155] It was pure fantasy then and now to argue that the efforts to establish an American episcopate was part of Secker's master plan 'to lock down upon us at home the Hierarchical Yoke, as well as to bend it to the necks of our brethren in the Colonies'.[156] '*Power* and *place*' simply were not 'the stakes for which Episcopalians contended throughout this ecclesiastical struggle'.[157] Rather, a matter of theological principle was at stake. Secker and the orthodox advocates for an American episcopate genuinely believed that an episcopal church was a rightly ordered church and that the Church of England was the most primitive, and thus the most pure, church in the world. If episcopacy was not the *esse* of the Church of England, it was certainly its *bene esse*.[158] Gilbert Burnet described a bishop as an official 'that shall have the chief Inspection over those whom he is to ordain, and over the Labours of those already placed; whom he shall direct and assist in every

---

[152] Perry, *Massachusetts*, p. 143: Cutler to SPG Secretary, 4 Jan 1724.
[153] Perry, *Pennsylvania*, p. 423: Craig to SPG, 7 Nov 1767.
[154] Rhodes House, Oxford, USPG B23 (no. 154): Graves to SPG, 4 May 1768.
[155] Doll, 'The Idea of the Primitive Church in High Church Ecclesiology', pp. 6–43; Gerardi, 'The Episcopate Controversy Reconsidered', esp. pp. 83–98.
[156] *PMHS* 99 (1987), p. 105: Francis Blackburne to Andrew Eliot, 23 Jan 1767.
[157] Bridenbaugh, *Mitre and Sceptre*, p. xii. Emphasis in the original.
[158] John Spurr, *The Restoration Church of England, 1646–1689* (New Haven, CT, 1991), pp. 132–65; Norman Sykes, *Old Priest, New Presbyter: The Anglican attitude to episcopacy, Presbyterianism and papacy since the Reformation* (Cambridge, 1956); and Robert D. Cornwall, *Visible and Apostolic: The Constitution of the Church in High Church Anglican and Non-Juror Thought* (Newark, NJ, 1993), pp. 105–15 examine the development of early modern Anglican theologies of episcopacy.

Thing; and who governs himself by the Rules of the primitive Church'; he was, Burnet contended, 'the likeliest Instrument both for propagating and preserving the Christian religion'.[159] Before his defection to the Church of England in 1723, Samuel Johnson wrestled with the issue of ecclesiology, and as early as 1719 recorded privately, 'I am firmly persuaded and am constrained from as good *as* evidences as the nature of the thing is now capable of ... firmly to believe that Episcopacy was truly the primitive and apostolical form of church government, and that the apostolic office was designed to be a settled standing office in the church to the end of the world.'[160] Henry Caner concurred. 'There are with us but three orders, bishops, presbyters, and deacons, according to the model of the pure primitive church, long before the lest step was made towards popery,' he declared in a riposte to Jonathan Mayhew.[161] A younger American primitive, Thomas Bradbury Chandler, likewise argued that 'as the Practice of the primitive Church was a faithful Comment on the Laws of Christ, and his Apostles, relating to the Government of the Church; so it is not so difficult a Matter, to discover what that Practice was': as it turned out, 'Episcopal Government obtained very early in the Church'.[162]

These orthodox American primitives were priests in a non-episcopal church in America. Their church polity was essentially that of the Congregationalists, and they knew it. This helps explain their fervour when promoting the need for an American bishops and the idealized tone that pervades their writing on episcopacy. Secker actually lived in a country where the Church was governed by bishops and was himself a practical thinker not always given to reveries on the purity of the primitive church. Nonetheless, he put obtaining an American episcopate near the top of his agenda once archbishop of Canterbury. 'This I have long had at Heart,' he reassured Samuel Johnson shortly into his archiepiscopate, 'and not only said, but written a great deal in favor of it ... Nor, unsuccessful as the Attempts have been, shall I ever abandon the scheme, as long as I live.'[163]

As it turned out, it was decade and a half *after* Secker's death before three Scottish non-juring bishops ordained Samuel Seabury the first American bishop. The failure to establish an American episcopate before then elucidates at least two salient points. To begin with, the Church's distinctive alliance with the English state came at a price. While it could widen the scope of the Church's influence, it could also severely circumscribe its range of options. In addition, it was clear that both the orthodox and the heterodox were part of larger, transatlantic intellectual communities and that the opposition to bishops in America was fuelled and nurtured by the heterodox in England. Indeed, the successful effort by the

159 Chandler, *An Appeal to the public*, frontispiece.
160 *SJ*, III, p. 5: 'My Present Thoughts Concerning Episcopacy', 20 Dec 1719. Emphasis in the original.
161 Caner, *A Candid Examination of Dr. Mayhew's Observations*, p. 88.
162 Chandler, *An appeal to the public*, pp. 7, 9.
163 LPL, MS 2589, f. 59: Secker to Johnson, 27 Sept 1758.

heterodox to block an American episcopate was their greatest victory during the eighteenth century in their ongoing battle with the orthodox. It was a proxy war in which an ecclesiastical superpower was humiliated by a numerically smaller, highly motivated force. And it was the Church's relationship with the state, not want of effort, which scuttled orthodox efforts to get an Anglican episcopate in America.

Thomas Secker worked doggedly, carefully, and wholly ineffectually during his episcopal career to bring off an American episcopate. He announced publicly his interest in the matter in his 1741 SPG sermon, following his friends George Berkeley and Martin Benson, who had themselves thrown their support behind an American episcopate in SPG anniversary sermons.[164] Secker's work rekindled interest in the subject of bishops and inspired supporters of the scheme.[165] Even after his death, the *London Chronicle* groused that Secker's SPG sermon had 'furnished the declaimers against the North American Colonies with the *root ideas* of defaming and episcopazing them'.[166]

By 1746, though, Secker was less than sanguine about the chances of getting bishops for America. 'Every thing looks very discouraging here, ecclesiastical & civil, domestick & foreign,' he lamented to Samuel Johnson in the aftermath of the Forty-Five, and while '[w]e are very blameable, in giving you no Bishops ... I see no prospect or amendment in that or any thing.' Nor did he see what he himself could do effectively to promote the cause. 'Being taken up, whilst in Town, with the Care of a parish which is too great for me, & having no Interest amongst the Great; I can attend the Society but little, & serve it still less,' he continued.[167] It was a reasonable assessment of his efficacy since, though a Newcastle and Hardwicke protégé, he was in royal disfavour at the time. His promotion to the deanery of St Paul's in 1750, however, signalled a return from the political wilderness, and he used the opportunity to press again for bishops in America.

Thomas Sherlock's translation to the bishopric of London in late 1748 occasioned Secker's renewed activity.[168] The origins and scope of the bishop of London's authority over America was a question that had vexed Sherlock's predecessors at Fulham Palace. Henry Compton, the Restoration bishop of London, had been the first holder of the office to appoint commissaries to act on

---

[164] Cf. George Berkeley, *A sermon preached before the Incorporated Society for the Propagation of the Gospel in Foreign Parts; at their anniversary meeting in the parish-church of St Mary-le-Bow, on Friday, February 18. 1731* (1732), p. 20; Martin Benson, *A sermon preached before the Incorporated Society for the Propagation of the Gospel in Foreign Parts; at their anniversary meeting in the parish-church of St Mary-le-Bow, on Friday, February 15, 1739–40* (1740), p. 24.

[165] Taylor, 'Whigs, Bishops, and America', p. 339.

[166] *London Chronicle* 34:1822 (18–20 Aug 1768), p. 169

[167] LPL, MS 1123/1, ff. 159–60: Secker to Johnson, 8 Mar 1746.

[168] Taylor, 'Whigs, Bishops, and America', pp. 339–44 provides the most reliable and succinct survey of the efforts from 1745 to 1750 to secure an American episcopate.

his behalf in the crown's plantations.[169] It was a practice generally followed but not closely questioned until Edmund Gibson's succession to the bishopric.[170] Gibson queried the legal foundations of the practice and the Attorney General and Solicitor General informed him that 'the authority by which the Bishops of London had acted in the Plantations was insufficient and that the ecclesiastical jurisdiction did neither belong to the Bishop of London nor to any Bishop of England but was solely lodged in the Crown by virtue of the Supremacy: and that the most proper way of granting to any person the exercise of such jurisdiction was by patent under the broad Seal'.[171] The crown subsequently granted Gibson a royal patent to exercise authority in the plantations, a patent which Sherlock later contended lapsed with Gibson's death. Sherlock's entry into office as bishop of London inaugurated a change in Fulham Palace's colonial religious policy, one that would both reopen the bishops debate *and* set back the cause by decades. Not the good soldier that Gibson was, Sherlock advocated instituting American bishops, and, when the government refused to establish them, simply sat on his hands, hoping to grind colonial religious life to a halt and force the government to support an American episcopate out of sheer necessity. It was a bold move that backfired completely.[172] How so? And what role did Secker play in the controversy stirred up by Sherlock?

In late 1748 and early 1749, Sherlock began to agitate behind the scenes for the government to reconsider the issue of an American episcopate. Newcastle, Hardwicke, and the rest of the Whig leadership wanted little to do with the matter and tried to ignore it. By early 1749, though, it came up for discussion during a meeting of the SPG. During a meeting devoted to considering the Church's role in the settlement of Nova Scotia, Secker himself drafted a paragraph in the Society's response to the Board of Trade urging the board to reconsider and support the application 'that the Society made some Time since for the appointing of Bishops ... in our Colonies in America'.[173]

Nothing material happened regarding the matter until almost a year later when the SPG met on 18 May 1750 to discuss again the need for American bishops. The English episcopal advocates for an American episcopate showed up in full force, with Benson chairing the meeting and Secker, Joseph Butler, and Thomas Hayter of Norwich prominently present.[174] The Society determined that Sherlock should draft an explanation of the scheme and that 2,000 copies would be

[169] Edward Carpenter, *The Protestant Bishop, Being the Life of Henry Compton, 1632–1713, Bishop of London* (1956), pp. 250–54, 262.

[170] Norman Sykes, *Edmund Gibson, Bishop of London, 1669–1748* (1926), pp. 369–75.

[171] Quoted in Edward Carpenter, *Thomas Sherlock, 1678–1761* (1936), p. 192.

[172] Ibid., pp. 193–94.

[173] Rhodes House Library, Oxford, SPG Journals 11, pp. 219–26: minutes of the SPG, 18 May 1750, quoted in Taylor, 'Whigs, Bishops, and America', p. 340.

[174] Taylor, 'Whigs, Bishops, and America', pp. 342–43; Carpenter, *Thomas Sherlock*, pp. 210–11.

distributed in the colonies. Because of opposition from the ministry, though, the matter was dropped at the Society's next meeting, on 25 May. The privy council had sent one of its clerks to inform Sherlock that his proposal was a non-starter, and Hardwicke was shocked that Sherlock had pressed the issue in the SPG, independently of the government. 'The Bishop of London upon the Message, of which I saw Your Grace's account, put a Stop to his proceedings at the Society for the propagating the Gospel, and ye affair stands adjourned *sine die*,' Hardwicke wrote to Newcastle. 'I cannot help but being a little surprised that a Man of his Piety and knowledge in business should pursue such an Affair in so improper an Assembly.'[175]

Horatio Walpole, not a member of the government but nonetheless someone who spoke for it, also wrote directly to Sherlock on 25 May, aiming to undermine the foundations of the episcopal scheme. 'Horace has writ his Lordship a long letter ... a Pamphlet against his whole Scheme,' Hardwicke let Newcastle know. 'This may not be amiss especially coming from one who is now no part of the Administration.'[176] Walpole's letter raised every conceivable objection to the project he could think of – Americans did not want bishops; former bishops of London had not agitated for one; American bishops risked provoking Dissenters at home and abroad, dividing the Church itself, and encouraging the growth of Jacobitism; and no one knew who would pay the bishops' salaries.[177] The episcopal response to Walpole came not from Sherlock, who was increasingly frail, nor from the cautious Archbishop Herring but from Secker.[178] His letter to Walpole was a vintage Secker performance, precisely worded, measured in tone, thoroughly discreet, and comprehensive in its rejection of every one of Walpole's arguments. Where Sherlock used sarcasm as a rhetorical weapon and surprise as a tactical one, Secker used the cool light of reason to expose the flaws in Walpole's argument and discretion to reassure the king's ministers that the orthodox were fully onside with them.[179] But it was a difference in style, not substance.

To Secker's way of thinking, Walpole's letter raised at least three important questions. Was the plan for an American episcopate reasonable? Would it grant the Church in America dangerous powers? And would American bishops destabilize either English or American political life? At the outset of his response to Walpole, Secker rehearsed the standard orthodox litany of reasons for bishops: they were needed to ordain, confirm, and supervise. The ecclesiological logic was

---

[175] BL, Add. MS 32721, f. 49: Hardwicke to TPH, 6 Jun 1750, quoted in Carpenter, *Thomas Sherlock*, p. 214.

[176] Ibid.

[177] Cross, *The Anglican Episcopate*, pp. 324–30: Walpole to Sherlock, 29 May 1750.

[178] L.W. Barnard, *Thomas Herring (1693–1757)* (Ilfracombe, 2006), pp. 66–67 points up Herring's equivocal stance on the issue.

[179] To this end, Secker left instructions that his letter to Walpole not be published until after his death, which accounts for its first public appearance in 1769. The original is to be found in LPL, MS 2589, ff. 44–56: Secker to Walpole, 9 Jan 1751.

wholly on Secker's side. How could the government support a functioning episcopal church at home but not in its colonies? How could it give its blessing to Moravian bishops in the North American colonies but not Anglican ones?[180] There was only one logically consistent answer. As the orthodox discovered during the mid eighteenth century, though, politicians have never seen intellectual consistency as a virtue in and of itself, and political exigencies always trumped ecclesiology. Secker knew as much, which is why he devoted the bulk of his letter to Walpole casting his argument for bishops in terms a government minister would appreciate by explicating the politics of an American episcopate.[181]

American bishops, Secker reminded Walpole, were to fulfil the spiritual, not the political, needs of American Anglicans. How could they do otherwise since 'all our temporal Powers and Privileges are merely Concessions from the State'?[182] If the government wanted to delimit the political powers of American bishops, it was fully within its right to do so. Furthermore, their installation in America would not pose a political problem at home for another reason: the very success of the Whig efforts to convince the parish clergy that it was an even more vigorous defender of the Church than the Tories. There would be no return to the days of Sacheverell because Anglican clergy during the mid eighteenth century were politically disposed to support the government.[183] 'Though too many both of the Clergy and the Laity are disaffected to the Government on one Account or another, yet of the former, even the lower Part are not near so generally possessed of the wild High-Church Notions, as they were,' reckoned Secker. 'Nor was a Time ever known, when the upper Part were so universally free of them.'[184] He also thought that Walpole wildly overestimated Dissenting opposition to the episcopal scheme. 'Now a few busy warm Men, are not the Body of the Dissenters,' Secker cautioned, and pointed out that notable English Dissenting leaders such as Benjamin Avery and Samuel Chandler had publicly removed their opposition to an American bishop.[185] Most importantly, rejecting the call for an American episcopate risked alienating the government's most loyal supporters by putting them in an untenable position. 'I apprehend, the Rejection of this Proposal will do the Government by far more Hurt amongst the Churchmen than it can possibly do them Good amongst the Dissenters,' Secker warned Walpole. Indeed, he turned Walpole's fears on their head, arguing that inaction would cause far more problems for the

---

180   Colin Podmore, *The Moravian Church in England, 1728–1760* (Oxford, 1998), pp. 228–65.
181   This argument does not vitiate Peter Doll's important point that Secker became, during the 1750s, the 'most articulate and persistent proponent' of the primitive argument 'that the colonial church as an independent spiritual society was entitled to and needed a complete polity': Doll, *Revolution, Religion, and National Identity*, p. 176.
182   Secker, *A Letter to ... Horatio Walpole*, p. 10.
183   Jeffrey S. Chamberlain, *Accommodating High Churchmen: The Clergy of Sussex, 1700–1745* (Urbana, IL, 1997).
184   Secker, *A Letter to ... Horatio Walpole*, p. 11.
185   Ibid., p. 22.

government than would installing bishops in America. 'When the Bishops are asked about it, as they frequently are, by their Clergy and others, what must they answer?,' Secker asked him.

> We cannot with Truth express Disapprobation of it, or Indifference to it. And if we did, we should be thought unworthy of our Stations. Must we then be forced to say, that we are all satisfied of the absolute Fitness, the great Advantages, the perfect Safety of the Thing, and have repeatedly pressed for it; but cannot prevail? Would not this both sadly diminish our Ability of serving the Government, by showing how little Credit we have with it; and make very undesireable Impressions on many Minds concerning the King, and those that are in Authority under Him; as incapable of being won by the Arguments or Intreaties of those, who have so strong a Zeal for them, to do an innocent Favour to the Church?[186]

Secker was right that it galled the orthodox to have the Dissenters' apprehensions trump orthodox Anglican ecclesiology. Yet this was not enough to turn the tide of government opposition.

Secker's elevation to archbishopric of Canterbury in 1758 offered fresh hope to supporters of the American episcopate. Herring had flinched at Sherlock's agitation, but Secker was, the orthodox believed, made of stouter stuff. Here was someone who had been a longstanding friend of the primitive American Anglicans and a vocal advocate of their most cherished dream. Secker assured the American primitives that he wanted an American episcopate, but warned them that they had to press the case according to the rules of the English political game. '[P]ushing it openly at present, would certainly prove fruitless and detrimental,' he cautioned Samuel Johnson in the fall of 1758. 'They alone are Judges of Opportunitys, who know the Dispositions and Influences of Persons and Parties which cannot be explained to others.' Part of the problem was Sherlock's 'unseasonable Step' of promoting the scheme openly. 'The time is not yet come for retrieving the Ground then lost,' Secker concluded.[187] Things had not changed by the next year, when Secker wrote to Robert Jenney, 'My Heart hath been much set for many years on forwarding a Provision for the Governm't & Discipline in our American Churches ... But at present, the only effectual Method, that of sending over bishops, cannot be proposed without doing Harm instead of Good.'[188] In late 1761, Secker continued to try to rein in Johnson from agitating too loudly for the bishops scheme. 'The right time to try is certainly when a peace is made, if circumstances afford any hope of success,' Secker counselled him. 'But this is a matter of which you in America cannot judge; and therefore I beg you will attempt nothing without the advice of the Society, or of the bishops.'[189]

---

[186] Ibid., pp. 26–27.
[187] LPL, MS 2589, f. 59: Secker to Johnson, 27 Sep 1758.
[188] LPL, MS 1123/II, f. 123: Secker to Jenney, 18 Jul 1759.
[189] SJ, III, p. 261: Secker to Johnson, 10 Dec 1761.

The end of the Seven Years War provided an opening. 'Probably our ministry will be concerting schemes this summer, against the next session of Parliament, for the settlement of his Majesty's American dominions,' Secker wrote enthusiastically to Samuel Johnson in March 1763, 'and then we must try our utmost for bishops'.[190] But, he warned Henry Caner, 'the less is said about the matter beforehand without doors the better'.[191] In the summer, Secker and Richard Trevor, the bishop of Durham, approached Charles Wyndham, the second earl of Egremont and the secretary of the state for the southern department, with drafts of plans for colonial bishops. 'His Answer was, that he had looked into some part, but had not had Leisure to read the whole,' Secker later informed Archbishop Drummond, 'And then he entered into Conversation with another person. This doth not look promising.'[192] Egremont died in 1763, to be replaced as the southern secretary by the reform-minded George Montagu Dunk, the second earl of Halifax.[193] 'Lord Halifax, is a friend of the scheme,' Secker wrote to Johnson, 'but I doubt whether in the present weak state of the ministry, he will dare to meddle with what will certainly raise opposition. I believe very little is done or doing yet toward the settlement of America; and I know not what disposition will be made of the lands belonging to the popish clergy in the conquered provinces.'[194] Nonetheless, he continued his behind-the-scenes work on behalf of the plan, until at the end of the spring of 1764 he could report, 'Indeed I see not how Protestant bishops can decently be refused us, as in all probability a popish one will be allowed, by connivance at least, in Canada'. Samuel Chandler and Lord Willoughby, the only English Dissenting peer, had not objected to the plan, and Halifax 'hath given a calm and favourable hearing to it, hath desired it may be reduced into writing, and promised to consult about it with the other ministers at his first leisure'. Despite these promising signs, 'what relates to Bishops, must be managed in a quiet, private manner'.[195]

As it turned out, even Secker's cautious optimism was misplaced, for nothing came of the plan. By the time Secker and Drummond 'had a long Conversation' with Lord Shelburne, the secretary of state for the southern department, in the spring of 1767 about American bishops, their suggestions were dead on arrival. 'I ... could make no Impression at all upon him,' Secker later recalled.[196] When William

[190] Ibid., p. 269: Secker to Johnson, 30 Mar 1763.
[191] Perry, *Massachusetts*, p. 495: Secker to Caner, 30 Mar 1763.
[192] BIHR, Bp. C&P VII/175/4: Secker to RHD, 13 Aug 1763.
[193] Marshall, *The Making and Unmaking of Empires*, pp. 76, 85, 171; W.A. Speck, 'Dunk, George Montagu, second earl of Halifax (1716–1771)', *ODNB*.
[194] *SJ*, III, pp. 277–78: Secker to Johnson, 28 Sep 1763. See also, Perry, *Pennsylvania*, p. 390: Secker to Jacob Duché, 16 Sep 1763.
[195] E. Edwards Beardsley, *Life and Correspondence of Samuel Johnson, D.D.* (New York, 1874), p. 281: Secker to Johnson, 22 May 1764. Cf. Kenneth W. Cameron (ed.), *The Church of England in Pre-Revolutionary Connecticut* (Hartford, 1976), pp. 127–28: Abraham Jarvis to Samuel Johnson, 30 July 1764.
[196] *Autobiography*, p. 58.

Willard Wheeler was in London in late 1767 to obtain his license from the bishop of London, he met with Secker, who explained to him why 'the Ministry were intirely aversed to send^g Bishops to America at present'. Among the reasons Secker cited, the most important was 'that as America seemed on the point of Rebellion & Independency, the Ministry were determined to retain every hold on America: that by necessitat^g the American Episcopalians to have recourse to Engl^d for Ordin^a they would be held in part. This hold would be lost if a Bp should be sent, the whole Hierarchy be erected complete in America.'[197] This government's explanation for inaction led the increasingly frail Secker to complain that 'political considerations should take the place of religious ones'.[198]

Secker's death marked a turning point in the episcopate controversy.[199] Opponents of American bishops thought it 'a shocking discouragement' to the episcopate's supporters. 'He without doubt, was the first mover, and great director, in all that has been done in this part of the world.' Charles Chauncy of Boston believed. 'Their hopes of success in their attempts were principally grounded on what, they imagined, he was able to do for them.'[200] By contrast, William Samuel Johnson urged his father not to blame Secker for doing too little to press the issue. '[T]he Court is not a scene for such good men to act in, and he wisely keeps himself to his own province.' Indeed, the younger Johnson informed his father, opposition to bishops 'is universal, and the common sentiment of all the leaders of all the parties, and that, perhaps, of all others in which they are most agreed'.[201] Shortly after Secker's death, William Samuel Johnson likewise warned his father not to expect much help from the new generation of metropolitan Anglican leaders. 'But from none of them, I fear, may religion in America expect that attention and aid which it has formerly had,' he counselled. 'The Church of England there should in fact think more of taking care of itself.'[202]

The scheme for bishops failed because the state did not support it. The king's ministers had put off reform of colonial policy for so long that by the time they attempted it in the 1760s, it caused a furore in the colonies. The ministerial instability that was the signal feature of British high politics during the 1760s made colonial religious reform even less likely, because to face down the vocal opponents

[197] Ezra Stiles, *Extracts from the Itineraries and other miscellanies of Ezra Stiles, D. D., LL. D., 1755–1794, with a selection from his correspondence,* ed. Franklin B. Dexter (New Haven, CT, 1916), p. 254.

[198] Massachusetts Historical Society, Boston, Hutchinson Transcripts, XXV.267: N. Rogers to Thomas Hutchinson, 2 July 1768, quoted in Marshall, *The Making and Unmaking of Empires,* p. 171.

[199] Carl Bridenbaugh, *The Spirit of '76: The Growth of American Patriotism Before Independence* (Oxford, 1975), p. 122 acidly suggests, 'Perhaps it was divine providence that took Archbishop Secker from this earthly scene and thereby permitted the issue of episcopacy to wither away.'

[200] D.O. Thomas and Bernard Peach (eds.), *The Correspondence of Richard Price. Volume I: July 1748–March 1778* (Durham, NC), I, p. 89: Chauncy to Price, 22 Mar 1770.

[201] Quoted in Beardsley, *Life and Correspondence of Samuel Johnson,* p. 317.

[202] Ibid., p. 322: William Samuel Johnson to Samuel Johnson, 12 Aug 1768.

of the American episcopate scheme required time, political calm, and ministerial continuity. With these in short supply during the 1760s, those who cast the king's colonial reform policies as an attack on political liberty quite easily cast American bishops as a threat to religious liberty.[203] Not surprisingly, those who battled against the bishops scheme also tended to be heterodox, just as the scheme's staunchest defenders drew from the orthodox. Indeed, the connections among the English and American orthodox and heterodox quite clearly show that the fight over bishops had as much to do with the religio-political future of England as it did with the situation in America itself.

During the mid eighteenth century, Thomas Secker stood as one of the leading orthodox churchmen of the age, someone to whom his fellow orthodox looked for leadership and to whom the heterodox looked with intense distrust, even dislike. In that defence of orthodoxy, Secker allied himself with the second generation of Hutchinsonians, clerics like George Horne, George Berkeley, jr., and William Jones of Nayland. This Hutchinsonian circle overlapped with other groups of orthodox divines, including those among the Lowth circle of biblical scholars and those defenders of clerical subscription to the Thirty-Nine Articles, such as Glocester Ridley, John Rotheram, Thomas Rutherforth, and Josiah Tucker. It is not surprising to find the American primitives closely connected, both intellectually and socially, with these groups of orthodox divines who would, during his archiepiscopate, orbit around Secker.

Samuel Johnson was particularly close to the second generation of Hutchinsonians, by way of his younger son, William, who died in June 1756 and had befriended them in England. A month before his death, William reported from Oxford that George Berkeley, jr., 'introduced us to a very valuable set of Fellows of several of the Colleges, Hutchinsonians, and truly primitive Christians, who yet revere the memory of King Charles and Archbishop Laud; and despise preferments and honors when the way to them is Heresy and Deism'.[204] His father evidently took seriously his son's recommendations, because in 1760, he asked Secker to name George Horne his successor at King's College.[205] He likewise thought highly of Jones of Nayland's defence of orthodox Christology in *Catholic Doctrine of the Trinity* (1756) and his explication of Hutchinsonian cosmology in *Essay on the first principles of natural philosophy* (1762).[206]

In 1766, Connecticut sent William Samuel Johnson, the elder son of Samuel Johnson, to England to represent the colony in a dispute before the privy council. The list of his companions while he was in England from 1767 to 1771 reads like a

---

[203] Bridenbaugh, *Mitre and Sceptre* makes this argument most fully and starkly.

[204] Beardsley, *Life and Correspondence of Samuel Johnson*, p. 205: William Johnson to Samuel Johnson, 25 May 1756.

[205] *SJ*, IV, pp. 59–60: Johnson to Secker, 15 Feb 1760.

[206] Beardsley, *Life and Correspondence of Samuel Johnson*, p. 291: Johnson to Horne, 1 June [1762]. Cf. B.W. Young, *Religion and Enlightenment in Eighteenth-Century England: Theological Debate from Locke to Burke* (Oxford, 1998), pp. 145–47.

who's who of the English orthodox – Secker, Robert Lowth, Thomas Newton, Richard Terrick, Daniel Burton, George Horne, Jones of Nayland, Beilby Porteus, and George Stinton, and George Berkeley, jr.[207] The younger American primitive, Thomas Bradbury Chandler, also fitted nicely into this transatlantic orthodox network after the appearance of his *Appeal to the Public, in behalf of the Church of England in America* (1767), a work which laid out the orthodox case for an American episcopate clearly, succinctly, vigorously, and controversially.[208] Among his friends were Lowth, Glocester Ridley, and Josiah Tucker,[209] and he wrote during the 1770s defending Secker's involvement in American religious affairs.[210]

Chandler and a number of other American primitives seem actually to have hoped that the younger George Berkeley would be named their first bishop. Berkeley's orthodox credentials were impeccable. Son of the noted philosopher and bishop of Cloyne, he was an erstwhile Hutchinsonian, a Secker protégé, an opponent of the anti-subscription campaign, and a zealous advocate of an American episcopate, even offering to do what he could to convince his friend, Lord Dartmouth (the secretary of state for the southern department), of the necessity of an episcopal presence.[211] The idea was Samuel Johnson's brainchild. Johnson's plan seems to have been to get Berkeley to America, hoping this would pave the way for him eventually to become bishop. 'It gave me very peculiar Satisfaction to find, that the Account, that had been given me by Mr. Tingley, of Dr. Berkeley's Intentions, was confirmed by your Letter,' Chandler wrote to Samuel Johnson in late 1770. 'The Residence of a Clergyman, of his Character and Disposition, for some Time in this Country, will certainly tend to forward an Episcopate.'[212] Charles Inglis concurred. 'I greatly approve your Scheme with Regard to Dr. Berkeley,' he reassured Johnson. 'It may be a Means in the Hand of Providence to accomplish what we so ardently desire ... The Doctor by all Accounts is a very worthy Man, & his Father's Character would undoubtedly help

---

[207] E. Edwards Beardsley, *The Life and Times of William Samuel Johnson* (Boston, 1886), p. 59.

[208] Samuel Clyde McCulloch, 'Thomas Bradbury Chandler: Anglican Humanitarian in Colonial New Jersey', in *British Humanitarianism: Essays Honoring Frank J. Klingberg*, ed. Samuel Clyde McCulloch (Philadelphia, 1950), pp. 100–23 is the only sustained scholarly treatment of Chandler.

[209] Episcopal Church Achives, Austin, TX, Hawks Papers, Box 2: Chandler to Samuel Johnson, 3 Sept 1767; *The Historiographer of the Episcopal Diocese of Connecticut*, XI, pp. 89–93: Chandler to Johnson, 5 Sept 1770; Kenneth Walter Cameron (ed.), *Anglican Experience in Revolutionary Connecticut and Areas Adjacent* (Hartford, 1987), pp. 130, 135. I am grateful to Bruce Steiner for alerting me to and providing me transcriptions of material from the Episcopal Church Archives.

[210] Thomas Bradbury Chandler, *A Free Examination of the Critical commentary on Archbishop Secker's Letter to Mr. Walpole* (New York, 1774) aimed to rebut Francis Blackburne, *A critical commentary on Archbishop Secker's letter to the Right Honourable Horace Walpole, concerning Bishops in America* (1770). See also, Chandler, *An Appendix to the American edition of the life of Archbishop Secker.*

[211] Beardsley, *Life and Times of William Samuel Johnson*, pp. 96–98: Berkeley to William Samuel Johnson, 10 Oct 1772.

[212] Episcopal Church Archives, Hawks Papers, Box 2: Chandler to Johnson, 14 Dec 1770.

to take off the Prejudices of Dissenters against his Person.'[213] November 1771 found Johnson writing to Berkeley asking for help in England, if his presence in America could not be secured. 'I am unwilling to give up all hopes of seeing you in America, at least of your being our first Bishop,' Johnson insisted, 'for then I could trust that we should set out upon the foot of true, genuine, primitive Christianity; and if you be not yourself the man, I beg you through your whole life strongly to interest yourself in our affairs, and so far as is possible to influence that we may have one or more Bishops, and that they may be true, primitive Christians.'[214]

Johnson died in 1772, before Berkeley or anyone else had become an American bishop. His dream was unrealized before his death, in large part, because the heterodox in both England and America claimed that American bishops were tools of popery and arbitrary government. It was a charge which useful to thwart orthodox reform during the mid eighteenth century, for it played to the fears of many colonial Americans, some of whose ancestors had left England in the early and mid seventeenth century to escape the Church of Bancroft and Laud.[215] Others in America saw bishops as a threat to their lay control over colonial religious life and as a tool to reassert the metropole's authority in colonial political life. At home, critics of the English church-state, particularly the Hollisite republicans and anti-subscription men, viewed the American bishops controversy as yet another example of religio-political authoritarianism. All of this made the government loath to do anything substantive to settle Anglican bishops in America, for fear of roiling the political waters by angering Dissenters at home and abroad.[216] England's ruling orders had not forgotten the mid seventeenth century or the age of Sacheverell. The battle over an American episcopate, then, was a battle over two competing notions of reform – the orthodox one, which aimed to bring primitive ecclesiology to America, and the heterodox one, bent on ensuring then an exclusively biblical ecclesiology. Both sought restoration, yet disagreed over what needed restoring.

What caused this fissure? In some sense, it was the still-festering sore of seventeenth-century wounds. It was common for opponents of American bishops to dredge up memories of the bad old days of Laud, when their forefathers had fled episcopal persecution in England for religious freedom in America. 'Did he never hear of the infinitely more distressed condition of great numbers that were deprived, fined, imprisoned, and, in other ways, most cruelly dealt with, in the days of those hard-hearted Arch-Bishops, Parker, Bancroft, Whitgift, and Laud?'

---

[213] Ibid.: Inglis to Johnson, 22 Dec 1770.
[214] Beardsley, *Life and Correspondence of Samuel Johnson*, p. 348: Johnson to Berkeley, 10 Nov 1771.
[215] Cf. Bradley, 'Anti-Catholicism as Anglican anticlericalism', pp. 67–92.
[216] Taylor, 'Whigs, Bishops, and America', pp. 331–56 rightly distinguishes between submission to a ministerial veto of religious reform proposals and abject political subservience; Anglican leaders, nonetheless, were chagrined at the failure to establish an American episcopate and some, like Secker, continued to press the issue, hoping ministerial resistance would subside.

Charles Chauncy asked rhetorically of Thomas Bradbury Chandler.[217] Even Secker's friend and political supporter, the second earl of Hardwicke, had told him 'when he proposed sending a Bishop, that the Americans left England to avoid Bishops'.[218] Winning the Seven Years War also produced a new set of challenges for the metropole and complicated religio-political dynamics across the Anglophone Atlantic world. The dynastic threat of Jacobitism had been a centripetal force for Protestants during the first half of the century, but the Jacobites' defeat during the mid 1740s led to a weakening of Protestant unity. The Seven Years War's conclusion further divided Protestants because the settlement required compromises, including ones over religion. In particular, the official lenience and latitude shown Catholics in Canada infuriated many Protestant Dissenters and encouraged them 'to look suspiciously on the Anglican elites who presided over the new tolerance'.[219] 'I am surprised that we have attended so little to the settling of a Popish bishop in Canada,' Andrew Eliot (1718–1778), of Boston's New North Church, complained to Thomas Hollis in 1766. 'I think the Church of England allows the validity of Popish, though not of Presbyterian, ordination. (If it comes from the sacred hands of a bishop, though is the professed offspring of the whore of Babylon, the mothers of harlots, it is well enough.) Our candidates for holy orders … need only take a little trip to Quebec, and they may be ordained to their satisfaction, and to the satisfaction of those who employ them.'[220] This was utter nonsense, but few believed more fully or spoke more forcefully or effectively to those visceral fears than the American episcopate's opponents, the most prominent of whom, like Eliot, hailed from Massachusetts and Virginia.

Jonathan Mayhew (1720–1766), one of episcopacy's most inveterate critics, served as minister of West Church in Boston. He was 'by temperament, an extremist, an instinctive controversialist, an indignant and militant Arian' whose thoroughgoing heterodoxy suffused his published work.[221] Benjamin Hoadly and Benjamin Avery lauded his *Seven Sermons* (1749), while his *Discourse concerning unlimited submission and non-resistance to the higher powers* (1750) was a 30 January sermon that railed against the Caroline union of church and state which, he insinuated, existed in his own time. 'God be thanked one may, in any part of the British dominions, speak freely … both of government and religion', lamented the author of the *Discourse*'s preface, 'and even give some broad hints, that he is engaged on the side of Liberty, the Bible and Common Sense, in

---

[217] Charles Chauncy, *The Appeal to the public answered, in behalf of the non-Episcopal churches in America* (Boston, 1768), p. 92.

[218] P.O. Hutchinson (ed.), *The Diary and Letters of His Excellency Thomas Hutchinson* (1883–86), II, p. 131.

[219] Stephen Conway, *War, State, and Society in Mid-Eighteenth-Century Britain* (Oxford, 2006), pp. 185–92, at p. 192.

[220] *CMHS*, 4th series (1858), IV, p. 400: Eliot to Hollis, 14 Nov 1766.

[221] Clark, *Language of Liberty*, p. 364.

opposition to Tyranny, Priest-Craft, and Nonsense, without being in danger either of the Bastile or the Inquisition'.[222] The chief threat to religious liberty came from resident bishops. 'People have no security against being unmercifully priest-ridden but by keeping all imperious Bishops, and other Clergymen who love to lord it over God's heritage, from getting their foot into the stirrup at all,' Mayhew argued.[223] 'In plain English, there seems to have been an impious bargain struck up betwixt the sceptre and the surplice, for enslaving the bodies and souls of men'.[224] He also excoriated those clergy who lamented Charles I's execution. 'And he was a martyr in his death, not because he bravely suffered death in the cause of truth and righteousness, but because he died an enemy to liberty and the rights of conscience, i.e., not because he died an enemy to sin, but dissenters,' Mayhew inveighed. 'For these reasons it is that all bigoted clergymen, and friends to church-power, paint this man a saint in light, though he was such a mighty, such a royal sinner; and as a martyr in his death, though he fell a sacrifice only to his own ambition, avarice, and unbounded lust of power.'[225] Church and state were, in Mayhew's eyes, allied to rob people of their religious and political liberties.

Mayhew came to Secker's attention during the early 1760s, when he led the heterodox side in a pamphlet war over the SPG's role in settled New England. In the spring of 1759, Henry Caner had written to Secker asking that East Apthorp (1733–1816) be named an SPG missionary in Cambridge to combat the theological heterodoxy succoured by Harvard.[226] 'Socinianism, Deism, and other bad Principles find too much Countenance among us', Caner groused. 'To prevent these and the like Errors from poysoning the Fountain of Education, it will undoubtedly be of great Service to erect a Church there, agreeable to the Desire of many of the Inhabitants, and to entrust the Conduct of it with a Gentleman who by his Doctrine and good Example may give a right Turn to the Youth who are educated there.'[227] Though 'apprehensive, that settling a Mission at Cambridge will raise a great Clamour', the Society nonetheless agreed unanimously to approve Apthorp's nomination hoping 'for much greater Good from his Abilities, Temper and Discretion'.[228] Soon after his arrival in Cambridge, Apthorp built an

---

[222] Jonathan Mayhew, *A discourse concerning unlimited submission and non-resistance to the higher powers: with some reflections on the resistance made to King Charles I. and on the anniversary of his death: in which the mysterious doctrine of that prince's saintship and martyrdom is unriddled: the substance of which was delivered in a sermon preached in the West Meeting-House in Boston the Lord's-Day after the 30th of January, 1749/50* (Boston, 1750), preface. Bernard Bailyn (ed.), *Pamphlets of the American Revolution, 1750–1776* (Cambridge, MA, 1965), pp. 204–11 contextualizes Mayhew's *Discourse*. See also, idem, *Faces of Revolution: Personalities and Themes in the Struggle for American Independence* (New York, 1990), pp. 125–36.

[223] Mayhew, *A discourse concerning unlimited submission and non-resistance*, preface.

[224] Ibid., p. 52.

[225] Ibid., pp. 52–53.

[226] John C. Shields, 'Apthorp, East (1733–1816)', *ODNB*.

[227] LPL, MS 1123/II, f. 104: Caner to Secker, 7 Apr 1759.

[228] Ibid., f. 125: Secker to Caner, 19 July 1759.

impressive parsonage – dubbed 'The Bishop's Palace' by Mayhew – and preached that 'a true church' was 'a guard and preservative against heretical opinions'. Indeed, a true church had no place for the heterodox among its ranks. 'Most of the depraved doctrines, that have corrupted and deformed religion, are so explicitly condemned in our public offices,' Apthorp insisted, 'that it is scarce possible for a disciple of Arius, or Pelagius, or any other haeresiarch, to shelter himself under the communion of that church, which so openly declares against their dangerous errors.'[229] It was, however, Apthorp's published declaration in 1763 that 'the primary and main intention of incorporating' the SPG was 'maintaining Episcopal Ministers in the Colonies, for the support of public worship among the English subjects in our own Provinces, in the most populous and settled parts of the continent, where they may be most useful', that finally drew Mayhew's fire.[230]

The ensuing flurry of pamphlets took place against the backdrop of the English privy council's disallowing of the charter for the New England missionary society, something which only magnified and aggravated the heterodox-orthodox divide.[231] In his initial response to Apthorp, Mayhew decried the Church of England, the orthodox, and the SPG. He asserted that it was Apthorp and his ilk, rather than William III who first chartered the SPG, who construed 'orthodox ministers' to be 'those of the English church in distinction from those of all the other churches in the world; and consequently to brand all the rest as heterodox'.[232] The SPG's original charter, Mayhew argued, made 'no distinction among Christians, except that of protestants and papists'. Instead, its 'grand object ... is, to promote Christianity, considered in opposition to atheism, infidelity and popery; not episcopacy and the liturgy of the church of England, in opposition to presbyterianism, &c'.[233] Nonetheless, the Society's original aims had, since the SPG's founding, been perverted to service a wholly corrupt church whose ecclesiology lacked biblical foundation. He lambasted 'the real constitution of the church of England; and how aliene her mode of worship is from the simplicity of the gospel, and the apostolic times'; 'her enormous hierarchy, ascending by various gradations from the dirt to the skies'; and 'what our Forefathers suffered from the mitred, lordly Successors of the fishermen of Galilee, for non-conformity to a non-

---

[229] East Apthorp, *The constitution of a Christian church illustrated in a sermon at the opening of Christ-Church in Cambridge on Thursday 15 October, MDCCLXI* (Boston, 1761), p. 20.

[230] East Apthorp, *Considerations on the institution and conduct of the Society for the Propagation of the Gospel in Foreign Parts* (Boston, 1763), p. 11. See also, Shields, 'Apthorp, East (1733–1816)', *ODNB*.

[231] Cross, *The Anglican Episcopate*, pp. 139–60; Charles W. Akers, *Called unto Liberty: A Life of Jonathan Mayhew, 1720–1766* (Cambridge, MA, 1964), pp. 166–97; Bernhard Knollenberg, *Origin of the American Revolution: 1759–1766*, rev. edn (New York, 1961), pp. 76–86; and Bell, *The Imperial Origins*, 166–85 examine the pamphlet war which attended the Mayhew-Apthorp controversy.

[232] Jonathan Mayhew, *Observations on the charter and conduct of the Society for the Propagation of the Gospel in Foreign Parts* (Boston, 1763), p. 22.

[233] Ibid., p. 28.

instituted mode of worship'.[234] Mayhew did not doubt that the Society wanted the Church of England to 'become the established religion' in America so that 'tests be ordained, as in England, to exclude all but conformists from posts of honor and emolument; and all of us be taxed for the support of bishops and their underlings'.[235]

Mayhew's assault on the Church was so trenchant and effective that Secker himself was drawn into the controversy in an anonymously published pamphlet which even Mayhew acknowledged met righteous anger with moderation.[236] 'The real conduct of the Society, with respect to provinces and parishes not Episcopal, hath been, to contribute towards supporting public worship and instruction amongst such members of the Church of England, as cannot in conscience comply with the worship and instruction of the other congregations in their neighbourhood, and yet cannot wholly maintain ministers for themselves,' Secker tried to reassure Mayhew.[237] He guaranteed his readers that the American bishops would perform purely spiritual, not political, functions.[238] Others among the orthodox were not so conciliatory. Though Henry Caner thought that Mayhew's *Observations* had 'insulted the Missions in General, the Society, the Church of England, in short, the whole national establishment, in so dirty a manner, that it seems to be below the Character of a gentleman to enter into controversy with him,' he nonetheless wrote a sharp reply.[239] Yet the orthodox made little headway in New England or England, for the colonial reforms of the 1760s made it seem to many American colonists that the king's government was actually trying to rob them of their religious and political liberties. In his last published work before he died of a stroke in 1766, Mayhew seamlessly conflated the efforts to establish an American episcopate and the imposition of the Stamp Act.[240]

---

[234] Ibid., p. 155.

[235] Ibid., p. 156.

[236] *PMHS* 69 (1956) p. 153: Mayhew to Hollis, 24 June 1764.

[237] Thomas Secker, 'An Answer to Dr. Mayhew's Observations on the Charter and Conduct of the Society for the Propagation of the Gospel in Foreign Parts', in *WTS*, IV, p. 522.

[238] Secker's private notes and public pronouncements confirm that the American episcopate's supporters envisioned only spiritual powers for bishops in the plantations. LPL, SPG Papers 10, ff. 177–79: Thoughts on the State of the Church of England in America, June 1764 (a document which accurately reflected the official mind of the Church of England's leadership) states unequivocally, 'No Coercive Powers are desired over the Laity, but only to regulate the behaviour of the Episcopal Clergy and Clerks of Parishes and to punish them according to the Law of the Church of England in case of Misbehaviour or neglect of duty; the directing and inforcing the Reparation of the Parsonage Houses and Churches, together with a due Provision of all such things as the Laws require for the decent and orderly Performance of Divine Service therein, should be also under this Jurisdiction.' Cf. LPL, MS 2564, ff. 260–62; Secker, 'An Answer to Dr. Mayhew's Observations'.

[239] Perry, *Massachusetts*, p. 489: Caner to Secker, 7 Jan 1763; Caner, *A candid examination of Dr. Mayhew's Observations*.

[240] Jonathan Mayhew, *The Snare Broken. A thanksgiving discourse, preached at the desire of the West Church, in Boston, N.E. Friday, May 23, 1766. Occasioned by the repeal of the stamp-act* (Boston, 1766), esp. pp. 17–18.

Jonathan Mayhew was not a lone voice decrying the English religio-political establishment. Rather, he was part of a transatlantic network of the heterodox, which included Thomas Hollis, Francis Blackburne, Caleb Fleming, Richard Baron, and Andrew Eliot, Mayhew's successor at the West Church in Boston.[241] Their correspondence shows quite clearly how religious issues (e.g., episcopacy) and political ones (e.g., subscription to the Thirty-Nine Articles) were 'integrated into a coherent conception which merged both'.[242] And the *bête noir* of this heterodox network was Thomas Secker.

Andrew Eliot thought that Secker and the orthodox wanted to bring off the union between the Roman Catholic and Anglican churches that William Wake had sought and failed to do. '[I]f I hear of a bishop sent to America, I shall fear there is a concatenation of causes and effects, and shall expect soon to hear that popery is tolerated in Ireland, then in England,' he fretted to Thomas Hollis. 'I hope in God it will never be established! But may not some future archbishop (we must not expect any such thing of the present!!!) again bring on the scheme of uniting the two Churches, the popish and the protestant, and become *papa alterius orbis*!' The orthodox ultimately aimed 'to increase their faction; to add to the number of Lord Bishops; to extend their episcopal influence; to subject the American dissenters to their yoke; to tyrannize over those who yet stand fast in the liberty wherewith Christ hath made them free'.[243] Elsewhere Eliot complained that 'Secker and the rest of the B-ps even, gladly encouraged and brought forward the Popish Episcopacy in Quebec'. In addition to being a papist sympathizer, Secker was likely a closet Tory, as well. 'Could Secker be in earnest for tory bishops?' Eliot wondered. 'Burton's panegyrick, betrays his high Oxonian domination and tyranny over conscience.'[244] Eliot believed that Secker's goal always was to impede religious reform, not to advance it. 'I hope in God the place will be filled with a person of more candor, and one who will not be so eternally contriving to advance the hierarchy,' he wrote to Hollis shortly upon learning of Secker's death, 'one who will improve his power and influence, to reform a church which, if it is not declining in wealth and grandeur, is evidently declining in piety and virtue – and not one who, like the last, will set himself to oppose every thing that looks like alteration or reformation.'[245]

Thomas Hollis (1720–1784) thought much the same of Secker. East Apthorp, he insisted, had been sent to America to be the archbishop's eyes and ears. 'The Return of Mr. Apthorp, that Spye upon your Land, must have been a thorough mortification to the A.B, who begat and sent him out such,' Hollis gloated to

[241] Bartholomew Schiavo, 'The Dissenter Connection: English Dissenters and Massachusetts Political Culture, 1630–1774' (Brandeis University Ph.D. thesis, 1976), pp. 465–520 anatomizes this network. I thank Professor James E. Bradley for this reference.
[242] Ibid., pp. 521–74, at p. 522.
[243] *CMHS*, 4th series (1858), IV, p. 411: Eliot to Hollis, 13 Nov 1767.
[244] Ibid., p. 450: Eliot to Hollis, 28 Jan 1770.
[245] Ibid., p. 432: Eliot to Hollis, 17 Oct 1768.

Jonathan Mayhew when Apthorp returned to England in 1765.[246] Elsewhere he mocked Apthorp as Secker's 'Understrapper and N.A. [North American] Privy Coucellor'.[247] The embodiment of orthodoxy, Secker was, Hollis thought, hypocritical, intolerant, and popish. 'I was going to have added, that I had had the honor to be acquainted with that prelate above twenty years, and apprehended myself to be not altogether unacquainted with his stile of writing and conversing,' he wrote to Mayhew shortly after Secker anonymously published is *Remarks on Dr. Mayhew's Observations* (1764). What followed was the heterodox catalogue of Secker's sins.

> Also, that since his elevation to the Primacy, and the observation that he left Popery unnoticed, widespreading, intolerant, overturning Popery, and yet prosecuted with bitterest severity, Anet, a poor old speculative Philosopher; that he shewed no hearty affection to Liberty of any sort, nor those men who loathed it; that he trod with glee the mired Court paths; and juggled for Fame with his own order who yet would never grant it him, knowing him well to be an Irregular and Interloper amongst them from the medical Tribe; I had declined my visits to him: and that now, on further observation of his plan and views in regard to America, and the extreme poorness of his conduct in having fixed a Spy upon you, for ever, *himself*, in the center of your Land; and his general actions and connections everywhere; I had determined ... to drop him wholly.[248]

Later that month, Hollis complained again that the 'Conduct of the Church of England in respect to Papists and Popery, appears to me to have been always strange or wicked, and never more strange or wicked than at this time'; Secker, he concluded, was skilled 'at the antient art or Mystery of Priestcraft'.[249]

Francis Blackburne (1705–1787), though an Anglican archdeacon, nonetheless shared the same fears as Mayhew, Eliot, and Hollis regarding American bishops, orthodoxy, and Secker. 'I have ever been of opinion that Episcopacy, as it is administered in our View, is a dead Weight upon Christian piety,' he wrote to Eliot in 1767. 'It is indeed impossible it should be otherwise, while it is encompassed with that pride and pomp, and Pharisaical Formality which exalts it so far above the Consideration of the spiritual wants and necessities of the Common Brotherhood.' Secker, the American episcopal scheme's most powerful advocate, stood at the head of a body of orthodox clerics who were enemies of religious liberty. 'I dread for my Country, the daily increasing influence and opulence of this order of men, affecting upon all Occasions a separate interest from the Public, and very visibly gaining that power and Consequence, which our wise forefathers had the Spirit to controul, and the good luck to Stifle in the Days of

---

[246] *PMHS* 69 (1956), p. 165: Hollis to Mayhew, 4 Mar 1765.
[247] Ibid., p. 190: Hollis to Mayhew, 19 June 1766. Of Apthorp's own retort to Mayhew's *Observations*, Secker noted, 'I corrected it & added largely to it.' In 1765, Secker awarded Apthorp the vicarage of Croydon: *Autobiography*, pp. 48, 51.
[248] *PMHS* 69 (1956), p. 146: Hollis to Mayhew, 4 Apr 1764.
[249] Ibid., p. 148: Hollis to Mayhew, 22 Apr 1764.

Laud and his Fellows,' Blackburne contended. 'The leading character of this Squadron has all the Artifice of a Jesuit, as well as the Laudaean Rancour against Christian Liberty.'[250] Elsewhere he lamented 'the dregs of Stuartine and Laudian Ecclesiastical Politics fermenting afresh in this country, after an interval of moderation which gave hopes ... that all that vile spirit had evaporated'.[251] No less than for the orthodox, the seventeenth century was never far from the forefront of the heterodox mind.

The same sorts of ideological commitments and intellectual networks at play in the New England opposition to Anglican bishops in America held in Virginia, as well. The Virginia episcopate controversy of the early 1770s has usually been seen as part of an effort of a laicized Church of England to protect its rights and privileges. This is surely correct, but it was also the case that the most vocal opponents of bishops were themselves heterodox opponents of orthodox religious reform. In 1771, John Camm, the erstwhile supporter of the Church's rights and privileges in the Parson's Cause, convinced James Horrocks, the bishop of London's Virginia commissary, to organize a clerical petition for an American episcopate.[252] That June Horrocks called a convention of the Virginia clergy to consider 'the Expediency of an Application to the proper Authority for an American Episcopate'. Only twelve of one hundred eligible clergy showed up, eight of whom supported a measure to petition George III to appoint a bishop in America. Leading the opposition to the petition were two of the four clergy in opposition, Samuel Henley and Thomas Gwatkin. Both faculty at the College of William and Mary, Henley and Gwatkin formally protested the vote, ostensibly for reasons of procedure and practicality, not principle.[253] For their efforts, the House of Burgesses resolved 'that the Thanks of this House be given to the Reverend Mr. Henley, the Reverend Mr. Gwatkin ... for the wise and well-timed Opposition they have made to the pernicious Project of a few mistaken Clergymen, for introducing an American Bishop: A Measure by which much Disturbance, great Anxiety, and Apprehension would certainly take place among his Majesty's faithful American Subjects'.[254]

At first glance, it appears that Henley and Gwatkin, unlike the New England Congregationalists and their English supporters, did not oppose episcopacy as such. There is reason to believe, though, that they were no less heterodox than Mayhew, Eliot, Hollis, or Blackburne.[255] Henley (1740–1815) studied at Caleb

[250] *PMHS* 99 (1987), p. 114: Blackburne to Eliot, 18 Aug 1767.
[251] Ibid., p. 105: Blackburne to Eliot, 23 Jan 1767.
[252] Cross, *The Anglican Episcopate*, pp. 226–40; Brydon, *Virginia's Mother Church*, II, pp. 346–61; Bridenbaugh, *Mitre and Sceptre*, pp. 314–23; and Isaac, *The Transformation of Virginia*, pp. 181–205 consider the Virginia episcopate controversy and its contexts in some detail.
[253] Thomas Gwatkin, *A letter to the clergy of New York and New Jersey, occasioned by an address to the Episcopalians in Virginia* (Williamsburg, 1772), pp. 6–8 reprints the protest in full.
[254] Quoted in Cross, *The Anglican Episcopate*, p. 235.
[255] Clark, *Language of Liberty*, pp. 342–47.

Ashworth's Dissenting academy before taking Dissenting orders. For two years, he served as the minister of a congregation at St Neots, near Cambridge, where he made the acquaintance of Bishop Edmund Law and John Jebb, both heterodox clerics.[256] With their support, Henley took Anglican orders in 1769 and a year later migrated to Virginia, where he assumed the professorial chair of moral philosophy at William and Mary. During the episcopacy controversy that ensued from his and Gwatkin's formal protest, Henley showed his heterodox colours. 'The episcopacy at large I have always opposed because it existeth only in the precincts of Rome,' he wrote in the *Virginia Gazette* during the summer of 1771.[257] The next year, in a sermon before the House of Burgesses, he explained the reasons for his anti-dogmatism. That the sermon was printed in England – just as the anti-subscription campaign there was nearing full bloom – suggests the degree to which the concerns he addressed in Virginia resonated across the Anglophone Atlantic world. 'If by Religion be meant the establishment of certain doctrines on the authority of the State; such doctrines, it is evident can produce no good effect, unless they are actually believed,' he argued. 'In reality, the most sacred dogmas would be but human prescriptions to him who had no conviction of their being divine.' Man-made dogmas should not be the litmus test of truth; rather, truth was to be judged solely by its rationality. 'If reason cannot produce assent, all other efforts must fail,' Henley posited. 'There can be no greater solecism than to suppose the possibility of forcing a belief.'[258] Compelling belief, though, was exactly what Henley believed the orthodox were intent upon doing. 'Among our more illuminated theologians it is no longer inquired whether a man be possessed [of] integrity and benevolence, but whether he is orthodox,' he lamented in 1774, ' … as though the inquiry at the last judgment would be are you Athanasian, or Arian, or Socinian'.[259] These views, and his heterodox Christology in particular, made Henley enemies in Virginia and explain why he was refused the rectory of Bruton Church, Williamsburg, in 1774.[260]

Thomas Gwatkin (1742–1800) was earlier in the field as an anti-orthodox author. A former Dissenter, educated at Jesus College, Oxford, and ordained into the priesthood in 1767, he too joined the staff of William and Mary's faculty, as professor of natural philosophy and mathematics.[261] While still in England,

[256] Fraser Neiman, 'Letters of William Gilpin to Samuel Henley', *Huntington Library Quarterly* 35 (1971–72), pp. 159–69.

[257] *Virginia Gazette* (8 Aug 1771), quoted in Ray Hiner, jr., 'Samuel Henley and Thomas Gwatkin: Partners in Protest', *HMPEC* 37:1 (1968), p. 42.

[258] Samuel Henley, *The distinct claims of government and religion, considered in a sermon preached before the Honourable House of Burgesses, at Williamsburg, in Virginia, March 1, 1772* (Cambridge, 1772), pp. 13–14.

[259] *Virginia Gazette* (17 Feb 1774), quoted in Hiner, 'Samuel Henley and Thomas Gwatkin', p. 44.

[260] Samuel Henley, *A candid refutation of the heresy imputed by Ro. C. Nicholas Esquire to the Reverend S. Henley* (Williamsburg, 1774).

[261] A.J. Willis (ed.), *Winchester Ordinations, 1660–1829* (Folkestone, 1967), II, p. 9; E. Alfred Jones, 'Two Professors at William and Mary College', *WMQ* 36:4 (1918), pp. 221–26; W.D.

Gwatkin had shown himself a champion of the heterodox and a harsh critic of Secker in two works countering Glocester Ridley's *Three letters to the author of The Confessional* (1768). Ridley, under Secker's close supervision and editorship, had written the three letters to rebut Blackburne's anti-subscription polemic, *The Confessional* (1766). In Gwatkin's second reply to Ridley, he likened Secker to Pope Clement XIII,[262] but it was in his first pamphlet that he witheringly criticized orthodoxy's champion. 'Under the mild Government of our present Primate, we have no reason to fear an undue exertion of Church authority,' he sarcastically averred. Nonetheless, it might be possible sometime in the future that 'another Laud should get possession of the primacy'. What kind of rule would such a man offer to the Church of England? And, how would he gain power? 'Let us imagine ... one directly opposite to the character of our present Archbishop,' Gwatkin urged his readers. This latter-day Laud would be 'a man in the early part of his life ... educated in the principles of liberty' and would 'by a course of free inquiry improperly conducted, ... be led to doubt of the truth, I will not say of revealed, but even natural Religion itself'. Having developed thus far in his views 'he should be so well satisfied with his new scheme, as to exert himself in making proselytes to it'. However, there would eventually appear before him 'the prospect of some temporal advantages, [and] he should be so miraculously converted to the belief of Christianity, as to enter into holy orders, and set up for a zealous defender of that Gospel he had before ridiculed and dispised'. Having to this point shown himself wholly unprincipled, the new Laud would 'by a dextrous accommodation to the times ... at length raise himself to the primacy of this kingdom'. Safely ensconced in Lambeth Palace he would then would proceed to 'shew his orthodoxy, by polluting himself with the persecution of a poor defenceless Infidel' and by employing 'the lowest arts to prevent the propagation of truth'. His 'whole conduct' would 'give the world reason to believe, that he considers Religion in no other light than a political engine'. At that point, 'we should ... be justly alarmed for our civil liberties, as well as the safety of the Protestant Religion'.[263] Once across the Atlantic, Gwatkin actually criticized Secker by name for his orthodoxy. 'How much the old spirit is left, let Secker's persecution of Annet, his illiberal treatment of the present Bishop of Carlisle, his conduct towards the truly learned and worthy Mr. Peckard, and the late expulsion of the six students from St Edmund's Hall, witness,' he argued in the *Virginia Gazette* in the summer of 1771. 'The violence of Secker is no secret.'[264] This was the very same litany of

---

MacRay, 'Honorary Oxford Degrees Conferred on New England Clergy in the Eighteenth Century', *Notes and Queries*, 7th series, VI (28 July 1888), pp. 61–62. I thank Bill Gibson for help with these references.

[262] Thomas Gwatkin, *Remarks upon the second and third of three letters against the Confessional* (1768), p. 43.

[263] Thomas Gwatkin, *Remarks upon the first of three letters against the Confessional* (1768), pp. 85–88.

[264] *Virginia Gazette* (18 July 1771).

Secker's sins adduced by Blackburne, Hollis, and Eliot. For Gwatkin as for others among the heterodox during the mid eighteenth century, orthodoxy was a sham: it was a blind adherence to irrational dogma by self-serving, ruthless churchmen wholly unmoored from principle. Orthodoxy threatened truth, and the orthodox were the enemy of both political and religious liberty. Episcopizing America, the heterodox argued, was but a symptom of a much larger problem – orthodoxy ascendant.

Thomas Secker understood orthodoxy's fortunes much differently. From his perspective, the orthodox were on the defensive, and he dismissed the heterodox charges of crypto-popery and tyranny as but means to an end. '[T]he Out-cry against [the orthodox clergy] as conniving at Popery is visibly a Pretence to serve a Turn,' he insisted. It was 'doubtless, both they, and the Church to which they belong, have their defects; but, Perfection is not to be attained in Human Affairs; and that striving for it with intemperate Eagerness hath often made things worse, but never better'.[265] Neither Secker nor the orthodox sought perfection in America – they hoped instead to reform the colonial Church of England, making it as best they could a reflection of their pure and primitive model.

The orthodox failed to get an American episcopate during the 1760s and1770s because the pressures of war were slowly de-confessionalizing English politics. Winning the Seven Years War both won the English a huge North American empire and burdened it with new problems of governance at home and abroad. To have granted the Anglican orthodox their wish for American bishops in would have destabilized both domestic and American politics because it would have angered the heterodox: John Adams, Samuel Adams, and John Wilkes, among others, ensured that England's governors realized just that.[266] What evidently mattered to the English state, then, was calm, not theological or ecclesiological consistency.

---

[265] *St. James's Chronicle* 982 (16 June 1767), writing under the pseudonym 'Irenicus'. Cf. *Autobiography*, p. 58.

[266] Bell, *A War of Religion* (chapter 8) demonstrates convincingly the effectiveness of the Sons of Liberty and Wilkes in ginning up heterodox political opposition to the English state over the prospect of an American bishop during the 1770s.

Chapter Eight

THE CHURCH AND CHURCHES ABROAD

On 6 October 1745, Secker addressed his parishioners at St James's, Westminster, on the dangers of popery, arbitrary government, and universal monarchy. Wars provoked crises of national and religious identity during the eighteenth century,[1] and they tended to give occasion for clerics to declaim the popish menace. In substance, Secker's sermon hardly distinguished itself from the many others which flew off the presses in 1745–46.[2] The Church of England was 'the most rational and worthy of God, the most humane and beneficial to men, the furtherest from being either tyrannical or burdensome, the freest from superstition, enthusiasm, and gloominess, of any in the world'. It had been 'established with such care, that the support of it is inseparable from that of the civil government'. Yet, he noted, those who dissented from it were wholly free to do so.[3] All of this, of course, contrasted markedly with the Church of Rome. 'No one instance can be given, that Popery ever spared Protestantism for any continuance, after it was able safely to oppress it,' Secker gravely warned his audience.[4] This was not warrantless fear-mongering, he reckoned, since James II had not so long ago trampled on the rights of English men and women in the cause of popery. 'Think then, all that love the church of England, all that believe the doctrines of the reformation to be the truth of Christ, what a condition it will be, either to profess and practice the falsehoods and impieties, of which you are so thoroughly convinced,' Secker inveighed, 'or to be driven from this, and every other place of God's public worship, into corners; nay, in a while, to be dragged out thence also, and sacrificed to that mother of abominations, which hath so long been drunken with the blood of the saints.'[5] To those who argued that 'Popery hath appeared milder of late than in former ages,' Secker countered with a litany of recent Catholic atrocities against continental Protestants. '[E]ven our days have known the executions of Thorn, and the banishments of Saltzburgh: and France, this very year, hath been persecuting and murdering our Protestant brethren for the profession of their faith,' he emphasized.

---

[1] Bob Harris, *Politics and the Nation: Britain in the Mid-Eighteenth Century* (Oxford, 2002); Kathleen Wilson, *The Sense of the People: Politics, Culture and Imperialism in England, 1715–1785* (Cambridge, 1995); Linda Colley, *Britons: Forging the Nation, 1707–1837* (New Haven, CT, 1992).

[2] Hannah Smith, *Georgian Monarchy: Politics and Culture, 1714–1760* (Cambridge, 2006), pp. 165–69; Françoise Deconinck-Brossard, 'The Churches and the '45', *SCH* 20 (1983), pp. 253–62.

[3] 'Sermon CXX. Preached on occasion of the Rebellion in Scotland on 6, 13 October 1745 [2 Samuel 10:12]', in *WTS*, III, p. 320. Secker had given a version of this sermon at St James's on 26 Feb 1744.

[4] Ibid., p. 323.

[5] Ibid., p. 324.

The lesson for the English was clear: should the Church of Rome 'regain so much of its ancient power, as would necessarily follow from prevailing here, it would soon resume its ancient fierceness in proportion'.[6] Popery, arbitrary government, and universal monarchy were inevitable if the Pretender snatched the English throne from the Protestant Hanoverians.[7]

Secker's sermon tapped directly into the language of the European 'Protestant interest', and with good reason.[8] From 1739 until 1763, England was at war almost continuously with the Catholic Bourbon powers. This turn to war impacted directly upon both national and religious identities, for as oppressed or displaced peoples across Europe sought English financial and military assistance, both church and state had to confront difficult questions.[9] How far could and should England go to fulfil her self-proclaimed role as the 'the Buttress of the Protestant Cause'?[10] Did that role abroad compromise the defence of the 'Constitution in Church and State' at home?[11] Was the Church of England catholic or national, Protestant or Anglican? What mattered most in the established Church's relations with non-English Protestants – ecclesiology, theology, or a common enemy? These were questions without easy answers. Yet the ways Secker and his contemporaries answered them cast stark light on the nature and the limits of orthodox reform.

Orthodox religious reform aimed primarily to restore the practices, principles, and ethos of the primitive church of the apostolic and patristic fathers. The signal

---

6   Ibid., pp. 325, 326. Cf. 'Sermon CXXXVIII. Persecution a Decisive Evidence of an Unchristian Spirit. Preached in the Parish Church of St Mary, Lambeth, November 5, 1758 [John 16:2–3]', in *WTS*, IV, p. 30, which likewise invokes the pogrom at Thorn (1724), the expulsion of Protestants from Salzburg (1731), French treatment of the Huguenots, and the Spanish inquisition as exemplars of popish atrocities against Protestants.

7   See, for instance, John Barker, *A sermon occasioned by the victory obtained over the rebels in Scotland, on the 16th of April, 1746* (1746), p. 19; Andrew Trebeck, *A preservative against popery. Being a new-year's-gift to his parishioners of St George, Hanover-Square* (1746), p. 12; William Wood, *Britain's Joshua: a sermon preached at Darlington, October 9, 1746; the day of public thanksgiving for the suppression of the late rebellion* (Newcastle upon Tyne, 1746), p. 16; John Denne, *A sermon preached in the parish church of St Mary, Lambeth, upon April 11, 1744. being the day appointed for a general fast* (1744), p. 8. John Robertson, 'Universal Monarchy and the Liberties of Europe: David Hume's Critique of an English Whig Doctrine', in *Political Discourse in Early Modern Britain*, eds. Nicholas Phillipson and Quentin Skinner (Cambridge, 1993), pp. 349–73 provides context.

8   Andrew C. Thompson, *Britain, Hanover, and the Protestant Interest, 1688–1756* (Woodbridge, 2006).

9   Tony Claydon, *Europe and the Making of England, 1660–1760* (Cambridge, forthcoming) argues convincingly for seeing the early 1760s as an axial moment in English international religious relations. I appreciate Dr. Claydon for allowing me to read portions of his book in advance of publication.

10   Anonymous, *An earnest address to Britons. Wherein the several artifices made use of by the emissaries of France and Rome, to corrupt the minds of the people, and to overturn our happy constitution, are explained, and laid open to public view* (1745), p. 22.

11   James Boswell, *Life of Johnson*, ed. George Birckbeck Hill (Oxford, 1934), IV, p. 29 records Dr. Johnson's umbrage with Secker's toast to the 'Constitution in Church and State', as opposed to the more traditional one to 'Church and King'.

feature of the early church was its unity and catholicity. Certainly heterodoxy existed in the early church, but orthodoxy was, depending on one's point of view, either preserved or asserted with the help of the state following Constantine the Great's conversion in the early fourth century. Yet just as the pressures of war had revealed the English state's scant interest in restorative religious reform in North America, so too did it cast stark light on the disunity and un-catholicity of the Church of England. Indeed, from the orthodox perspective, the eighteenth century was as much an age of anxiety as it was an age of reform.

I

England lived under the threat of invasion during the mid eighteenth century, and Ireland had long been feared as a staging ground for foreign incursions. The memories of the Irish rebellion of 1641 likewise reverberated in English memory, serving as a salutary reminder of what popery unbridled was capable of in the British Isles.[12] Ireland, then, was a source of concern for the English government. The island was also, from the orthodox perspective, a house of horrors. Like England, Ireland was a confessional state with the Church of Ireland as its established church.[13] But this established church was, for all intents and purposes, merely a Protestant sect, so outnumbered was it by Catholics (who comprised roughly three-quarters of the populace) and Ulster Presbyterians (who significantly outnumbered members of the established Church). At the turn of the eighteenth century, the bishop of Meath concisely and devastatingly enumerated the Church of Ireland's problems: '1. want of ministers; 2. want of Protestants; 3. the great pluralities and non-residence of the clergy who are there; 4. the ruinous condition and want of churches in that kingdom'.[14] Here was the nightmare scenario of what the Church of England might become in grotesque reality on the far side of the Irish Sea.

Secker learned something about religion in Ireland from his friend, George Berkeley, who served as bishop of Cloyne for nearly two decades.[15] The reports

[12] Ethan Shagan, 'Constructing Discord: Ideology, Propaganda, and English Responses to the Irish Rebellion of 1641', *JBS* 36:1 (1997), pp. 4–34; Jacqueline R. Hill, '1641 and the Quest for Catholic Emancipation, 1691–1829', in *Ulster, 1641: Aspects of the Rising*, ed. Brian MacCuarta (Belfast, 1993), pp. 159–71.

[13] Alan Ford, James McGuire, and Kenneth Milne (eds.), *As By Law Established: The Church of Ireland since the Reformation* (Dublin, 1995), esp. pp. 131–86; S.J. Connolly, *Religion, Law and Power: The Making of Protestant Ireland, 1660–1760* (Oxford, 1992), esp. pp. 144–97.

[14] John Brady, 'Remedies Proposed for the Church of Ireland (1697)', *Archivium Hibernicum* 22 (1959), pp. 163–73, at p. 164.

[15] There were rumours afloat in 1746 that Secker himself would be offered an Irish see: BL, Add. MS 39311, f. 52: Martin Benson to Secker, 28 Oct 1746.

which the Whig orthodox dean of Kilaloe, William Henry, sent to Secker during the 1760s only confirmed his view of the grim state of Irish religious affairs.[16] When the Hearts of Oak in the north and the Whiteboys in the south protested against required tithing to the Church of Ireland, for instance, Henry excitedly wrote to him, 'There is an absolute necessity, that something very Effectual should be Done, and that Immediately to prevent not only the Ecclesiastical, But even the civil constitution from Being Dissolved.'[17] Likewise when George Stone, archbishop of Armagh, died in 1764, Henry feverishly worried that 'the very Existence of the protestant Religion in our present Constitution Depends at this time on the choice ye shall make of a proper primate'.[18] Henry found in Secker someone all too willing to buy his morbid diagnosis.

Secker agreed with Henry that popery posed the greatest threat to Ireland; that it was a disease which, if left unchecked, could spread to England; and that the established Church of Ireland was the surest prophylaxis against popish contagion. 'The kingdom of Ireland is blessed by Providence with all the means of prosperity; and yet the bulk of the people are in a condition very lamentable,' Secker bemoaned in 1757. Though 'the door of Christian freedom is open to them, they continue in thick darkness, voluntary slaves to absurd superstitions. Attached with servile awe to the lowest emissaries of the See of Rome, they imbibe even the dregs of its errors.' While in the thrall of popery, the Irish posed a threat to England because they offered foreign invaders a proximate staging ground. 'Therefore, till the generality of the Irish are brought to be protestants, the English are not safe', and he likened Protestant proselytization there to 'carrying the war ... into our enemies' head-quarters'.[19] Indeed, Secker worried privately that the England risked becoming like Ireland. 'I am sincerely concerned for Ireland,' he wrote to Hardwicke in 1763, 'but cannot help but thinking further, how possible it is, that a Spirit, somewhat of the same kind, may rise here also. Men of no principles, and actuated only by present Interest, or wild notions, are capable of any thing. And how large a proportion of them there is, of all ranks, in this Nation: and how little Likelihood of Union against them.'[20] These fears coloured the Church of England's relations with its Irish first cousin.

---

16 Neal Garnham, 'Henry, William (d. 1768)', *ODNB*. Secker actively politicked for Henry to get the Kilaloe deanery: LPL, Secker Papers 2, f. 229: Secker to George Montagu Dunk, 2nd earl of Halifax, 22 Oct 1761.

17 LPL, Secker Papers 2, ff. 255–56: Henry to Secker, 2 Nov 1765. See also, J.S. Donnelly, 'Hearts of Oak, Hearts of Steel', *Studia Hibernica* 21 (1981), pp. 7–73; idem, 'The Whiteboy Movement, 1761–65', *Irish Historical Studies* 21 (1978), pp. 20–54.

18 LPL, Secker Papers 2, ff. 234–37: Henry to Secker, 20 Nov 1764. See also, BL, Add. MS 32963, ff. 399–40: TPH to Secker, 14 Nov 1764.

19 'Sermon CXXXVII. The Pernicious Effects to a Nation of Ignorance and Idleness; and the Happy Consequences of Knowledge and Industry. Preached before the Society for Promoting English Protestant Working Schools in Ireland, April 27, 1757 [Proverbs 9:6]', in *WTS*, IV, pp. 1–2, 6, 14.

20 BL, Add. MS 35607, f. 74: Secker to Hardwicke, 20 Sept 1763.

There were times when Irish needs and English ones were at variance, a difference which itself highlighted the essential Englishness of Secker's orthodox reform vision. The conflicting forces at play shine through clearly in a February 1768 letter from Secker to Frederick Hervey, bishop of Derry. Hervey had been working with the 'moderate' Catholic Committee to draft an oath of allegiance appropriate to Irish circumstances. A prominent segment of Irish Catholics had, during the mid eighteenth century, come to accept the revolution settlement, the Protestant establishment, and the need for close relations with England.[21] Recognizing this, Hervey hoped that a new oath of allegiance might inculcate Gallican ideas, reduce Rome's influence, and strengthen the Church of Ireland.[22] 'My object is to leave your faith entire but to secure your allegiance to the present government and to make you independent of all foreign jurisdiction whatever,' he wrote to one Irish Catholic in 1767.[23]

Proposals to liberalize the penal laws against Roman Catholics, though, made the Francis Blackburnes and Thomas Hollises of the world – always quick to draw clear lines of connection between orthodoxy and popery – froth at the mouth.[24] Hervey's proposals, then, boxed the orthodox into a corner: they could do little but take a hard line against the bishop of Derry's proposed new oath and against penal law relaxation more generally. 'No one can be a heartier Friend to the Civil Toleration of all religious opinions & practices, which are not very prejudicial or dangerous to Civil Society,' Secker assured Hervey. 'But I look on the Church of Rome as peculiarly formidable to Protestant States, and especially to these Kingdoms. For it claims absolute Authority over the very minds of men: it is a powerful Body, united under one Head: its Adherents are numerous even in England, much more in Ireland: its Emissaries are disciplined to exact Obedience, zealous to advance its Interests, skillful by Instruction & Experience how to do it: and for that purpose the genuine members of this vast Community are always ready to use Force & Fraud, when it shall be requisite.'[25] As such, he concluded, 'a Protestant State hath no Security against Papists, but from Want of Ability in them, & especially in its own Popish Subjects, to overturn it'. Nowhere did this hold truer than in Ireland, where Catholics far outnumbered Protestants.

---

[21] Jacqueline R. Hill, 'Popery and Protestantism, Civil and Religious Liberty: The Disputed Lessons of Irish History, 1690–1812', *PP* 118 (1988), pp. 96–129, at pp. 105–06.

[22] S.J. Connolly, 'The Church of Ireland and the Royal Martyr: Regicide and Revolution in Anglican Political Thought, c.1660–c.1745', *JEH* 54:3 (2003), pp. 484–506 demonstrates that the Church of Ireland's identity was not solely the product of anti-Catholicism.

[23] Quoted in Gerard O'Brien, 'Hervey, Frederick Augustus, fourth earl of Bristol (1730–1803)', *ODNB*.

[24] See, for instance, Francis Blackburne, *Considerations on the present state of the controversy between Protestants and Papists in Great Britain and Ireland* (Dublin, 1770).

[25] Public Record Office of Northern Ireland, D 2798/5/6: Secker to Hervey, 25 Feb 1768. Unless otherwise noted, the quotations in this paragraph and the next are taken from this letter.

How, then, should Irish Catholics be treated? 'Our Language to them must be thus,' Secker insisted, 'We will never molest You, provided you attempt not to convert Us; but let our people alone, or expect no Favour from us. And we must so far to make the Threatening good, that they shall be sure to find themselves Losers by such Attempts.' Secker thought that the problem, not the solution, was disciplinary laxity, and he complained that Irish religious and government leaders lacked the will to impose the penal laws which curtailed the legal rights of Irish Catholics: 'The present Laws against papists, are so far unexecuted,' he groused, 'that they have by Connivance all the Liberty, with respect to their Worship, which they want.' Perhaps it would be alright to repeal 'the severer part of the Laws...as no longer necessary, though not as originally unjust: but so as that still they may in some Degree lie at our Mercy, not we at theirs'. Nonetheless, Secker wrote to Hervey, Irish Catholics 'should have no Laws in their Favour, which they can abuse to our Disadvantage: and we should have Laws in our Favour, by which we can repress any Attempts of theirs with more Rigour, than I hope we shall ever chuse or need to exercise'. In the end, however, he feared that the Church of England's heterodox critics would latch on to any loosening of the penal laws' severity as yet further proof of orthodoxy's essential popery: 'any proposals, made by English Bishops, that could bear but the smallest Appearance of being favourable to papists, though proceeding from the sincerest purpose of securing the Establishment in Church & State against them, would raise a Clamour against us, that we should not be able to withstand'.

A revised Catholic oath of allegiance finally came to pass in 1774, against the opposition of many bishops. The English government, though, had noted the way in which the Quebec Act had disposed Canadian Catholics to more enthusiastic support for the colonial government; it hoped that some relief from the penal laws would have a similar effect on Irish Catholics and would enable the English state to mobilize Catholic manpower for the army.[26] In this instance, then, the demands of war trumped those of confessional continuity and uniformity. It was also the case that anti-Catholicism's ability to forge Protestant solidarity, both within the British Isles and across Europe, waned markedly in the last half of the eighteenth century.[27] The obliteration of Jacobitism as anything but a political language of opposition in the Forty-Five's aftermath and the thumping defeat of France in the

---

[26] Jacqueline R. Hill, 'Religious Toleration and the Relaxation of the Penal Laws: An Imperial Perspective, 1763–1780', *Archivium Hibernicum* 44 (1989), pp. 98–109; Philip Lawson, *The Imperial Challenge: Quebec and Britain in the Age of the American Revolution* (Montreal and Kingston, 1989).

[27] Nigel Aston, *Christianity and Revolutionary Europe, c.1750–1830* (Cambridge, 2002), p. 12; Colin Haydon, '"I love my King and my Country, but a Roman catholic I hate": anti-catholicism, xenophobia and national identity in eighteenth-century England', in *Protestantism and National Identity: Britain and Ireland, c.1650–c.1850*, eds. Tony Claydon and Ian McBride (Cambridge, 1998), pp. 33–52; idem, *Anti-Catholicism in eighteenth-century England, c. 1714–80: a political and social study* (Manchester, 1993). But cf. Colley, *Britons*, pp. 11–54.

Seven Years War increasingly made armed Catholicism a non-issue at home and abroad, however much the irrational fears of papists-under-the-bed might have fired the combustible imaginations of Blackburne, Hollis, and their heterodox kindred. Anti-popery's diminishing virulence, in turn, altered the calculus of the Church of England's relations with churches abroad, for it highlighted intra-Protestant divisions both within and without England.[28]

II

Both centrifugal and centripetal forces were at play in the eighteenth-century Protestant religious world. The transatlantic evangelical revival, for instance, highlighted common religious impulses and needs while at the same time cracking open confessional fissures.[29] So too did the Church of England's connections to the larger Protestant world tug in a number of different directions. Since the Reformation, English bishops had long been interested in fostering closer relations with Protestant churches in Europe.[30] This was given particular urgency in the late seventeenth century, when the Catholic Counter-Reformation looked poised to take back much of the ground lost during the Protestant Reformation.[31] Especially menacing was Louis XIV, who aimed to expand France to her 'natural' borders and to extirpate Protestantism within those borders. His aggression and success frightened Protestants, who thought he aimed to set up a 'universal monarchy'.[32] Many Europeans looked to England as 'the refuge and protectoress of distressed nations'; and among contemporaries in the Protestant world, the Church of England 'enjoyed a chorus of admiration which, if not quite unanimous, far exceeded anything which has since come her way'.[33] In England, Henry Compton,

[28] J.C.D. Clark, 'Protestantism, Nationalism, and National Identity', *HJ* 43:1 (2000), pp. 249–76 and Brian Young, 'A history of variations: the identity of the eighteenth-century church of England', in *Protestantism and National Identity*, pp. 105–28 highlight some of the faultlines within British Protestantism.

[29] G.M. Ditchfield, *The Evangelical Revival* (1998); W.R. Ward, *The Protestant Evangelical Awakening* (Cambridge, 1992); Michael J. Crawford, *Seasons of Grace: Colonial New England's Revival Tradition in its British Context* (Oxford, 1991); John Walsh, 'The Origins of the Evangelical Revival', in *Essays in Modern English Church History, in memory of Norman Sykes*, eds. G.V. Bennett and J.D. Walsh (Oxford, 1966), pp. 132–62.

[30] W.B. Patterson, *King James VI and I and the Reunion of Christendom* (Cambridge, 1997); Hugh Trevor-Roper, 'The Church of England and the Greek Church in the time of Charles I', *SCH* 15 (1978), pp. 213–40.

[31] R. Po-Chia Hsia, *The World of Catholic Renewal, 1540–1770* (Cambridge, 2005).

[32] Steven Pincus, 'The English Debate over Universal Monarchy', in *A Union for Empire: Political Thought and the British Union of 1707*, ed. John Robertson (Cambridge, 1995), pp. 37–62.

[33] Edmund Burke, 'Speech on Lord North's Budget', 18 May 1774, quoted in Daniel A Baugh, 'Great Britain's "Blue-Water" Policy, 1689–1815', *International History Review* 10:1 (1988), p. 44; W.R. Ward, 'The Eighteenth-Century Church: A European View', in *The Church of*

bishop of London (1676–1713) was foremost among those who welcomed and helped the Huguenot refugees who fled France after Louis revoked the Edict of Nantes in 1685.[34] William Wake, archbishop of Canterbury (1716–1737), likewise maintained extensive contacts with continental Protestants – and, indeed, with the Gallican Church – hoping to forge either church unions or bonds of communion.[35]

The spirit of pan-European Protestant unity and ecumenism shrivelled up in the mid eighteenth century, though. Since the Restoration, the English had considered themselves as part of the 'Protestant international' and, indeed, as members of 'Christendom'.[36] The 1760s, however, marked a turning point, after which 'the players in the great international game no longer kept up the pretence of playing on confessional principles'.[37] Yet the Church of England continued to maintain extensive relations with churches abroad, as much from necessity as from choice, and foreigners went first to the archbishop of Canterbury, who was for them the face of the Church of England. During his archiepiscopate, Secker served as fundraiser and dealmaker for foreign Protestants; he never agitated for – nor even expressed a desire for – church union.[38] Yet if he was no Wake, Secker's

England, c.1689–c.1833: From Toleration to Tractarianism, eds. John Walsh, Colin Haydon and Stephen Taylor (Cambridge, 1993), pp. 285–98, at p. 285. See also, Hannah Smith, 'The Idea of a Protestant Monarchy in Britain, 1714–1760', *PP* 185 (2004), pp. 91–118.

34 Sugiko Nishikawa, 'The SPCK in Defence of Protestant Minorities in Early Eighteenth-Century Europe', *JEH* 56:4 (2005), pp. 730–48; idem, 'Henry Compton, Bishop of London (1676–1714) and foreign Protestants', in *From Strangers to Citizens: The integration of immigrant communities in Britain, Ireland, and colonial America, 1550–1750*, eds. Randolph Vigne and Charles Littleton (Brighton, 2001), pp. 359–65.

35 Norman Sykes, *Daniel Ernst Jablonski and the Church of England: A Study of an Essay towards Protestant Union* (1950); idem, *William Wake, Archbishop of Canterbury, 1657–1737* (Cambridge, 1957), I, pp. 252–314; II, pp. 1–88; and idem, *From Sheldon to Secker: Aspects of English Church History, 1660–1768* (Cambridge, 1959), pp. 105–39 make much of Wake's ecumenism. But cf. Stephen Taylor, 'Wake, William (1657–1737)', *ODNB* for a salutary reminder that Wake's search for a church union 'should not be regarded as a precursor to the ecumenical movement of the twentieth century. Rather, it was another means of shoring up the church's defences in response to the threats from Arianism and Socinianism, from latitudinarianism among the clergy and from the liberal religious policies of some whig politicians.'

36 Claydon, *Europe and the Making of England, 1660–1760*, conclusion.

37 W.R. Ward, *Christianity under the Ancien Régime, 1648–1789* (Cambridge, 1999), p. 239. But cf. Thompson, *Britain, Hanover, and the Protestant Interest*, pp. 229–37.

38 Secker's first documented dealings with foreign Protestants came in 1752. 'I gave Sir Luke Schaub for French Protestants £20 & allowed the Committee for them to meet at the Deanery, till they could find a fitter Place': *Autobiography*, p. 30. Bodleian, MS Rawlinson J.4 251, f. 252 contains a newspaper clipping with the following announcement: 'Dom Dominicus Bonaventura, Native of Italy, and Baron of Spilery, abbot of St Mary in Prato, Notary and Apostolick Notary, Chaplain of Honour to the King of the Two Sicilies, and Knight of the Order of St Salvator, having had the Grace to find out the Errors of the Romish Church, has willingly embraced the true Protestant Religion, and has had the Honour to be receiv'd by the Right Rev. Father in God the Lord Bishop of Oxford [i.e., Secker]; and did likewise to his greatest Comfort and Satisfaction, receive the Holy

dealings with foreign Protestants nevertheless forced him and the orthodox within the English church to confront fundamental questions of identity.

The orthodox willingly helped those continental Protestants who refused to accept the Church of England's ecclesiology, liturgy, and theology, but only so long as they did not seek a permanent home in England.[39] Protestants whose churches were damaged during war often sent representatives to London to solicit financial aid. Many (such as the churches in Hagen or in Custrin in the Newmarch) sought English help to rebuild churches destroyed during confessional wars with the French.[40] Sometimes even foreign rulers wrote to English authorities on behalf of their Protestant subjects to request financial assistance.[41] In such cases as these, rather than dole out money directly from the Treasury, the English government tended instead to support royal briefs, which got printed in English newspapers and which publicized the predicament of Protestants in Catholic Europe.[42]

The most brazen applicants went so far as to threaten bad publicity for the Church of England if aid was not forthcoming. In 1757, for instance, representatives from the church in Thorn in Polish-Prussia, site of one of the century's most well-publicized anti-Protestant pogroms, appealed to the English bishops to help them raise money in England to rebuild their church. Archbishop Herring pled 'reasons of Health' for not spearheading an episcopal fund-raising effort, but he revealed privately to Secker 'the plain Truth' of his diffidence. 'I am unwilling to come into any measure of assistance on that Head, but on the subject of a Brief by publick application,' he insisted. 'There it will very well become the Bps & the clergy too to exert themselves, but to call out the Bps to shew themselves on this occasion to any large & exemplary purpose, wth regard to more than one of them will be as hard upon their circumstances or their modesty as a small contribution will be of no consequence, & the Petitioners will expect a large one.'[43] Perhaps sensing that Herring was stalling, Thorn's emissary, Samuel Luther Geret, warned Secker of the consequences to the Church of England's reputation if aid were not forthcoming. 'I will add, that, since no Man abroad will believe, that in England I should have so quite entirely cried in vain for Help for the poor

---

Sacrament, with the Congregation, at St James's Church, the 17th of May, being Whitsunday. 1741.'

[39] W.R. Ward, 'Anglicanism and Assimilation; or Mysticism and Mayhem in the Eighteenth Century', in *Crown and Mitre: Religion and Society in Northern Europe Since the Reformation*, eds. W.M. Jacob and Nigel Yates (Woodbridge, 1993), pp. 81–91 discusses the problems eighteenth-century European states faced assimilating religious minorities.

[40] Hagen: LPL, MS 1122/II, ff. 56–58, 64–65, 70, 71–73; Custrin: LPL, MS 1122/II, ff. 103–05. See also, Anonymous, *The case of the unhappy people of Custrin, in the New-Mark, in the Electorate of Brandenburg, since the invasion of the Russians in 1758* (1759).

[41] LPL, MS 1122/III, f. 37: Secker to Prince of Nassau Saarbruck, 24 June 1761.

[42] See, for instance, *Lloyd's Evening Post, and British Chronicle* (4 Sept 1758, 13 Dec 1758), pp. 217, 564.

[43] LPL, MS 1122/II, f. 39: Herring to Secker, 4 Feb 1757.

Members of Christ at Thorn, I shall be obliged immediately after mine Arrival in Holland, to publish in Several Languages The Acts of my Commission in England,' he not so subtly threatened Secker, 'and therefore [I] wish, that I…may not be constrained myself to confess publickly, that our Miscarriage in England is owing to the Bishops.'[44] In general, though, foreign supplicants were far less brash than Geret and did quite well through the briefs.

Protestant universities in Catholic nations also sent emissaries to England with cap in hand. The most successful was the University of Debreczen in Hungary. In the 1750s, the court of Vienna sought to cut off the oxygen to the Hungarian Protestant cause by withholding the salaries of professors at Debreczen, where Protestant ministers and teachers were educated. The university sent agents to London, including Stephen Wespremi and Nicholas Sinai,[45] and by 1759, the English bishops and universities had raised £590 to supplement the salaries of the Debreczen professors.[46] Secker himself would consistently help Hungarian Protestants.[47] At the end of his life, for instance, he gave 10 guineas a year to the Debreczen professors and to Johannes Uri, an Hungarian specialist in Oriental languages. Uri went to Oxford on Secker's recommendation in 1766 to prepare a catalogue of the Bodleian's Oriental manuscripts for the Clarendon Press.[48] Indeed, Secker proved to be a generous benefactor to several impoverished Protestant émigrés in England. Besides Uri, he granted considerable sums to a French Protestant agent's widow, to a Portuguese ex-Catholic Anglican convert named Francisco Xavier de Oliverya, to a pseudonymous Greek priest from Amsterdam named Nectarius, and to 'one Pap a poor Hungarian who came to spend a Year at Oxford on a mistaken Imagination that he might be maintained there; & am to give him 10 [guineas] more, if he finds Encouragem't to stay out the Year'.[49]

There were times when giving financial assistance promised to fulfil a number of English political and religious objectives at once. In 1763, for instance, agents for a proposed Protestant colony at Philippen in Moldavia arrived in London to ask for financial help to get the colony up and running. Secker was initially unenthused, warning the earl of Halifax in early May that '[t]hese applications

---

44 Ibid., f. 47: Geret to Secker, 4 April 1757.
45 There appears to have been some initial mistrust between the two agents, though, for Sinai needed Secker to write a letter to the Debreczen professors to refute Wespremi's claims that he had been a negligent fundraiser in England: LPL, MS 1122/I, f. 235: Edward Bentham to Secker, 25 July [1759?].
46 LPL, MS 1122/I, f. 234: John James Majendie's memo on Debreczen, 28 July 1759. The fund would grow to over £3,000 and in 1951 it was still administered by the SPG: H.P. Thompson, *Into All Lands. The History of the Society for the Propagation of the Gospel in Foreign Parts, 1701–1950* (1951), p. 40.
47 But cf. LPL, MS 1122/II, f. 136: Secker to College of Enyed, 29 Mar 1763.
48 *Autobiography*, pp. 51, 52, 168.
49 Ibid., pp. 48, 49, 51, 69, 157, 161, 165. Secker's Greek correspondence with Nectarius can be followed in LPL, Secker Papers 7, ff. 241–66.

seem likely to increase' and noting that the 'people of England … have generally a Brief read to them every month, & contribute very scantily towards rebuilding our Churches here at home, will not receive at present, so well as might be wished, a proposal for building a Church & a School in Nonse in Moldavia: a Country, which most of them have never in their Lives heard named'.[50] By June, though, he had warmed considerably to the idea of a Philippen brief because he saw in it a number of potential benefits to the cause of pan-European Protestantism and to England, in particular. If the Philippen colony thrived, it 'may prove a place of Refuge to other suffering Protestants, especially in Hungary and Poland,' Secker wrote to Halifax. 'And the Liberty granted them to exercise their Religion in this place may become a precedent for granting the same to Protestants in other parts of the Turkish Dominions.' While this would surely be good, in and of itself, a self-sustaining Protestant refuge in eastern Europe might also staunch the flow of supplicants to England and serve as an example to other European Protestants of what they could do for themselves. A thriving colony also might encourage Catholic monarchs to show their Protestant subjects 'a milder Treatment at home' for fear of losing them to places like Philippen. This, too, promised to retard the number of those seeking English financial assistance.[51]

Secker's fingerprints were all over the official royal brief for Philippen, which was issued in February 1764 and which reiterated each of the points he had made to Halifax the previous June. Tellingly, it also described the situation of the Philippen Protestants in a way sure to register a particular confessional point in England. The brief reported that the prince and council of Moldavia had recently issued a charter to the Philippen colonists 'whereby their Liberties both Civil and Religious are secured to them and to their Descendants, with Licence for holding Lands in Property, and for erecting Churches and Schools, as to them shall seem meet; and a total Exemption from the Jurisdiction of the Greek Church, which is the Established Religion of the country'.[52] This sounded very much like the legal situation of Protestant religious nonconformists in England. The brief concluded that 'by settling this Colony, a Door is opened for the Propagation of pure Christianity, in those regions from which it hath been banished for many Ages past, and where now it is probable it will get a solid Footing, and spread itself both among the Turks and the Members of the Greek Church'.[53] Two important points are made here, ones that run straight through all of Secker's reforming efforts. First, the brief implies that evolutionary reform, not its revolutionary evil twin, is

---

[50] LPL, MS 1122/III, f. 142: Secker to Halifax, 7 May 1763.
[51] Ibid., f. 155: Secker to Halifax, 10 June 1763.
[52] *Notes and Queries*, 8 series, IX (30 May 1896), p. 421.
[53] Ibid. Cf. LPL, MS 1122/III, f. 155: Secker to Halifax, 10 June 1763, in which Secker suggests, 'And such as go to settle there, not only may be instrumental in suggesting to the Members of the Greek Church, which is a very superstitious one, Ideas of a purer Christianity than they now profess, but also may contribute something to shew it in a more favourable Light to the Mahometans themselves.'

normative. It further implies that evolutionary reform naturally enables a return to 'pure Christianity', the sort associated with the primitive Church of the apostolic and patristic fathers. This royal brief for Philippen was to be read from every pulpit in every parish in England, and Secker was not the sort of person to let an opportunity like that pass without taking advantage of it to make a polemical point.

Sometimes the Church of England's public reputation demanded that Secker expend considerable political capital to help persecuted foreign Protestants. In April 1761, for instance, Jean Louis Gibert (d. 1773), a Huguenot cleric, arrived in London to ask the English government to help French Protestants 'from the Hardships, which they now suffer'd on account of their Religion'.[54] Gibert hoped that the English would demand that the French grant a general toleration for all Protestants in the war's aftermath. Otherwise, he hoped that George III 'wd furnish them with money to come over into England'.[55] Secker consulted the king's ministers before advising Gibert that a demand for toleration would only bog down any negotiations to end the war and might even incite the French to impose harsher penalties on native Protestants. Instead, Secker recollected, 'His Majesty directed me to say in His Name, that both Humanity & Religion disposed him to pity & relieve them, but that he thought nothing could be attempted by him without Danger of hurting them, whilst they continued in France; but that as soon as they had quitted it, they should have every Mark of his Protection & Favour & Bounty.'[56] It was proposed that the group should escape to England, reassemble, and then depart for America where it would establish a colony. After meeting with Secker on 23 April 1761, Gibert returned to France, not to be heard from again until early January 1763 when a letter announced Gibert's imminent arrival in England.[57]

The Peace of Paris and George III's earlier promises had spurred Gibert to action. 'On this, as soon as the Peace was made, M. Gibert came over with some hundreds, & more were coming,' Secker recalled later.[58] Upon learning the news, Secker immediately alerted the earl of Egremont, one of the secretaries of state, adding that Gibert's refugees were 'well worth having'.[59] Egremont told him to take up the matter with the Treasury; by the time Secker contacted Bute on 31 March, Gibert had just arrived in London to help settle arrangements for his followers who remained in Switzerland.[60] The timing was not propitious for Gibert

54 LPL, MS 1122/III, f. 170: Secker's notes on a meeting with Gibert, 24 April 1761.
55 *Autobiography*, p. 47.
56 LPL, MS 1122/III, f. 170: Secker's memorandum to Gibert, 24 April 1761.
57 Ibid., f. 174: M. Gautier to Majendie, Dec 1762.
58 *Autobiography*, p. 47.
59 LPL, MS 1122/III, f. 176: Secker to Egremont, 6 Jan 1763.
60 Ibid., f. 184: Secker to John Stuart, 3rd earl of Bute, 31 Mar 1763.

because Bute's 'retirement' from office during the first week of April left the ministry in the hands of George Grenville.[61]

George III's new prime minister was intent on cutting costs, but his grip on power was tenuous, something Secker exploited when lobbying for Gibert's cause. From the outset, Grenville expressed his reluctance to offer financial aid to Gibert's Huguenots. Grenville 'seems backward to engage in it, & very apprehensive that it may be an immediate Expence upon the Crown,' Secker wrote to John James Majendie, a French émigré and intermediary for many French Protestants. 'But wn I reminded him that the King had by the Advice of his Ministry given his word two years ago, he said he wd speak to his Majesty. And so will I too on Wednesday next, God Willing, if I find that Mr. Grenville hath not or that no good Effect is produced by it.'[62] In the end, Grenville tried to short-circuit the matter behind the backs of both the archbishop and the king by contacting Gibert directly and ordering him 'to stop the disembarking of the French Protestants for wm he is concerned, till the means of their subsistence shall be regulated; but not intimating how or when such Regulation is to be made'. After learning from Gibert of Grenville's duplicity, Secker demanded a private joint-audience with the king, explaining that '[t]his appears to me [so] unsuitable to the assurances wch I have in the Kings name by his Order two years ago, that I shall think my self guilty of neglecting my Duty to his Majesty, unless I remind him of them'.[63] The Church of England's reputation was at stake.

Secker initially outflanked Grenville. George III welcomed Gibert and the French refugees 'to stay in England, till a proper Destination abroad can be found for them. And these may in the mean time be maintained out of the public money allotted for the Relief of Prisoners'.[64] The king also gave the refugees £1000 out of his own pocket.[65] George III, however, cautioned those Huguenots still in France to remain there until proper provision for them could be lined up in England. 'By this he doth not mean to discourage them from the Intention of becoming his Subjects, which he is very desirous that they should,' Secker emphasized.[66]

Yet Grenville continued to drag his feet. Gibert's group was to settle in Plymouth until transport on to America could be secured for them. John James Majendie was also to secure the financial assistance of the Plymouth French community, who would advance the refugees money against credit from the Treasury. On 19 May, Secker wrote to Grenville, informing him that a Plymouth

---

[61] LPL, MS 1122/III, f. 186: Bute to Secker, 8 April 1763; ibid., ff. 189–90: Grenville to Secker, 11 April 1763.

[62] Ibid., f. 193: Secker to Majendie, 17 April 1763. Secker later recollected, 'But, as [Gibert's followers] were all poor; not being allowed in France to sell any part of their real or even personal Estate, Mr. Grenville was afraid of the Expence, for which there was no fund': *Autobiography*, p. 47.

[63] LPL, MS 1122/III, f. 197: Secker to Grenville, 25 April 1763.

[64] Ibid., f. 198: Secker's memorandum to Gibert, 29 April 1763.

[65] Secker gave them £52–10–0: *Autobiography*, p. 47.

[66] LPL, MS 1122/III, f. 198: Secker's memorandum to Gibert, 29 April 1763.

merchant had volunteered to administer the disbursement of funds to Gibert and his followers and requesting an immediate response.[67] Charles Jenkinson assured Secker that he was handling the matter while Grenville was away, but that he could not locate the relevant papers.[68] The matter regarding the Plymouth merchant was not resolved until Grenville returned to town in late June and ordered an immediate disbursement to Gibert's group.[69] Secker had learnt that he needed to monitor the situation closely or Grenville would simply do nothing. So, July found him confirming with Jenkinson about the precise terms of payment to the refugees, while October saw him complaining to the earl of Halifax about the miserable conditions in which Gibert's group was living in Plymouth.[70] It was not until 2 January 1764 that Gibert's group finally set sail from Plymouth, arriving in South Carolina four months later where they established the successful colony at New Bordeaux.[71]

Grenville's utter lack of enthusiasm for Gibert's refugees cannot solely be put down to the financial straits in which the English found themselves at the end of a long and expensive war. Surely the prime minister reckoned that encouraging the flight of French Protestants after, rather than before, the war with France was an investment of questionable merit. In truth, though, it was not just the Treasury which Secker had to monitor: Gibert and the his group caused him his share of headaches, as well. In late December, Majendie informed Secker that 'a Spirit of Division is got among them, and ... many are dissatisfied with Mr. Gibert, who is accused of by them of carrying Things with too high a Hand. We are actually labouring to prevent the Evil from spreading.'[72] Just after the group had decamped for South Carolina, Majendie wrote back to Secker with only slightly more encouraging news. 'I have done all I could (and the other Trustees likewise) to bring them to a proper temper & hope that during the voyage they will make such reflexions as will considerably abate a ferment, which will be very prejudicial to the community, should they carry it with them to America,' Majendie reported.[73]

While every effort was made to relieve those who sought aid from England, neither Secker, the Church, nor the state was able to assist all who sought financial aid. Most often, the parlous position of the nation's finances during the 'Second Hundred Years War' was blamed. In 1757, for instance, Archbishop Herring explained to Secker his decision to discourage a group of Nuremburg

---

67   BL, Stowe MS 119, f. 159: Secker to Grenville, 19 May 1763.
68   LPL, MS 1122/III, ff. 208, 209: Jenkinson to Secker, 19, 20 May 1763.
69   Ibid., f. 210: Grenville to Secker, 25 June 1763.
70   Ninetta S. Jucker (ed.), *The Jenkinson Papers, 1760–1766* (1949), pp. 170–71: Secker to Jenkinson, 21 July 1763; Joseph Redington (ed.), *Calendar of Home Office Papers of the Reign of George III, I: 1760–1765* (1878), no. 1046: Secker to Halifax, 21 Oct 1763.
71   Arthur Henry Hirsch, *The Huguenots of Colonial South Carolina* (Durham, NC, 1928), pp. 38–43. As late as January 1765, the Treasury was still delaying payment to the refugees: BL, Add. MS 38204, f. 43: Majendie to Jenkinson, 23 Jan 1765.
72   LPL, MS 1122/III, ff. 236–37: Majendie to Secker, 10 Dec 1763.
73   Ibid., f. 238: Majendie to Secker, 6 Jan 1768.

Protestants from seeking a royal brief. 'I cannot think it right for us, to drane out our own purses to build Churches for the Protestants in Germany, when our Cathedrals & other of our Churches are in so visible decay, & when so many so frequent & so necessary Charities are call'd for at home,' he wrote to Secker, '& more peculiarly excepted from the Bps, who must suffer great inconveniences fro' answering the unreasonable expectations of some men or be hurt in point of reputation by the malign reflections of their Enemies.'[74] Secker echoed Herring's sentiments two years later when he complained about requests from the prince of Hesse Damnstadt for English aid to help rebuild war-damaged churches in his principality: 'If Germany is so impoverished by the wars so is this nation dreadfully. And we want money very much to build & repair Churches for our selves at home & for our fellow subjects in America.'[75] Particularly during a war, financial considerations like these mattered; but it was actually questions of ecclesiology, liturgy, and theology which most consumed the orthodox when dealing with émigré congregations in England.

III

While Anglican ecclesiology privileged episcopacy, the orthodox had, since the Reformation, argued that hostile political circumstances prevented most Continental Protestant churches from having bishops.[76] This allowed the orthodox to avoid 'unchurching' those Protestants living in Catholic states which were bent upon establishing confessional uniformity. By the mid eighteenth century, though, this rationalization no longer worked, since by then it had become evident that many Continental churches would never adopt episcopacy. Secker, in turn, worried what message native English religious nonconformists might take from the bishops' countenance, even support, of foreign Protestant congregations. In particular, he worried that they would demand full civil liberties since the Church of England supported and provided relief for those from abroad who worshipped in non-episcopal churches. For this reason, he tried subtly, but firmly, to compel foreign congregations to follow the liturgy spelled out in the Book of Common Prayer and to come into communion with the established Church. The chief weapon in his arsenal was money.

Financial assistance for émigré Protestants came primarily from three sources. Sometimes the government granted an annual payment from the civil list.

[74] LPL, MS 1122/II, f. 40: Herring to Secker, 4 Feb 1757.
[75] Ibid., f. 208: Secker to Majendie, 19 Dec 1760.
[76] Norman Sykes, *Old Priest and New Presbyter: Episcopacy and Presbyterianism since the Reformation with especial relation to the Churches of England and Scotland* (Cambridge, 1957), pp. 69, 81–82. See also, Peter B. Nockles, *The Oxford Movement in Context: Anglican High Churchmanship, 1760–1857* (Cambridge, 1994), p. 146.

Alternatively, Parliament might offer one-time grants-in-aid to those seeking financial assistance. More commonly, though, relief came from royally sponsored church briefs, and letters patent issued from the king authorizing collections to be made in all parishes for specified charities. London also teemed with foreign agents whose primary task was fundraising.[77]

Soon after moving into Lambeth Palace, Secker began receiving letters from émigré French Protestants and their agents in England, especially John James Majendie. The eldest son of a late seventeenth-century refugee Huguenot minister, Majendie took Anglican orders and rose to prominence as tutor to Queen Charlotte and her two oldest sons, as the preacher at the French chapel in the Savoy, and as a prebend of Windsor.[78] Among other prominent resident supporters of the French Protestant community in London were Louis Dutens (1730–1812),[79] Benjamin DuPlan (1688–1763),[80] Jacques Serces (1707–1761),[81] Jean Des Champs (1707–1767),[82] and César De Missy (1703–1775).[83] One of the most frequently discussed issues between these French agents and Secker was the operation of the Royal Bounty, established in the late seventeenth century to aid destitute French Protestants refuged in England. Their work on the Bounty demonstrates the ways the Church of England's leadership battled religious heterodoxy, even among those taking refuge in England from religious persecution elsewhere.

Following the Huguenot flight after the revocation of the Edict of Nantes, the English provided relief for them through a variety of *ad hoc* charitable means.[84] This brought only limited relief to the destitute refugees, though, and in November 1695, William III reminded the House of Commons of the 'miserable circumstances of the French Protestants who suffer for their religion' and urged the body 'to provide a supply suitable to these occasions'.[85] In April 1696, the House responded by adding to the civil list an annual bounty of £15,000, with £12,000

77 Raymond Smith (ed.), *Records of the Royal Bounty and Connected Funds, the Burn Donation, and the Savoy Church in the Huguenot Library, University College, London* (1974), pp. 1–2.

78 Robert Hole, 'Majendie, Henry William (1754–1830)', *ODNB*.

79 H.R. Luard, 'Dutens, Louis (1730–1812)', rev. Elizabeth Baigent, *ODNB*; Louis Dutens, *Mémoires d'un voyageur qui se repose, contenant des anecdotes historiques, politiques et littéraires, relatives à plusieurs des principaux personnages de ce siècle* (Paris, 1806).

80 *Autobiography*, p. 165.

81 Frédéric Gardy (ed.), *Correspondance de Jacques Serces* (1956).

82 Jean Des Champs, *The Life and 'Mémoires Secrets' of Jean Des Champs (1707–1767), Journalist, Minister, and Man of Feeling* (1990), ed. Uta Jassens-Knorsch (1990), pp. 9–61.

83 Ibid. p. 307, fn. 306.

84 Between 1681 and 1694, charitable donations totalling £90,174 were collected for the Huguenots in Anglican churches on the order of the English monarchs: Roy A. Sundstrom, 'French Huguenots and the Civil List, 1696–1727: A Study of Alien Assimilation in England', *Albion* 8:3 (1976), p. 221.

85 Quoted in Roy A. Sundstrom, 'Aid and Assimilation: A Study of the Economic Support Given French Protestants in England, 1680–1727' (Kent State University Ph.D. dissertation, 1972), p. 54.

designated for the laity and £3,000 for French ministers. The money for distressed clergy was either granted directly to individual clergymen or, more commonly, to individual congregations to help them supplement their minister's salary. In 1726, George I reduced the grant to £8591, with £6872.6s for the laity and £1718.4s for eligible clergy. The Royal Bounty would remain funded at this level until the turn of the nineteenth century.[86]

The administration of the Bounty fell to three groups. The Lords Commissioners – comprised normally of the archbishop of Canterbury, the bishop of London, the lord mayor of London, and others appointed by the Crown – oversaw the administrative process. The members of the French Committee were refugees chosen by the Lords Commissioners and actually distributed monies from the bounty. Finally, the work of the French Committee was audited by the English Committee, a supervisory board comprised of prominent Englishmen and French refugees.[87]

The job of distributing the £15,000 annual grant belonged originally to the French Committee. In November 1739, though, the Lords Commissioners established a separate Ecclesiastical Committee, comprised of four French ministers and a lay treasurer, whose sole function was to administer the funds to the ministers.[88] The Church of England, by way of its representation on the Lords Commissioners, tried to use the Ecclesiastical Committee to promote conformity to Anglican liturgical forms among the Huguenot churches.

The Bounty payments were chronically late. In February 1759, Majendie offered Secker his 'unfeigned Thanks...for the Steps you have taken for obtaining the Payment of his Majesty's Bounty in behalf of the Protestants in France'.[89] Nonetheless, the payments do not appear to have been released from the Treasury regularly, for Majendie wrote to Secker in January 1764, 'the poor French Refugees are greatly distressed by the Suspension of His Majesty's Bounty, there being more than a Year due to them, & their Landlords beginning to seize on their goods'.[90] Evidently Secker was unable to get the Treasury to disburse the Bounty funds because July found Majendie bemoaning to Charles Jenkinson the fate of 'the poor French Protestants of this Kingdom, who suffer greatly from so long a suspension of His Majestys usual Bounty, whereof a whole Year is now due'.[91]

When thanking Secker in early 1759 for his help securing tax-exempt status for the Bounty, Majendie raised a point that cut to the heart of the Ecclesiastical Committee's work and purpose. 'I must beg Leave to inform your Grace that a

---

[86] Smith (ed.), *Records of the Royal Bounty*, p. 37.
[87] Sundstrom, 'Aid and Assimilation', pp. 56–60.
[88] The original members of the Ecclesiastical Committee were Rev. Paul Covenent, Rev. Stephen Abel Laval, Rev. Isaac Jean Barnouin, Rev. John Peter Stehelin, and Peter Tirel serving as treasurer. John James Majendie served on the Ecclesiastical Committee from 1749 to 1784: *Records of the Royal Bounty*, pp. 38, 40.
[89] LPL, MS 1122/II, f. 98: Majendie to Secker, 11 Feb 1759.
[90] LPL, MS 1122/III, f. 238: Majendie to Secker, 6 Jan 1764.
[91] BL Add. MS 38203, f. 34: Majendie to Jenkinson, 12 July 1764.

Meeting of the Ecclesiastical Committee, lately held to draw up the new List for your Grace's signing,' he wrote to Secker, '...at which meeting neither the Revd. Mr. Serces nor myself could be present, on account of Illness, it had been resolved, contrary to the established Rules & Practise observed hitherto, to introduce into the said List a nonconforming congregation with a Pension of £20 pr annum.'[92] Isaac Jean Barnouin, minister of the nonconformist French church at Southampton, was the ringleader of the committee,[93] and what ensued from Majendie's complaint to Secker was a debate which evidenced the ambivalence orthodox Anglicans felt about the refugee Huguenots: while Secker wanted to help them, he did not at the same time wish to promote Protestant nonconformity in England.

In May 1759, Barnouin wrote to Secker to ask whether 'there is any Clause, wherein some particular priviledges have been granted of their Churches that should conform to the Church of England, whereby those that should not conform should be excluded from all benefits arising from thence?'[94] Under the terms of the act establishing the Bounty, conformist congregations had received payments to help them pay their clergy (7, 8 William III, c. 30, 31). While individual nonconformist clergy could receive Bounty funds, nonconformist congregations were barred from receiving grants to help them hire clergy. But the origins of the policy were murky, so that there were no clear legal barriers to opening the Bounty's coffers to nonconforming congregations.[95]

Barnouin directly challenged whether it was legal to deny Bounty funds to nonconformist French congregations.[96] He pointed out that there was no written or, to his knowledge, implicit prohibition against funding the nonconformists. 'After this Nation had [since Edward VI's reign] received...with so much humanity the French Protestants', it would be hard to believe that William III and Parliament 'would have excluded these same Protestant Churches from the Benefices of the bounty Granted for the support of the French clergy in General.' Appealing to a history of amicable inter-confessional relations, he noted furthermore, that 'the Divines of the Church of England have always, ever since the time of the Reformation held a friendly Correspondence with the Churches of

92 Ibid., f. 115: Majendie to Secker, 29 Jan 1759.
93 Barnouin served as minister of the French Church at Southampton from 1736 until 1797: Edwin Welch (ed.), *The Minute Book of the French Church at Southampton, 1702–1939* (Southampton, 1979), pp. 8–9.
94 LPL, MS 1122/II, f. 119: Barnouin and Thomas DuBisson to Secker, 1 May 1759.
95 John Pinnington, 'Anglican Openness to Foreign Protestant Churches in the Eighteenth Century', *Anglican Theological Review* 51:2 (1969), pp. 143–44.
96 The appeal probably resulted from a dispute earlier in the year among French Committee members regarding the issue (LPL, MS 1122/II, ff. 115–16: Majendie to Secker, 29 Jan 1759). Secker's notes on the subject furthermore suggest that Barnouin had raised a similar issue with Archbishop Herring in 1750 only to have it rejected (LPL, MS 1122/II, ff. 123–25: Thomas Secker's observations on French Nonconformist Churches' Claim to Share Queen Anne's Bounty, 8 May 1759).

France; have always looked upon their Ministers as Brothers & have always put a great difference between them, and those they call schismaticks'.[97] Why, also, he wondered, would the government have established pensions for nonconformist French churches in Ireland but not intend relief be granted to those attending nonconformist French churches in England. Meeting with Secker in person a week later, Barnouin went even further, contending 'that most of the French Protestants who come over, are averse from the Church of England, & many of them think it almost as bad as the Church of Rome'.[98] It was hardly prudent for Barnouin to tar the Church of England with the brush of popery and then to ask the archbishop of Canterbury's help in securing support for its detractors: there was little Secker could do to silence Blackburne when he made these sorts of charges, but he wielded the power of the purse over someone like Barnouin.

Barnouin's appeal to Secker was timed to coincide with his petition to the Ecclesiastical Committee to grant Bounty monies to his French nonconformist congregation in Southampton. Interestingly enough, the application was forwarded to the Committee by latitudinarian Benjamin Hoadly, bishop of Winchester. Not surprisingly, Hoadly recommended funding Barnouin's congregation. 'I have enquired thoroughly into it; & am fully convinced that the granting it would be for the public good, the Interest of Religion,' Hoadly wrote to Majendie.[99] Equally unsurprising was Secker's opposition to Barnouin's scheme.

Secker rejected Barnouin's arguments primarily on the grounds that they would unnecessarily encourage religious heterodoxy in England. To begin with, he worried about the scope of the Bounty's activities, because it potentially offered support even to nonconformist ministers.[100] He thought it was 'less advisable to give to nonconformist congregations, than to others, because it tends to discourage a needless separation'. Indeed, since most French Protestants in England were not recent refugees, Secker believed they had had ample time and opportunity to conform. 'And few of the Fr. Laity,' he argued, 'have Objections of Conscience against the Service of the Established Church to which they have now had sufficient time to reconcile themselves.'[101] Barnouin would resign from the Ecclesiastical Committee when Secker refused to expand benefaction, but Secker steadfastly held that the Bounty should be used not just to aid those legally qualified but also to promote conformity to Anglican liturgical forms among resident French Protestants.[102] When replacing Barnouin on the Ecclesiastical

97 LPL, MS 1122/II, f. 119: Barnouin and Thomas DuBisson to Secker, 1 May 1759.
98 Ibid., f. 127: Secker's notes on a conversation with M. Barnouin, 9 May 1759.
99 Ibid., f. 121: Hoadly to Majendie, 17 April 1759.
100 LPL, MS 1122/II, f. 130: Secker to Majendie, 19 May 1759: 'The substance of what I said to M. Barnouin was only, that I should have been fearful of extending it [the Royal Bounty] so far, had the proposal been made in my time; and therefore should be more unwilling to extend it further, & take in the Nonconformist Congregations also.'
101 Ibid., f. 125: Secker's observations on French Nonconformist Churches' Claim to Share Queen Anne's Bounty, 8 May 1759.
102 Ibid., f. 167: Barnouin to Secker, 21 Jan 1760.

Committee, Secker took care to appoint someone who would promote these aims, and it is not surprising that all three French ministers nominated to fill the position served conforming French churches in London.[103]

The guidelines for administering the Bounty to French Protestants, then, provided one way for Secker to encourage conformity among the French émigrés in England, and it appears that the Committee followed those guidelines to the letter,[104] and this determination to adhere strictly to the guidelines extended even to requests from eminent persons. In 1759, for instance, the duke of Grafton asked Secker to grant Bounty funds to an impoverished cleric named Viel, 'a Frenchman by Birth & a minister here'.[105] Poor, married with three children, and in Anglican orders, here was a French refugee cleric who seemed to fit ideally the Bounty's purpose. Secker soon passed Grafton's request along to Majendie, asking him to see whether Viel qualified under the Bounty's terms.[106] Majendie reported that prior to taking Anglican orders, Viel had been a Roman Catholic priest in France and thus was restricted from receiving Bounty aid under George II's 1729 strictures.[107] In turn, Secker denied Grafton's request, though he granted Viel money out of his own pocket 'as I have done for sev'l years past, & shall do with more pleasure in time to come, on account of your Graces good opinion of him'.[108] The rules for the Bounty protected the Church of England and to bend them for Grafton would, to Secker's way of thinking, have opened the door to nonconformist mischief.

Secker's response to a petition from a group of German Lutherans wishing to build a chapel on the outskirts of London likewise illustrates his wariness regarding foreign Protestants in England, for while wanting to grant them the right to construct, he also sought to ensure that he did not encourage religious heterodoxy. In late October 1762, George III forwarded to Secker a petition from German Lutherans in Whitechapel.[109] Seeking the king's approval to build a chapel, at their own expense, on Little Alie Street in Goodman's Fields, Whitechapel,[110] the petitioners contended that their great distance from the German-speaking Lutheran chapels in central London prevented them, 'especially in Wintertime, when the Days are short and the Season inclement...from hearing the Word of

---

103 Ibid., ff. 169–170: Majendie to Secker, 24 Jan 1760. Revs. Rocheblave, Jean Des Champs, and Maury served, respectively, the French Royal Chapel, the Savoy Church, and St Martin's Orgars.
104 For example, see petitions from Anne Gonslave (LPL, MS 1122/II, ff. 74, 76, 78), M. DeFlandrin (LPL, MS 1122/II, f. 133), and M. Montbrun (LPL, MS 1122/II, ff. 187, 189).
105 LPL, MS 1122/II, f. 96: Grafton to Secker, 28 Jan 1759.
106 Ibid., f. 97: Secker to Majendie, 8 Feb 1759.
107 Ibid., ff. 98–99: Majendie to Secker, 11 Feb 1759.
108 Ibid., f. 100: Secker to Grafton, 15 Feb 1759.
109 LPL, MS 1122/III, f. 108: Egremont to Secker, 21 Oct 1762.
110 John Southerden Burn, *The History of the French, Walloon, Dutch, and other Foreign Protestant Refugees Settled in England* (1846), p. 240.

God and performing their Religious Duties'.[111] Secker's response is telling. He approved granting them a license to build a chapel and perform services in German according to the Lutheran liturgy, but only 'provided the petitioners are genuine Lutherans, and not followers of the late Count Zinzendorf; concerning which it may be proper, that the Ministers of the present Lutheran chapels should be consulted, and should certifie'.[112] He bore no animus towards genuinely Lutheran Germans in England, but he was clearly worried about religious heterodoxy potentially posed by German Moravians to the religious and civil order.[113]

A sense of the conflicting pressures when dealing with foreign Protestants shines through in Secker's response to petitions for relief of French galley slaves. In 1761, John James Majendie wrote to Secker with a list of people who 'were condemned to the Gallies in France, on no other account but for having been present at a religious Assembly, held by the Protestants of Languedoc, in 1756'.[114] Secker subsequently asked Joseph Yorke to gather together for him a list of all the French Protestant galley slaves, but nothing came of the matter for another year.[115] Then, in November 1762, Secker replied to Yorke in a letter which laid bare his anxieties. The émigré French Protestants had repeatedly requested that peace negotiations at the conclusion of the Seven Years War should include a demand by the English that Protestants in France be granted toleration. This, to Secker's way of thinking, was a non-starter because 'it cannot be imagined ... that the Fr. King will suffer his behaviour to his own Subjects to be regulated by articles in a Treaty with any of his neighbours'. George III was willing to 'give them the kindest Reception if they found their way into his dominions', but believed 'that asking Favours for them in France might provoke the Governm't there to treat them worse, or might produce improper Requests in return for Favours to papists here'. Protestants in France might be 'unhappy sufferers' on account of their religion, but they would not get the archbishop of Canterbury's help if it meant reciprocity for Roman Catholics in England.[116]

---

[111] LPL, MS 1122/III, f. 106: Petition of the King's German Lutheran Subjects, 19 Oct 1762.
[112] Ibid., f. 110: Secker to Egremont, 22 Oct 1762.
[113] Colin Podmore, *The Moravian Church in England, 1728–1760* (Oxford, 1998), pp. 246, 287–88 points out that Secker was not opposed to the 1749 Moravian Act but that his hostility to the Moravians developed sometime after the early 1750s.
[114] LPL, MS 1122/II, f. 27: Majendie to Secker, 4 May 1761.
[115] LPL, MS 1122/III, f. 66: Yorke to Secker, 1 Sept 1761.
[116] Ibid., f. 114: Secker to Yorke, 18 Nov 1762. Nevertheless, Secker went on to say that the case of the galley slaves 'imprisoned ... for their Religion is different' and asked Yorke to report to M. Royer that 'I have several times mentioned this matter to the King: & he hath now directed orders to be sent to the D. of Bedford to make the strongest instances for the Release' of them.

IV

In the spring of 1768, by which time his body was being ravaged by the cancer which would soon kill him, Secker helped organize a royal brief for the Vaudois Protestants, and the very last thing he recorded in his autobiography was a gift of 10 guineas to 'Mr. Finnman who came to beg for money for building a Reformed Church in one of the Dutchies of Mecklenberg'.[117] Despite these shows of generosity, though, he had not changed his mind about the inherent risks in the Church of England's ties to foreign Protestants. In 1767, the Artillery Church, a French nonconformist chapel in Bishopsgate, London, asked John Moore, lecturer of St Sepulchre's, to preach an anniversary sermon commemorating the repeal of the Edict of Nantes.[118] Before accepting the offer, Moore had his father, himself rector of St Bartholomew the Great, approach Secker about the matter. Though advising against accepting the invitation, Secker referred Moore to Richard Terrick, who as bishop of London had direct episcopal jurisdiction over foreign congregations in London. Terrick, however, saw no prohibition to accepting the invitation, and there the matter rested until the Artillery Church's minister, Jacob Bourdillon, wrote to Secker arguing that ordained Anglican ministers should be able to conduct services in French nonconformist churches. Clearly Moore had told Bourdillon of the archbishop's initial qualms about his preaching the anniversary sermon, and Secker's response to Bourdillon points to the ambiguities faced by orthodox Anglicans when dealing with foreign Protestants in England.

After more considered reflection, Secker accepted Bourdillon's argument that ordained Anglican ministers faced no canonical barrier to *preaching* in nonconformist churches. He agreed that neither the relevant Edwardian and Caroline statutes nor the seventy-first canon which Bourdillon had cited prohibited Church of England clergy from preaching in the nonconformist churches. Neither did he see any prohibition in English canon law forbidding them from leading religious services in private houses.[119] 'I see no other Law, that hath any Appearance of putting a Negative on Mr. Moore,' he concluded.

Yet this was as much as Secker was willing to concede, and he rejected wholly Bourdillon's argument that ordained Anglican clergy might conduct religious services in nonconformist chapels. He reminded Terrick that every ordained Anglican clergyman had 'subscribed a Promise at their Ordination, that they would use the Form in the Common Prayer Book prescribed, in the publick Prayer & Administration of the Sacraments, & none other'. And here he explicitly drew the connection between French nonconforming churches and native English dissenting ones. 'But if a man uses, perhaps alternately, our form in one

---

[117] *Autobiography*, pp. 68, 69.
[118] LPL, Secker Papers 7, ff. 227–30: Secker to Terrick, 23 Sept 1767. Unless otherwise noted, the Secker quotations in the following three paragraphs refer to this letter.
[119] *Anglican Canons*, p. 363 (Canon 71 of 1603).

Congregation, and a different Form or none in another, & explains his Subscription to mean only, that he would use the established Liturgy as often as he officiated in the established Church: surely this is taking a considerable Step further,' he reckoned. 'Were he to divide himself thus between the established Church and an English dissenting congregation, it would be universally condemned. So far indeed the Cases differ that the Dissenters were of our Church, & Separated themselves from it; & the French, not. But the Interpretation of the Subscription Promise might be extended equally to both Cases.' He insisted furthermore that 'there is no more Reason, why a Foreigner, not episcopally ordained, shd be allowed to administer the Sacrament in the Church of England, than why an Englishman, not episcopally ordain'd should'.

John James Majendie tried to convince Secker that 'those Foreign Protestants … coming from abroad, & settling in this kingdom … ought surely to be considered in a very distinct light from what we view our Separatists in'.[120] He need not have bothered, for Secker was not to be dissuaded. In part, his intransigence reflected his belief that foreign Protestants in England were often proving more of a nuisance than anything else. 'I am very sorry for every new Instance of Unreasonableness & Wildness in a Body of Men, to whom I most heartily wish well. But indeed increasing Pain hath worn me out to such a degree, that making any Remarks or Reflexions on any thing is beyond [my] power,' he wrote to Charles Jenkinson in January 1768.[121] More importantly, though, Secker's ambivalence to them reflects his concerns about the Church of England. Secker worried that assisting churches abroad would nourish heterodoxy, encourage religious separatists, and further undermine the established Church's place in English society. It would, in other words, emphasize the un-catholicity of the Church of England. The spectre of disunity haunted Secker, and it could not be purged from his mind. So, he died, as he had lived, filled with certainty and wracked by anxiety. Yet that was what it meant to be an orthodox reformer walking down a path toward a destination which could never be reached.

---

120   LPL, Secker Papers 7, ff. 239–40: Majendie to Secker, 31 Oct 1767.
121   BL, Add. MS 38206, f. 22: Secker to Jenkinson, 28 Jan 1768.

EPILOGUE

'He is indeed to Us *Ultimus Romanorum*, the last of those Great and Good Men with whom we have been connected,' the earl of Hardwicke wrote to his brother on learning of Thomas Secker's death.[1] The end came in the late summer of 1768. Secker had spent the entire year in agonizing pain, suffering from what his physicians thought was rheumatism. Though Secker tried to hide his discomfort from family and friends, he confided to his doctors that 'the Pains were so excruciating that unless some Relief could be procured, he thought it would be impossible for human Nature to support them long'.[2] On Sunday evening, 31 July, he lay on a couch in Lambeth Palace's picture gallery, attended only by his two doctors and a servant. Around eight o'clock, he 'found himself suddenly sick, called for a Bason, was raised from the Couch, and attempted to retch, but could not; at that very instant, he felt a most dreadful Pain in his right Thigh, and cried out most lamentably'.[3] His right femur, eaten away by cancer, an autopsy would later reveal, had snapped in half. He died three days later in an opiate haze.

Secker left behind explicit instructions for his funeral to be 'as private as possible', and the only people admitted into St Mary's, Lambeth, on 9 August for it were family members, chaplains, servants, and a very few others. Beilby Porteus performed the service, after which the large elm coffin containing Secker's corpse was taken outside and placed in an unmarked leaden vault within the wall of an arched hallway between the parish church and the archiepiscopal palace. Yet no one now knows exactly where Secker's remains lie because he 'particularly directed that no Epitaph shall be put up for him either at Lambeth or elsewhere'.[4] The only public monument to him today is a worn black slab, etched barely visibly with his name and dates, in the floor at the entrance to the Museum of Garden History.

The Museum of Garden History, of course, used to be St Mary's, Lambeth, and just about where Porteus preached Secker's funeral sermon now sits a café. For nearly a millennium, St Mary's was a functioning parish church. A freefall decline in congregation numbers, though, prompted its deconsecration in 1972, and the former church was slated for demolition in 1976 before the museum trust saved it from destruction.

Quite obviously England has changed dramatically in the two and a half centuries since Secker's death, and, indeed, the fate of St Mary's is emblematic of

---

[1] BL, Add. MS 35632, f. 211: Philip Yorke, 2nd earl of Hardwicke to Charles Yorke, 9 Aug 1768.
[2] Porteus, *Life of Secker*, p. 87.
[3] Bodleian, Eng.misc.b.46, f. 46: A.C. Ducarel's account of Secker's death and burial, 17 Aug 1768.
[4] Ibid., f. 47. See also, LPL, MS 1719, ff. 28–29: Funeral expenses of Thomas Secker, 1768.

those changes.[5] Somewhere along the way, the nation became, by almost every conceivable standard, secularized and de-Christianized.[6] 'At the start of the twenty-first century the vast majority of people do not to go church and only the children of churchgoers go to Sunday school', one prominent sociologist of secularization reckons. 'Christian ideas are not taught in schools, are not promoted by social elites, are not reinforced by rites of passage, are not presented in a positive light in the mass media, and are no longer constantly affirmed in everyday interaction.'[7] Its parish churches emptier and emptier by the year, the Church of England yet retains its nominal establishment status, but church and state are now effectively separated.[8]

If asked, historians of the eighteenth century would likely tell you that the hundred or so years after 1688 marked the beginning of the end of Christian England, not because it is a proposition which many have sought to prove,[9] but because it is simply assumed that secularization is an historical inevitability. Religion is *supposed* to decline to the point of disappearance as societies modernize: what else could it do, after all? Put another way, *secularization* is the 'master narrative' of English religious history and is the protagonist in England's ineluctable march to modernity.[10] Most historians simply take for granted that the

---

[5] Callum Brown, *The Death of Christian Britain: Understanding Secularisation, 1800–2000* (2001), p. 4.

[6] Jeremy Morris, 'The Strange Death of Christian Britain: Another Look at the Secularization Debate', *HJ* 46:4 (2003), pp. 963–76 incisively and succinctly surveys the historiography of its subject.

[7] Steve Bruce, *God is Dead: Secularization in the West* (Oxford, 2002), pp. 63–73, at p. 73. Sociological scepticism about secularization theory is, however, robustly expressed in Callum G. Brown, 'The secularisation decade: what the 1960s have done to the study of religion', in *The Decline of Christendom in Western Europe, 1750–2000*, eds. Hugh McLeod and Werner Ustorf (Cambridge, 2003), pp. 29–47 and idem, 'A Revisionist Approach to Religious Change', in *Religion and Modernization: Sociologists and Historians Debate the Secularization Thesis* (Oxford, 1992), pp. 31–58.

[8] Edward Norman, 'Church and State since 1800', in *A History of Religion in Britain: Practice and Belief from the Pre-Roman Times to the Present*, eds. Sheridan Gilley and W.J. Sheils (Oxford, 1994), pp. 277–90. But see S.J.D. Green, 'Survival and autonomy: on the strange fortunes and peculiar legacy of ecclesiastical establishment in the modern British state, c. 1920 to the present day', in *The boundaries of the state in modern Britain*, eds. S.J.D. Green and R.C. Whiting (Cambridge, 1996), pp. 325–40.

[9] Notable exceptions include Blair Worden, 'The question of secularization', in *A Nation Transformed: England after the Restoration*, eds. Alan Houston and Steven Pincus (Cambridge, 2001), pp. 20–40; Roy Porter, *The Creation of the Modern World: The Untold Story of the British Enlightenment* (New York, 2000), esp. pp. 205–29; Kaspar von Greyerz, 'Secularization in Early Modern England (1660–c.1750)', in *Säkularisierung, Dechristianisierung, Rechristianisierung in neuzeilichen Europa*, ed. Hartmut Lehman (Göttingen, 1997), pp. 86–100; and C. John Sommerville, *The Secularization of Early Modern England: From Religious Culture to Religious Faith* (Oxford, 1992).

[10] Jeffrey Cox, 'Provincializing Christendom: The Case of Great Britain', *Church History* 75:1 (2006), pp. 120–30; idem, 'Master narratives of long-term religious change', in *The Decline of Christendom in Western Europe*, pp. 201–17. More generally, see, Allan Megill, '"Grand

eighteenth century witnessed the birth of the modern and that, in consequence, religion mattered less then than it had previously.[11] Subjects which do not fit easily into that big story are either ignored or discredited as anomalous.

Orthodox church reform is just one of those subjects. Yet it actually tells us quite a lot about the eighteenth century which complicates the big story of England's modernization and secularization. In particular, the *idea* of orthodox church reform highlights the era's continuities with early modernity. Others have noted that the meaning of *reform* – and of *church reform* in particular – changed significantly during the 1780s.[12] The conception of orthodox church reform before then was symptomatic of an era in which most thought that God operated providentially, in which England was supposed to be the 'new Israel', in which church and state were thought to be organically conjoined, and in which societal change was understood and managed with reference to the past. Before the 1780s, orthodox church reformers might have aimed to defend durable Christian truths and Anglican liturgical forms against heterodoxy, but they nevertheless shared fundamental assumptions with religious and political liberalizers: both looked to the past for solutions to present problems, both looked to reform through restoration. This almost universal belief in the necessity of restorative reform hardly seems consonant with *modernity*.[13]

What, then, accounts for the altered meanings of reform after 1780? In no small part, the *outcome* of eighteenth-century orthodox reform illuminates some of the processes which fundamentally transformed Thomas Secker's England and helps to explain the timing of the conceptual sea change. If eighteenth-century England remained a religious society to the marrow of its bones, the wars it fought

---

narrative" and the discipline of history', in *A New Philosophy of History*, eds. Frank Ankersmit and Hans Kellner (Chicago, 1995), pp. 151–73.

[11] For an important examination of the causes and consequences of the secularized historiography of eighteenth-century Britain, see B.W. Young, 'Religious History and the Eighteenth-Century Historian', *HJ* 43:3 (2000), pp. 849–68. See also, Brad S. Gregory, 'The Other Confessional History: On Secular Bias in the Study of Religion', *History and Theory* 45:4 (2006), pp. 132–49.

[12] Joanna Innes, '"Reform" in English public life: the fortunes of a word' and Arthur Burns, 'English "church reform" revisited, 1780–1840', in *Rethinking the Age of Reform: Britain, 1780–1850*, eds. Arthur Burns and Joanna Innes (Cambridge, 2003), pp. 71–97, 136–62.

[13] Zygmunt Bauman, 'Modernity', in *The Oxford Companion to the Politics of the World,* 2nd edn, ed. Joel Krieger (Oxford, 2001), p. 551 succinctly defines *modernity* as 'the age marked by constant change–but an age aware of being so marked; an age that views its own legal forms, its material and spiritual creations, its knowledge and convictions as temporary, to be held "until further notice" and eventually disqualified and replaced by new and better ones. In other words, modernity is an era conscious of its historicity. Human institutions are viewed as self-created and amenable to improvement; they can be retained only if they justify themselves in the face of the stringent demands of reason–and if they fail the test, they are bound to be scrapped. The substitution of new designs for old will be a progressive move, a new step up the ascending line of human development.' See also, idem, *Legislators and Interpreters: On Modernity, Postmodernity, and Intellectuals* (Cambridge, 1987).

nevertheless chipped away at the foundations of the confessional state. Indeed, neither rationization nor urbanization nor industrialization did nearly so much as war to transform eighteenth-century England and the fortunes of its established Church. It did so in two complementary ways. Firstly, the crisis which engulfed Europe from 1789 until 1815 unleashed forces which threatened established churches and confessional states throughout the West. Attempts to restore the old order after Waterloo could not squelch questions about the need for state-sponsored Christian churches and, indeed, about Christianity's centrality to Western European society.[14] These questions had particular purchase in England because of religious liberalization, itself a second effect of war and one well advanced by the end of Secker's life. In the aftermath of the Glorious Revolution and in preparation for war with France, the English Parliament passed the Toleration Act (1689), which allowed for a measure of religious pluralism, and allowed the Licensing Act to lapse in 1695, which enabled a torrent of anti-clerical and anti-religious literature to flood into the public sphere. Initially, wrong-footed by these liberalizing measures, the established Church of England had almost regained the full measure of its former standing by the 1730s. Yet successive wars against the Catholic Bourbon powers of Europe and the British colonists of North America cracked intra-Protestant fissures wide open, catalyzed the rehabilitation of Catholicism in England, enabled the dramatic growth of Protestant nonconformity, and corroded the theoretical and legal ties which bound together the established church and state.[15] The repeal of the Test and Corporation Acts (1828) and Catholic Emancipation (1829) were not the product of an unforced surrender but the logical conclusion of the confessional state's erosion since the end of the Seven Years War, after which it became increasingly clear that 'the continuance of the Establishment [was] of grace, not of right'.[16] Insofar as

---

[14] Jeremy Morris, *F.D. Maurice and the Crisis of Christian Authority* (Oxford, 2005), esp. pp. 3–18.

[15] See, for instance, Stephen Conway, *War, State, and Society in Mid-Eighteenth Century Britain and Ireland* (Oxford, 2006), pp. 170–92; idem, *The British Isles and the War of American Independence* (Oxford, 2000), pp. 239–66; G.M. Ditchfield, 'Ecclesiastical Legislation during the Ministry of the Younger Pitt, 1783–1801', *Parliamentary History* 19:1 (2000), pp. 64–80; idem, 'Ecclesiastical Policy under Lord North', in *The Church of England, c.1689–c.1833: From Toleration to Tractarianism*, eds. John Walsh, Colin Haydon, and Stephen Taylor (Cambridge, 1993), pp. 228–46; Colin Haydon, *Anti-Catholicism in eighteenth-century England, c. 1714–80: a political and social study* (Manchester, 1993); David Bebbington, 'The growth of voluntary religion', in *World Christianities, c.1815–c.1914 (The Cambridge History of Christianity, VIII)*, eds. Sheridan Gilley and Brian Stanley (Cambridge, 2005), pp. 53–69.

[16] Norman Sykes, 'Memorandum in Church and State in England since the Reformation', in *Church and State: Report of the Archbishops' Commission on the Relations Between Church and State* (1935), I, p. 300. Cf. J.C.D. Clark, *English Society, 1688–1832: Ideology, social structure and political practice during the ancien regime* (Cambridge, 1985), pp. 349–420 and idem, *English Society, 1660–1832: Religion, ideology and politics during the ancien régime* (Cambridge, 2000), pp. 16, 501–64.

eighteenth-century orthodox church reform's achievements fell short of its aspirations, they did so because the state did not, or could not, support it.

John Henry Newman (1801–1890) certainly appreciated the fact that the English state was an inconstant ally of orthodox reformers. Newman's religious worldview was actually not so very different from Secker's.[17] Dogma formed the foundation of both his and Secker's theology and churchmanship. '[M]y battle was with liberalism,' Newman recorded in his *Apologia Pro Vita Sua*, and 'by liberalism I mean the anti-dogmatic principle and its developments.'[18] Both men believed that the Church of England was catholic, both thought it was a *via media* between Rome and Geneva, and both took a high view of the sacraments. 'I was confident in the truth...that there was a visible Church, with sacraments and rites which are the channels of invisible grace,' Newman recollected. 'I thought that this was the doctrine of Scripture, of the early Church, and of the Anglican Church.'[19] So too did both hold 'the Pope to be Antichrist' and believe that 'the Church of Rome was bound up with the cause of Antichrist by the Council of Trent'.[20] Newman, like Secker, advocated restorative reform, not transformative reform, and he, like Secker, laid the greatest blame for English society's problems on human moral failings rather than on institutional imperfections.[21]

In the interim between Secker's death and the publication of the Tracts during the 1830s, the dogmatic truths of the catholic Church of England had not changed. But nineteenth-century orthodox churchmen debated how best to defend them. For Secker it had been axiomatic that church and state were allied, indeed in union, and that restorative religious reform was only possible with the state's help. Having witnessed what they believed to be the state's 'apostasy', Newman and the Tractarians contended that the Church of England's relationship with the state was at once erastian and corrupting and, thus, that the state was an impediment to restorative religious reform.[22] The debate which he and the Tractarians sparked during the 1830s and 1840s over the proper relation of church to state in England and over the English Church's core identity both

---

[17] Peter B. Nockles, *The Oxford Movement in context: Anglican high churchmanship, 1760–1857* (Cambridge, 1994) elucidates the genealogy of high churchmanship from the mid eighteenth century through to the mid nineteenth century.

[18] John Henry Newman, *Apologia Pro Vita Sua, Being a History of His Religious Opinions*, ed. Martin J. Svaglic (Oxford, 1967), p. 54.

[19] Ibid., p. 55.

[20] Ibid., p. 57.

[21] On this theme, see Edward Norman, 'Newman's Social and Political Thinking', in *Newman after a hundred years*, eds. Ian Kerr and A.G. Hill (Oxford, 1990), pp. 153–73.

[22] But see Peter B. Nockles, 'Newman and Early Tractarian Politics', in *By Whose Authority? Newman, Manning and the Magisterium*, ed. Vincent Alan McClelland (Bath, 1996), pp. 79–111; idem, '"Church and King": Tractarian Politics Reappraised', in *From Oxford to the People: Reconsidering Newman and the Oxford Movement*, ed. Paul Vaïss (Leominster, 1996), pp. 93–123.

revivified the institution and ultimately doomed its long-term fortunes by opening up doctrinal and ecclesiological divisions which eventually proved to be unbridgeable.[23] In 1845, Newman left the Church of England for the Church of Rome, which he believed was the true home of Christian orthodoxy. Relatively few Anglicans swam the Tiber with him, and within the Church of England that he abandoned, internal divisions soon fathered external weaknesses. For the last century and a half, internecine war between dogmatists and anti-dogmatists has riven the English Church and the institution has seen its prestige and authority plummet to depths which neither Secker nor Newman could ever have imagined.[24] The results of these correlated developments are to be found in the Museum of Garden History, in whose entranceway lies an almost wholly unnoticed monument to one who was the unlikely embodiment of eighteenth-century England's age of reform.

[23]   Sheridan Gilley, 'The Oxford Movement Reconsidered', in *Prejudice in Religion: Can We Move Beyond It?*, ed. Peter Cornwell (1997), pp. 19–34 and idem, 'The Church of England in the Nineteenth Century', in *A History of Religion in Britain*, pp. 291–305. But see Arthur Burns, 'The Authority of the Church', in *Liberty and Authority in Victorian Britain*, ed. Peter Mandler (Oxford, 2006), pp. 179–200 for a more sanguine view of the nineteenth-century Church of England's fortunes.

[24]   S.J.D. Green, 'The Strange Death of Puritan England, 1914–1945', in *Yet More Adventures with Britannia: Personalities, Politics, and Culture in Britain*, ed. William Roger Louis (2005), pp. 185–209 anatomizes an important, and related, change in twentieth-century English cultural and social mores.

BIBLIOGRAPHY

This bibliography confines itself only to manuscript and printed primary sources: full details of all secondary sources are to be found in the footnotes.

1. Manuscript Sources

Ann Arbor, MI: William L. Clements Library
Lord Shelburne Papers
Sir Henry Clinton Papers

Austin, TX: Episcopal Church Archives
Hawks Papers (Box 2)

Aylesbury: Buckinghamshire Record Office
Sir George Lee Papers (D/LE/C/4/26–27, D/LE/B/1/10)

Bedford: Bedfordshire and Luton Archives and Record Service
Wrest Park (Lucas) Papers (L30/6/1–2, L30/9/1–8)

Belfast: Public Record Office of Northern Ireland
Hervey/Bruce Papers (D/2798/5/6)

Cambridge, MA: Houghton Library, Harvard University
Thomas Hollis's MS Diary (MS Eng 1911)

Cambridge: Westminster College Library
Papers of Selina, Countess of Huntington (E/3/1/2–5, 9)

Charlottesville, VA: Alderman Library Rare Books Room
George Green Shackelford Manuscripts (MS 3525–s)

Devonshire: Chatsworth House
Thomas Secker correspondence, 1760–1763 (1st series, 609.0–3)

Durham: Durham Record Office
Composition tithe book of rectory of Houghton, 1724 (EP/Ho 466)

Farmington, CT: Lewis Walpole Library
Horace Walpole Papers (Commonplace Books)

Kew: The National Archive
State Papers Domestic, George II (36)

London: British Library
Additional Manuscripts

4291, 4317–4319, 4475 (Thomas Birch Papers)
5817 (William Cole Papers)
6043 (Thomas Secker's Parliamentary Papers)
11275 (Nathaniel Forster Papers)
15935 (A.C. Ducarel-Browne Willis Correspondence)
19864 (Sir William Bentham Papers)
32722–33072 (Newcastle Papers)
35586–36269 (Hardwicke Papers)
39311–39316 (Berkeley Papers)
37682 (Taylor Papers)
38203, 38204, 38206 (Liverpool Papers)
42560 (Thomas Warton Papers)
46839 (Miscellaneous)
61668 (Blenheim Papers)
Egerton Manuscripts
3437, 3439 (Holdernesse Papers)
2446 (Miscellaneous Papers)
Stowe 119 (Miscellaneous Papers)

London: Dr. Williams's Library
Account of the Dissenting Academies from the Restoration of King Charles II (MS 24.59)
Francis Blackburne Correspondence (MSS 12.45, 12.52, 12.53)

London: Lambeth Palace Library
VV 1/4/5/22 (Vicar General Records)
MS 1119 (Faculty Offices & Lord Hardwicke's Marriage Act)
MS 1120 (Queen Anne's Bounty)
MS 1121 (Sons of the Clergy)
MSS 1122/I-IV (Foreign Protestants)
MSS 1123/I-III (American Colonies)
MSS 1124/I-III (Society for the Propagation of the Gospel)
MSS 1130/I-II (Royal Court)
MS 133 (Account of Archbishop Wake's MSS)
MSS 1134/I-VIII (Visitations of the Diocese of Canterbury and Peculiars)
MS 1155 (Visitor of All Souls, Oxford)
MSS 1349–1350 (Secker Papers)
MS 1373 (Letters and Papers, 18th century)
MS 1483 (Secker's Account Book, 1758–1768)
MS 1719 (Miscellaneous letters & papers, 18th century)
MS 2165 (Guardbook, miscellaneous letters & papers)
MS 2185 (Howley Papers)
MS 2214 (John Nichols Papers)
MS 2547 (Miscellaneous Papers)
Secker's Cabinet
MSS 2559–2562 (Interleaved Bible, 1722–3, annotated by Secker)
MSS 2564–2569 (Notebooks of Thomas Secker)
MSS 2574–2575 (Secker's commentary on the Book of Daniel)
MS 2576 (Papers concerning the establishment of bishops in America, 1712–77)
MS 2577 (Remarks by Benjamin Blayney on passages in the Old Testament)
MS 2578 (*Biblica hebraica*, annotated by Secker)
MS 2589 (Church of England in the American Colonies, c. 1723–85)

BIBLIOGRAPHY

MSS 2590–2594 (Notebooks of Thomas Secker)
MSS 2595–2597 (Miscellaneous notes by Thomas Secker)
Herring Papers 2 (St. Paul's Cathedral, 1750s)
Thomas Secker Papers
      Secker Papers 1 (America)
      Secker Papers 2 (Bible & Ireland)
      Secker Papers 3 (Canterbury Diocesan Papers)
      Secker Papers 4 (Metropolitical Papers)
      Secker Papers 5 (Dispensations)
      Secker Papers 6 (Miscellaneous)
      Secker Papers 7 (Charities, case papers & other correspondence)
SPG Papers
Fulham Papers
MSS TR 9, 10, 12, 14, 20, 31, 34, 35, 36 (Archbishops' Estates)
MSS TS 5, 140 (Archbishops' Woods)

London: Westminster Abbey Library
Zachary Pearce Papers (Muniment 64617–64651, 65203)

London: Westminster City Archives
St. James's, Westminster vestry agenda book, 1712–1750 (D 1759, D1760)

New Haven, CT: Beinecke Rare Book and Manuscript Library
Papers relating to Catherine Talbot, 1694–1804 (Osborn Papers MSS 53)
Thomas Secker's Housekeeper's Diary, 1744–1746 (Osborn Collection C.291)
Osborn MSS File Folder 13280, 13281

New South Wales: Mitchell Library
Thomas Haweis's MS Autobiography

Nottingham: University of Nottingham, Hallward Library
Portland Papers (PW F 7505, 8246–8248)
Newcastle (Clumber) Collection (Ne C 1080)

Oxford: Bodleian Library
I.A. Dumay's Observations on Kennicott's MSS (MS Kennicott e.43)
Browne Willis Papers (MS Willis. 43)
Notes on Oxford University (MS Top. Oxon.e. 13)
A.C. Ducarel's account of Secker's death & burial (MS Eng. misc.b.46, ff. 27–28)
Miscellaneous Secker correspondence (MS Eng.misc.c.436, ff. 9–26, Eng.lett.c.60, ff. 1–2, Eng.lett.c.574, ff. 67–73)
Thomas Secker's personal account book, 1747–1758 (MS St. Edmund Hall 55)
Counsel's opinion in dispute with official to the archdeacon, 1738 (MS Top.Oxon.c.209)
Richard Rawlinson Papers (MS Rawlinson 4 4.251)
Edmund Gibson-William Nicholson Correspondence (Add. MS A.269)
Robert Lowth's copies of Secker's notes on Isaiah (MS. Eng.th.c.94.doc)

Oxford: Codrington Library, All Souls College
Founder's Kin, 1761–1762 (Injunctions, Mandates, Letters 261–262)

BIBLIOGRAPHY

Oxford: Rhodes House Library
SPG Correspondence: Connecticut, 1759–1782 (USPG B23)

Oxford: Oxford University Press Archives
Orders of the Delegates of the Press, III (1758–1794)

Sheffield: Sheffield City Library
Thomas Secker's Letterbook (Bagshawe C.330)

York: Borthwick Institute of Historical Research
Robert Hay Drummond Papers (Bishopthorpe C. & P. VII 109, 215; VIII 175)

2. Printed Primary Sources

2.1 CORRESPONDENCE, DIARIES, MEMOIRS, ETC.

Mary Bateson (ed.), *A Narrative of the Changes in the Ministry, 1765–1767* (1898).
E. Edwards Beardsley, *The Life and Times of William Samuel Johnson* (Boston, 1886).
———, *Life and Correspondence of Samuel Johnson, D.D.* (New York, 1874).
Francis Blackburne, *Memoirs of Thomas Hollis* (1780).
James Boswell, *Life of Johnson*, ed. George Birckbeck Hill, 4 vols. (Oxford, 1934).
Peter D. Brown and Karl W. Schweizer (eds.), *The Devonshire Diary. Memoranda on State of Affairs, 1759–1762* (1982).
Edmund Calamy, *An Historical Account of My Own Life with Some Reflections on the Times I have Lived in (1671–1731)*, ed. John Towill Rutt, 2 vols. (1830).
Henry Caner, *Letter-book of the Rev. Henry Caner, SPG Missionary in Colonial Connecticut and Massachusetts until the Revolution: A Review of His Correspondence from 1728 through 1778*, ed. Kenneth W. Cameron (Hartford, CT, 1972).
Jean Des Champs, *The Life and 'Mémoires Secrets' of Jean Des Champs (1707–1767), Journalist, Minister, and Man of Feeling*, ed. Uta Janssens-Knorsch (1990).
William Coxe, *Memoirs of the Life and Administration of Sir Robert Walpole, Earl of Orford*, 3 vols. (1800).
G.M. Ditchfield and Bryan Keith-Lucas (eds.), *A Kentish Parson: Selections from the Private Papers of the Revd. Joseph Price Vicar of Brabourne, 1767–86* (Stroud, 1991).
George Bubb Doddington, *The Political Journal of George Bubb Doddington*, eds. John Carswell and Lewis Arnold Dralle (Oxford, 1965).
Earl of Egmont, Historical Manuscript Commission, *Diary of the First Earl of Egmont (Viscount Percival)*, 3 vols. (1923).
David Fairer (ed.), *The Correspondence of Thomas Wharton* (Athens, GA, 1995).
Thomas Gibbons, *Memoirs of the Rev. Isaac Watts, D.D.* (1780).
Thomas Gray, *Correspondence of Thomas Gray*, eds. Paget Toynbee and Leonard Whibley, 3 vols. (Oxford, 1935).
Jack P. Greene (ed.), *The Diary of Colonel Landon Carter of Sabine Hall, 1752–1778*, 2 vols. (Charlottesville, VA, 1965).
Robert Harris (ed.), *A Leicester House Political Diary, 1742–3* (1992).
Francis L. Hawks and William Stevens Perry, *Documentary History of the Protestant Episcopal Church in the United States ... Connecticut* (New York, 1864).

BIBLIOGRAPHY

Thomas Hearne, *Remarks and Collections of Thomas Hearne*, 11 vols. (Oxford, 1885–1921).

John, Lord Hervey, *Some Materials Towards Memoirs of the Reign of King George II*, 3 vols., ed. Romney Sedwick (1931).

Peter Orlando Hutchinson (ed.), *The Diary and Letters of His Excellency Thomas Hutchinson*, 2 vols. (1883–86).

Countess of Ilchester and Lord Stavordale (eds.), *The Life and Letters of Lady Sarah Lennox, 1745–1826* (1901).

Samuel Johnson, *Samuel Johnson: His Career and Writings*, eds. Herbert and Carol Schneider, 4 vols. (New York, 1929).

William Jones, *Memoirs of the Life, Studies, and Writings of the Right Reverend George Horne, D.D., Late Lord Bishop of Norwich. To which is added His Lordship's own collection of this Thoughts on a variety of great and interesting subjects* (1795).

Ninetta S. Jucker (ed.), *The Jenkinson Papers, 1760–1766* (1949).

Aubrey N. Newman (ed.), 'Leicester House Politics 1750–60: From the Papers of John, Second Earl of Egmont', in *Camden Miscellany*, 4th series, 23 (1969), pp. 85–228.

John Henry Newman, *Apologia Pro Vita Sua, Being a History of His Religious Opinions*, ed. Martin J. Svaglic (Oxford, 1967).

John Nichols, *Illustrations of the literary history of the eighteenth century. Consisting of authentic memoirs and original letters of eminent persons; and intended as a sequel to the Literary anecdotes*, 8 vols. (1817–58).

——, *Literary anecdotes of the eighteenth century; comprizing biographical memoirs of William Bowyer, printer, F.S.A., and of many of his learned friends; an incidental view of the progress and advancement of literature in this kingdom during the last century; and biographical anecdotes of a considerable number of eminent writers and ingenious artists; with a very copious index*, 8 vols. (1812–16).

Geoffrey F. Nutall, *Calendar of the Correspondence of Philip Doddridge D.D. (1702–1751)*, Historical Manuscripts Commission JP 26 (1979).

Montagu Pennington (ed.), *A Series of Letters between Mrs. Elizabeth Carter and Miss Catherine Talbot, from the Year 1741 to 1770: to which are added, Letters from Mrs. Elizabeth Carter to Mrs. Vesey, between the Years 1763 and 1787*, 2 vols. (1808).

William Stevens Perry (ed.), *Historical Collections relating to the American Colonial Church*, 5 vols. (New York, 1969).

Joseph Redington (ed.), *Calendar of Home Office Papers of the Reign of George III, I: 1760–1765* (1878).

Herbert and Carol Schneider (eds.), *Samuel Johnson: His Career and Writings*, 4 vols. (New York, 1929).

Thomas Secker, *The Correspondence of Thomas Secker, Bishop of Oxford, 1737–58*, ed. A.P. Jenkins (Oxford, 1991).

——, *The Autobiography of Thomas Secker, Archbishop of Canterbury*, eds. John Macauley and R.W. Greaves (Lawrence, KS, 1988).

William Smith, *Life and Correspondence of Rev. William Smith, D.D.*, ed. Horace Wemyss Smith, 4 vols. (Philadelphia, 1880).

Ezra Stiles, *Extracts from the Itineraries and other miscellanies of Ezra Stiles, D. D., LL. D., 1755–1794, with a selection from his correspondence*, ed. Franklin B. Dexter (New Haven, CT, 1916).

D.O. Thomas and Bernard Peach (eds.), *The Correspondence of Richard Price*, 3 vols. (Durham, NC, 1983).

Leonard Twells (ed.), *The lives of Dr. Edward Pocock, the celebrated orientalist, by Dr. L. Twells; of Dr. Zachary Pearce, Bishop of Rochester, and of Dr. Thomas Newton, Bishop of Bristol, by themselves; and of the Rev. Philip Skelton, by Mr. S. Burdy* (1816).

BIBLIOGRAPHY

Margaret Maria Lady Verney, *Verney Letters of the Eighteenth Century from the MSS at Claydon House*, 2 vols. (1930).

Gilbert Wakefield, *The memoirs of the life of Gilbert Wakefield* (1792).

Horace Walpole, *Memoirs of King George II*, ed. John Brooke, 3 vols. (New Haven, CT, 1985).

———, Horace Walpole, *Memoirs of the Reign of King George the Third*, ed. G.F. Russell Barker, 4 vols. (London, 1894).

———, *The Yale Edition of Horace Walpole's Correspondence*, ed. W.S. Lewis, *et al.*, 48 vols. (New Haven, CT, 1937–83).

William Warburton, *Letters from a late eminent prelate to one of his friends* (Kidderminster, 1793).

John Wesley, *The Works of John Wesley, Letters II, 1740–1755*, ed. Frank Baker (Oxford, 1982).

Philip C. Yorke, *The life and correspondence of Philip Yorke, Earl of Hardwicke, Lord High Chancellor of Great Britain*, 3 vols. (New York, 1977).

2.2 PAMPHLETS, SERMONS, and CONTEMPORARY PUBLICATIONS

Anonymous, *An account of the ceremonies observed at the coronation of the Kings and Queens of England* (1761).

———, *The case of the unhappy people of Custrin, in the New-Mark, in the Electorate of Brandenburg, since the invasion of the Russians in 1758* (1759).

———, *Old covenanting and true Presbyterian layman, A true copy of a genuine letters, sent to the Archbishop of Canterbury, by eighteen Presbyterian ministers, in America: with some remarks thereon in another letter to the congregations of the said ministers* (Boston, 1762).

———, *An earnest address to Britons. Wherein the several artifices made use of by the emissaries of France and Rome, to corrupt the minds of the people, and to overturn our happy constitution, are explained, and laid open to public view* (1745).

———, *Some observations upon the present case of the Dissenting interest, and the case of those who have lately deserted it: wherein something further is suggested for its support and strengthening, occasioned by some late pamphlets concerning the decay of that interest* (1731).

East Apthorp, *Considerations on the Institution and Conduct of the Society for the Propagation of the Gospel in Foreign Parts* (Boston, 1763).

———, *The constitution of a Christian church illustrated in a sermon at the opening of Christ-Church in Cambridge on Thursday 15 October, MDCCLXI* (Boston, 1761).

Antoine Arnauld, *Logic, or, The art of thinking in which besides the common, are contain'd many excellent new rules, very profitable for directing of reason, and acquiring of judgment, in things as well relating to the instruction of a man's self, as of others, in four parts ...* (1696; originally published in 1662).

The form and order of the service that is to be performed, and the ceremonies that are to be observed, in the coronation of their Majesties King George III and Queen Charlotte in the Abbey Church of S. Peter, Westminster on Tuesday the 22d of September, 1761 (1761).

J.B., *The Church of England's complaints to the Parliament and against I. Careless non-residents II Encroaching pluralities. III. Unconscionable simony. Loose prophaneness. V. Undue ordination. Now reigning among her clergy ...* (1737).

John Bacon, *Liber Regis* (1786).

John Barker, *A sermon occasioned by the victory obtained over the rebels in Scotland, on the 16th of April, 1746* (1746).

BIBLIOGRAPHY

John Beach, *A Modest Enquiry into the State of the Dead, by which it appears to the enquirer that there is no intermediate state, but the resurrection immediately succeeds death* (Boston, 1755).

William Bell, *A defence of revelation in general, and the gospel in particular; in answer to the objections advanced in a late book, entitled, The Morality of the New Testament digested under various heads &c. &c. and subscribed, a rational Christian* (1766).

Martin Benson, *A sermon preached before the Incorporated Society for the Propagation of the Gospel in Foreign Parts; at their anniversary meeting in the parish-church of St. Mary-le-Bow, on Friday, February 15, 1739–40* (1740).

Edward Bentham, *A letter to a fellow of a college. Being the sequel of A letter to a young gentleman of Oxford* (1749).

——, *A letter to a young gentleman. By a tutor, and fellow of a college in Oxford* (Oxford, 1748).

George Berkeley, *The works of George Berkeley, D.D. late Bishop of Cloyne in Ireland*, 2 vols. (Dublin, 1784).

——, *A sermon preached before the Incorporated Society for the Propagation of the Gospel in Foreign Parts; at their anniversary meeting in the parish-church of St Mary-le-Bow, on Friday, February 18. 1731* (1732).

Francis Blackburne, *The works, Theological and Miscellaneous, ... of Francis Blackburne ... With some account of the life and writings of the author, by himself, completed by his son, Francis Blackburne, L.L.B., and illustrated by an appendix of original papers*, 7 vols. (Cambridge, 1804).

——, *An historical view of the controversy concerning an intermediate state and the separate existence of the soul between death and general resurrection, deduced from the beginning of the Protestant Reformation to the present times. With some thoughts, in a preferatory discourse, on the use and importance of theological controversy*. 2nd edn (1772).

——, *A Critical Commentary on Archbishop Secker's Letter to the Right Honourable Horatio Walpole, concerning Bishops in America* (1770).

——, *Considerations on the present state of the controversy between Protestants and Papists in Great Britain and Ireland* (Dublin, 1770).

——, *The Confessional; or, a full and free inquiry into the right, utility, edification, and success, of establishing systematical confessions of faith and doctrine in Protestant churches*, 3rd edn (1770).

——, *A critical commentary on Archbishop Secker's letter to the Right Honourable Horace Walpole, concerning Bishops in America* (1770).

——, *Remarks on the Revd. Dr. Powell's sermon in defence of subscriptions, preached before the University of Cambridge on the commencement Sunday 1757. Wherein the latitude said to be allowed to subscribers to the Liturgy and Articles of the Church of England, is particularly considered* (1758).

——, *A serious enquiry into the use and importance of external religion. Occasioned by some passage in the Right Reverend the Lord Bishop of Durham's charge to the clergy of that diocese ... in the year MDCCLI* (1752).

Richard Blacow, *A letter to William King, LL.D. Principal of St. Mary Hall in Oxford. Containing a particular account of the treasonable riot in Oxford in Feb. 1747* (1755)

Richard Bland, *A Letter to the Clergy of Virginia* (Williamsburg, 1760).

Benjamin Blayney, *Jeremiah, and Lamentations. A new translation with notes critical, philological, and explanatory* (1784).

Richard Burn, *Ecclesiastical Law*, 3 vols. (London, 1763).

Gilbert Burnet, *A Discourse of the Pastoral Care*, 4th edn (1736).

BIBLIOGRAPHY

Joseph Butler, *The Works of Joseph Butler, D.C.L., late Lord Bishop of Durham*, ed. Samuel Hallifax (New York, 1860).

———, *The Analogy of Religion* (1798; originally published 1737).

Henry Caner, *The Firm Belief of a Future Reward a powerful motive to obedience and a good life: a sermon preached at Christ Church in Boston, August 20. 1765. At the funeral of the Rev. Timothy Cutler, D.D ... .* (Boston, 1765).

———, *A candid examination of Dr. Mayhew's observations on the charter and conduct of the Society for the Propagation of the Gospel in Foreign Parts* (Boston, 1763).

Thomas Bradbury Chandler, *An Appendix to the American Edition of the Life of Archbishop Secker: containing His Grace's letter to the Revd. Mr. Macclanechan, on the irregularity of his conduct; with an introductory narrative* (New York, 1774).

———, *A Free Examination of the Critical commentary on Archbishop Secker's Letter to Mr. Walpole* (New York, 1774).

———, *An Appeal to the public, in behalf of the Church of England in America*, 2nd edn (1769).

Charles Chauncy, *The Appeal to the public answered, in behalf of the non-Episcopal churches in America* (Boston, 1768).

Thomas Church, *An appeal to the serious and unprejudiced: or, a second vindication of the miraculous powers, which subsisted in the first three centuries of the Christian Church* (1751).

———, *A vindication of the miraculous powers, which subsisted in the three first centuries of the Christian church. In answer to Dr. Middleton's Free enquiry ... With a preface, containing some observations on Dr. Mead's accounts of the Demoniacs, in his new piece, intituled Media sacra* (1750).

William Chillingworth, *The religion of protestants a safe way to salvation* (Oxford, 1638).

[Ralph Churton], *A letter to the Lord Bishop of Worcester, occasioned by his strictures on Archbishop Secker and Bishop Lowth in his Life of Bishop Warburton now prefixed to the quarto edition of that prelate's works* (Oxford, 1796).

John Conybeare, *A defense of reveal'd religion against the exceptions of a late writer, in his book, intituled, Christianity as old as the creation, &c.* (Oxford, 1732).

———, *The case of subscription to Articles of religion consider'd. A sermon preach'd at the triennial visitation of ... John, Lord Bishop of Oxford, held at St. Mary's, in Oxford, on Tuesday, July 20th. 1725* (Oxford, 1725).

John Denne, *A sermon preached in the parish church of St. Mary, Lambeth, upon April 11, 1744. being the day appointed for a general fast* (1744).

———, *A discourse on the nature, design, and benefits of confirmation* (1737).

Philip Doddridge, *The Works of Rev. P. Doddridge, D.D.*, 10 vols. (Leeds, 1802–10).

David Durell, *Critical remarks on the books of Job, Proverbs, Psalms, Ecclesiastes, and Canticles* (Oxford, 1772).

John Eachard, *The Works of John Eachard*, 3 vols. (1773–74).

———, *The grounds and occasions of the contempt of the clergy and religion inquired into* (1670).

Alexander Geddes, *Doctor Geddes's address to the public, on the publication of the first volume of his new translation of the Bible* (1793).

———, *Dr. Geddes's General answer to the queries, counsils, and criticisms that have been communicated to him since the publication of his proposals for printing a new translation of the Bible* (1790).

James Glazebrook, *The practice of what is called extempore preaching, and the propriety and advantage of that mode of public instruction urged and supported, by arguments deduced from scripture authority, primitive example, historic facts, and the very nature of the office* (Warrington, 1794).

BIBLIOGRAPHY

[Strickland Gough], *An enquiry into the causes of the decay of the Dissenting interest* (1730).

G. Gregory, *Sermons*, 2nd edn (1789).

P.J. Grosley, *A tour of London: or, new observations on England, and its inhabitants ... . Translated from the French by Thomas Nugent, LL.D., and fellow of the Society of Antiquaries*, 3 vols. (Dublin, 1772).

Thomas Gwatkin, *A letter to the clergy of New York and New Jersey, occasioned by an address to the Episcopalians in Virginia* (Williamsburg, 1772).

———, *Remarks upon the second and third of Three letters against the Confessional by a country clergyman* (1768).

———, *Remarks upon the first of three letters against the Confessional* (1768).

Edward Hasted, *The History and Topographical Survey of the County of Kent*, 4 vols. (Canterbury, 1797–1801).

Samuel Henley, *A candid refutation of the heresy imputed by Ro. C. Nicholas Esquire to the Reverend S. Henley* (Williamsburg, 1774).

———, *The distinct claims of government and religion, considered in a sermon preached before the Honourable House of Burgesses, at Williamsburg, in Virginia, March 1, 1772* (Cambridge, 1772).

Richard Hill, *Pietas Oxoniensis: or, a full and impartial account of the expulsion of six students from St. Edmund Hall, Oxford* (1768).

Benjamin Hoadly, *The common rights of subjects, defended: and the nature of the sacramental test, consider'd. In answer to the Dean of Chichester's vindication of the Corporation and Test Acts* (1719).

Richard Hooker, *Of the Laws of Ecclesiastical Polity*, ed. Arthur Stephen McGrade (Cambridge, 1997).

George Horne, *An apology for certain gentlemen in the University of Oxford, aspersed in a late anonymous pamphlet*, 2nd edn (1799).

———, *Considerations on the projected reformation of the Church of England. In a letter to the right honourable Lord North* (1772).

———, *A fair, and candid, and impartial state of the case between Sir Isaac Newton and Mr. Hutchinson* (Oxford, 1753).

David Hume, *An Enquiry concerning Human Understanding*, ed. Tom L. Beauchamp (Oxford, 2000).

Richard Hurd, *A discourse, by way of general preface to the quarto edition of Bishop Warburton's works* (1794).

Absalom Hurley, *Non-Residence Inexcusable; or, the Monitor Admonished: in a Letter to Dr. Free, on the occasion of his Elaborate Harangue, delivered to the London clergy at their annual festival, held on the 15th of May last, at Sion College* (1759).

William King, *A Proposal for publishing a poetical translation of the Rev. Mr. Tutor Bentham's Letter to a young gentleman of Oxford* (1749).

———, *A poetical abridgement, both in Latin and English, of the Reverend Mr. Tutor Bentham's Letter to a young gentleman of Oxford* (1749).

Vicesimus Knox, *Christian philosophy: or, an attempt to display the evidence and excellence of revealed religion* (1795).

Samuel Johnson, *A dictionary of the English language ... The eleventh edition* (1799).

John Jones, *Free and candid disquisitions relating to the Church of England, and the means of advancing religion therein. Addressed to the governing powers in church and state; and more immediately directed to the two Houses of Convocation*, 3rd edn (Dublin, 1750).

William Jones, *Remarks on the principles and spirit of a work entitled the Confessional* (1770).

Benjamin Kennicott, *The annual accounts of the collation of Hebrew MSS of the Old Testament* (Oxford, 1770).

BIBLIOGRAPHY

———, *The state of the printed Hebrew text of the Old Testament considered*, 2 vols. (Oxford, 1753).

———, *The duty of thanksgiving for peace in general, and the reasonableness of thanksgiving for our present peace. A sermon preach'd at St. Martin's in Oxford, before the mayor and corporation, on Tuesday, April 25, 1749. Being the day of thanksgiving for the general peace* (1749).

John Leland, *A View of the principal deistical writers that have appeared in England in the last and present century, with observations upon them, and some account of the answers that have been published against them. In several letters to a friend* (1754).

Robert Lowth, *Isaiah. A New Translation* (1778, 1779, 1795).

Bernard Mandeville, *The Fable of the Bees*, ed. Philip Harth (1970).

Jonathan Mayhew, *The Snare Broken. A thanksgiving discourse, preached at the desire of the West Church, in Boston, N.E. Friday, May 23, 1766. Occasioned by the repeal of the stamp-act* (Boston, 1766).

———, *Observations on the charter and conduct of the Society for the Propagation of the Gospel in Foreign Parts* (Boston, 1763).

———, *A defense of the observations on the charter and conduct of the Society for the Propagation of the Gospel in Foreign Parts, against an anonymous pamphlet, falsly intitled, A candid examination of Dr. Mayhew's Observations, &c.* (Boston, 1763).

———, *A discourse concerning unlimited submission and non-resistance to the higher powers: with some reflections on the resistance made to King Charles I. and on the anniversary of his death: in which the mysterious doctrine of that prince's saintship and martyrdom is unriddled: the substance of which was delivered in a sermon preached in the West Meeting-House in Boston the Lord's-Day after the 30th of January, 1749/50* (Boston, 1750).

[William McClenachan], *A Letter, from a clergyman in town; vindicating himself against the malevolent aspersions of a late pamphleteer letter-writer* (Philadelphia, 1764).

James Merrick, *Annotations on the Psalms* (Reading, 1768).

———, *The Psalms, translated or paraphrased in English verse* (Reading, 1765).

Conyers Middleton, *A vindication of The free inquiry into the miraculous powers, which are supposed to have subsisted in the Christian church, &c. from the objections of Dr. Dodwell and Dr. Church. By the late Conyers Middleton, D.D.* (1751).

———, *A Free Inquiry into the miraculous powers, which are supposed to have subsisted in the Christian church, from the earliest ages ... by which is shewn, that we have no sufficient reason to believe, upon the authority of the primitive fathers, that any such powers were continued to the church, after the days of the apostles* (1748).

Henry Nettleship (ed.), *Essays by the late Mark Pattison, sometime Rector of Lincoln College*, 2 vols. (Oxford, 1889).

William Newcome, *An historical view of the English biblical translations: the expediencey of revising our present translation: and the means of executing such a vision* (1792).

———, *An attempt towards an improved version, a metrical arrangement, and an explanation of the prophet Ezekiel* (1788).

———, *An attempt towards an improved version, a metrical arrangement, and explanation of the twelve minor prophets* (1785).

John Henry Newman, *An Essay on the Development of Christian Doctrine*, ed. Charles Frederick Harrold (1949).

[Richard Newton], *Pluralities indefensible. A treatise humbly offered to the consideration of the Parliament of Great-Britain. By a presbyter of the Church of England* (1743).

Thomas Nowell, *An answer to a pamphlet, entitled Pietas Oxoniensis, or, a full and impartial account of the expulsion of six students from St. Edmund-Hall, Oxford. In a letter to the author* (1768).

298

BIBLIOGRAPHY

Peter Peckard, *Subscription. Or historical extracts* (1776).

——, *Observations on the doctrine of an intermediate state between death and resurrection: with some remarks on the Rev. Mr. Goddard's sermon on that Subject* (1756).

——, *Farther observations on the doctrine of an intermediate state, in answer to the Rev. Dr. Morton's queries* (1757).

Thomas Phillips, *The history of the life of Reginald Pole* (1764).

Alexander Pope, *Imitations of Horace and An Epistle to Dr. Arbuthnot, and the Epilogue to the Satires*, ed. John Butt (New Haven, CT, 1953).

Thomas Randolph, *An answer to a pamphlet, entituled, Considerations on the propriety of requiring a subscription to articles of faith* (Oxford, 1774).

——, *An answer to a pamphlet entitled Reflections on the impropriety and inexpediency of lay-subscription to the XXXIX articles, in the University of Oxford* (Oxford, 1772).

——, *The reasonableness of requiring subscription to articles of religion from persons to be admitted to holy orders, or a cure of souls, vindicated in a charge delivered to the clergy of the diocese of Oxford, in the year 1771* (Oxford, 1771).

Glocester Ridley, *Three letters to the author of The Confessional* (1768).

——, *A review of Mr. Phillips's History of the life of Reginald Pole* (1766).

John De La Rose, *A Funeral Sermon Occasion'd by the death of the Reverend Mr. Timothy Jollie, Late Pastor to the Congregational Church at Sheffield* (1715).

Thomas Rutherforth, *A defence of a charge concerning subscriptions, in a letter to the author of the Confessional* (Cambridge, 1767).

——, *A vindication of the right of Protestant churches to require the clergy to subscribe to an established confession of faith and doctrines in a charge delivered at a visitation in July MDCCLXVI* (Cambridge, 1766).

——, *A second vindication of the right of Protestant churches to require the clergy to subscribe to an established confession of faith and doctrines in a letter to the examiner of the first* (Cambridge, 1766).

Henry Sacheverell, *The Political Union. A discourse shewing the dependance of government on religion in general: and of the English monarchy on the Church of England in particular* (Oxford, 1702).

Santorio Santorio, *Medicina statica: being the aphorisms of Sanctorius, translated into English with large explanations. Wherein is given a mechanical account of the animal œconomy*, ed. John Quincy (1712).

Thomas Secker, *Lectures on the Catechism of the Church of England; with a Discourses on Confirmation*, ed. Beilby Porteus and George Stinton, 8th edn (1799).

——, *A Sermon on Confirmation. A New Edition* (1795).

——, *The Works of Thomas Secker, L.L.D., late Lord Archbishop of Canterbury: to which is prefixed a review of his life and character*, ed. Beilby Porteus, 4 vols. (Edinburgh, 1792).

——, *Nine sermons preached in the parish of St. James, Westminster, on occasion of the war and rebellion in 1745*, 2nd edn (1771).

——, *A Letter to the Right Honourable Horatio Walpole, Esq.; written Jan 9, 1750–1* (1769).

——, *Sermon preached before the University of Oxford, at St. Mary's, on Act Sunday ... July 8, 1733* (Oxford, 1733).

Thomas Sharp, *Mr. Hutchinson's exposition of Cherubim, and his hypothesis concerning them examined: in three discourses. Wherein also what hath been advanced by some late writers, in support of his doctrine, is occasionally considered* (1755).

——, *A review and defence of two dissertations concerning the etymology and Scripture-meaning of the Hebrew words Elohim and Berith* (1754).

——, *Two dissertations concerning the etymology and scripture-meaning of the Hebrew words Elohim and Beerith. Occasioned by some notions lately advanced in relation to them* (1751).

Gregory Sharpe, *A letter to the Right Reverend the Lord Bishop of Oxford, from the Master of the Temple. Containing remarks on some strictures made by His Grace the Late Lord Archbishop of Canterbury in the Revd. Mr. Merrick's Annotations on the Psalms* (1769).

William Smith, *Discourses on Public Occasions in America* (1762).

——, *A discourse concerning the conversion of the heathen Americans, and the final propagation of Christianity and the sciences to the ends of the earth* (Philadelphia, 1760).

Abraham Taylor, *A letter to the author of An enquiry into the causes of the decay of the dissenting interests. Containing an apology for some of his inconsistencies; with a plea for the dissenters, and the liberty of the people. To which is added, a short epistle to the reverend Mr. Gough* (1730).

D'Blossiers Tovey, *Anglia Judaica: or the history and antiquities of the Jews in England, collected from all our historians, both printed and manuscript, as also from the records in the Tower, and other public repositories* (Oxford, 1738).

Andrew Trebeck, *A preservative against popery. Being a new-year's-gift to his parishioners of St. George, Hanover-Square* (1746).

Josiah Tucker, *An apology for the present Church of England as by law established, occasioned by a petition laid before Parliament, for abolishing subscriptions, in a letter to one of the petitioners*, 2nd edn (Gloucester, 1772).

Gilbert Wakefield, *Memoirs of the life of Gilbert Wakefield* (1792).

Isaac Watts, *The Works of the Rev. Isaac Watts, D.D.*, 9 vols. (Leeds, 1812–13).

[Francis Webb], *The morality of the New Testament digested under various heads, comprehending the duties which we owe God, to ourselves, and to our fellow-creatures. With an introduction to Deists; ... The whole concluding with observations on a late treatise, intitled, the doctrine of Grace, written by Dr. Warburton ... By a rational Christian* (1765).

Noah Welles, *The real advantages which ministers and people may enjoy especially in the colonies, by conforming to the Church of England; faithfully considered, and impartially represented, in a letter to a young gentleman* (Boston1762).

Thomas Wintle, *Daniel, an improved version attempted* (Oxford, 1792).

William Wood, *Britain's Joshua: a sermon preached at Darlington, October 9, 1746; the day of public thanksgiving for the suppression of the late rebellion* (Newcastle upon Tyne, 1746).

2.3 ECCLESIASTICAL RECORDS

T.M. Blagg, *The Parish Registers of Shelton, in the county of Nottingham, for the years 1595–1812* (Worksop, 1900).

Gerald Bray, *The Records of Convocation*, 20 vols. (Woodbridge, 2006)

——, *Tudor Church Reform: The Henrician Canons of 1535 and the Reformatio Legum Ecclesiasticarum* (Woodbridge, 2000).

——, *Anglican Canons, 1529–1947* (Woodbridge, 1998).

Mellen Chamberlain (ed.), *A Documentary History of Chelsea, Including the Boston Precincts of Winnismmet, Rumney Marsh, and Pullen Point, 1624–1824*, 2 vols. (Boston, 1908).

R.E.G. Cole (ed.), *Speculum dioceseos lincolniensis sub episcopis Gul: Wake et Edm: Gibson ad 1705–1723* (Lincoln, 1910).

James F. Cooper, jr., and Kenneth P. Minkema (eds.), *The Colonial Church Records of the First Church of Reading (Wakefield) and the First Church of Rumney Marsh (Revere)* (Boston, 2006).

John Fendley (ed.), *Bishop Benson's Survey of the Diocese of Gloucester, 1735–1750* (Bristol, 2000).

Kenneth Fincham (ed.), *Visitation Articles and Injunctions of the Early Stuart Church. Volumes I-II* (Woodbridge, 1994, 1998).

Jeremy Gregory (ed.), *The Speculum of Archbishop Thomas Secker* (Woodbridge, 1995).

John R. Guy (ed.), *The Diocese of Llandaff in 1763: The Primary Visitation of Bishop Ewer* (Cardiff, 1991).

John Le Neve, *Fasti Ecclesiae Anglicanae, 1541–1857. VIII: Bristol, Gloucester, Oxford, and Peterborough Dioceses,* compiled by Joyce M. Horne (1996).

———, *Fasti Ecclesiae Anglicanae, 1541–1857. I: St. Paul's, London,* compiled by Joyce M. Horne (1969).

John Le Neve and T. Duffus Hardy, *Fasti Ecclesiae Anglicanae* (Oxford, 1854).

H.A. Lloyd Jukes (ed.), *Articles of Enquiry Addressed to the Clergy of the Diocese of Oxford at the Primary Visitation of Dr. Thomas Secker, 1738* (Banbury, 1957).

S.L. Ollard and P.C. Walker (eds.), *Archbishop Herring's Visitation Returns, 1743* (Wakefield, 1928–29).

Mary Ransome (ed.), *The state of the bishopric of Worcester* (Leeds, 1968).

———, *Wiltshire Returns to the Bishop's Visitation Queries, 1783* (Devizes, 1971).

Stephen Taylor (ed.), *From Cranmer to Davidson: A Church of England Miscellany* (Woodbridge, 1999).

W.R. Ward (ed.), *Parson and Parish in Eighteenth-Century Hampshire: Replies to Bishops' Visitations* (Winchester, 1995).

———, *Parson and Parish in Eighteenth-Century Surrey: Replies to Bishops' Visitations* (Guildford, 1994).

Edwin Welch (ed.), *The Minute Book of the French Church at Southampton, 1702–1939* (Southampton, 1979).

2.4 PERIODICALS

Gentleman's Magazine
Lloyd's Evening Post, and British Chronicle
London Gazette
Monthly Repository of Theology and General Literature
St. James's Chronicle
Virginia Gazette

INDEX

303

INDEX

INDEX

INDEX

INDEX

INDEX